D0752715

THE BLOOD ROAD

By the Same Author

Combined Fleet Decoded: The Secret History of American Intelligence and the Japanese Navy in World War II

The Hidden History of the Vietnam War

Keepers of the Keys: A History of the National Security Council from Truman to Bush

Presidents' Secret Wars: CIA and Pentagon Covert Operations from World War II Through the Persian Gulf

Valley of Decision: The Siege of Khe Sanh (with Ray W. Stubbe)

Pentagon Games

The Soviet Estimate: U.S. Intelligence and Soviet Strategic Forces

The Sky Would Fall: The Secret U.S. Bombing Mission to Vietnam, 1954

THE BLOOD ROAD

The Ho Chi Minh Trail and the Vietnam War

JOHN PRADOS

John Wiley & Sons, Inc.

New York · Chichester · Weinheim · Brisbane · Singapore · Toronto

This book is printed on acid-free paper. ∞

Copyright © 1999 by John Prados. All rights reserved
Published by John Wiley & Sons, Inc.
Published simultaneously in Canada

No part of this publication may be reproduced, stored in a retrieval system or transmitted in any form or by any means, electronic, mechanical, photocopying, recording, scanning or otherwise, except as permitted under Sections 107 or 108 of the 1976 United States Copyright Act, without either the prior written permission of the Publisher, or authorization through payment of the appropriate per-copy fee to the Copyright Clearance Center, 222 Rosewood Drive, Danvers, MA 01923, (508) 750-8400, fax (508) 750-4744. Requests to the Publisher for permission should be addressed to the Permissions Department, John Wiley & Sons, Inc., 605 Third Avenue, New York, NY 10158-0012, (212) 850-6011, fax (212) 850-6008, E-Mail: PERMREQ@WILEY.COM.

This publication is designed to provide accurate and authoritative information in regard to the subject matter covered. It is sold with the understanding that the publisher is not engaged in rendering professional services. If professional advice or other expert assistance is required, the services of a competent professional person should be sought.

Library of Congress Cataloging-in-Publication Data:

Prados, John.
   The blood road : the Ho Chi Minh Trail and the Vietnam
War / John Prados.
      p.   cm.
   Includes bibliographical references (p.   ) and index.
   ISBN 0-471-25465-7 (cloth : alk. paper)
   1. Vietnamese Conflict, 1961–1975—United States.   2. Ho Chi Minh
Trail.   I. Title.
DS558.P74   1998
959.704'3373—DC21   98-9340
                                                                       CIP

Printed in the United States of America

10 9 8 7 6 5 4 3 2 1

TO NATASHA

who came with me
to see
how things work

Each of us carried in his heart a separate war
which in many ways was totally different,
despite our common cause.

—BAO NINH
The Sorrow of War

CONTENTS

List of Maps   xi

Introduction   xiii

Chapter 1
"Plainly a Gateway to Southeast Asia": *1954–1960*   1

Chapter 2
Ants and Elephants: *1961–1962*   21

Chapter 3
The Watershed: *1962–1963*   43

Chapter 4
The Battle Joined: *1963–1964*   61

Chapter 5
Dark Road Ahead: *1964–1965*   91

Chapter 6
The World and The 'Nam   123

Chapter 7
Squeezing Hanoi: *1965–1966*   139

Chapter 8
Indian Country: *1966–1967*   181

Chapter 9
Forks in the Road: *1967*   205

Chapter 10
Fire in the Night: *1968*   241

Chapter 11
Pinball Wizards: *1968–1969*   267

Chapter 12
A Strategy of Force: *1969–1970*   287

Chapter 13
No Plug in the Funnel: *1971*   311

Chapter 14
The Road Turns South: *1971–1975*   351

Afterword   381

Notes   383

Index   410

LIST OF MAPS

Map	Pages
Indochina Mountains	6
Area of The Trail	12
The Trail, 1964	87
Trail Extensions in 1965 (Showing U.S. Road Watches)	114
Mu Gia Pass Area	189
Trail Extensions, 1966–67 (Showing U.S. Road Watches)	192
The Demilitarized Zone Area (Showing McNamara Line)	216
Invasion of Laos, February–March 1971	337

INTRODUCTION

As the Vietnam War took its course through the 1960s and 1970s, almost every American became familiar with the name "Ho Chi Minh Trail." An American nickname in truth, taken from the idea of a passage through difficult country plus the identity of the leader of the Democratic Republic of Vietnam, known this side of the Pacific as North Vietnam, the Ho Chi Minh Trail is a staple in accounts of the progress of the war. No story on the balance of forces arrayed on the sides of the conflict could be complete without reference to the Ho Chi Minh Trail, and there were obligatory allusions to it in explanations of why the constant stream of powerful strikes against the adversary had not brought him down. Today, in the third decade since the end of the Vietnam War, claims that we failed to consider cutting the Ho Chi Minh Trail are among the leading contenders for arguments that the Vietnam War might have turned out differently. In fact, taken to an extreme, there are some who argue that American victory would have followed the cutting of The Trail.

These are undoubtedly important assertions. Yet for all the consequence invested in the arguments, there has been very little effort to understand the actual content of these claims. During the war, practically no one investigated in depth just where The Trail came from, few knew what it added up to, and everyone kept their eyes on the daily details of battle rather than on the sinews that made war possible. Since the war, advocates of cutting The Trail as a perfect strategy have paid little attention to the measures actually taken in pursuit of that goal during the Indochina conflict.

The Trail undeniably lay at the heart of the war. For the Vietnamese of the North it represented much more than a term in a strategic equation. Calling it the "Truong Son Strategic Supply Route" after the Vietnamese name for the mountain range that bisects the Indochinese peninsula or, more simply, the Old Man's Trail for a guide who helped surveyors lay out its early course, the Ho Chi Minh Trail embodied the aspirations of a people. For Hanoi and its soldiers, the dream of reunifying Vietnam required going south—to the South Vietnam that America defended, an artificial division of Vietnam created by international agreement in 1954. Things such as supplies, ammunition, and weapons could be sent South by boat, to land along the Vietnamese coast or sail into Cambodian ports, but only overland was it possible for men and women to head South and join in combat. Creating The Trail would be necessary, and building The Trail or hiking it became the central experience for a generation of Vietnamese from the North. The juxtaposition of their efforts to open and sustain The Trail, with American and South Vietnamese attempts to close it, tells a powerful story.

What was done to close The Trail? What things to keep it open? It seemed important to find out. The story is much more complex than appeared at first, involving not only nations at war but also their allies, not just soldiers but also political movements, and not just battle action but secret strategic debates as well. Through it all there was the physical accomplishment of creating The Trail, a struggle of men and women against nature. Forging The Trail meant channeling passages through a hostile land, turning pathways into roadways, then roads into highways. Ultimately the Ho Chi Minh Trail would comprise twelve thousand miles of roads and paths laid in the face of a potent nature and an increasingly violent and systematic series of American efforts to prevent this very achievement. Almost a hundred thousand Vietnamese and Laotians worked on this ambitious project at its height; many paid the ultimate price. Today there are seventy-two military cemeteries filled with the remains of people who toiled on The Trail, perished under the bombs, or expired from disease, exhaustion, animal bites, storms, and all the other challenges of a harsh land. Tigers and elephants were sometimes more dangerous than American airplanes. Rain often threatened to wash away the labor of months or even years. This effort needs to be better understood in the West.

Most accounts of the Vietnam conflict center on some single aspect, or they sketch a broad canvas of the period. In none of them is there a coherent treatment of The Trail, whose flow of men, women, and the apparatus of war became the lifeblood of our adversary's struggle. This gap has prevented a full appreciation of diplomatic and political developments as well as battles and campaigns, a surprising number of which relate directly to strategies of opening, or countering, The Trail. Our knowledge of the trauma that was Vietnam can be considerably improved by inquiring into the whole question of The Trail.

The story of The Trail is at the same time the tale of Vietnam's borders with Laos and Cambodia, and of the Demilitarized Zone that separated the two Vietnams. To the North Vietnamese, going South meant crossing borders or the zone, once if entering Laos, twice if going into Cambodia or back across the Vietnamese border into South Vietnam. A centerpiece of Hanoi's strategy would be a constant effort to preserve the ability to cross these borders and make the travel easier. To the South Vietnamese, Hanoi crossing the border was the nightmare, for that meant the struggle for the South was on. American strategists, steeped in the fashionable theory of counterinsurgency, saw the border in terms of the role of bases in guerrilla warfare. The strategists insisted that guerrilla success absolutely required an outside base, as North Vietnam could be by using The Trail. Conversely, sealing the borders would isolate the guerrillas in South Vietnam. To play on Mao Zedong's formula for guerrilla warfare, which saw the guerrilla as a fish swimming in the sea of the population, sealing the border would drain the sea, after which the rebel fish could simply be mopped up.

Borders also assumed growing importance for another group, the anti-war movement in the United States. Thinking, after 1968, that America was on its way out of Vietnam, the passion of activists was inflamed when the Nixon administration attacked across borders into Laos and Cambodia. Nixon's target in those attacks would be Hanoi's supply system—The Trail and its base areas.

In a number of ways, The Trail thus meant much to a great many people. By following these various threads, moreover, it is possible to look at the Vietnam experience from many sides, avoiding the narrowly focused battle histories, atomized individual accounts, and overly general visions of the past. The Trail serves as metaphor and microcosm of the Vietnam War. *The Blood Road* will record the sides to that story, from the trials of Vietnamese soldiers in the wild, to the heroism of Americans trying to save their buddies against impossible odds, to the desperation of antiwar activists who feared that a conflict out of control spelled doom for a great nation, to the machinations of diplomats and generals scheming to get their way. This book is the tale of a fulcrum that turned the balance in the Vietnam War.

I have used a wide array of sources to produce this work. The largest single compilation of material has been formerly secret records of the U.S. government. Some of these were obtained through the Freedom of Information Act, others by an identical procedure used at record centers called Mandatory Declassification Review. Although *The Blood Road* contains a great deal of fresh material from this process, I must nevertheless reiterate a complaint heard widely from scholars and journalists: the declassification procedure remains too cumbersome, too stilted, too arbitrary, and positively ridiculous in the ways many of the exemptions allowed by law are utilized. Until there are sanctions enforceable against bureaucrats who wield their "secret" stamps too freely, and bulk release of masses of records that are being withheld, the full sweep of America's history will remain shrouded in a cloak of darkness.

A number of collections of U.S. records were used in the course of this research, and I wish to acknowledge the help I received at all of them. These include the National Archives, where John M. Taylor and his aides continue to demonstrate peerless knowledge of important holdings. Also of key importance have been the various presidential libraries, which form branches of the National Archives and Reference Administration. At the John F. Kennedy Library, help was furnished by Stuart Curly, Michael Desmond, and Ronald Whealon. At the Lyndon B. Johnson Library I am indebted to Regina Greenwell, Linda Hansen, and Shellyne Eickhoff, as well as former archivists David C. Humphrey and Nancy Smith. At the Richard M. Nixon Library Project of the National Archives, personnel also were very helpful. At the U.S. Army Military History Institute, important assistance came from Richard J. Sommers, John Slonacker, and Pamela Cheney. William Hammond and

Graham Cosmas from the Army's Center for Military History kindly answered relevant questions. Roger G. Miller from the Office of Air Force History did the same.

There are important collections of U.S. records that are held outside government, including useful compilations of formerly classified documents. Research assistance on this project came from Malcolm Byrne and William Burr at the National Security Archive. At the Archive of the Vietnam War invaluable aid was provided by Bruce Cammack, Michael D. Lerner, James Ginther, and Danette Owens.

In addition to documents, I have used oral histories and interviews, memoirs, relevant secondary sources, and current periodicals. Oral histories came from the archival sources already enumerated. Interviews have been conducted by myself or others. Both are listed following this narrative. Published works were consulted at the Library of Congress; the Columbia University Libraries; Wheaton Regional Library and other branches of the Montgomery County Library system and the Takoma Park Library, all of these in Maryland; and the Martin Luther King, Jr., Library of the District of Columbia. Librarians and others at all these facilities helped without stinting.

For help with particular source materials of their own or others I wish to thank Robert K. Brigham, Kevin Bowen, Tim Brown, Timothy N. Castle, John M. Carland, Jack Kull, George McT. Kahin, Theodore Mataxis, Douglas Pike, D. Gareth Porter, James R. Reckner, Lewis Sorley, Roger J. Spiller, and Karen Turner. Vital shoulders to cry on, logistical assistance, or other help came from Roothee Gabay and Marvin Dollison, Bill and Abbot Kominers, Ellen Pinzur, Thomas Powers, and Scott Wallace.

I want to take this occasion to thank my agent, Russell Galen, who has been with me through thin and thick.

Finally, I owe a debt to my first reader, perhaps the toughest of all, Jill Gay. Each of these people was vital in producing what you are about to read; all of them contributed to the fine qualities of this book. All its errors and omissions are mine alone.

—John Prados
Washington, D.C.
July 31, 1996

CHAPTER 1

"Plainly a Gateway to Southeast Asia"

1954–1960

For a time Comrade Phong became the watchmaker of Dien Bien Phu. Driver of a truck used to drag heavy cannons up the difficult roads to this mountain valley, Phong had less to do once the artillery got their guns into caves and deep dugouts. Phong acquired the tools of a watchmaker and set himself up in one of the caves to fix timepieces. Huu Mai, political officer of a front-line Viet Minh battalion, met Phong when he stumbled into the watchmaker's cave while walking among the antiaircraft positions. Mai's watch had broken; he missed it sorely, for Mai's job was to keep his unit on schedule whenever engaged in operations. Mai had tried everything to get his watch fixed, down to making deals with supply drivers who hauled from the big bases in the rear. Nothing worked. Red tape or lack of spare parts blocked every repair scheme. Now Mai met Phong.

Comrade Phong took the watch and agreed to fix it. He told Mai to come back in four days and lent him a replacement. Mai felt grateful. Four days later he got the watch back, but not from Phong. The artillery had gotten orders to move to fresh positions. Phong went to help. The morning fog cleared, with trucks and gunners on the move in plain sight of the enemy. The vehicle in front of Phong blew up under fire; by veering his truck dangerously, Phong managed to avoid the wreck and reach his destination. He succeeded on a second trip, too. On the third try the enemy brought Phong down. Huu Mai heard the story when he went for his watch, remembered Phong through all the adversities of the campaign, and recounted it later for posterity.

This was the big battle at last, a defining moment for heroes and knaves, for empires and independent nations. Dien Bien Phu became the final act of the French war in Vietnam. In the mountain valley, snug up against the border of Laos, both sides risked everything in a cataclysmic bid for victory. The French fought to preserve Vietnam as part of what they called the

French Union, a liberalized incarnation of a colonial empire. Their Vietnamese opponents, known at that time as the Viet Minh, fought for independence and the reunification of their country, which had been divided under French colonial rule.

The battle at Dien Bien Phu should have been impossible. For the French that mountain valley lay two hundred twenty miles from their command center at Hanoi, the intervening land wholly controlled by the Viet Minh. The French depended on technology. They used airplanes to fly supplies and reinforcements to Dien Bien Phu; relied on tanks and artillery to defeat any Vietnamese who attacked; and, before that, on warplanes to prevent the Viet Minh from even concentrating in the uplands. French intelligence was reading a significant portion of the Viet Minh radio messages. The French were formidable; they had many reasons to expect success. Holding Dien Bien Phu, the French command believed, would bar the door to Laos.

The Viet Minh were also far from their supplies—150 miles—and, unlike the French, had little technology. What the Viet Minh had was people like Phong, determined and numerous. There was some artillery, which, if it could ever be gotten up into the mountains and supplied continuously with ammunition, could cause a great deal of trouble. There were some trucks that could pull guns, like those of Phong's unit. But the roads were poor, in many places little more than tracks, and all were watched by the French air force with its infernal technology.

Throughout what the Vietnamese later called their "anti-French war," the Viet Minh always laid stress on people, depending on them for the mobility of the army. Typically the peasants in villages along the path of marauding armies were dragooned to work as porters, carrying for a week before returning home. Since the amount a man or woman could carry was limited, and because the porters had to eat, too, only a small portion of a load would actually be delivered. The turnover in porters was huge. It has been estimated that to feed a 10,000-man Viet Minh division on the march for twelve days, 50,000 porters were necessary. In one campaign northeast of Hanoi in 1950 there had been 130,000 porters, while 95,000 had worked with the Viet Minh in 1953 when they first operated in Laos.

Dien Bien Phu involved the largest Viet Minh field army yet, and its remoteness meant the old ways could not suffice. Viet Minh commander General Vo Nguyen Giap assembled 55,000 troops for the battle. There were not enough villagers in all the sparsely populated mountains of northern Vietnam to furnish porters to such a force. The solution lay in creativity. The Vietnamese, then as later, adapted simple technologies for ambitious roles. Bicycles could negotiate all but the worst mountain tracks. With extra suspension plus widened handlebars fitted with pallets, the bicycles could carry three hundred to four hundred pounds, ten times the load of a porter. Even with two peasants as a team to walk the bike, the amounts moved were much greater than before; the porters delivered more than they consumed. For the first time, supply arrivals could be calculated in tons, not pounds.

At the same time, the Vietnamese set about improving the roads. These were smoothed, widened for trucks, and given bypasses at places where bridges could be bombed out or roads blocked by rock and obstacles. Some 20,000 tribesmen and peasants worked on the last stretch of road alone. General Giap also diverted two engineer regiments to road improvement, at key moments used replacement soldiers en route to the battle, and added some of his front-line infantry when required. The result was good enough for trucks like Phong's. This was striking, especially given the fact that there had been no regular vehicular traffic over these roads since 1945, and in view of the Viet Minh's complete dependence on manual labor for heavy construction work.

In addition, the French were completely aware of what these Vietnamese were trying to do. The French air force set about frustrating that goal, flying from fields at Hanoi and nearby Haiphong, sometimes from as far south as Da Nang,* or from aircraft carriers in the Gulf of Tonkin. French aircraft bombed places they estimated the road could not be bypassed, or the planes flew along above the roads, shooting machine guns and automatic cannons when they encountered Viet Minh supply columns. The Vietnamese countered with deception and defenses. Viet Minh convoys hid during the day, moving mostly at night, concealing parts of the road under canopies of foliage where the tops of trees were tied together. As for defenses, by the end of 1953, French intelligence detected four times as many antiaircraft gun positions in northern Vietnam as there had been a year earlier.

Dien Bien Phu became a struggle between French attempts to shut the supply lines and Vietnamese ones to keep them going. Defending routes or laboring on them were a core of 23,000 Viet Minh; moving supplies were 800 trucks and 75,000 porters. Hundreds of tons of French bombs failed to stem the flow. Arrival of those supplies meant that General Giap's artillery could close the airfield at Dien Bien Phu, greatly restricting *French* supplies and reinforcements, while Giap's infantry battered the perimeter of the French fortress. Gradually the French were strangled until, on May 7, 1954, their last positions fell to the Viet Minh.

The French people were not passive observers of these events. Frustration and war-weariness led many Frenchmen to demand an end to the fighting. There were antiwar demonstrations in Paris, Lyons, Marseilles, and elsewhere. At the Arc de Triomphe in Paris, when the French prime minister arrived to lay a wreath in memory of war dead, Indochina veterans jostled him. Negotiations on Indochina at Geneva, greatly affected by the fall of Dien Bien Phu, resulted in agreement for a French withdrawal. Hanoi would become capital of the new Democratic Republic of Vietnam.

*During French colonial times this city on the central Vietnamese coast was called Tourane. Americans knew it as Da Nang, the name given by the Saigon government after the French war. We avoid confusion by utilizing this form throughout.

* * *

Issues left behind from the French war had much to do with America's Vietnam war. Ho Chi Minh defined the French struggle as that of an elephant with a tiger. The elephant would be immensely powerful, but the tiger would not stand still, lurking in the jungle by day to emerge at night. Others, such as the novelist Jean Lartéguy, preferred the simile of the ant, and that proved peculiarly appropriate both at Dien Bien Phu and in the American war. The elephant would be capable of stamping ants to death by the thousand. But the ants would pursue their goal with a purposefulness that would drive the elephant to distraction, then defeat. The elephant would tire and be overwhelmed. Ants. No more, no less. The French fighting in Indochina never believed it. Then came Dien Bien Phu. Ants.

Americans forever insisted that their involvement in Vietnam would be nothing like that of the French. The United States was not out to acquire colonies, so colonialism was not a factor. Busily denying any similarities, Americans failed to learn from the Franco-Vietnamese war, including its metaphors. This was true in 1955, in the immediate aftermath of Geneva, when Washington collaborated with a new government in the southern part of the country, now styled South Vietnam. It remained true in 1965, when South Vietnam seemed at the point of collapse. In 1955 Washington and South Vietnam evaded the provisions of the Geneva agreements providing for reunification of Vietnam and universal elections within two years. In 1965 Washington stood at the brink of active military intervention to shore up the faltering South Vietnamese government.

Analogy to the French experience proved rather important in 1965, when Washington decided to move to full-scale war in Indochina. Lyndon B. Johnson, president of the United States, had been in the thick of the Dien Bien Phu crisis, as a key American legislator at the moment when American air strikes were suggested as a means to save the French. LBJ saw the French defeat. George W. Ball, one of President Johnson's senior diplomatic advisers in 1965, opposed any American decision for war on the basis of arguments drawn from the French failure.

President Johnson, assailed with doubts, would be reassured by his national security adviser, McGeorge Bundy. Attempting to derail Ball's logic, "Mac" Bundy questioned whether France in 1954 was at all a "useful analogy" for the United States in Vietnam in 1965. According to Bundy, France had been "a colonial power seeking to reimpose its overseas rule, out of tune with Vietnamese nationalism, deeply divided in domestic opinion, politically unstable at home, the victim of seven years of warfare—the last four marked by military engagements on a scale far greater than anything yet encountered by the United States." Mac would come to rue those words, as would one of his key allies in this round of bureaucratic infighting, Secretary of Defense Robert S. McNamara. In 1965 neither of them questioned whether the American citizen was any more "in tune" with Vietnamese nationalism than had been the French. In a 1995 memoir, however, McNamara proceeded to argue that the Vietnam War became a tragedy for America precisely due to a failure to appreciate Vietnamese nationalism. But in 1965, before this introspection, McNamara sided with Mac Bundy's analysis that the United States remained politically strong and had options not available to the French in 1954. Lyndon Johnson accepted their thinking.

Like top American leaders, military men, diplomats, and intelligence officers, with a few notable exceptions, resisted the notion that the United States had anything to learn from the French experience. Thinking themselves innovators, Americans evolved many of the same tactics and techniques the French had used before them. This became ironic as the American war progressed, for Ho Chi Minh and his generals faced much the same problem as they had at Dien Bien Phu—the necessity to support warfare on remote battlefields—and their solution would be identical. As the indigenous guerrilla resistance in South Vietnam gained momentum, rekindled as early as 1958–1959, the situation increasingly commanded Hanoi's attention. At the time of Geneva a number of the Viet Minh in the South had elected to go North to the Democratic Republic of Vietnam. Now it seemed important in Hanoi to get those Southerners back into South Vietnam. Hanoi's device for doing so would create a fulcrum upon which hung the balance of the American war in Vietnam.

South Vietnamese president Ngo Dinh Diem had little good to say about French rule in Vietnam. Take roads, for example. Diem once told American officials that the French built roads in the interior only to serve their rubber plantations. There had been no meaningful development of transportation for the nation. Diem's remarks are not surprising, considering he had beat out a French-backed *coup d'état* in 1955 and that Diem's lack of a French colonial background was the strength that brought him to power in Saigon. The French had not only failed to build roads, they also had never provided the equipment necessary to maintain those that existed. "Every new road," Diem said, "opens up Vietnam economically and provides more benefits to the people." Meeting with Americans in Saigon and Washington, and with World Bank officials, Diem's agents constantly harped on bulldozers and dredges. Scooping out paths, reclaiming land to make them, as well as new Mekong River delta passages, seemed to be Diem's vision of the new Vietnam.

Ngo Dinh Diem could talk roads militarily, too. For the South Vietnam of that era, before the great guerrilla threat, the main danger was supposed to be a conventional attack down the spine of the Indochinese peninsula. Such an attack could come straight across the Demilitarized Zone (DMZ), or it could angle through Laos and Cambodia (see Map 1). Diem pushed for the improvement of Route 9, the lateral road behind the South Vietnamese side of the DMZ, as well as Route 14, a major thoroughfare in the Central Highlands, the most likely target in case Hanoi attacked farther to the south. Diem's army, the Army of the Republic of Vietnam (ARVN), kept

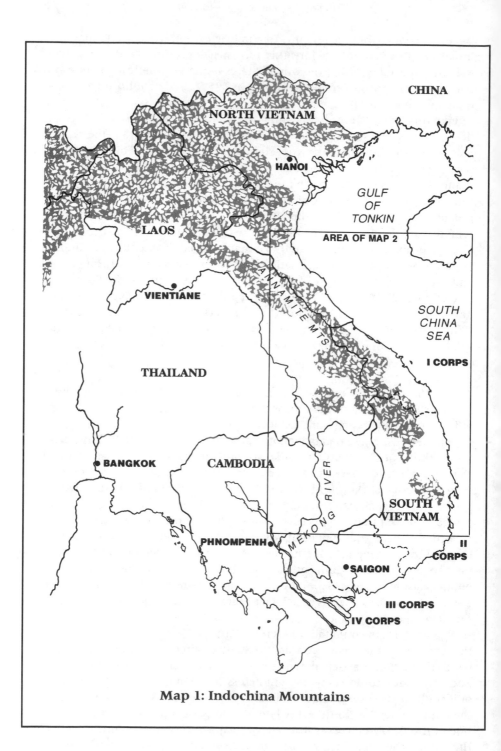

Map 1: Indochina Mountains

6

two of its seven divisions below the DMZ, and another pair of these scarce units in the Highlands. In April 1960, when the question was the location of a new regimental base camp in the highlands, Diem involved himself directly with the American military advisory group, advocating a specific site in Kontum Province over another that was backed by a river. When Saigon learned that guerrillas were beginning to gather in areas along the Cambodian border, in late 1959 and 1960, Diem told the Americans he needed a road paralleling that border, which meant a construction project from the Gulf of Siam to the wilderness of the Central Highlands.

One of President Diem's pet projects, in the summer and fall of 1959, was a road linking Kontum with the Laotian provincial capital of Pakse. A river town on the middle Mekong, Pakse was the economic engine of lower Laos, dominating trade on the water as well as that of the upland tribes inhabiting the Bolovens Plateau. Pakse was home to one of the three schools in Laos offering a postprimary education, and to one of the most accessible airfields. The market town had good road links with the Bolovens and north and south in the Mekong River valley. Diem's vision was a road connecting Attopeu, at the eastern base of the Bolovens, with Route 14 in the Central Highlands. Only thirty miles separated the two places, and there was already a trail capable of improvement that entered South Vietnam in the vicinity of Dak To. The problem, Eisenhower administration officials told Diem's chief of staff, was that the bulk of the roadwork would be in Laos, and neither the Laotians nor United States aid had funds for such a project. Diem's road came to naught, victim of the realities of America's then-meager interest in Southeast Asia.

The dream, however, went on to become a nightmare. Diem and his successors wrestled with the thought that the other side, Hanoi, might complete the road and make it a boulevard to the overthrow of Saigon. Their apprehension was justified: it was a process that began immediately. Soon Saigon was detecting movements of persons and equipment through the Laotian panhandle southward. They understood that this could only be sustenance for the Viet Cong movement.

Expressions of concern showed in American exchanges with the South Vietnamese. The specter of a Hanoi march on Saigon colored thinking for the duration of the conflict. Perhaps the first words of terror were those of Nguyen Dinh Thuan, Diem's chief of staff, visiting Washington in April 1960. Thuan told U.S. diplomats of guerrillas infiltrating into South Vietnam from lower Laos, and of others carried past the DMZ in boats. The traffic had to be stopped. Thuan attributed Viet Cong successes to this support. His remarks reinforced concerns expressed by Diem himself, meeting the American ambassador before Thuan's trip. President Diem stressed the need to block Northerners crossing into South Vietnam—by building roads, airstrips, and waterways in inaccessible places along the borders.

At lunch on April 8 with the deputy director of the Central Intelligence Agency, Nguyen Dinh Thuan went farther in his dark recitations. Thuan told Charles P. Cabell and other CIA officers that lower Laos had gone "completely rotten." During French days the phrase Thuan used, *complète-ment pourri*," had been regarded with particular fear. Nguyen Dinh Thuan, not to say Ngo Dinh Diem, would have been especially concerned to learn what North Vietnamese prime minister Pham Van Dong had told the French consul in Hanoi a few months before. "You must remember we will be in Saigon tomorrow," Pham had said in September 1959, then repeated, "we will be in Saigon tomorrow." No one then knew how much lay behind that declaration.

Only those who made the decision can say what really happened in Hanoi. Everyone else is a mirror watcher. In Washington and the American press, some saw Hanoi's choice to back rebellion in South Vietnam as a result of struggle between pro-Chinese and pro-Russian factions of the ruling Lao Dong (Vietnam Workers') Party. Others viewed events as a competition between intellectual and agrarian party members; or the military versus the politicians; or said that none of this truly mattered. Whatever the actual cleavages among the authorities, the fact remains that Hanoi's choice came in the face of rival demands for scarce resources in the wake of the 1954 Geneva agreements.

Tonkin and the southern panhandle, the nucleus of what became the Democratic Republic of Vietnam (DRV), had been heavily damaged during the French war and were not well developed even before it. Construction—Lao Dong ideologues called it "socialist rehabilitation"—and investment became keys to the future of the republic. This led to the disastrous land reform of 1955–1957, when forced collectivization, army security measures, and plain disorganization killed or starved 55,000 peasants, especially in the DRV panhandle, Ho Chi Minh's own birthplace. The glaring need for investment in North Vietnam also gave Hanoi reasons to reach out to China and Russia, each on one side of a deepening hostility transcending their political affinity.

Anything that happened in South Vietnam—even violation of the Geneva commitment to reunification of Vietnam—took place against the backdrop of the demands of development. Hanoi discounted in advance the failure to hold stipulated free elections by 1956. A Lao Dong Party plenum that April, several months ahead of the Geneva deadline, recognized that the schedule set in the agreement would not be met, that a new timetable was necessary, but that rural reconstruction remained the main priority. The Lao Dong specifically rejected violence as a strategy. A half dozen party convocations over the next several years reemphasized the needs of North Vietnam, advising southern cadres to bend their efforts to organizing peasants in the villages of South Vietnam.

The Saigon government did not just sit back to wait for things to happen. Military operations aimed at former Viet Minh were easy to tag on to those against armed religious sects that had threatened the leadership of Ngo Dinh Diem. Specially targeted operations began in December 1955—there would be some activity of this kind under way somewhere in South Vietnam, at *all* times, *for the next twenty years*. The very phase "Viet Cong" originated during this period, a contraction of the words for Communist and the nation, *Viet Nam Cong San*, a pejorative label. Between late 1957 and early 1959 the Viet Cong lost half or more of all those killed, missing, or arrested in the years since Geneva. It has been estimated that attrition cut the ranks of southern cadres by two thirds, from 15,000 to 5,000. Regional party committees in the Far South and, in 1958, the central regional committee as well, appealed to Hanoi for instructions to resume former guerrilla ways. After mid-1958, Lao Dong party histories affirm, local cadres made practically no headway in South Vietnam.

Despite all pleas from the South, as late as December 1958 DRV prime minister Pham Van Dong still declared prospects improved for peaceful reunification, supposedly due to a more relaxed international climate. The DRV offered to negotiate arms reductions with Saigon, but the Diem government dismissed such diplomacy as propaganda. In retrospect it seems that the pressure on Hanoi to act on the cadres' problems had become intolerable and that a final gambit was being made to avoid confrontation with Diem. Hanoi's dilemma was further sharpened in that its ally in Laos, recently forced out of government, had also begun to beg for assistance.

Just a month later, a new Vietnamese party conference adopted a resolution calling for support to the revolution in the South. "Resolution 15," this product of the fifteenth plenum of the Lao Dong Party, amounted to a decision to help the Viet Cong even if that meant fighting Diem's South Vietnamese army. Not only that; by now the United States had become well established in Saigon. Pham Van Dong did not care. There was surprising vehemence in the words Pham uttered to a Western diplomat, who promptly passed them along to Washington. Firmly and evenly Pham Van Doing had said, "We will drive the Americans into the sea."

It was a Tuesday, a few months after "Resolution 15," that Colonel Vo Bam sat in his office, plodding through the monotony of the day. Bam was anxious to get through the routine—it was Ho Chi Minh's birthday, May 19, festivities had been prepared. A supply specialist with the Ministry of Defense, Vo Bam was senior enough to be invited to some of the more interesting receptions. Suddenly the telephone rang on his desk. Colonel Bam found himself summoned to the Party Central Military Committee. There Bam found Major General Nguyen Van Vinh, a permanent member of the committee. After a few moments exchanging pleasantries and light banter, Vinh got down to business.

"Under instructions from the Political Bureau and on behalf of the Party Central Military Committee," General Vinh declared, "I hereby entrust you with the task of organizing a special military communication line to send supplies to the revolution in the South and create conditions for its development."

Colonel Bam was startled at this mandate and impressed with its seriousness. He began to take out his notepad to record the specifics of his assignment, only to be stopped by Vinh.

"Don't take notes," said the general. "From now on, you'll have to commit to memory all briefings about your work."

The supply line was to be created outside the normal chain of command, and directly under the Central Military Committee. Nguyen Van Vinh told Vo Bam the committee would put him in contact with people and units necessary to the mission, that the men who would work for him (no more than five hundred to start) were to be selected from Vietnamese who had regrouped to the DRV after Geneva, and that any weapons had to be taken from stocks captured from the French during the 1945–1954 war. The words "special trail" were used, and General Vinh envisioned this as an avenue to move not only arms and medical supplies but also soldiers and cadres. Initially The Trail was to be confined inside the borders of Vietnam proper; that is, it had either to cross the Ben Hai River or another sector of the Demilitarized Zone separating the two Vietnams.

Vo Bam had fought during the anti-French war in Annam, the central portion of Vietnam, an area the Viet Minh had called "Interzone 5," which made him familiar with the terrain now become the DMZ. Being a veteran of many unusual assignments, Bam was also familiar with the requirements of special operations. Bam began that very afternoon with a further briefing from an old Interzone 5 commander, Tran Luong, now in charge of helping build the Viet Cong under supervision of DRV Politburo member Le Duan. Luong told Vo Bam the immediate need for 1959 was to move 7,000 weapons, including light machine guns, and 500 persons, among them soldiers up to the rank of lieutenant colonel. Again Luong put emphasis on secrecy.

"This route must be kept absolutely secret," Luong ordered. "It must not be allowed to become a beaten path—that is, not a single footprint, cigarette butt, or broken twig may be left on it after the men's passage."

Vo Bam began by selecting his driver and was given a Vietnam People's Army (VPA) command car, a GAZ-69 of Russian manufacture. He used the vehicle to visit various VPA military zone commanders as well as those units composed of Southerners. Only commanders and their political officers were told the purpose of the visits. Colonel Bam soon chose the VPA 305th Division to furnish his initial manpower.

Stationed north of Hanoi and the Red River delta, the VPA 305th Division (some sources identify it as a brigade) numbered among six large Vietnam People's Army units created after Geneva and formed from the 90,000 Viet Minh who had regrouped to the DRV. The 305th had originally been stationed in the Vietnamese panhandle—an area important to Vo Bam—but had moved to the more northerly base as early as February 1956. Division commander Colonel Nguyen Minh Chau and his political commissar, Colonel Nguyen Duong, conducted vigorous jungle training, combat tactics, farm construction, agricultural work, and military modernization. Vo Bam's assignment would take away a significant portion of their manpower, yet the unit commanders did not mind—as the VPA organizer recalled, he had only to mention his purpose was to help the comrades in the South, and all objections melted away.

Nguyen Danh was a political officer with the division when Colonel Bam visited in May 1959. Danh liked to look at the brick houses perched on the hillsides north and east of Phu Tho, the division base; he thought them a romantic and beautiful tableau, perhaps also a symbol of permanence and stability. He had been admiring that vista when called to the commander's office, where he found his political officer in the anteroom. The commissar introduced Danh to another colonel, a man from Hanoi, Vo Bam. It soon became clear that Bam's orders represented the end of stability and the beginning of a great adventure, for Nguyen Danh was to help open The Trail.

Political officer Danh and a friend, unit commander Chu Dang Chu, were given the pick of the division's personnel and settled on 308 men for a new VPA 301st Battalion, the first formation assigned to the Central Military Committee's secret operation. The 301st members were issued uniforms different from those of the VPA—pajamalike costumes, Vo Bam recounts—and scored village flea markets for backpacks, canteens, and other items left over from the French war. Chu and Danh marshaled their men within a week and got them aboard a train to Thanh Hoa. From there the 301st moved by truck to Vinh Linh, a village on the Ben Hai River just above the Demilitarized Zone. Headquarters of the VPA 341st Division, then busy cutting firewood, Vinh Linh at first seemed to hinder the assignment. Men of the 301st were obliged to chop wood also, but matters were quickly straightened out, and the wood details continued just for physical hardening as Vo Bam's confederates awaited the results of preliminary scouting parties.

Colonel Vo Bam personally came to Vinh Linh to study the situation. Among others he met with two Viet Cong comrades from the South named Hanh and Quyet, who briefed Bam on conditions in Quang Tri and Thua Thien Provinces below the DMZ. Vo Bam began with the idea that supplies would be handed over to the Viet Cong at a point north of the Ben Hai (see Map 2), but Comrade Hanh swiftly disabused the Hanoi colonel of any such notion. The Viet Cong had no porters, scouts, liaison men, or rice to feed them, Hanh argued, so leaving weapons where the Viet Cong would have to move them would be no better than giving nothing at all.

Vo Bam quickly revised the plans. Initially men were to enter South Vietnam and follow Route 9, the road past Khe Sanh, which links the Vietnamese coastal plain with the Mekong River Valley at Savannakhet in Laos. Southern cadres worried, however, that Saigon's soldiers patrolled Route 9 day and night, and that Protestant missionaries with the Bru tribesmen around Khe Sanh would discover the 301st Battalion supply parties and betray them to local ARVN commanders. Vo Bam knew that during the anti-French war leaders of Interzone 5 had created a supply line called the

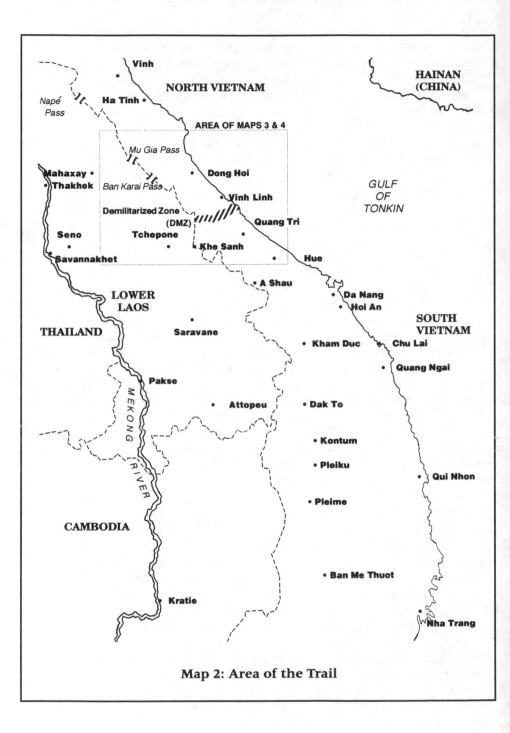

Map 2: Area of the Trail

"Reunification Trail" along the western boundaries of Vietnam from the Central Highlands north. Something like that now seemed necessary, although Bam worried that ARVN possessed a "fairly dense network" of outposts in the region and sent police spies to watch the borders. A few trips a year, well organized and carefully prepared, could work. In June 1959 Bam planned a system that would cross Route 9 and leave it behind, with weapons actually handed over to the Viet Cong at a point three "stations" farther south. There would be nine such stations, or way points, at which infiltration parties could halt and rest, two of them inside the DRV and the others successively farther south.

Equipping infiltrators with local clothes and possessions, palm hats to pajamas, stories and dialects, became the rule as The Trail system took root. But even at the beginning there was great care taken by the *bo dois*, the VPA soldiers, who were making the supply marches down The Trail. The relay stations were nothing more than clearings in the woods, and these had to be changed every few days to prevent the South Vietnamese from discovering their presence. Supplying the *bo dois* on the march, as at Dien Bien Phu, was an exceedingly thorny problem. At first Chu Dang Chu's unit resorted to starting each stage by carrying only rice to the next relay station. Then they would *march back* to pick up their load of weapons or ammunition—each man carried a bundle of four rifles or a forty-four-pound box of ammunition. The first infiltration down The Trail began on June 10, 1959. It was the height of the rainy season in this part of Vietnam, which usually lasts from June through September. The *bo doi* had nothing more than sheeted plastic over his head to keep out the rain, and it was the same sheeted plastic the VPA soldiers used to cover their tracks whenever they crossed a road, such as Route 9. General Nguyen Van Vinh had approved Vo Bam's recommendation that The Trail cross Route 9, and the North Vietnamese were going to make sure those supplies reached the Viet Cong. Nevertheless, the first Trail mission proved a miserable affair.

Determination paid off. On August 20, Hanoi received a message from the South that said simply, "ALL GOODS DELIVERED SAFELY." Later, the detailed report added an account of the meeting between the 301st Battalion patrol and a member of the standing committee of Interzone 5, a meeting at the head of the A Shau valley, a point roughly a hundred miles' march from Vinh Linh. This supply trek at the height of the rainy season marked the beginning of what became infamous during the Vietnam War as the "Ho Chi Minh Trail."

None of the *bo dois*, neither Vo Bam the careful planner, nor the operators Chu Dang Chu and Nguyen Danh, nor their scouts, laborers, security men, or liaison personnel, knew they were creating in the wilds of the Demilitarized Zone a road to Saigon. What began here grew more important than anyone could have dreamed that high rainy season. The trailblazers focused on their immediate world, the grueling necessity of taming the wilderness, the special demands of doing everything in secret. So careful were the North Vietnamese they restored the leaves on the ground to their previous pattern to mask their passage.

L e Duan was only one among Hanoi's leaders mightily pleased when Vo Bam completed his first mission to succor the Viet Cong. Soon afterward, on September 12, Vo Bam's unit was given a name, the 559th Transportation Group, the numerals being those of the month and year the orders were issued to help the South. More elements of the Vo Bam plan were adopted by the Central Military Committee, including the need to have a seaborne finger to the infiltration system. Hanoi now created a parallel Transportation Group, to handle movement by sea. Near Dong Hoi a fresh secret unit, the 603rd Battalion, began building boats that could pass for typical South Vietnamese fishing craft. Unfortunately for Hanoi, there was just no way to disguise the impact of its help for the Viet Cong. Actual discovery of a VPA presence in the South could only be a matter of time.

The trailmakers worried about standard security matters. One was the South Vietnamese Army's patrols along Route 9 below the Demilitarized Zone. This was a false issue, for the ARVN did nothing more than sporadic patrolling into this country, and Saigon had stopped maintaining Route 9 itself. The westernmost district, the one that included the coffee plantations of Khe Sanh, mostly sold its coffee to the markets at Savannakhet, at the Laotian end of Route 9. Another Hanoi worry, avoiding use of equipment attributable to the DRV, would be obviated because the South Vietnamese, once they discovered infiltration, would be in no doubt whence it came. The main effect would be to delay the day Saigon had concrete evidence of a North Vietnamese presence.

Meanwhile, Vo Bam again visited Chu Dang Chu's 301st Battalion zone to measure progress of the supply effort. Colonel Bam traveled with one of the columns to see conditions for himself. The 301st Battalion main base was at a village called Khe Ho, west of Vinh Linh. There was also an alternate center disguised as a state cattle farm at Bang, in westernmost Quang Binh Province. Chu's 301st had a dozen platoons, several manning posts extending through the DRV, most of the rest distributed on the network into South Vietnam. A few consisted of scouts, reserves, and selected specialists. There were seven way stations inside South Vietnam.

Vo Bam's infiltration party walked four days just to reach the last relay station before the DMZ. That part of the inspection was easy, since within the Democratic Republic the Chu unit had the use of trucks, thirty horses, and three elephants to move food and the heaviest equipment. Crossing the DMZ and Route 9 was done at night, and the infiltrators watched breathlessly for a long time before setting out. Like the others, Bam trod over a sheet of plastic, which the patrol then reeled up behind them. Bam found the "stations" were merely places where people had agreed to meet. Colonel Bam returned to Hanoi convinced the 301st Battalion needed more men to work effectively. Hanoi readily agreed.

Disaster struck near Khe Sanh early in 1960. North Vietnamese parties were accustomed to cutting across Route 9 there, where coffee plantations permitted a concealed approach to the road that was not too arduous. One night the men of Station 5, worn out from a lengthy trek, marched through a plantation but left behind a bundle of four French-made MAS-36 rifles. The next morning the woman owner of the plantation and her overseer, walking their grounds, found the lost rifles. South Vietnamese troops moved to Khe Sanh and began a regiment-sized clearing operation. The 559th Group instantly halted all infiltration activity.

For Hanoi the halt could not have come at a worse time. The Lao Dong Party stood on the verge of deciding to support creation of a National Liberation Front (NLF) in South Vietnam. Southern guerrilla forces were recovering from recent losses, and had picked up their pace of kidnappings and assassinations of Diem government local officials. Le Duan, Politburo member for the South, advised that the Viet Cong had become strong enough to carry out guerrilla warfare in South Vietnam's Central Highlands, but could move to open armed struggle in the region of the DMZ and the old imperial capital of Hue.

Hanoi's leaders gave new orders when Colonel Vo Bam reported on the obstacles facing the 301st Battalion. It was Le Duan who suggested finding a passage that would not attract Saigon's attention. Vo Bam realized a supply route could also run down the *western* side of the Truong Son mountain range, the Annamites, entering South Vietnamese territory from Laos, avoiding all the problems of DMZ infiltration. Such a route simply required going through the panhandle of lower Laos. By January 1961 southern organizer Tran Luong could tell Vo Bam he had instructions to clear the idea with the Laotian Communist Party.

While political decisions were made, the 559th Group continued to solve practical difficulties. One of the biggest was ensuring weapons arrived in good condition despite monsoons or other weather and physical conditions. The group took over a former French post in Kim Lu village at the edge of Hanoi. With a central blockhouse and some smaller bunkers, Kim Lu became the warehouse for supplies to The Trail. As for weapons in good working order, Vo Bam's group, about to begin experiments, heard that a cache of old French weapons had just been found that the former adversaries had left behind; these could be used for the new guerrilla movement. The 559th asked for some of the guns and ammunition, then analyzed how these had been packed. Vo Bam's men carefully packed some of their own equipment the same way, then deliberately dropped the boxes into the waters of an isolated river. Fished up a month later, the bullets and guns were found in fine condition. There was no rust. Vo Bam had solved his packing problems.

In early 1961, with approval from the Laotian Communists, Hanoi made its final decision to extend The Trail into Laos. Vo Bam's transport group would march in behind a major Vietnam People's Army foray that removed any threat from Royal Laotian Army outposts in the region. The Dien Bien

Phu campaign happened to be the closest available model to what the VPA was about to do. There was also a parallel in the French war for a military drive through lower Laos. That was the 1953–1954 march of two Viet Minh regiments through Laos into Cambodia. The troops had crossed the Annamite Mountains, trekked through lower Laos, and finally entered northern Cambodia. The path taken by this expedition—passes used, staging areas, water points, roads and trails followed—provided the first kernel of knowledge the VPA used to create its Ho Chi Minh Trail, known in Vietnam as the "Truong Son Strategic Supply Route." Once Vo Bam and the other VPA unit commanders called for the earlier records, the data were revealed to them. Vietnam People's Army combat units duly swept into lower Laos in the spring of 1961. Major Laotian army garrisons were left in place, but the countryside between them passed into the hands of the North Vietnamese.

Leaders of the 301st Battalion soon reconfigured The Trail to pass through Laos. Conditions were harsh and remained so. Nguyen Danh spent three years with the 301st, suffering through the forest clearing "stations," miserable monsoons, the malaria, the constant hunger. There were no houses, tents, or even roofs, except at the base camps in North Vietnam. Food invariably consisted of rice and salt, nothing more. Letters home were collected but once a month, and were trekked back to the post office at Quang Binh; replies posted to bo dois on The Trail were returned care of the postmaster at Quang Binh. Exchange of a letter could take a season or more. Yet morale stayed high. Danh and the other men of the 559th Transport Group felt they were liberating the South.

The weapons and supplies beginning to filter around Vietnam's Demilitarized Zone were not all that much for desperate southern cadres beset by President Diem's troops. By Nguyen Dang's own account the first shipment could not have amounted to more than a few hundred rifles plus ammunition. Among an active Viet Cong resistance movement of perhaps 5,000, spread throughout South Vietnam, the effect was psychological more than anything else. Arrival of new weapons had a direct impact only in the regions where the equipment was distributed—below the DMZ and in the provinces just south—Thua Thien, Quang Nam, Quang Ngai, and those of the Central Highlands. There the Viet Cong made a start with raids on outposts and isolated units of the ARVN.

As early as January 1960 the American consul at Hue encountered widespread fear when he visited Kontum in the highlands. The chief of Kontum's northernmost district told the consul that within a three-week period Viet Cong had persuaded to move or forcibly ejected several tribal villages in his area. The Kontum Province militia chief and the district boss both felt the Viet Cong were establishing a big jungle base in the mountains beyond the point where Route 14, the high road through the Central Highlands, wound to its end. The American official tried to see for himself, but could not reach the village at the end of the road, because a militia unit

Thus it proved ironic when South Vietnamese tried to recruit Montagnard Ranger companies for a border force. U.S. documents of the period disclose several instances of Vietnamese officials expressing contempt for the very peoples they expected to bring to the defense of their flag. It was much more likely the Montagnards would be attracted by the siren songs of men palpably different from Vietnamese. And so it proved to be.

By 1961 it was the Viet Cong who were making inroads among the hill tribes. One Montagnard had been made a vice president of the National Liberation Front. He headed a popular front movement designed to incorporate Montagnards into the resistance. Already two Viet Cong battalions in Quang Ngai Province were composed mostly of tribal volunteers. David A. Nuttle, an American and civilian expert with International Voluntary Services (IVS), had developed a strong interest in the hill tribes and saw the Liberation Front making its inroads. A private relief organization such as IVS could do little, but Nuttle visited one tribe, the Rhadé in the highlands above Ban Me Thuot, and returned determined to get something done. Nuttle felt the United States ought to counter the NLF initiatives, and he took the idea to an American he knew in Saigon.

Nuttle's Saigon contact was Gilbert Layton, a marine colonel on loan to the CIA as chief of paramilitary operations for the Saigon station. Layton saw merit in Nuttle's argument that Montagnards might well respond to a security program clearly linked to the United States rather than the Saigon regime. The two cooked up the concept of a village defense program funded by the CIA, while Nuttle appeared before Ambassador Nolting's mission council to argue that population relocation and other methods being discussed, such as mining the trails, would not work in the mountains or with the Montagnards. William E. Colby, CIA station chief, backed the program and guided it through the bureaucratic maze. One key hurdle was gaining the acquiescence of Diem's brother, Interior Minister Ngo Dinh Nhu.

At length all agreed there could be a pilot project to show whether a countrywide program was feasible. A village of the Rhadé tribe northeast of Ban Me Thuot was selected for the experiment. In October 1961 Nuttle, a CIA officer, and an army Special Forces medical expert traveled to meet the village elders. While the medic treated assorted ailments, Nuttle and the CIA paramilitary officer attempted to convince the elders during a tribal council session that lasted for more than two weeks. Nuttle, who had helped the Rhadé with agricultural projects, hunted and fished with them, and earned the distinction of a tribal name, was the key figure in winning Montagnard trust.

The CIA got help from the U.S. Army's Special Forces beginning in early 1962. Teams of Green Berets came to South Vietnam, initially from U.S. bases on Okinawa. Captain Ron Shackleton and half of Detachment A-113 became the first Green Berets involved in the village defense program. The team stayed in a CIA safe house in Saigon and then flew up to Ban Me Thuot in an unmarked C-46 aircraft with a Nationalist Chinese crew.

Village defense in the highlands became a spectacular success story. More and more surrounding villages were incorporated in a defense zone. By April 1962 there were already 975 Rhadé soldiers protecting 14,000 villagers. The program quickly spread to all of South Vietnam's corps areas, recruiting other tribes, minorities, and religious sects. By mid-1962 U.S. embassy officials were appealing for an extra 400 tons of rice to feed more than 100,000 Montagnards in protected settlements. Ngo Dinh Nhu visited the protected zone and pronounced himself impressed. South Vietnamese interest was confirmed when ARVN became much more assertive about its prerogative, teaming its own Special Forces, the LLDB (Luc Luong Dac Biet), in each camp, with command vested in the ARVN Special Forces team leader.

The National Liberation Front quickly took notice of the CIA–Special Forces Montagnard program. In June a Viet Cong unit attacked a village that had joined the Montagnards but had yet to be provided with anything more than its own weapons. North Vietnamese and Liberation Front sensitivity about the Montagnard program was dramatically demonstrated by the battle, for after the tribesmen defeated the Viet Cong assault using just bows and arrows, traps, and knives, the Viet Cong came back two days later with decisively superior force. They took the village and massacred every male. The NLF show of force backfired, however, when the Sedang tribe was infuriated by the Viet Cong action and rallied to the CIA paramilitary force in even greater numbers. There were soon two battalions of Sedang "mobile strike forces," the name given to more heavily armed Montagnard units that operated from the Special Forces camps and backed up the village defense militias.

The mobile strike forces became the backbone of the Montagnard program. Bill Colby of the CIA christened them "Civilian Irregular Defense Groups" (CIDGs), and thus they would be known through most of the war, even when the Montagnard program was taken out of the CIA and put squarely into Special Forces. The tribesmen were called "strikers" or simply CIDGs. Usually there were several CIDG companies in a mobile strike force. Green Berets often led the CIDG patrols in the field, with Vietnamese LLDB counterparts commanding in name but not necessarily in battle. Special Forces and CIA also acquired a taste for the fighting prowess of certain tribes, such as the Nung, who originated from the Vietnamese-Chinese border region and had been stalwarts of the Viet Minh during the anti-French war. Special Forces created extra scout units of these Nung under direct American command to stiffen the CIDGs and carry out long-range patrols, such as watches on The Trail. There were 300 Nung scouts by 1963, together with 6,000 CIDG strikers and 19,000 village militia.

For Washington the evident success of the Montagnard program was one of the most promising developments of that time. An alternative pacification program in the lowlands, called Operation Sunrise and involving population resettlement in strategic hamlets, an effort pushed by Ngo Dinh Nhu, had opened to fanfare but then ground to a halt in a morass of corruption and lack of initiative. In September 1962 General Taylor told a meeting of the NSC Special Group (CI) that there had to be better coordination between the Montagnard irregulars and the South Vietnamese Army. This was achieved by Operation "Switchback," which transferred the CIDG program to the U.S. Army, specifically Special Forces. The potential was considerable. As the State Department's deputy chief of the interagency Vietnam task force put it in a comprehensive trip report of December 1962, "As the Montagnard trail watchers and strike forces get into action, I think we will get a better picture of what is happening on the plateau. If all goes well, these forces may in fact pretty well stop infiltration across the highlands." On another occasion General Paul D. Harkins, commander of the new Military Assistance Command Vietnam (MACV), remarked when meeting President Diem that with the Montagnards plus recently opened Special Forces camps at Aloui and Ashau in the Annamite foothills, North Vietnamese access across the border would certainly be blocked.

Among those not convinced, however, was President Ngo Dinh Diem. This became apparent when Maxwell Taylor met with the Saigon leader. According to the cabled account of their September 11, 1962, conversation, Diem "expressed doubt that, by themselves, [Montagnards] could be entrusted with defense of borders and spoke at length of their child-like nature and lack of initiative and leadership qualities." Taylor countered that even if only effective as guards, the Montagnards "would help considerably in solution of [the] border problem."

On the other side of the Lao border there were similar programs, as well as the same doubts and debates. In lower Laos resided a variety of tribes whose members spoke languages that were variants of Mon or Khmer. Laotians called them Lao Theung—this was a descriptive term or classification, not the name of a tribe. The pejorative name was "Kha." As early as 1960 Green Berets in Laos with Project White Star had made efforts to organize units of irregulars from the tribes with some success. A dozen companies of Lao Theung were under arms by 1962 as part of the Army's Project Pincushion, funded by the CIA. Later there was a direct CIA effort called Project Hardnose, which tried to capitalize on the ethnic mobilization to create scout teams to radiate into the Hanoi-controlled hinterland.

The Lao Theung had little sense of ethnic identity or nationality, however. Until French times, tribal villages had not even had headmen, and even in the 1960s, tribesmen regularly migrated as itinerant laborers. Some Lao Theung had a reputation for timidity and placidity. Moreover, the Pathet Lao had already made inroads among the Lao Theung, and both Savannakhet and Saravane Provinces had elected Pathet Lao candidates who were Lao Theung to the Laotian National Assembly. A Lao Theung would number among the senior Pathet Lao leadership right into the 1970s. The old man who served as guide for Colonel Vo Bam in the original VPA survey party that had set up The Trail had been a Lao Theung.

Green Beret advisers as widely distributed as Joe Garner, at Paksane, and William T. Craig, near Savannakhet, attest to the difficulties of working with the tribes. Their problems were complicated by corruption among lowland

Lao officers who held commands in the districts, and by the rapid rotation of the Americans, who served only six months before leaving. William B. Rosson, then a colonel and one of the army's true Southeast Asia experts, visited the Bolovens Plateau during this period to inspect the Lao Theung irregulars and came away convinced the units were worthless.

Nevertheless, both the army and the CIA continued to push the Lao Theung toward involvement. Units were created, and some became relatively effective. It was as a result of this effort that the Green Berets got their first direct look at North Vietnamese troops on The Trail. This happened during a July 1962 patrol led by Captain Jerry King. The scouts were in the jungle, only about six miles from Tchepone, looking for a suitable campsite, when they heard noises behind them. Suddenly a force of Vietnam People's Army soldiers appeared, marching up the track the Lao-American patrol had just stepped off of. King estimated Vietnamese strength as the better part of a battalion. The VPA promptly halted, then bedded down for the night themselves, leaving King's patrol no alternative but to stay right where they were. The Americans and their companions spent a terrifying night before the VPA *bo dois* moved off the next morning.

This encounter near Tchepone could be seen as a metaphor for the dance of death the United States and the DRV were beginning along The Trail. Pirouetting around each other, Washington and Hanoi had yet to land telling blows, but they were coming closer every day. In fact, events in Laos led Washington almost to make the open intervention some had advocated in 1961. It would be characteristic of the Vietnam War that this new push for intervention came in the context of another negotiated accord neutralizing Laos.

For months on end, while the Kennedy people tried to energize Ngo Dinh Diem's government, the president also tried to dampen the crisis in Laos. He sent Democratic patrician Averell Harriman to Geneva to participate in multilateral negotiations about Laos. The administration's goal, according to Secretary of State Dean Rusk, was "we wanted an agreement that produced a neutral but independent Laos, an 'island of peace' in Southeast Asia that would be a buffer zone." Harriman, whom the president regarded as a sovereign entity, had the patience to endure hundreds of repetitive speeches and make some of his own. Likened to a crocodile, who could lie quiescent on a riverbank for hours on end, Harriman had been known to turn off his hearing aid when it seemed appropriate. That happened when CIA officials tried to explain to him why there could be no Laotian agreement because of their plans for the country. Actually John F. Kennedy had soured on the agency's favorite, Laotian general Phoumi Nosavan, and it was the president's willingness to countenance a renewed neutralist government of Laos that made it possible for Harriman to negotiate at all.

At least Geneva was a pleasant setting for diplomatic drudgery. Its lakes sparkled on a clear day, glistening in the vibrant mountain air of Switzerland, and there seemed no dearth of nice restaurants and Swiss hospitality. In fact, the main recollections of both Harriman's top assistants concern ambience. William H. Sullivan, the professional diplomat on Harriman's delegation, took some Russians to a piano bar late at night, after dinner at his apartment. As the diplomats partied, Sullivan learned the next day, the Russian spy apparatus in Geneva had gone frantic in fear their diplomats were defecting, and had even invaded Sullivan's apartment.

Chester L. Cooper's moment came near the end of the conference. He and Sullivan went to a Chinese reception held to mark success in the negotiations. Cooper, Harriman's CIA specialist, had spent World War II with the Office of Strategic Services in China and had tried to learn the language. Now, suddenly, Chinese foreign minister Chen Yi spoke earnestly to Cooper for a good half hour, having dismissed their interpreter after mistakenly deciding the CIA man's wartime Chinese was current enough to understand their tête-à-tête. Cooper stood rooted to the spot, unable to disengage himself from the private talk, even though he could not understand a word that was said. Many other diplomats, curious as to what Chen Yi was telling this American, drifted over to hear the talk Chet Cooper could not understand. Cooper cringed at the thought of the reporting cables all those diplomats would send home after the party.

"Ave" Harriman, who came from one of America's railroad mogul families, had been governor of New York State, and also had been Franklin D. Roosevelt's ambassador to the Soviet Union during the final years of World War II, had a fine eye for receptions. The ones at Geneva were the sincere celebrations of people who thought they had accomplished something. The major advances in fact were made during the spring and early summer of 1962. In structure, the new Geneva accords were partly a series of political actions, partly a set of declarations and international agreements.

In late June, Laotian prince Souvanna Phouma presented a new national unity cabinet to the king. Souvanna also joined his Laotian Communist cousin, Prince Souphanouvong, and their relative Prince Boun Oum, representing General Phoumi, in a declaration of nonbelligerence. Then the Souvanna government declared its neutrality, recognized by the Geneva powers in a document of July 9. That was followed by an international agreement on July 23 that prohibited foreign military aid to Laos, promised that foreign troops would be withdrawn from the country, and pledged to respect Laotian neutrality. Dean Rusk joined Harriman in signing for the United States. The Democratic Republic of Vietnam was also a signatory of the agreement, as were both China and the Soviet Union.

These diplomatic developments occurred in tandem with certain military actions in Laos itself. The provisional cease-fire in effect since the early months of John Kennedy's presidency would be punctuated by lapses, some triggered by the Pathet Lao, others by Phoumi forces. The most serious fighting began in January 1962 at Nam Tha in northern Laos. Pathet Lao, with North Vietnamese advisers from VPA Group 959, besieged a large garrison loyal to Phoumi Nosavan. The siege continued for several months, during which Harriman visited Laos in company with William Sullivan, meeting with Souvanna, Souphanouvong, and Phoumi as well. Shortly after Harriman's departure, the Pathet Lao attacked again. Most of Phoumi's troops ran away; the rest put up little resistance. The battle rendered an abject demonstration of the consequences of failure to reach a settlement.

In Washington, the fall of Nam Tha spelled crisis. As in 1961, President Kennedy prepared to signal his determination by sending marines to Thailand's side of the Mekong, plus putting warships in the South China Sea. There followed a rerun of the debate over implementation of SEATO Plan 5, too. Now ensconced at the head of the State Department's Policy Planning Council, Walt Rostow pressed for occupation of lower Laos by U.S. troops. He urged other forceful actions as well. Commenting on State Department intelligence immediately after the demise of the Lao garrison, Rostow told Roger Hilsman, State's chief intelligence official, that the United States "must put forces opposite Hanoi" and that "we must be prepared to go ahead and not just bluff." Dr. Rostow's notion of a suitable signal, according to Hilsman, involved the U.S. Air Force counterinsurgency unit Jungle Jim. This secret unit, and its companion covert bomber force Farmgate, were in South Vietnam ostensibly to train Vietnamese pilots.

"Jungle Jim ought to go quietly to North Vietnam," Hilsman noted of Rostow's idea, "and take out some railroad tracks . . . and [in Laos] plaster Tchepone."

Advocates of Plan 5 Plus, the lower Laos occupation, pushed hard in the dickering in Washington. With Walt Rostow's aggressive rhetoric he lost key allies, among them Maxwell Taylor, who now expressed doubt as to the suitability of Plan 5 or its more radical variant. On the other hand, some military officers, especially in the air force, supported the forceful option. President Kennedy kept the option alive at a White House meeting on May 10. After another such session two weeks later he had McGeorge Bundy sign NSAM-157, which ordered preparations for the eventuality of a breakdown in the Laotian cease-fire. One of the two major items to be planned was the "holding and recapture of the panhandle of Laos from Thakhek to the southern frontier with Thai, Vietnamese, or U.S. forces."

Roger Hilsman later wrote, describing U.S. deliberations in this episode, "The debate was taut and tense, and some of the participants may have succumbed to feelings of vindictiveness."

One blow in Washington's bureaucratic war would be a study just finished by the RAND Corporation and that Hilsman circulated. The paper argued that unless Laos was defended forward—at the Annamite chain, right along its border with Vietnam—the Pathet Lao and Hanoi could pour in so many troops they would challenge any practicable defense. Separately, as director of State's Bureau of Intelligence and Research, Hilsman concurred in a Special National Intelligence Estimate prepared at the CIA. That estimate predicted that the occupation of lower Laos, and other, even more forceful policies, would almost certainly lead to new intervention on the other side by either or both the Soviets and the Chinese.

Dean Rusk prepared for military action to defend the Mekong valley. Rusk saw that as contributing to the Geneva negotiations by backing the diplomats with military muscle. Also, if the valley and its big towns like Pakse and Savannakhet were to be lost, there would be little to save through negotiations anyway. Willingness to countenance action made Rusk a potential ally to advocates of going beyond SEATO Plan 5. State Department contingency plans existed in draft form by the end of May 1962. They included language for a congressional resolution, similar to the Tonkin Gulf Resolution of 1964, authorizing the president to resort to armed force in Southeast Asia.

Ironically, it would be the Pentagon that blocked these energetic measures, even though the Joint Chiefs were on record with the opinion that U.S. troops could save South Vietnam. Secretary of Defense Robert S. McNamara worried about military commitment in Indochina, given the Berlin crisis in Europe plus plans to strengthen U.S. forces in NATO. McNamara was also acutely aware that Thailand, through which U.S. troops in Laos would have to be supplied, lacked necessary transportation means. The JCS themselves favored a defense of all Laos—a larger solution—over any limited effort to fight in the Mekong valley.

These matters were thrashed out in early June, even as Souvanna Phouma and the Lao politicians put in place the elements of a new Geneva accord. The crucial meeting took place in Rusk's seventh-floor conference room at the State Department on June 12. Secretary McNamara mollified Rusk with the statement that he and the Joint Chiefs shared the concern for the Mekong "but felt it was unwise militarily to introduce U.S. forces for the sole purpose of occupying the valley." McNamara wanted to prepare a base for intervention in Thailand by building ports, roads, and railroads, using Pentagon money and army engineer units. The process would take six to eight months. There can be no doubt McNamara was correct—without this measure none of the force options would be physically possible. By the time the Thai improvements were made, however, the moment for U.S. intervention had passed.

In the meantime, McNamara would proceed with planning—as long as it remained planning—for military contingencies. These included bombing Laos, implementing Plan 5, the SEATO plan plus occupation of lower Laos, or portions thereof. As for the even more aggressive courses favored by those such as Walt Rostow, McNamara told the June 12 meeting, "The Defense Department is not currently pursuing the plan for an amphibious operation [against] North Vietnam at Vinh."

A session with President Kennedy the next day confirmed this basic stance. Intelligence presented JFK with a rather bleak picture, and he proved relieved not to have to make any decision about dispatch of U.S. troops at this time. The result was that the Geneva talks took their course, and fresh agreements eventuated.

The net effect of the Geneva negotiations would be to leave each side in the Laotian civil war in control of the areas they already had. In lower Laos that left the Pathet Lao and Vietnam People's Army in possession of The Trail. Hanoi's march South continued. Lower Laos, the Central Highlands, and the provinces of I Corps more and more became an arc of conflict, a fulcrum from which hung the issue of the Vietnam War.

Souphanouvong, the notorious Pathet Lao "Red Prince," had studied during the French colonial period to become a civil engineer. Eventually employed in public works, Prince Souphanouvong had actually supervised construction of parts of Route 9. In effect this gave the Vietnam People's Army access to detailed knowledge of the lay of the land in this area, while Bui Tin and others furnished knowledge of the people. Hanoi would not be blessed with such ideal circumstances in all the areas its Trail would have to reach. Moreover, much as had happened at Tchepone when the more westerly paths were being established, reaching into Vietnam's Central Highlands or the Laotian-Cambodian-Vietnamese triborder region meant outstripping the supply capacities of VPA units making the first treks into these regions.

It is not surprising that the VPA again turned to its 919th Military Air Transport Squadron. Starting in late March 1962 the VPA made flights into the triborder region and the Central Highlands, some close to South Vietnamese bases at Pleiku, with the apparent mission of parachuting supplies, personnel, or both to Viet Cong units in these areas. The flights were detected and tracked intermittently by American and South Vietnamese radar. American aircraft were unable to catch the planes from Hanoi, however, even after deployment of jet interceptors capable of rapid response. The purpose of the North Vietnamese flights remained a mystery.

In contrast there could be no doubt that the National Liberation Front forces throughout the arc of conflict were growing steadily more powerful. The Viet Cong attack on the Sedang tribe may have been a political fiasco, but it was also a clear token of gathering strength. The Geneva agreements brought no respite. Although all foreign forces were supposed to evacuate Laos under the accords, Hanoi withdrew only a handful of its troops, and those were mostly Group 959 advisers to the Pathet Lao. Colonel Vo Bam's Transport Group 559 remained in place, as did the VPA infantry screening The Trail. The march of infiltration groups down The Trail slowed but did not stop.

Washington expected no less. At the State Department, Roger Hilsman's intelligence analysts described the situation in an assessment for Averell Harriman that September. The report described U.S. Army estimates of VPA troop strength in Laos—the army found some covert withdrawals, but estimated Hanoi forces had been reduced only from 9,000 to about 7,500. Two VPA battalions had recoiled only as far as the Annamite mountain passes; in fact, one planted itself right at the Mu Gai Pass. In lower Laos an estimated two VPA battalions retained previous positions.

The most creative speculation as to the reasons why two VPA units remained around Saravane in lower Laos was advanced by Diem's brother Ngo Dinh Nhu. The occasion was a visit by the U.S. commander in chief in the Pacific in October 1962. Nhu told the visiting Americans he believed the People's Army units wanted to enter South Vietnam, except for some individuals who preferred to return to Hanoi, and that this was against the wishes of DRV leaders. Russia's agreement at Geneva not to provide further supplies for VPA forces in Laos, Nhu argued, complicated the situation by forcing Hanoi to supply these troops, which it did not want to do. Nhu believed Hanoi had previously decided these troops were not reliable, ordering them to Saravane as a sort of holding area. Nhu claimed the VPA units had sent emissaries to discuss their problems with him. However, other than this conversation with Admiral Harry D. Felt, there is no evidence the VPA troops around Saravane were anything except what they seemed, a screening force behind which Vo Bam was building his supply network.

There *were* indications, on the other hand, that Hanoi's supply arrangements for southernmost Laos were just beginning to function. The South Vietnamese had been sending scout teams into Laos since 1960, run out of Nha Trang by Colonel Tran Khac Kinh, deputy commander of ARVN Special Forces (this may have been where Nhu got the information he retailed to Admiral Felt). The program had been promising enough that before the end of 1961 the CIA had three paramilitary experts attached to it. In any case, in early 1963 in the Bolovens area, one of Kinh's teams was captured by the North Vietnamese. The ARVN radio operator was forced to transmit to headquarters, asking for supplies, many times more supplies than the commando team would ever have needed. The radioman managed to include a secret indicator showing he was working under duress. Nha Trang headquarters responded that the supplies would be sent; then the Americans arranged for air strikes on the coordinates. As a result, the VPA battalion suffered losses, and the ARVN commandos were able to escape. The South Vietnamese managed to reach the Laotian airfield at Attopeu, where they were picked up and brought to safety. These events demonstrated that while Hanoi was building up, The Trail was far from perfected.

In the Central Highlands the Green Berets were building up, too. Indeed, this 1962–1963 phase can be portrayed as a race between buildups. Strike forces and CIDG camps sprouted all over I and II Corps areas, and even north of Saigon in the III Corps area. More camps and strikers meant more American Green Berets to train and lead the CIDG units. Before 1963 was out, the Special Forces would have thirty-six field units called "A-Detachments"; four "B-Detachments," or command elements; and a "C-Detachment" logistics and support unit. The latter, with one of the command elements, was located on the Vietnamese coast at Nha Trang in II Corps. Nha Trang became headquarters of Special Forces Group Vietnam (Provisional), later the 5th Special Forces Group, the Green Beret high command. At this time there were 674 Green Berets assigned to the command, most of them with the Montagnard program.

In the meantime, on January 3, 1963, the Special Forces camp at Plei

Mrong, near Kontum, became the first to be attacked by the Viet Cong. The camp had been established a couple of months before, and a village defense program initiated just days prior to the battle. The action appears to have been an effort to disrupt Special Forces recruiting among the Jarai tribe. The Plei Mrong attack came while half the camp's strikers, plus a mobile strike force, were away on patrol. As became a feature of many similar battles, the attacking NLF must have had help from the inside, for someone had cut key barbed-wire barriers before the assault began. South Vietnamese commanders at II Corps headquarters refused to commit the available reserve at Kontum. Despite these disadvantages Plei Mrong managed to hold out through the night, and the Viet Cong faded away with the dawn. Four American Special Forces men were among the total of about 150 casualties in the action.

Plei Mrong would be the opening chord of an intricate contest with military, political, and psychological dimensions. During 1963 Viet Cong forces probed or shelled Special Forces camps with mortars some 94 times, they tried to infiltrate camps 11 times, and there were 374 contacts between CIDG units and the enemy. Throughout this period the CIA continued its transfer of executive authority over the Montagnard program to the army, completing the process in July. Also phased out was the old border patrol concept, responsibility for which officially passed to Special Forces in November. By then there were 76 posts along South Vietnam's periphery, manned by 3,860 troops. Special Forces consolidated these into about two dozen border projects that, in July 1964, employed more than 200 Green Berets leading 11,250 strikers. The border surveillance camps became a recognized feature of the Vietnam War.

Standard procedure for the Montagnard program was for Special Forces to open a camp where local conditions were desirable, recruitment possibilities were great, or the location was such that a military presence was necessary. Green Berets would move in with ARVN counterparts, make contacts among local tribesmen, and mobilize a village defense force and maybe some CIDG units. The Special Forces camp could be maintained indefinitely or closed out if the training mission were completed, local security deteriorated too much, or the troops were called away for some other purpose.

The border surveillance camps were maintained as a string of listening posts and launching points—*sonettes*, as the French would have put it. Most of the border camps were maintained over a long period, or at least until Special Forces were almost driven from them. Khe Sanh, a post to block Route 9 in from Tchepone, was opened as early as August 1962. Kham Duc, astride a key access to the coastal plain in Quang Tin Province, was opened in September 1963. A Shau and A Ro, blocking the paths to Da Nang and Hue, opened in March and June 1964, respectively. These were significant bases, radiating into the hinterland, or "Indian country," as Americans came to term it. Khe Sanh, for example, was garrisoned by five CIDG companies and a Nung platoon, an aggregate of about 750 troops. Kham Duc held more than 1,250 soldiers, including a mobile strike force. The only one of these camps ever to close would be A Ro, located so remotely in the Annamite foothills that Green Beret efforts there were very unproductive.

An unexpected factor also entered into the calculation. That was the overthrow of Ngo Dinh Diem by a military coup in November 1963. Over time the ARVN generals reached the point where they felt they could not stomach Diem anymore, and in the summer of 1963 they received encouragement from the U.S. government. The incessant talk of a coup, which had become a Saigon art form, reached fruition with the November 1 coup, followed the next day by the assassination of Diem and his brother Nhu. Hardly three weeks later, in Dallas on November 22, President John F. Kennedy was himself assassinated, with the result that new hands took over both the United States and South Vietnamese governments. Hanoi quickly realized that, whatever contempt he inspired, Diem's political stature was not matched by any of the South Vietnamese generals or their oligarchic allies. Thus the aftermath of the Diem coup seemed to Hanoi a moment of opportunity.

In December 1963 the Ninth Congress of the Central Committee of the Lao Dong Party took place in Hanoi. Le Duan and his pro-Chinese colleague Truong Chinh addressed the congress and advocated a party resolution that represented the culmination of earlier discussions about The Trail and its future. The resolution asserted that "We must have the capability to check and defeat the enemy in his 'special war.'" Hanoi's specific strategy was "to conduct a protracted war, relying mainly upon our own forces, and to combine political struggle and armed struggle," building gradually to a "general uprising," a mass popular revolt against Saigon's rule. A military buildup was implied in the resolution's determination to "build and develop . . . forces to gain victories in a short time." The resolution also adopted the most recent Le Duan line, emphasizing warfare ("armed struggle plays a direct and decisive role") over political action. In that respect,

> South Vietnam's mountainous area [the Central Highlands and Annamite chain] occupies an important strategic position. It offers favorable conditions for us to conduct a protracted struggle even in the most difficult situations. This is the area where we can build up a large armed force and annihilate many enemy troops. . . . We can also use the mountainous area as a stepping-stone to expand our activities to the lowlands.

Again, expansion of NLF forces was implied in this concept, and hinted once more where the resolution referred to the task for the DRV: "The North must bring into fuller play its role as the revolutionary base for the whole nation."

Right through 1963, as the CIA later observed, Hanoi had sent not only military and also political, security, economic, financial, and education specialists, but "essentially all the infiltrators were South Vietnamese who had been relocated in [the] North." That was about to change. Hanoi had determined to expand its objectives, and that entailed improving The Trail. Soon there was intelligence that Hanoi's engineers had restored the old French airstrip at Chavane in the Bolovens Plateau. There were also reports that the VPA's 919th Transport Squadron was running as many as four aircraft a day into Tchepone. At the same time, the United States and South Vietnam were rapidly building up their forces as well, and the Green Beret Montagnard program was an especial thorn in Hanoi's side. The situation was ripe for escalation; in fact, battle was about to be joined.

CHAPTER 4

The Battle Joined
1963–1964

Walt Rostow was known as a man of ideas. For several years before the 1960 elections Rostow had been a member of John F. Kennedy's personal brain trust. Rostow's best-known book, *The Stages of Economic Growth*, provided a theory that accounted for lagging development of the nations, many of them former colonial possessions, of Latin America, Africa, Asia, and the Middle East. Rostow also coined the term "new frontier" that Jack Kennedy adopted for a campaign slogan. Walt had a particular interest in Latin America and was undoubtedly gratified when President Kennedy created the Alliance for Progress to stimulate the countries there and made the southern hemisphere a showcase for the Peace Corps, of American volunteer assistants. Rostow was, and remained, an enthusiastic promoter of these programs through the Kennedy administration and beyond.

It is ironic that whereas Rostow promoted construction on one continent, he pushed equally hard for destruction on another. The Rostow who advised confrontation in Southeast Asia, the man of the Taylor-Rostow report and of SEATO Plan 5 Plus, was no aberration. Rather, his approach reflected a different side to the man of ideas. During the Eisenhower administration he had served as consultant to the Central Intelligence Agency, the army, and the National Security Council on psychological warfare and Cold War competition. He had a role in initiatives after the death of Stalin and disarmament proposals of the middle 1950s, always with a view to showing up the rigidities of communism. Rostow had been consulting on national security when limited-war theorists were concocting the practice of combining military and diplomatic maneuvers, an approach later given the name "coercive diplomacy." The policy of the United States with respect to North Vietnam was quintessential coercive diplomacy, and Rostow participated with gusto.

As the months wore on, however, Walt Rostow's place in the scheme of things changed. His visit to Vietnam with the Taylor-Rostow mission was almost the last function he performed as deputy national security adviser. In late November 1961, less than a year into the Kennedy presidency, the president reshuffled his foreign affairs lineup. Secretary of State Dean Rusk got a new deputy, George McGhee, a seasoned career diplomat who had previously headed Rusk's ideas unit called the Policy Planning Council. McGhee was Rusk's choice for chief policy planner, and had held the job only a few months when Kennedy's changes vacated the position. Rusk initially resisted JFK's offer of Rostow, but the choice *was* a logical one, and there was no gainsaying the president's determination to have his own man with a watching brief at State. Walt Rostow was happy to have an opportunity to reach beyond the day-to-day headaches of security affairs. At the Policy Planning Council he could put his hand to shaping broad approaches.

The change suited Walt Rostow just fine. Alternatives had been his business for many years, for the forty-four-year-old Rostow had been a crafter of options most of his professional career. The theories he espoused as a professor at the Massachusetts Institute of Technology were couched in terms of good and better alternatives for national economic development. These ideas he had honed in the years immediately following World War II, when Rostow had been a State Department economics planner for Germany and Austria, and after that an expert under the Swede Gunnar Myrdal at the Economic Commission for Europe. During the war itself Rostow had been engaged in determining optimum ways of applying airpower against Germany as a target analyst for the Eighth Air Force, and an Office of Strategic Services economist.

Not only was communism bad by Cold War lights, but also experience taught Rostow that immediate action was preferable to action later. The lesson of Munich—and here was one place where Walt Rostow held beliefs like Dean Rusk's, and where the two built their affinity for one another— was that waiting meant a more terrible war. Walt had been in England at the time of Munich, at Oxford, and he had had a front-row seat on pre-1939 debates over how to face up to the Fascist dictators. Common belief in the Cold War era was that fascism and communism were merely different forms of totalitarianism. As a nation labeled Communist, North Vietnam was infected by this plague. Looking for measures of coercive diplomacy that could be applied to the Vietnamese situation, Rostow worked from beliefs that precluded questioning assumptions.

George Ball, one of Walt's senior colleagues in Rusk's State Department, once told an interviewer that "Rostow took a position very early on and spent a good deal of time defending it." Similarly, David Halberstam, chronicler of the foibles of John Kennedy and Lyndon Johnson's best and brightest, found that insiders joked about "Air Marshal" Rostow or Walt's "SEATO Plan Six." One of Walt's academic brethren, Lucien Pye, another MIT professor whom Rostow considered a fellow soul on the subject of Vietnam, actually told a class one day, "You know, you don't sleep quite so well anymore when you know some of the people going to Washington."

Within weeks of arriving in Washington with the new Kennedy people, while he remained with the NSC staff, Walt Rostow made his views quite plain. Walt discussed Communists with a class at the U.S. Army Special Warfare School at Fort Bragg.

"They are the scavengers of the modernization process," Walt told the graduating Green Berets. "Communism is best understood as a disease of the transition to [economic] modernization."

Rostow adopted his view on Vietnam even before the Taylor-Rostow mission. He did not modify that view during years under Rusk at State. A review of Walt's memorandums for the period reveals considerable concern over lower Laos, the dangers of infiltration from the North, constant pressure for aggressive action, and an optimism that a whiff of grapeshot, as it were, would solve the whole problem. It was as if the United States, at this early point in the Vietnam conflict, was in a position to inflict a Dien Bien Phu on Ho Chi Minh.

Suggesting language Jack Kennedy could use at a May 1962 presidential news conference, Rostow would have had the president say, "I believe it is in the common interest that the leaders in Hanoi cease their aggression south of the Seventeenth Parallel." The very next day he told State's intelligence director that planes from the covert U.S. air unit in South Vietnam should go "quietly" and bomb Tchephone, as well as take out railroad tracks in North Vietnam. In language for a draft speech he apparently wrote in 1962, Rostow had the president declare he was sending American planes to leaflet Hanoi and areas of North Vietnam while other U.S. aircraft struck previously designated military targets. Jack Kennedy made no such speech, but Rostow's files are full of appreciative notes from colleagues. Some of them take the line that the rest of the government had gotten stuck trying to get to Rostow's level, and needed a crisis to make real changes in policy.

Another Rostow technique was to use seemingly alarming numerical comparisons. The policy planner did this with The Trail in November 1962, when Walt was arguing for military action in Laos to enforce the 1962 Geneva accords. In that case he took recent intelligence that in one month 500 North Vietnamese soldiers had trekked down The Trail. Rostow then postulated that Hanoi infiltrated *at least* that many *every* month (a figure well in excess of U.S. intelligence estimates, including retrospective ones). To measure the true impact of guerrillas, Walt went on, you needed to look at the burden on the counterinsurgent, the South Vietnamese. Rostow proposed that 15 or 20 soldiers were necessary to counteract the impact of each infiltrating guerrilla (military planners generally held 10 to 1 as a standard ratio for adequate security forces in relation to a guerrilla army). Dr. Rostow then concluded that the burden of Hanoi's infiltration was the equivalent of adding 7,500 men a month to the South Vietnamese military; that would have amounted to 90,000 a year (coincidentally, one option then before the Kennedy administration was whether to fund a 100,000 increment in ARVN forces).

Walt Rostow put this assessment in a November 28, 1962, memorandum to Secretary Rusk that was ostensibly about "Mikoyan and Laos"— that is, the Soviet responsibility for implementing the provisions of the 1962

Geneva arrangement. In February 1963 Rostow sent a copy of the same memorandum to Averell Harriman, then assistant secretary of state for the Far East. On Independence Day, July 4, Rostow sent Rusk a further paper that made a new version of the numerical argument and added, "It is evidently Ho's policy to sop up the improved performance in South Vietnam by this cheap device." By far the biggest thing to happen in Saigon in 1963 was the coup d'état that overthrew Ngo Dinh Diem and murdered him plus his brother Nhu. Dr. Rostow took that occasion, November 1, to draft a paper to which he attached yet another copy of the original "Mikoyan and Laos" paper. This time Rostow's circle included not only Rusk but also Harriman, Hilsman, Robert Johnson, and George Ball. Except for Ball, all of them had seen Walt Rostow's infiltration argument before.

The aggressive tenor of Dr. Rostow's advice on Southeast Asia is also widely displayed. Rostow would fasten upon particular options and come back to them repeatedly. Occupation of the Mekong valley, in the first years, was one of them. Forcing compliance with Geneva and thereby getting Hanoi out of lower Laos, thus halting infiltration, became a constant Rostow theme. On Independence Day 1963, Walt went so far as to assert that "if we are to have a showdown with Ho (and, implicitly, Mao) on this matter, we should bring it about before the Chinese Communists blow a nuclear device."

During the Diem coup, Rostow reiterated his argument that Ho Chi Minh was getting by on cheap alternatives—Hanoi's strategy "is explicitly based on the fact that he has been able to keep the war going at little cost." Rostow sounded the alarm, but also made a promise:

> [I]t is difficult, if not impossible, to win a guerrilla war with an open frontier. . . . A cessation of infiltration would not end the war in a day; but I am confident that, without steady support, the strictly domestic aspects of the Viet Cong effort could be dealt with in a reasonably short period of time.

Such generalizations were mixed with references, divorced from political or historical perspective, to numerous guerrilla wars and revolutions since World War II. In this particular case the Greek Civil War was held up as the example. In February 1964 Dr. Rostow asked that open borders be made the object of U.S. action. Again employing his alarming projection of the burden of guerrilla ratios, Rostow wrote that "the problem of the illegal crossing of frontiers is made critical by the extraordinary economics of guerrilla warfare."

At the apex of Rostow's recipe was direct action against the North. Again the theme is woven through Dr. Rostow's work from very early on. Typically, on January 10, 1964, Rostow warned Secretary Rusk that "forces are converging which might well produce the greatest setback to U.S. interests on the world scene in many years." The proper response? "I return . . . to the concept of a direct political-military showdown with Hanoi." To William

P. Bundy, transferring from the Pentagon to State as the new assistant secretary for the Far East, Rostow insisted he had "advocated that we adopt a program of politico-military showdown." Again to Bundy, "(only)," on May 19: "*we could trigger a North Viet Nam operation any time we were ready to go.*" When Secretary of Defense McNamara listed intervention as an alternative in his reports to the president, Walt chimed in, referring to the "McNamara Option Three (or Rostow) policy." During early June Rostow supplied another draft presidential speech justifying forceful action, and on June 11 he wrote Bill Bundy, "diplomacy can only be truly effective once the President is committed to a confrontation."

Walt Rostow's aggressive posture eventually got him in trouble with Lyndon Baines Johnson, who came to the presidency in November 1963. Facing an election in 1964, President Johnson wanted to project a measured but firm attitude toward Vietnam, in contrast to the shrill, increasingly hysterical rhetoric of Republican candidates. Without implying particular U.S. measures, Johnson tried to warn Hanoi in a speech, saying North Vietnam had engaged in a "deeply dangerous game." Walt Rostow had been talking to journalists over several weeks, and some, among them the influential Joseph Alsop, read Rostow's remarks and Saigon rumors as an implicit threat of action against Hanoi. The upshot became an angry presidential phone call to Rostow, then in Aspen, Colorado, on March 4, 1964.

Lyndon Johnson's call got Walt out of the bathtub, where he was no doubt relaxing after a busy afternoon on the slopes. LBJ wanted to know what reporters Rostow had been talking to, advised the idea man not to talk to reporters anyway, then made a second point:

"The President doesn't know the position of the administration," Johnson said about Vietnam policy, "so you can't know it."

Dr. Rostow apologized profusely for the "misunderstanding," insisting he had not been trying to sandbag LBJ into any position, but within State he continued to press his preferences. In 1962 Rostow had advocated "limited" military options directly linked to The Trail and Hanoi's infiltration South. Walt Rostow returned to this theme in early 1964, to suggest maneuvers that could gain leverage for the United States should there be a new international conference to revisit the Geneva accords on Laos.

The military scenario Dr. Rostow proposed turned out to be quite explicit:

> We should begin a series of unacknowledged attacks against installations in the panhandle [of Laos] such as Muong Nong, Muong Phine and eventually [the] Mu Gia [Pass], at the North Vietnamese–Lao border. We can certainly drag out the preliminaries for such a Southeast Asian conference while these actions are in train. Once we agree to the conference itself, we could then slide our attacks across into the truck marshalling yards in North Vietnam, the assembly points . . . and similar logistics targets directly associated with the North Vietnamese infiltrations.

A further coercive signal could be timed to coincide with the initial visit to Hanoi by Canadian Blair Seaborn of the International Control Commission. That would be a second ("unacknowledged") attack—evidently the first had already been carried out by CIA-supported Hmong special guerrilla units—at the major Vietnam People's Army staging base in northern Laos.

During this same period, while the State Department was preparing secret instructions for Seaborn, who had agreed to deliver a message to Hanoi, Walt Rostow contended that "our only real choice in Laos is a vigorous response now, as against a much greater commitment later, unless we are prepared to accept the loss of all of Laos." The policy planner recommended that U.S. troops be put into the Mekong valley. It was in the last days before the departure of Seaborn that Rostow penned, in a memo suggestively titled "The Trigger: A 'Dear Brutus' View," his disturbing declaration that the United States could have a North Vietnam operation anytime it was ready to go.

On May 24, 1964, Walt Rostow contributed a lengthy analysis of possible "intermediate ranges of military action." Here Rostow charged that the perception of contemplated military moves as large, open-ended commitments was an obstacle to decision. He therefore favored smaller moves "directly related to the problems at hand . . . that could be readily terminated." The first possibility, "which has often been discussed," was bombing of the supply routes, The Trail. A second initiative could be the insertion of commando teams "to mine roads and bridges." The next level on the escalation ladder was "a screening force based on Route 9, from the Mekong to the sea, blocking all major movement and obstructing infiltration by individuals." An alternative could be airborne raids to occupy Trail segments for short periods, or there could be "a more enduring occupation of key terrain through an airhead operation of perhaps division size." Such a force could patrol extensively around itself to cut additional infiltration routes and "would offer several attractions."

Almost the identical phrases appear in the planning documents that preceded the French Army decision to occupy Dien Bien Phu.

In 1964, ten years after Dien Bien Phu, Walt Rostow's notion of a suitable objective for an airhead to block The Trail was Tchepone: "The political static of putting a division in Tchepone would be no more than for putting a battalion or two along the Laos bank of the Mekong." American troops could depend on the nearby airfield for their supplies while radiating into the surrounding area.

Ten days after his floating the idea of a Tchepone operation—in fact, on June 6, 1964, the day an American warplane was first shot down over Laos—Walt Rostow sent an extensive paper on Southeast Asia direct to President Johnson. Once more using his proposition (built on guerrilla force ratios) that infiltration made warfare cheap for Hanoi, Rostow pressed his case. "Unless U.S. forces are located in the Laos corridor, below the seventeenth parallel," Dr. Rostow wrote, "that corridor will continue to be used as a major route of infiltration."

In his retrospective work that is partially a memoir, *The Diffusion of Power*, Walt Rostow continued to profess the ideas he had at the time. He went so far as to reprint the bulk of the "Mikoyan and Laos" memorandum of 1962. Among passages *left out* of that published version are those in which Rostow advocated "a serious politico-military scenario designed to force the issue of infiltration," and an entire postulated series of events leading to "initially modest" air attacks on "selected North Vietnamese targets"—in this case, transport and power stations. Rostow also chose to delete a sentence from his conclusion of 1962: "No such scenario should be set in motion unless we are clear that we are prepared to back our play to the limit."

The context of Rostow's actions is also significant. For example, "Mikoyan and Laos" went to Dean Rusk the day before Rusk and the president were to meet Soviet foreign minister Anastas I. Mikoyan. Walt's main point at the time, aside from forcing the issue of The Trail, was to get the administration to pressure the Soviets to force Hanoi's withdrawal from Laos.* The Rostow memorandum also followed immediately on an incident over Laos in which an Air America supply plane was shot down by Pathet Lao forces.

Retrospectively, Rostow writes that this November 1962 paper was the *first time* "in almost a year" he formally addressed Southeast Asian problems. That is not accurate. Walt had taken an active role in May 1962 discussions over intervention in Laos, including repeated papers sent to Rusk on North Vietnam and Laos, and a draft presidential speech. Recipients of Rostow comments on Vietnam or Laos between November 1961 and that month in 1962 also included President Kennedy, Harriman, and the then ambassador to South Vietnam, Frederick Nolting, who received a list of recommendations for action worked up by Rostow's staff. Walt wrote Nolting on September 9, 1962: "I do have the personal feeling, based on the indicators I have seen, that we may in the next few months be approaching the real turning point of the struggle."

Other Rostow contributions to the policy debate on Southeast Asia show similar evidence of close calculation. He repeatedly circulated the "Mikoyan and Laos" paper, each time to a wider circle of officials. In terms of timing,

*At a summit conference in Vienna in the summer of 1961 Soviet leader Nikita S. Khrushchev had told John Kennedy that Laos ought not to be an issue between the superpowers. Thereafter, meeting in Rome that fall, Averell Harriman and Russian diplomat Georgi Pushkin reached a private understanding that the Soviet Union would help enforce a Laos agreement. This understanding lay behind American acquiescence in the Geneva accords of 1962. The Russians, to our present knowledge, never did live up to their part under the Pushkin understanding. It is not known whether the Pushkin negotiation was not authorized by Moscow, whether Moscow could not deliver Vietnamese performance, or if Moscow simply made no effort to enforce the Geneva accords. However, the Royal Laotian government, faced with Pathet Lao intransigence, also did not comply with the accords, and the United States, discounting North Vietnamese compliance, covertly continued to support its Hmong paramilitary army.

Harriman got a memo just before heading for London to try setting up meetings with Soviet officials, in an attempt to demand Moscow enforce on Hanoi compliance with the Geneva accord. Not only did Rusk get one the day before his scheduled meeting with Mikoyan, he also received another Rostow paper, on Independence Day. More Rostow missives were penned on the occasions of the Diem overthrow, the coup that brought to power General Nguyen Khanh, the shoot-down of the first U.S. combat aircraft over Laos, and the Gulf of Tonkin incidents. Like a bulldog, Walt Rostow took a position and would not let go. He was determined to be heard. "I regarded continued use of the infiltration trails as a firebell in the night," Rostow recounts in *The Diffusion of Power.* In pursuit of a U.S. response, Dr. Rostow's advice, far from what is expected of a policy planner, often got quite tactical.

This Rostow tendency again manifested itself when U.S. destroyers in August thought themselves under attack off the Vietnamese coast. That was a night of firebells, and Walt Rostow happened to be at the White House then, too, where Mac Bundy asked him to help presidential speechwriter Horace Busby with a speech LBJ intended to use at Syracuse University the next day. Rostow pulled out the draft speech he had sent President Johnson with his long memorandum in June, a draft that articulated a policy of not permitting privileged sanctuaries in this war. For the president's speech in Syracuse, Rostow helped with overblown Cold War logic. "The challenge we face in Southeast Asia today," President Johnson would say, "is the same challenge that we have met with strength in Greece and Turkey, in Berlin and Korea, in Lebanon and Cuba." The president's peroration, sounding very much like the Rostow draft, was this: "There can be no peace by aggression and no immunity from reply."

In the immediate aftermath of the navy's assertion that its destroyers had been attacked a second time in the Gulf of Tonkin, Rostow restricted himself to commenting upon Hanoi's supposed motives in this action, but within days he was back to his preferences. On August 10 he sent a fresh memorandum to Secretary Rusk. Here Dr. Rostow argued it was "worth considering whether we should not put a substantial U.S.-[South Vietnamese] force to operate out of the Tchepone area, to be supplied by Route 9 (and the Tchepone airfield) from the Vietnam side." Walt Rostow's stream had become a drumbeat.

W alt Rostow did not make his arguments in isolation. There were plenty of people of influence in Washington, Honolulu, Saigon, and Vientiane. Any number held similar points of view. Henry Cabot Lodge, ambassador in Saigon during 1963–1964, favored strong action, and an actual program of covert operations against Hanoi had been put in place. Dean Rusk also took a hard line, as did McGeorge Bundy at the National Security Council and Maxwell D. Taylor, chairman of the Joint Chiefs of Staff. If there was a Vietnam option that suffered from lack of defenders it was not Rostow's offensive action, it was withdrawal, which, when mentioned at all, was held up as the horrible alternative that must compel action.

Moderate voices were few and belonged to less exalted officials or ones not listened to. George Ball is the most frequently remembered dissenter on Vietnam policy during this period. Ball was Rusk's undersecretary; he had witnessed the French debacle at Dien Bien Phu as a lawyer working with the French on economic integration of Europe. Ball, writes Robert McNamara, "was recognized as having a strong European bias" so that "Dean, Mac, and I treated his views about Vietnam guardedly." The two H's—Harriman and Hilsman—both relative moderates, were progressively eased out of power. Hilsman, too closely identified with the Kennedys, had also made many enemies, particularly in the months before the Diem coup. Harriman's presence worried Lyndon Johnson, who sent the New York Democrat off as ambassador-at-large in the summer of 1965.

Also leery of Harriman was the State Department's desk officer for Laos and Cambodia, Norman B. Hannah. His recollection is that Harriman and Hilsman crafted an approach that sanctioned violation of the Geneva accords on Laos on the basis of some tacit understanding that Vietnamese involvement would not exceed that which existed in July 1962. But intelligence from Hilsman's unit at State would be among the first to indicate that Hanoi was not pulling out of Laos. These reports, considered at a high level in the Kennedy administration, led to the hedged policy of observing Geneva on the surface while secretly pursuing the CIA's paramilitary operation with the Hmong. Whatever the tacit understanding, it lasted no later than the summer of 1963, when the president decided to expand the CIA secret army. Hannah believes the fundamental flaw in U.S. Southeast Asian policy was to have fought the war in South Vietnam, that not fighting in Laos was "the key to failure." Unfortunately, the Kennedy administration's repeated deployments of U.S. forces to Thailand, to backstop the Mekong River line, had confirmed by 1963 that it was physically and logistically impossible to prosecute a major war in Laos. Still, Hannah and Rostow are representative of that camp who urged purposeful force in 1963–1964, and it was that view which prevailed.

A reasonable gauge of Washington's direction is what happened to Hannah's opposite number, State's desk officer for Vietnam at this time, Paul M. Kattenburg. One source for the expertise applied by Harriman and Hilsman, who had been a fellow student at Yale, Kattenburg had Indochina experience going back to 1949. Visiting Saigon after the overthrow of Diem, the desk officer concluded that the game was up, the bottom had fallen out of the South Vietnamese effort. When he said as much, not even Hilsman would shield Kattenburg, who lost his key function of acting for State at the Interdepartmental Working Group on Vietnam and got shifted to a sinecure. Paul was out as soon as Bill Bundy, who had crossed swords with him before, took over from Hilsman. The Vietnam dissenter went to the Policy Planning Council for two years before the mast of Walt W. Rostow.

"There was still no consensus among President Johnson's advisers," recalls McNamara of those days. At a meeting with LBJ late in 1964, the former secretary of defense notes "the substantial split among his military advisers." Yet the differences were not about broad directions but the quantity of force and pace of escalation. Max Taylor clarifies much in writing: "There was a wide range of opinions as to the proper timing of either tit-for-tat reprisal bombing or the initiation of a sustained air campaign to induce Hanoi to cease its aggression." Paul Kattenburg later wrote that the decision "was over a year . . . in preparation."

The biggest question mark in the equation was Lyndon Baines Johnson. By his own account LBJ involved himself most intensely in the passage of the Civil Rights Act of 1964 and laying foundations for the safety-net measures that became the "Great Society" and the "War on Poverty." The president insisted that "during my first year in the White House no formal proposal for an air campaign against North Vietnam ever came to me as the agreed suggestion of my principal advisers." Secretary McNamara, however, had had such an option in his draft report following a March 1964 visit to Saigon. Some historians believe McNamara removed the option at the behest of the president, who privately told him the recommendations should not contain such a plan. The 1964 elections loomed over everything. LBJ wanted no trouble that might cloud his chances. The most suitable alternative for those who cried out for energetic action became a major initiative against Hanoi's infiltration, a battle against The Trail.

Aside from President Johnson, it was Robert McNamara who figured as the biggest player in Vietnam strategy, and McNamara's position was also a key mystery. When he recalls divided counsel among LBJ's cohorts, it is partly himself to whom McNamara refers. One day Mac Bundy marveled at the irony that Dean Rusk, the top diplomat, favored a military solution, while McNamara, the senior military manager, advocated diplomacy. Notes the secretary of defense, "This irony said much about the deeply vexing problem we faced."

In McNamara's March 16, 1964, report to the president, he pointed up the difficulties of marshaling a case to justify overt action against North Vietnam. McNamara also observed the Saigon government needed to consolidate its base prior to any such campaign. "On balance," the secretary of defense concluded, "I recommend against initiation at this time of overt [South Vietnamese] and/or U.S. military actions against North Vietnam."

On the other hand, McNamara's recommendations did not even mention withdrawal, and quickly dismissed any possibility of neutralizing Indochina, a solution France proposed at that time. The net effect was that the Department of Defense proposed *only* alternatives to improve the situation in South Vietnam; and, aside from measures to maximize Saigon's military strength, the sole detailed prescription offered by Robert McNamara was a five-point program for sealing the borders of Vietnam.

Accounts of these events by both McNamara and George Ball agree on one thing: Lyndon Johnson, far from a confident warmaker, was agonized and uncertain. LBJ could have gone either way. But the evident worsening of the situation in Vietnam seemed to require some decision, and McNamara's management style created an appetite for options. The situation was ripe for men of *ideas*, figures like Walt Whitman Rostow.

The fact is that far from a voice crying out in the wilderness, Rostow was in the mainstream of U.S. thinking in 1964. Walt had already ordered a study of the "Rostow thesis," the notion that "by applying limited, graduated military actions reinforced by political and economic pressures . . . we should be able to force [a] nation to reduce greatly or eliminate altogether support for . . . insurgency." Headed by Robert H. Johnson, Rostow's staff man for Southeast Asia, the preliminary study indicated that Washington would not be able to apply the Rostow thesis to Cuba and Latin America, but might best do so in Indochina. Walt took this to Rusk, and a wider interagency group formed, also under Bob Johnson, to study how Rostow's thesis might work in Vietnam.

Bob Johnson worried about this study because it clearly anticipated escalation. Like Paul Kattenburg and some others, Johnson opposed escalation and saw the war, if not already lost, as something to be decided in the villages of the south, not by *force majeure*. Among an interagency panel, Johnson's opinion could easily have been submerged or overridden by objections. The final result turned out not too bad from his standpoint, however. Partly because the rush of events prevented agencies from formally approving his paper, partly because Johnson ended up drafting key passages himself, he felt the paper struck the right tone.

Titled "Alternatives for Imposition of Measured Pressures Against North Vietnam," the paper proved satisfactory to hawks because it concluded that escalation could achieve psychological effects in Saigon while demonstrating U.S. determination. The issues analysis, however, based on over two dozen topic studies, found that Hanoi probably could not be dissuaded from backing the NLF, and that its counter to U.S. moves must be to increase help to the Viet Cong. Furthermore, Johnson notes, "the report recognized that the United States would have serious problems both in convincing the American public and others that escalation was justified and prudent."

Meanwhile, the parent group of this committee, the Interagency Working Group on Vietnam, labored on plans for more energetic actions. Situated directly within Dean Rusk's office, under Michael Forrestal and then William H. Sullivan, the unit came up with detailed scenarios plus the earliest versions of a congressional resolution to be used to secure LBJ's political flanks as he forged ahead. Yet a third stream of advice came from Saigon, where Henry Cabot Lodge advocated military action against the North as a way for Saigon strongman General Nguyen Khanh to solidify backing for his regime.

There were at least two problems with all the schemes for purposeful action. The first was the diplomatic dilemma—the United States would be moving toward major military action without ever exploring other means of resolving the imbroglio. A reconvening of the Geneva conference could have forced Russia, in its capacity as a Geneva cochairman, into some enforcement of the accords of 1962 if not those of 1954. The United States resisted this because France was sure to propose the neutralization of Indochina. Moreover, ongoing American activities in Laos, particularly those of the CIA, could become violations issues themselves. As Robert H. Johnson puts it, "negotiations therefore were seen, in the context of the assumed U.S. strategy, more as a problem than as an opportunity." Johnson's boss agreed wholeheartedly—Walt Rostow consistently argued that the United States should attend an international conference *only* if that were being held to mark Hanoi's final compliance with the 1962 accords.

Even discussing a possible international conference, Rostow kept in mind his preference for action: As he put it to Dean Rusk in February 1964, "It will be more difficult for us to produce a Dien Bien Phu for Ho [Chi Minh] during a conference than it was for Ho in 1954."

That memo had been marked "For The Secretary ONLY."

While avoiding an international conference, the United States decided to make a direct approach to Hanoi, not to resolve differences but as a warning. Canadian diplomat Blair Seaborn, who could travel freely to Hanoi as a member of the International Control Commission, agreed to carry out the mission. He would make several visits to Hanoi during 1964 and 1965 and was received at various times by senior Vietnamese leaders.

Seaborn carried a set of talking points developed by the State Department. Their tone was tough, even harsh: "U.S. policy is to see to it that North Vietnam contains itself and its ambitions within the territory allocated to it by the 1954 Geneva agreements." The Canadian's instructions affirmed that Washington was "prepared" to engage in "alternative courses of action with respect to North Vietnam" to stop the war in the South, and that it might initiate "action by air and naval means." The carrot was a reference to possible foreign aid if the war ended. Washington was sure, Seaborn was asked to say, that Hanoi could stop the war in the South if it chose to do so. The Canadian could review for the Vietnamese the forces available to the United States versus those of Hanoi or nearby in China.

In Hanoi on June 18 Seaborn met with Prime Minister Pham Van Dong. The message conveyed as intended. Pham Van Dong laughed.

"We shall win!" Pham shot back.

But the Vietnamese leader also declared that Hanoi did not intend to provoke the United States and would not "enter" the war—here Hanoi's leaders made an apparent distinction between infiltration of the South and a conventional military invasion. Given the ambiguities introduced by the original failure to complete implementation of the 1954 Geneva accords, and the restriction of aid to the Liberation Front (Southerners returning to the South and equipment that was primarily from old French stocks), Hanoi could make a plausible argument its actions were restrained. The December 1963 party plenum decisions to send bigger weapons and more cadres on an improved Trail had not yet been carried out to the degree they could be detected by the Americans. If the war could be kept at this level Hanoi might win through without Washington being able to justify further escalation. An invasion, on the other hand, would directly challenge the United States and play to American strength. Invasion would also challenge Saigon, whose army had been specifically designed to fight a conventional war. There is every reason to believe Pham Van Dong's disavowal of any intention of making an invasion.

Meanwhile, Pham insisted on a "just solution," which included reunification of Vietnam plus a U.S. withdrawal. Vietnam, however, could be a neutral country, like Cambodia was at that time. Should there be a direct confrontation, Pham Van Dong saw little chance for the Americans.

"If war is pushed to the North," Pham suggested in his lyrical French, "we are a Socialist country, one of the Socialist countries, you know, and the people will stand up."

For Washington, that was it, precisely; the second problem with planning for aggressive war. What response ought to be expected from North Vietnam's allies? That problem lay just under the surface in many Washington debates on Indochina policy.

The role of China in the Vietnam War remains one of the darker corners of that frustrating story. Washington never ignored Hanoi's allies in its deliberations on strategy in Indochina, and both the CIA and the State Department intelligence were in the forefront warning of options that might trigger Chinese intervention. Intelligence regularly reported both public and private hints from Beijing and Hanoi. Pham Van Dong's exclamation to the Canadian Seaborn simply became the latest piece to the puzzle. In Hanoi there was a strong pro-Chinese wing within the Lao Dong Party, believed to be in the ascendancy since at least early 1962. Le Duan, mastermind for the South, figured among the leaders of the pro-Chinese faction. Further, Hanoi regularly invoked the specter of China. Party newspaper *Nhan Dan* and Radio Hanoi, in February 1964, both carried a statement that if the United States attacked, it would have to fight "not only with North Vietnam but also with China, or eventually with the Socialist camp as a whole." Ho Chi Minh personally gave an interview in April in which he declared that Hanoi had "powerful friends ready to help."

A formal Special National Intelligence Estimate (SNIE) compiled by the U.S. intelligence community and written by the CIA's Office of National Estimates laid out the basic trends in June 1963. The SNIE concluded: "The Chinese and North Vietnamese seek a quicker victory through the application of military as well as political pressure . . . Hanoi has considerable initiative and freedom of action." A February 1964 special estimate stated that "dramatic new Chinese Communist intervention in Vietnam or Laos is unlikely" but put this in the context that Viet Cong military and political prospects had improved considerably. Had the Americans attacked into Laos, the outlook would be far different. Another CIA analysis, a March 1964 SNIE, observed that "the DRV probably could not sustain large-scale military involvement, such as open invasion, without a considerable increase in

Chinese Communist or Soviet aid." At the same time, however, the CIA believed Hanoi was capable of expanding infiltration on its own resources, up to regular forces of battalion size.

In May 1964, with U.S. planning for action outside South Vietnam in full swing, the CIA produced an SNIE on that specific issue. The special estimate concluded that China and Russia would both support Hanoi's protests in the event of U.S. "preparatory and low-scale actions." The SNIE's reasoning on the Chinese ran like this:

> Communist China almost certainly would not wish to become involved in hostilities with U.S. forces. It would accordingly proceed with caution, though it would make various threatening gestures. There would probably not be high risk of Chinese Communist ground intervention *unless* major US/GVN [i.e., South Vietnamese] ground units had moved well into the DRV or Communist-held areas of northern Laos, or possibly, the Chinese had committed their air and had subsequently suffered attack on . . . bases in China.

This view by intelligence authorities was *more optimistic* than that held in some other quarters in Washington, and may be related to the fact that CIA director John McCone personally favored strong action against Hanoi.

Thomas L. Hughes, the director of State's Bureau of Intelligence and Research (INR), who followed Hilsman, recalls that this last special estimate, SNIE 50-2-64, actually papered over differences among the intelligence community. Hanoi's *will* might be affected by the coercive measures considered in Washington, but the DRV could take retaliatory *actions*. Nothing on the plate was going to affect its capabilities. It was State intelligence that reported comments of a senior Chinese official ("in all probability Chou En-lai") printed the day before the Gulf of Tonkin incident began. The official went to great length to insist that China wanted no war, but then continued, "We would feel threatened only if, perhaps, the United States would send their 'special warfare' . . . toward the north, if they attacked North Vietnam. . . . This would directly endanger the stability of our border and of the neighboring Chinese provinces. In such a case we would intervene."

One of INR's best analysts on China was Allen S. Whiting, who had been a State Department representative on Bob Johnson's panel that grew from the "Rostow Thesis." Alert to nuances from Beijing, Whiting detected several Chinese warnings on Indochina, of which he later wrote. Calling for reconvening the Geneva Conference on June 24, Chinese foreign minister Chen Yi remarked, "The Chinese people absolutely will not sit idly by while the Geneva agreements are completely torn up and the flames of war spread to their side." On July 1 the Peking newspaper *People's Daily* printed an editorial linking America in Southeast Asia with earlier efforts with the Nationalist Chinese to destabilize China. Calling this the People's Republic of China's "300th serious warning," *People's Daily* questioned, "Do you intend to embark on an adventure such as extending the war? We would like to ask the U.S. rulers: Have you pondered carefully what consequences such an adventure would bring about?"

On July 6 Chen Yi dispatched a formal letter to North Vietnamese foreign minister Xuan Thuy, which, for effect, the Chinese released to the press. Referring to U.S. extension of the war and threats of bombing as well as naval and air blockade, the letter read: "China and the DRV are fraternal neighbors closely related like the lips and the teeth. The Chinese people cannot be expected to look on with folded arms in the face of any aggression against the Democratic Republic of Vietnam." There were more *People's Daily* editorials and then, on the tenth anniversary of the 1954 Geneva agreements, another official statement. "China has not sent a single soldier to Indochina," Beijing declared. "However, there is a limit to everything. The United States would be wrong if it should think that it can do whatever it pleases."

Within days the Gulf of Tonkin incident occurred, and with it, a U.S. retaliatory air strike on Hanoi's naval bases. That brought a further Beijing statement: "U.S. imperialism went over the 'brink of war' and made the first step in extending the war." Worse followed: "Aggression by the United States against the Democratic Republic of Vietnam means aggression against China."

Privately Zhou Enlai and the People's Liberation Army (PLA) chief of staff asked Hanoi to survey its military needs. During the evening of August 5 came a meeting at PLA headquarters of army, navy, and air force leaders with the commander of the Beijing military district. The PLA went on alert. The next day came a recommendation that the 7th Air Corps deploy close to the Vietnamese border, with the 12th Air Division and the 3d Antiaircraft Division to Nanning and a navy fighter division to Hainan Island. Based on its intelligence, on August 10 Washington announced that MiG-15 and MiG-17 jet fighters had been detected on North Vietnamese airfields for the first time. Spokesmen passed this off as a routine, long-awaited development.

Several airfields in southern China were improved and new ones constructed. At one location a hundred miles from the DRV-PRC border, the Chinese built a complete facility identical to an airfield nearby that already existed. American analysts speculated the purpose of creating such a duplicate facility was to provide for a different command (the Vietnamese) to work in their own language. Through the air war that followed, this base, Peitun-Yunnani, gave Hanoi's air force a bolt-hole, a sanctuary untouchable to U.S. forces. Meanwhile, in January 1965, Vietnamese and Chinese air forces held joint air exercises in the border region.

By that time the radar net in southern China had been greatly extended and furnished modern equipment, its ninety-four sets almost three times as many as available at the time of Tonkin Gulf. The Chinese also sent in their most modern jets, MiG-19s. Previously these aircraft had alternated between fields in Manchuria and those opposite Taiwan. The increase in Chinese military activity became palpable. U.S. intelligence tracked these developments with a watching brief. By the end of 1965, notes INR's Tom

Hughes, "Chinese intentions and capabilities were a source of brooding interest, and accounted for most of the disagreements" in the national estimates.

Washington policymakers were no more blind to the Beijing-Hanoi relationship than the intelligence people. In fact, awareness of the Chinese potential became a limiting factor in American decisions. Concern became open enough that in February 1964 Secretary McNamara asked the Joint Chiefs of Staff for their opinion of the scale of military action the Chinese could mount. The chiefs' response, in their paper JCSM-174-64, proved unsettling reading. They believed that the People's Liberation Army could move and support up to 13 infantry divisions during dry season; PLA air could be as much as 400 jet fighters and 125 bombers. Saigon could not fight a force like that, and no option was feasible that could counter such an intervention. Cross-border operations, actions against The Trail, were the lowest common denominator, something that might be done with the least chance of bringing in the Chinese, *provided* those activities were not on too great a scale.

On this question, as on some others, Walt Rostow held rather more exuberant views of the possibilities, as well as starker visions of the dangers of inaction. In June 1963 Dr. Rostow argued that enemy success in Laos would be seen as "essentially a Chinese Communist enterprise" and the worst thing possible for moderates in the Sino-Soviet dispute. It was a month later that Rostow advised Dean Rusk that the United States ought to seek a showdown "with Ho (and implicitly, Mao)" before China exploded a nuclear device. On February 15, 1964, Rostow wrote Rusk, "I assume . . . that Ho and Mao are now operating very closely and, indeed, engaged in a plan to warn us of escalation should we move north." Rostow knew the dangers: "A substantial war with North Vietnam would require the Chinese Communists to introduce into Hanoi aircraft and, perhaps, troops." In March, Rostow believed U.S. planning should consider "what role nuclear weapons might play" since these could be necessary if the Chinese intervened massively. In May, Walt held out a U.S. occupation of lower Laos, the Tchepone area, as something that could "help deter use of [Chinese] and North Vietnamese conventional forces."

On several occasions Dr. Rostow repeated that the United States ought not to move without being prepared for a maximum adversary response, but in his heart Rostow did not believe in that possibility. In a major paper for President Johnson on June 6, 1964, Dr. Rostow argued:

> Mao's basic doctrine has always been: When the enemy advances, withdraw; when the enemy weakens, attack. He has good reason to live by that doctrine now, given the weakness of his armed forces; his increasing dependence on overseas food and other critical supplies from the Free World; the vulnerability of his atomic installations to air attack; and the fact that he is engaged not merely in a struggle with Moscow within the Communist movement, but in a systematic effort

to widen his trade and other ties with the rest of the world. All of this argues that, as in the Quemoy-Matsu crisis of 1958, he will find a way to withdraw if he judges us able and willing to hold firm.

This was the same memorandum in which Rostow told LBJ that *the* critical calculation *"must be your judgment that war must be faced if necessary."* Walt italicized every one of those words.

This was not exactly what President Johnson wanted to hear, not in the year of the Great Society, especially not in an election year. Whenever the subject of bombing North Vietnam came up, China reared its head; LBJ recalled that one or another of his advisers usually mentioned the risk of Chinese intervention. More than once Johnson brought it up himself. Rusk also raised the danger that the Russians might move on Berlin or in the Middle East. The constant concern fueled by The Trail also remained: pressure against the North might lead Hanoi to invade South Vietnam. "Our goals in Vietnam were limited," President Johnson wrote. "I wanted to keep them that way." An attack on The Trail, something less than Walt Rostow's scheme for occupying Tchepone, looked like just such a limited option. That was *on.* That was what Lyndon Johnson accepted. One region of Indochina was in for a great deal of trouble.

Bob McNamara made one of his periodic visits to Saigon in December 1963. Circumstances seemed pregnant. There was new leadership in both Saigon and Washington. President Johnson wanted a fresh look by someone he trusted; there was the question as well of nudging the military junta in Saigon. Hanoi had reconsidered its strategy, and though the conclusions of the party conference were not yet known in detail, statements in the northern press and on Radio Hanoi promised increased support for the National Liberation Front. For its part, the NLF had begun making foreign contacts and setting up diplomatic missions with help from the Democratic Republic of Vietnam. On the ground the NLF remained strong, the South Vietnamese preoccupied with Saigon politics.

The moment was an important one from the standpoint of American military action. Frustrated at the apparent lethargy of the South Vietnamese, Americans pressed for more direct participation. In the matter of activities outside South Vietnam, this agitation had come to fruition. For two years the CIA had helped Saigon with a covert project to insert agents and intelligence teams inside North Vietnam. None of the operations carried out had been successful. The agents and teams had been captured by Hanoi's security forces. Many were "turned" or "doubled," induced to work for the DRV to deceive Saigon, in effect, "played back." Agent losses were significant and growing—more than 200 before the end of 1963. A total of 123 agents or commandos were lost that year, the peak of disaster for Project Tiger, the secret CIA program to penetrate North Vietnam.

The Trail became an early target of the intelligence program due to the need to develop knowledge of infiltration from North to South. Tiger teams were sent to both the coastal provinces Vietnamese passed before starting down The Trail, and the mountain vastness of the Annamites. As early as June 1961 Team Echo had been parachuted into Quang Binh Province, immediately above the DMZ. Echo had been the fourth secret mission for the CIA-Saigon effort, and but the second by a group or team. By 1963, of several dozen forays to the DRV, about a third had been aimed at the Vietnamese panhandle.

Project Tiger tried to come up with new data on The Trail, in fact, immediately prior to Secretary McNamara's December visit, when Team Ruby parachuted into the North close to the Mu Gia Pass. Within hours the unit of seven commandos was under attack; within a day, captured. The team's best radio operator was executed. There would be no intelligence.

Information that *was* available, however, alarmed Robert S. McNamara. "The situation is very disturbing," he reported. "Current trends, unless reversed in the next two to three months, will lead to neutralization at best and more likely to a Communist-controlled state." McNamara noted infiltration by both land and sea. In Saigon he examined "various plans providing for cross-border operations into Laos," but none seemed very good. "On the scale proposed," Secretary McNamara told President Johnson, "I am quite clear that these would not be politically acceptable or even militarily effective." He wanted U-2 aerial photography of the entire Lao-Cambodian border of Vietnam as a prelude to a new round of planning.

This Pentagon view dovetailed with opinions expressed by Leonard Unger, U.S. ambassador to Laos. Unger cabled on December 14 to warn that asking for Laotian agreement to a cross-border program would create political difficulties for Souvanna Phouma, attempting to rebuild a coalition. Proceeding without Lao permission meant even worse problems once the activity became known. Ambassador Unger also believed no program ought to be begun prior to aerial reconnaissance to better define the target. As for scouting on the ground, the CIA's Project Hardnose, to whose expansion the Laotians *had* agreed, could do the job without the complications. Besides threatening the Geneva accords on both local and international planes, the program, Unger warned, would lead Hanoi to respond: "WE BELIEVE POTENTIAL IMPORTANCE OF ROUTES IS SUCH THAT [the North Vietnamese] WOULD MAKE MAJOR EFFORT INCLUDING COMMITMENT REGULAR DRV TROOPS IF REQUIRED TO PREVENT LOSS OF THIS PROTECTED ACCESS TO SOUTH VIETNAM (AND CAMBODIA), INCLUDING ITS NORTHERN NEXUS AROUND TCHEPONE."

Washington split the difference, accepting Unger's political analysis but giving the Pentagon some of what it wanted. There had been a meeting on December 6 wherein State agreed to furnish its assessment of the consequences of ground probes into Laos. The resulting paper contained the same warning as Unger's cable, but State went on to concede Washington could inform the Laotians *sotto voce* rather than seek approval, which would be more likely anyway if there were an understanding on the subject between the South Vietnamese and the Laotians. In a subsequent phase the scout patrols could begin. State then proposed a mechanism for political control of the missions.

More acceptable were plans for "graduated military pressure" against the North, ordered by a November conference at Honolulu, then coordinated by MACV planners and CIA's Bill Colby. In Saigon, McNamara reviewed this Operations Plan 34A-64, or OPLAN 34A, then pronounced the plans "prepared as we requested and . . . an excellent job," from which he wished to select options offering "maximum pressure with minimum risk." General Victor H. Krulak, the marine heading the unconventional-warfare directorate at the Pentagon, led a group that distilled 34A into a form President Johnson approved for implementation beginning in February 1964.

Unknown to history until now is the MACV companion plan, 34B-64, which focused specifically on the cross-border mission. As Unger's commentary showed, OPLAN 34B aroused opposition in the Vientiane embassy. There were also objections raised at CINCPAC in Honolulu. On December 21, just after returning from Saigon, Secretary McNamara in fact decided *against* 34B cross-border operations, instead relying on CIA's Project Hardnose. But that determination did not survive. By March 1964 the tide was running the other way.

As part of the planning for OPLANs 34A and 34B, the Central Intelligence Agency in Saigon and MACV command reviewed forces required. As early as November 14, 1963, these headquarters made joint recommendations. Peer de Silva, the CIA chief of station, agreed to turn over to MACV its mountain scout program and border surveillance assets. The ARVN Airborne Rangers, then comprising 540 soldiers (mostly ethnic Vietnamese), could be incorporated easily into ARVN Special Forces. The Rangers had only carried out their function (of acting in support of intelligence patrols or as strike forces to back up forays into Laos) "to a limited degree." The Rangers usually participated in conventional ARVN operations instead. In addition, the CIA's Combat Intelligence Team program had another 650 individuals. They were already being absorbed into the CIDG forces, and MACV could control them, too. That would "enhance U.S. management and control of these assets," and MACV would be "in [a] better position to systematize command and support of these irregular units." The proposal was that responsibility for paramilitary action into lower Laos pass to MACV effective December 1, 1963.* Concerning North Vietnam, if the commando effort were retained at existing size, it should be kept within the CIA. If Project Tiger expanded to the coercive instrument envisioned by OPLAN 34A, and "if the U.S. government is prepared to accept a reduction in plausible deniability to the level of discreet

---

*As the joint Embassy-CIA-MACV cable put it: "It would be unnecessarily complicated either to try to establish an entire separate set of assets and launching sites for cross-border operations or alternatively to negotiate the availability of such assets for cross-border missions on an individual basis" (CAS Cable 2440, November 14, 1963).

overt operations," then the task could better be done by the Military Assistance Command Vietnam.

This latter proved to be the decision. In Saigon, MACV set up an entity euphemistically called the Studies and Observation Group, MACSOG, or, for short, SOG. Under Colonel Clyde Russell, SOG had a small staff in Saigon with its activities conducted by "sections"—an air command at Nha Trang, a maritime section at Da Nang, and a ground section that became a center for field activities. Initially SOG consisted of just a few dozen Americans, but it soon grew tentacles throughout Vietnam. When the United States flipflopped and decided to proceed with cross-border operations into Laos after all, MACSOG became the agency responsible.

Meanwhile, McNamara's demand for aerial photography of the border would be met swiftly. Under the code name Trojan Horse, a detachment of U-2 planes from the Strategic Air Command began taking the pictures early in 1964. Better maps would be one result. But the pictures brought disturbing intelligence—for the first time the United States received evidence of road-building along The Trail, including pictures of heavy construction equipment.

Robert McNamara returned to Saigon in March. He saw the U-2 pictures then, and they were sent to the National Security Council shortly after his return to Washington. The pictures served to dispel doubts about the need for robust cross-border interdiction. That McNamara personally involved himself in this quest is revealed by what happened to SOG's Colonel Russell during the defense secretary's visit. Russell and Special Forces Vietnam commander Colonel Theodore Leonard were summoned to meet the brass; they encountered McNamara with General Maxwell Taylor, General William C. Westmoreland, Ambassador Henry Cabot Lodge, and Ambassador Leonard Unger.

"Out of a clear blue sky," Colonel Leonard recalls, "I was asked how soon I could begin operations into Laos."

The Green Beret officers tried to pin down the brass on what was the intention here, just what was the mission, the forces. "Nobody had enlightened me or tied it to our planning," says Leonard. Fortunately he had had World War II experience in Italy sending scout parties across the lines to eyeball German supply roads; the brass had something like that in mind. Tchepone and Muong Nong were mentioned; clearly The Trail had become the object.

Green Beret officers insisted they could not promise tangible results unless Americans participated.

"I agree with you," McNamara replied. "However, Mr. Rusk does not at this time feel that we should risk the exposure of American forces in an area that they're not supposed to be in."

In fact, though Vietnamese were now to carry out this program, Special Forces and SOG were not permitted even to mention the subject to the ARVN Joint General Staff before further word from the U.S. government.

Action moved to Washington, where Dean Rusk joined McNamara and

President Johnson for a session of the National Security Council on March 17. This NSC meeting featured detailed discussion of cross-border operations as well as the notion of "graduated" pressures on Hanoi. After the meeting the president approved National Security Action Memorandum (NSAM) 288, the policy document that governed U.S. strategy through the crucial period 1964–1965. The sole disquieting note was Max Taylor's statement that the Joint Chiefs, though accepting the concept, felt that "action against North Vietnam might be necessary to make effective the program recommended by Secretary McNamara."

The NSAM-288 scheme included a variety of border control measures that led to open-ended efforts. One point was to add low-altitude flights over Laos by photo plans when needed to supplement U-2 photography. McNamara's conversations with MACV were reflected in NSAM-288's approval of "Vietnamese cross-border ground penetrations into Laos, without the presence of U.S. advisers or resupply by U.S. aircraft." Also approved was "expansion of the patrols into Laos to include use of U.S. advisers and resupply," which seems to contradict the last alternative, but apparently reflects a distinction between combat unit forays, in the first instance, and reconnaissance patrols. Further actions included "hot pursuit" across the borders, and the use of South Vietnamese (not yet U.S.) forces for "air and ground strikes against selected targets in Laos." Up to a hundred soldiers could participate in "routine" cross-border missions; operations of battalion size or larger would be coordinated between the U.S. embassies in Saigon and Laos, with final approval in Washington. Coordinating with Laos, in a sop to Ambassador Unger's warnings, meant the United States would seek acquiescence of the Lao government.

While observers such as Norman Hannah, now CINCPAC's political adviser, considered the requirement for Laotian approval a formula for doing nothing, in fact at this precise moment Prime Minister Souvanna Phouma presided over a secret agreement between his own military and the South Vietnamese. Laotian general Phoumi Nosavan and ARVN general Nguyen Khanh signed the instrument, which provided free passage of the border to ARVN units, along with intelligence-sharing between these two armies.

At that time South Vietnamese out-of-country operations were the province of the Special Branch of the Liaison Service. Until Diem's demise this unit had been under direct control of the president, and had existed since January 1959. Special Branch unit "Atlantic" in Hue mounted patrols across the DMZ or into Laos. Unit "Pacific," at Da Nang, conducted agent and commando operations by sea into the Democratic Republic of Vietnam. There was also a staff in Vientiane, "Comete," to coordinate with the Laotian government; element "Hercule" in Savannakhet, headed by an ARVN colonel with four men pretending to be civilians; and station "Alto" in Bangkok. Paris was the location of unit "Venus," supposed to collect information about Hanoi's activities in France, as well as recruit Vietnamese there and infiltrate them into the DRV. In 1963 there had been an abortive plan to establish intelligence units in Hong Kong and Tokyo as well. With the Laotian-Vietnamese secret agreement Saigon's Central Intelligence Organization added a small unit at Pakse.

A typical relationship was that between Hercule and the command of Laotian Military Region 4. According to the Laotian chief of staff of this region at the time, while the Laotians passed along all their intelligence regarding The Trail, "my [staff] received nothing in return that would help us against the [North Vietnamese] who opposed us in the panhandle." Nevertheless, the Laotians would be loyal to their agreement—when MACSOG sent a U.S. officer in mufti to Savannakhet, with the idea of arranging American missions into Laos, the man was promptly arrested and expelled from the country as *persona non grata*.

In any case, the Khanh-Phoumi secret agreement, and later additional understandings, provided the framework for military actions in lower Laos over many years. Under it as well, the South Vietnamese assumed responsibility for supplying the Laotian infantry unit (BV-33) at Ban Houei Sane, so beleaguered by Hanoi's Trail garrisons. At Vientiane, Souvanna Phouma also approved reconnaissance flights, later armed escort for those flights, any number of bombings, and the various cross-border forays that developed. There is little evidence of the Laotian leader rejecting *any* American suggestion for action during the war years. This may have been due to solicitous U.S. diplomats in Vientiane, but it suggests another reason why Washington would remain steadfastly reluctant to overturn the 1962 Geneva agreements, which underlay the political compromise keeping Souvanna in power.

In the meantime, on April 30 the National Security Council received detailed data on Hanoi's construction along The Trail. In behalf of the Joint Chiefs, General Taylor had already sent over the concept for cross-border patrols toward Tchepone that he and McNamara discussed in Saigon, together with a recommendation that MACV be permitted to begin concrete preparations with the South Vietnamese. Concerned over the latest intelligence, the State Department abandoned previous opposition, while the White House had no problem with the mission. On May 5 the Joint Chiefs of Staff cabled an authorization to Saigon.

It would be Special Forces Vietnam, not MACSOG, that finally carried out the cross-border mission. Colonel Leonard had already talked informally with ARVN counterparts. The Vietnamese felt they needed thirty days to find the right men for the commando teams. Now Washington was giving Leonard thirty days to prepare the entire mission. Americans would not be allowed to participate.

To carry out this foray Leonard created a unique unit he named Project Delta. The unit would have its own secure compound within the growing base complex at Nha Trang, with separate security forces, everything very hush-hush. The long-term concept was to form commando teams for scouting and larger strike forces to back them up, but for this first mission, code-named Leaping Lena, only scout teams would be used. Donald Duncan was one of the young Special Forces sergeants assigned to Project Delta to work with the Vietnamese. Duncan recounts that, at first, everything went swimmingly, with Delta expenses being paid out of CIDG funds, free beer supplied, and agreement on lump-sum payments to the Vietnamese completing training and on return from the mission.

Sergeant Duncan began to have doubts when Special Forces was obliged to pay bonuses for each field training mission or parachute drop, things that were supposed to be part of the normal routine. Then came news that no Americans would be along for Leaping Lena. The original idea of teams composed of two Americans and four Vietnamese had to be scrapped in favor of slightly larger eight-man all-Vietnamese commando teams. There were desertions from the Delta camp and more petty grievances—at one point the commandos refused to go on unless given better watches and wool sweaters. The Vietnamese had seemed dedicated before, and some of them had had experience in the Leaping Lena operating area, but the American stand-down sapped their morale.

Beginning on June 24 Leaping Lena was mounted ("launched" became the term of art in Vietnam) out of Nha Trang. There were five teams of Vietnamese Special Forces (LLDB); their commander showed up drunk at the airplane to bid them farewell. The men parachuted, using smoke jumper techniques to land in the tree-studded terrain of the Annamites. Another Project Delta Green Beret, an Army sergeant named Ted B. Braden, who had been a pioneer in high-altitude, low-opening (HALO) parachute methods, had struggled to bring at least a few of the LLDB team members to proficiency. Unmarked planes flown by South Vietnamese pilots carried the teams, one of which dropped the first day, followed by three on June 25 and the last on July 2. Two of the scout teams went in north of Route 9, the others below that road, toward Muong Nong.

Though the Leaping Lena teams were supposed to range their assigned areas for up to a month, that never happened. One of the teams disappeared and was never heard from at all, and a second was captured when it blundered into an enemy-held village. The remaining teams made radio contact but were missing after various intervals. During the final stage, Leaping Lena helicopters made two flights daily, scouring the countryside for signs of the teams. One helicopter even entered Laos to search the road from Muong Nong up toward Tchepone, flying so low the crew could use a hand-held camera to photograph people standing in their doorways. The flight encountered no trucks, hostile forces, or movement, and was not fired at. There were no scouts.

At length a few returned, with the climax coming when one team crossed the border near Khe Sanh and encountered a People's Army battalion doing the same thing. Toward dark, as the Leaping Lena team awaited its helicopter pickup, the VPA saw them and a firefight ensued, with more South Vietnamese losses. The operation was terminated on July 9. Only five commandos made it back to friendly positions.

For Sergeant Duncan, Leaping Lena showed that the importance of the Ho Chi Minh Trail had been grossly exaggerated. The Vietnamese losses on a mission on which Americans had not been permitted also brought strong guilt feelings. Recalls Duncan, "This was the one thing, if I had to single one out, that made me really start questioning our role in Vietnam."

Colonel Leonard felt disappointed at the Leaping Lena intelligence but consoled himself that the reports were "much more than we had prior to that time." Survivors reported company-size units, new roads and trails that showed on no map but that were being used by truck convoys, and Pathet Lao guards at bridges and culverts. The scouts discovered the VPA had apparently cleared out villagers from a swath of terrain on the Laotian side of the border, the same way ARVN had done within Vietnam. They were sure the enemy were from Hanoi because the adversaries were clothed in the kinds of uniforms issued by the Vietnam People's Army.

As early as 1961 the strength of Hanoi's 559th Transportation Group has been estimated at about 2,000 *bo dois*. Vietnamese sources put the 559th at double that size three years later. With its decision to improve The Trail, Hanoi began sending down engineers for the construction, their units amounting to another 1,000 men. With mobilized porters and local labor, plus security troops and a minimum of two Pathet Lao battalions, Hanoi's resources had become significant and were growing.

By this time most of the figures who would play key roles in the building of The Trail had taken their places onstage. Vo Bam soldiered on, but became deputy in an expanded command under General Phan Trong Tue, former minister of communications and transport in the DRV government. Tue's civilian engineers were drafted with him to provide specialists for what arguably became Hanoi's biggest public works project. Dong Sy Nguyen, a Quang Binh native who had trained as an architect and construction engineer, was chief of the Military-Civilian Department of the VPA General Staff. He would later succeed Tue on the Truong Son artery itself. Bui Phung worked tirelessly on so many aspects of the construction he acquired a reputation among Northerners as the "builder" of The Trail. General Tran Sam, a vice minister of defense and director of the General Rear Services Department, procured necessary equipment and became Hanoi's leading expert on foreign military assistance. Together with unnumbered thousands of men and women who toiled to make roads out of trails, and trails where none existed, these individuals exerted major unseen influence on the Vietnam War.

The heart of the Truong Son system, pumping supplies to the South like blood coursing through the body, were the porters. There were two kinds of porters upon whom the system relied. As during the French war, there were local villagers impressed to carry loads a relatively short distance. This predominated within the DRV during the early years, as well as for supply movements within South Vietnam. Both men and women were impressed, over time increasingly the latter, as young men were drafted into the VPA or the NLF. Eventually older men comprised the bulk of males as porters.

Villagers suffered the privations and dangers of The Trail, yet their stories are hardly known.

The Laotian hinterlands west of the Annamites were sparsely populated to begin with, and the VPA moved many villagers away. Here People's Army soldiers furnished the motive force. Transport units came to be attached to each way station for short hauls, extraordinary supply movements, and shipments intended for the stations themselves. There were also units that moved loads the full distance to their destinations, especially as the VPA began to depend on bicycles, and trucks increased the volume of supply flows. The bicycles came to be called "steel horses"; truck drivers were known as "pilots of the ground."

Nguyen Viet Sinh knew nothing of the machinations in Saigon and Washington and he never met Vo Bam, but the decisions at those exalted levels affected him intimately. Sinh was a *bo doi* in one of the transport units and made dozens of treks down The Trail between 1959 and 1964, contributing no fewer than 1,089 workdays during that time. At first he carried, on his back, loads of 80 to 100 pounds, and he walked more than 24,000 miles. As the war progressed, Sinh began using a "steel horse," without which the record he set would not have been possible—personally hauling 55 tons of supplies. The steel horses with their lengthened handlebars, strengthened frames, and platforms carried loads of 220 to 330 pounds. Vietnamese favored French-made Peugeot or Czech Favorit bicycles. One Favorit bike, frame number 20220, held the record for hauling loads totaling more than 100 tons in a two-year interval. The individual record for a bicycle load, made in 1964 by *bo doi* Nguyen Dieu, was 924 pounds. The record previously set, at Dien Bien Phu, had been 724 pounds. According to a member of the commission Hanoi used to evaluate its options for expansion, under the impact of the steel horses, by 1964 the capacity of The Trail had risen to 20 or 30 tons a day.

As important as supplies were, Hanoi continued to send the men. In 1964 they were still primarily Southerners and individual specialists, though this shortly changed. An indication of the revised strategy would be the VPA's resort to both southern and northern Vietnamese as infiltrators. Around the time of the Tonkin Gulf incidents, for example, Captain Bui Long Bac trekked South after ten days' leave. Bac, not only a Northerner but also a trainer of infiltrators, was old-line People's Army, having gotten his own basic training with the Chinese in 1950–1951. His connection to the South resulted from service with the 325th Division in the anti-French war, when that unit fought in lower Laos, central Vietnam, and Cambodia. Bac hiked the full length of The Trail with the 621st Infiltration Group, to become executive officer of a regiment, and later a staffer at regional command headquarters.

With northern Vietnamese heading South in increasing numbers, it could only be a matter of time until the secret got out. In fact, American sources record gaining their first evidence of northern *bo dois* among the infiltration flow in October 1964.

The most important Vietnam People's Army figure to make his way down The Trail that year was General Nguyen Chi Thanh. Often seen as Giap's main competitor for the high command, Thanh was aligned with the pro-Chinese faction of the Lao Dong, *and* he was an expert in political-military action, having directed the apparatus with which the Viet Minh tried to demoralize North Africans and black Africans in the French Expeditionary Corps during the 1945–1954 war. Nguyen Chi Thanh was not from the North, however. He had been born in a village outside Hue. French colonial authorities had arrested Thanh twice. Lao Bao figured among the prisons in which Thanh had been held, as did Ban Me Thuot. By 1964 Nguyen Chi Thanh had been a member of the Hanoi Politburo for fourteen years. "My domain has always been the human spirit," a defector had heard him say.

General Thanh's specialties are suggestive of Hanoi's strategy in 1964, which embraced a full spectrum of "struggle" (*dau tranh*) that could range from military to political. The mix of elements became the crucial decision. Le Duan expressed a certain *dau tranh* formula in assigning the fifty-year-old Thanh to the South. The dispatch of General Nguyen Chi Thanh confirmed Hanoi to be serious about stepping up its war. Never before had there been a senior officer of the Vietnam People's Army in any kind of command capacity in the struggle in the South. The appointment of a VPA regular officer also suggested, if it did not promise, that Hanoi would soon back up its commitment to the South with real military muscle. We still lack the sources to know exactly how much the National Liberation Front knew at this moment about Hanoi's intentions, but from what is known of the Lao Dong's December 1963 decision about The Trail and the South, we do know that Hanoi had in fact made its decision to expand the war.

In the middle of the expanding Vietnamese corridor (see Map 3), soon to reach fifty miles wide, the Laotians were in no doubt as to what was happening. As early as the summer of 1963 they reported truck movements as far south as Muong Phine and Muong Nong—that was past Tchepone. Colonel Thao Ma's Royal Laotian Air Force (RLAF) had its main base outside Savannekhet, at Seno. They did a good deal of flying in the Route 9 area. The RLAF estimated that Tchepone was held by at least a thousand VPA *bo dois* plus another five hundred Pathet Lao. Colonel Ma also reported more flights by Russian-built IL-12 and IL-4 cargo aircraft. The RLAF credited Hanoi's 919th Air Squadron with landings at Tchepone and with air drops of cargo near Muong Nong, Muong Sen, and at simple way stations. Ma wanted to use his American-furnished T-28 fighter-bombers to hit these targets. Leonard S. Unger, ambassador to Laos, managed to get the United States to deny the use of U.S.-supplied aircraft for this purpose, and for a time the possibility of bombing was averted. But the option formed one of four assembled in the fall of 1963 by CINCPAC, then Admiral Harry D. Felt, to neutralize infiltration. Others included battalion-size and division-size forays coordinated between the Laotians and the South Vietnamese. The Laotians were to capture Muong Phine and Tchepone from the west.

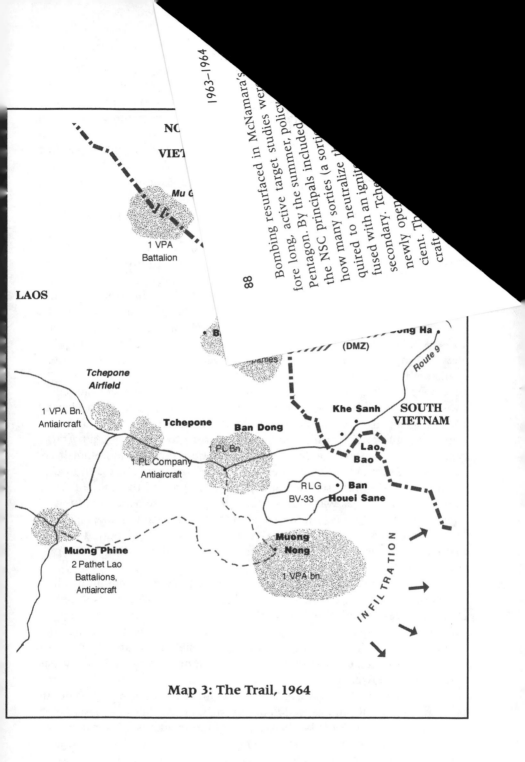

Mu G...

1 VPA
Battalion

LAOS

88

Bombing resurfaced in McNamara's...
fore long, active target studies wer...
Pentagon. By the summer, policy...
the NSC principals included...
how many sorties (a sorti...
quired to neutralize t...
fused with an ignit...
secondary. Tche...
newly ope...
cient. Th...
craft...

B...

...ng Ha

(DMZ)

Route 9

...anies

Tchepone
Airfield

1 VPA Bn.
Antiaircraft

Tchepone

Ban Dong

Khe Sanh   SOUTH
VIETNAM

1 PL Bn.

Lao
Bao

1 PL Company
Antiaircraft

RLG
BV-33

Ban
Houei Sane

Muong Phine

2 Pathet Lao
Battalions,
Antiaircraft

Muong
Nong

1 VPA bn.

INFILTRATION

Map 3: The Trail, 1964

options in the spring of 1964. Be-
being made in Honolulu and at the
documents sent to President Johnson and
specific lists of Trail targets and notations of
equals one flight by one airplane) would be re-
them. The plan was to use napalm (jellied gasoline
r) as the primary munitions; explosive bombs would be
pone would be allotted 68 sorties, Muong Phine 30. For a
d area such as Muong Nong, 10 sorties were deemed suffi-
Mu Gia pass, the JCS supposed, could be neutralized by 14 air-
orties.

Intelligence for this exercise in target planning also furnished disquieting indications. Antiaircraft emplacements were spotted in lower Laos for the first time—four guns at a camp outside Muong Phine.

These Joint Chiefs of Staff contingency plans were drawn up for South Vietnamese or American (FARM GATE) planes. President Johnson rejected the idea at that time, but decided to permit the Laotians to use their planes for strikes in lower Laos. During the final months of 1964 Thao Ma's pilots flew 750 sorties against The Trail. Intelligence was optimistic, but the effect could not be measured.

General Ma's Laotian plans struck most of the targets envisioned in Washington's contingency plans for The Trail. Ma personally led a flight of four T-28s against a storage area just south of the Mu Gia on October 14. Another flight hit the post at the pass itself. Also bombed were a barracks near Tchepone, assorted bridges and road junctions, and the more northerly Nape pass. Secretary McNamara approved release of extra T-28s from U.S. surplus stocks to increase RLAF muscle. On the ground the Laotian Army planned an attack eastward across Route 9 to recapture Muong Phine and then Tchepone, but this evaporated when ARVN refused to make a parallel attack westward from Khe Sanh. General Westmoreland reported that an array of factors prohibited Saigon from trying such an offensive until some-time in 1965.

Possibilities that Trail attacks might induce intervention by Hanoi's allies were discounted by the CIA. Director John McCone gave Langley's view in a July 28, 1964, paper: "We believe that none of the Communist powers in-volved would respond with major military moves designed to change the nature of the conflict." Laos began to seem feasible from an international standpoint—sweet, even—but the subtext remained that the adversary was threateningly powerful.

Meanwhile, another prong of the effort against The Trail would be put in place by the ground studies section of MACSOG. This coincided closely with the eclipse of Project Tiger by the Gulf of Tonkin incidents. Fewer than two weeks after the destroyer fracas, General Westmoreland's MACV command finished plans for cross-border incursions in conjunction with the South Vietnamese. The ARVN would call cross-border missions "An Dung" opera-tions; they would be under Lieutenant Colonel Ho Tieu's Liaison Bureau, an intelligence organ of the Joint General Staff. The Vietnamese Special Forces leader, General Doan Van Quang, made private arrangements for them in secret meetings with the Royal Laotian military.

Missions would depart from one of three "launch sites"—Khe Sanh, Kham Duc, and Kontum. Khe Sanh would become base for a backup strike force of four airborne ranger companies, later to be supplemented by an ARVN paratroop battalion. The Leaping Lena (soon Project Delta, and then MACSOG) scout teams would range up to twelve miles into Laos. All the launch sites would have detachments (100-man companies of Nung strikers) to follow up scout reports or to rescue beleaguered mission teams. Although an intended focus on Tchepone and Route 9 was ruled out, for political reasons of the moment, the overall scheme was implemented.

The final months of 1964 brought another round of behind-the-scenes deliberations in Washington. Plans for bombing were at the center of the debate. In November, when Viet Cong shelled the American air base at Bien Hoa, and again in December, when saboteurs set off a bomb at a Saigon hotel housing American advisers, the Joint Chiefs recommended bombing. Theirs were not the only voices. At the State Department, the Vietnam desk officer prepared what he called "Option V," a classic formulation of the idea of coercing Hanoi by airpower and seapower, which he saw as "a logical follow-on of the draft Seaborn message," and an alternative that would "at the same time minimize the risk of high casualties which I foresee coming out of any ground operations in the Lao panhandle."

Adopting the notion, advanced by Walt Rostow, that the Democratic Republic of Vietnam was no longer a guerrilla movement but a nation-state with national vulnerabilities to match, State argued, "We could develop a series of actions jointly with the [South Vietnamese] which would keep the DRV permanently at general quarters while spreading alarm and despondency among its personnel and raising serious doubts among its population." The concept was to strain Hanoi's governmental machinery. In this way the United States could duplicate the DRV tactics in South Vietnam without the use of guerrilla forces "for which we have no parallel." Thus, "We would not be obliterating targets but rather needling Hanoi." For example, "we would seek occasions to tempt the DRV naval forces into action against the [South Vietnamese] naval forces with the intention of taking appropriate occasions to hit them with U.S. air if they came out." In general the notion was to strike bridge, railways, ports, factories, levees, coal mines, and river craft.

The degree to which Washington thinking was shifting at about this time is suggested by the reaction of Mike Forrestal, who had been on the National Security Council staff, where he had resisted projects for escalation. Forrestal went to State in the spring of 1964, to head the interagency group on Vietnam that Paul Kattenburg had been kicked out of. Now Forrestal saw the "Option V" idea as something Washington could do *before* real negotiations and *until* stronger measures became necessary.

At the highest level, however, Dean Rusk, though strongly supporting efforts in Vietnam, rejected bombing. This was true in August and September 1964, and remained true that December, as both Rusk himself and Lyndon Johnson attest Bob McNamara and Mac Bundy were wavering due to the apparent necessity to do *something* to shore up Saigon's flagging morale. President Johnson sided with Rusk.

In the various military options papers that kept coming up there was another alternative, one seen as much less sensitive than bombing. That was cross-border operations. It was something everybody could agree on. Bombing remained controversial, and President Johnson continued to resist it, but he accepted the principle of an attack on The Trail. In Washington, Saigon, Hanoi, even in Tchepone, no one could know what a dark road lay ahead.

CHAPTER 5

Dark Road Ahead
1964–1965

On the night of November 1, 1964, Viet Cong mortarmen crept past the guards along the perimeter of the big Bien Hoa air base, north of Saigon, then set up their weapons. For a half hour they rained destruction on the place, long the seat of FARM GATE, the covert U.S. Air Force bomber unit. The barrage walked up and down the flight line, explosions ringing in the ears of airmen, jarred from sound sleep to seek cover desperately. Having finished with the airplanes, for good measure the Viet Cong went on to mortar the barracks. When the smoke cleared, four Americans and two South Vietnamese lay dead, with another seventy-two Americans and five Vietnamese wounded. Every American B-57 jet bomber on the base had either been damaged or demolished, as had a number of other aircraft. This was the first time the Viet Cong had ever aimed an attack squarely at Americans, and a signal that U.S. support for Saigon would not be devoid of costs.

As at Tonkin Gulf, in the wake of Bien Hoa, U.S. commanders asked for reprisal air strikes on North Vietnam. Washington proved more cautious. On the brink of his election, Lyndon Johnson merely ordered studies, but the restraint would be double-edged, as LBJ's minions reacted in anger. Previously many Washington officials had insisted that Saigon needed to put its own house in order before there could be stronger application of American force. Bien Hoa suddenly made the issues seem different. John T. McNaughton, assistant secretary of defense and a key aide of McNamara's, summarized the new consensus on November 6: "Action against North Vietnam is to some extent a substitute for strengthening the government in South Vietnam." The Viet Cong could be reined in by a Hanoi subjected to American pressures. As McNaughton put it, "A less active VC (on orders from DRV) can be matched by a less efficient [South Vietnam]. We therefore should consider squeezing North Vietnam."

McNaughton's term "squeeze" soon became a favorite among cognoscenti. His policy group, which LBJ had created following Bien Hoa, talked over all the elements of an action policy. One was the Laotian Air Force T-28 strikes; the McNaughton group noted preparations to hit more targets, including the Tchepone area. There was discussion of flights by U.S. aircraft over lower Laos (operation Yankee Team), and of the status of the CIA's Project Hardnose, running patrols against The Trail from the Mekong valley side. Planners considered more cross-border operations from Vietnam, but after Leaping Lena, General Westmoreland had reviewed the progress of MACSOG and reported he felt little could be accomplished before 1965, so there was nothing to be done there. There was extensive talk of the 34A activity and Tiger forays to North Vietnam. Only George Ball favored making no changes. According to William P. Bundy on November 7, "the working group is agreed that our aim should be to maintain present signal strength and level of harassment, showing no signs of lessening of determination."

Change was in the air. The possibility of a sustained bombing effort, going beyond simple reprisals, was bruited about. The Joint Chiefs of Staff for the first time talked of having American troops in Vietnam to protect the air bases. Policy planner Walt W. Rostow noticed the shift, and made a fresh sally on Vietnam in which he argued that the signal was more important than any damage to Hanoi, and that a ground force commitment of some kind had become essential for the next stage in Vietnam; "we are putting forces into place to exact retaliation directly against Communist China."

A few weeks after Lyndon Johnson's election, by a substantial margin; on November 23, 1964, Dr. Rostow revisited Vietnam strategy and advocated three critical moves. The most important, as he saw it, would be reinforcement of the U.S. Pacific command with "massive" forces—"to deal with any escalatory response, including forces evidently aimed at China as well as North Vietnam." The *first* item on the Rostow menu, however, was "introduction of some ground forces in South Vietnam and, possibly, in the Laos corridor." Walt returned to the point in discussing accommodation with Hanoi: "It is because we may wish to maintain pressure for some time to ensure their compliance that we should think hard about the installation of troops not merely in South Vietnam . . . but also in the infiltration corridor of Laos."

President Johnson did not accept this advice in decisions made early in December, but LBJ nevertheless crossed a Rubicon of sorts. Though Johnson pressed his advisers with earnest questions about political stability in Saigon, he began to argue the South Vietnamese were too weak to handle Hanoi on their own. Without much thought, the president here rejected the option of permitting Saigon to rise or fall of its own weight. Existing programs now could only be the first phase; with extras added on, the American military effort would expand tremendously. Johnson's decisions, implicit at a White House meeting on December 1, quietly moved the United States into a shooting war in Southeast Asia.

Among the add-ons supplementing America's Vietnam effort would be operation Barrel Roll, the first sustained air campaign of the war. The Trail became the target of this initiative, even before the inception of the regular bombing of North Vietnam. The Barrel Roll aircraft missions were innocuously called "armed reconnaissance," conveying the impression that American planes were simply scouting and could shoot back if fired on. Actually, Barrel Roll planes carried full weapons loads and were to attack any worthwhile target they encountered. Phase One actions were to be initiated within thirty days.

A paper prepared on December 2 stated U.S. intentions baldly: "We will join at once with the South Vietnamese and Lao Governments in a determined action program aimed at DRV activities in both countries and designed to help [South Vietnamese] morale and to increase the costs and strain on Hanoi." The plan provided both for intensification of Laotian air force missions "especially in the corridor areas and close to the DRV border," and also that "U.S. armed air reconnaissance and air strikes will be carried out in Laos, first against the corridor area and within a short time against . . . other infiltration routes." Laotian leader Souvanna Phouma agreed to permit the U.S. attacks on December 10. In Washington, a committee reporting to the National Security Council would select two segments of The Trail every week that would be subjected to armed reconnaissance strikes. Fifteen U.S. Air Force planes from Da Nang carried out the first mission, on December 14, 1964, and a dozen Navy planes made the second attack three days later.

In Washington on December 19 the action committee duly met to review Barrel Roll missions to be carried out over a two-week interval. National Security Council staff member Chester L. Cooper reported to Mac Bundy, "It was agreed to continue our stone-walling tactics with respect to information on these flights." The idea that war in Laos could be conducted in secret was no figment of some reporter's imagination.

To close out the year, on December 30 a flight of A-1H fighter-bombers from the carrier U.S.S. *Hancock* ran a typical armed reconnaissance mission along Route 9, then past Muong Phine, down Route 23 toward Saravane. They found no traffic to attack. Instead the planes bombed a cluster of buildings that looked suspicious.

American force was committed; the mailed fist was readily visible to the *bo dois* who worked The Trail. But Hanoi was not above to cave in. The CIA had been correct observing, in several special estimates, that the DRV felt itself in a strong position. Hanoi would persevere. Its signal, or at least that of the Viet Cong, came on Christmas Eve. That day in Saigon a bomb exploded at the Brink Hotel, quarters for some of the American officers in the city. Two Americans died and more than a hundred Americans, Australians, and South Vietnamese were injured. In the field, during the second week of December the Viet Cong overran an ARVN battalion command post south of Da Nang. Over the new year, in their first recorded multiregiment attack, Viet Cong hit the ARVN post at Binh Gia, then fought a pitched battle against South Vietnamese relief forces. Clearly the Viet Cong had lost no combat power.

Colonel Theodore C. Mataxis returned to Pleiku dog tired late that afternoon. It was a Sunday, February 7, 1965, but this had not kept Mataxis, senior adviser to ARVN's II Corps, from visiting battalions stationed around Ban Me Thuot. The colonel left his helicopter at Pleiku's airfield and motored to the American advisory compound, roughly four and a half miles north of the town. Dinner and a couple of drinks and then Mataxis tumbled into his bunk. In the darkness before dawn Mataxis suddenly awoke, startled by the sound of explosions. Viet Cong were attacking both his MACV compound and the Pleiku air base. It was chaos.

Leader of an infantry battalion in World War II, a regiment in Korea, Mataxis became familiar with Vietnam as an aide to General Maxwell D. Taylor during the latter's stint on the Joint Chiefs of Staff. Now Taylor was the ambassador, and Mataxis, too, had come to Vietnam. At Pleiku, the colonel doubted the security provided by his ARVN counterparts, and had arranged for his Americans to take turns on perimeter duty. On February 7–8 that proved fortunate for some at Pleiku—one of the guards, Jesse Pyle, though himself killed, fired on the Viet Cong in time to keep them from placing demolition charges against the barracks building. The enemy threw their explosives onto the roof instead, but that diminished the impact of the blast. More Viet Cong simultaneously attacked the air base.

Just by coincidence, another American at Pleiku that night was well-known cartoonist Bill Mauldin, come to visit his son, a pilot with the Army's 52nd Aviation Battalion. Mauldin, renowned for his sketches of soldier life in World War II, wanted to draw pictures of Montagnards. "I didn't know there was going to be a war and besides I am too old for that stuff anymore," Mauldin later recounted. When the attack began at 2:00 A.M. Mauldin, staying with battalion commander Lieutenant Colonel John C. Hughes, jumped out of bed in his underwear and ran for a bunker behind the quarters, but ended up helping the wounded. Confusion abounded. At the airfield control tower Americans who saw demolition charges exploding beneath helicopters and light aircraft could not get through to the command post, so they called the fire department. Still, within minutes three helicopters were airborne in support of the defenses. The tower also got an Air Force C-123 diverted from its flight to Saigon—wounded at the airfield were evacuated within three hours of the attack. Pursuers managed to get the Viet Cong unit commander and one of his mortar section leaders, and documents found on the bodies confirmed that, as Mauldin put it, the Viet Cong were "professionals"; in fact, "down from the North on a planned mission to do the job."*

Eleven aircraft and helicopters were destroyed at the base. Of Colonel Mataxis's men at the MACV compound, 8 died and a whopping 104 were wounded.

---

*General Dang Vu Hiep, political officer to the People's Army command involved, reports that the Pleiku strike was carried out by a detachment of just thirty men, who were presented medals for their heroism in the battle. Vietnam today celebrates February 7 as the day the North came to aid the South in the struggle for reunification.

Pleiku brought a crunch for Washington's war planners, who had been wrestling with projects for a new phase of engagement. Still searching for a way to cope, President Johnson had sent national security adviser McGeorge Bundy to Saigon to hammer out a fresh strategy. Bundy and Bob McNamara had been telling LBJ that reprisal bombings—"tit-for-tat" strikes in the argot of that day—were losing their effect, and both were backing sustained bombing. Now Bundy was in Saigon at the very moment of Pleiku. He and Max Taylor went to General Westmoreland's MACV headquarters first thing in the morning to see the reports, and Mac immediately telephoned the White House with advice to mount a reprisal against the DRV. President Johnson happened to be meeting with his National Security Council when the call came through. He quickly approved.

Meanwhile, Taylor and Bundy flew to Pleiku themselves to survey damage. Though Bundy, when back in Washington, told reporter David Halberstam that "Pleikus are like streetcars," at the real Pleiku he was sickened. Colonel Mataxis showed the visitors to the barracks. There, on one bed, was brain tissue from a victim whose head had been torn open. Bundy looked pale and had to go outside. The others found him leaning weakly against the wall, holding his stomach.

Flying back to Washington, McGeorge Bundy compiled a paper for the president that called for "sustained reprisal" against Hanoi.

The Viet Cong carried out a sustained campaign of their own in the II Corps region. Colonel Mataxis likens it to the famed Tet Offensive several years later. Operating along the provincial boundaries, the Viet Cong cut off every province in the region from every other. At Qui Nhon on February 10 they set off another bomb at an American barracks whose floors collapsed one on top of another. It took three days just to dig out the victims.

Viet Cong units blocked Route 19, the main access to the Central Highlands from the central Vietnamese coast. The Americans countered, bringing eight of the Farm Gate A-1E fighter-bombers into Qui Nhon even though that field was considered anything but secure. The planes flew up to three sorties a day in their attempt to blunt the Viet Cong offensive. One day they caught two Viet Cong battalions crossing Route 19 between Pleiku and Qui Nhon and had a field day; on another the Viets damaged two battalions of the ARVN 40th Regiment even though it was backed up by armored personnel carriers. The overall situation was very troublesome.

Lyndon Johnson's reprisals were carried out just as surely as the Viet Cong attacks. The afternoon of February 7, the day of Pleiku, brought a strike by forty-five planes from the carriers *Hancock*, *Coral Sea*, and *Ranger* on the barracks at Dong Hoi, just above the DMZ. One A-4C jet was shot down; the Vietnam People's Army announced it had recovered the body and effects of pilot Edward A. Dickson. After the Qui Nhon bombing there was a hundred-plane raid from the carriers against Chap Le, also north of the DMZ. Lieutenant Robert H. Schumaker was shot down and became a prisoner of the Vietnamese. Both pilots were of attack squadrons from the

Coral Sea. Both targets were staging bases for The Trail. American blood had been drawn in the air battle against The Trail.

Judging Lyndon Johnson by his memoir, which lavishes many pages on his deliberations over the reprisal raids but just one paragraph to his decision for an air campaign, the president thought he was not breaking any new ground when he approved Rolling Thunder on February 1. This campaign scheme comprised much more than a retaliatory strike, and led to sustained bombing the like of which had never been seen. Actually, at the February 10 meeting of the National Security Council (NSC), Johnson had gone along with Bob McNamara when the secretary of defense talked about "phase two" military actions in Vietnam pretty soon, *even* if there was *no* Viet Cong terrorism. LBJ expressed concern mostly about the need to avoid leaks, and whether there were targets within South Vietnam that could be substituted for going to the North.

The matter of retaliation was a key diplomatic issue, because the United States knew that Russian prime minister Alexei Kosygin was on his way to visit Hanoi with a high-level Soviet delegation. Bombing the DRV while a top leader of its sustaining ally was in town could be very provocative. At the NSC George Ball argued for a smaller strike and won that concession, but it would be a palliative. Vice President Hubert Humphrey and U.S. expert on the Soviets Llewellyn Thompson both favored delaying any response until after Premier Kosygin had left Hanoi. Lyndon Johnson not only rejected their advice and sided with his military, but was so angry at Humphrey that for several years afterward President Johnson froze his own vice president out of his innermost deliberations on national security. There was no specific NSC discussion of the Rolling Thunder decision itself. President Johnson's approval came in the form of a memorandum from on high. There can be no doubt that LBJ at that moment was satisfied with actions proposed to him and confident of U.S. military power.

At Honolulu the commander in chief Pacific (CINCPAC), Admiral U.S. Grant Sharp, was just as confident of his capabilities, and would be the man in actual charge of the bombing campaign. His orders from the Joint Chiefs of Staff called for the first air attacks to be made February 20, but political unrest in Saigon forced several postponements, and the initial mission occurred on March 2, 1965. The delays frustrated Sharp, adding to his growing sense that, while his forces might be capable, his mandate was erratic due to Washington's uncertainties. Whatever the perspective from Honolulu, site of CINCPAC headquarters, President Johnson in quick order made a series of decisions driven by the bombing that greatly deepened U.S. involvement. These decisions to defend enclaves reflected LBJ's trust in his military advisers. When the set of enclaves expanded and MACV began talking about a maneuver element, the die was cast for a big war. Westmoreland's reinforcement requests soon attained large proportions—44,000 men, then 75,000, then 100,000 or more. Vietnam was going to be a war, not a country.

Ambassador Taylor watched as Lyndon called the shots. Back for consultations, Taylor opposed major ground forces for the moment but found Johnson tough to restrain: "I soon sensed that, having crossed the Rubicon on February 7, he was now off for Rome on the double."

Another of the administration's March 1965 choices would be to order MACSOG to proceed with a cross-border campaign to watch and pressure The Trail. This operation clearly represented the complement on the ground to the now-ongoing bombing of Laos, as well as the Rolling Thunder bombing of the Democratic Republic of Vietnam. Creation of a launching site at Kham Duc Special Forces Camp became just one of SOG's practical arrangements. Before preparations were complete, Colonel Russell left the Studies and Observation Group, to be succeeded by Colonel Donald D. Blackburn.

Unusual provisions for SOG were necessary due to its place among American action units in Vietnam at this time. Colonel Blackburn's group intended to carry out activities in a country (Laos) in which it was not located and that, from the standpoint of American diplomacy, remained under the control of the U.S. ambassador there. At the same time, the Studies and Observation Group was embedded in a military command, MACV, which had no actual dominion over it. Instead, Blackburn's chain of command stretched directly to Washington, where he answered to the Joint Chiefs of Staff through their special assistant for counterinsurgency and special activities (SACSA). The SOG chieftains would typically keep General Westmoreland informed of their operations, and often got him to plead their case for more men or authority, but MACV could only ask for things; it could not demand them.

This unique system survived the conference held at Honolulu late in April 1965 that set basic ground rules for the American war in Vietnam. That meeting confirmed that Westmoreland would run the ground war inside South Vietnam, CINCPAC would have responsibility for air matters, and so on. The conference also set basic outlines for Rolling Thunder: The DRV was to be coerced by an air campaign whose purpose was *not* primarily to inflict damage.

Specific adjustments for SOG were also discussed, as they were in Washington and at the meeting of the Southeast Asia Coordinating Committee (SEACOORD), a body composed of senior officials of the U.S. embassies and military commands in Vietnam, Laos, and Thailand. The group served as a sort of local high council. The April SEACOORD meeting heard a CIA proposal to expand the Hardnose paramilitary operation, which featured patrols by primitive Lao tribesmen. Langley pushed the effort as part of a larger package of initiatives Director John McCone suggested to LBJ as the agency's contribution to the war. At SEACOORD and afterward, the U.S. ambassador to Laos, William H. Sullivan, proved skeptical about the CIA project. Sullivan told Westmoreland, "It is far-fetched to think of storming the Ho Chi Minh Trail with a bare-bottomed bunch of these boys." The military were at SEACOORD with a proposal of their own for initiation of MACSOG cross-border forays into Laos. Any storming of The Trail would be in Bill Sullivan's country and on his watch. It was Sullivan who would be facing Souvanna Phouma asking for permission. Just what Sullivan thought mattered a great deal.

Those who delighted later in making jibes about Bill Sullivan the field marshal would have been surprised to hear that the urbane diplomat had indeed learned from a proconsul, perhaps America's greatest. For two years during the Korean War, Sullivan knelt at the feet of Douglas A. MacArthur, as a State Department representative assigned to the Far East supreme command. That had been a heady time and marked the beginning of a series of plum assignments that had Sullivan as an adviser to the Mediterranean regional commander for the North Atlantic Treaty Organization, a senior diplomat in Holland, and a member of the U.S. delegation to the United Nations.

Sullivan came to Laos only by indirection. Except for his first diplomatic tour, a junior post in Thailand in the late 1940s, Bill had no Southeast Asian experience. His major preoccupations in the 1950s concerned the Japanese Peace Treaty; Europe; and at the United Nations, China, where membership for the People's Republic was opposed by the United States. Sullivan's own recollection is that until the beginning of 1961, when he was asked to make suggestions on Laos for a transition report for John Kennedy's people, he never had anything to do with the place. Sullivan had had the State Department's Burma desk for a short time, but that by no means qualified him on Laos.

What did happen for William Sullivan was Averell Harriman. The latter was touring world capitals as a roving ambassador when Kennedy tapped him to be chief negotiator on Laos at Geneva. Dean Rusk attended the opening session but left, saddling Harriman with an entourage of more than 120 diplomats and military experts, some quite senior and willing to get in the way. Harriman liked room to move, needed someone who knew the State Department from the inside, and he had been impressed with a paper Sullivan had written during the preparatory effort. When objections surfaced that Harriman had many Foreign Service officers senior to Sullivan, and that therefore Bill could not serve as deputy chief of the delegation, Harriman sent home everyone who ranked higher than William H. Sullivan. Before long Sullivan knew a great deal about Laos.

Two key concepts in the Geneva negotiations, words that would continue to reverberate through the Indochina war and after, were "neutralization" and "partition." Different people meant different things by neutralization, but it was a key goal to restore to Laos the political stability that neutralization in 1954 had brought. Given the strength of various Laotian factions, not simply the Pathet Lao, but also General Phoumi Nosavan's faction and the military neutralists under another officer, Kong Le, many felt neutralization could not be achieved without partition. In turn, partition bothered some, because a formal territory could be seen as sanctioning a victory by Communists. Bill Sullivan squared the circle by playing down the significance of territorial integrity. "Laos," he told a later interviewer, "was really more of a geographical expression than it was a state that had rigid boundaries."

William Sullivan and Averell Harriman crafted a Geneva accord sufficiently ambiguous to be agreed by all parties, which meant that afterward it was ambiguous enough to dissatisfy everyone too. Laos retained its territorial integrity, for no divisions of territory were stipulated. At the same time, Laos was partitioned, for no procedure was provided to reintegrate the nation. Souvanna Phouma's government, with which Washington could work, was confirmed in its power.

As one of the architects of this compromise, Bill Sullivan became a player on Indochina policy and remained so for almost a decade. Sullivan acted for Harriman when the latter was elevated to assistant secretary of state for the region, headed interagency groups on Indochina, and participated in such esoteric exercises as the "Sigma" games, simulations of the Indochina crisis held by the Joint Chiefs of Staff. By early 1964 the forty-one-year-old Sullivan was special assistant to Dean Rusk for Vietnamese affairs.

Bill Sullivan was in Washington during the key period of 1964 when plans were being crystallized. In fact it was Sullivan, together with Mike Forrestal, who drafted an early version of a congressional resolution for authority to conduct military operations in Southeast Asia. That June, when Johnson ordered Yankee Team reconnaissance flights over Laos, then sent air force strike planes to retaliate when one of the photo missions was fired on, Sullivan witnessed an example of the miscarriage of U.S. military efforts in the war. Planes struck the antiaircraft position as ordered, and the air force sent the White House aerial photographs of the damage it proudly displayed on the conference table in the Cabinet Room. LBJ ordered a second retaliation after a similar incident; now the air force remained silent. When LBJ pressed, he learned that this time the strike had missed by as much as forty miles—the Air Force had hit a different antiaircraft position that was similarly located in an old fort from the French period. LBJ mouthed some frothy Texas comment about air force proficiency and accuracy, but Bill Sullivan carried the lesson to a place he would soon have to employ it.

During this period Sullivan was shuttling between Washington and Saigon, for Maxwell Taylor had insisted on having Bill as executive secretary when he set up shop as ambassador. The Tonkin Gulf affair provided Sullivan another demonstration of the foibles of military action. Doubts about whether a second North Vietnamese boat attack really had happened resonated with Sullivan, who had been a destroyer sailor in World War II. During the Normandy invasion Sullivan's ship covered one flank of the amphibious armada, one the Germans struck with some of their torpedo craft. There had been a night surface battle that went on for some time, and at one point his destroyer was shooting at her own wake. The similarities to what happened off the Vietnamese coast on August 4, 1964, gave Sullivan pause.

In World War II there was military experience aplenty for young

Americans, and William H. Sullivan had gotten his share. His destroyer had fought German submarines in the North Atlantic and Mediterranean, been at D-Day, and the squadron had subsequently been sent to the Pacific. Sullivan's ship fought in the Okinawa campaign and survived, though hit twice by Japanese suicide planes. Despite the fact that none of the dozen destroyers in the original squadron was lost prior to Normandy, only two ships made it through the war unscathed. That was a lesson, too. Then there had been Sullivan's grandstand seat with MacArthur during the Korean War and his experience with NATO. Bill Sullivan was not without qualifications to be a field marshal.

Robert McNamara threw a party at his home one night for the Washington officials being sent to Saigon. Lyndon Johnson dropped by in an impromptu show of esteem for Max Taylor and the new Saigon team, Sullivan and U. Alexis Johnson. There were jokes about who else stood to be fed into the maelstrom—Bobby Kennedy's name came up. Sullivan seemed slightly out of place; he knew he was already in line to be appointed to Laos. Rusk had asked him if he wanted the job one day—Vientiane was a hardship post that most in the Foreign Service could refuse—and Sullivan had acceded. The assignment with Taylor was strictly temporary duty. Leonard Unger, the current ambassador, extended his own tour to accommodate Taylor's desire to have Sullivan at his side. On November 25, 1964, President Johnson nominated William H. Sullivan for ambassador. The Senate approved without qualm. Bill Sullivan arrived in Vientiane early in December.

By April 1965 there had been time to become acclimated, and to renew acquaintances with the Laotian characters first met during the Geneva negotiations. Ambassador Sullivan's courtly manner irritated some but pleased others. A graduate of Brown University with a master's from the Fletcher School of Law and Diplomacy, he definitely had the candlepower to understand Laos. All this made the SEACOORD meeting at Bangkok in April 1965 especially important for Sullivan, as it would be his first foray into the field in the Vietnam War.

The Honolulu meeting and that of SEACOORD in Bangkok discussed the same plans; their talks marked a long step forward for America into the Indochina war. Those involved included Admiral Sharp of CINCPAC; Ambassador Taylor and General Westmoreland from Saigon; and from Washington, Secretary McNamara, his assistant John T. McNaughton, JCS chairman General Earle Wheeler, and diplomat William P. Bundy. The group firmed up management, enshrined SEACOORD, and sanctioned the autonomous position of MACSOG.

General Harold K. Johnson, the army chief of staff, had visited Saigon about a month earlier and worked up a plan for ground forces that he took to the Joint Chiefs. Johnson recommended a multinational enterprise, an anti-infiltration force to block the neck of Indochina at the seventeenth parallel, using five divisions from the United States and its SEATO allies, plus another in a mobile role behind the barrier. Tactically, the formula repeated previous schemes for blocking Route 9, and that road would have been the lateral route for supply of the barrier. When staffed out, the Johnson plan proved to have extravagant engineering and logistics requirements, with massive construction necessary on Route 9, and estimates of up to 18,000 engineers plus 10,000 locals to labor on the lines of communications or supply the force.

Westmoreland viewed the anti-infiltration force as desirable, but, he writes, "I saw no possibility of getting authority to form it and overcoming inherent logistics problems in time to have the needed effect." The plan also proved too ambitious for the JCS, which scaled back the option to require three divisions of troops. The JCS concept remained only a concept; at Honolulu, conferees focused on a much smaller troop deployment. Westmoreland favored one army brigade around Bien Hoa and a division to fight it out in the Central Highlands. Officials at Honolulu settled on a program of nine U.S. battalions—the equivalent of one army division—plus three battalions from South Korea (down from a full division) and one from Australia. As Westy recalls, "While accepting the strategic goal of breaking the enemy's will by denying him victory in the South, nobody saw any immediate hope of drastic improvement in the ground war."

The JCS and MACV plans were taken to Bangkok and briefed to SEACOORD members there. This was the same meeting that heard the CIA proponents of Project Hardnose and the cross-border planners who wanted to unleash MACSOG. William H. Sullivan not only took a dim view of Hardnose, as already quoted, he also had doubts about large deployments, given the parameters of Washington plans and the air campaign already in progress. Ambassador Sullivan told Washington on April 21 that the "Lao believe our methodical bombardment of North Vietnam is correct and will produce results." Sullivan feared massive troop deployments would be interpreted "as evidence of panic" and warned "this atmosphere can be very infectious." Moreover, the Vientiane proconsul cautioned, deployments would cause the Lao to reexamine their belief that the United States had no colonial or neocolonial ambitions.

While Sullivan worried about major ground forces, he was willing to go along with cross-border operations with certain conditions. Under a Studies and Observation Group scenario proposed on March 27, there would be several phases of operations. In the first, teams would be launched from either the Mekong valley or the Vietnamese side of the border, would engage Hanoi's troops "only to avoid capture," and would stay for periods of up to ten days. In a second phase the ten-man mission teams would loiter in Laos for up to three weeks, and in the final phase there would be deep penetrations of Laos and missions of up to twelve months' duration. The SOG concept specifically provided that "U.S. personnel will be imployed [sic] in both air support and ground advisory role where feasibel [sic]." The operation quickly acquired the code name Shining Brass. Provided SOG avoided air drops of Americans north of Route 9, and that teams entered by land, Ambassador Sullivan was willing to support the activity.

General Westmoreland felt the strictures Sullivan wanted would prevent the success of Shining Brass. There were huge physical obstacles to overland movement; if air and helicopter entry were not permitted, Westmoreland would prefer to cancel Shining Brass altogether, he cabled Admiral Sharp and the JCS on May 12. If it were done Westy's way, MACV agreed to restrict initial operations to the two small sectors the Vientiane proconsul recommended. On July 5 Westmoreland forwarded a detailed mission plan under which two SOG teams would launch from Kham Duc to points inside the Vietnamese border, then reconnoiter into Laos. Washington resisted approval pending Ambassador Sullivan's agreement. Meanwhile, Sullivan also showed other signs of hardheadedness, such as on July 14, when he cabled Washington to warn against expanding tribal Hmong operations in northern Laos, shifting to an offensive mode against the Pathet Lao, without additional policy review.

Convincing the Vientiane proconsul came to seem a matter of importance. The CIA did its part; from the Mekong valley the agency began to send Lao Theung recruited under Hardnose to act as road-watch teams along The Trail. By June five such teams were in place, three just under the Mu Gia Pass and the others in the vicinity of Muong Phine. The Laotian government helped, too: on June 21 Sullivan and his air attaché visited General Thao Ma at the headquarters of the Royal Laotian Air Force in Savannakhet. Ma showed Sullivan his own intelligence on The Trail and explained how twice recently he had requested strikes by Barrel Roll jets, which, when they arrived overhead, had been unable to find the road beneath them.

Leaving headquarters, Ambassador Sullivan had gone to Laotian Mobile Group 18, which had just captured Pathet Lao territory that straddled The Trail. The Laotian commander, Colonel Nouphet, took his visitors there by helicopter. Sullivan reported:

> Both [the] Air Attaché and I, despite our several years experience in this part of the world, were astounded by what we found. The "trail," even in this rainy season, was a thoroughly passable road. We drove two jeeps over it for more than a mile. It would have easily accommodated 4 × 4 trucks. Yet nowhere on this road, except for two very limited areas, was it open to the sky. Even flying over it slowly with a helicopter, the road was not discernible from above. The Air Attaché took several photographs demonstrating the cancer. . . .
>
> It seems clear to me, from this experience, that significant quantities of logistics can still be moving over routes which General Ma and his men have so meticulously plotted out for us but which our strike aircraft are unable to discern.

Laotian planes, Sullivan reported, had flown literally hundreds of sorties, "mostly at tree-top level," to find the roads, way stations, and truck parks. General Ma had a good fix on two passages from Muong Nong to the Vietnamese border, and his pilots had occasionally seen truck convoys on them.

The evidence clashed with opinions Ambassador Sullivan continued to express, including during his July visit to Washington, when he told offi-cials that incursions into Laos involving American soldiers could lead to collapse of the 1962 Geneva accords. If Americans were captured it would be especially damaging, and there was a danger of an open-ended commit-ment developing from the scout missions.

Another potential cross-border project Sullivan opposed for similar rea-sons. This was operation Golden Eagle, which would have involved Green Berets and Thai Special Forces, working from Thailand, moving to the Bolovens Plateau of lower Laos and making raids on The Trail from there. Sullivan discovered that the Laotian generals in the panhandle disliked Thais intensely, and this became yet another reason to oppose the opera-tion. Golden Eagle never flew, though eventually many SOG patrols against The Trail would be launched from Thailand.

Intelligence evidence and problems with the air campaign eventually forced Bill Sullivan's hand. Several bombing errors in September under-lined the need for better intelligence, while a successful photo flight at mid-month revealed even greater concentrations of Vietnam People's Army troops and supplies near the border. From Hawaii, Admiral Sharp pressed hard for ground patrols out Route 9, and asked Westmoreland to run his initial missions into that area once Shining Brass got the go-ahead. The proconsul in Vientiane could see the stakes as well as anyone. By the end of August Bill Sullivan was on board. Thereafter followed quiet diplomatic contacts with Souvanna and discussions in Washington. Finally, on the af-ternoon of October 12, top-secret JCS dispatch 3924 clattered off the teleprinters: "Higher authority approved the concept for Shining Brass in principle and the execution of Phase I." Ground teams and bombers, in combination, were about to challenge the Vietnam People's Army in its lair. How good were the men who made up the commandos would have a lot to do with the success of the overall effort. Finding those few good men, and preparing them, became a major task for MACV's Studies and Observation Group.

About twenty miles east of Saigon, Long Thanh village would have much to do with both Laos and North Vietnam despite its location very far from either. This resulted from Long Thanh's role as a center for the Studies and Observation Group (SOG), where Americans and Vietnamese Special Forces trained reconnaissance teams for cross-border operations. Back in 1943 the Japanese had built an airstrip at Long Thanh and a minor base there. Later South Vietnam used the strip and road net for a base of its own. The place had been given to exotic activities in 1963, when the CIA handed over its paramilitary activities to the U.S. military. The agency had used Saigon safe houses to prepare teams for Project Tiger, while CIDG training had been done at existing Montagnard camps. The military intended to expand both initiatives; a more ample facility became necessary. The South Vietnamese agreed.

In March 1963 the ARVN high command assumed direct control of Long Thanh. Restyled the "Quyet Thang Training Center," over the next year Long Thanh whipped into shape seven companies of "civilian combatants"—whether Montagnard strikers, rangers, Tiger teams, or others goes unrecorded. By 1964, especially after the Leaping Lena debacle, it was apparent the success of cross-border pressures depended on more skilled fighters for even more dangerous missions to come. Even as Project Delta qualified the scouts for that reconnaissance to Tchepone, MACSOG confronted the dilemmas of forging a new training system. More Green Berets were needed. The Pacific Command in Hawaii was asked to send an A detachment of Army Special Forces, plus officers for a headquarters, for the specific task of preparing and controlling the cross-border mission. On May 28 MACV also reported it had formed a unit at Nha Trang, on the central Vietnamese coast, for the planning and execution of "ARVN Special Forces operations in Laos."

Extra Green Berets arrived in the summer of 1964 and went straight to Long Thanh. The camp was quickly being improved. When Vietnamese LLDB instructors first arrived, demolitions classes had had to be carried out in a decrepit ammunition depot. Colonel Russell of SOG felt the demolition range barely existed; he also commented, "The firing ranges were totally inadequate to teach anybody to do anything with weaponry. The communications setup was extremely poor." The MACSOG commander proved as unimpressed as his Vietnamese trainees. With American prodding, before the end of 1964 a crash construction program refurbished Long Thanh to house about 250 recruits plus their ARVN and American instructors. Extended and paved with asphalt, the old airstrips eventually accommodated planes as big as the C-130. The strip acquired the radio code name "Bear Cat."

Formally, Long Thanh belonged to the South Vietnamese Army. Aside from the LLDB who worked with Americans, all the ARVN troops at Long Thanh came from the Strategic Exploitation Service, an intelligence arm of the general staff.* Colonel Tran Van Ho was in charge. A banker before entering the army, Ho had been around long enough to get some CIA experience, and as a lieutenant colonel took over the STD on the eve of its 1964 expansion. Though relatively uncorrupted, Colonel Ho proved malleable

---

*Because nomenclature changed several times during the war, and because Long Thanh represented one end of the pipeline feeding soldiers into the battle of The Trail, the names have to be disentangled and a common one adopted. Tran Van Ho, and many of the other people running these programs, remained the same throughout the period. The Liaison Bureau, which actually ran the missions, was a semi-independent organ of the ARVN Joint General Staff, but was related to Vietnamese Special Forces (LLDB) and the former 1st Observation Group. The group and bureau were folded into the Exploitation Service, which, in mid-1965, became the Strategic Technical Section. In 1967 this became the Strategic Technical Directorate (STD) of the Joint General Staff. To avoid confusion, only the last name will be used from here on.

and not very ambitious. These qualities enabled Ho to survive all the South Vietnamese *coups d'état* but also had other consequences. For one, though convinced the Tiger missions into the DRV were useless, Ho caved in to SOG when Americans pressed to continue them. Another consequence was that Colonel Ho, also in charge of reliability investigations for recruits, quickly developed a large backlog and never pushed his investigators to finish inquiries faster. Slow granting of security clearances became a major MACSOG headache.

Vietnamese recruits came from many places. Noncommissioned officers and men from ARVN front-line units—for example, the 22nd Division in the Central Highlands—were a regular manpower resource. The ARVN camp commander at Long Thanh, Colonel Ho Thieu, had long service in the South Vietnamese airborne branch, and used his contacts to furnish a stream of men drawn from paratroop and ranger training programs. Civilians were recruited directly into the Strategic Technical Directorate. Finally there was the LLDB, which provided occasional recruits as well as instructing the volunteers. Certain specialists, such as aircrews and pilots for STD planes and helicopters, or officers for coastal vessels, were nominated by their parent armed services.

Beyond security clearances there were other problems at Long Thanh. Disappointment at the primitive facilities proved strong at the beginning. Some complained recruits for Tiger missions and those for Laos were being compromised by mixing them together. A commando team leader who arrived at Long Thanh in late 1963 later observed to an American that the pooling "told us you didn't care about the secrecy anymore." Vietnamese began to desert in 1964, when the average number of recruits at Long Thanh stood at 190, and desertions were running at about a dozen a month.

More prosaic but equally important were the numerous differences among Vietnamese cadres. According to Lieutenant Colonel William C. Carper III, American senior adviser at Long Thanh from November 1964 to August 1965, Ho Thieu never imposed discipline effectively. "If you had a . . . problem," Carper recalled, "the matter was taken up with Colonel Ho's staff and usually the man was . . . placed in Saigon in another job or in Da Nang or Nha Trang . . . he was just moved out of the way and the pot stirred once more." A couple of the teams sent to North Vietnam in Carper's time were well selected, but most recruits had come from the Saigon area. Said Carper, "These personnel were highly mercenary and pretty unreliable and certainly not motivated." One difficulty was that recruits came to Long Thanh as civilians and believed they were not subject to regulations. Americans also expressed concern that counterparts were not well qualified and that, in general, Tran Van Ho's unit "did not provide enough depth in instructor[s]."

The training attempted to duplicate at Long Thanh what Americans learned in Special Forces school at Fort Bragg. First were almost three months of introductory courses on weapons, tactics, communications, medicine, psychological operations, and the like, in addition to parachute training.

During the second portion, trainees specialized in one of these skills. That would be followed by a month of field exercises. In 1965 the CIDG unit that provided guards for Long Thanh lost almost a third of its strength to desertion—much better-paying jobs were nearby, in Saigon. This weakened protection of the camp. The MACSOG and STD trainers compensated by conducting many of their field expeditions—three- to five-day patrols—in the Long Thanh area. Patrols gave recruits confidence, improved security around the base, acquainted everybody with the surroundings, and helped instructors find volunteers who could be made team leaders.

Colonel Carper came away convinced the Vietnamese could be good commandos. They were effective as medics, Carper observed, very good on the radio, and "they could navigate and function in the jungle in a highly successful manner," although "some of their shooting wasn't of the best." Carper felt, "The biggest problem . . . was in developing leadership and teamwork."

Despite obstacles, the preparation of Vietnamese moved ahead, and presently some teams were ready to go. For Carper that brought the worst time of all. What had made Sergeant Duncan feel guilty in the Leaping Lena mission—that Americans were not allowed to go into battle with their Vietnamese teams—Carper saw very differently. It was an impediment if instructors went into the field because it retarded the training. Yet Americans needed to go along to keep the loyalty of their commandos. The dilemma "did curtail my operations as far as the . . . North was concerned." Carper had to improvise. He knew things would be better if he had separate cadres of Americans for instructors and for missions, but at that time Special Forces had trouble just providing enough Green Berets for 5th Group, much less SOG needs. Eventually demand was met; one to three Americans and six to nine Vietnamese made up the usual team. The moment a team moved from its staging area to an airfield for a mission frequently brought crisis. That was when poor leadership surfaced, Carper discovered: "when it came time to launch on numerous occasions teams would refuse to go." It was "one hell of a job" to get commandos to board airplanes. One way or another the SOG and STD officers usually prevailed.

There were different problems with Vietnamese Air Force people. The first crop of pilots were fabulous airmen, not surprising since they were personally selected by then–air force leader Nguyen Cao Ky. It was Ky himself who, in 1961, flew the first CIA-inspired Tiger mission to the North, and he knew just how hard the flights were. To avoid detection a plane had to hug the ground or the surface of the sea, flying at night, both of which made navigation extremely difficult. The altitude also gave precious little margin when mountains or rocks reared up. The usual approach, directly up the mountain valleys of the Truong Son range, staying on the Laotian side of the border until the last minute, gradually became studded with antiaircraft defenses as well.

Air Commodore Ky led a squadron of the Vietnamese Air Force (VNAF) and from this chose most of the early mission pilots. But Ky was a politically engaged general, and 1964–1965 was the height of South Vietnam's bout of coup fever. Within the space of thirteen months there were no fewer than seven *coups d'état*. Nguyen Cao Ky stood in the thick of this action, and often it was VNAF planes that turned back an attempt or gave coup forces their key assist. The pilots of Ky's squadron were also his primary coup intervention unit. They were so good they flew both the C-47, a transport, and the A-1, a fighter-bomber. Loyal only to Nguyen Cao Ky, pilots sent up for some infiltration flight repeatedly hightailed it for Saigon at Ky's first whisper of need.

Clyde Russell of SOG felt completely frustrated with the air wing. He needed crews permanently in place at Nha Trang who could move a scout team from Bear Cat to a mission area. Russell saw Ky several times to work out the mechanics of VNAF support. Each time Air Commodore Ky assured MACSOG that everything would be fine. Each time nothing changed. Finally the VNAF began sending a trickle of airmen to Nha Trang, but now the Americans found the quality of crews dropping precipitously, to the point that some Vietnamese crews were judged incapable of flying the simplest, in-country missions. The crews also had to be checked out on a new airplane, the C-123 "Provider," which became the mainstay of SOG activities. That posed another difficulty for Americans, who themselves lacked instructor pilots with the proper clearances to work with SOG. The problem would be solved by training U.S. airmen already at SOG, then having them instruct the Vietnamese on the C-123. Over time the VNAF improved its contributing unit, the 83rd Special Operations Group, finally one of South Vietnam's best. Colonel Russell and his successors also pressed to have an American air wing directly attached to MACSOG and that, too, would come to pass.

As the Studies and Observation Group invented itself, the supply system became one final headache. Terry K. Lingle, a navy lieutenant, arrived at SOG headquarters to manage supplies in November 1964 and found almost no accountability. "There was no actual control over any of the supplies as far as I could tell other than the fact that they were locked in a warehouse," Lingle remembered. This may have carried over from the largesse in the CIA's setup, in which no one had to sign for anything or track it either. All the Americans, both officers and enlisted, had keys to the warehouse. The SOG leaders were entirely focused on getting their unit in gear and bent a deaf ear to pleas to back up the supply officer. An army major who first headed the warehouse complex could not make the system work, and Lieutenant Lingle had to be sent out to relieve him.

Terry Lingle discovered his logistics people were not experienced enough to maintain an inventory. Some supply specialists were drinking heavily, even during duty hours, with Vietnamese women who worked at the center. Throughout SOG the Americans indulged friends by granting them favors, including access to supplies. Lieutenant Lingle also found that the officer he relieved had been living with a woman right in the complex, and when the major left, a top sergeant took up with the same woman in an apartment nearby. This man would later be hauled before investigators looking into the theft of supplies from the warehouse. Even from the mundane standpoint of personnel assignment, it turned out most Americans assigned to the complex were parachute riggers, not supply specialists. "I don't believe," Terry Lingle concluded, "that supply discipline, as such, actually existed at MACSOG."

Undoubtedly, Lieutenant Lingle's opinion resulted partly from his navy perspective, unfamiliar with the freewheeling style of Special Forces. Both SOG and 5th Special Forces Group needed many things that did not appear in standard military inventories. The Counterinsurgency Supply Office on Okinawa, and a side arrangement with the CIA, played critical roles in this exotic procurement. Over time considerable progress occurred. Nevertheless, as late as 1967 Colonel John K. Singlaub, then heading SOG, believed the system had been overtaken by events. Colonel Harold R. Aaron, leading the 5th Group at the same time, felt there was too much duplication in supply. Thus problems persisted. Meanwhile, in 1965, when the lease expired on SOG's Saigon center at 10 Nguyen Minh Chien Street, the owner refused to renew. The Studies and Observation Group had to move its warehouse.

Through 1964 the SOG system handled an average of fifty tons of matériel a month. Major construction projects were at Long Thanh; at Nha Trang, where SOG built an upscale barracks for VNAF pilots, who were complaining about their quarters; at Saigon, location for a covert radio station; and at Da Nang, site for naval base facilities for operations 34A and Tiger. In 1965 the SOG construction related directly to the attack on The Trail—a launch pad for cross-border missions built at Kham Duc CIDG camp, and a command post for the same purpose at Camp Fay, the SOG base outside Da Nang.

Despite setbacks, American and South Vietnamese forces were gathering to hurl themselves on The Trail. In the border provinces and the Central Highlands, the 5th Special Forces Group held the line with its Montagnards. Though political chasms opened between the tribes and the Saigon government, forces were considerable. In September 1965 there were more than 1,300 Americans in the 5th Group, leading 24,400 strikers, a mobile strike force of 1,900, and 25,000 local defense militia. Project Delta had become a going concern, showing its prowess on battlefields in the Central Highlands. The Studies and Observation Group had begun hitting North Vietnam with 34A maritime operations and was about to take the field in Laos with Shining Brass. Its strength, too, was considerable: about 2,500 secret warriors, including 336 Americans, plus another 370 Vietnamese, Taiwanese, and Nungs (not to mention a sprinkling of CIA officers, perhaps 15 by one count). There were more than 1,800 people in Colonel Tran Van Ho's Strategic Technical Directorate. All this was in addition to ARVN regular units and the Americans, South Koreans, Thais, and Australians beginning to arrive in great numbers. On the other side of the hill, however, Hanoi itself had decided to escalate the war.

* * *

No matter how hard the decisions to be made, it was a little easier because of the surroundings. The French had had an eye for a place, and at Hanoi they had put their main administrative complex along the southern shore of the Grand Lac. The breezes were the best, enriched by the pleasant Botanical Garden. The Quai Clemenceau ran along the nearby Red River. The road led to the Doumer Bridge, named for a liberal French governor of Indochina, and spanned the Red River. There was an airfield just across the river, at Gia Lam. The French built their Government General building in the Botanical Gardens, and their Citadel stood right above the bridge and housed the military command.

When the Viet Minh took over Hanoi following the French war, many of the buildings did not even change function. Ho Chi Minh's presidential palace was the old colonial administration building, the Citadel still had the Ministry of Defense, and the Central Committee and the Ministry of Foreign Affairs were nearby. So were the embassies. The old Sûreté was the Security Ministry, and the Vietnamese had a foreign intelligence service center tucked away inside the Citadel complex. Perhaps the nicest quarters were those of the Radio Intercept Research Section at Thuy Khue, right on the Grand Lac. Until Hanoi's leaders rocked under the bombs of Rolling Thunder, they certainly faced none of the dangers of *bo dois* on The Trail.

Vietnamese leaders did not hesitate to raise their stake in the South. Exactly when they made their choice is still shrouded in the mists of history, though there are signs of a policy change scattered about. Hanoi decided to intervene on a large scale with its Vietnam People's Army (VPA). Hanoi made its move at about the time of the Gulf of Tonkin incident, perhaps a little before. It was in August 1964 that the People's Army assembled 400 men for Infiltration Group 53, which it sent down The Trail to Quang Tri. That was not unusual, but the difference was that the group *stayed together,* to become the 808th Battalion, instead of being broken up to cadre other units.

It was a short step from sending a combat unit to sending a major formation, and Hanoi soon made that decision, too. In the fall the VPA 325th Division began a regime of especially tough training. In due course orders to move came from the Citadel. According to Saigon sources, those orders came as early as April 1964. If so, the preparation period was quite extended. Components of the division began to gather in Quang Binh Province, north of the DMZ. Some units had made previous forays into Laos in support of The Trail; some manned small garrisons or screened the DRV border against South Vietnamese commando teams. It was November before the *bo dois* began to trek South. The 95th Regiment was the first to leave, skirting the DMZ, crossing into Laos where it met the border, then reaching Route 9 and marching to Tchepone. The unit then made its way to the region where Laos, Cambodia, and Vietnam share the border. By February 1965 the 2,000 *bo dois* of the 95th were in place opposite the Central Highlands. On February 15, People's Army troops ambushed an ARVN unit moving on

Route 19 near Pleiku. Nguyen Trong Hop of the 95th's 6th Battalion was captured that day and became the first prisoner ever taken from the VPA 325th Division.

The 101st Regiment began its own infiltration in mid-December, following the same route. It halted at Dong Hoi for a new issue of equipment but then was on its way. By December 20 the regiment was marching through Laos. It, too, made for the Central Highlands, but made for Kontum Province, arriving in February 1965. On March 8 the 101st Regiment entered combat, ambushing an ARVN military convoy twelve miles west of Dak To. During March the 1,200 *bo dois* of the regiment attacked at least three posts. Saigon identified the 101st Regiment after Nguyen Van Doanh of the 2d Battalion defected to the ARVN at Kontum on March 23.

The American bombers were too late to catch these major VPA movements. Navy planes from the *Coral Sea* made the first interdiction strike on the Mu Gia Pass on February 28. There were ten A-1H Skyraiders and fourteen jets, A-4C Skyhawks, accompanied by two photo planes. The planes dropped bombs that ranged from 500 to 2,000 pounds, some set to detonate as long as six days later. This attack, and the Air Force hit on the Napé Pass on March 3, were on the Vietnamese side of the border, but the following week Souvanna Phouma approved a list of U.S. interdiction targets that included the passes, and on March 21 planes from the carrier *Hancock* struck the Laotian side of Mu Gia. The infiltration corridor was now being cut by a new initiative, Steel Tiger, to distinguish it from air action in northern Laos, which remained the goal of Barrel Roll.

These American attacks missed the 325th Division's last regiment, the 18th, since it crossed the Laotian border at the western end of the Demilitarized Zone. This was a close thing, however, for the 1,500 men of the 18th did not begin moving until March 15, were at Dong Hoi on March 17, and briefly entered Laos on March 20, swinging back into Vietnam beneath the DMZ. Had the United States detected the move, it could easily have been this regiment, not the Mu Gia, that was struck the next day. The 18th Regiment in Quang Tri Province posed a direct threat to the U.S. Special Forces camp at Khe Sanh. In June the regiment moved farther south, into Quang Nam Province, and elements of the 18th participated in a rocket attack on the Da Nang air base on July 1.

Vietnam People's Army moves demonstrated not only that Hanoi was serious about the war but also showed that its effort was as yet still rather weak on the ground. The dispersion of the 325th Division over many provinces of South Vietnam made it impossible to do much more than stiffen the Viet Cong. In fact, the VPA's dilution of its division's strength was even greater because other divisional elements were converted directly into Viet Cong formations. Staffs cadred new units; weapons units were diverted to serve the needs of the command of Interzone V. The 325th Division had not been that powerful to begin with, its biggest weapons being 82-mm mortars and 75-mm recoilless rifles. Nevertheless, news of the VPA troops fighting in the South, which became known in Washington in short order, would be an important catalyst in President Johnson's decision to dispatch major U.S. ground forces to Vietnam.

Meanwhile, the Steel Tiger bombing had little discernible effect on VPA supply movements. Road-watch teams below the Mu Gia Pass reported 185 trucks driving south in December 1964. In February, when teams were in position 27 days of the month, they counted 311 trucks headed south and 172 going north. In March the figures were 481 and 658, respectively. The pass was bombed in both those months. In April, again with teams on station for almost the entire month, 640 trucks were counted driving south, and 775 to the north. In all, between December 1964 and May 1965, 2,294 Vietnamese trucks were seen moving south and 2,492 in the opposite direction. Aerial photographs for the first time showed gasoline tanker trucks on The Trail—clear evidence that Hanoi intended a major expansion of capacity.

By June, when the monsoon began, the United States had flown more than 4,000 interdiction sorties in Steel Tiger. Besides snakes and tigers, The Trail now held even more perils. In a typical case, a VPA battalion had to detrain and hide out in a state farm in Thanh Hoa, then move only by night. Father south there was another train for a few miles, but almost all the bridges had been bombed out right down into Quang Binh; ferry crossings that replaced the bridges were especially dangerous because of U.S. planes on armed reconnaissance. Local residents appeared anxious about bombing when asked to provide lodging. One village was bombed three times while the infiltrators were in its vicinity. On Route 12, approaching the Mu Gia Pass, bridges had been replaced by underwater causeways for men and trucks. One company actually got caught and suffered casualties to air strikes. Despite such accounts, it was the monsoon that shut The Trail to motorized movement.

Through the monsoon season Hanoi shifted to an intense focus on improving The Trail. The leadership clustered around the lakes must have decided about the time Lyndon Johnson announced initial marine landings and an enclave strategy. Major General Phan Trong Tue, minister of transport and communication in the DRV government, recalls that it was in April when he received the call to come to the Central Party Commission. General Tue had just finished hosting a conference of the socialist bloc's international railway association. Tue took delegates to see the damage inflicted by U.S. bombers around Ha Long Bay, one of Vietnam's natural wonders and a frequent destination for visitors. Upset by the destruction, Tue knew Hanoi was secretly helping the Liberation Front in the South, for it was his ministry that built the disguised junks and steel-hulled transport vessels Hanoi's navy used to carry supplies by sea. Given a coconut from the southernmost point of Indochina as a memento, to preserve the secret arms shipments General Tue had had the tree planted in an anonymous village rather than the front patio of his ministry. Tue also knew that the American and South Vietnamese naval patrols were choking off the sea route. Destruction of a hundred-ton ship on a run to the South a couple of months before signaled that a new way had to be found to increase supplies to the South.

Arriving at the Central Party Commission, Phan Trong Tue found General Giap, who promptly informed him of the decision of the Politburo to expand The Trail. Warlord Giap asked General Tue to assume command of the 559th Group in addition to his duties with the transportation ministry. April 1965 marked the beginning of a long headache for Phan Trong Tue.

General Tue was new to The Trail, though walking it had long been among his dreams. As a young political officer in the South, Tue had heard of a route from Tonkin early in the war against the French. He had wanted to visit his native village, where his mother had just returned after release from prison. On a later trip to the North, Tue had had to go by sea due to the pressures of time. Only in 1955, when he led People's Army border troops around Vinh Linh, just above the DMZ, did Phan Trong Tue get his first direct exposure to the lore of The Trail. In 1959 and 1960, just prior to his appointment to the ministry of transportation, Tue had supervised a buildup of security forces in the Vinh Linh region that was specifically intended to protect the early 559th Group camps. Once Tue had felt it necessary to blow up a bridge in the DMZ to prevent international control commission observers from discovering the secret of Hanoi's supply route.

Phan Trong Tue recounted much of this story at the meeting he held of 559th Group leaders to review progress on The Trail. Colonel Vo Bam would remain with the group as deputy commander. Another colonel, Vu Xuan Chiem, who had been with Tue in a French prison, became deputy political officer behind Tue himself, who held both the command and political posts. Colonel Dieu headed the engineer corps, while Colonel Vu Van Don ran the transport service staff. The officers quickly agreed on a reorganization of the 559th to carry out expansion of The Trail. To manage the work General Tue usually spent afternoons at 559th Group headquarters on Ly Dam De Street in Hanoi, following mornings at the ministry ordering creation of new units needed on The Trail. That both organizations were physically located in Hanoi greatly simplified the work.

In the field the 559th Group's forces were put into units by geographical area, essentially one of three sectors that corresponded to divisional commands. Limited personnel at the old way stations were increased by engineer, construction, communications, and air defense troops. The old transport units of porters were now assigned to regular stations. More infantry came to defend the stations, which finally amounted to real base areas and which would be called *binh tram* units. Fresh motorized units became the backbone of the transportation effort. On the main road of the first line, the assigned truck units totaled 245 vehicles, and there was also an independent company with 95 more.

The Trail benefited from Phan Trong Tue's appointment because his ministry of transportation controlled resources for building roads as well as for traveling on them. The units initially sent to Laos to widen existing roads and open new ones consisted of more than 1,000 specialists, with another

1,500 young volunteers and about 30 pieces of mechanized equipment. Felling trees behind them, to pave the roads and permit passage in the face of monsoons, were 300 more engineers and 2,000 volunteers, many of them women from Ha Tinh Province. Their work would be considered so valuable that, later in the war, Minister of Defense Vo Nguyen Giap personally traveled to visit the women's volunteer units to thank them for their labors.

People's Army troop movements began in earnest in July. At that point there were four VPA regiments in the South, consisting of the 325th Division plus the independent 32nd Regiment, which had arrived opposite Pleiku Province in January or February. Now regiment after regiment, and many smaller units as well, departed the DRV. Before the year was out, seven more regiments—almost 12,000 *bo dois*—had joined the trek. The People's Army sent another 8,000 soldiers in smaller infantry and sapper units, more than 10,000 replacements, plus divisional staffs and other odds and ends. The VPA began sending specialized units, too, such as the C100 Sniper Company (130 men), the 711st Group (300 men) of tank specialists, and the 7th Signal Battalion.

The flow of Vietnam People's Army reinforcements included units capable of improving The Trail itself, perhaps amounting to 4,500 *bo dois* in the second half of 1965. These comprised four new engineer battalions, several transport companies, and, most significantly, at least eight antiaircraft units. Truong Son commander General Phan Tong Tue supplemented his 70th Transportation Group (sector) with two new entities, the 71st and 72d, each of which was responsible for extending The Trail into new parts of South Vietnam. Road construction (see Map 4) progressed apace, as did improvement of routes inside the DRV. By the end of 1965 there were probably 10,000 to 12,000 Vietnamese directly involved in maintaining or expanding the Truong Son network in Laos and Vietnam, an estimated 6,000 porters, and an unknown number of troops in a security role. There were also 80,000 laborers at work on transportation routes in the southern part of the Democratic Republic, including about 21,000 working on roads and bypasses between Vinh and Ha Tinh, and 6,000 dredging rivers and estuaries.

Hanoi's resolution was shown in other ways, too, particularly by manpower policies of the Vietnam People's Army. Before the war the term of service for *bo dois* had been three years. In 1961 this was actually reduced to two years, but the term reverted in 1962. In 1964, ominously, the VPA stopped discharging people altogether. Service was to be for the duration. Draft calls had been twice a year, but were increased to three times annually in 1964, and by late 1965 Vietnamese of the DRV were being drafted at any time. Not only were wartime needs driving draft calls, but also the urgency of the battlefield began affecting training. A later survey of 125 VPA soldiers captured during 1965, of whom all but 13 were draftees, showed that more than half of the *bo dois* had less than a year of service and fully a third fewer than six months. As for unit infiltration training, that had varied from up to two months in the case of one People's Army battalion, down to none at all.

Map 4: Trail Extensions in 1965

◆ Allied "Roadwatch" Teams, June 1965
—— Road in use Jan. 1, 1964
━━ Road Constructed by Sept. 1, 1965

While Hanoi girded itself for war, National Liberation Front and VPA forces remained on the offensive in the South. One element of their strategy was a campaign of pressure against the Special Forces camps behind the Vietnamese border. Another was the attacks in II Corps, the Pleiku shelling among them. Several district towns in the highlands had to be abandoned. In the lowlands the ARVN suffered another defeat at Ba Gia, where a full battalion was decimated.

Le Duan wrote anew to local cadres in the South in May. "The war of aggression in the South is being gradually 'Americanized,'" declared Hanoi's political mastermind. "The war of destruction against the North is being stepped up. . . . We must show our determination to rely on our own forces, and fight for our cause and for the glory of present and future generations."

In Washington, demands grew for even greater commitments of U.S. ground forces. Despite misgivings among some Americans there was a bandwagon effect in public opinion. In late July Lyndon Johnson made his momentous decision to forge ahead in Vietnam. Polls showed that 61 percent of Americans supported the president. LBJ gave Westmoreland what MACV was asking for—the airmobile division, the army's First Team, with plenty of other forces to round it out. Troop strength would increase to 175,000. Westmoreland shifted to an offensive stance. More men would follow as needed, President Johnson said. Saigon was asking for 100,000. Vietnam had become a big war. Westy intended to throw the First Team, actually called the 1st Cavalry Division (Airmobile), right into the highlands. This would be the arena for the first big fight, and the *bo dois* were arriving there just as fast as any Americans.

An early casualty of the struggle on the border would be the surveillance post at A-Ro. Situated in the foothills at the head of the A Shau valley, A-Ro fell of its own weight, or perhaps the lack thereof. This site had been a favorite of "Hanging Sam" Williams and opened during Lionel McGarr's time as MAAG chief. By 1965 they were long gone, and General Westmoreland had much more interest in the coast, where he was landing an expeditionary force, and in the Central Highlands, where battles raged. The military role of A-Ro began to be questioned by the U.S. command in Saigon.

To add to its difficulties, the A-Ro camp suffered from numerous defects. The place had been carved into the top of a hill, and its perimeter enclosed the airfield, which meant the strip was as small as could be imagined, not properly graded, and too narrow. The air force refused to land fixed-wing aircraft at A-Ro, and the only army plane that alighted there could never get off the ground again. The local tribes were Katu and took little interest in the war. Patrols sometimes found their huts in the forest but hardly ever saw any tribesmen. Americans had to import CIDG units for the garrison, but since Montagnard strikers were most effective in their own tribal lands, that did little for this beleaguered camp. A-Ro proved dicey at best. On April 24, 1965, its fortifications were blown up, the post abandoned.

There were also times South Vietnamese or Americans got in the licks. Out of Khe Sanh, for example, an October 1964 patrol had crossed the Lao border, found a People's Army company camped out, and shot their bivouac to pieces. The patrol brought back hard evidence, including VPA gear and ID cards. There were other patrol actions, too, and Green Beret Pete Morakon, who served at Khe Sanh with detachment A-101, was convinced the People's Army began to pay attention to Khe Sanh because it was a thorn in their side. By late 1965 the situation in the district had become tense. Nancy Costello, a civilian missionary for Wycliff Bible Translators, considered it too dangerous to make her rounds. Evidence was that VPA units were no longer just passing through on their way somewhere else. A new Green Beret commander arriving that October saw one of his own strikers sighting in a machine gun on the team house.

Farther south in Thua Thien, that summer the South Vietnamese came up with intelligence of a major enemy supply center and made a big sweeping operation. As it happened, Interzone V indeed had two depots in the La Hap area, along with the supply command for its whole sector. The VPA officer who had recently taken charge recounted there were as many as 4,000 tons of supplies at risk. In a battle that lasted several days, *bo dois* were able to keep losses to a minimum. The Americans followed up with destructive raids by B-52 heavy bombers. Colonel Hong Ky relates that the huge bombers collapsed every shelter but destroyed only 20 barrels of gasoline and a few supplies. In view of the combat power of the B-52s, the VPA officer considered the damage a success.

So much for I Corps. In II Corps the situation, bad as it had been earlier in 1965, only got worse. American intelligence learned that Viet Cong units were relocating from the coast to the foothills of the Central Highlands, and the United States confirmed the presence of People's Army regiments. Among the discoveries were indications that Hanoi exercised direct control and that headquarters—in effect, divisional commands—had been created to manage many regiments at a time. The pace of fighting picked up starting in June. A district town west of Pleiku was overrun and lost, followed by another in Kontum. On July 7 the VPA took Dak To, north of Kontum, but were driven out after a day. Mortars harassed many outposts, including Kontum itself. Action in the Highlands forced Saigon to send reinforcements into II Corps, including a two-battalion task force of Vietnamese marines and ARVN's airborne brigade, with four paratroop battalions under it.

A major battle now took place southwest of Pleiku, at the Special Forces camp of Duc Co. Just seven miles from the Lao border, Duc Co guarded the one road Diem had completed that almost reached that goal. In a basin, the approach to its airstrip came in over a high ridge. Its triangular perimeter smaller than that of a football field, Duc Co's garrison numbered a few hundred CIDGs, an ARVN Special Forces team, and Captain Richard B. Allen's Green Beret detachment A-215. From the end of June, when a nearby district town fell, Duc Co was considered endangered.

At Pleiku, ARVN II Corps command post, everyone worried about a mountain fastness called the Chu Pong, which lay beyond Duc Co and straddled the border. No one had any idea how many *bo dois* might be in those hills, though mortar craters all around the camp testified to the threat. Opinions were more optimistic at the headquarters for the 24th Special Tactical Zone, which had tactical responsibility for Duc Co. These differences led to an unusual scouting mission in the sector.

At Nha Trang the 5th Special Forces Group had expert scouts in its Project Delta. Major Charles A. Beckwith held the command. "A lot of guys went to Vietnam just to get their ticket punched," General Henry Emerson recounted. "But I only knew ten or twelve who were 'certified'—who were really going after it. Charlie was one of them. He was always willing to take risks." Known as "Chargin' Charlie," Beckwith, a dynamic officer, proved a Special Forces disciple. He volunteered for Vietnam following the one-year course at the army's Command and General Staff College. Colonel Bill McKean of the 5th Group put Beckwith in charge of B-52, the detachment that ran Delta.

Charlie Beckwith breathed new life into Project Delta, demoralized from the Leaping Lena failure. It became an elite unit, ultimately the equivalent of a battalion. Beckwith created larger combat platoons to beef up the scouts who had proven so vulnerable in the reconnaissance to Tchepone. The teams themselves were led by Americans from Beckwith's B-52 detachment, a major gain over the composition of the patrols sent on the failed cross-border operation. Moreover, inside South Vietnam, Project Delta could count on much better helicopter support from the Vietnamese helicopter unit assigned to special operations.

Duc Co became a Delta mission. In July, Major Beckwith was tapped to scout two trails that ran back into the Chu Pong but intersected the road, Route 19, behind Duc Co. "This was Indian country," Charlie Beckwith recalls. "Bad. We were supposed to put teams on the ground and report enemy sightings back to II Corps." In Vietnam barely a month, Duc Co was Beckwith's second mission. Chargin' Charlie decided to go along to see how the Vietnamese commandos did in the field. The Vietnamese chose a good hideaway to stay the night, a thicket on a hill. The scene was calm enough that, before dawn, a tiger walked up to rest in the grass nearby. This incident terrified Beckwith but convinced him that if tigers were at play, the North Vietnamese must be far away. The three-day tour was uneventful except for the tiger, and the Vietnamese H-34 pilot who came to get them was sharp enough to pick up their landing zone just by the flash of a mirror. Beckwith's scout team was back at Nha Trang before dinner. The Delta reconnaissance may have been a source of the optimism of ARVN leaders at Pleiku.

The usual way Delta teams operated was to have a look around before a major offensive. In Beckwith's case, too, II Corps planned an action around Duc Co. A two-battalion ARVN Airborne task force came to Pleiku in early August. The whole situation on the border was dramatic enough to attract the attention of Associated Press reporter Peter Arnett, who went to Duc Co to report from the Green Beret camp.

When the ARVN Airborne checked with 24th Zone command for their orders, they were told to clear the Duc Co sector. The paratroopers were supposed to sweep the camp perimeter and move out to the border, following it for a distance before swinging back to Duc Co. The order could have been written by an American staff. But the senior adviser to the task force found out that virtually everything in the order that was critical to the operation was also wrong. The promised air support was impossible to secure in the time left before execution; artillery was nonexistent; the designated backup unit, a ranger battalion, had just come in from the field and had dispersed on leave; and the intended landing zone was a clearing on headquarters maps that did not exist in the jungle.

Senior adviser to the Vietnamese paratroopers was another American who attained later fame, H. Norman Schwarzkopf, who would lead Coalition forces in the 1990–1991 war with Iraq. In 1965 Schwarzkopf was an army captain and the man at the receiving end of the faulty Duc Co plan. It proved the beginning of an extended mission from hell. Captain Schwarzkopf advised rejection of the concept, and his ARVN counterpart did exactly that.

The reluctance of the vaunted ARVN airborne task force led to a late-night confrontation at the downtown Pleiku mansion of General Vinh Loc, commander and virtual warlord of II Corps. Ted Mataxis remembers the session as a staff meeting, II Corps following up on the airborne's comments on the battle plan. Colonel Mataxis was still top American adviser to the corps commander. Schwarzkopf recalls the meeting as an inquisition, practically a court-martial. He was prodded about the airborne's rejection of the plan, told there were no enemy in Indian country, and even had his competence challenged. Schwarzkopf stood his ground, Mataxis tried to relieve him, then the dispute went up the chain of command. The chief adviser to ARVN airborne forces, Schwarzkopf's boss, flew up from Saigon to review the issues. After seeing the operations plan, he upheld Schwarzkopf. To make things even more plain, he took the opportunity to stage a promotion ceremony, pinning new insignia on Norman Schwarzkopf, whose elevation to major had just come through.

Pleiku revised its plan, and the airborne task force eventually landed right at Duc Co. Despite preparatory air strikes by Skyraiders, ships among the forty-helicopter transport lift came under fire as they landed. Far from there being no enemy in Indian country, the 32d Regiment of the Vietnam People's Army was investing Duc Co. Colonel Dinh Khanh of the 32d had 1,800 bo dois under arms. The 3d and 8th airborne Battalions of Schwarzkopf's ARVN task force had fewer than 1,000. Of the Green Beret officer he met upon landing, Schwarzkopf writes, "I don't think I'd ever met a happier man . . . we represented his salvation."

Salvation remained far away. Things became hairy when the airborne began its sweep. On the first day there was an encounter with some enemy within a couple of miles of the border in which the paratroopers took losses. Helicopters refused to lift out the bodies; Major Schwarzkopf won the loyalty of his ARVN charges when he threatened a pilot to get the job done. On the second day, moving back toward Duc Co, the paratroopers were startled by the sound of a mortar shell being inserted into a tube, the start of a firefight. Most of the force got back to Duc Co, but radio revealed that part of the 3d Battalion were lost in the jungle. Major Schwarzkopf went out and brought them back, then went out again when it became clear that yet a smaller party had been separated also, and it needed help to come in.

Back in Duc Co began a siege that went on for the better part of two weeks. Peter Arnett landed from the helicopter of an intrepid pilot of the Army's 52d Aviation Battalion, which still flew from Camp Holloway at Pleiku. "I was the first off," Arnett remembers, "but it turned out to be safer on the chopper. Shells blasted around us almost immediately." The camp consisted of "rusty barbed-wire defenses," and after dawn Arnett could see "a sorry mess: the roofs ripped from the wooden administration shacks and barracks, and sandbagged defenses torn apart and ragged, their contents spilled onto the ground."

The reporter met Major Schwarzkopf. "The truth is we're sitting ducks here," Arnett quotes the major saying, "the Viet Cong can hit us any time they like."

Bo dois besieged Duc Co for ten days. During that time supplies came by parachute drop, and many fell inside VPA lines. Half the Montagnard strikers deserted. The airborne suffered forty dead and twice that number wounded. No one would fly in to evacuate the wounded until Lieutenant Earl S. Van Eiweegen, doing the bar circuit in Pleiku, heard of Duc Co's plight and insisted. His twin-engine transport, a C-123, just made it. Lingering only long enough to pick up the ARVN wounded, Van Eiweegen's plane still took mortar damage and more than twenty small-arms hits. He nevertheless flew the wounded all the way to Saigon. At Duc Co demoralized CIDG strikers stopped fighting and just hung around the camp.

At Pleiku the 24th Special Tactical Zone, whose American adviser was Lieutenant Colonel Edward B. Smith Jr., set up a relief column. Forces allotted by II Corps included the ARVN 3d Armored Task Force, a small unit with a company of M-41 tanks, one of armored personnel carriers, and a couple of guns. Much more powerful was the Vietnamese marines' Task Force Alpha, composed of the 1st and 5th Marine Battalions. The group was making its way toward Duc Co when the marines ran into a Vietnam People's Army battalion dug in along the road. When the South Vietnamese stopped, another VPA battalion came out of the jungle to hit their rear. Major William G. Leftwich Jr., American adviser to the Vietnamese marine task force, rallied the Vietnamese.

Colonel Mataxis watched the firefight from a helicopter above. Mataxis knew how the war was changing—this battlefield vigil was only the latest of a dozen since that night in February when Pleiku had been attacked. Among the first senior U.S. officers to be shot down in a chopper—because Vietnamese counterparts refused to heed his warnings in one of the highlands battles—Mataxis was able to call on air support or commit his

U.S.-controlled Eagle Flight of Montagnard troops. He worried about the highlands. Before, an ARVN company had always been enough to get the Viet Cong to melt away. Now II Corps was running actions more than ten times that big, and the adversary stayed to fight. When Mataxis came up with his first evidence of Hanoi's regular army in the highlands, MACV had refused to accept it, so the data had been passed to the CIA. Here, beneath the adviser's helicopter, battle still raged, though II Corps had the equivalent of six battalions already involved in the Duc Co business. The Vietnam People's Army *bo dois* were emerging from the woods in whole platoons, trundling heavy weapons and all. It looked like World War I.

Ted Mataxis sent out a call for American troops, and General Westmoreland responded by ordering up his first big unit, the 173d Airborne Brigade, recently arrived in Vietnam. In an airlift of 150 sorties, the 173d reached Pleiku. By then Major Leftwich and the big column on Route 19 had overcome the VPA ambush, but the American paratroopers occupied a critical pass on the road behind the relief force, and sent small heliborne patrols into clearings all around the area. The relief column pressed onward, arriving at Duc Co to break the siege.

This battle brought the proverbial fifteen seconds of fame to Duc Co. Peter Arnett had gone, but a new crop of reporters descended. So did Colonel Mataxis and General Westmoreland, who briefed the journalists on the battle of Duc Co. Schwarzkopf, who survived the siege and who had been pressed to come up with some estimate of enemy killed the brass could use to brag, was annoyed that men who knew nothing of the realities were now posing as experts on the action. Schwarzkopf had one more brief spat with Mataxis but found the senior adviser mostly solicitous.

Westmoreland was another matter. The general emerged from a meeting at one point to praise marine major Leftwich, telling reporters Leftwich was the best adviser in Vietnam. Later, finding a circle clustered around Schwarzkopf, Westy broke up the proceedings, saying he needed to speak with the major privately. "Please get the microphones out of here," Westy had said, "I want to talk to this man."

After an awkward silence, General Westmoreland then asked Norman Schwarzkopf, "How's the chow been?"

The ARVN airborne adviser, who had been existing on a diet of rice and raw jungle turnips gathered on dangerous sallies by his Vietnamese paratroopers, was stunned. The best Schwarzkopf could manage was, "Uh, fine, sir."

Then Westy came back with, "Have you been getting your mail regularly?"

Schwarzkopf assumed so, though, of course, nothing like mail was ever delivered at Duc Co.

Westmoreland ended the séance with a simple, "Good, good. Fine job, lad."

Norman Schwarzkopf resented being called a lad, and the rest of the exchange didn't please him very much more. As a general and U.S. field commander in another war, Schwarzkopf was notorious for his short fuse and fierce temper, in fact acquiring the nickname "Stormin' Norman." Schwarzkopf dates the emergence of his temper to the battle of Duc Co.

Other than Stormin' Norman's temper, the legacy of the Duc Co battle was one of the 3d Armored Task Force's M-41 tanks, disabled near the Special Forces camp; the tank was considered not worth towing back to Pleiku. Instead the tank was dragged into the Duc Co perimeter and dug in, its turret gun henceforth part of the camp's defenses. The VPA 32d Regiment faded into Indian country, the Chu Pong, where more People's Army units were arriving off The Trail daily. The VPA were soon ready to renew their offensive, but this time MACV, the ARVN Joint General Staff, II Corps, everybody, knew they were there. General Westmoreland determined to do something about it. The Cav, his First Team, was already on its way. Westy had plans for his 1st Cavalry Division (Airmobile), but he did not have a free hand. Freedom of action was going to be affected by what was happening in many other places. Beijing, Moscow, and Washington would be as important to Vietnam as Saigon. So would Los Angeles; Detroit; and Peoria, Illinois.

CHAPTER 6

The World and The 'Nam

As Americans began to find themselves in Vietnam, thousand upon thousand, they developed a language all their own. This was a commonality, binding comrades thrown together from diverse lives and experiences, not different from the practice in other wars in other times and other places. In World War II soldiers had called themselves "GIs," a play upon the jargon term of that day for "government issue" food, clothes, and equipment. While the tag GI was still favored by journalists, the soldiers of Vietnam called themselves "grunts." Vietnam itself became "The 'Nam." Everything else was "The World." Going home upon completing a tour of duty was returning to The World. More and more things that happened everywhere else—in The World—were going to affect the lives of the men and women in The 'Nam. The terms came to feel right, oddly appropriate in a reality in which so much seemed to be wrong.

In actuality the language of the Vietnam War would be exactly descriptive. Things that happened in China, in Russia, internationally, and in the United States exercised a direct effect on the war. A true understanding of the Vietnam experience is impossible without putting The World in its context in The 'Nam. Indeed, as far as The Trail is concerned, developments in The World were central to what did and did not happen in the battle for The Trail. Prior to immersion in that battle, therefore, The World needs to be set in key relief.

Before Vietnam became a shooting war, before Beijing made the decisions on military assistance that it did in consequence of the Gulf of Tonkin, Chinese leaders already spoke of their relationship with Hanoi as an alliance of "brotherly comrades." Despite historical animosities, that ideological tie continued and deepened under pressure of the Vietnam conflict. After Tonkin Gulf, Beijing took protective measures along its border with Vietnam and increased its shipments of military goods to Hanoi. In 1965 the ties between the People's Republic of China and the Democratic Republic of Vietnam rose to a new level.

Visits of top leaders and delegations provide a clear window into the evolution of a military alliance. As early as June 1964 Mao Zedong had told the Vietnam People's Army chief of staff, General Van Tien Dung, "Our two parties and countries must cooperate and fight the enemy together. Your business is my business and my business is your business . . . [we] must deal with the enemy together without conditions." That July Chinese foreign minister Zhou Enlai and a delegation talked in Hanoi with both Vietnamese and Laotian Communist leaders. In a joint message to Hanoi just after the Tonkin Gulf incident, Zhou and the Chinese army chief of staff asked the DRV to survey requirements and report its needs. Without getting everything it wanted, Hanoi got some of what it needed.

On April 8, 1965, the Chinese tracked U.S. Navy planes over Hainan Island, and four MiG jets scrambled in an attempt to intercept. Chinese sources report the planes were not to shoot unless fired upon; the American aircraft did open fire. Zhou Enlai was briefed that night. Shortly afterward Chinese naval and air forces, previously under instructions to avoid combat with Americans, were ordered to attack when U.S. planes intruded. On April 12 Chinese air forces were warned to stand by for possible large-scale military action.

The day of the air intrusion, Vietnamese Party official Le Duan and Defense Minister General Vo Nguyen Giap were in Beijing for high-level discussions with the Chinese. Their aid was the best Hanoi was getting, both in quantity and quality. The Vietnamese asked for even more help, including engineer troops and air force pilots. Chinese leader Liu Shaoqi told the Vietnamese that Beijing was determined to render every assistance. "It is our policy that we will do our best to support you," Liu had said. "The initiative will be completely at your disposal."

General Giap continued talks directly at the military staff level. On April 17, with Giap still in Beijing, the VPA staff cabled a request that Chinese engineering troops be sent to Tonkin Gulf offshore islands to construct defenses. The Chinese created a "Corps of Railway Services." Its first deployment was a unit to Hon Gay, a district just across the Vietnamese border known for its offshore islands. A "Chinese People's Volunteer Engineering Force" also formed to furnish the construction resources the Vietnamese wanted. The sides signed a formal agreement on April 27, and that and subsequent additions specified more than a hundred projects with which China would assist the Democratic Republic of Vietnam.

In related action, on April 2, 1965, Foreign Minister Zhou Enlai asked the president of Pakistan to convey a communication to Lyndon Johnson. Zhou promised that China would not start a war with the United States, but warned that if war came, Beijing was prepared; the United States would not be able to withdraw, and no policy of mere bombing would suffice. "We will unhesitatingly rise in resistance and fight to the end," Zhou declared. "Once the war breaks out, it will have no boundaries."

A month later Ho Chi Minh himself visited China—it was a secret visit—and met with Mao Zedong. The talks took place on May 16, not in Beijing, but in Changsha, capital of Mao's boyhood province, where the Chinese

Communist Party leader stopped to exchange his deluxe private train for a car en route to the interior. Mao's trip was part of a maneuver against party opponents in a power struggle. Ho Chi Min's mission was to request new aid. Ho spoke of the burden of The Trail, of the rugged land, and of forging the necessary roads and tracks. Vietnamese could do it, Ho assured Mao, if the DRV could divert resources from the northern part of the country. Chinese troops could make up for the ones Hanoi sent South. Ho wanted help on a dozen roads north of Hanoi. Mao agreed.

In early June General Van Tien Dung followed up, flying to Beijing to meet with the Chinese chief of staff. They coordinated plans for several options. If the South Vietnamese attacked the DRV using U.S. naval and air support, China would give similar forces to Hanoi. If American forces engaged directly in the North, the PLA would become the Vietnam People's Army's strategic reserve. The generals completed preparations for PLA engineer units to enter Vietnam. The Chinese formed a policy group for Indochina, and a committee of managers to oversee the actual programs, under the chairmanship of the People's Liberation Army chief of staff.

The 1st Division of People's Volunteers was a railway unit. It would have the longest service in the DRV. Composed of six regiments, it would be joined by two more in the summer of 1968. One of the division's major projects would be the rail line that followed the Red River valley down to Hanoi. By 1966 Yen Bay, the town where this line crossed the border, became a huge complex, more than 200 buildings, hardened command bunkers, antiaircraft guns dug into the surrounding hills. Before the last elements of the unit left Vietnam in 1970, the division would have built 14 tunnels, 39 bridges, 20 railroad stations, and 70 miles of new track. The Chinese also repaired and maintained 217 miles of existing rail lines.

On June 6, three weeks ahead of the railway troops, the 2d Division of People's Volunteers began crossing into the DRV, initially to work on defenses and communication systems at eight points along the Tonkin Gulf coast and on fifteen offshore islands. The division included three engineer regiments, a hydrology brigade, a maritime transport detachment, a truck transport regiment, a communications engineering unit, and several antiaircraft elements—in all, 12,000 PLA troops. The commander was invited to Hanoi and was received warmly by Vietnamese leaders, including Ho Chi Minh, Pham Van Dong, and General Giap.

Military capabilities in the form of antiaircraft units from the Chinese armed forces also entered the DRV. A Chinese Navy antiaircraft regiment was one of the earliest to deploy, its men told to wear white shirts to distinguish them from the VPA regulars. The 61st and 63d Divisions of the antiaircraft troops of the PLA were requested by the Vietnamese General Staff on July 24. They began to enter on August 1. Four days later the 61st set up its initial fighting positions—at Yen Bay. Their first engagement with a U.S plane occurred on August 9. The 63d Division first fought at Kep, a base of Hanoi's air force, on August 23. On both dates Chinese sources maintain one American plane was shot down. The tally through the Rolling Thunder campaign, again according to the Chinese, was 2,154 fights, in which 1,707 American planes were shot down and 1,608 damaged.*

At a minimum the United States obtained a partial picture of these developments. U.S. intelligence detected the movement of the headquarters of the PLA 2d Division into Vietnam in the last week of June. In late July, analyzing limited data when available, the Watch Committee of the U.S. Intelligence Board noted: "Available evidence to date . . . continues to indicate . . . probable primary association with military logistic operations from Communist China into the DRV or to Southwest China. Our evidence is now much stronger that several of these entities are located in northeastern North Vietnam." By October 17 the CIA was reporting "a possible change" in China's "overall military posture in this area," including deployment of an additional regiment of jet fighters to Hainan island. As of October 20 the CIA was projecting PLA troop strength in the DRV at 15,000 to 20,000 and was aware of the 2d Division's "border defense/coastal security mission." Langley also remarked, "In late June, a high-level probable logistics authority [deleted] was detected moving from the Kwangsi area of south China to the [Hon Gay region]." Additional movements of what could be railway engineers were noted that could raise Chinese strength to 30,000 to 35,000. Ominously, the CIA reported Chinese contingency plans, "possibly beginning in April," to further reinforce the PLA forces: "The number could be relatively high, perhaps as many as several hundred thousand." Beijing's moves were obviously no surprise in Washington.

Throughout this period, which coincided with President Johnson's agonizing over his decision to send large numbers of ground troops to South Vietnam, U.S. intelligence produced a steady stream of Special National Intelligence Estimates (SNIEs) on probable responses to American action options. At the inception of Rolling Thunder an SNIE predicted a "fair chance" Beijing would introduce "limited numbers of Chinese ground forces as 'volunteers.'" There was a possibility of "more extreme Chinese reactions—such as introduction of large-scale ground force combat units . . . though we think this unlikely in the early stages."† The State Department's intelligence unit dissented, believing the chance "is considerably higher than is estimated." An amplifying special estimate circulated in Washington a week later added, "We think it unlikely that the Chinese or DRV would respond to U.S. air raids by air attacks on U.S. aircraft carriers or South Vietnamese airfields." The SNIE also doubted the possibility of any "sneak attack on an aircraft carrier by an unidentifiable Chinese submarine."

In April 1965 the intelligence community was asked for an SNIE on reactions to a program of U.S. air attacks directly against China. The CIA-led

---

*U.S. records indicate that a total of 922 American aircraft were lost during Rolling Thunder, a figure that includes all losses to Hanoi's own air defenses, which undoubtedly accounted for the majority of shootdowns.

†At the time the CIA estimated there were 200,000 to 250,000 PLA troops within 200 miles of the Vietnamese border.

consensus continued to predict a less than even chance of Chinese air attacks on the U.S. bases or ships, though they would try to defend themselves, as well as "put the United States under various new pressures to halt all bombings." The more likely Chinese reaction was starkly posed: "If they had not already done so, Chinese Communist forces would probably move into North Vietnam. Chinese or additional DRV forces would probably move into northern Laos. The DRV armed forces, with Chinese support, would probably open an offensive against South Vietnam. Thailand would [also] be threatened." In June, when the CIA obtained evidence that Chinese military units were in fact moving into the DRV, the conclusions in this SNIE must have seemed right on the mark.

Indeed, during June the CIA was instructed to estimate reactions to a U.S. program of attacks against air defenses in the DRV, including airfields and newly appeared surface-to-air missile sites. The SNIE concluded: "It is likely that Hanoi would request—and that the Chinese would provide—additional support, e.g., ground equipment and personnel for air defense purposes or engineering help for constructing and repairing airfields." That exact thing was happening at that moment in Hanoi and Beijing.

As President Johnson moved toward dispatching major ground forces to South Vietnam, in late July he asked for an SNIE on reactions to this deployment. This time U.S. intelligence stated its belief that the Chinese *would not* intervene overtly but increase support to Hanoi of types they were already providing. This American understanding paralleled almost exactly the secret decisions made in Hanoi and Beijing. The CIA understood also that a U.S. invasion of the North would force an intervention on Beijing, and that, too, concorded with the understandings between the Communist allies.

In September the intelligence community produce an SNIE that centered on the plan to cut off Hanoi from the South by blocking Route 9. The estimate assumed a U.S. force of three divisions manning the block. According to the intelligence community, this option would create a huge mess: China "almost certainly would counter in the northwest [of Laos] by supplying personnel and equipment to augment Communist capabilities there and expand Communist control into areas close to the Thai border." That would permit infiltration of Thailand to bypass the Route 9 block. If the Americans remained around Route 9, the Chinese would be unlikely to move to large-scale intervention, *but* the increased PLA presence in northern Laos would induce the government to ask for U.S. troops there as well, giving provocation to the Chinese, who would send more troops of their own.

The impact on the Chinese, according to SNIE 10-10-65, would have been disturbing enough. But that was only the beginning. Hanoi, U.S. intelligence judged, "would almost certainly learn that a major U.S. operation was being planned" and could undertake limited offensives to preempt it. Once the U.S. operation was under way, Vietnam People's Army units could engage "at specific points where [they] would have local advantage." Even in place, the Route 9 block would not prevent Hanoi from efforts to infiltrate some cadres through Laos, or even greater numbers through Thailand.

One Hanoi option that went untreated in the special estimate was inherent in the terrain here in the neck of Indochina. The U.S. force on Route 9 would inevitably be depending upon that road for its supplies, and the single lateral route remained vulnerable to a Vietnam People's Army attack from across the Demilitarized Zone (DMZ). To protect this flank American generals would be under considerable pressure to mount an ancillary invasion of North Vietnam above the DMZ. This would be backing into a Chinese intervention because it would activate the contingency Hanoi and Beijing had previously agreed on.

Finally there was the matter of the Laotian government. "We believe," the SNIE concluded, "that the chances are less than even that Souvanna could be persuaded to make . . . a request [for the Route 9 invasion]." Most other Lao leaders, "including the King," said the estimate, "would be likely to share Souvanna's misgivings." A successor regime that overthrew Savanna "would be seen by most of the world as a U.S. puppet."

The various SNIEs of 1965 were littered with footnotes that indicated the dissent of one or another U.S. intelligence agency. Thomas L. Hughes, a director of State's Bureau of Intelligence and Research, wrote later that the troop deployment SNIE "splintered the intelligence community" and that in another, in December, "China was very much to the forefront, and in that estimate we had splits all over the place." Not least among the dissenters, Hughes himself rejected an entire SNIE on reactions to an expansion of the bombing in September 1965. State also became the sole agency to take exception to the Tchepone–Route 9 estimate, but in that case its amendment was to *increase* the stark pessimism of the SNIE, advising that China should be expected to send whole troop units to Laos, not simply advisers or cadres.

Dean Rusk, Hughes recalled in an interview three decades later, always reserved his harshest rhetoric for the Chinese, even during years when Russia became Hanoi's biggest arms supplier. Referring to the perception that he had had a hawkish position on China, at a 1989 luncheon in his honor, where Rusk sat next to Tom Hughes, the former secretary of state blurted out, "I am not the village idiot!" Hughes worried that all the footnotes damaged the credibility of U.S. intelligence during this period, but comparing Chinese actions vis-à-vis Hanoi with what the SNIEs predicted demonstrates a close correlation.

Nonetheless, the Hanoi-Beijing relationship remained a delicate one, and already contained seeds of its demise. The compromise strategy the Vietnamese adopted at the end of 1965, embodied in a party document known as Resolution 12, did not go far enough in meeting Beijing's preferences. The Vietnamese were ready to fight the protracted war China favored, but they were also far more willing to mix guerrilla tactics with conventional ones. That displeased Beijing.

Whatever happened later, in 1965 the People's Republic was involved in the Vietnam War. Chinese moves were carefully calibrated, but also offered the potential for a much greater level of intervention. The CIA knew of these Chinese moves, and addressed them in the light of the very measures being considered in Washington. Neither Lyndon Johnson nor any other American leader could afford to act in contempt of our estimates of Beijing's position. The China factor continued to have real weight in The 'Nam.

If the specter of Chinese intervention was not enough to concern Americans, there would also be the danger Russia posed. For years the Soviet Union had followed a low-key approach toward Hanoi. Aid and trade had been modest, and under Nikita Khrushchev Moscow's prime interest lay in improving relations with Washington. Russia's first (1955) assistance treaty with Hanoi provided only 400 million rubles, while Soviet aid plus low-cost loans through the next decade added just 320 million more. During that decade 2,500 Russians traveled to Vietnam, and only 4,500 Vietnamese were trained in the Soviet Union. But Khrushchev's American gambit expired in the missile gap, the U-2 affair, and the Bay of Pigs; Vietnam's struggle fit nicely within the Russian leader's concept of wars of national liberation.

In Hanoi the Russian embassy compound was about the same size as the Chinese one and but a couple of blocks away. At first the Chinese embassy buzzed with activity while the Russian one seemed somnolent. Ambassador Karozov told Moscow the Vietnamese were very close-mouthed; Soviet diplomats often suffered in ignorance. Repeatedly the embassy reported deliberate efforts by Hanoi to conceal aspects of its situation. Afraid of being sucked into an intervention, the embassy counseled caution.

With a widening split between Russia and China, which had begun to accelerate out of Moscow's orbit in the late 1950s, Khrushchev started to have a problem in Hanoi. The Vietnamese could choose to side with either party to the dispute, while the Soviet Union and the People's Republic needed to compete for influence worldwide. Hanoi constantly used this position between Moscow and Beijing to manipulate each for the DRV's own benefit. In 1962, when China fought a short, sharp border war with India, Hanoi criticized Russia's lukewarm support for Beijing. A year later, a CIA special estimate noted that Hanoi seemed to maintain independence amid the Sino-Soviet dispute although having a certain sympathy for Beijing.

The pressures on Khrushchev to demonstrate Russia's value as an ally were highlighted by the Gulf of Tonkin incident. Just a few days before, a delegation of National Liberation Front envoys had met Soviet party official Boris Ponomarev to plead for aid (in U.S. dollars) along with antiaircraft and antitank guns. When Tonkin Gulf occurred, Moscow had not decided. Khrushchev first learned of the consequent American bombing of the DRV from the press. Furious, he sent an angry protest to President Johnson.

A new ambassador went to Hanoi that September. Ilya Scherbakov had been minister counselor to the Soviet mission in Beijing. His appearance in Hanoi suggested that, in Vietnam at least, Russia and China might cooperate amicably. In the meantime Khrushchev, weakened politically by agricultural failures and the Cuban Missile Crisis, was overthrown. Successors to the mantle of authority were Leonid I. Brezhnev, Party secretary, and Alexei N. Kosygin, prime minister of the government. The new collective leadership moved closer to Hanoi. In December 1964 Russia permitted establishment of a National Liberation Front diplomatic mission in Moscow. The Soviets also entertained a delegation led by Pham Van Dong, come to consult on the conflict with the Americans. Moscow arranged that Prime Minister Kosygin would return the visit, continuing these discussions while on his way to see Mao Zedong in Beijing.

The Kosygin trip proved vital to Russia, not only for the talks with Hanoi but also precisely because of the Sino-Soviet split. There was a fresh Russian leadership, after all, and Moscow wished to see if rapprochement could work. More internationally minded and technically adept than Brezhnev, Alexei Kosygin seemed the man to show Russia's better side. An indicator of Leonid Brezhnev's personal interest was the presence on the delegation of Yuri V. Andropov, the leader's deputy for relations with foreign Communist parties. Senior generals of the Soviet military were also along for the trip. Hanoi and Beijing would be successive stops on an important diplomatic sounding mission.

Washington showed itself entirely aware of the Soviet calculation. On February 1, 1965, with the Kosygin expedition at its outset, Tom Hughes's analysts at the State Department wrote of Moscow "seeking to wean Hanoi away from Beijing." The Bureau of Intelligence and Research argued: "A major purpose of Moscow's more vigorous involvement in Southeast Asia is to shake the DRV's close association with Beijing." The CIA agreed. A paper from the Office of Current Intelligence the same day observed that the announcement of the Kosygin trip "underscores both the USSR's desire to regain influence with the North Vietnamese and its concern over the possibility of escalation in the Indochina conflict." A few days later, State Department analysts opined, "At a minimum, the Soviets probably intend to introduce a significant supply of military hardware, including advanced antiaircraft equipment and the like."

Vietnam's own actions on the occasion of the Kosygin visit are of some historical significance. Hanoi showed every indication of enthusiasm, with the newspaper *Nhan Dan* printing a welcoming notice the same day Moscow announced the forthcoming trip. Upon his arrival Kosygin received a fine reception. Then, with the Russian delegation in Hanoi, the Viet Cong suddenly staged their bloody attack on the American air base at Pleiku. That event put the matter of reprisal before President Johnson. Kosygin's whole pitch to the Vietnamese would be trumped by Johnson's tit-for-tat bombing. American bombers struck twice while the Kosygin visit continued, visible evidence to Hanoi that Soviet weapons could not prevent its becoming a victim. The bombings were a slap in the face for Moscow.

This episode conditioned relations among the Communist powers through the remainder of the Indochina war. Russian observers uniformly condemn Washington's actions of those days. Georgi K. Arbatov, director of Moscow's main institute studying the United States, and adviser to many successive Russian leaders, writes this: "It so happened that the Americans started bombing . . . when the new head of the Soviet government was there. And this of course led to another increase in mistrust and hostility. I think this was either [a] very serious mistake by the American government or a calculated provocation aimed at testing the mettle of the new Soviet leaders."

Anatoli Dobrynin is even more instructive on the impact of Kosygin's trip. Russia's ambassador to Washington, having arrived there on the eve of the Cuban Missile Crisis, Dobrynin remained through the tenures of six American presidents and four Soviet leaders. According to him, "Kosygin bitterly resented the bombing that had taken place while he was in Vietnam and turned against Johnson, although previously he had been more favorably disposed toward him in Kremlin meetings."

Washington did not cross eyeless into Indochina. At Lyndon Johnson's deliberations on reprisal bombing after Pleiku, the matter of Kosygin's presence in Hanoi came up. Diplomat Llewellyn Thompson suggested bombing be postponed at least until Kosygin left Vietnam; Vice President Hubert Humphrey opposed it altogether. President Johnson not only went ahead, he also kept Humphrey out of later high-level national security meetings, *and* LBJ followed within days with his approval of the sustained-bombing campaign Rolling Thunder.

If Pleikus *were* like streetcars, the United States ought to have waited for another one.

The provocation and timing of the Viet Cong attack at Pleiku and those that followed, if crafted by Hanoi, effectively trapped the Soviet Union in a delicate situation, complete with top Russian leaders on hand to serve as hostages against direct American attack. If the Viet Cong took this action in defiance of Hanoi, a predominantly southern Vietnamese Communist faction had succeeded in manipulating Hanoi, Russia, *and* the United States in a way that affected the outcome of the Vietnam War. If Pleiku merely represented mindless or local revolutionary violence, then truly fateful tragedies occurred that day.

The latest evidence on this point comes directly from the Vietnamese command for the Central Highlands. General Dang Vu Hiep, political officer in the region from 1965 through the end of the war, spoke on this matter to an international conference of former officials, military officers, and scholars, held in Hanoi in June 1997. According to Hiep, the timing of the Pleiku attack was purely coincidental and no provocation had been intended. Americans were not specifically targeted; rather, Pleiku was attacked simply because it was the seat of the ARVN II Corps command, and Qui Nhon because it constituted a key coastal supply base. The assignment was given to a unit that, given the necessity to plan and practice the attack, had complete freedom to choose its moment. Not only did the People's Army not know McGeorge Bundy was visiting Vietnam, but also General Hiep asserts the officers of his command did not even know who Bundy *was*. Hanoi would suffer much from the escalation that inexorably followed Washington's perception of Pleiku as a dagger aimed at the United States.

At the time of Johnson's reprisal bombings, Dean Rusk went to Ambassador Dobrynin with his most sincere assurances—the air strikes aimed only to influence Hanoi, Washington had no desire to sour relations with Moscow, all of that. But the assurances fell on deaf ears. Moscow and Hanoi signed new agreements for aid and military advisers. Vietnam and, Dobrynin thought, Cuba, continued to bedevil Soviet-American relations. "The situation was absurd," the ambassador recalls. "On the one hand the Soviet leaders were well aware of the game the Vietnamese were playing and cursed them behind their backs . . . but in the last analysis it was ideological dogmatism in Moscow that inexorably drove our country along a faulty and wanton course." Brezhnev would be among the more avid swearers, and he was a man known for his salty language, but as long as Moscow remained wedded to its demonstration of solidarity, there was nothing to be done. Of the Vietnamese, Dobrynin writes, "They were doing their utmost to foster enmity between Washington and Moscow."

One of Kosygin's goals for the following stage of the trip, a visit to China, had been to coordinate with the Chinese on aid to Vietnam. That portion of the mission ended in failure. Moscow and Beijing each held on to its own piece of the Indochina conflict, jealously eyeing the other. The Russian aid flow that began with the Kosygin visit continued past the end of the war. Heavy freight for Hanoi crossed China in sealed boxcars, to be reloaded at the Vietnamese border, for China's railways used a standard gauge and Vietnam's a metric one. On one pretext or another, Beijing halted Soviet trains several times during the war. Russian did better with ships sent directly to Haiphong.

Types of military aid were up for discussion between Hanoi and Moscow. In April 1965 Le Duan went to Russia on party matters, but also talked of military affairs. As Lao Dong Party general secretary, he had excellent knowledge of conditions in the insurgency and those along The Trail. General Vo Nguyen Giap visited Moscow soon after the Party delegation. By June the air defenses of the DRV began to bristle with Soviet-made surface-to-air missiles (SAMs). The first site appeared near Hanoi, but others soon sprouted. American military commanders pressed for authority to bomb the SAM sites.

The Vietnam People's Army, naturally, had no troops familiar with the technical complexities of SAMs, and it took time to instruct crews. During the interval, evidence now suggests, Russian troops manned the SAM sites, and Soviet experts of many kinds flooded into the Democratic Republic. The closeness of the military relationship, and any casualties among the Soviets that resulted from American actions in the war, inserted two new factors that could trigger foreign intervention alongside Hanoi.

North Vietnamese air defenses quickly became a focus of the American air campaign. From April 1965, when U.S. photo planes brought back the first evidence of SAM sites under construction, the war effectively assumed a new guise. American intelligence looked at the implications of the SAMs in two special estimates. Their effect was discounted—the CIA felt the Russians would continue to give SAMs to Hanoi no matter what the United States did. President Johnson duly authorized an air strike concentrating on SAMs shortly after the first U.S. plane was lost to a missile, on July 24, 1965. From that day raged a secret war between Russians and Americans inside North Vietnam.

Colonel G. Lubinitsky of the Russian air defense troops fought in the DRV with one SAM unit in 1965. He recalls shooting down three American planes and an unmanned reconnaissance drone. Lubinitsky claims his SAM battalion launched forty-five missiles and obtained twenty-three hits. "The most impressive moment," recounted Sergeant N. Kolesnik, "was when the planes were downed. All of a sudden through this dark shroud an object you couldn't even see before comes down in a blaze of shattered pieces." The United States used electronic countermeasures to outfox the SAM radars, and missiles to attack them. The Russians built fake SAM sites and dummy SAMs to decoy American strikes.

Hanoi's public figures for 1965 are that 346 American planes were shot down in the first six months, with another 488 downed in the last half of the year. Proliferation of SAM sites continued; by the fall of 1966 U.S. intelligence counted 130 SAM batteries in the Democratic Republic of Vietnam. Soon the sites were appearing down the Vietnamese panhandle, protecting the approaches to The Trail.

Whatever they were, Russia's casualties in Vietnam deepened its stake in the war. Hanoi continued to play off Moscow against Beijing. A good example is the case of the Vietnam People's air force. One of the more persistent DRV demands of the Chinese would be for air intervention, planes and pilots, "volunteers" if necessary. Though Beijing promised favorable consideration, they never furnished this aid. Harking back to its experience in the Korean War, China adopted the "Andung model," under which planes had to be based across the border, in sanctuaries in China that were off-limits to the Americans. Beijing supplied only air defense troops. Hanoi turned to the Russians instead. Instructors, some pilots, seven dozen jet fighters, and ten IL-28 light bombers became the first fruits of this initiative. Russian assistance became the mainstay of the DRV's air force.

Russian activity steadily broadened and increased. By 1967 more than 1 billion rubles' worth of military equipment had been sent to the DRV. Russian shipments of all types to Vietnam that year amounted to more than 1.8 billion rubbles. The number of Soviet military advisers was generally estimated in the West at about a thousand; in the fall of 1968 a Soviet publication revealed there were several times that number of Russian cadres in North Vietnam.

Events in Hanoi's relationship with Moscow were important for The Trail in two ways. First, direct involvement of Soviet interests heightened the possibility that Russia might opt for open military intervention, or respond by creating a crisis for the United States elsewhere in the world. Washington's leaders, if not its admirals and generals, had to keep that danger constantly in mind. Second, Soviet aid helped Hanoi operationally, extending the air defenses to the Vietnamese panhandle and later to lower Laos as well. This activity primarily involved antiaircraft and SAM units; only much later did Hanoi use aircraft down South.

Former Russian foreign minister Andrei Gromyko, in a memoir published in the West in 1989, furnishes a sour view of Washington's policy. Gromyko recounts that the 1966 congress of the Communist Party of the Soviet Union, with a Hanoi delegation in attendance, adopted a resolution that socialist countries would give the DRV the support necessary to enable it to sustain the Indochina war. Writes Gromyko dryly, "This declaration ought to have been taken seriously."

The last analysis shows that China and Russia were and remained real constraints on American strategy in Vietnam. President Johnson guided himself accordingly; his generals were never able to do everything they wanted, for that reason. Yet even as this international headache continued, a domestic political element began to enter the equation. American politics became unsettled, with The 'Nam a locus of the abscess, and foreign criticism of U.S. actions added to dissent. If Beijing and Moscow were a headache, the antiwar movement would become a migraine.

Like many who came after them, the three Americans were charmed by Hanoi. Among the first to visit that forbidden place during the war, the three stayed at the Reunification Hotel (Thong Nhat), the former Hôtel Metropole of French colonial days, a four-story structure that featured big rooms and a fine bar. Somewhat seedy at the end of 1965, serving weak beer, the Thong Nhat nevertheless was right downtown, not far from the Botanical Gardens and DRV government offices the guests would frequent. The Vietnamese gave the Americans a tour that became standard for visitors to Hanoi—stops at places hit by the bombing, sessions with Lao Dong Party officials and front groups, a meeting with an American prisoner, trips to museums extolling Vietnamese resistance and nationalism. Tom Hayden found a pleasant restaurant to supplement the Thong Nhat, one right on the Lake of the Revolution—typically, Vietnamese had been prohibited from eating there during the colonial period. Were it not for the destruction visible at every hand, and the manhole bomb shelters on every street, Hanoi would have been enchanting.

The three Americans were in Hanoi for ten days over the New Year of 1966. It was a time when Lyndon Johnson had ordered a pause in the Rolling Thunder campaign, so no U.S. bombers appeared overhead. President Johnson sent diplomats, and even some private citizens all over the world—to sixty-five countries—in search of contact with Hanoi. While these LBJ initiatives, which many saw as a farce, were completely fruitless, the three Americans in Hanoi on their own initiative made the very connections Johnson had been striving for.

Several times the guests were told they might meet with Ho Chi Minh, but Ho's schedule remained in flux; that never came off. The Americans *did* meet with Pham Van Dong, however, at the DRV government house in the Botanical Garden. That Pham came out of his office, stood under the portico as they arrived, and came to greet them is an indication of the importance the Vietnamese attributed to this occasion. Unaccompanied, wearing a scarf against the blustery wind, the prime minister hurried down the steps, shook their hands, and led the Americans into the building. Pham Van Dong sat for an interview and supplied written answers to previously tendered questions.

Hanoi's message, calculated to appeal to world public opinion, nevertheless gave nothing away. "The U.S. aggressors are going against history," said Pham. "In spite of their economic and military strength, in spite of their tricks and maneuvers, they will fall." The DRV prime minister told the visitors they should ask President Johnson, if they saw him, why America had to fight Vietnam. "Nobody wants war," Dong concluded, "but we must have independence. The highest sentiment is fraternity. This age is the age of that sentiment. That is why it is clear the United States war . . . will be defeated."

Lyndon Johnson never received the Americans who had gone to Hanoi, and some of Pham Van Dong's statements were clearly disingenuous. He had, for instance, maintained that only Southerners were fighting for the National Liberation Front in the South, something that might have been true a year earlier but could not be after Hanoi's decisions in 1964–1965. President Johnson had made a speech at Johns Hopkins University that spring, offering the carrot of economic development of the Mekong River basin but threatening the stick of force, and Hanoi had countered with a four-point peace proposal. The four points represented a repackaging of what Pham Van Dong had privately told the Canadian Blair Seaborn. Now Johnson's peace offensive in conjunction with the Christmas bombing pause was also aimed at the public—Dong told his interlocutors that American diplomats had not made *any* direct contacts with Hanoi's. This pattern became characteristic of peace efforts through the next six years, with the sides holding incompatible goals, mouthing appealing rhetoric, and going about their military business. Hanoi and Washington were talking past each other, aiming their words at a wider audience.

Thus the visit of the Americans to Hanoi proved sterile as a gambit in a peace process. The trip was significant in another way, however, as a sign of the growth in the United States of political opposition to the Vietnam War. The three Americans who made this journey—Herbert Aptheker, Staughton Lynd, and Thomas Hayden—represent a snapshot of what would come to be known as the antiwar movement. At this moment in time the antiwar movement had not become a major political obstacle, but it was already gathering force; President Johnson's decision to commit major combat units set the stage for growing confrontation.

Herbert Aptheker came from the traditional Left, increasingly called the "Old" Left to distinguish it from the "New" Left youth of the 1960s. This was the Left of the Communist Party of the United States of America (CPUSA), and Aptheker himself was a well-known Marxist theoretician. The invitation to Hanoi materialized when Aptheker, attending a conference in Eastern Europe, was approached by Vietnamese Party members attending the same meeting, who asked if he might be interested in coming to the DRV together with a couple of other Americans opposed to war in Vietnam. Aptheker favored negotiations and had argued the point both publicly and to his daughter Bettina, a student activist at the University of California at Berkeley, and he was happy to serve as catalyst here.

Staughton Lynd would be the first recruit; he personified another traditional political movement in America, the pacifists. Old enough to remember the isolationists in pre–World War II America, Lynd had come of age just as the French war in Vietnam began, and at the time of Dien Bien Phu he had been in the U.S. Army, worrying about whether he was about to be sent to fight in Indochina. A Quaker, Lynd responded to the pacifist causes of the 1950s, including the "Ban the Bomb" movement against nuclear weapons and atmospheric nuclear testing. He became enmeshed in the civil rights movement, having observed events in the American South from the perspective of a history instructor at a woman's college in Atlanta. Lynd directed the "Freedom School" initiative of 1964, in which civil rights workers banded together to help African Americans meet the artificial literacy requirements set in many places to prevent their registration for voting. At the time of Aptheker's invitation to Hanoi, Lynd had become an assistant professor at Yale and editor of *Liberation*, a pacifist journal.

Lynd's civil rights connection is a key tip-off to where a lot of the antiwar movement was coming from. John F. Kennedy and Lyndon B. Johnson had a good deal to do with the mobilization that occurred, both through their actions and their failures to act in civil rights matters. Kennedy's call to youth in his 1961 inaugural address betokened a politics of hope and of action, in contrast to the widely perceived lethargic fifties. By 1965 the Civil Rights Act that JFK proposed and LBJ had pushed through Congress not only marked advances for African Americans but also reinforced the notion that activism was appropriate and could have real political impact. The linkage between activism on the civil rights front and on Vietnam is further shown by Lynd's initial suggestion for the third American to go on the Hanoi trip, Robert Moses, a civil rights activist who had been on the front lines in Mississippi. "You've got to learn from the South," Moses told an audience at Berkeley, "if you're going to do anything about this country in relation to Vietnam."

Berkeley in fact became a touchstone of the antiwar movement, but its first furor rose directly from civil rights—university administration and city actions against student supporters of the Congress for Racial Equality. The campus demonstrations, protests, and controversy of the "Free Speech" movement at Berkeley over 1964–1965 confirmed the right to organize. The tactic of the "teach-in," debating issues and providing information for participants, flowed from the Free Speech movement but swiftly became a favorite of antiwar activists. Berkeley's Vietnam Day teach-in during the spring of 1965 would be one of the biggest, attended at different times by 10,000 to 30,000 people.

Tom Hayden, the third man to make the Hanoi trip, came from this culture of youth. Though older than student activists such as Bettina Aptheker, Hayden held similar beliefs. Just out of college, he had been active and engaged enough to participate in the founding of the group known as the Students for a Democratic Society (SDS) and had worked on its major theoretical tract, the "Port Huron Statement." Hayden had also gone to Mississippi during the civil rights struggle, and at the time of the Hanoi invitation was working as a community organizer in Newark, New Jersey.

There were so many linkages among activists on different issues that what became known as the antiwar movement cannot be understood in isolation, but only as part of a larger social and political mobilization. The activists themselves emphasized this, constantly drawing together the different issues of their struggle. Staughton Lynd, Bob Moses, and Tom Hayden were exactly emblematic of the New Left, a movement of passion in an era of hope that now seemed threatened by war in Vietnam.

Some argue that the antiwar movement was ignorant, but, in fact, it knew more about Southeast Asia than many supporters of U.S. official policy. Opinion survey data from the University of Michigan in 1965 showed that about a quarter of all Americans did not even know there *was* a war in Vietnam. The administration's white papers and public statements had not built support for the war so much as provide a focus for debate. Polls showed support for President Johnson, but that support was soft, and the opposition increasingly vocal. Robert McNamara's memoir of Vietnam laments that there were no experts telling the administration that Ho Chi Minh could be an "Asian Tito," a Communist leader following an independent path aligned neither with Moscow nor Beijing. In fact there were any number of speakers at the teach-ins of 1965 explicitly making that point.

Lyndon Johnson might have succeeded in forging a consensus had he engaged the dissenters, argued out the issues, and come to a more or less open compromise. Johnson was a consensus president, so there was at least a possibility he might have adopted that course. Instead LBJ tried to outmaneuver the dissenters, ordering bombing pauses and grandstand diplomatic ploys, but prohibiting McGeorge Bundy and other government spokesmen from appearing at the teach-ins to debate the policy. These efforts were designed to avoid lending credibility to the antiwar movement, but the result was that the opposition could seize on each apparent contradiction in Washington's actions to call the whole progressively into question. In the end it would be LBJ himself who was openly tagged with having created a credibility gap. Amid the burgeoning numbers of youth, the myriad linkages of issues the activists called upon, and the stumblings of Washington, the opposition to Vietnam deepened. The antiwar movement grew slowly, but it grew.

A line of sorts was crossed as early as November 1964, when the War Resisters' League called for immediate withdrawal of all U.S. troops and military aid to Vietnam. Protest demonstrations rarely included more than a few hundred, but they were becoming a constant. When Johnson went ahead with Rolling Thunder, the protests began to get bigger and more vociferous. A major march on Washington was laid on by SDS, which was remarkable because activists in that organization previously had rejected the mass march as a useless tactic. On April 17, 1965, the peace march took place. According to Kirkpatrick Sale, chronicler of SDS history, this became the biggest peace protest in U.S. history to that date. Organizers optimistically anticipated up to 10,000 participants; crowd estimates at the march ranged from 15,000 to upward of 25,000. A similarly large crowd demonstrated in New York that October, and the Pentagon also saw its first demonstration in 1965.

Aside from the big marches there began to be a panoply of small, even tiny, acts of resistance that could not be enumerated, even in a narrative centered entirely on the antiwar movement. Picketing of banks and corporations involved in Southeast Asia, of draft boards and military induction centers, of military bases, and leafleting of bus and subway stations were just a few of these actions. Teach-ins added to the numbers of protesters. Equally troubling from Washington's perspective, agitation against American involvement in Vietnam began to appear in other countries. The big demonstration in October 1965 was billed as an International Day of Protest; picketers began to be seen in England, France, Germany, Sweden, and elsewhere.

These things happened even as President Johnson, in search of a military solution, dispatched troops, planes and ships to Southeast Asia. The military problems of actually prosecuting the war began to be matched by a political headache at home and abroad. Hanoi caught on quickly and proved adept at playing the international audience. The 'Nam and The World became different theaters in a single conflict. There would come a moment when the international factors, The World, would impinge directly on the battle of The Trail. Factors that brought about that phenomenon were already in play. The way to avoid that eventuality was to win the war on the ground, and Lyndon Johnson and his generals did their best to do that. The immediate focus of their effort would be South Vietnam's Central Highlands and, behind them, The Trail.

CHAPTER 7

Squeezing Hanoi
1965–1966

Come the end of July 1965, Fort Benning, Georgia, was a scene of total pandemonium. "The Word," when it comes, is rarely a complete surprise to a soldier, and there had been plenty of scuttlebutt at Benning since before Independence Day, when a ceremony at the fort's stadium marked the dissolution of the army's experimental 11th Air Assault Division and creation of the 1st Cavalry Division (Airmobile). Vietnam was the hottest conflict on the horizon at the time, plus being the one where helicopter mobility could be the key. Many soldiers who had no access to the classified knowledge that Secretary of Defense McNamara, the chief of staff, General Johnson, MACV commander Westmoreland, and the president had and who were all discussing the prospective commitment of the Cav, were aware that big things were in store for the unit.

Major General Harry W. O. Kinnard, division commander of the Cav, was a pioneer in the heliborne assault tactics his unit innovated. Relying on mass employment of helicopters, the 1st Cavalry possessed a unique ability to sustain both a very high tempo of operations and a high rate of response to fresh orders or intelligence. The helicopter also freed Kinnard's sky soldiers from the constraint of the front line. The 1st Cav could leap over the lines to strike in the enemy rear. These tactics worked brilliantly in war games and on paper, but no one had ever built or run a division-size integrated air-ground unit in the army before the assault division. Harry Kinnard conjured a support structure to maneuver infantry in tandem with helicopters and artillery, as well as planning how to move the force to a military theater and supply it once there.

Much was promised of the Cav and much, in fact, rode on the smoothness of the division's deployment to Vietnam. Harold K. Johnson had the most invested in the move; the army chief of staff had been to Vietnam that spring and since then had advocated a series of measures, including sending the Cav. General Johnson spoke with Kinnard before the troops began to ship out, and the army chief of staff expressed strong views on how the division ought to be used in Vietnam.

Major General Kinnard had more experience than anyone, having run the division in its incarnation as the 11th Air Assault, an experiment for the Continental Army Command. The army decided the unit was both feasible and necessary for counterinsurgency warfare, and some argued there should be as many as five airmobile divisions. Others favored three, which happened to be the size of the XVIII Airborne Corps, the army's strategic reserve. General Kinnard embraced the airmobile concept, shepherded it across these shoals, and continued to be very concerned that his unit's performance validate the push for these novel forces and tactics. That required they be properly used on the battlefield. As Fort Benning bustled, his troops marshaled, and equipment was loaded on ships at ports on the Atlantic and Gulf Coasts, General Kinnard went ahead to Vietnam by plane and met William C. Westmoreland.

Fort Benning had been talking long enough about the Cav's prospective mission that Kinnard's operations staffers were able to complete no fewer than five contingency plans for the First Team. The most radical concept would have had the 1st Cavalry base itself in Thailand and conduct raids against the Ho Chi Minh Trail throughout lower Laos. Not coincidentally, the use of an airmobile division in Laos had been the scenario used in early 1962 for one of the army's first war-game tests of the impact of a large air-ground formation in combat.

Doug Kinnard put his ideas to Westy when the two met at MACV headquarters on August 29. An advance party of Kinnard's people had already been in Saigon more than three weeks, handling the myriad details of inserting this big new force into the country. General Westmoreland had his own notions about the airmobile division, and had already gotten into an argument with Pacific Theater commander Admiral Grant Sharp. Both agreed that the 1st Cavalry should be committed along the central Vietnamese coast—Qui Nhon was selected early as the port of entry—but CINCPAC wanted the Cav to operate at first in the coastal and foothill areas before leaping into the Central Highlands. As for Westmoreland, since before the spring visit of army chief of staff Harold Johnson, Westy had been arguing that the primary problem was the Central Highlands, and he wanted Cav troops right in there. Westy's engineers assembled extensive analyses to show that An Khe, a town in the foothills, could handle the 600 to 800 tons a day of supplies the airmobile division would need. According to Admiral Sharp, Ambassador Taylor and the JCS agreed with his own view of the situation, and his concerns "were nothing more than those of prudence with respect to logistical support . . . and consistency with regard to utilizing our forces to first secure our base areas." After the An Khe study, CINCPAC decided its ideas and Westmoreland's were compatible after all. At that point MACV had taken another reinforcement, the 1st Brigade of the 101st Airborne Division, arriving at Cam Ranh, and thrown it into a clearing operation to seize An Khe and prepare for the Cav.

The encounter at MACV headquarters on August 29 seems to have been a difficult session. Kinnard later told Army interviewers that Westy had pointed to a map on the wall and talked about how he needed each brigade of the Cav in a different place. Kinnard asked to respond, then discussed the synergistic advantages of using his division together, along with General Harold K. Johnson's desire for an anti-infiltration force or a unit to screen the border. William Westmoreland's notes on the discussion are worth quoting here:

> General Kinnard's ideas on how his division would be employed are not realistic to the environment in Vietnam. I am sure that he will reorient his thinking after he has had an opportunity to see at first hand the nature of the conflict. He was under the misapprehension that he could use his division to secure the Laotian border in the highlands; a mission he feels his command could accomplish. I pointed out to him that this is a task probably beyond the capability of his division but I would give him time to judge this for himself.

Harry Kinnard countered that General Creighton W. Abrams, then vice chief of staff of the army, had urged him to encourage MACV to use the Cav to stop infiltration in lower Laos. Then came Westy's response: "Such a plan was not in the cards in the foreseeable future because of complex political and other considerations." As for Harold Johnson's troop cordon plan,

> I pointed out that this is a much discussed plan but, in my opinion, completely impractical in the foreseeable future. This discussion served to point out the difficulty that senior officers, who have not served in Vietnam, experience in attempting to understand the situation and the practical problems faced by our military units in fighting the Viet Cong and countering the well-developed infiltration from the north.

The novel option of sending the Cav into Thailand to attack The Trail from there was also rejected. Westmoreland permitted Kinnard to fly on to Bangkok and discuss this possibility with Major General Richard S. Stilwell, but the latter also cited Thai sensitivities and political obstacles and nixed the plan. Westmoreland had his way. The 1st Cavalry Division went into the Central Highlands, as MACV wanted, but Westy permitted Kinnard to fight with his division all together. The impact of the Cav in a combat environment, as will be seen, would be awesome.

Before that moment came a succession of mind-bending riddles to solve as the First Team surmounted each obstacle in the way of moving itself to Vietnam. The simple mechanics of the move were a major difficulty. Lieutenant Colonel Edward C. Meyer, deputy commander of the Cav's 3rd Brigade and later, as a general, army chief of staff, subsequently wrote, "The Army hadn't moved a full division and all of its equipment overseas since the Korean War. And the Army had never moved a division with over four hundred aircraft." In fact the move involved 470 aircraft, not to mention

16,000 men, 3,100 vehicles, and 22,800 tons of supplies. Four aircraft carriers plus more than a dozen troop transports and cargo ships were necessary to load it all.

Some of the Cav's difficulties were simply mundane. The supply depots of the U.S. Army did not have enough jungle fatigues in stock to issue a set to everybody in the division. Those who could not get new uniforms had to make do. Stores around Benning suddenly found their shelves emptied of dark green dyes. It is said for weeks afterward, even once the First Team had left for Vietnam, the sewage water of Columbus, Georgia, and nearby Phenix City, Alabama, ran a dark greenish color.

The route to the Far East lay through the Caribbean—Lieutenant Colonel Kenneth D. Mertel, commanding the 1st Battalion, 8th Cavalry, was disappointed to see so little of Cuba. His ship passed within miles of Guantánamo Bay but stayed well to sea, then on to the Panama Canal and across the Pacific. Mertel tried to emphasize physical conditioning for his men, but was relieved when the ship stopped at Honolulu for a day and the troops could stretch their legs ashore. Robert Mason, a pilot with Company B, 229th Assault Helicopter Battalion, recalled: "The trail from our hatchway back through the interior of the ship to the mess hall was like a jungle path through piles of boxes, bags, coils, barrels, cases, and Hueys." Mason played a lot of chess, and he remembers the late afternoons and sunsets. Specialist 4 Steve Yarnell of the 1st Squadron, 9th Cavalry, recalls a sickening, over-crowded voyage: "it seemed like the guy [who bunked] above you always had his hind end stuck in your face, and you had your hind end stuck in somebody else's face." Though incredibly hot below decks, military police on Yarnell's ship kept chasing the men inside, even at night, when the ocean breeze freshened.

Colonel Mertel understood better than most what to expect when the convoy arrived off the Vietnamese coast. Ken Mertel had been in Qui Nhon as an American adviser in 1963; he remembered it as a quiet little seaport village with an airstrip barely big enough to land a twin-engine plane. That was still Qui Nhon in 1965—the Cav had to unload across the beach, or onto lighters to make the shore. Kinnard moved his division up to An Khe as quickly as he could. By then battle loomed; the Central Highlands were in peril once more.

As soon as the call came in, Charlie Beckwith knew his easy time was nearing an end. Beckwith had moved Project Delta to a district north of Qui Nhon, radiating scout patrols into the surrounding countryside but finding very little. The call was from the deputy commander of 5th Special Forces, who wanted to have a look around, probably because Delta was coming up empty-handed. The weather was foul, fog with low clouds and heavy rain, not at all good for helicopters, and Major Beckwith thought he was off the hook when he told the man that the only way in would be by parachute. Instead, Lieutenant Colonel John Bennett jumped right in. Bennett duly noted the little that was going on and promptly ordered Beckwith back to base. But before Charlie Beckwith could move Delta, late in the afternoon of October 19, 5th Group changed the orders and Delta had a mission again. Shortly before dark the Vietnam People's Army had begun attacking the Special Forces camp of Plei Me; now Delta was to reposition itself at Pleiku, anticipating a II Corps response.

Plei Me represented the opening shot of what Hanoi would call its "Winter-Spring Campaign" (*dong xuan*) of 1965–1966. This was no casual sally but a calculated flexing of the military muscle Hanoi was pushing down The Trail. New regiments made the offensive possible; new staffs, which the VPA called "field fronts," directed them. The Tay Nguyen Front, with its strength in the Chu Pong massif, was to fight in the Central Highlands. Major General Chu Huy Man led this front.

Hanoi's selection of Chu Huy Man to command in the Central Highlands was another sign of the political sophistication it applied to this war. Man was Hanoi's Montagnard, born in 1914. He became one of the earliest Viet Minh, joining a peasant rebellion in 1930. Imprisoned by the French at Kontum, Man learned the Central Highlands the hard way. Joining the People's Army in August 1945, Man soon became a regiment commander, and thereafter the party and the VPA constantly used Man in posts where his minority knowledge paid off. General Man had been at Dien Bien Phu as political commissar for the VPA 316th Division, a unit composed primarily of Montagnards. Under the DRV he served as both political and military leader of the Tay Bac, an upland minority region. Chu Huy Man had been a member of the party's central committee since 1951, and from 1960 he sat on the government's national defense council. During 1962–1964 General Man headed the section of the VPA General Political Department responsible for Montagnard policy in the South. Chu Huy Man trekked South himself in 1964, passing through his native Vinh, where he had risen from a landless peasant family. Man's first assignment was as deputy commander of the 5th Interzone. Soon after, the People's Army set up the Tay Nguyen Front under Man's charge.

The VPA plan for the Plei Me attack had the newly arrived 33rd Regiment make the assault while the 32nd, of Duc Co fame, came down from the Chu Pong to set an ambush for the inevitable relief column. The plan proved simple and carefully prepared, with General Man's subordinates issuing their own orders as early as October 12. The *bo dois* left the Chu Pong four days before the battle. "The secret of our troops' movement had been kept so well," says a Vietnamese account, "that on the previous night a scout patrol of the Saigon army starting off from Plei Me had . . . disappeared without a trace in the jungle."

In fact, Captain Harold Moore's Special Forces Detachment A-217 had sent out a big combat patrol, to get it stuck in the jungle nine miles from the camp when the attack began. The CIDG strikers had marched right past the *bo dois* investing Plei Me without encountering them. The safety of this patrol remained a headache for Green Berets throughout the first night of battle.

Plei Me was a border camp at the edge of the valley of the Ia Drang river ("Ia," the local word for river, will be used hereafter). Two outposts and five night patrol positions protected the main camp. Beginning at 10 P.M. on October 19 the 33rd Regiment opened an assault on the southern outpost. Though that position fell, Plei Me was initially saved by rapid air intervention, a hefty 637 sorties. The People's Army assault collapsed so abysmally that the regimental commander never bothered to send in his reserve battalion.

For the first five days of the siege the Army aviation unit at Ban Me Thuot furnished the only helicopter support at Plei Me. The 155th Assault Helicopter Company flew all night, one of its ships even rescuing a fighter-bomber pilot who went down nearby. Captain William H. Zierdt of the 155th saw "tracer fire you could land on. The camp was being attacked in waves. Our guns flew a steady shuttle from Pleiku—reload then back on station." At one point Zierdt listened on the radio to the fifty-man patrol and their American sergeant caught outside Plei Me, who marked his position with lights at about 3 A.M. the first night of the action. The patrol was never heard from again.

At Pleiku, Ted Mataxis, on the final days of his tour as II Corps adviser, argued with General Vinh Loc over the ARVN reaction. Colonel Mataxis pressed for all available troops, but Vinh Loc decided he would not make such a large commitment. Only the 21st Ranger Battalion would go, as part of a task force almost identical to the one used in August to succor Duc Co. It was this move that led to the orders for Major Beckwith's Delta unit to head for Pleiku.

Project Delta returned from its scout mission on October 20. Charlie Beckwith rested the teams that had been out with him, but left for Pleiku with fifteen Americans and two companies of the ARVN 91st Airborne Ranger Battalion. Beckwith's bosses wanted him to parachute into Plei Me; at II Corps Colonel Mataxis rejected that idea as impractical. Officers went back and forth over sending Delta by helicopter until 5th Group leader Colonel William McKean, who had flown up from Nha Trang, convinced Mataxis that II Corps ought to divert the choppers it had already slated for an operation in the lowlands. Beckwith stayed up most of the night scanning maps in search of a suitable landing zone (LZ), and the next morning he and "Bulldog Bill" McKean flew out early to inspect the one chosen. The LZ had to be close enough to Plei Me for Delta to reach the camp without exhaustion, but enough away to avoid tipping off the VPA. The officers settled on a clearing about three miles to the northeast. As they surveyed this place, the gunship escorting them suddenly lost its rotor, fell away into the jungle, and exploded. Major Beckwith thought it a bad omen.

Back at Pleiku, Beckwith got his Vietnamese and Americans on their helicopters. The lift began to deposit Delta at its LZ at about 9 A.M. They progressed slowly until afternoon, when one of the American troops encountered a *bo doi* carrying a box of shells for 75-mm recoilless rifles. Beckwith's ARVN counterpart identified the man's body as a soldier from the People's

Army, not a Viet Cong. Seeing as a battle with the VPA now impended, the ARVN decided to turn back, but Delta pressed on toward Plei Me, and the ranger commander finally changed his mind and rejoined. The column made it to the Special Forces camp on the morning of October 22, running pell mell down the road the last couple hundred yards. Chargin' Charlie, like Norm Schwarzkopf at Duc Co, found the Plei Me camp a mess and decided to assume control.

As Charlie Beckwith painfully hacked his way into Plei Me, at Pleiku ARVN lieutenant colonel Nguyen Trong Luat assembled forces for an expedition but got orders from Vinh Loc merely to "simulate the imminent approach of a relief column." General Loc awaited reinforcements from the lowlands, both ARVN and U.S., and wished to take no chances. Luat had a company of M-41 tanks, another of M-113 armored personnel carriers, a battery of 105-mm guns, some engineers, and the 21st Rangers. His task force advanced down Route 14, then the track that led a dozen miles off it to Plei Me.

The simulation, if such it was—for Vinh Loc is the author of this self-promoting account—proceeded with the grim inevitability of a Greek tragedy. Luat, according to an Associated Press reporter, could even point out on a map the exact place where an ambush would occur. Colonel Luat put fighting patrols out on both sides of the road. Hanoi's *bo dois* had expected that—the tactical order issued eight days before by the VPA declared that the ARVN battle formation could operate elements more than half a mile off the road and could intersperse infantry with armor. The Saigon troops were expected to arrive one or two days after initial attacks on Plei Me. Luat showed up exactly on schedule.

When the Vietnamese road convoy reached the indicated place, it was late in the afternoon of October 23. The front of the forty-two-truck assemblage stopped at a roadblock backed by dug-in *bo dois*. When Luat called a halt, the rear of his convoy got hit by another VPA battalion. The ARVN supply column, the tail of Luat's formation, suffered grievous losses, including two armored cars and two gasoline tanker trucks, half the ARVN cannon, and a dozen other vehicles heavily damaged. The overland effort stalled.

At Plei Me, now with no relief in sight, the emergency paralleled the siege of Duc Co. Major Beckwith wanted to hunker down and concentrate on improving the defenses, but 5th Group's "Bulldog" McKean gave him a direct order to get outside the wire and sweep the surrounding area. The ARVN airborne rangers tried, but were barely beyond the camp gate when *bo dois* opened fire. Fourteen were killed, among them the rangers' American adviser.

There were no more sorties from Plei Me.

Airpower saved the camp in Beckwith's opinion. Support ranged from flare ships at night to air strikes and supply aviation. It also proved fortunate that the Delta troopers included its operations officer, who became a skilled forward air observer, and McKean's regimental sergeant major. The first night, Chargin' Charlie feared for the camp. He had Americans visit all

Plei Me's machine-gun positions to reassure defenders. There was shelling from heavy mortars and recoilless rifles but no assault. The initial airdrop fell outside the camp perimeter. The second would be all ammunition, and there would be other problems, too. One pallet load landed on top of two soldiers and killed them; another hurtled through the roof of the mess hall. Beckwith raised eyebrows when he called for a case of whiskey, but he got that too, with the third parachute drop. In aerial activity around Plei Me twenty planes suffered damage; three aircraft and a helicopter were shot down.

At II Corps headquarters General Loc was reluctant to send in his reserves. But the emergency only got more serious. Finally he resorted to the Americans: If MACV would take responsibility for the security of Pleiku itself, II Corps would send in its last ranger battalion, plus another ARVN infantry unit brought from Kontum. This resulted in orders for the 1st Cavalry Division (Airmobile) to move into Pleiku and maneuver as necessary in the Central Highlands. Those orders triggered what became known as the battle of the Ia Drang valley.

The action began with the Vietnamese. The Special Forces camp of Duc Co sent a company of CIDG strikers to march to Plei Me. Meanwhile, the two fresh battalions joined Colonel Luat, who broke through the People's Army ambush. Colonel To Dinh Kanh, Luat's *bo doi* adversary, withdrew his 32nd Regiment. Luat's relief force resumed its progress. On Beckwith's third day at Plei Me, the radio squawked with news that the armored convoy would arrive that afternoon. A transport helicopter brought in an artillery observer to call down a barrage of fire ahead of the task force. The first tanks clanked into view as the sun went down over Indian country. It was October 25.

The following morning the Luat task force tried to make a sweep outside Plei Me, the same job that had led the airborne rangers into trouble, and with the same result. Luat moved without incident until his tanks and carriers encountered an obstacle they could not cross. When the ARVN units turned to retrace their steps, one ran into a battalion of the People's Army 33rd Regiment. The South Vietnamese suffered more than a hundred casualties, including 30 killed; they claimed to have killed 150 VPA soldiers.

Five *bo dois* were captured at Plei Me. They identified the People's Army unit as the 3rd Battalion of the 33rd Regiment. One of the prisoners, a rallier who deserted on October 20, described how he had been drafted as a porter, and had had to carry loads of rice, dried fish, and powdered milk from a warehouse across the Cambodian border to a depot a few miles from the Chu Pong. Porter columns of a hundred men were making the trip three times a day. People's Army commander Chu Huy Man was clearly up to something serious.

Charlie Beckwith and his closest Delta comrades considered themselves lucky to get out of Plei Me without a scratch. In Pleiku afterward Beckwith visited the air force forward controllers to render his personal thanks. In only a few days Delta was wanted back at Pleiku to support 1st Cavalry Division operations. This time Major Beckwith's counterpart, the South Vietnamese officer commanding the 91st Airborne Rangers, refused the mission. Delta sent the reconnaissance teams that had sat out the Plei Me battle.

The 2nd Battalion, 8th Cavalry led off the American–South Vietnamese riposte with an air assault onto the slope north of Plei Me on October 26. They were merely the first wave of a considerable offensive mounted against the Chu Pong. The ARVN's Joint General Staff reinforced Pleiku with nearly a division worth of elite troops, a two-battalion Vietnamese Marine task force; plus an ARVN Airborne brigade headquarters with two forces totaling five battalions under command. On the American side, General Kinnard of the Cav shuttled his airmobile brigades through Pleiku, and they executed one combat assault after another into the foothills of the Chu Pong. The fighting would be the most intense of the war to date. Kinnard and his First Team were on the cutting edge of battle.

Some called it a classic calvary pursuit action, but there were plenty who would remember this battle as sheer hell. It began as General Chu Huy Man's *bo dois* broke contact at Plei Me and faded into the jungle. William Westmoreland was in Pleiku that day, and he visited the forward LZ the Cav had air-assaulted to disengage the Special Forces camp. A Cav brigade headquarters was already up to control the action, and Westy conferred with its leaders, the division commanders, and Major General Stanley R. Larsen, overall commander of American troops in the II Corps region. General Westmoreland turned to Larsen. "Give Kinnard his head," Westy said.

The pursuit began with one of the Cav's very novel units, Lieutenant Colonel John B. Stockton's 1st Squadron, 9th Cavalry. Stockton's was a combined unit that featured helicopters for scouting, some for fire support, plus riflemen who could land to check out reports or fix the adversary in place until larger forces arrived. Beginning on October 26 the "Headhunters," as they began to call themselves, combed the area of Plei Me and the Chu Pong in search of the Vietnam People's Army. They found several targets that were hit by artillery fire or air strikes. There was no direct engagement until November 1, when one of the Headhunter scouts spotted some *bo dois* among trees in the valley of the Drang River. A nearby Headhunter rifle platoon helicoptered in and ran into a regular hornet's nest. It turned out they had found a VPA field hospital halfway between Plei Me and the People's Army base in the Chu Pong. The 2d Battalion of the 33d Regiment had halted at the hospital to lick its wounds after Plei Me.

With the energy and ferocity that became its trademark, the Cav fed in portions of three different infantry battalions, with help from artillery and gunship helicopters. Hanoi's troops were heavily outgunned. Steve Yarnell, one of the soldiers who had had such an unpleasant time on his troop ship crossing the Pacific, was a rifleman with the Headhunters. "They say the creek, I called it a ditch, ran red with blood that day, and it did. It was one of the most eerie sights that I have ever seen," Yarnell recalled. The Americans overran the hospital and captured forty-four *bo dois*, many patients previously wounded at Plei Me. It was the biggest haul of North Vietnamese prisoners during a single tactical encounter in the Vietnam War.

Gary Massey was another Headhunter infantryman, with C Troop of 1/9, and his unit scored with an ambush two nights later. A VPA company—the troopers counted ninety *bo dois*—came down a track right into their fire zone. Massey heard the enemy talking and singing. The Americans devastated the hapless North Vietnamese, then pulled back to their LZ, only to be attacked almost immediately by the rest of the VPA battalion. The Headhunters were saved by a night air assault—the Cav's first—bringing in part of the 2nd Battalion, 12th Cavalry. Every slick in the lift took hits during the landing.

Colonel Stockton was sent on to a Saigon staff job after this fracas, for he had been under orders not to engage without clearance from the brigade commander. By now, however, Headhunter scouts from Duc Co camp were ranging all over the Chu Pong.

Scout pilot David Bray, following a jungle trail he had discovered, crossed the border, headed west. On the Cambodian side, Bray recounts, "I flew right through camp after camp of North Vietnamese. We passed them so fast . . . they had no chance to shoot at us. My observer was busy noting mortar positions, stacked weapons . . . numbers of men, et cetera." Bray's superiors feared he would be court-martialed if his report went up the line as presented, for Americans were not supposed to be in the other countries of Indochina, particularly neutral Cambodia. Bray's report went in as if he had seen all this with binoculars while flying along the border.

The engagement most identified with the Battle of the Ia Drang began on the morning of November 14, when Lieutenant Colonel Harold G. Moore's 1st Battalion, 7th Cavalry air-assaulted an LZ called X Ray, fourteen miles west of Plei Me. Moore's battalion sported the heraldry carried to a famous encounter in another Indian country by George Custer's 7th Cavalry in 1876. Within hours of landing, one of Moore's companies saw People's Army troops. One platoon chased the *bo dois* so far into the jungle it became isolated from the main force. Then the VPA attacked.

According to People's Army documents captured a year later, though the 33rd Regiment had suffered crippling losses in the siege of Plei Me, General Chu Huy Man ordered a renewed offensive. General Man depended on a fresh regiment, the 66th, just arrived from The Trail. These forces were about to move when Moore's 1/7 Cavalry lifted into LZ X Ray. Instead of hitting Plei Me, the VPA went at the Cav troopers from three directions. Moore's pursuing company would be temporarily cut off while its isolated unit was caught even farther afield, becoming the Lost Platoon of the Ia Drang battle.

Landing Zone X Ray would be an epic of stark terror and human survival against the odds. When a rescue column reached the Lost Platoon on the second day, November 15, the battered survivors were afraid even to stand up. The Cav continued to feed troops into LZ X Ray, first two companies of 2/7 Cavalry, then an entire battalion, the 2nd of the 5th Cavalry, the latter overland from a new LZ nearby. After a final assault early in the morning of the sixteenth, the People's Army disappeared. Colonel Moore marched back from X Ray with most of a brigade under command. The cost was bitter on both sides—79 Americans killed and 121 wounded; 834 *bo dois* dead on the field with 1,215 estimated killed by artillery and air strikes. Moore cut back the body count figure to 634 to account for confusion and the fog of war, but the higher figure would be the one given the public by MACV.

Whatever the People's Army losses, they were moving forward, not back. General Man's deputy, Lieutenant Colonel Nguyen Huu An, who was leading the VPA soldiers in the action, sent a reserve battalion ahead and hit some companies of 1/5 Cavalry, who ran into the VPA as both sides hacked through the jungle. The battle for what became known as LZ Albany would be even more expensive than X Ray. American losses were put at 151 killed, 121 wounded, and 4 missing; VPA losses were put at 403 on the battlefield and another 100 estimated. In this case, to judge from weapons captured that amounted to the complement for a full battalion (212 individual weapons, 39 light and 3 heavy machine guns, 6 mortars, and 8 rocket launchers), the People's Army unit involved (the 8th Battalion of the 66th Regiment) must have been decimated.

The intensity of the fighting in the Ia Drang startled MACV. Visiting Cav wounded at a hospital in Qui Nhon, General Westmoreland got the feeling that he had not heard the full story in his own briefings from the responsible field commanders. Westy quickly sent his operations chief, Brigadier General William E. Depuy, up to Pleiku to survey the situation in II Corps. Depuy was among the army's best experts on the art of military operations, and would later be responsible for a revolution in American military doctrine that led directly to victory in the Persian Gulf War of 1991. At Pleiku Depuy learned that the Ia Drang was high and not fordable, its waters fast with runoff from the Chu Pong watershed. Westy worried because both the 1st Cavalry Division and the ARVN General Reserve forces were in II Corps in reaction to Plei Me, and now there were serious losses among the Cav. Not only was wear on the American division a factor, General Westmoreland notes, but also "a bloody nose for the ARVN general reserve would be adverse to government morale." Bill Depuy recommended that the counteroffensive phase of the Ia Drang battle be confined to the north bank of the river. This was the side of Pleiku and the Special Forces camps, and the choice was very logical. A sweep past Duc Co to the Cambodian border became the MACV-JGS strategy. The only problem with that strategy was that it left the Chu Pong entirely to the enemy. Indian country was real; there were places the army and the Saigon forces could no longer sustain themselves. That was a result of The Trail.

Saigon's sweep became the counteroffensive campaign. The 1st Cavalry Division deployed a brigade at Duc Co, one reinforced with extra elements. For a time Harry Kinnard had another brigade forward around Dak To, north of Kontum, where Montagnard country was also very unsettled. A

Vietnamese Marine task force of two battalions stayed in II Corps as part of the counteroffensive, and there was the 1,000-man combat team that Colonel Luat returned to Pleiku. The most important new force, however, would be the ARVN Airborne.

Emergency orders went out as Major Norman Schwarzkopf was half asleep in his room at Saigon's Manor quarters. The adviser to the ARVN Airborne was told to get out to Tan Son Nhut airfield as quickly as he could. Schwarzkopf had just turned in after a big meal of beer and curried chicken, but he hustled out to the base, to find paratroopers already lining up outside planes. Schwarzkopf went with one of two ARVN Airborne task forces, an unusually strong one of three battalions. Two more battalions were with the other force, and an Airborne brigade controlled operations in coordination with II Corps.

The ARVN Airborne flew to Duc Co, its red dirt strip so painful to Major Schwarzkopf. The brigade was under Colonel Ngo Quang Truong, Airborne chief of staff and right-hand man to its commander. Truong always got the toughest missions, and now he had the biggest force, about 2,000 paratroopers. They were supposed to prevent Chu Huy Man's troops from getting back into Cambodia. The five ARVN battalions received support from the 2nd Brigade of the Cav and from the 52nd Aviation Battalion of the U.S. Army.

The night of November 17 at Duc Co, Norman Schwarzkopf watched with wonder as Colonel Truong opened his map case and described exactly how the battle would unfold. Truong wanted Major Schwarzkopf to arrange artillery fire the next day for a particular target and time. The airborne colonel then ordered two battalions to blocking positions as contacts occurred the way Truong had predicted. Air Strikes caught VPA *bo dois* in the act of massing to attack in the center. Here is the account of a platoon leader of the People's Army 32nd Regiment from his captured diary:

> I have just been assigned as platoon leader for a few days when suddenly enemy airborne troops were thrown into the vicinity of our location. We began to move at midnight on November 18. We kept on moving to get out of the enemy encirclement on the next day . . . we were ordered to be ready for an attack. . . . The enemy must have recently bombed the area because the ground was marked with large craters. We could not help becoming anxious. We had just dispersed when suddenly enemy aircrafts [sic] appeared again and strafed into our position.

One of Truong's blocks was craftily placed along the Cambodian side of the border, and the Airborne Brigade committed the two battalions of the second task force on November 20 and 22, just as the 32nd Regiment became trapped. Lieutenant Bui Van Cuong, a political officer with the 33rd, surrendered to the ARVN soldiers. The Airborne claimed 265 enemy killed and ten weapons recovered from the sweep to the head of the Ia Drang valley.

An important role in the battle was played by the awesome bombardment firepower of the B-52 bomber. Strikes by these huge jets began in June 1965 under the code name Arc Light. The early ones were approved at the highest levels in Washington, and that included Plei Me. The B-52s usually struck in groups of six or nine; about a dozen Arc Lights were carried out in the Ia Drang, for a total 96 sorties dropping 1,795 tons of bombs. To give one example, 18 bombers on November 16 dumped 344 tons of munitions along the southeastern slopes of the Chu Pong.

Chu Huy Man fought on in the South throughout the war. American intelligence analysts were not much impressed with his prowess but, after 1965, their biography summaries began to say General Man was especially adept at division-size operations—exactly the dimension of the Ia Drang battle.

Hanoi's legions undoubtedly suffered tremendous losses and that met Westmoreland's concept of imposing a cost on the enemy. If the flow of People's Army troops and supplies could be cut to less than what was needed to replace losses, Westy's attrition strategy might ultimately win the war. But Hanoi made gains, too—before it was simply not known whether *bo dois* could fight Americans. At Ia Drang the People's Army stood in the face of the First Team. The portent was that Hanoi could sustain the conflict. In the new kind of war that emerged, reinforcements and supplies hung in the scale against losses. The fulcrum of this delicate balance would be The Trail. What was done to close The Trail became more important than ever.

Though a key target, Hanoi's lifeline would never become an easy mark. The main arteries of The Trail lay behind the border, and between the American and South Vietnamese bases and the border were mountains and dense jungle, all of it dominated by the Viet Cong and the VPA. All that area continued to be considered "Indian country," where American troops maneuvered at their peril. Almost the only Americans who made getting into Indian country their business were those of the Studies and Observation Group (SOG), becoming active at this very moment, beginning with a reconnaissance team called Iowa.

Quietly flown up to Kham Duc and then turned loose into the hills, Reconnaissance Team Iowa moved out smartly into Indian country. The first scout unit fielded by SOG, Team Iowa became the advance guard for a newly invigorated assault against The Trail by land, sea, and air. Beginning on October 8, Team Iowa made its initial patrol, really more of a dry run into territory that was a little dangerous but still comfortably inside the Vietnamese border. The three-day foray went smoothly, with Iowa calling in one target that led a flight of jets to strike a suspected People's Army bivouac. The team returned to claim credit for the destruction of three huts, eight buildings, and numerous sheds.

After this dress rehearsal, Reconnaissance Team Iowa worked out of Kham Duc and made itself the terror of Indian country, as SOG commenced action on operation Shining Brass. Bad weather held up Iowa for several days, but on October 18, just as Chu Huy Man's *bo dois* were taking their places around Plei Me, Iowa jumped off, moving forward to Dak To. The team began to feel its way out to the Laotian border, through hills the ARVN regulars refused to tread. Iowa consisted of eleven South Vietnamese led by several SOG Americans. They were carried aboard a VNAF CH-34 helicopter escorted by two strike aircraft and a forward air controller (FAC). The team was inserted in a clearing about two and a half miles from their intended target area.

On the second day of the patrol Team Iowa ran into some *bo dois* they could not hide from, and there was a short exchange of fire. The Vietnamese team leader, at the head of the column, was shot before he could take cover. The incident marked the beginning of a SOG legend, Master Sergeant Richard J. Meadows. With a clear mastery of fieldcraft, Meadows kept Iowa out for three more days, completed the mission, and got to an LZ where the team was lifted out on October 23. A week later, on the basis of Sergeant Meadows's information, thirty-seven fighter-bombers would be sent at a VPA camp; their bombs ignited fires and more explosions.

Sergeant Meadows was a soldier's soldier, not only skilled but careful as hell. In the Korean War Meadows had been the youngest GI in the U.S. Army to make master sergeant. That he remained an enlisted man was partly by choice but also because Meadows had nothing more than a ninth-grade education—bored with school, fascinated with the military, Dick had run off to join the army soon after World War II. Dick Meadows had been in some hot places, including the Panama riots of January 1964, where his wife had been trapped at home in the most dangerous area during an outbreak of mob violence. Sergeant Meadows and a buddy had driven directly through rioting Panamanians to protect their endangered families.

In the army Richard Meadows became an early volunteer for Special Forces. He was an expert parachutist, including high-altitude and competition jumping. Meadows also prided himself on his self-taught knowledge; the sergeant used vocabulary peculiar to much more highly educated people. He gravitated quite naturally to MACSOG, and with Team Iowa Dick Meadows showed himself meticulous as well. Before every foray, Sergeant Meadows made a sand model of the area, which the scouts used to go over the plan and memorize key terrain. This careful preparation brought Reconnaissance Team Iowa home from every Shining Brass mission conducted under Dick Meadows, who would eventually hold unchallenged the SOG record for bringing back live prisoners—thirteen *bo dois*, some of them from North Vietnam itself.

Not every one of the Studies and Observation Group's Americans was a Dick Meadows, but plenty of them were very good. In some quarters SOG acquired a reputation as a collection of loose cannons and flaky spooks, but many of its missions were quite effective. The third patrol, by Reconnaissance Team Alaska against a target called Alpha-1, was compromised when one of the SOG men was seen, but posted the biggest payoff yet, a People's

Army camp with dozens of buildings, caves, and weapons positions that kept seventy-eight aircraft busy for a full week. Before the end of the year Alaska had made another patrol, and teams Idaho, Kansas, and Dakota had made one each. Related missions into North Vietnam by all-Vietnamese teams continued with little more success than previously. On November 19, for example, SOG moved Team Romeo from Long Thanh to Khe Sanh, from where three choppers took the commandos to a landing zone in the DRV's Quang Binh Province, where there were reports that the North Vietnamese were building roads to another mountain pass, the Ban Karai, which could supplement the Mu Gia and Nape passages. Romeo landed at the wrong place, wandered for days, starved, then took some prisoners and discovered that the People's Army was already looking for them. Team Romeo would be ambushed and captured in its turn on January 14, 1966, its radio operators forced to broadcast home in a North Vietnamese deception scheme.

The main weakness SOG warriors perceived as 1966 opened was a lack of larger intervention forces to exploit scouts' discoveries or rescue beleaguered teams. Along with the intervention capability, expansion of the geographic domain of Shining Brass became the issue for command decision. From the beginning Admiral Sharp pressed for a focus along Route 9 toward Tchepone. From Vientiane, Ambassador Sullivan resisted such a high-profile tactic. Westmoreland proved willing to go for targets Sullivan accepted just to get SOG up and running. In 1966 Westmoreland won approval for an operations zone within which SOG could work without special approval. At first this would be just three miles deep. Larger operations or deeper ones were coordinated among Vientiane, MACV, CINCPAC, and Washington. Cross-border missions into Cambodia were planned using the code name Daniel Boone. The Studies and Observation Group also began setting up platoon-size "Hornet" forces and company-size units ("Havoc") to back the reconnaissance teams. There could also be battalion-size "Haymaker" forces, and SOG recruited three battalions of Nung strikers to compose these intervention forces. The reconnaissance teams were called "Spike" groups, and twenty of them were in action by mid-1966.

Under Colonel Donald D. Blackburn, in 1966 the Studies and Observation Group grew to a total strength of perhaps 3,500. Aside from maritime activities and those under project Footboy, the new tag for missions against the North, SOG averaged eleven Spike team patrols a month in Shining Brass. At a given moment there were usually three teams in the field. The first Hornet Force intervention occurred on April 16; thirteen of these exploitation operations followed that year, including some in September and October to help recover downed American aircraft flight crews. The latter kind of operation, code-named Bright Light, began in 1966 and became a staple of SOG effort.

In support of SOG, its air wing flew 442 missions in South Vietnam alone during 1966, carrying 13,893 passengers and 2,450 tons of cargo. There were also substantial levels of helicopter activity by VNAF, which usually carried the SOG troops, and the U.S. Army, which flew escort and support. Missions were inserted by the Vietnamese, and six to ten VNAF choppers would be assigned to Shining Brass at a time. During a typical operating period, July 18 through September 26, there were about thirty-six operations, including three patrols by Hornet forces and a patrol where a Spike team was reinforced by a Hornet force. During that time army gunship helicopters flew 101 sorties to escort the infiltration or exfiltration flights, and 83 more in close support of Shining Brass teams on the ground in Laos. The air support reflected the great and continuing danger of the missions. In late July, Spike team Montana was virtually annihilated, with one American and a Vietnamese killed plus another American and two more Vietnamese missing. On an October mission immediately to the west of the DMZ, where the VPA's earliest trails entered South Vietnam, three more Americans disappeared and only the team interpreter came back. Eight of the nine October patrols required emergency lift-out by helicopter. Two Americans were missing in action from another Spike team west of the DMZ in early December.

To work for the ultra-hush-hush Studies and Observation Group was to exist in a classified state of being, but to be killed or be missing in Laos was especially unfortunate, since no American troops were supposed to be in that country. From Vientiane, Ambassador William H. Sullivan kept vigilant watch on everything to do with the cross-border missions, and he registered disagreement as often as approval. Sullivan attempted to preserve the secrecy of the war in Laos at all costs. In April he cabled Washington his strong rejection of the "philosophy that any U.S. spokesman, 'if pressed,' has to admit anything. Spokesmen are paid to say what they are told. . . . The press can speculate all it wants ,but there is no, repeat no need for U.S. officially to confirm anything which is contrary to our national interest."

A typical Spike mission was the patrol of Reconnaissance Team Ohio, carried out from May 24 to 28. The team found the Laotian side of the Chu Pong replete with rice graneries, abandoned villages, campsites that had been used by large units, and several well-traveled tracks. On the fourth day, hearing noises, the SOG troopers hid in the jungle. Fewer than twenty-five yards away passed a People's Army force of 250 men. Aside from burning huts, killing pigs, and calling in air strikes, Team Ohio captured several *bo dois*. Two said they were from the VPA 32nd Regiment. Before the end of Ohio's patrol it had been helped by 37 aircraft, including B-57 bombers; F-4, A-4, and A-1E fighter-bombers; and UH-1B gunships.

One of the biggest SOG operations of 1966, naturally completely unremarked in public, began after the November loss of an A-1G fighter-bomber west of Saravane. All three crewmen parachuted from the plane, and the pilot and copilot were found. There was an eight-day search for the crew chief. A SOG recovery team of 40 men was inserted by HH-3 choppers of the 20th Air Commando Squadron, and that force was subsequently increased to 150 troops. The search group was further reinforced by a 175-man Laotian unit plus a CIA-led special guerrilla unit of 70 more.

The bread and butter of Shining Brass remained its effort to pinpoint targets on The Trail for air strikes. Five different missions during 1966 found enemies considered so critical they were struck by the high-flying B-52 bombers, purveyors of invisible death. There were myriad other strikes by tactical air. As far back as August, General Westmoreland noted in a dispatch that Shining Brass had sent no fewer than nine Spike teams into Laos along the Quang Tri provincial border, patrols that would have launched from Khe Sanh. The Spike teams discovered a supply depot five miles south of Route 9, plus a major infiltration pathway that crossed the Vietnamese border a few miles north of that road.

Meanwhile there had been another key intelligence development when, in March, the Laotian Air Force reported a new trail up from Cambodia, linking with the existing trails in Laos. Colonel Blackburn and his successor, Colonel John K. Singlaub, put a good deal of effort into getting data on this new network, which the Laotians dubbed the "Sihanouk Trail" and the Americans Route 110. Blindly at first, several Arc Light strikes were flown against Route 110. Then, in August, Dick Meadows and Reconnaissance Team Iowa brought back evidence from this area.

From August 7 to August 9, Sergeant Meadows operated against a target called India-4. When VPA troops passed them, Meadows pulled out a snapshot camera he had been carrying and took pictures. Meadows then borrowed an 8-mm movie camera his assistant leader, Chuck Kearns, had brought along on a lark, and made movies as well. Team Iowa found sheds containing several VPA 75-mm mountain guns in shipping packs. Before calling planes to demolish the site, Meadows removed the breach block of one and took it with him. Twenty-three strike aircraft and fourteen helicopter gunships finished off the storage site and other Iowa-designated targets. When Team Iowa returned with two prisoners in addition to its other finds, Colonel Singlaub took Meadows with him to brief Westmoreland personally during one of the SOG chief's weekly meetings with MACV's commander. Sergeant Meadows put the enemy 75-mm breach block on Westy's desk. It was the most concrete evidence imaginable, and also the first hard intelligence that Hanoi was sending artillery guns to the South. Copies of the patrol's still photographs were given by the South Vietnamese to the International Control Commission on October 27 to substantiate Saigon's charges that Hanoi's regular troops were taking part in the war. Westmoreland, mightily impressed with Dick Meadows, helped Singlaub in a successful campaign to get Meadows a battlefield commission to officer's rank. Beyond that, it was clear Hanoi's challenge had assumed major proportions. For Westmoreland, there was some comfort in that the Studies and Observation Group was far from the only arrow in his quiver.

Where the Shining Brass scout teams, for all their ingenuity in carrying the war to The Trail, really played in minor key, the brass and percussion of the campaign against Hanoi became the air effort. From the beginning the goal of the bombing had been to coerce Hanoi through a process of destroying both the North's economic infrastructure and its shipments of troops and supplies down The Trail. The Rolling Thunder operation sought to achieve that goal in the DRV itself; Steel Tiger did the same directly against the People's Army in lower Laos. A conventional ground operation under which The Trail would be severed by an invasion of Laos also figured on the wish list of many American commanders and officials. The ideal of squeezing Hanoi was to be met through violence. Whatever restrictions were imposed, the fact is that the level of violence was enormous.

Two basic kinds of activity characterized U.S. air efforts, specifically targeted attacks for which pilots were briefed in advance, and armed reconnaissance, in which planes could attack anytime they found targets of designated types within agreed patrol areas. The bombing of a bridge is a typical prebriefed target—for example, the "Dragon's Jaw" bridge spanning the Song (river) Ma at Thanh Hoa, which had been completed only in 1964 and which represented the gateway to the DRV's panhandle, the top of the funnel leading to The Trail. Trucks, troop columns, boats, and railroad cars would be the objects in armed reconnaissance, though pilots were usually given secondary targets to hit if they found no moving targets. The great majority of air sorties—by some counts as much as 80 percent—were armed reconnaissance flights.

Conduct of the Steel Tiger campaign over Laos featured new types of missions as well. While Steel Tiger represented a smaller proportion of the air effort than Rolling Thunder, both were actually different aspects of an integrated attempt to squeeze Hanoi. It is important to realize that even as the considerable attacks enumerated here were occurring, an even greater scale of bombardment with the same objective was in progress on the Vietnamese side of the Truong Son Mountains.

The Trail became an immediate focus of the air campaign. Tchepone, given its role as a People's Army cantonment and transit center, was hit early and repeatedly. No longer satisfied with the Laotian Air Force's interdiction effort, CINCPAC set its 2d Air Division the task of blocking The Trail. On April 8, 1965, just a few days after a major strike on Mu Gia Pass, the Tchepone airfield was the primary target. On April 12, Secretary McNamara, with the interdiction effort still in its earliest stages, was already closeted with the Joint Chiefs of Staff to look for ways to increase effectiveness of the bombing. The Vietnamese were not going to stop, and on April 18 there was a suggestion of the increasing VPA capability—in the fact that navy pilots saw trucks in Laos with eight to ten in one convoy, sixteen to twenty-two in another. American air commanders pursued their plans for a systematic effort, and by the end of April some 791 sorties had been flown in Steel Tiger.

With the Americans beginning to hit hard in southern Laos, it was nevertheless true that Hanoi stood at the cusp of greatly increased capability of its own. The rapid buildup and dispatch of Vietnam People's Army units to the South that occurred in 1965 was possible only because of Hanoi's labor improving The Trail over the preceding year.

The quantum leap in capability that occurred coincided almost exactly with the calendar, as the stories of two VPA soldiers illustrate. Huong Van Ba was a People's Army officer who left for the South with the last wave of the "southern" infiltrators, when Hanoi was just beginning to send combat units. Ba was a captain with an artillery unit and deputy commander of the forty-five men from his unit who made up the infiltration group. Down through Thanh Hoa and Dong Hoi they traveled by truck, the flatbeds covered by canvas, stopping only at deserted places. Crossing the Ben Hai River and the western edge of the DMZ, they left their trucks behind and began to march, the most grueling part of the trek—the Truong Son—right at the beginning. Men sickened and died along the way. Ba was mortified when his good friend Captain Tran Chanh Ly sat down to rest at one of the way stations but lay dead at the end of the break. Only seven or eight men made it all the way to the Saigon region without reporting sick or worse, and the journey took three months.

About a year later, an unnamed *bo doi* traveled to lower Laos with another VPA infiltration group. By now the entire trip could be made by truck. The *bo doi*'s truck "convoy" hardly deserved the name—there were only two or three vehicles for most of the trip—but the difference was striking. This soldier's journey took fewer than two weeks, and though his convoy was threatened by American fighter-bombers no fewer than six times, on each occasion the trucks pulled off the road and evaded attack. No one died during the trip. As a matter of policy for Hanoi, this kind of infiltration was far more sustainable than the costly overland marches down The Trail. In 1965, however, resources and weather limited Hanoi's supply network. Marching soldiers still could move when monsoons stopped the trucks. Thus CIA's road-watch teams in Laos, who reported no truck traffic at all between the Mu Gia and Muong Phine that June and July, nevertheless counted 22,000 troops passing them during the summer.

The Project Hardnose CIA road watchers continued to have difficulty working against The Trail. Hardnose was run out of Nakhon Phanom, Thailand, by a pair of CIA officers. From 1962 to 1964 these were Mike Duell and Richard Holm. A linguist who spoke Thai and Mandarin Chinese as well as French, Holm was the chief. He had served previously in the Congo, where he survived a fiery crash in a light plane and then nine days trapped in the wreckage before his rescue by a CIA Cuban mercenary. Project Hardnose itself suffered similar misfortune on October 12, 1965, when an Air America H-34 helicopter carrying the two CIA officers who succeeded Duell and Holm crashed in the jungle while on a familiarization flight. Both CIA officers apparently died in the tragedy, although only one, Mike Malony, has ever been identified. The CIA road-watch program nevertheless persevered, hampered by the fact its patrols of Lao Theung tribesmen could only walk in or helicopter to the locations where they monitored The Trail.

American commanders sought to halt both the enemy trucks and marching parties. In May, when Ambassador Sullivan forced a temporary halt in Steel Tiger as a result of bombing errors that killed Laotian soldiers and civilians, U.S. fighter-bombers attacked 179 trucks on The Trail and estimated destroying 51 of them. In fact, about half of *all* missions conducted in the Steel Tiger area by June were armed reconnaissance. Using the other approach, striking specified targets, U.S. officers selected "choke points," places whose destruction would interrupt roads or key passages in ways difficult to bypass. The Truong Son mountain passes were obvious selections, and both the Mu Gia and Nape passes were on the list in the summer of 1965, when Steel Tiger inderdiction concentrated on nine choke points. In combat action typical of this period, on July 16 and 17 F-105 fighter-bombers dropped 18,000 pounds of munitions on each of the two passes.

Another way to increase the destructiveness of the bombing was to use the biggest bombers. From an early date Laos would be an operating area for the B-52 jets. Political obstacles in Vientiane, and uncertainties in Washington, delayed application of Arc Light in Laos but did not prevent it. In one of its Special National Intelligence Estimates, the CIA looked at the implications of B-52 raids and decided that, except for North Vietnam, Arc Light could be used in Southeast Asia more or less with impunity. In Washington, President Johnson had a committee review proposed Arc Light strikes, composed of his national security adviser, the secretary of defense, and an undersecretary of state. In the wake of the Ia Drang battle, that group decided to permit Arc Lights in Laos against a VPA base area MACV had proposed for attack. The first Arc Light in Laos took place on December 10, 1965, using twenty-four B-52s. This strike also featured the first use in Southeast Asia of cluster bombs, weapons that separated on impact into many small bomblets that could subsequently explode like land mines.

The political value of the particular way Bill Sullivan handled the Laotian prime minister also became manifest that month. When the B-52 attack was reported in the press, along with news that air activity in Laos was being intensified, Souvanna Phouma termed the reports a fabrication. Since Souvanna had approved U.S. bombing originally, and in mid-November also approved the planned increases, and since the Laotians were now relaxing some previous restrictions on the U.S. air campaign, the conclusion must be that Souvanna was willing to go along with and even protect the U.S. military activity in Laos. Had there been an overtly pro-American leader in power in Vientiane, the likelihood is that with a modicum of effort the Pathet Lao and Hanoi could have made that government disintegrate. At a minimum, American attention would have been pulled to northern Laos, and the campaign against The Trail could have ground to a halt.

Northern Laos was not the only war front that beckoned. To judge from his retrospective memoir, as well as the report on the war in Vietnam he released in conjunction with Westmoreland, which hardly mentions Laos, Admiral U.S. Grant Sharp remained far more interested in freedom of action against the DRV. The Joint Chiefs of Staff had broader interests, but they backed Sharp's calls for lifting restrictions on the air campaign. Some other officials were of like mind, notably Walt W. Rostow, who argued on the basis of political-military war games in Washington that "air and other direct pressure on the North is a critical variable." In September 1965 Rostow sent Dean Rusk a memorandum proposing that Rolling Thunder concentrate on the DRV's transportation system, on fifty or so critical choke points and maintain those cuts, while also perhaps cutting points between Hanoi and the Chinese border. Beyond this transportation focus Rostow, and some others, were already pressing for an "optimum" use of airpower—to destroy the DRV's oil refining and storage capacity to bring the economy (and the transportation system) to a halt.

It would be Walt Rostow whom President Johnson appointed, in February 1966, to succeed McGeorge Bundy as his national security adviser. In the wake of Rostow's emergence in this key White House position, the committee to review Arc Light strikes lost its importance as a restrictive mechanism.

During the last three months of 1965 there were more than 4,000 attack sorties in the Steel Tiger area, followed by 8,000 in January 1966 and more than 5,000 the following month. Over the same period there were approximately 15,000 fighter-bomber sorties in Rolling Thunder. Claims for destruction in 1965 included 1,500 boats, euphemistically termed "waterborne logistics craft," 650 railroad cars, and 800 trucks in Rolling Thunder, along with more than 100 trucks (and 115 damaged) within Laos. Aircraft dropped 315,000 tons of bombs over Southeast Asia that year. This represented a major effort.

The ferocity of the air campaign was such that the United States, superpower that it was, came close to running out of the bombs it depended on the most. Stocks of munitions were soaked up by the strikes, to such a degree that by the spring of 1966 even MACV and the 2d Air Division were forced to recognize this as a major problem. When Deputy Secretary of Defense Cyrus Vance visited Saigon at that time, he was told that the air force had fewer than three quarters of the bombs, and just one third of the cluster bomblets, necessary to strike the existing list of approved targets. In a five-day period in early April, just prior to the Vance visit, the air force had been unable to fly almost 400 possible sorties because there were no bombs for the planes. This problem was alleviated only by the United States *buying back* from Germany bombs previously sold to that country; by more sharing of stocks between the navy and the air force; by reducing numbers of bombs given to Laos in military aid; and by sending out aircraft only partially loaded, a practice the military hated for good reason. Had the air war in Southeast Asia been freed of all restrictions, which some former participants would have preferred, it still could not have been waged effectively because the military themselves could not furnish the means to conduct it.

One way to maximize the return from what was available was to send the aircraft against targets immediately upon their discovery. This was the practice with close air support in South Vietnam, where forward air controllers (FACs) in propeller-driven light aircraft acted as dispatchers, sending heavier jets and bombers against targets they discovered or were told of by observers on the ground. The procedure was extended to Laos under a program code-named Tiger Hound, beginning in 1965. General Westmoreland was enthusiastic about the possibilities, and recounts that the name evoked aggressiveness (Tiger) and an ability to smell or track the enemy (Hound). At meetings of the regional review group, the Southeast Asia Coordinating Committee, Westy pressed for Tiger Hound beginning in July 1965. At first General Thao Ma of the Laotian Air Force resisted this new U.S. program, on the ground that American FACs were not going to see any more than his own pilots, but this objection gradually melted away.

Tiger Hound became a kind of aerial complement to SOG's Shining Brass on the ground; indeed, the two wound up linked by a procedure under which Spike teams could ask FACs for instant air strikes. Another similarity between the programs was their launching points—Tiger Hound's operating sites were Khe Sanh, Dong Ha, Kham Duc, and Kontum. Most of these places were perfectly familiar to the men of the Studies and Observation Group. Tiger Hound's main base, Da Nang, was also locale for the northern field command of SOG. With a small staff unit in Saigon, Tiger Hound mirrored the Studies and Observation Group in every aspect of the way its mission was performed in the Vietnam environment. Unlike Tiger Hound (it always remained a tiny special unit), SOG ultimately became the equivalent of a division command. In fact, the whole Special Forces function of unconventional warfare was big business in military terms in Vietnam, and the 5th Special Forces Group was regarded as a corps command. It was Westmoreland, not anyone else, who wrote the efficiency reports about the 5th Group commander. Efficiency reports on the SOG chief came directly out of the Joint Chiefs.

The strong air force orientation was perhaps the most significant limitation on Tiger Hound. There were the usual difficulties with the Lao, but these were less important than the problems existing within the air force itself. "There were two ways to do a thing," recalls one Da Nang veteran of that period, "the right way or the air force way." It would be months before there was an easy way for SOG patrols to call on the air assets right around them. On its own flights, the air force set altitude and load requirements that often impaired effectiveness. Sometimes Tiger Hound FACs had to orbit too high to see well; at others the fighter-bombers had to fly so high they were lucky to hit anything at all. The jets, soon to be called "fast movers" in the argot of the battle for The Trail, had to act in a split second to make a strike at speed. Pilots who violated restrictions to come in lower went home to face a tongue-lashing or worse. The air force of the Vietnam era was run for the Strategic Air Command, the private fiefdom of General Curtis E. LeMay, then air force chief of staff. The bomber jockeys flew at high altitude all the time and saw nothing wrong with it; the Tiger Hound FACs, soon to be known as "Ravens," and the fast-mover pilots, thought otherwise.

Whatever its drawbacks, Tiger Hound was serious competition to the B-52s for the best thing going in 1965–1966 in the battle for The Trail. Formed under air force colonel John F. Groom, Tiger Hound initially used army planes, O-1E "Bird Dogs," to spot targets for the fast movers. Captain

Roy C. Dalton was posted to RLAF headquarters at Savannakhet for special liaison with the Laotians. The first flight of a Hound Dog—the radio call sign the Ravens used—came on December 5. The next day air force C-123 aircraft began dropping defoliant chemicals along the shoulders of Route 9 and other roads to improve visibility for the Ravens and strike pilots. There were 800 Tiger Hound sorties in December 1965, then 3,500 in January 1966. Action was plentiful.

It was either Tiger Hound or the irritation provided by SOG's Shining Brass forays that led to the first direct action for the Khe Sanh camp. Run by Special Forces Detachment A-101, Khe Sanh's garrison included an ARVN LLDB detachment, two companies of Nungs, and two companies of CIDG strikers. Nearby there was a battalion of the ARVN 1st Division and an artillery element of two 105-mm howitzers. The Studies and Observation Group had a launching point at Khe Sanh, and for Tiger Hound the air force added a detachment of four pilots with two 0-1 Bird Dogs.

The LLDB camp commander was in the habit of summoning everyone for a flag lowering at sunset each night, and on the evening of January 3, 1966, just as the ceremony ended, People's Army *bo dois* began to shell Khe Sanh with 122-mm mortars. It was the largest weapon yet seen in VPA hands in the war. The shell pattern raked over the camp. People's Army firing positions were out of range of both Khe Sanh's own 81-mm mortars and the ARVN 105-mm guns. Before the shelling ended there were thirteen dead and fifty or sixty wounded. One of the Bird Dogs at the airstrip had been demolished.

Over the preceding weeks, strikers had been finding greater and greater People's Army presence in the hinterland. Enemy strength in the Khe Sanh region was estimated at two full regiments. If CIDG patrols were to be believed, the *bo dois* were fresh VPA troops with brand-new equipment, some still packed in shipping crates. This is consistent with what we know about Hanoi's buildup in the South, and it is also an indication of the growing strength and depth of the People's Army dispositions around Tchepone. Another hint of the VPA–Pathet Lao power position lay in the fact that Green Berets and local advisers were now getting the impression that the Laotian troops of Bataillon Volontaire 33 at Ban Houei Sane had reached some private accommodation with the *bo dois*.

Equally disturbing were signs that the Chinese had something to do with all this activity. A patrol near Khe Sanh had found a body alleged to be a Chinese officer, and after the January 3 mortar attack, it was reported that Chinese was heard on radio circuits in the Khe Sanh area. During the Plei Me–Ia Drang battle it was also reported that a Chinese was captured. Trains said to be full of Chinese troops were mentioned in CIA reports from Hanoi. Precise data still lack, but it is plausible that the Chinese People's Liberation Army would have wanted its own picture of the Vietnam War and could have sent observers to witness combat at first hand.

Meanwhile, Tiger Hound carried the war to Indian country. The planes encountered convoys, troop columns, and fixed targets they fed to the Lao and got onto approved lists. There were twenty-nine of these fixed targets as of December 5, but already sixty-nine by January 12, 1966, and of those, fifty-six had already been struck. Opposition was such that ten planes, both Ravens and fast movers, were hit during the initial months, and four were shot down. A major loss was Lieutenant Colonel David H. Holmes, Tiger Hound detachment leader, shot down over Laos on March 15. Special Forces prepared a rescue mission, but it was canceled by higher authority. Holmes was later presumed dead.

So successful was the Raven–strike plane combination that it was extended into the part of the DRV just above the Demilitarized Zone under a program called Tally Ho. Several base installations for The Trail were located in the Tally Ho area of operations, which stretched from the DMZ up to Dong Hoi, encompassing the approaches to the Mu Gia, a new crossing at Ban Karai, the old trail at the west side of the DMZ, and the defense district of Vinh Linh. Tally Ho got under way in late July 1966, and in its first week scored a major success with the destruction of a huge supply depot not far from Vinh Linh. More than 100 tons of ammunition were destroyed by bombs or in secondary explosions. The rainy season in Laos plus the requirements for Tally Ho temporarily reduced Tiger Hound to only a couple dozen sorties a month, but toward the end of the year it was back up to speed, accounting for 1,300 of the aircraft flights in Laos during November 1966 and 1,600 the following month. Tally Ho lost its independent identity in early 1967, being folded into the routine of the Rolling Thunder campaign.

The Strategic Air Command of the air force also played its part in Laos, with some eighty-four Arc Light strikes before the end of 1966. The most important ones were directly at Mu Gia Pass, which was bombed after Westmoreland pressed Ambassador Sullivan at a SEACOORD meeting in March 1966. There were B-52 attacks on both sides of the border at Mu Gia in April, June, and again in December 1966. These were maximum-effort strikes using thirty or more huge bombers.

Air efforts against The Trail continued to run afoul of Laotian sensibilities, though the United States sometimes pleased the Laotians as well. In March 1966, when the VPA and the Pathet Lao threatened Laotian Army troops holding Attopeu, American air intervention saved the day. On February 23, on the other hand, misguided attacks by two flights of F-105 fighter-bombers hit a village near Route 9 and wrecked the headquarters of the Laotian Army's Mobile Group 15. That same unit had been victim of another mistaken U.S. air strike, in 1965. Following this incident the Lao clamped more restrictions on air activity over lower Laos, including some that forced planes to fly at higher altitude around certain towns.

A notable advance in authority came in November 1966, when Vientiane approved the suggestion that U.S. aircraft have blanket approval to attack any vehicle they found moving within 200 yards of a road throughout the Steel Tiger zone of Laos. It so happened that Bill Sullivan was in the hospital at the time of that decision. Senior aide Emory Swank signed off on the recommendation in the ambassador's name.

America's air campaign in 1966 was a highly destructive affair. Over Laos that year there were 48,000 attack sorties plus 10,000 for combat support. Rolling Thunder added 81,000 attack sorties with 48,000 combat support flights. Explosives expended amounted to 440,000 tons, of which 52,000 tons fell specifically on Steel Tiger (and 123,000 on the DRV). Destruction claims in Rolling Thunder included 2,067 vehicles destroyed (2,017 damaged), 1,095 railway cars (1,219 damaged), and 3,690 boats (5,810 damaged). The barons who masterminded this vast effort could hardly believe Hanoi did not capitulate to this squeeze, that it would not be coerced. In search of greater impact, of "optimum" effectiveness, they resorted to every scheme imagination or science could devise. The unbelievable would be exactly what happened. The intelligence reports from Indian country were quite clear; there was no surprise. Hanoi was *still* on the march.

The mainstay of Hanoi's supply efforts through the early years of the American war remained the bicycle—French models were preferred, but Polish and Czech designs were also used. Their frames specially strengthened, the bicycles could haul hundreds of pounds, as illustrated here. This bicycle is loaded with three 50-lb. rice sacks plus a 75mm recoilless rifle. (Author's collection)

Vietnamese Central Highlands west of Pleiku, from which People's Army troops emerged to attack Duc Co and fight in the Ia Drang valley. The total absence of roads, trails, or anything man-made gives an idea of the difficulty of the country; the mountain fastness of the Annamite chain proved even more rugged. (U.S. Air Force photo)

Taken through the barbed wire of the Special Forces camp at Duc Co, this picture shows troops of the 1st Cavalry Division (Airmobile) loading for an air assault on January 14, 1966. (U.S. Army photo)

At the People's Army War Museum in Hanoi: This photgraph illustrates the range of weapons the U.S. brought to bear in Vietnam. Against the backdrop of an SA-2 anti-aircraft missle of Russian origin, the display of American bombs includes a napalm tank, 500-, 750-, two types of 1,000-, and several kinds of 2,000-lb. bombs. (Author's collection)

Attacked by People's Army units which pretended in their communications to be agricultural sites, Camp A Shau would be overrun. On March 12, 1966, two days afterwards, this reconnaissance photo demonstrates the almost complete destruction of the Special Forces camp's facilities. (U.S. Air Force photo)

Reconstruction of a typical hut at a way station on the Ho Chi Minh Trail. The major functions of the stations are all illustrated: automotive repair, medical aid, food and water, rest and relaxation. (Author's collection)

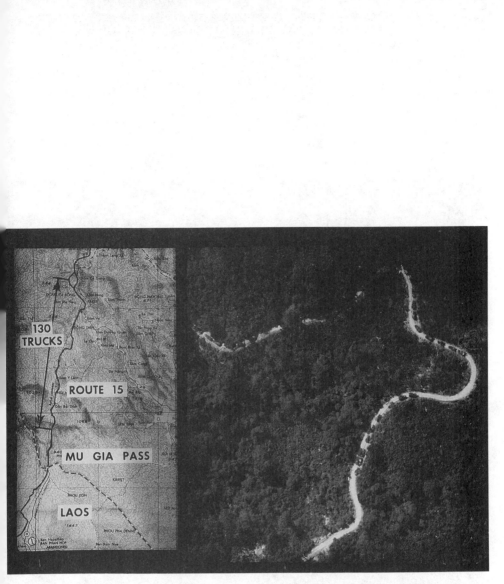

People's Army truck convoys heading up Route 15 to the Mu Gia Pass, February 9, 1967. This air reconnaissance montage shows 26 of the 130 fully loaded trucks counted by photo interpreters. The previous day another 75 trucks had been counted. (U.S. Air Force photo)

Closeup of a Chinese truck captured during the invsion of Laos. Note the removal of glass windows (to prevent shards and fragmentation if hit) and improvement of the front bumper. Markings on the left side of the hood on this truck identified its origin as the "Nanking Auto Company." (U.S. Army photo)

A People's Army convoy underway through the bombed and defoliated wilderness the "Pinball Wizards" created along the Ho Chi Minh Trail. Note the panel built over the hood of the lead truck for shade, camouflage, and for use as a weapon platform. (photo from the Institute for Military History, Vietnam)

Taxicab used in Saigon as a decoy on the night of Tet, 1968. Volunteer Nguyen Tan Mieng drove this taxi up to Gate 051 at Tan Son Nhut air base in the initial stage of the attack. Only the specialists and replacements who arrived down the Ho Chi Minh Trail enabled the People's Army and the Viet Cong to recover after the offensive. (Author's collection)

Artifacts of The Trail: tools used by engineers assigned to the 968th Division of the People's Army; a map case; and most importantly, a poem and songbook of the Truong Son produced in 1970 by *Binh Tram* 33, the people responsible for The Trail from Tchepone south to Muong Nong. (Author's collection)

Reconstruction of a typical center for radio communications at a way station along The Trail. The barrel just outside the radio hut could catch rainwater. (Author's collection)

The 1969–1970 issue of the magazine *We'll Win*, published by the 71st Engineer Battalion of *Binh Tram* 33. (Author's collection)

A selection of the American electronic sensors used to acquire data for relay to the "Pinball Wizards." (Author's collection)

American weapons disarmed and recovered by Vietnamese of the 559th Transportation Group along The Trail. From left to right: chemical cannisters, gravel mines, alarm signals, primer for a magnetic bomb. (Author's collection)

A June 1971 aerial view of U.S. installations at Nakhon Thanom, Thailand. In the foreground is the Infiltration Surveillance Center (Task Force Alpha), home of the "Pinball Wizards." (U.S. Air Force photo)

Grunts of the 1st Battalion, 501st Infantry, 101st Airborne Division northwest of Quang
Assigned to support the Laotian invasion through operation "Dewey Canyon II," these An
ican soldiers are about to be lifted into battle by UH-1D helicopters. (U.S. Army photo)

Khe Sanh, 1971. A restored airfield became a key supply link for American and South Vie
namese forces operating against the Ho Chi Minh Trail. This view shows U.S. Army radar a
tactical navigation facilities at the end of the runway. Beyond them an Air Force C-130 tran
port is on its final approach to the base. (U.S. Air Force photo)

An American soldier takes time for a shower under the waterfall in the Rao (river) Quan that lay just below the southern edge of the Khe Sanh combat base; February 12, 1971. (U.S. Army photo)

In the battle zone in Laos: southeast of Hill 31, the detritus of a battle ARVN lost. Surrounded by bomb craters and the ruts from their tracks which show how they had manuevered, two People's Army PT-76 tanks lay destroyed and derelict. (U.S. Air Force photo)

109 512 U S A F   SA-2 SITE   5 JULY 73

MISSILE LAUNCHER SHEDS

KHE SANH AFLD 2.5 NM

By 1973 the tables were turned. Not only were there People's Army surface-to-air missile (SAM) sites protecting The Trail, this July 5, 1973, reconnaissance photo shows a SAM site actually inside South Vietnam, at Khe Sanh itself. (U.S. Air Force photo)

Relics of war: A collage formed by various parts of American warplanes shot down over North Vietnam at the People's Army War Museum, Hanoi. (Author's collection)

CHAPTER 8

Indian Country
1966–1967

On the American frontier in the nineteenth century, Indian country had been a constantly diminishing quantity. There had been many tribes to start with, and Indians covered all the land, but they had been pressed back by the settlers. Ranchers, sheep herds, gold diggers, their numbers only augmented by the arrival of the railroads, trimmed away at Indian country. This would never be the case in the Vietnam War, in which People's Army domination of the hinterland, the new "Indian country" in the argot of the war, started strong but stayed that way. If anything, the dynamic in Southeast Asia in the 1960s and 1970s proved the opposite of what it had been on America's frontier. Hanoi was not pressed, it was pressing. The ants were continuing their march.

In Laos, along The Trail, the valleys resounded, day after day, with the sounds of marching men and, at night mostly, speeding trucks. There were other noises, too—the sounds of road clearing and repair, of bulldozers, picks and axes, and of trumpeting elephants. The cacophony hardly ceased.

Hanoi had sent a wave of regulars South during 1965, but that flow expanded right through the heavy bombing of the next year. It was February 1966 when the People's Army 18B Regiment, the first of the new year, passed the Vietnamese border. Not far behind, having just crossed the Truong Son range, came the 24th. Fifteen more People's Army regiments, plus a plethora of smaller units, including engineers, antiaircraft, and artillery, trekked South that year. The troops in these units numbered almost 30,000 *bo dois*, more than half Hanoi's total infiltration for the year. Through most of 1967, replacements dominated on The Trail, though even then, several new VPA regiments came through during the first part of the year.

Preparing the men and managing this flow amid the violence of American countermeasures would have challenged the greatest of military commanders. The Vietnamese leadership had their failings, but they brought considerable energy and improvisational skill to the task. In fact, the story of The Trail is at once a tale of dedication and *bo dois'* ad hoc solutions to difficulties.

Bamboo became a secret weapon. People's Army ingenuity may well have determined victory.

Improvisation was married to system in Hanoi's effort, and the combination would be set early. With Hanoi's decision to send regulars South, the old system of infiltration training became outdated. The Vietnam People's Army began recalling former enlisted men in 1964 and officers the next year. This plus the influx of draftees and volunteers was more than the VPA could handle. There was refresher training for reservists and recalled soldiers, basic training for inductees, and specialized training of all kinds required in addition to infiltration preparations. Beginning in 1965 the VPA formed several new training units and also started to carry out some training for new *bo dois* in all its field combat units.

Because of weather patterns that reversed themselves on the two sides of the Annamite Mountains, the People's Army gradually developed a routine of two cycles of training a year. In the summer and fall, when monsoon rains soaked The Trail in Laos, *bo dois* received their basic and infantry training, leaving for the South from December through May or June. Vietnamese selected for more specialized training as sappers, artillerists, communications personnel, and so on, would undertake a second cycle of advanced training, only then moving on to the infiltration centers and hence the South.

The stream of *bo dois* and cadres who made up the flow down The Trail trained with a series of People's Army units in camps throughout the DRV. One of the most active was Unit (Doan) 32, which evolved from the People's Army 320th Division and became known to U.S. intelligence as the 320B Training Division. In the French war the 320th had been the division of the Delta—the Red River Delta in those days—and it had participated in all the French battles south and west of Hanoi. The locale of its biggest campaign, Hoa Binh, became the 320th's garrison after the war. Deputy command of the division had been one of Van Tien Dung's last troop assignments before Dung became a power on the VPA General Staff. In 1965 Doan 32 remained in Hoa Binh when it began to train *bo dois* for the war in the South.

Doan 32 eventually ran seven subordinate units in a dispersed area. It instructed for signalmen, gunners, and infantry and had courses that ranged from three to eight months. Later in the war, when American bombers hit the first infiltration center (Xuan Mai), and the 338th Division moved South to Thanh Hoa, Doan 32 created a detachment to refurbish the damaged base and resume the training there. Judging from U.S. intelligence reports, Doan 32 by itself accounted for a significant fraction of the flow down The Trail. Intelligence traced seven of the 1965 infiltration groups to Doan 32, in all amounting to 3,500 *bo dois*. In 1966, however, the training unit sent 40 groups South for a total of 22,000 soldiers. The overall estimate for *all* VPA infiltration for 1966 was 55,300. Even measured against all "possible" North Vietnamese infiltration, for which the 1966 estimate was 86,100, Doan 32 was a notable contributor. Moreover, the unit's trained groups included many regular units—at least 5 full regiments during 1966.

When the 320th Division sent its own 48th and 52nd Regiments South, both passed through the finishing schools of Doan 32. Through 1967 the unit trained another 30 groups (2 were regiments) numbering more than 14,000 *bo dois*.

Toward the end of 1966, as Hanoi reached full stride in its move to South Vietnam, American intelligence assembled a mosaic of the People's Army *bo doi*. Part of that study involved a survey of almost 800 infiltrators in U.S. or ARVN custody. The survey data reveal an interesting snapshot of the People's Army in the field at the height of the war. There can be no doubt that Hanoi's was a peasant Army—with more than 11 percent of the DRV's population, Hanoi and Haiphong together accounted for only 3.7 percent of the survey population. This was also a professional army—more than half of the *bo dois* had more than a year in the military, and most in excess of two. The percentages even grew, overwhelmingly, in late 1966, though the concentration shifted to *bo dois* with thirteen to eighteen months' service. Fully 83 percent of officers and 19 percent of enlisted men were members of the Lao Dong Party, while another 11 percent of officers and 68 percent of enlisted men were affiliated with youth groups.

Single Vietnamese made up about half of the People's Army in this 1966 snapshot. Surprisingly, those married with children—30 percent—outnumbered married Vietnamese without families by almost two to one. More than 90 percent of the People's Army soldiers practiced ancestor worship or were Buddhists; fewer than 5 percent were Catholic. Hardly any VPA soldiers were without education, at least two years' worth; most *bo dois* had four to seven years' schooling; only 6 percent of infiltrators had nine or more years of education. The provinces of the Vietnamese panhandle, beginning with Nam Dinh at the edge of the Red River Delta, pumped the lifeblood of the Vietnam People's Army. With slightly more than a quarter of the DRV's population, the panhandle provinces furnished no less than 64.4 percent of the soldiers. Nghe An alone proved the source of a quarter of the *bo dois* who would be infiltrated, captured, and surveyed. Americans often assumed that the jungle and mountains were a natural habitat for the *bo dois*, but as the MACV intelligence study observed, "the vast majority of . . . infiltrators are from the coastal and delta lowlands. . . . They are no more accustomed to the hardships of the highlands than are ARVN American troops." The *bo doi*'s trek South "is usually his first contact with unfavorable terrain and climate."

Through late 1966, as Hanoi's regular regiments left for the South in increasing numbers, elements in the survey data also indicate the VPA approaching the full stretch of mobilization. The average age of VPA soldiers captured was falling. Through most of the period, more than 40 percent of the *bo dois* had been old enough to have fought in the French war, a percentage that fell before the end of 1966, even though men recalled to service—16 percent of the total by then—almost doubled. During the same interval the number of eighteen- and nineteen-year-olds tripled and began to match the number of older soldiers. The percentage of volunteers also shrank, to fewer than a fifth.

Volunteer or draftee, the data indicate that the People's Army soldier trained carefully. Though some *bo dois* left for the South with little or no training, not until the 1969–1970 period did these individuals appear in significant numbers. Men and women were grouped in "cells" of three that worked together and watched each other. Except for a dinner break and "siesta" of perhaps two and a half hours, a typical day featured classes and training exercises from 6:30 A.M. to 5:00 P.M., and after supper there would be sessions with political officers from seven to nine o'clock. The officers kept watch on the cells and led the "criticism-self-criticism" sessions that the People's Army used as exhortation, punishment, and even entertainment. For the most part *bo dois* were instructed in weapons and squad, platoon, and company tactics. Ambush and assault were taught most frequently. People's Army training did much to make the *bo dois* seem the purposeful ants that Western observers fancied them to be.

Like the regiments of Colonel Lam's 320th Division getting their toughening for The Trail with Doan 32, even the full units—especially these units—passed through the training system before marching South. Upon completion of preparations there were usually leave, light duty, parties, or other entertainment before departure. Both combat units and groups of individual replacement soldiers then received new identities, *doan* numbers, by which they would be known on The Trail. *Bo dois* received a full issue of equipment, including medicines to fight the many dangers along the way. At the DRV border the *bo dois* would receive numbers of their own, on "infiltration passes" that served as their identification in the South. Then the *doans* would be loosed into the stream of troops and equipment feeding the war in the South.

Nam Dinh, at the edge of the Red River Delta, stood as the major city of Nam Ha Province. Nam Ha itself, on the coast of the Tonkin Gulf, was among those provinces providing fewer recruits for the People's Army. One, more accurately an officer draftee, was Tran Danh Tai. Unusual in several ways, Tai married a city girl, had no children, and lived in Hanoi. After a decade in provincial schools, Tai had gone on to Hanoi Medical School. Tai was twenty-five when he finished in December 1964, and his young brother, sister, and parents were all very proud. Though his diploma would not be issued until the spring, in January Tran Danh Tai got orders to report to the VPA's Medical Studies institute.

Situated at Ha Dong, just west of Hanoi, the institute provided surgeons and technicians for the People's Army. Student doctors lived in barracks, four to a room; the technicians in large communal quarters. Several hundred attended; the usual course of instruction lasted a year. This was the moment of Hanoi's big commitment to the South, however, and its effect on Tai would be that his class was sent out after just six months. Commissioned a lieutenant, Tran Danh Tai went to Nghe An Province, birthplace of Ho Chi Minh, where Tai mustered into the 18th Medical Battalion, hospital unit of the 325th Division. By that time the division's three original regiments had all left for the South, so there was not a lot to do at the hundred-bed hospital.

In late November 1965 Lieutenant Tai received new orders, to report to the 95B Regiment, a new unit forming under the division's command. It turned out that the 95B was about to take The Trail to war. While the regiment started its physical toughening and preparations, Tai and others from the medical company left immediately, in a convoy of ten vehicles. They were considered high-priority personnel. The convoy departed a base in Ha Tinh on January 11, 1966. A week later they entered South Vietnam, having escaped any air attack. Lieutenant Tai brought four trucks of medical supplies to a way station, where he set up a clinic. About a month later, Doan 300 arrived. This infiltration group posed as "Agricultural Site 10," but in reality it was an infantry division commanding several regiments on hand or marching South, among them Tai's own 95B unit. The Vietnam People's Army wanted to clear the flanks of The Trail, sweeping away American and ARVN troops on the Vietnamese side of the Annamites, Laotians on the other side. Lieutenant Tai became part of that endeavor.

Nestled against the Laotian border, at the head of a valley that led northeast toward Hue, was the A Shau Special Forces camp. Its location made the camp a potential launch point for SOG patrols against The Trail. Conversely, the A Shau valley was a fine avenue of approach to Hue, and People's Army supply depots were already in this area. People's Army commanders had little difficulty concluding that the Green Berets and their CIDG strikers had to be cleared out of Camp A Shau. At first, lack of sufficient combat troops prevented attack, but that changed in February 1966 as the 95B Regiment arrived down The Trail, 2,000 fresh *bo dois* ready to test wills with the Americans. Colonel Tran led the regiment, known as "Worksite I" to the officers masquerading as Agricultural Site 10. They reinforced Tran with an extra battalion and sent the regiment to take camp A Shau.

Enemy intentions were telegraphed when a defector went over to the Americans, who also found documents hinting something was up. Camp commanders asked for more troops, but ARVN's I Corps rejected this request. The security of this sector had been in increasing jeopardy for months, and ARVN had already forced the withdrawal of two smaller border camps in the area. Captain John D. Blair IV, heading Detachment A-102, asked for help from Green Beret bosses and got some. "Bulldog Bill" McKean sent a company of Nungs from the mobile strike force to A Shau on March 7. Colonel McKean would have used more, but A Shau could not fit any more troops. Captain Blair had three companies of CIDG strikers, and there were some civilian laborers and post exchange girls, in all about 50 civilians and close to 400 Montagnard, Nung, Vietnamese, and American troops.

Patrols and ambush parties found nothing, yet on the evening of March 8

Colonel Tran's *bo dois* probed Camp A Shau's defenses. Late that night they began shelling A Shau with 82-mm mortars. Before dawn, Tran hit with a two-company ground assault. The initial attacks were repulsed, but A Shau, entirely dependent on air support, seemed in grave danger. One "Puff the Magic Dragon" (AC-47) gunship was shot down after making a single pass, while a marine chopper sent to retrieve wounded was crippled upon landing. Mountain fog and low overcast hampered the planes helping A Shau.

Supplies were a further problem. None arrived until a couple of C-123s dropped down through the cloud cover, guided by the A-1E fighter-bomber piloted by air force captain Bernard D. Fisher. He flew repeatedly over A Shau during the battle. When his unit commander, Major Wayne D. Myers, sustained heavy damage to the aircraft that forced a crash landing, Fisher went in right behind, landed at A Shau in the face of intense machine-gun fire, and rescued the downed aviator. For this act of bravery Captain Fisher earned the Congressional Medal of Honor, the first such decoration awarded to an air force man in the Vietnam War.

Seven Green Berets and roughly 100 Nungs and strikers escaped from A Shau overland. Together with wounded and others evacuated by air, about half of A Shau's defenders survived. But the combat also turned out to be expensive for the VPA—it was surgeon Tran Danh Tai's hospital that treated the A Shau casualties. Tai received more than 200 wounded from the battle; his aid station could not move for more than a week after the fight, until the wounded regained strength for the march. Nevertheless, the Vietnamese *bo dois* ended up in undisputed control of the A Shau valley.

The action at A Shau cleared The Trail's eastern flank of an irritant. While the Special Forces camp had existed, scout patrols and intervention units from SOG and the ARVN commandos had had easy access to the heart of the People's Army supply network. Without A Shau the patrols had to make difficult airborne insertions or march in from the coastal plains, which were effectively too far away to permit activity in the region of the Laotian border. Vietnam People's Army commanders, in overrunning Camp A Shau, won important freedom from interference for The Trail. From the VPA standpoint, however, interference from the west, from the Lao side of the Annamites, also posed a problem. The Bolovens Plateau had a number of Laotian government garrisons, including the bases of Attopeu and Saravane. The People's Army determined to clear this flank of The Trail as well.

Six more VPA battalions gathered to menace Attopeu, at the edge of the Bolovens. This town, a key market center, contained a garrison of the FAR—the Royal Laotian Army. The Lao had three battalions at Attopeu. Until spring 1966 it had been a quiet post, benefiting from an informal truce with the Pathet Lao and the VPA. Now the People's Army smashed one of the battalions outside Attopeu, killing several senior officers, a sharp signal of the changing times. On the night of March 3 the VPA made a pitched attack, and only the intervention of two American AC-47 gunships prevented the fall of the Lao base. The "Puff" aircraft, lumbering C-47s heavily armed with rapid-fire machine guns and cannons, were credited with denting the People's Army maneuvers. Some enthusiasts spoke of AC-47s neutralizing as many as 100 to 250 of an 800-man enemy force.

The *bo dois* subsided. But FAR troops were not inclined to maneuver beyond their big bases, such as Attopeu. Even when, prodded by the Americans, FAR began to recruit irregulars it called "Special Guerrilla Units" (SGUs) and new militia, the whole area of lower Laos was covered by nothing more than 1,500 SGU soldiers plus an equal number of local militia. That would not be until 1970, and then it was little challenge to the security forces on The Trail. Attopeu's main importance became as a receiving point for road-watch teams manning observation posts along the People's Army and Pathet Lao transport lines. The Sihanouk Trail and the network from the North that terminated in the Central Highlands and Chu Pong could be watched best from Attopeu, which eventually had a half dozen observation posts associated with it. Until 1971 the People's Army would tolerate Attopeu, making do with any inconvenience U.S. and FAR operations caused them.

Toleration meant that the *bo dois* did what they could to sweep away the road-watch teams and resist the SOG patrols without necessarily exercising close physical control over every inch of the countryside. On occasion this meant the People's Army conducted sweeps along the roads in exactly the same fashion as ARVN and American troops within South Vietnam. In late March and early April 1966, for example, the People's Army cleared away hostile eyes below the Mu Gia in a systematic campaign. Four Lao Theung SGUs or CIA road-watch teams were either attacked or maneuvered out of their positions; one of them had been in place for only two days. A Lao who reached safety with another SGU recounted that the VPA had captured everyone else in his unit, while one SGU was not heard again on the radio for more than two weeks.

The operations of ARVN's Strategic Technical Directorate also frequently aimed at putting a watch on The Trail. An objective of special interest was Ban Karai Pass, a new Truong Son crossing the People's Army began to use in early 1966. That summer, and again in the fall, South Vietnamese commando teams (Hector I and II) were landed near Ban Karai on the Vietnamese side of the border. The first team was able to survive in the mountain fastness—for the Ban Karai area was a true wilderness—for about a month. Hector II, launched from Udorn, Thailand, on September 13, was not on the ground more than five minutes before being captured by security forces.

Only forewarning and a first-rate security system enabled the People's Army to police The Trail with such success, especially since the VPA itself was not all that technologically advanced. Until late in the war runners and messages were the norm, higher commands mostly used field telephones, and human observers had no help from such instruments as radar or seismic detection. The People's Army innovated simple but effective communications techniques; guns, for example, were used by small *bo doi* patrols to signal other units along the border. Shots alerted nearby forces anyway, and the number of shots, their pattern, or other characteristics could be used to convey meaning.

If anything, the border patrols of the People's Armed Security Force were even less well equipped than the Vietnam People's Army. The *bo dois* of the security force actually did most of the patrolling; they were *like* the VPA but not *of* the People's Army, traveling through rough country lightly armed. The Armed Security Forces were an element of the DRV's Ministry of the Interior and had existed from an early date. Their numbers were estimated at 30,000 to 100,000 as early as 1964, but they had to patrol many miles of remote and mountainous borderland. A couple of security force battalions had gone into Laos with the earliest wave of VPA forces and had been there ever since. The 923rd and 925th Border Battalions were accepted on the MACV order of battle from the mid-1960s. In 1969 the 927th Border Force "battalion" was identified as being a formation that *ran* battalions, five of them, at widely separated points in lower Laos. There were ultimately perhaps 10,000 to 12,000 border troops among The Trail's defenders.

The other major components of the security forces were those furnished by the 559th Transport Group of the People's Army. General Phan Khac Tue's Truong Son command divided its domains in Laos and northeastern Cambodia into regions managed by subordinate units called *binh trams*. Each had main camps and satellite way stations and was responsible for everything in its area, from the care and feeding of troops, to extension of the roadway and repair of damage, to keeping the trucks on schedule. The *binh trams* ran the antiaircraft defenses, provided the local security, and arranged the transportation of VPA units and supplies. Each came to have attached porters and guides, transportation units, infantry; and the units adapted to their local circumstances. Intelligence estimates of the size of a *binh tram* hovered between 1,000 and 2,000 soldiers. The 559th Group commanded eleven *binh trams,* and in 1967 it was estimated to be using 7,000 porters plus local laborers.

A critical if not typical *binh tram* was the unit at Mu Gia Pass. Even before the war there had been a border post here, and with the inception of The Trail, Binh Tram (BT) 1 took over this area. Especially during the period before trucks could drive all the way into Laos, unloading and repacking supplies had been a key function, and BT 1 had two full transportation battalions to meet its responsibilities. There was also the 25th Engineer Battalion, which, with local labor, improved the crossing. At first only the simple, narrow Route 12 crossed at Mu Gia, reaching the village (*ban*) of Na Phao on the Laotian side. Before long the engineers added a bypass that reconnected with Route 12 at Ban Lang Khang (Map 5). As the war heated up and Hanoi determined to improve The Trail, BT 1 added a third, extensive bypass with several crossovers that trucks could use to get past blockages in the road. An airstrip at the southern end of the Mu Gia, at Ban Pha Nop, completed the complex, all of which was repaired as often as American air strikes succeeded in cratering it.

Obviously the air threat was a major problem for Binh Tram 1, and its air defenses eventually far outweighed ground security, provided by a single

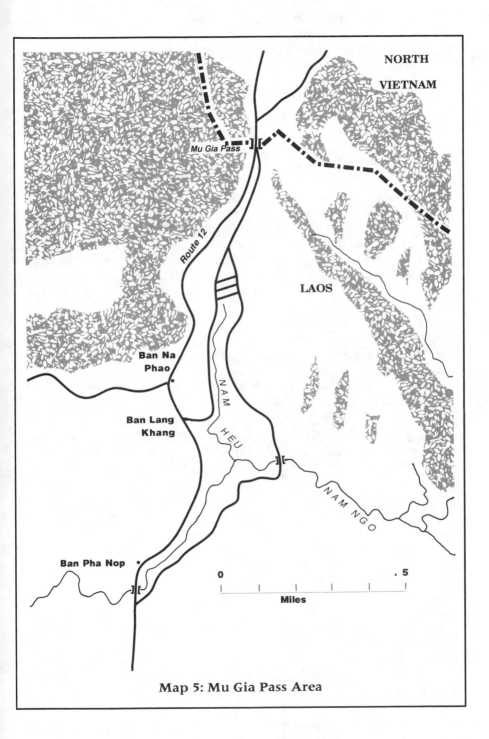

NORTH

VIETNAM

Mu Gia Pass

Route 12

LAOS

Ban Na
Phao

Ban Lang
Khang

NAM HEU

NAM NGO

Ban Pha Nop

0   . 5

Miles

Map 5: Mu Gia Pass Area

rifle battalion. In April 1966 U.S. intelligence evaluated the Mu Gia area as having almost ninety occupied antiaircraft positions, including 50 containing larger-caliber guns (37 mm, possibly some 57 mm). After a round of Arc Light strikes on both sides of the pass had brought more detailed aerial photography of the area, in June 1966 the Seventh Air Force raised its estimate of antiaircraft positions in the BT 1 area to no fewer than 302 sites. There was no doubt that the Mu Gia position had become a major flak trap.

In contrast to the flak-heavy BT 1, on the Route 9–Tchepone corridor the *binh trams* developed somewhat differently. That zone was also a major supply transhipment point, so Binh Tram 32 at Tchepone featured two transport battalions of its own, while there was another just a few miles away, with BT 33 at Ban Dong. The latter village, forwardmost outpost of the VPA disposition along Route 9, became the nerve center for the People's Army security net along the Vietnamese border. Binh Tram 33 included three security battalions and two engineer units—it was managing major road construction—and was the only BT in the 559th Group to have its own signal battalion. This suggests that Ban Dong had become an important command post for *bo dois* operating against Khe Sanh and the DMZ. The Tchepone–Ban Dong complex became known to U.S. intelligence as Base Area 604. In mid-1966 it was estimated to contain fourteen manned antiaircraft positions equipped with at least twenty-seven 37-mm guns and almost two dozen machine guns. Troop strength was put at six battalions plus two regiments of People's Army regulars.

The VPA regulars positioned themselves across the border from Khe Sanh. That fact, or other intelligence, led General Westmoreland to fear a People's Army attack, and MACV ordered strengthening of Khe Sanh. Among the initiatives was the stationing of U.S. Marines at a combat base there, a big sweep called operation Virginia, and a visit from Project Delta, which for a couple of weeks in October saturated the sector with its recon patrols. After Delta's departure, SOG plus the marines' own 3d Force Reconnaissance Battalion kept up the pressure. Bequeathing its old haunts to the marines, Special Forces moved even closer to the border, to a hamlet called Lang Vei, where it built a new CIDG camp.

In April 1967 marines encountered *bo dois* of the 18th Regiment in the hills above Khe Sanh, triggering a major battle. Two U.S. Marine battalions slugged it out with the People's Army, who were forced back in more than a week of intense fighting. The VPA struck again when its 95C Regiment attacked Lang Vei on the night of May 3–4. Viet Cong among the CIDG's Bru tribesmen helped the *bo dois* with key information about the defenses. With help from marine artillery at Khe Sanh, Lang Vei held out successfully. Contemporaneous marine sources relate the assault on Lang Vei to the DMZ battle at Con Thien then in progress, but it is likely that, for the People's Army, the security of The Trail was the real issue. Like the previous actions at A Shau and Attopeu, destroying U.S. outposts around Khe Sanh reduced the potential threat to The Trail.

South of Khe Sanh and just across the Lao border stood Ban Houei Sane, with its Laotian Army enclave. The Laotians did little to disrupt The Trail and were not much bothered themselves, except, paradoxically, by the Americans. U.S. aircraft mistakenly bombed Ban Houei Sane at least twice, with losses to the 33d Volunteers and their families. Laotian government protests, investigations by the U.S. embassy in Saigon, and fallout therefrom, became another spark in the ongoing dispute between Ambassador Sullivan in Vientiane and MACV over permissible activities in lower Laos.

South and east of Ban Houei Sane rose the mountain known as Co Roc; behind it the People's Army had another depot area, around Muong Nong. Here, too, were the paths to the head of the A Shau valley. This would be known to American intelligence as Base Area 611. Two *binh trams* worked this complex. Between them the way station units had a single transport battalion, two of engineers, and two security battalions plus one of regular infantry. The heavy engineer presence is significant, for the VPA were extending their road network into the A Shau. Opposite the Central Highlands, the *binh tram* feeding the Chu Pong massif was BT 37, which contained one battalion each of engineers, transport specialists, security men, and infantry.

To cover Cambodia and directly assist the National Liberation Front, Hanoi set up an entire new transportation group equivalent to the 559th. Eventually called the 470th, the group in Cambodia had its own collection *binh trams*, way stations, and operating units.

Work on The Trail, Hanoi's lifeline to the South, remained the heart of Vietnamese activity in Laos. During the dry season from September 1965 to March 1966 the *binh tram* labor forces added new roadway at a rate of 60 miles a month, for a total of 415 miles. Highlights included opening the new route into Laos through Ban Karai Pass, as well as motorable roads all the way to the Sihanouk Trail and the Cambodian border. By then the basic network was in place. From the start of the 1966 monsoons through the fall of 1967, most additions were new bypasses around critical points such as road junctions or river crossings. More efforts also had to be diverted into repair of damage inflicted by bombing. During that period only about 80 miles of new roadway are estimated to have been added to The Trail. The rivers themselves were pressed into service in the effort to move supplies. By then The Trail (see Map 6) was already fairly extensive.

During these middle years General Tue and his engineers started pushing their network right into South Vietnam. In late 1967 and through 1968, the 559th Group shifted to a strategy of maintaining existing roads and adding improvements while investing major resources in construction that crossed the border. In the spurt of building, U.S. intelligence estimated 246 miles of new or improved roadway were added between October 1967 and April 1968. Americans were intensely aware of some of these activities. Marines at Khe Sanh, for example, dubbed one route going in to the north of them the "Santa Fe Trail." But that road turned out to be just one of four People's Army construction projects on both flanks of the Americans at Khe Sanh.

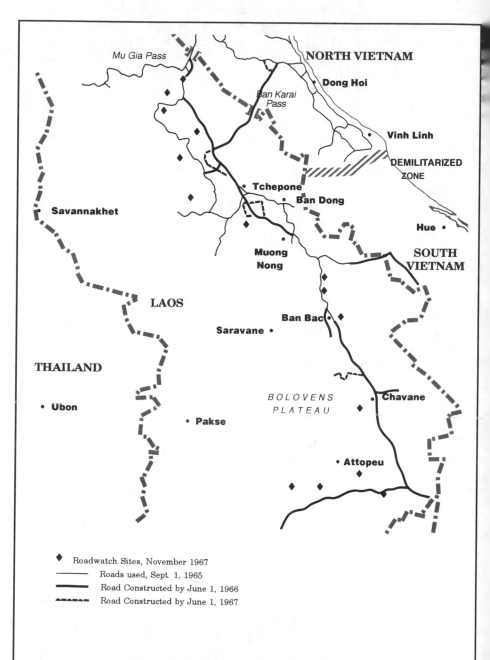

Mu Gia Pass

NORTH VIETNAM

Dong Hoi

Ban Karai
Pass

Vinh Linh

DEMILITARIZED
ZONE

Tchepone

Ban Dong

Savannakhet

Hue •

Muong
Nong

SOUTH
VIETNAM

LAOS

Ban Bac

Saravane •

THAILAND

BOLOVENS
PLATEAU

Chavane

• Ubon

• Pakse

• Attopeu

♦ Roadwatch Sites, November 1967
——— Roads used, Sept. 1, 1965
—— Road Constructed by June 1, 1966
■━■━■ Road Constructed by June 1, 1967

Map 6: Trail Extensions in 1966–67

In the A Shau sector, Binh Trams 42 and 43 put a road across the border that eventually gave them a link on the Vietnamese side, as well as connecting with the Saigon government's Road 547 in the valley. The trailmakers then kept pushing their road like a tentacle, directly east, toward Da Nang.

Probably the most extensive construction during this period would be a project that pushed the Sihanouk Trail into Vietnam near Dak To. Branches of that new road led toward Kontum and Pleiku. The big battle of Dak To in the fall of 1967, which drew in more than a division of People's Army *bo dois*, fighting the U.S. 173d Airborne Brigade and 4th Infantry Division, coincided with the new road building. Additional tip-offs to Hanoi's strategy were the fact that it created a new B-3 Front command to oversee the Central Highlands and sent General Hoang Minh Thao to lead it. In a pattern typical of People's Army command relationships, General Thao supplanted Chu Huy Man, who then soldiered on as the B-3 Front chief of staff.

Work on The Trail continued, on more and more minute segments, more sophisticated bypasses and storage facilities; and there was always the need for repair, reconstructing blown bridges and culverts, clearing landslides, and filling bomb craters. As the network to maintain became longer and the new roadway extended into the mountainous Vietnamese borderland, labor use actually fell. In 1967 the Central Intelligence Agency estimated the number of construction workers on The Trail at 23,000. By January 1968 that estimate was down to 11,500 men and women. The driving factor was not the length of roadway being constructed but the introduction of mechanized equipment. The CIA, which admitted it could not locate the VPA equipment and could not be sure of accurate numbers, nevertheless projected the 559th Group as using twenty bulldozers, eleven road graders, three rock crushers, and two steamrollers during the 1967–1968 dry season. The amounts of equipment would only increase over time.

Nevertheless, over the length of the war, people formed the soul of The Trail. Their stories reek of hardship, sacrifice, and sadness, but strength, too, and a determination to get to the South. Vietnamese writer Dao Vu tells of the women Nhuan and Ngu and the sapper Chu, whose task was to maintain road section 308–500. The characters run from intruding fighter-bombers and toil to fill craters before the passage of scheduled convoys. Vinh Linh villager Nguyen Thanh Mai knew such women; she recalls:

> I also had girlfriends who went to work in the forest to build the Ho Chi Minh Trail. They were young and beautiful and smart. They stayed in the forest for ten, fifteen years, and when the country was liberated and they came back, they were over thirty. In our country, they were already old. They had no skills, because they had had no time for learning, and nobody to fall in love with them. They had lost their youth. Truly these girls had given their lives for their country.

Women served as porters, as laborers, in medical clinics, in the antiaircraft units and engineers. At night, when the trucks tried to drive with a minimum of illumination, women at bridge crossings and other critical locations dressed in white and became human road markers. Day after day, women with the *binh trams* were assigned to comb the jungle to mark the bodies of people killed by the planes, wild animals, or tragic accidents.

People's Army historians prefer to write of The Trail in heroic terms, and Vietnam has not published much in the way of realistic accounts of life in the Truong Son command. Vietnamese have turned to fiction and poetry to recount the trials of The Trail. A flavor, but just a flavor, of this has reached the West. Nguyen Quang Sang, a writer who marched The Trail as a *bo doi* in 1966, said in the mid-1980s, "The period of writing about the trail's glorious victories is over." Similar is the comment of eleven-year Truong Son veteran Pham Tien Duat: "So many facts about the Ho Chi Minh Trail have never been revealed: the difficulties; the sorrows, the sacrifices, even the failures. All of the books extolling the trail as a great victory are highly exaggerated."

Plentiful are Vietnamese who bear the scars of The Trail, and they are not limited to writers. Que, who retired as a colonel in the People's Army, had been a member of one of the Truong Son command's security units. Thirty years later Que was enduring bouts of heavy-headedness he connects with having hit his head against a rock when buried in the blast of an American bomb. Many, many veterans recall terror at the B-52 Arc Light attacks, which truly came close to rolling thunder. Mrs. Hong, a woman volunteer with the construction units, served from 1965 until 1968, until she lost both arms to the B-52s and returned to her native province. She numbered among the lucky ones. Like so many others, she met and loved a soldier passing through: "He went South, and I got injured. I went away and never told him, but after the war, in 1976, he went to my native land to find me."

What made Mrs. Hong lucky was that her soldier remembered and came back. More typical was the pattern where lives separated by war remained severed; families, friends, lovers, mourning lost relationships but getting on with life. Thus, in a 1972 short story, Minh Loi writes of the *bo doi* and girl guide he loved, how they went to different fronts once she joined an anti-aircraft unit, and how he often thought of her afterward. In Bao Ninh's 1991 novel *The Sorrow of War*, the loss of love and innocence, symbolized by a march away, the trek down The Trail, leads to a broken later life in which idealized memories can never be re-created. A classic expression of the same theme occurs in "A Division Commander's Story" by Nguyen Duc Mau. In this story a People's Army division commander loses touch with his teenage sweetheart only to discover, thirty years later, that the soldier dating his daughter and likely to become his son-in-law is really the son of his lost first love.

Certainly the people of The Trail suffered many hardships and tragedies, and there is a natural tendency in the West to downplay the effort Hanoi made in its propaganda to romanticize and render heroic the common coin of experience, which was death and destruction. A good example here is

Quang Binh Province, in particular its Vinh Linh district, which lay just above the DMZ. Articles in the DRV press and radio reports repeatedly extolled the virtues of the people here. Artillery units at Vinh Linh were credited with astounding achievements, coast defense troops with turning back virtual South Vietnamese invasions. In the spring of 1966 Hanoi even published a monograph titled *With the Fighters of Quangbinh-Vinhlinh*, which reported, among other things, that "traffic goes on"; "rice grows better than ever"; and that scientific and artistic achievement continued apace. In the twin fights of boosting production and opposing the Americans, Vinh Linh and its province were models Hanoi felt other parts of the DRV should emulate.

"Between two fights," editors Vu Can and Nguyen Khac Vien wrote, "life resumes its normal course and continues its advance. The U.S. Air Force has been unable either to sow panic or disrupt the course of historical evolution. There lies its biggest failure."

Reality was more prosaic, though tragic, too. As a nine-year-old resident of Dong Hoi, Mrs. Nguyen Thanh Mai, her family, and other survivors of the first bombings went to live in nearby forests—and stayed ten years. "We were bombed nearly every day," she recalls. At Vinh Linh itself the villagers were reduced to living in caves, and even women and young people carried rifles to shoot back at the fighter-bombers. "The people of Vinh Linh are farmers, and still went to the fields to work every day," says Mrs. Nguyen Thi Thiet. "When the planes came they escaped to the tunnels right by the fields. . . . I lived seven days a week underground."

Vinh Linh villager Nguyen The Chat was exactly right. "They bombed so much here because it is the border between North and South," Chat said. "The Americans wanted to stop the transportation of weapons and supplies." Of the fourteen people in Chat's family, ten died under the bombs. Vinh Linh and Quang Binh formed the main parts of what the American air planners called "Route Package 1." The area included the approaches to both the Mu Gia and Ban Karai passes. The very first American reprisal bombings (those while Kosygin visited Hanoi in 1965) had been in Route Package 1, and it continued to be the biggest U.S. target up through the termination of Rolling Thunder in March 1968. Even then, Washington would end its attacks on the northern DRV but single out Quang Binh—with the panhandle provinces up to Thanh Hoa—for further bombing.

The Americans aimed to interdict the approaches to The Trail. It was the American air strategy, not simply Bob McNamara's construct but an agreed concept, that the purpose of the campaign was to raise the cost to Hanoi of conducting war in the South. The distribution of the actual attack sorties carried out from the beginning of 1967 through March 1968—the end of the Tet Offensive—shows a quite purposeful exercise of interdiction options. Route Package 1 would be the most blasted region of the Democratic Republic of Vietnam. Every month it got at least 3,000 attack sorties except at the very height of Tet, when U.S. effort was, understandably, diverted to the South. Even in the months of the most concentrated U.S. campaign directly against the Hanoi-Haiphong complex, June to August 1967, that area received fewer than one third of the U.S. attack sorties flown against Route Package 1 (about 4,600, as against almost 15,000). Quang Binh Province and RP 1 were the targets of 50,000 airplanes in 1967, almost half the *total* of *all* U.S. attack sorties against North Vietnam. There were another 9,000 flights targeting RP 1 in the first quarter of 1968, by then 60 percent of the overall U.S. effort, which no longer had to be restricted because of numbers of bombs.

Quang Binh did not include the approaches to Napé Pass, or those to northern Laos, so there was at least one alternative to interdicting the DRV's panhandle besides the focus on Route Package 1. That involved sealing off the DRV provinces of Ha Tinh, Vinh, and Thanh Hoa. The records of 1967–1968 air operations make it clear that this alternative was attempted at the very beginning of the period, and again in May and June 1967. At the latter time American air commanders were already shifting to Hanoi-Haiphong, so the concentration marked time while the new assault was prepared. Through all of 1967 there were fewer than 30,000 U.S. attack sorties in the provinces represented by these route packages.

The bare bones of statistics leave out the reality of the technique practical Americans innovated to increase the destruction of Rolling Thunder. Beginning with Mu Gia, all the Arc Light strikes in North Vietnam fell on RP 1. Vinh Linh and hamlets along the DMZ could be subjected to naval shell fire and long-range artillery in addition to bombing. President Johnson rejected that in 1967, but the option would be exercised in due course. Then there was the forward controller-assisted strike system that became program Tally Ho. The range of the slow movers (FACs) restricted this method to the Quang Binh region. The success of Tally Ho was also established within days of the beginning of FAC sorties over RP 1 when bombers led by ravens blew up a huge People's Army supply dump a few miles from Vinh Linh. Not since the early days of Rolling Thunder, when U.S. Air Force officers exulted at destroying a VPA ammunition depot (beneath Mu Gia Pass) that contained a significant portion of the DRV's entire ammunition stock, had there been a more "lucrative" target.

Another aspect of the U.S. air campaign in Southeast Asia was the intelligence side. Unmanned drones, U-2 and SR-71 strategic reconnaissance planes, and a variety of low-level photography or electronic reconnaissance planes flew every day. Lyndon Johnson, it is said, rejected the recommendation once brought to him to end Lucky Dragon, the program of U-2 flights over Vietnam. In 1967, in some of the few Vietnam SR-71 flights that were piloted by the CIA, photos answered LBJ's questions about whether Hanoi was importing ground-to-ground missiles. But the pictures showed something else, too—ants on the march. The *bo dois* continued South. Some 8,600 troops infiltrated during March 1967, the month of peak movement during the first half of the year. In that month there were about 8,500 attack sorties in Rolling Thunder, perhaps 5,100 of them in Route Package 1. That meant almost one aircraft attack mission *for every People's Army infiltra-*

tor. Since the average attack sortie delivered several tons of munitions, often assisted by ravens or other technical means, it was clear that air interdiction was not a success.

As Vo Bam, by then a retired general, put it in the 1980s: "The Americans made the correct choices about where to bomb the road, but they were not very effective." There *was* great tragedy connected with The Trail, and no doubt it became the crucible for a generation, but Hanoi's wartime propaganda was not entirely wrong. It was an accomplishment to keep The Trail open; the balance of forces in the South was preserved. Hanoi could now calculate that balance and attempt to manipulate it. This fact took the war to a new level. For their part, Hanoi's enemies also reached new levels in their efforts to break the lifeline South.

Spearhead of the assault on The Trail remained the Studies and Observation Group, during this period under Colonel John K. Singlaub. About as unconventional as officers could get in the U.S. Army, Singlaub—"Jack" to his friends—was one of a small elite in the American military who slid between regular service and assignments with the Central Intelligence Agency. Ironically, in Singlaub's case, this had arisen from efforts during World War II to make a career for himself *in* the military by converting his reserve commission to a regular one. Volunteering for a hush-hush mission, Jack found himself in the Office of Strategic Services, America's wartime CIA, and wound up parachuting into France as a "Jedburgh" commando. As the war closed, he was in China, still with OSS, and led a team that freed camps of Allied prisoners on the island of Hainan. Jack also helped train commando teams of Vietnamese—Viet Minh, in fact, since for a brief moment at the twilight of that war it had been U.S. policy to cooperate with Ho Chi Minh's forces against the Japanese.

Within months of returning to the U.S., the young officer was back in intelligence, and he returned to China with the organization that succeeded OSS and became the CIA. From the perspective of a U.S. consulate in Manchuria and from CIA headquarters, Singlaub witnessed the Chinese civil war and the early years of the Franco-Vietnamese conflict. During the Korean War, Major Singlaub trained rangers for American divisions at the front, then went to Seoul with the CIA paramilitary activity in Korea. He finished up as a battalion commander, winning the Silver Star for one night's work in 1953, when Jack's unit outfought the PLA in one of those scrappy fights among the hills that so characterized the last months of the war. In Vietnam in the 1960s Colonel Singlaub would be among a handful with experience in paramilitary operations in all three of America's recent wars.

Jack Singlaub also believed in what he was doing and was a brave fellow. Exposure to Mao Zedong's brand of communism in Manchuria and Korea defined Jack's hatred for the enemy. He had extra reason because the Red Chinese intervention in Korea, when it came, resulted in a slaughter of a force led by Don Faith, Singlaub's buddy from Fort Benning. As for bravery, Jack had plenty of medals on top of the Silver Star—twenty-nine over a span of three decades, including two French awards of the Croix de Guerre as well as the Purple Heart, the U.S. award for a combat wound.

As he rose in rank and responsibility through the 1950s, Jack Singlaub had led one battle group of a U.S. division assigned to NATO, had an office in the Pentagon, and had been an instructor for the Command and General Staff College. Probably most important from the standpoint of Vietnam, however, was Singlaub's assignment as a troop commander and then staff officer with the 101st Airborne Division during the time it was commanded by General William C. Westmoreland. When Jack did go to Saigon he would have a friendly relationship with the MACV chief.

In the wake of the Ia Drang battle, with Colonel Singlaub looking ahead to a Vietnam tour as adviser to an ARVN infantry division, he was called one day into the office of General Harold K. Johnson. The Army chief of staff bluntly told Singlaub he was changing the colonel's orders to command of SOG, and he rejected Jack's objections that he wanted a regular, not an unconventional, assignment in this war.

As a result, the Studies and Observation Group had the best leader possible. Colonel Singlaub reached Saigon in April 1966. By then Shining Brass was up to speed, with forays three miles into Laos not needing any further approval. Westy and SOG would both push at that restriction; in February 1967 President Johnson widened the free action zone to a depth of twelve miles. A month later the code name for the Laos operations changed to Prairie Fire.

Colonel Singlaub led the Studies and Observation Group at a key moment in the war. General Westmoreland's anti-infiltration campaign had swung into full gear. Singlaub's SOG, with such special-warfare units as Project Delta, the Mike Forces, the marines' Force Reconnaissance battalions, and Navy SEALs, plus airpower, represented the cutting edge of the effort to shut down The Trail. If ever the South was to be sealed off, this was the moment. Westmoreland actually believes that interdiction succeeded—he writes that between the bombing and SOG activities The Trail would nearly be closed by late 1966. People's Army trailmaster Vo Bam, in contrast, maintains that the longest interval during the whole war that The Trail actually had to close was two days.

Jack Singlaub proved active, energetic, and smart. For example, the early SOG missions showed People's Army security to be quite effective. A few months after Singlaub's arrival, Spike team Montana was virtually wiped out; that fall most scouts needed emergency evacuations. Firefights happened on, or right next to, the landing zones. Colonel Singlaub decided that dependence on helicopters for landing and recovering the Spike team was a key weakness in SOG methods. For an alternative, Singlaub encouraged adoption of a shoulder harness rig linked to a balloon by a lead wire that could be scooped up by an airplane in flight, to pick up a person on the ground. To answer concerns about the danger of this apparatus, Singlaub held a demonstration at Camp Long Thanh at which he was the first man to use the gear. Later, on The Trail, Spike teams often used the harness gear to spirit away captives, almost always ensuring very talkative prisoners afterward. As for getting teams into their objectives without choppers, Singlaub favored the HALO technique, and made sure two of SOG's Spike teams were trained in high-altitude, low-opening-parachute methods. One of the high-altitude teams was Iowa, led by Dick Meadows. Colonel Singlaub had jumped with the army sport parachute team and knew Meadows and some other experts. Billy Waugh, a HALO-trained parachutist with SOG, recalls doing several HALO drops a month.

Another SOG change that Jack Singlaub ushered in had to do with communications. The Spike teams relied on frequency modulated (FM) radios, which broadcast by line of sight. In Laos the high hills cut short the range of transmission. In both Laos and Cambodia, where Singlaub began running missions under project Daniel Boone, there were few U.S. radio posts close to the areas of operations. Singlaub saw the need for a radio relay station. One day Ken Sisler, a junior officer with the Spike teams, whom Jack had known in the States as a Reserve Officers' Training Corps (ROTC) cadet, came in with news of a perfect relay site. It was a mountain tall enough to see into all those deep valleys, but so narrow and steep it could hardly be climbed and would be virtually impervious to artillery or mortar fire. Sisler had pictures, and showed how a helicopter landing pad could be prepared with minimal effort. A HALO-qualified parachutist, Captain Sisler was convinced he could drop onto the peak.

Colonel Singlaub sent Sisler's Spike team to the pinnacle rock for a couple of weeks, during which they prepared the site. That began the routine—SOG would deploy a team for two weeks at a time, to sit atop this mountain and communicate with their buddies on patrol in the valleys below. Sisler's peak would be called "Eagle's Nest" and touted as one of the year's significant developments by the 1967 command history for SOG. Stationing the teams required special procurement of cold-weather gear and materials for the site. That, too, made Eagle's Nest unusual. The SOG commander wanted to see for himself; one day, leaving behind all rank insignia and identification, Singlaub hitched a chopper ride to Eagle's Nest. He lunched with the Spike team on post and watched the sorts of things they did, peering into the countryside at the places where various patrols had had trouble and so on. Singlaub's presence was a violation of security protocols, prohibiting exposure to possible capture of anyone who knew the things the SOG commander did. General Westmoreland would be nonplussed, to say the least, when Jack reassured him that Eagle's Nest could not be captured and that Singlaub had verified that by personal reconnaissance.

Jack Singlaub proved correct—Eagle's Nest never was captured. The People's Army quickly figured out what was up and soon put units at the foot of the pinnacle, but their own successes were at harassment. The VNAF chopper bringing Colonel Singlaub for his visit was shot at by 37-mm flak guns but was out of the line of fire before they could draw a good bead. Machine guns harmlessly hit the rock face or missed altogether, artillery shells' flat trajectories made impact on the pinnacle almost impossible, while the small area of the peak made the same true for mortar bombs. Many times the VPA tried to scale Eagle's Nest, but their troops were shot up and blown apart by grenades rolled down on them. Singlaub estimates that hundreds of *bo dois* died in the effort to do something about SOG's observation post.

The radio relay was not only effective, it also became more necessary than ever. In 1967 the Studies and Observation Group mounted 187 missions by Spike teams and 68 with Hornet forces in Prairie Fire alone. Even during the summer monsoon the Spike team patrols continued, though larger forays fell to a low level. Operations into Cambodia with Daniel Boone added another 99 Spike teams launched (though only 63 actually entered Cambodia) beginning in July. Evasion and escape of downed air crews and other prisoners under Bright Light remained a continuing SOG interest and Singlaub constantly kept two Spike teams on alert for rescue missions. The pace was such that SOG was typically using four times the number of helicopters it had averaged the previous year. Through 1967 a total of twenty-three of those helicopters were shot down.

Studies and Observation Group resources to carry out these activities were also commensurately greater. Counting Vietnamese and other personnel, the secret campaign into Laos, Cambodia, and the DRV was the concern of about 1,000 Americans and 9,000 others. There were twenty-five Spike teams and thirty-six Hornet forces. Company-size "Havoc" forces and battalion-size "Haymaker" units were not yet completed, but each of SOG's three regional commands was authorized two of the former, and SOG as a whole was asking to recruit three Haymaker forces. Seven more Spike teams would be added during the year. Air cargo transported by SOG doubled over 1966 levels. The Prairie Fire operations entailed almost $5 million in direct expense, while the cost of Footboy into North Vietnam stood at about three times that amount. Costs for Daniel Boone were being picked up by the 5th Special Forces Group.

Jack Singlaub did well with Westy, and SOG retained generally good relationships with other commands until partway through Singlaub's tenure, when Colonel Francis J. Kelly took over the 5th Special Forces Group. "Splash" Kelly may have been intent on making waves simply to put his mark on the 5th Group, for he also replaced key subordinates over inconsequential disputes. However, Kelly had a program of his own that would compete with SOG. This was the idea of using Mike Force battalions on extended missions into Indian country. These "Blackjack" operations would be confined to South Vietnam, but the concept was similar to Havoc and Haymaker in SOG's repertoire, and some of *those* SOG missions took place within South Vietnam. Singlaub, for example, carried out certain patrols north of Kontum at the request of the 4th Infantry Division. There may have been more than secrecy involved when Kelly, in a monograph about Green Berets written for the army after the war, never so much as mentioned the Studies and Observation Group.

In any case, Colonel Singlaub's difficulties with the 5th Group arose over personnel, and SOG's classified state of being had a lot to do with the problem. The way Studies and Observation Group assignments were handled, soldiers volunteered Stateside and were sent to Vietnam with orders directing them to the 5th Special Forces. That was for cover purposes, however, and orders had an asterisk in them, which meant the person should be sent on to SOG. Meanwhile, SOG's personnel requests were folded into Special Forces and made to seem part of those for the 5th Group. Personnel staffs at Nha Trang and Saigon were perfectly aware of the arrangement, which, according to Colonel Singlaub, worked without a hitch until the arrival of Frank Kelly. After that, when someone who looked good arrived with SOG orders, 5th Group would instantly send them on to some border camp, where they were effectively submerged in the Green Beret system. If SOG inquired, it would be told the individual concerned had never arrived. These difficulties were not worked out until June 1967, when Kelly left for a new assignment. Under his successor, Colonel Jonathan F. Ladd, the headache disappeared.

Problems with the 5th Special Forces were clearly to be avoided. After all, 5th Group remained the main recruiting grounds for SOG. Again SOG's highly classified status permitted all sorts of rumors to circulate that could be detrimental to finding the good men who were needed. Jim Morris was a thirty-year-old officer on his second tour when he ran into an acquaintance from Okinawa now with SOG. A public information officer who was helping put out *Green Beret* magazine, Morris nevertheless knew nothing of SOG but the rumors, which was doubly ironic since he had been with Detachment A-322 at Kham Duc in 1964, just before that place became a launch site for SOG missions. In any case, the rumor was that SOG couldn't depend on volunteers because its losses were at *200 percent* a year. In fact, Prairie Fire causalities in 1967 numbered 42 Americans killed, 104 wounded, and 14 missing plus more than 300 indigenous losses. Certain army, marine, and air force specialists or aviation crews might not be included in these figures, not to mention CIA contract people and losses for Footboy in the DRV, but the total did not look anything like the rumor.

This did not mean, however, that there were no really expensive sallies. A tactic that Westmoreland introduced in 1967 provided the occasion for many such incidents. This was the SLAM operation, with the acronym standing for "Seek, Locate, Annihilate, and Monitor." The mechanism for annihilation was to be Arc Light plus any other air or artillery firepower that could be brought to bear on targets identified by intelligence, including communications intercepts and overhead reconnaissance. The Studies and Observation Group's role would be to monitor, to go in after the strike, and to see what had been accomplished. Since SLAM aimed at the biggest concentrations of troops around, that could make for trying moments. This was not the case during SOG's first SLAM sortie, carried out over three days at the end of January 1967. It would not be the case at Con Thien, a marine strongpoint below the DMZ, where VPA forces were so thick no one made any pretense at scouting outside the perimeter wire. It would be true, however, at objective "Oscar 8."

This particular SLAM turned out to be the only Hornet Force operation that June. The target was a point at the head of the A Shau valley; radio traffic analysis had indicated so many messages flowing through this place that some suspected Oscar 8 to be the command post for the entire Ho Chi Minh Trail. Actually the target may have been associated with Binh Tram 34 at Muong Nong or Binh Tram 42 at the border. Intelligence estimated that a full VPA regiment occupied the area. Oscar 8 was a valley 1,500 feet above sea level surrounded by mountains of 3,000 to 4,500 feet. The B-52 attack, originally planned for eighteen bombers, was cut back to just four aircraft when carried out on June 2.

Behind the bombers, SOG was deploying an eighty-man Hornet Force from its forward operating base at Khe Sanh, but everything imaginable went wrong. Thunderstorms, high winds, and low clouds forced postponement of the ground element of SLAM for hours, into the late afternoon. Five marine and nine VNAF helicopters, escorted by four gunships, carried the ground troops, and were put down on the LZ after a scout helicopter surveyed the target area. Their estimate that the VPA had been destroyed proved wrong. The SOG troops were engulfed in a fierce battle. Efforts the next day to get them out halted after one helicopter was destroyed on the LZ and another badly damaged. Major Richard E. Romine, the downed pilot who had also been formation leader the previous day, ended up the senior officer on the ground and took over the defense of Oscar 8. Survivors could only lift out on June 4 after a major air armada gathered over the landing zone. Marine Romine won the Navy Cross for his brave air sorties and the ground battle, but only about fifty of the SOG troops and chopper crews made it back. Master Sergeant Ronald J. Dexter of Spike team Illinois, nine of his ten Vietnamese, and at least that number of Nungs were missing in action. Dexter is now believed to have been killed in captivity by People's Armed Security Forces as the prisoners made their way back up The Trail into the DRV. The fate of three marine airmen remains unknown; one other was repatriated in 1973.

More SLAM attacks occurred during 1967, including half a dozen full-series SLAM efforts and three more "Shock" campaigns, featuring cooperation with the Laotians, that took place outside the Steel Tiger zone. The number of B-52 sorties over southern Laos that year would be 1,711, almost three times the level of 1966 and better aimed by virtue of SLAM. Records for SOG show that by late October, two years after the first Spike teams entered Laos, a total of 929 B-52 and 3,413 fighter-bomber missions had been directed by SOG teams. Nevertheless, a CINCPAC team evaluating the utility of the Studies and Observation Group argued at about this time that SOG could be less effective than pure air operations such as Tiger Hound; worse, Tiger Hound coverage had been curtailed over certain areas for extended periods (up to three weeks), so the Spike teams could have a clear field to play on.

Officers with the Studies and Observation Group tended to see their difficulties more as flowing from restrictions placed on them by such friendly antagonists as Ambassador William H. Sullivan. Commenting about the area of The Trail behind the Chu Pong massif, for example, one SOG veteran told Pentagon investigators that he understood major People's Army supply bases had been discovered there in early 1967 but counteraction only became possible once Sullivan relaxed his structures. In fact, this region and the Sihanouk Trail were a major focus of the 1967 SLAM attacks.

There were also things that the Studies and Observation Group could do simply because it *was* on the ground and other forms of power were not. For one thing, SOG could bring in prisoners, and did bag twenty-six *bo dois* during its first two years. Another SOG initiative was part military, part psychological; this was sabotaging VPA supplies to make *bo dois* distrust their own supply system. Under project Eldest Son, shells, rigged to burst when fired, were inserted into enemy ammunition stockpiles. There were many variations on this theme. In one case, Singlaub recalls, a Daniel Boone team ran into a rice cache that amounted to almost 100 tons. It was more useful to doctor the stock with chemicals that made the rice inedible than attempt to destroy it, which often brought VPA reaction and pursuit.

Nevertheless, the effectiveness question was one that participants could never disentangle from that of restrictions, and Bill Sullivan continued to be seen as the culprit. Jack Singlaub got a kick out of one of the SEACOORD meetings he attended at Udorn in 1967. As usual, Ambassador Sullivan was there, along with General Westmoreland, and Ambassador to Thailand J. Graham Martin. Like Sullivan, Martin had the reputation of being an imperious sort. Singlaub saw them as "strong-minded American ambassadors with Napoleonic ambitions." At Udorn that time, Westy left the meeting in between the two ambassadors. Outside were airmen with their cameras to take pictures of the potentates.

"Well, Westy," said Ambassador Sullivan, making light of the moment, "looks like you've got quite a few fans over here."

The MACV commander shot back, "Oh, no, Bill. This is just the first time they've ever seen a four-star general escorted by two field marshals."

The game was played as if only American actions mattered, as if what happened in Indian country depended simply on what was done to cut The Trail. Westmoreland, and others, still had cards to play on the strategy of interdiction, and on the devices employed to raise the cost of infiltration. But what occurred in Indian country was not simply a dependent variable in some algorithm or model. Hanoi's strategy made a difference, too. The struggle for a strategy defined the problems of Saigon and Washington, while a new strategy in Hanoi was soon going to transform the Vietnam War.

CHAPTER 9

Forks in the Road

1967

The mantle of a field marshal was one Bill Sullivan carried rather heavily. He might have conceded arrogance and toughness, but never supposed he was going to outgeneral the generals. Another, who carried that mantle more lightly, planning policies or military strategies with equal enthusiasm, was Walt Whitman Rostow. A rising star in Washington at war, Rostow, whom we have seen already at the State Department, moved over to the White House in early 1966 as national security adviser to Lyndon Johnson. Through all the years under Dean Rusk, not to say those with the president, Walt kept pushing at the envelope of policy, trying to aim it in his preferred direction. If asked, Dr. Rostow would have explained that, since everyone knew his views and made allowances for them, it was perfectly all right to argue his preferences.

LBJ's selection of Rostow was significant. In late 1965, when McGeorge Bundy told the president he was tired and needed to work outside government, Johnson had his pick of national security experts for the White House job. Exuberance was not the issue. The NSC staffer who acted in Mac Bundy's stead once Mac left, Robert Komer, was at least as exuberant as Rostow. The president was also perfectly aware of Walt's preferences, which he had seen on paper numerous times and which, as recounted, had occasionally caused real political difficulties for Johnson. The only possible conclusion is that LBJ *wanted* Walt, *with* his policy preferences, over the others who might have come instead.

For his own part, Walt Rostow remained the man he had been, a "working stiff, not a thinker," as he liked to see himself. But this stiff advocated as hard as any general, and at least as hard as any economist, which Rostow was by discipline. The most salient strategic debate was the direction of the air campaign. Here, in keeping with Rostow's early focus on zeroing in on the Democratic Republic of Vietnam's economy, Walt favored systematically bombing the DRV's oil import, storage, and refinery capacity, reasoning that the loss of the oil would cripple the DRV's war effort. Short of that strategy, which LBJ had not accepted in 1965, Rostow wanted a focus on a small number of choke points along the infiltration routes, with a maximum effort to keep those cuts in place.

As the debate had evolved through 1966 Dr. Rostow eventually got his way. President Johnson approved the Rolling Thunder program proposal that summer permitting the oil strikes. The strikes were made, and the DRV's oil capacity would be substantially reduced. The result? No observable difference. This was for both Hanoi's prosecution of the war and its infiltration, which rose in spite of dependence on gasoline-powered trucks for The Trail. The next panacea, favored by the air generals and with which Rostow aligned himself, was a program of direct attack on Hanoi and Haiphong. Again the observable results were negligible. Armed reconnaissance, the staple of the air campaign, continued throughout and, as already seen, it, too, had few apparent results.

Walt Rostow, arguing for air attacks years before Rolling Thunder and Steel Tiger ever began, would not be fazed by their lack of success. Instead, Walt pulled other options out of his hat as talk within the U.S. command increasingly turned to ground alternatives. In this Rostow found an ally in William C. Westmoreland, who developed several plans for ground operations outside South Vietnam. Another ally was ARVN general Cao Van Vien. The chief of Saigon's Joint General Staff had proposed a strategy of isolating the South by means of a defended corridor across lower Laos in 1965. Meeting with President Johnson at Guam in February 1966, Vien renewed the suggestion and added that five ARVN divisions could do the job. It was a bid to set the parameters for the next round of U.S. budget decisions on what level of ARVN expansion to fund. Walt Rostow had previously worked that side of the policy street, and had once favored putting an ARVN division right across the center of the corridor at Tchepone.

General Westmoreland's projects had grown from thoughts about exploitation after the Ia Drang battle. The early 1966 version, Westy notes, was one of the plans he was most proud of during his MACV years. Called Full Cry and developed by Harry Kinnard with Green Beret Arthur ("Bull") Simons, this concept provided for the 1st Cavalry Division (Airmobile) to leap over the Laotian border and create an airhead at Attopeu, following that with jumps up the Laotian panhandle to Saravane, then finally Savannakhet. Simultaneously the 3d Marine Division would attack west from the DMZ, crossing Route 9 through Tchepone to Savannakhet. Such an attack would have created the corridor of which General Vien spoke. Pressure on Hanoi's forces would have been maintained by the ARVN pushing up the A Shau valley, and the U.S. 4th Infantry Division attacking on the ground west of Pleiku-Kontum. Once the neck of Indochina had been severed, an ARVN force could be put across Route 9 to hold the block.

This was an ambitious concept and more than Lyndon Johnson would sanction. Military experts talked of three American divisions, and the answer was the same. Johnson didn't go for that either. In Laos, Ambassador Sullivan told a U.S. senator that he feared the estimate of forces was too low. Sullivan reported, "I said I doubted they could develop [an] airtight plug anyway. . . . I doubted that ground troops constituted the answer."

In truth there were numerous problems with the Full Cry concept. One was that the focus on the neck of Indochina would very likely necessitate a collateral flanking attack against Hanoi's troops north of the DMZ. Such an attack raised the danger of active intervention by Chinese or Soviets. On the technical side there were questions as to whether it would be possible to airlift sufficient supplies into a Laotian airhead to support the 1st Cavalry Division effectively. At Attopeu and in the Bolovens plateau there were only five airfields, several of them mere dirt strips. The Cav had had trouble during the Ia Drang battle in using more than a single brigade (albeit reinforced) at the front, even though the four airfields around Pleiku were much better developed than those in Laos. There was also a question as to the amount of help to be expected from Thailand. Westmoreland nevertheless appears confident in his memoir that the Full Cry plan would have worked. From what we now know of Hanoi's troop movements at this moment in the war, the attack would have been going up against the crest of a major wave of VPA deployment. Full Cry would have been a big gamble, and would have led to a battle royal in lower Laos.

Westmoreland tabled Full Cry in November 1966 but had few expectations. In a later dispatch to Admiral Sharp, Westy frankly admitted that execution of the plan could only be a "remote" possibility, because "it involves deploying across international borders." Rather than give up, MACV ordered studies of smaller Laotian invasions, named High Port and Fire Break. The latter provided for a combination parachute drop and heliborne assault, plus a corridor across Route 9. At MACV headquarters, more than once Westy exhorted his staff to speed up the invasion plans. Unfortunately, MACV's own study of the Fire Break idea found it "not practical at this time in view of the cost of the effort required and in light of stated national policy."

Again there was no giving up. The sequel, in early 1967, provided for a division-sized thrust out Route 9 to Tchepone, almost exactly what Walt Rostow had pressed for several years earlier. General Westmoreland attached the option of the Laos invasion to his request for fresh forces to be sent to Vietnam, as an attack that could be carried out with the new units. Though the identity of interest between Westmoreland and Rostow seems almost palpable, in fact they proved to be in quite different places. The mind of Lyndon Johnson became the battleground in the next stage of the Vietnam policy debate.

The most important alternative to invasion of Laos was an invasion of the Democratic Republic of Vietnam (DRV). In 1967 this would be Walt Rostow's preference. Rostow preferred to go for the jugular, betting the Soviets and the Chinese would do nothing even if the United States made amphibious landings on the Vietnamese coast. Aside from the danger of intervention, key drawbacks in Rostow's concept flowed directly from its virtues. An invasion would have plugged The Trail, but it also offered the target of American units placed directly across a path already sustaining a major flow of forces. In particular, since Rostow wanted to invade around Vinh, somewhat farther north than Quang Binh Province, and because he wanted to go in enough strength to "hold the area hostage" to force a DRV withdrawal from Laos and the South, Soviet and Chinese responses should not have been discounted. Equally bad, Hanoi's defense would have been simplified, for the People's Army would have been closer to its bases and the United States without a major port to supply its forces.

In addition, the possibility of an invasion of North Vietnam was obvious, and if Hanoi somehow had missed it, they had been reminded. Aside from mentions in the public debate, Saigon generals and politicians had threatened invasion of the North when it suited them. In addition, certain agents and commandos lost in the North by CIA and MACSOG had been briefed to say if captured, that they were precursors to an invasion. Colonel Singlaub of SOG even considered it an achievement of his command in psychological warfare that the DRV's fears of an invasion had been raised.

Hanoi did notice the threat. As early as summer 1966, the People's Army in Quang Binh was strengthened by a full division, which then marched right through the DMZ into the South. General Westmoreland and U.S. Marine commanders believed they had driven back the VPA troops, but the result was a buildup in which Quang Binh, especially Vinh Linh district, was greatly reinforced. American intelligence soon found itself compiling reports on why the DRV had built this strong force across from I Corps. With 1967 the Con Thien battle accentuated U.S. concerns.

In the fall of 1965, Australian journalist Wilfred Burchett had asked Ho Chi Minh about invasion speculation in the American press. "The idea reminds me of a fox with one foot caught in a trap," replied Ho. "He starts leaping about trying to get out, and—pouf—he gets a second one in another trap." Burchett also put this question to General Giap, who answered fiercely, "Let them try! We would welcome them where we can get at them with modern weapons. . . . But they will also find themselves caught up in People's War. The whole people are united as they were under our ancestors, and invaders will find every village a hornets' nest."

In January 1967 Giap addressed a group studying defense measures to be taken by the VPA Third Military Region. Discussing the role of militia, Giap focused directly on an invasion: "It is necessary to prepare local troops and self-defense militia in all fields and make them ready to collaborate with regulars to defeat enemy troops on the mainland from the very beginning." That included "setting up a reserve force so that, when required, the regular force can be supplemented quickly," as well as creating fortified "combat villages." In this way "We can create favorable conditions for preparing ourselves for defeating all adventurous acts of the U.S. aggressors, including a situation in which they daringly use their infantry to attack the North."

General Giap returned to this matter in late 1967 in the series of articles eventually published as the book *Big Victory, Great Task:* "We have adequately prepared ourselves and are ready to deal destructive blows . . . if they adventurously send infantry troops to the North." The similarity of these statements suggests Hanoi's message was partly aimed at Washington.

After the war, in 1983, General Nguyen Xuan Hoang, chief of the People's Army historical office, told American writer and former marine William Broyles that of the myriad different escalation scenarios, "the landing would have been the most foolhardy. We knew we could easily defeat as many as a hundred thousand men there."

General Westmoreland himself had misgivings about invasion. Westy used to meet every so often with Douglas Pike, one of the embassy's foremost experts on the adversary, and at one of those sessions the issue came up. An invasion would be impossible for all sorts of reasons, in Westy's view. The MACV commander pulled out a map and began lecturing, about weather, using up all the shipping in the western Pacific, and other factors, Pike recalls. In fact, a Joint Chiefs of Staff study of the project to deploy a corps-sized force to Vietnam, which was Westmoreland's troop request, found that two thirds of the large landing ships (LSTs) in the Pacific plus thirty-six more LSTs operated by the Military Sea Transportation Service were already in Southeast Asia furnishing vital supply services to MACV. The navy as a whole had only enough shipping to lift less than two division/ wings of marines, and more than 20 percent of it was already in use.

None of the intelligence or opinions dissuaded Walt Rostow. When Westmoreland visited Washington in April 1967 the talk of alternatives came to a head at a key White House meeting. In the Cabinet Room, using a map of Southeast Asia on an easel, Dr. Rostow painted a picture of a brilliant amphibious coup such as at Inchon in the Korean War—Westy had made the identical comparison to Doug Pike—to cut off Hanoi from the South. Rostow recalls this as one of only two times during his White House years that he intervened directly in a Cabinet-level discussion. Westmoreland heard Dr. Rostow make the point that the new forces must be committed so they gained a spectacular advantage. In an attack above the DMZ, the United States could wipe out many People's Army troops and supplies.

Rostow recounts his April 27 briefing this way: "On balance, I thought this a more effective way to proceed than going into the difficult terrain of Laos during the dry season, which, in any case, lay half a year or more in the future." General Westmoreland commented that MACV had studied such an operation, and had contingency plans for an invasion, which would be militarily feasible and could produce significant results, "if the political risks were considered acceptable." That was a big if. Worse, the weather for an invasion in the Gulf of Tonkin was perfect *at that very moment*, and since no preparations had been made, and the new forces were not in place, it would be spring or summer *a year hence* before any invasion could be executed. Rostow's account is misleading where it says that Westy referred simply to "weather factors that would affect the timing of such an invasion and . . . the forces required."

Walt Rostow records that LBJ said nothing, merely taking it all in and continued "chewing over the problem for many weeks." Westmoreland is more direct: "No one around the table, to include the President, expressed any great enthusiasm for the operation, and the discussion died with only Rostow and me participating." The JCS had studied an invasion, however, both Rostow's ambitious Vinh alternative and the amphibious hook above the DMZ. The Joint Chiefs' study of moving a corps-size force to Vietnam had two options under which a division or two of marines would sail with their battalions combat-loaded aboard transports. But the Joint Chiefs showed that gathering this force would adversely affect the global U.S. military posture, while some equipment requirements could not even be met before fiscal 1969 or 1970. Helicopter units, engineers, and artillery battalions were especially problematical. General Earle Wheeler advised the president to mobilize reserves.

To President Johnson the requested reinforcement by more than two divisions, which would increase MACV from 470,000 to 640,000, looked like something other than an "optimum force," as General Westmoreland called it.

LBJ seemed troubled: "When we add divisions, can't the enemy add divisions? If so, where does it all end?"

Westy conceded Hanoi could add to its armies—up to four more divisions—but asserted the VPA could not supply all those troops.

The president then asked, alluding to China and the Soviet Union, "At what point does the enemy ask for volunteers?"

"That is a good question," Westmoreland replied.

In addition to the international risks, invasion of either the DRV or Laos came freighted with political costs. As General Wheeler knew, the force levels could not be met without national mobilization. In an undeclared and politically controversial war, Lyndon Johnson was not going to go into the 1968 election with that weight on his shoulders. Westmoreland understood this dimension, as shown by his remarks here and on other occasions. Westy had also offered a "minimum essential" reinforcement option, some 50,000 men, but warned victory would take two years longer that way. The president did not care. Johnson's refusal drove members of the Joint Chiefs of Staff to the brink of rebellion, but LBJ's intransigence had deep roots.

Nevertheless, though General Westmoreland heard nothing like approval at the April 27 meeting with the president, he came away determined to preserve the invasion options. As Westy put it, "I will proceed to work out alternative courses of action in the event the Administration decides to pursue a different strategy."

One MACV substitute was a series of plans collectively named York. These were to clear the border from the vicinity of Pleiku all the way up to Khe Sanh, with the possibility of a thrust across into Laos as a sequel. The follow-up, El Paso, provided for a much bigger attack across Route 9, ending at Tchepone, dwarfing a predecessor plan known as High Port. Such an operation would have had very definite logistics implications, however. Standard Army planning factors suggest that a force of the size foreseen in

El Paso needed roughly 2,350 tons a day for a Laos invasion. The northern I Corps area did not have anything like that amount of surplus capacity. The C-130-capable airfield at Khe Sanh would be at maximum load handling just 300 tons a day and also would have to support the garrison there.

Everything depended on the mountain road, Route 9. That thoroughfare remained so primitive that a truck convoy could not even turn around anyplace in the portion from Ca Lu to Khe Sanh, and it was in disrepair in any case. Trucks supplying a Laotian invasion would have been at the mercy of weather, too, and the People's Army could have put the whole invasion force in a sack with a single successful ambush on Route 9. The closure of that road in early August, after the VPA ambush of a much smaller artillery convoy on July 21, 1967, well illustrated the dangers. Marines had to use more than a battalion of troops just to disengage that convoy. Captain Richard D. Camp, commanding Lima Company of the 3d Battalion, 26th Marines, recalls Route 9 at this time as "real Indian country," with jungle growing right to the edge of the road. Air supply ruled at Khe Sanh until the spring of 1968.

Secretary McNamara's analysis of the Laotian invasion option, contained in his May 19, 1967, memorandum on Vietnam policy, shows that this understanding is not merely retrospective:

> *Ground actions in Laos* are similarly unwise. Le Duan, Hanoi's third- or fourth-ranking leader, has stated the truth when he said "the occupation of the Western highlands is a tough job but the attack on central and lower Laos is a still tougher one. If a small force is used, the problem remains insoluble. The U.S. may face a series of difficulties in the military, political and logistics fields if a larger force goes into operation. In effect, an attack on central or lower Laos would mean the opening of another front nearer to North Vietnam, and then the U.S. troops would have to clash with the North Vietnamese main force." In essence, a brigade will beget a division and a division a corps, each calling down matching forces from North Vietnam into territory to their liking and suggesting to Hanoi that they take action in Northern Laos to suck us further in. We would simply have a wider war, with Souvanna back in Paris, world opinion against us, and no solution either to the wider war or to the one we already have in Vietnam.

None of the forks in this road led in any desirable direction.

Years later, Admiral Elmo R. Zumwalt, former U.S. naval boss in Indochina, returned to Vietnam and visited his adversaries. On two occasions Zumwalt discussed might have beens with Vo Nguyen Giap. Based on their exchanges about what actually did happen at Khe Sanh, Admiral Zumwalt came away convinced that General Giap would have liked nothing better than to have a bunch of U.S. divisions out on a limb in Laos, at the end of a long supply line back to Da Nang.

Meanwhile, Westmoreland preserved not only the Laos mission but also the North Vietnam operation as active contingencies. In August 1967 MACV proposed an amphibious plan nicknamed Butt Stroke, and at CINC-PAC Admiral U. S. G. Sharp drafted his own version. The two disputed who ought to lead such an invasion, but it would have involved some of MACV's finest troops: the 1st Cavalry, a marine division, an ARVN airborne brigade, and a two-battalion task force of Vietnamese marines. In Washington, making preparations for an invasion but *not* carrying it out was also suggested as a way to deceive Hanoi. Aides to national security adviser Rostow warned, however, that Hanoi would not be fooled unless invasion preliminaries were so realistic that "it could be extremely difficult for the president to decide not to carry through."

Walt Rostow's picture of Lyndon Johnson in 1967, that LBJ chewed on his strategic dilemma but said nothing, obscures more than it enlightens, because it implies the choice lay between invasion options or doing nothing. In fact there was a third option, to create a "barrier" against infiltration, across the DMZ and Laos to the Thai border. Politically and diplomatically, the barrier strategy worked within the framework Washington had already accepted. The real choice in 1967 was between invasions entailing risk and controversy, or a technical solution containing no apparent escalation. The barrier, suggested by Robert McNamara, would be derided later as the "McNamara Line," but Lyndon Johnson's choice had been an easy one. It became the foundation for U.S. actions in Indochina over several years.

Above all else, the "McNamara Line" represented a technological solution to a physical problem, the problem of curbing Hanoi's Trail network. In this the solution mimicked the man, for Robert Strange McNamara was very much a technologist. Partly as a matter of rationality—imagining solutions to intractable puzzles—and partly from convenience, leading-edge technology often figured in McNamara's proposals. He would likely see it differently, simply as problem-solving, but there always remained a fissure between Bob McNamara's visions and others' appreciations of them. With a penchant for climbing mountains to claim mastery over the Earth, Bob had a more relaxed image of himself than often came across. The calculating technologist, cold and crafty, ruthlessly putting his imprint on the Pentagon and U.S. military, made many enemies during his time in government. The loss of Mac Bundy especially disturbed McNamara, who felt it as a grievous privation even though they had not always agreed.

McNamara saw Mac Bundy as frustrated with the war, with Lyndon Johnson's behavior, and with the ways things got done in Washington. Again, impressions recorded in a memoir could easily have applied to the writer, for McNamara's own actions betrayed discomfort with Vietnam policy. The notion of a barrier came from the secretary of defense's own ruminations on the impossibility of blocking The Trail. Midwives to the concept were a group of private academic advisers who met with McNamara before the end of 1965. According to former NSC staffer Carl Kaysen, by then returned to the Harvard faculty, "RSM" loved the idea and just wanted a proposal. In March 1966 McNamara asked the Joint Chiefs to assess the effectiveness and engineering feasibility of "an iron-curtain counterinfiltration barrier across northern South Vietnam and Laos from the South China sea to Thailand."

American military officers were never enthralled by the barrier concept. As early as November 1965 the operations chief of the Joint Staff had assailed a DMZ barrier as militarily impractical as well as a "visible, fixed, long-term" violation of the 1962 Geneva accords. The Joint Staff prepared a paper in April 1966; the concept provided for a cleared path, or "trace," five hundred yards wide, from which all vegetation had been removed, sowed with mines or other devices. The trace was to parallel the north side of Route 9 and have barbed-wire entanglements along its perimeters. Behind the trace would be an electrified fence, and behind that, watchtowers or bunkers for observation of the barrier area. Reserve bases would be located at intervals along the 225-mile length of the barrier. A less developed barrier system would also be placed along the south side of Route 9 for a total length of 120 miles to protect from rear attack at key points.

The barrier designed by the Joint Staff required three full divisions plus the renovation of Route 9 to move materials for the men and their project. The planners concluded that the barrier would need two to four years to complete, with requirements for 271 battalion-months of engineering work, and 206,000 tons of construction materials. The study obviously saw the concept as a difficult one, and it argued that the forces necessary could be better used in other ways, since the barrier could only obstruct large units and did nothing to halt infiltration by sea or through Cambodia.

Not surprisingly, General Earle Wheeler railed against the barrier system. In his memorandum 1353–66 of April 18, Wheeler maintained that the effort needed to create it would be a dangerous diversion of forces. General Westmoreland, Admiral Sharp, the Pacific army and fleet commanders, and the top U.S. officer in Thailand all opposed the barrier.

In the summer of 1966 the Institute for Defense Analysis studied the barrier concept once more. This summer study by the so-called JASON Group was completed and sent to McNamara at the end of August. The civilian scientists gave a different reading of the prospects based on a more technological configuration. Instead of a troop force all along the line, the JASON version combined ground and air barriers with defenses limited to those under the DMZ, and a remote-controlled block on the Laotian side of the border, enforced by aircraft, artillery fire, and area-denial weapons such as mines. The Laos block would be roughly sixty miles wide to reach the Mekong valley, and twenty-five miles deep to catch Hanoi's infiltrators in a kill zone. The JASON Group believed the barrier could be emplaced within a year, and be maintained at a cost of some $800 million annually.

McNamara sent the JASON summer study to Earle Wheeler for comment but did not tarry for the Joint Chiefs' response. On September 15 McNamara ordered that a barrier be designed and installed in one year, and established a Pentagon unit to handle the project. Joint Task Force 728 was headed by army lieutenant general Alfred D. Starbird, a senior research and engineering specialist. Secrecy was layered around the project like an onion, with the Starbird unit being given a cover name, the "Defense Communications Planning Group," the project itself cover designations for the ground portion and the air denial portion of the barrier operation. The whole was given the nickname "Practice Nine." The hush-hush Starbird unit found itself a secret headquarters that was no more than an old Quonset hut on one of the military reservations in Washington, D.C.

Belatedly, two days after McNamara's directive setting up the barrier program, the Joint Chiefs went on record that the effort would be acceptable only as an addition to, and not in place of, other military programs.

This was not the way Secretary McNamara viewed the barrier, and it also would not be Lyndon Johnson's position. On January 6, 1967, McNamara asked LBJ to approve a National Security Action Memorandum (NSAM) that gave the barrier the highest possible priority for defense expenditures and authorizations. President Johnson had Walt Rostow sign the resulting document, NSAM-358, on January 13. The NSAM was a presidential decision document, the first on any aspect of Vietnam in many months and, if organization for pacification is excluded, the first NSAM on Vietnam strategy since the ancient days of 1964, before there ever was a ground war in Vietnam. Lyndon Johnson had stopped issuing presidential directives, and while NSAM-358 may have focused on budget priorities, there are plenty who say that budget *means* policy.

Thus in April, when Westy came to Washington, D.C., to press for new forces and authority to invade Laos, and when Rostow pushed for the DRV invasion, the president had already approved McNamara's technological barrier to infiltration. LBJ knew the generals were against it but went ahead anyway. This was a technical fix, something he could do without sending more troops, and without doing anything in Laos the United States was not already doing.

With the almost studied irony that infuses so much of the Vietnam experience, Ambassador Sullivan and the diplomats in Vientiane were moving ahead to obtain Laotian permission for the barrier at the exact moment Westmoreland in Washington pressed to invade that country. South Vietnamese air marshal Nguyen Cao Ky, now prime minister of a government led by General Nguyen Van Thieu, had been told about the barrier and in Saigon he surfaced the idea as his own. In consequence a Laotian general drew Sullivan aside during a ball at the capital, Luang Prabang, and bid him step into the royal enclosure. There the ambassador found Souvanna Phouma, who asked for more precise information: "Specifically he wanted to know if we intended to attempt to seal the DMZ hermetically. Were we going to clear a strip, put in minefields, barbed wire, control towers, etc., 'line the Iron Curtain.'" If so, Souvanna wanted to know if the barrier was going to extend all the way to the Thai border.

Sullivan replied there were studies of such a project and preparations in hand to install it—he had been with Westmoreland the day before in Da Nang, where they were briefed on Practice Nine—but that Ky's remarks were premature. Over the next few days the exchange evolved, as Dean Rusk first told his ambassador that the United States did not want to leave a false impression but also did not yet wish to reveal details of the barrier, and that extension of any such system to the Laotian border with Thailand "remains an open question." Prime Minister Ky's comments let the cat out of the bag publicly, making the barrier a subject for media attention. Souvanna Phouma, Saigon officials, and MACV officers were soon being asked about the prospects. On April 21 Sullivan called on Souvanna to give him Washington's line on the project but also to ask the Laotian leader to desist from public comment. This limited cooperation shifted to collaboration on May 15, when Ambassador Sullivan sought Souvanna's formal approval for the barrier in lower Laos.

Sullivan was in for a surprise: All of a sudden the Laotian prime minister launched into a detailed discussion of how the barrier should be constructed and where it ought to go. Souvanna crossed to his wall cabinet and opened a relief map stacked there, indicating where he thought the barrier could best be placed—through the hills below the DMZ, diagonally across the edge of the DMZ at its Laotian end to a point above Tchepone, and so on. Souvanna repeated something he had said before, to Sullivan, to Laotian generals, and to reporters, that no one should expect the barrier to be "watertight." It was a point the Joint Chiefs of Staff in Washington had themselves made. On Souvanna's desk was the current issue of *Newsweek* magazine, which happened to contain an article about the idea for a barrier following Route 9.

Bill Sullivan summed up, "I was treated to a rather startling performance."

Once more Souvanna Phouma not only condoned U.S. operations but also took a hand in the effort to attain maximal effect. Neutralist that he was, Souvanna remained a valuable ally.

As the diplomats sought necessary approvals, the military continued to resist. Joint Chiefs of Staff (JCS) memoranda made the point that Practice Nine was going to divert forces from other tasks; JCS studies, as well as plans at MACV and CINCPAC, all assumed new forces would be sent to Vietnam to install and man the barrier. Original plans were modified by General Starbird at the end of 1966, and McNamara ordered minor changes to accommodate the JCS just before he recommended top priority to the president. In late January 1967 the MACV requirements plan for the barrier was finished; it was forwarded to Admiral Sharp, then sent to Washington.

In its new incarnation, the barrier would start from the coast below the Demilitarized Zone (DMZ) (see Map 7). There, where People's Army troops had infiltrated before and could do so again, it would include strongpoints of company-size backing up the trace plus observation towers. At key terrain features would be even bigger bases manned by full battalions. The positions would be spaced more widely in the Annamites and foothills, where

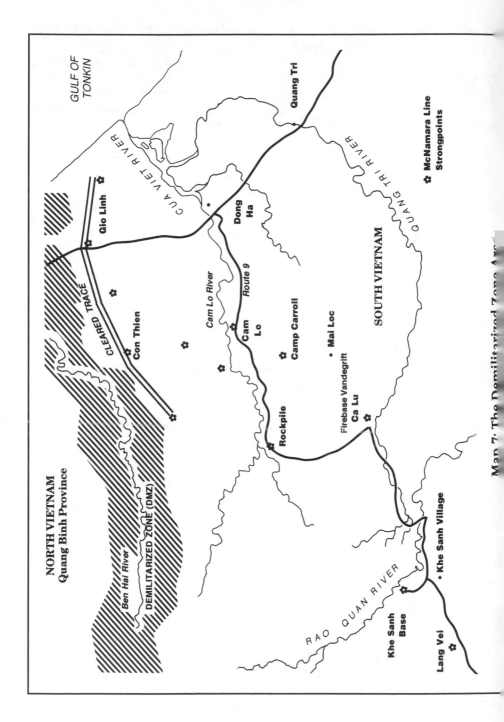

Map 7. The Demilitarized Zone Area

bases would protect defiles or passes columns of troops might easily use. This "strongpoint obstacle system" would be the Dye Marker portion of the barrier; Muscle Shoals would be the Laotian segment, not held by troops at all, but maintained and reseeded by aircraft and by SOG. Even so, MACV anticipated a force requirement of a division plus an armored cavalry regiment, of which one brigade and additional specialists, a total of 7,700 personnel, were needed right away. The brigade was supposed to be a down payment on the full force, which was built into the troop deployment proposals Westmoreland carried to Washington that April.

The instructions finally issued told CINCPAC and MACV to conduct barrier operations with forces in hand, though the stipulated armored cavalry regiment *would* be sent to Vietnam, arriving in early 1968, and would in fact be deployed in the I Corps area. Other costs of the barrier were more easily handled, such as the programmed $1.6 billion in research and development, the $600 million needed to build a command center, the sensors, munitions, and other equipment. In Washington on March 8 McNamara ordered Starbird to procure materials for a system to cost $3 billion to $5 billion overall. Before long the secret Joint Task Force 728 had placed orders for more than 5 million 32- and 72-inch fence posts and 200,000 spools of barbed wire (roughly 50,000 miles' worth). Within Vietnam the barrier would require the use of about 23,000 acres of land and make necessary relocation of 13,000 to 18,000 villagers.

Westmoreland, Bill Sullivan, U. S. Grant Sharp, and even Walt Rostow if he cared to inquire, knew the score a month before the White House session with LBJ. At Da Nang on March 17 the marines, responsible for the barrier's land component, held a briefing to inform ARVN I Corps commander General Hoang Xuan Lam. Westy ordered his marine chief, General Lewis Walt, to work with Lam on the final plan. But Walt objected to Practice Nine on the grounds that it would soak up his entire 3d Marine Division, the key force along the DMZ. Westmoreland knew this, but there was little he could do. The installation of the barrier became the subject of Marine plans 11-67, that June, and 12-67 in September. Before the end of the year 757,520 man-days and 114,519 machine-hours had been invested in Practice Nine construction. As with cross-border operations, the code name for this project changed after its revelation, first to Illinois City, then, in July, to Dye Marker.

Some of the scientific people working the problem were no happier than the marines. Richard S. Greeley, a chemist for the Mitre Corporation, consultants to the Pentagon, calculated that for Hanoi's supply forces to be destroyed on The Trail by air attacks targeted under the barrier's sensor array, seven discrete sets of events would have to occur. The overall probability of this succession Greeley initially put at no better than 20 percent. Because of pressures on the Starbird unit to produce, when Mitre briefed the electronic barrier portion of the project to the DCPG's science advisory committee, Greeley raised his probability assessment to 70 percent and relied on the argument that barrier detection represented a sort of laboratory experiment.

In the summer of 1967 modified antisubmarine acoustic devices, small cluster bomblets, and communication and display equipment were assembled for field tests, first in Florida at Eglin Air Force Base, then at Pot Lid, a jungle-warfare proving ground in Panama. Despite indifferent results, when *some* passing trucks triggered some sensors, the barrier concept was judged workable, and the Pentagon quickly ordained its use in the war. A Mitre Corporation scientist went to Thailand to supervise emplacement of Muscle Shoals, the electronic portion of the barrier system. A town in Thailand with an airfield and just across the Mekong was chosen for the "infiltration surveillance center." The remote sensing devices were to furnish a steady stream of data to indicate Pathet Lao and People's Army movements, repeated through relay aircraft, which the center would process and display for commanders.

By late December a crew of about 450 Thai workers had built a complex for Task Force Alpha, the surveillance center unit, at Nakhon Phanom. For cover it would be called the "Communications Data Management System." Alpha received the nickname Dutch Mill, and a unit number as well, all to confuse anyone who might get curious. Eventually 400 air force and other technicians and managers worked for Alpha, which called targets based on its readouts, summoning attack planes and command aircraft to hit the targets the data generated. The core staff comprised fewer than a dozen, including specialists on both acoustic and seismic sensors, tactical experts, and people from military and scientific laboratories. Dick Greeley, who came to Nakhon Phanom as the initial manager of the core battle staff, discovered a few days after his arrival that General Starbird wanted a final inspection and was already on the way.

The last test proved a disaster. Acoustic sensors bounced off the baked mud of dried-up paddy land at Nakhon Phanom, and when a couple of sensors did finally dig themselves into the ground, they sent no signal as airmen stomped the ground nearby trying to activate them. However, the failure had resulted from a simple error in setting radio frequencies, and the sensors later fed their information back successfully. Starbird declared Muscle Shoals a success, and the system went to war. Chemist Greeley, on the other hand, recognized that there were key problems in knowing the physical location of deployed sensor arrays, and in the prevalence of false readouts. In addition, the IBM model 1401 computer that was supposed to process the data had barely been put online, and represented relatively small computing power anyway. The difficulties were ultimately not completely solvable, and frustration grew; Greeley recalls, "the more I struggled the less effective the system seemed." Within a year, frustration drove Greeley out of military work altogether; later he focused on environmental matters at Mitre.

Air delivery or emplacement by Prairie Fire teams were the preferred means of deployment for the sensors, because it was crucial to have accurate records of the location of sensors. Aside from the sonobuoys there were seismic detectors, chemical sniffers, traffic counters, and simple radio relays that broadcast sounds near them. Sensor technical difficulties delayed activation of the system until December 1967 for the antipersonnel array around Tchepone and the DMZ (called Dump Truck) and until January for Mud River, a wider antivehicle array. Air force brigadier general William P. McBride became commander of Task Force Alpha.

In Vientiane that summer, CINCPAC staff officers let Bill Sullivan in on their plans for the sensors and minefields of the barrier. They anticipated a bigger U.S. presence on the ground than Sullivan had understood. In Washington, McNamara was about to go to LBJ with the recommendation that Prairie Fire sorties be permitted in battalion strength (the "Phase III" of that operation). Previously, Sullivan had deliberately refrained from telling Souvanna Phouma that Prairie Fire units were to have *any* role in the barrier, on the notion that this aspect of U.S. activity could be minimized. Now SOG forays would be larger than ever.

Ambassador Sullivan fired off a cable to Dean Rusk, acidly offering his own job to the military briefer but warning that if things were to be done as outlined, the CINCPAC staffer "had better bring another 200,000 U.S. troops with him to 'pacify' the area he wants to occupy." That was effectively a comment on the Laos invasion proposals as well. In his inimitable style, Sullivan concluded: "I am disappointed that messages of this type are permitted to move in official channels and receive wide dissemination. It is the sort of thing which is giving marijuana a good name."

In the patchwork of muddled thinking that passed for strategy in Vietnam, everybody was right though everyone was wrong. Westy and the Joint Chiefs were right that the McNamara Line would not stop all infiltration, and that it could not be held with the troops available. Bob McNamara was right to criticize Laos invasion proposals. Bill Sullivan was right to question the line that would separate an antiseptic "barrier" across lower Laos from an attempt at close occupation of territory.

On September 7 in Washington, Secretary McNamara held a news conference at which he discussed Dye Marker. The resulting public attention led to the "McNamara Line" colloquialism. In his passage on this subject in *A Soldier Reports*, William Westmoreland writes as if Dye Marker had been abandoned, though no public notice would be given. In fact the barrier was never abandoned. This had major importance for the marine combat base at Khe Sanh, where a role emplacing the barrier, plus Khe Sanh's potential as launchpad for an invasion of Laos, Westy's other preference, became the twin rationales for the continued holding of that place. In turn the Americans at Khe Sanh attracted growing attention from the Vietnam People's Army.

Hanoi's *bo dois* were beginning to react to the barrier strategy, too. At first the hottest sector was down in the coastal plain. The initial set of fourteen watchtowers, put up for soldiers to keep an eye on the trace, were all blown up just as promptly by the VPA. The People's Army also fought a major battle around Con Thien, one of the outposts of the strongpoint obstacle system. Unprecedented use of artillery and new large-caliber guns marked Hanoi's fight. On the U.S. side, the 1st Battalion, 9th Marines suffered such heavy causalities at Con Thien that they became known as "The Walking Dead." Up in the Annamites, *bo dois* soon encountered strange new American contraptions—the sensors of Muscle Shoals. Audio feeds on some sensors broadcast the play-by-play as *bo dois* argued over who would have the privilege of shooting up the machines. Soon enough, though, the responses became more sophisticated. Soldiers from the *binh trams* drove herds of animals up and down the paths to fox seismic sensors; chemical ones were defeated by buckets of urine hung in trees; sound sensors could simply be picked up and moved to where they were useless. The battle of The Trail became a contest between technology and ingenuity.

Perhaps the finest example of technology as strategy on this fork of the Vietnam road was the attempt to harness the weather and the land to defeat the enemy. Like the barrier idea, this was something managers such as McNamara found technically sweet. There were two components in the attempt to enlist nature in the service of war. One was to induce flooding by making rain, the other to use rain to make mud. Flooding affected The Trail directly by preventing passage during short periods, then creating longer-term obstacles with washed-out bridges and roads. The soil operation aimed at making choke points on The Trail even harder to transit by converting roadbed into bottomless mud.

Again, like the sensors and new munitions used in the barrier, enlisting nature formed part of the wizard war that backed up the Allied forces in Southeast Asia. Donald F. Hornig, science adviser to President Johnson, and William G. McMillan, who performed the same function for MACV, were constantly on the lookout for creative technical ideas to better fight the adversary. Hornig formed an ad hoc Vietnam panel of the Science Advisory Committee, which he headed. Indeed, Stanford physicist Sidney Drell, who chaired the ground warfare subcommittee of the unit, and IBM scientist Richard R. Garwin, played important roles in the barrier project. Colonel Singlaub of SOG fame recalls Dr. McMillan as a great help to him.

The weather war was based on innovations in chemistry by scientists at Dow Chemical Corporation, which had also been a force in creating Agent Orange and other chemical defoliants used in Vietnam and Laos. Chemists at Dow developed a compound marketed in the United States under the trademark Calgon and used in detergents. With a few changes the compound could, having loosened soil, retain its moisture, creating mud. In the iron-rich Annamites, the mud would be very sticky indeed. Another chemical, silver iodide, with which meteorologists were experimenting to make rain, also found its place in the war. Used in America to attempt relieving droughts in farmland, or to draw the teeth of hurricanes before they reached shore, in Vietnam the vision was to flood The Trail.

Early Calgon experiments occurred in Laos in 1966. One recollection of the effect is provided by Fred Locke, a pilot with marine Medium Helicopter Squadron 265, who flew missions for SOG among his other duties. One day Locke was briefed for a flight out to the Tchepone area, which he remembers well because of the juxtaposition of what he was told at the briefing and what actually happened. It was soon after the surgeon general of the United States had made his first finding that smoking was harmful to health, and part of the briefing was devoted to telling the pilots to give it up. Then the briefer casually admonished the chopper pilots to be sure not to ask for air strikes against friendly elephants.

"I'm beginning to wonder if this is Disneyland," Locke remembered, but he was supposed to be the flight leader, and he had to ask how they were supposed to tell the friendly elephants from the enemy ones. Sure it was a setup, Locke was surprised when the briefers explained that the "enemy" elephants would have their bellies tinged red from the clay mud of The Trail.

"I'll be doggone if we didn't see a whole bunch of elephants and they did. We're talking *Lost Weekend*, I know—the 'pink elephants.' But there they were, right in front of me!"

The mud operation, code-named Commando Lava, began in a major way in May 1967. The mudmaking chemicals were dropped in sacks by large C-130 aircraft on choke points near Tchepone and, farther south, along the Sihanouk Trail. Admiral Sharp, Secretary McNamara, the Joint Chiefs, and other Washington officials all approved. Also waxing enthusiastic was Ambassador Sullivan. The operation was timed to begin shortly before the onset of the monsoon season in Laos, with the notion that Calgon would magnify the impact of the rains. The "chelating" chemicals became a subject of discussion at the SEACOORD meeting in Udorn on May 27. As Sullivan gleefully reported, "If we could combine these techniques with [rainmaking] . . . perhaps within [the] concept of Practice Nine, we might be able to make enemy movement among the cordillera of the Annamite chain almost prohibitive. In short, chelation may prove better than escalation. Make mud, not war!"

The Commando Lava experiments continued in June, with mudblocks attempted in the A Shau valley, where Marine Force Reconnaissance patrols were able to check the results, and in Laos. Through the summer, aerial photography and patrols confirmed that *binh tram* road crews merely laid logs and bamboo matting at especially muddy places in exactly the same fashion as they did at points not attacked by chemicals. Commando Lava failed to live up to Bill Sullivan's high hopes, while Westmoreland called off the chelation operation on October 21, before the Laotian monsoon season even ended.

Rainmaking went by the code name Popeye, at least during its experimental phase in 1966. A team from China Lake, the Naval Ordnance Testing Station in California's Mojave Desert, brought the chemicals and trained Seventh Air Force crews to dispense them using flare pistols. The potential for floods in Laos and the likelihood that the Lao would refuse to believe Americans could cause rain led Sullivan to keep the initiative quiet, not informing Souvanna Phouma. Nevertheless, Popeye was considered successful, to be resumed on a larger scale beginning on March 20, 1967, as

Project Compatriot. This top-secret operation was considered so sensitive it was reported weekly, "eyes only," directly to President Johnson. Walt Rostow added cover memos with his usual rosy commentaries.

At the end of May and the beginning of June, for example, the Compatriot cloud-seeders concentrated primarily on the routes from Mu Gia and Ban Karai to Tchepone, and on the People's Army transportation routes near Attopeu, including the approaches to the Vietnamese border opposite Dak To and Kham Duc. The monsoon had just begun, and by June 9 Sullivan was reporting from Vientiane, "Vehicle traffic has ground virtually to a halt. . . . Our road-watch teams report that in many stretches . . . ground water has already reached saturation point and standing water has covered roads." The ambassador expected to redeploy his road-watch and air interdiction forces to counter bicycle and human porter traffic. In the comment appended to this cable for LBJ's benefit, Walt Rostow added, "The rainy reason has arrived in Laos, with wholesome results."

What was unusual about the 1967 monsoon season was that rainfall would be *scarce* in northern and western Laos. This damaged the rice crop and seedbeds normally laid at this time of year. Ambassador Sullivan probably felt events justified his earlier reluctance to tell the Lao about the rainmaking. Fortunately, there was a cover—Sullivan reported that "all knowledgeable Lao" blamed the monsoon pattern on the recent Chinese atmospheric test of a hydrogen bomb.

A separate facet of Compatriot was a plan to flood out the Song Ca inside the Democratic Republic of Vietnam. Inundating this river system would wash out Hanoi's main transportation artery in the funnel down to The Trail, especially the approaches to the passes south of Vinh. This JCS proposal did not receive unqualified support, however. In late May Don Hornig told Rostow the president should seek more information on the expected military impact before approving this initiative. Hornig anticipated flooding would cause health and sanitation hazards for the young, aged, and infirm, as well as food shortages. Even though a leak from participants was not likely, he judged exposure as probable, Hornig wrote, for these reasons:

> 1. The unusual cloud formations have been repeatedly observed on Saigon weather radars. So far this attention has been diverted by ascribing them to "early monsoon conditions."
>
> 2. The clouds can be observed from weather satellites which are non-classified and may arouse the curiosity of the meteorological community.
>
> 3. The fact that we are going ahead with [another, public] program on the basis of apparently flimsy backup evidence has led to speculation that we "know something" which has not yet appeared.

Dr. Hornig expected revulsion in meteorological circles and loss of esteem by "our highly disaffected general scientific community" and also foresaw "potential damage to our world position."

President Johnson nevertheless went ahead to approve extension of Compatriot into the DRV. The Joint Chiefs issued the order on July 11, 1967. Rainmaking over North Vietnam continued through November 1968, and the program as a whole went on until July 1972. All this time the rainmaking stayed under close White House control. It was in 1971, with Henry A. Kissinger the national security adviser, that Compatriot peaked, with expenditure of almost a quarter of the chemical canisters used in the entire effort. In all the rainmaking involved some 2,602 aircraft missions that used 47,409 containers of silver iodide.

Despite this effort, rainmaking had marginal impact in the war. There would be just one drop of supply activity recorded on The Trail that officials could link directly to rain, and that happened to coincide with a typhoon that inundated Laos. Short of that, *bo doi* improvisation proved a match for American science. All those schemes Bob McNamara found seductive kept coming up sterile. As the war dragged on, McNamara could not help but see the mounting political challenge, something with the potential to push the United States down an entirely different fork in the road.

As the war progressed, its issue never resolved by technology on the battlefield, political protest deepened. A crucial moment in the unraveling of the Diem regime during 1963 had been the self-immolation of a Buddhist monk in Saigon. Horrible on its face, the burning had catalyzed opposition to Ngo Dinh Diem. A parallel event in Washington during 1965 failed to trigger an eruption in the antiwar movement, which continued a slow but steady incremental growth, but it nevertheless confronted Robert McNamara with the depth of feeling in America on Vietnam.

Norman R. Morrison was an officer of the Stoney Run Friends Meeting in suburban Baltimore. Contrary to the image of college students out to beat the draft, Morrison was beyond draft age, a thirty-two-year-old father of three. Born in Pennsylvania, raised a Presbyterian, and once a student at the College of Wooster, Morrison's previous commitment had been to the civil rights movement. He was a friend of Staughton Lynd and was impressed by Lynd's visit to Hanoi amid the rising violence of war. On November 2, 1965, Morrison traveled to Washington. He had written to his congressman, he had read of the Vietnam terror, there had to be more he could do. That afternoon Morrison appeared on the steps at the river entrance to the Pentagon, a place just forty feet from Secretary McNamara's window. Dousing himself with kerosene, Morrison struck a match and expired in fierce flames and a haze of smoke. He had been clutching his eighteen-month-old daughter, and bystanders shouted to him to save her. Morrison tossed the toddler to one who rescued her. In a statement, Mrs. Morrison declared her husband had sacrificed his life "to express his deep concern over the great loss of life and human suffering caused by the war in Vietnam."

Bob McNamara was meeting in the office as the Quaker pacifist took his life on the steps outside. The commotion brought McNamara to the window, but not until ambulances were already on the scene and medics were swathing the corpse in blankets. McNamara saw the commotion, the crowd, the haze of smoke drifting away. Of the Morrison suicide, McNamara recounts: "I reacted to the horror of his action by bottling up my emotions and avoiding talking about them with anyone—even my family." Bob knew that his wife, Marg; his three children; and even the wives and children of several Cabinet colleagues, shared Mr. Morrison's antiwar views.

This wrenching event on the Pentagon's steps took place even as, in Vietnam, Hanoi's *bo dois* laid siege to Plei Me and then faced the Cav at the Ia Drang. For the week of November 13 the Department of Defense announced the deaths of 86 Americans. It was the highest toll of the war so far. In the following week's announcement, coincident with the fight at Landing Zone X Ray, the Pentagon admitted no fewer than 240 battle deaths. After that the numbers began to pile up, week after week, in a mind-numbing current of sadness enshrined one day on a black marble wall on the Washington Mall.

General Westmoreland naturally put the best face imaginable on Ia Drang. "I consider this an unprecedented victory," Westy told the press. It was. But the losses were as unprecedented as the gains. Author Thomas Powers has written, "The effect on the antiwar movement was electric." As for unprecedented victory, battle after battle, right down to the events of Tet 1968, would be claimed to be successes of this kind. The string of assertions, in the face of a war situation that to the public appeared quite static, became as mind-numbing as the toll of losses. In the long run the combination would be devastating.

Politicians' business was to keep their finger on the pulse of public opinion. Neither William Westmoreland nor Robert McNamara were politicians. Lyndon Baines Johnson was. The president's public and private comments evince rising concern about attitudes on Vietnam, and his actions clearly demonstrate an attempt to counter the trend. The notorious "bombing halt" of thirty-seven days over 1965–1966 was born in just such an effort.

President Johnson also needled his own subordinates, and closely monitored their public contacts, both to keep them on the reservation and to get them out in public, building support for the war policy. At the time of the big national teach-in, a publicly televised debate held on May 15, 1965, LBJ had prevented Mac Bundy from participating for the administration, but he supported Mac's consolation appearances at Harvard and in another televised debate. McNamara's appreciation of LBJ's desire for the top team players to get out there in support is part of the reason the secretary of defense himself mouthed the phrase "McNamara's war" at one of his news conferences announcing Vietnam initiatives.

Johnson was not the only politician, however, and there were others to warn him of a political prognosis grown increasingly bleak. In particular, Arkansas senator J. William Fulbright, long an intimate Johnson ally, became increasingly alarmed. Fulbright was the powerful chairman of the Senate Foreign Relations Committee, and felt he had been slighted during the spring of 1965, when LBJ ignored his advice and intervened in the Dominican Republic. At the beginning of 1966, when the administration asked for more foreign aid for Saigon, Senator Fulbright held public hearings on American involvement in Southeast Asia. By this time a majority on the Foreign Relations Committee, which in the 1960s excised greater influence on U.S. foreign policy than it has since, were already concerned about or openly against the war.

Bill Fulbright set the tone himself the day Dean Rusk first came to testify. "Something . . . is wrong or there would not be such a great dissent," said the senator, "that is evidenced by teach-ins and articles and speeches by various responsible people. I do not regard all of the people who have raised these questions as irresponsible. I think it is our duty . . . to try to clarify the nature of our involvement there . . . and whether or not the ultimate objective justifies the enormous sacrifice in lives and treasure."

One of the tragedies of Vietnam is that the executive branch of the U.S. government saw its aims as being of such importance that the goals excused it from confronting questions of this sort. Methods of manipulating public opinion—"spin-doctoring" in the argot of a later age—became endemic during Vietnam and did a great deal to convince Americans that their government was not to be trusted. The techniques of propaganda, innovated for war against a foreign enemy, were played back at home. Of a piece with this, as Fulbright biographer Randall Bennett Woods reveals, after these Vietnam hearings in early 1966 President Johnson quietly instructed J. Edgar Hoover, then head of the Federal Bureau of Investigation (FBI), to try to produce evidence that his old friend Bill Fulbright was either a Communist agent or a dupe.

At the hearings themselves, Secretary of State Rusk played the lead role for the administration. "It is not McNamara's war; it is not the United States' war," Rusk intoned, "it is Ho Chi Minh's war. Maybe it is Mao Tse-tung's [Zedong's] war in terms of the support he has given." Rusk would be questioned about China by senators concerned, as the administration secretly was, about the probability of Beijing's active military participation in Vietnam. He does not appear to have answered these questions at all, at least in public session. Instead Rusk maintained a hard line on China: "It is the policy of Beijing that has greatly stimulated Hanoi and has apparently blocked the path toward a conference." The reference was to a renewed Geneva conference—Rusk's assertion stood reality on its head. It had been a primary aim of U.S. policy to *prevent* a Geneva conference *unless Hanoi was defeated*, while Beijing had been calling for just such a negotiation.

Meanwhile, the notion that dissent could be handled as a public relations matter, by dismissing protesters as irresponsible, disruptive elements, did grave though invisible damage to the Johnson administration. Since dissent was construed as not "serious" for far too long, the administration neglected its failure to build public consensus behind policy. In part it was seduced by the fact the strategy seemed to work—public opinion polls continued to show majorities for the war, while antiwar protesters found it very difficult to get a hearing in American media. In fact, opinion was soft because of the missing consensus, and the mind-numbing aspects of the war gradually undermined what support there was. With each revelation of manipulation of the law or the news from Vietnam, protesters were further enraged while supporters grew more perplexed.

Failing to engage his opposition, Lyndon Johnson failed to create a synthesis of policy. Instead he did such things as set up a new interagency committee to control information—a subject for a National Security Action Memorandum—or encourage prominent Americans to go to Vietnam and be given "the tour" by MACV and the U.S. embassy. The procession included Democratic stalwarts such as Clark Clifford, Republicans such as Richard Nixon and George Romney, and chameleons such as Henry Kissinger. In Washington, LBJ began a series of White House meetings where members of Congress were invited for background briefings. The briefers were Dean Rusk and Robert McNamara. Rusk recalls that over 1966 and 1967, in groups of thirty, "Lyndon Johnson covered the entire Congress in those meetings."

Bob McNamara writes that he began to waver on the war during this period, but there were reasons both inside and outside the president's councils for that. On the inside, the secretary of defense had been told, right after the Ia Drang "victory," that MACV needed 400,000 troops by the end of 1966 and possibly 200,000 more in 1967. Political instability in Saigon had increased, pacification was stalled, ARVN desertions were up, and intelligence estimated The Trail could handle two hundred tons of supplies a day—"*despite* heavy interdiction bombing"—more than Hanoi needed for the most intense fighting. "The U.S. presence rested on a bowl of jelly," McNamara says, it "shook me and altered my attitude perceptibly." No wonder the secretary of defense favored an electronic barrier. His attitude cannot have been improved when Westmoreland, having been denied the 200,000 reinforcements the year before, came back in the spring of 1967 to ask for 214,000.

Outside government was the mounting opposition. Louis Harris poll data found that while Americans still supported LBJ on Vietnam, by early 1966 a majority wanted an honorable way out. Between the end of 1965 and mid-1966 those expecting the conflict to drag out increased from 54 to 72 percent. McNamara felt the heat. Given honorary degrees in 1966 by New York University and Amherst College, some faculty and students at both places walked out on McNamara during commencement ceremonies. In Seattle that summer, the defense secretary was waiting to board his plane when a man approached him and screamed "Murderer!" There was a similar incident in Aspen, and a near-confrontation with a crowd of protesters at Harvard.

It is instructive that Lyndon Johnson's memoir *The Vantage Point* presents an account of making Vietnam strategy in 1966 and 1967 as if no antiwar opposition existed. LBJ's recounting of recommendations and decisions has an odd air of unreality for this very reason. In fact, some of the things Johnson did were intended to create the appearance of movement or to generate dynamism precisely to counteract the growth of pessimism on the war. President Johnson's summits at Guam and Manila, and his visit on the spur of a moment to U.S. troops at Cam Ranh Bay, formed part of this effort, which never produced the results he would have wished.

LBJ may have pretended in memoirs that the antiwar movement did not exist, but it had concrete impact on Johnson the president. During John Kennedy's years in the White House, Americans lacked any perception of a government systematically misleading them. That perception and the antiwar movement grew in tandem, and the growing malaise can be associated with an increase in threats to the president. In Kennedy's time, Secret Service files listed 700 individuals considered to have threatened the president, and the service was receiving 100 tips a month. In mid-1967 the threat file contained 1,800 names, and intelligence items ran to 7,000 a month; mail containing threatening statements, by itself, stood at substantially above 1,000 pieces a month in early 1968, a tenfold increase. During the fiscal year ending in June 1967, a total of 425 persons were arrested for making threats against the president, more than four times the rate of 1965.

Lyndon Johnson's travel patterns show the direct impact of the controversy over the war. A visit to Syracuse was canceled when student demonstrators were found preparing containers of urine to throw. In Australia the president's motorcade actually would be pelted with red paint. LBJ virtually stopped traveling except under tightly controlled conditions, such as to the LBJ Ranch outside Johnson City, Texas, to military bases, or on foreign trips. Of forty trips President Johnson made during 1967, fully twenty-eight were insulated from the public in this way. During Johnson's last year in office his record would be even worse, with more than half his total trips just to the LBJ Ranch. Vietnam politics drove Lyndon Johnson practically into seclusion.

Through the middle years of the conflict, when conditions were getting this bad, President Johnson was actually enjoying the *best* support he would have. Opinion poll measurements of Johnson's handling of the war and LBJ's performance as president still showed majority support. Through much of 1966 antiwar demonstrations remained small and attracted little media attention. Nevertheless, inside the White House, Walt Rostow was telling LBJ he needed a "Gettysburg Address." When the 1966 congressional elections came, Johnson's Democratic Party lost every House of Representatives seat it had gained upon his election two years before, plus several Senate seats to boot.

Other fissures were also beginning to show as support for Johnson's Vietnam policy became ever more brittle. More troops under Westmoreland in Vietnam meant increased draft calls in the United States—30,000 in July 1966 became 46,000 that October—and spurred resistance to the conscription system. By 1967 there would be mass burnings of draft cards, even a public collection of cards that activists then tried to turn over to Justice Department officials. In the summer of 1966 veterans joined in dissent—several dozen participated in a march from Valley Forge to Washington. In February

1967 the magazine *Ramparts* published an article by former Green Beret Donald Duncan that contained the first public revelation of the Leaping Lena cross-border operations into Laos, as well as allegations regarding American and South Vietnamese torture of prisoners. In April veterans of the Vietnam fighting constituted themselves as Vietnam Veterans Against the War (VVAW), a group that Duncan and many more would join. That February a crowd of 2,500 women protesters marched on the Pentagon.

Mass demonstrations returned in the spring of 1967 as President Johnson considered Westmoreland's and Walt Rostow's strategy proposals. On April 15 in New York City a crowd of more than 200,000 rallied against the war, while 50,000 marched in San Francisco. The crowd figures were conservative, and a new solidarity between the antiwar and civil rights movements was denoted by the fact the New York rally was addressed by Martin Luther King Jr. and other African American leaders. Opponents of the antiwar movement tried to discredit the mass protests with demonstrations of their own, and organizers called for a New York rally on April 29, confidently predicting 100,000 would attend. Only 7,500 prowar demonstrators showed up, while a repeat performance by embarrassed organizers still drew just 20,000 on May 13.

In mid-April the Pacific Theater commander, Admiral U. S. Grant Sharp, gave a press interview castigating dissenters for encouraging Hanoi and damaging the overall U.S. position. A similar sally came from General Westmoreland, speaking to the American Newspaper Publishers Association at the Waldorf-Astoria Hotel in New York on April 24. In that speech, and in an address to a joint session of Congress, Westy offered bright pictures of the situation in Vietnam. Military commanders did everything they could to win freedom of action in the war.

The net result proved problematical, as would be a further round of efforts to mold public opinion in the fall, directly masterminded by Walt Rostow through something he called the "Vietnam Information Group." In meetings of senior administration officials, elaborate plans were laid to publicize favorable data, counter adverse stories in the media, and leak secret materials that seemed to support Washington's claims. Graphic charts General Westmoreland used privately for key briefings in late 1967 were quickly massaged, reproduced, declassified, and given to the press. This included information on combat actions, capture of VPA and Viet Cong men and weapons, pacification statistics, supply deliveries to South Vietnam, and more. The president and Rostow bought limited public backing, but through extravagant claims that left them vulnerable to discovery.

Over the short term, opinion poll results showed some improvement. In May 1967 Harris Poll data had Americans divided about equally between efforts to attain military victory or, alternatively, mutual withdrawal. In July George Gallup's polling organization released results demonstrating Americans opposed any large troop increase in Vietnam by 61 to 29 percent. By then only a third continued to approve Lyndon Johnson's handling of the war.

In this touchy climate the president had been handed military options that might trigger war with the Chinese, Russians, or both; drive those hostile powers into each other's arms; and result in much higher American casualties. The risks were both diplomatic and political. As CIA director Richard Helms put it to a later interviewer, "Johnson was constantly concerned about whether or not the Chinese might come into the war." The same applied to Russia. The military and Rostow wanted freedom of action. On May 19 Robert McNamara went on record with his extensive analysis refuting the claims made for the next set of reinforcements. The secretary of defense advised sending only "minimum essential" forces to Vietnam, ruling out escalation. Though McNamara's rejection may have given LBJ political cover for his decision, there is little reason to suppose President Johnson would have sided with the Joint Chiefs, Westy, Sharp, and Rostow, even without McNamara's negative advice.

On August 3 President Johnson announced he was approving dispatch of an additional 55,000 soldiers to Vietnam—the minimum essential—and he also asked for a 10 percent surcharge on federal income taxes to pay for the war and his social programs. This attempt to manage the alternatives satisfied no one. The Joint Chiefs wanted national mobilization and backed Westmoreland. The antiwar movement saw another increment of force, and its fury intensified. Americans at large feared for their pocketbooks with the tax increase.

Antiwar leaders answered with a mass march on the Pentagon on October 21. More than fifty thousand demonstrators rallied in Washington, crossed the Potomac, then moved onto the grounds, nervously defended by troops brought up from Fort Bragg. The crowd included young and old, veterans, women, and local groups from many places. One CIA officer among the marchers kept running into people from the agency and from the Pentagon itself. A military official had the same experience. Another ran into his brother, who lived in another city and whom he had never known to express opposition to the Vietnam War.

A sometime McNamara speechwriter, now at work on the massive review of Vietnam decisions that became known as the Pentagon Papers, Daniel Ellsberg also marched that day. Ellsberg wanted to get a better view of the crowd, so he used his Department of Defense identification to cross the lines of military police and enter the building. He went up to the room the Pentagon Papers analysts had been using, which stood right next to Robert McNamara's office. Still not satisfied with what he could see, Ellsberg opened the door to McNamara's room. Inside there was a secretary at the window and, in the shadows next to her, McNamara himself. The secretary of defense invited Ellsberg in to have a look, then turned to resume his vigil. McNamara was quiet, brooding; he said nothing.

Almost two decades later, Bob McNamara recalled the moment for writer Paul Hendrickson:

> Can you imagine? Christ, yes, I was scared. You had to be scared. A mob is an uncontrollable force. It's terrifying. Once it becomes a mob all the leaders are useless. It was a mess. But there was no question I would be up there. You don't delegate something like that. I was up there with Cy Vance and Warren Christopher and General Buzz Wheeler. . . . They did it all wrong. I mean, the marchers. The way to have done it would have been Gandhilike. Had they retained their discipline, they could have achieved their ends. My God, if 50,000 people had been disciplined and I had been the leader I absolutely guarantee you I could have shut down the goddam place.

That day proved an epiphany for McNamara. On November 1, not very long afterward, he handed President Johnson a memorandum advising that the bombing of North Vietnam be halted, the war contained at existing levels and handed over to Saigon forces, and negotiations opened. McNamara's days were numbered; shortly after that, LBJ nominated him to head the World Bank. The former secretary of defense is still not sure whether he quit or was fired.

As for the lack of discipline among the marchers, that was a constant feature of antiwar actions, and a direct consequence of the movement's alliance among a bewildering array of interest groups and causes. The inclusiveness contained potential for mob action, to be sure, but much more often it was a recipe for amorphous, even aimless actions, calm rallies rather than days of rage. Small, coherent groups, as the Vietnam Veterans Against the War would later demonstrate, could maintain discipline and take purposeful action, but the movement as a whole remained a manifestation of political will, not an army, ignorant or otherwise.

Lyndon Johnson tried to dismiss the opposition and cut it down, much as he suspected adversaries (or friends) such as Bill Fulbright of being Communists or dupes. LBJ went to Dick Helms and demanded the CIA report on whether Hanoi or other Communists controlled the antiwar movement. A massive CIA study sent to President Johnson on November 15 could find no such ties, only associations between individuals and others who might be in the enemy camp. There was no question of leadership. Not satisfied, LBJ demanded another study, and an even more detailed examination by the CIA reached the same conclusion. Nevertheless, the FBI, the Secret Service, the CIA, and the U.S. Army continued to follow and even harass the movement. This was a poor precedent for future American politics.

In fact there was no possible way Hanoi could have directed the disparate, inchoate rainbow of constituencies that made up the antiwar movement. Nevertheless, it *was* in Hanoi's power to do things, in Vietnam, in the war, that would affect the antiwar movement as much as Lyndon Johnson.

Hanoi had come to that fork in the road. As Washington wrestled with its Vietnam strategy, so did Hanoi. The result proved explosive.

Hanoi propagandists were fond of saying that all Vietnamese were brothers. That truism could not be denied; in fact, sometimes it struck very close to home. Take Vo Nguyen Giap, for example. The general, defense minister of the Democratic Republic of Vietnam and renowned military strategist from the time of the anti-French war, hailed from Quang Binh Province, that place that was the object of so much of the American interdiction campaign. Giap's home village, Kien Giang, also happened to be birthplace of Ngo Dinh Diem, Hanoi's erstwhile enemy, and as a boy Giap had attended a school run by the Ngo family. In the Vietnam People's Army, one of Giap's major competitors was General Nguyen Chi Thanh. They, too, shared a commonality—during French colonial times both had been convicts held at Lao Bao prison, a facility between Khe Sanh and Tchepone on Route 9. When observers consider Khe Sanh and what happened there, it is not usually noted that Giap had personal knowledge of that part of the country.

The two generals would be major players in Hanoi's deliberations on strategy. Unfortunately, that is about as much as we know for certain, even at this late date. There is no authoritative source available on decisionmaking within Hanoi's inner sanctum, and Western reconstructions of events are inevitably clouded by our limited sources. Nevertheless, Hanoi's choices had important implications for The Trail and the whole future of the war and need to be reviewed.

In many accounts the Vietnamese decision is viewed in very simple terms: There was one faction favoring a long war, a "protracted" conflict. That is pictured as the pro-Chinese faction, since Beijing had counseled Hanoi to extend the war until the time China would be armed and equipped to join in. Another faction favored the Soviets. That group supposedly favored large-unit warfare, and General Nguyen Chi Thanh is known to have advocated such a style of military operations. Hanoi's decision would be expressed in a resolution adopted by the twelfth plenum of the Lao Dong Party Central Committee, a meeting held in December 1965.

Actually, Hanoi's strategy was a mixed one and far more complex than this suggests. Coming on the heels of the Ia Drang battles, which convinced the People's Army that its troops could face Americans in the field, the problem at that time was to construct an approach to continue the war despite the U.S. intervention. To follow the Chinese model meant deemphasizing regular forces, confining activities to guerrilla operations. But against the massive combat capability weighing in on Saigon's side with the addition of American ground troops, Hanoi feared danger to the Viet Cong. A defeat for the Liberation Front would cripple the guerrilla effort. On the other hand, regular troops in the South could draw off the Americans and permit the guerrilla war to proceed.

The party document expressing the December 1965 decision, called Resolution 12, provided for seeking victory within a relatively short time. Since Hanoi often spoke in terms of decades, sometimes even centuries, Western observers have frequently interpreted this to mean that a decision for protracted war had resulted. Since Vo Nguyen Giap was thought to favor that strategy, observers picture Resolution 12 as a triumph for him. Conversely, Hanoi's decision of early 1967 that led to the Tet offensive is seen as a win for Nguyen Chi Thanh's preferred course of reliance on the People's Army.

There are several features that must lead to questioning this version of Hanoi's decisions. In the first place, Resolution 12 embodied a compromise, not a pure strategy, using General Thanh's VPA regulars as a shield behind which Giap's protracted war could continue. Moreover, Hanoi's next choice, for Tet, was no rational selection made in some non-value-laden environment. Personalities and politics were involved, both at the time, and in retrospect, in the presentation of historical data. The casting of General Giap, for example, does not ring true: Giap is numbered with Hanoi's pro-Soviet faction in typical Western analyses, yet his protracted-war strategy amounts to the Chinese preference. Meanwhile, General Thanh was pro-Chinese, and regarded as an expert on political, not conventional, warfare. As for personal competition, that between Giap and Nguyen Chi Thanh is the one usually noted, but there were others. General Van Tien Dung, People's Army chief of staff, was intensely competitive with Giap, and there is evidence that in connection with operations in 1972 and 1975 Dung gave accounts that tried to minimize Giap's contributions. Dung and Nguyen Chi Thanh both served on the Lao Dong Party's Political-Military Commission, which excluded Giap. Le Duan and Le Duc Tho, top Party figures on the commission, used that body to centralize control over the war in the South. According to Bui Tin, after 1963 they dominated. General Dung was part politico—he had been commissar of the 320th Division—and saw alliance with Duan and Tho as a ticket to the top. The ambitious son of a tailor from a village on the outskirts of Hanoi, Dung had little education and would have had indifferent prospects without powerful patrons.

At the political level, Le Duan faced the need to moderate between the demands of those who advocated an emphasis on political struggle and those favoring emphasis on military struggle, as well as the question of what to do about negotiations with the United States. Prime Minister Pham Van Dong, heir apparent to Ho Chi Minh, remained more moderate than either Duan or Le Duc Tho, and was beginning to favor a negotiation, at least to test the waters. General Thanh, of course, advocated what became the Tet Offensive, backed by other senior generals in the South, such as Nguyen Van Vinh and Tran Do, both of whom had been sent down The Trail like Thanh himself. Aside from personality questions, there was thus a war versus peace issue in 1967. Hanoi needed to demonstrate battlefield prowess to stake its claim in negotiations.

There was also a theoretical aspect to the debate over strategy. Vietnamese revolutionary theory, drawn from Party ideologist Truong Chinh, had always maintained that revolutionary warfare would proceed through the stages of guerrilla operations, then mobile operations, culminating in a general offensive and general uprising of an energized people. Vo Nguyen Giap in his own theoretical contribution *People's War, People's Army* used a similar typology. The general offensive and general uprising represented a chance to combine political and military elements of Liberation Front and DRV forces; it was not an either/or proposition. Rather, a central question in Vietnamese strategy would always be to identify the moment when it was propitious to move to the higher level of war. General Giap would not have resisted a review of strategy on that issue.

There was an additional issue of alliance diplomacy in Hanoi's decision that remains shrouded in the mists of history. Although the DRV had been very successful in playing off its Chinese and Russian allies against each other, the game was getting harder all the time. The Sino-Soviet conflict had sharpened, putting more pressure on Hanoi to take sides, thereby threatening its aid from one country or the other. Also, it now appears that the relationship with Beijing had passed its peak in 1966. In that year the Chinese protested when a Soviet ship making for Haiphong was allegedly given preference over Chinese craft, and Beijing also made open and formal its refusal to provide aircraft to fight alongside the Vietnamese. Toward the end of the year China began to withdraw some of its troops from the DRV on the pretext that their mission had been accomplished. By 1967 it had to be apparent in Hanoi that only a limited period of time was left to move to a general counteroffensive that still had Chinese support. Le Duan and Le Duc Tho, who were identified with the pro-Chinese faction in Hanoi, had to be even more conscious of this aspect of the strategic problem.

Actually, in terms of the mysteries residing in Hanoi's decision of 1967, any alleged differences between Generals Thanh and Giap pale beside the Chinese question. After all, the Chinese had been advocating protracted warfare most vociferously—it was Mao Zedong's original concept—and they could be expected to look dimly on a Hanoi decision to pass to an attempt at general uprising. As stalwarts of the alliance with Beijing, Le Duan and Le Duc Tho were moving against their own political interests in deciding for Tet.

This leads back to General Giap's position in the strategy debate. Not only had Vo Nguyen Giap been considered pro-Soviet from an early date, but also the Americans had taken steps to freeze him into that political stance. One of the Saigon commandos the CIA had sent into the North in 1962 had been told to implicate Giap as a foreign agent, recruited in Moscow either by the Russians or the CIA itself. The commando was duly captured and re-tailed his story. Coincidental or not, the ascendancy of the Le Duan–Le Duc Tho committee had begun at about that time. In 1967 a decision to mount a general uprising that weakened the Chinese alliance would eclipse the power of the Chinese faction. It was in General Giap's interest to press for this strategy, not to mention that his theory of revolutionary warfare provided for such a stage of conflict. "For us, you know," Giap told journalist Stanley Karnow years later, "there is never a single strategy."

Typical accounts of Hanoi's decision for Tet assume Giap remained wholly committed to protracted war. The question is perhaps colored by the series of articles the general published in the fall of 1967, collected into the book *Big Victory, Great Task*. The Western press reporting on those articles—in *Newsweek*, the *New York Times*, *The Economist*, and elsewhere—took the line that Hanoi's Giap was making a paean for protracted warfare. Subsequently Giap's arguments have been construed that way. But there is both internal and external evidence to cast doubt on this version.

First, the internal. It is correct that *Big Victory, Great Task* extolls the value of protracted warfare; it was from those statements that the media derived their take on the articles and book. Part of Vo Nguyen Giap's aim in the series was to validate past practices, and previously guerrilla methods, protracted war among them, had been the staple of Viet Cong and VPA tactics. Giap's book is structured in five parts; almost all his references to protracted war occur in the earlier sections that describe the evolution of the Vietnam conflict. The phrase "protracted war" hardly appears in the prescriptive, final section of *Big Victory, Great Task*.

In addition, a number of the arguments Giap's book contains should be seen as suggestive of the Tet strategy of a go-for-broke offensive. General Giap postulates that the United States had been trying to confine Vietnam within a limited-war framework; though Giap does not actually say so, a counter would be to escalate the level of fighting. Giap does write extensively about artillery forces and other special troops not necessary in guerrilla warfare. *Big Victory, Great Task* contains numerous exhortations to coordinate political struggle, guerrilla and conventional operations. Giap further notes that revolutionary forces have constantly sought fighting methods capable of developing all their strength. Both of these features suggest change to come. In pregnant phrasing, General Giap writes that "The present time is the era of revolutionary storms."

What does appear in *Big Victory, Great Task* is a strong sense of forces in motion and necessary timing. Giap is aware of President Johnson's decision to send 55,000 more troops to Vietnam; this dates the writing to August 1967 or later. Also mentioned is the possibility the Americans might commit another 100,000 or 200,000 men, both figures Westmoreland and MACV had used as more desirable reinforcement levels. Giap shows an appreciation of the need to move before major changes in the balance of forces. Perceptively, Hanoi's general notes, "the present mobilization level has far exceeded initial U.S. forecasts and is at sharp variance with U.S. global strategy," and "the American imperialists are at a crossroad." Combined with Giap's intimation of revolutionary storms, there is a clear expression of a sense of opportunity here, plus a consciousness of near-term risk in the growth of American forces.

It is now generally accepted that Hanoi's decision for an offensive originated in 1965, was discussed by the Politburo in May 1967, and was confirmed by the thirteenth plenum of the Central Committee a month later. Hanoi's most authoritative statement on the matter is that presented to an international conference of former officials and scholars that met in June 1997 to consider the missed opportunities of the Vietnam War. Speaking before delegates who included Robert McNamara, former Washington officials and military men, and historians, Ambassador Nguyen Khac Huynh explained that Hanoi had laid down its basic objectives for the Tet offensive in April 1967 and that the People's Army had completed detailed plans by July. The main objective would be to win a major victory by attacking all the big southern towns and cities. According to Huynh, a focused battle along the border, such as at Khe Sanh, did not figure in the planning. Hanoi imagined three possible scenarios: a major success forcing the United States to accept the DRV's conditions to end the war; a moderate victory that would reduce hostilities against the North by forcing the enemy to concentrate upon South Vietnam; or a limited success, which could be positively dangerous if it triggered a more virulent U.S. reaction, expanding the war into Cambodia and Laos, or into the DRV itself.

The text of Lao Dong Party plenum Resolution 13, adopted in June 1967, alluded to the ambitious plans and has since been at the heart of many debates over whether Tet took the Americans by surprise. In any case, Giap's articles appeared in September 1967, not as an entry in an ongoing debate over whether there ought to be an offensive, but as an acquiescence in and justification for the policy already adopted. Giap knew what the decision was. If one insists on the old view that Giap's book represents advocacy for protracted war, it is then necessary to argue that the general was dissenting from established policy, which is not likely; or that he was exhorting a course with which he disagreed, also not very probable. The logic is straightforward only if Giap is seen as laying groundwork for a course with which he agrees.

Now, a word about other external evidence. As it transpired, Hanoi and the Liberation Front suffered enormous losses as a consequence of this decision. Hanoi's deliberations thus contain a tragic element. Had General Giap *opposed* the strategy of a major offensive, that fact would have been virtually impossible to suppress, and also would have been reflected in a resurgence of Giap's voice in Hanoi's military councils in the months after Tet. Neither at the time nor later is there any statement by Giap in the record that he disagreed with the Tet strategy, and the record is also devoid of others making such a claim in his behalf. General Giap's influence compared to that of such other officers as Van Tien Dung also did not increase; he remained a largely ceremonial figure.

In *Big Victory, Great Task*, Vo Nguyen Giap observes that American forces made up the core of those deployed against the NLF and the VPA and that heavy defeats for the Americans "will have a very great adverse effect on the puppet armed forces." Giap's book even contains passages detailing strengths and weaknesses of the 1st Cavalry Division, the U.S. Marines, and other combat units. At Dak To in the Central Highlands on November 6, an American infantry company of the 173rd Airborne Brigade captured a document that turned out to be a copy of the B-3 Front's directive for the conduct of a winter-spring offensive. The top task set by General Hoang Van Thai matched Giap's prescriptions: "To annihilate a major U.S. element in order . . . to destroy or disintegrate a large part of the puppet army."

My view is that the purpose of *Big Victory, Great Task* was to give all those People's Army political commissars background material to help them prepare the troops for what lay ahead. It all sounds very much like the recipe for an offensive, one before all those new American forces arrived; one, in fact, at Tet.

A final point to clinch this argument emerges from a cable to Washington sent from Paris in November 1968. The cable recounts the remarks of Hanoi's diplomatic mastermind Le Duc Tho to an informant at a private dinner at that time. "The decision to stage the Tet offensive," Tho told the informant, "was taken only after extensive debate in the Central Committee, with Giap favoring action."

Generals Giap and Thanh may have differed on the shape of an offensive (though they probably did not), but the execution was definitely Giap's. For one thing, Nguyen Chi Thanh was dead. In connection with the deliberations in Hanoi, General Thanh left his headquarters in Cambodia and flew from Phnom Penh to participate. In Hanoi, some say after too much revelry, Thanh suffered a heart attack. He expired in a military hospital early in July.

According to Le Duc Tho in 1968, the initial concept for the offensive had simply been to capture Hue, hold it, then declare the Liberation Front as a provisional government. The plans soon became much more ambitious, with attacks all around the country and a bid for a general uprising. To prepare for this major offensive involved everything from recruiting new spies to practicing troops in carrying out their activities in coordination with *bo dois* of many different units. Preliminaries included a series of battles along the borders of South Vietnam. First, in the fall of 1967, came a fight at Loc Ninh, near Saigon. Then there was Dak To in the Central Highlands. People's Army troops seemed to mass along the Demilitarized Zone as well, threatening Con Thien and Khe Sanh. The pattern would be strikingly similar to that at Dien Bien Phu, where the main action had been preceded by diversions in northern and central Laos, in central Vietnam, and in Cambodia. At Dien Bien Phu General Giap had unquestionably been in charge.

Vo Nguyen Giap knew that the preparations for an offensive on so grand a scale could not be carried out without the Saigonese and Americans detecting some of them. The trick was to give them something else to believe in. The border battles started this deception in a minor key, but threatening Khe Sanh perfected it. Khe Sanh remained the biggest, best-armed Allied combat base on the flank of The Trail. Hanoi had, in 1966, shown itself to be highly sensitive about the security of its Truong Son network. It was not much of a calculation for Giap to see that a People's Army move against Khe Sanh would appear very credible to the Americans. Moreover, Giap *needed* The Trail for his Tet offensive. Without the supplies he could stockpile from The Trail and the fresh *bo dois* he would push down it, there could not be any great attack. If General Giap mounted a deception at Khe Sanh, and it achieved any real success, that would only improve Hanoi's overall chances at Tet. To a considerable degree, therefore, the battle of Khe Sanh happened only because of the proximity of that place to The Trail. Thus over the final months of 1967 an important little byplay took place between the Vietnam People's Army, struggling to set up for the big offensive, and the Americans working, as always, to close off The Trail.

As Hanoi made up its mind, Washington continued the effort to emplace an air-ground barrier that would block The Trail. Giap's book had something to say about that, too: "No well-fortified barrier can avoid collapsing in the face of our people's strength." In building the barrier, General Giap believed, "U.S. troops would become more scattered and would be trapped in an inert and defensive situation." That very thing occurred at Khe Sanh, western terminus of the ground portion of the McNamara Line, where operations into Indian country became fewer and farther between as the People's Army encroached on the base. The marines sent an extra battalion to reinforce the place toward the end of 1967, and more troops would follow.

On Thursday, November 9, Washington's top-secret war wizards came directly to Khe Sanh's outlying strongpoints. General Alfred D. Starbird and his aides, including MACV scientists, visited Hill 881 South. With them went General Robert E. Cushman, commanding all marines in Vietnam. Starbird and Cushman supervised creation of the air barrier Muscle Shoals, supposed to start west of Khe Sanh and follow Route 9 to the Mekong valley. Marines on the hill, the northernmost point in Vietnam occupied by U.S. forces, saw the generals gesticulate, pointing at their maps and at places in Indian country. Starbird left Vietnam, but a group from the Defense Science Board followed him a couple of months later to evaluate the latest arrangements. Ironically, the scientists' airplane arrived over Saigon's Tan Son Nhut airport just as the VPA attacked it on the night of Tet. The barrier had not stopped the offensive. The plane was forced to divert and ended up landing in Thailand.

Another facet of Khe Sanh activity involved communications intelligence. A detachment of the marines' 1st Radio Battalion, the first in the area for more than two years, moved to Hill 881 South in November. These radiomen intercepted messages from People's Army units and *binh trams* along The Trail, and used special antennae to localize the transmitters. There were indications confirmed by the radiomen's reports to the National Security Agency, that Hanoi had begun movement of General Hoang Dan's 304th Division down The Trail. In December signals intelligence detected General Sung Lam's 320th Division following the same route. Dan's division trekked directly through Tchepone to the border southwest of Khe Sanh; Lam's marched to a position at the corner formed by Vietnam's border with Laos and the DMZ.

Road-watch teams and aerial observation by forward air controllers (FACs) picked up the same People's Army movements and detected a very large volume of supplies as well. There was more. A single battalion of the 308th Division started for the South in October 1967; the bulk followed in the first several months of 1968. The People's Army used the division's 38th Artillery to strengthen the forces ranged opposite Khe Sanh, 100 guns, mortars, and rocket launchers of the 68th Artillery. By mid-1968, when a sergeant of the 308th Division was captured southwest of Khe Sanh, the Americans had confirmation that the entire division had been involved.

Intelligence figures for infiltration do not show the huge numbers for the end of 1967 claimed later by some critics, but the estimate of 21,000 for the last three months still included important combat units. As the People's Army moved into the 1968 campaign the figures mushroomed, with almost 23,000 infiltrators projected in January alone. The destinations of infiltrators also showed Hanoi's strategy and the effects of continued combat. In 1967 Tchepone and the A Shau proved the destinations for about 15 percent of VPA traffic on The Trail, while the Mekong and Cambodian base areas, where the Liberation Front was strong, accounted for fewer than 10 percent. During 1968 the I Corps share of infiltrators grew to about a fifth of the total, but *more* than that were being sent to the Far South. Vietnamese sent to the Saigon region more than doubled through the period, and the reversed trend continued through 1969 and 1970.

The increases in infiltration were palpable, not only to the machine spies but also to the road-watch teams. Efforts to physically monitor Hanoi's traffic on The Trail were already in high gear in 1966. During the period October 1966 to February 1967, for example, road-watch teams were active along The Trail on 116 of 150 days. The teams manned eight stations and had very good coverage of some route segments, such as the Sihanouk Trail and the Ban Bac area. Tchepone was under periodic observation. By late 1967 there were fifteen active road-watch sites, but People's Army and Pathet Lao security had improved to the degree that coverage of Tchepone was no longer possible. There were still several road-watch teams on the routes to the Truong Son passes, however, especially the Mu Gia. That September ground teams reported 201 trucks on the move, exceptionally close to the 256 sighted by air reconnaissance; then sightings ballooned. In October air scouts reported 992 trucks, many en route from Ben Karai Pass toward Tchepone. Emphasis shifted to the Mu Gia–Tchepone route for the first part of November, and both routes were in heavy use through the end of the year. Air reports identified no fewer than 4,235 trucks in November 1967, and even the road watchers picked up 695, an unprecedented number.

The density of traffic brought more and more air strikes in an endless progression. On the parts of the Trail in the Tiger Hound operating zone, air controllers had a very busy time. The FACs directed strike aircraft credited with destroying 271 vehicles and damaging another 170 during the last three months of 1967. That was a tenfold increase over preceding months. The climax came in a thirty-six-hour period on January 17–18, 1968, started by a pair of FACs that took off from Da Nang at night, about 2:00 A.M., and used light-intensifying "Starlight Scopes" to survey Indian country. Some fifty miles southeast of Tchepone, near the site of a very successful previous attack (March 1966), the Ravens found a group of five trucks. They summoned a B-57 bomber, then eleven successive sets of fighters, *then* spotted a truck park near the points already struck, which received the attentions of fifteen more flights of aircraft before it was all over. The bomb damage assessed totaled thirteen trucks destroyed and more than 130 secondary explosions. The Ravens, call signs "Covey 642" and "Covey 673," turned for home and a solid "Well done!"

Another notable attack, this one directed by communications intelligence on a Vietnam People's Army headquarters in the Muong Nong–Co Roc sector, was carried out as a B-52 strike in late January. The target was believed to be a high-level VPA command, perhaps the "Khe Sanh Front," which American intelligence believed in but whose existence has never been confirmed by Hanoi (the VPA reports that it had a Route 9 Front in lower Laos). After some haggling between MACV and the air force, the strike was carried out as a morning Arc Light by thirty-six jet heavy bombers, followed by an evening reprise using nine more B-52s. That added up to more than 1,000 tons of munitions. Westmoreland reported that Vo Nguyen Giap may have been in the headquarters. That was not true. Hanoi's commander at Khe Sanh was General Tran Qui Hai, formerly Van Tien Dung's assistant on the VPA General Staff.

The sortie numbers describe the awesome fury of this aerial assault on The Trail: 2,300 flights during October; 3,700 in November; 5,800 the next month; and more than 7,200 in January 1968, without even counting navy and marine air activities, for which figures are not yet available.

Still, for every attack made, for each truck or troop column struck by the marauding knights of the air, more columns and convoys got through. The People's Army effort also became more robust than ever. One *bo doi*, captured in the Far South a couple of months later, reported having been carried aboard helicopters for one leg of his trek. There were more specialized units as well, such as the 2d Battalion of the 426th Sapper Regiment, which marched down The Trail to positions close to Da Nang, which Hanoi had plans to attack at Tet. Indeed, Hanoi's great decision of 1967 had moved the Vietnam conflict past a fork in the road from which there would be no turning back.

CHAPTER 10

Fire in the Night
1968

The words "Dien Bien Phu" roll off the tongue easily, melodiously, with a grace that belies the horror of that place, the misery and suffering that occurred there. There was heroism at Dien Bien Phu, and drama in that the battle marked the passing of the French era in Indochina. The drama, no less than the lyrical quality of the words, led musicians Ritchie Havens and Eric Clapton to use Dien Bien Phu and its stark image in songs of the 1970s and 1980s. It was Lyndon Johnson whose Texas twang made the least mellifluous use of these words: listening to his generals explain how they were going to thrash Hanoi at Khe Sanh, LBJ finally said with a rasp, "I don't want any damn Dinbinphoo!"

Battle at Dien Bien Phu had been decisive; in a neat sort of way that battle clearly separated the time the French were prepared to fight the Vietnamese from that when they could fight no more. What happened in 1968 would be different. There was nothing neat about Vietnam that year, not at Khe Sanh, not at Saigon, or Pleiku, or any of the other places scarred by the vicious combats of what became known as the Tet Offensive.

Hanoi's idea was to attack everywhere, all over South Vietnam, all at the same time. Such an extensive array of preparations was necessary for this offensive that it was inevitable American or ARVN intelligence would discover some of them. The genius in Hanoi's plan was to give the Americans an interpretation *they* would believe in for what the People's Army was up to. Americans believed in Dien Bien Phu. The Joint Chiefs of Staff warned of an "aerial Dien Bien Phu" if they were not allowed to do certain things with the bombing. Policymakers such as Walt Rostow speculated about the possibilities of inflicting a Dien Bien Phu on Hanoi. Press briefers in Saigon constantly harked back to that key battle of 1954 in extolling the results of this or another battle or program. There were more references to Dien Bien Phu whenever Americans tried to explain why their war was not going to be like that of the French. Officers and grunts in the field remembered Dien Bien Phu when they encountered terrain of a certain kind, as had the Green Berets under siege at Duc Co in 1965. Dien Bien Phu was plausible.

An attempt by Hanoi to trigger a decisive battle, in the pattern of Dien Bien Phu, could be expected.

Not least of those who believed in Dien Bien Phu was the American commander in Vietnam. General William C. Westmoreland had been arguing that his strategy had pushed the enemy past a "crossover point" at which People's Army and Viet Cong losses exceeded their replacement ability. That meant the VPA and the Liberation Front either had to fight on from a position of diminishing strength or make a go-for-broke bid to regain the upper hand. To seek a decisive battle was a logical gambit. Westmoreland, who also knew Nguyen Chi Thanh's supposed preference for large-scale operations, figured this strategy fit that mold. A Dien Bien Phu was plausible indeed. Moreover, Westy had been secretary to the General Staff of the U.S. Army at the time of the real Dien Bien Phu.Thus he had had an intimate vantage point from which to observe that decisive battle and its impact on such American generals as Matthew B. Ridgway and James W. Gavin.

Not only was there a strategic rationale for a Dien Bien Phu, there also was a venue: Khe Sanh. General Westmoreland had been specifically worried about a Dien Bien Phu in the context of Khe Sanh since at least 1966, when he had the U.S. Marine commander in I Corps contrast the earlier French battle with the situation at Khe Sanh. Americans who went to Khe Sanh often thought of the Dien Bien Phu comparison right away, for the lay of the land was the same, with an upland plateau, in this case, surrounded by high hills and distant mountains. Two important histories of Dien Bien Phu, the books by Bernard B. Fall and Jules Roy, were just current at the time, and were widely read by Americans in Vietnam, including Westmoreland, Khe Sanh commanders and marines, and the journalists who covered the battle. Hanoi could hardly miss the connection Americans so frequently made between Dien Bien Phu and Khe Sanh. A deception built on American belief in a Dien Bien Phu became both plausible and easy to orchestrate.

Khe Sanh would never have happened if that base had not been so close to The Trail. As the crow flies, barely twenty-five miles separated Americans at Khe Sanh from People's Army soldiers at Tchepone. The same factors that made Khe Sanh desirable as a place from which to implant sensors for the McNamara Line also made it a prime target for any VPA attempt to clear the flanks of The Trail. In his *Big Victory, Great Task*, General Giap had expressed an interest in wiping out a large contingent of Americans, and Khe Sanh seemed an excellent place to do it. Proximity to The Trail meant that Giap could switch from deception to battle array at will. Major VPA formations assumed positions near Khe Sanh and gave teeth to the notion that Hanoi sought battle. Mesmerized by the *bo dois* opposite, MACV focused more and more on the immediate threat to Khe Sanh and less on the overall contours of Giap's activities. The U.S. Marines had their gaze fixed on Khe Sanh by mid-December 1967, when they began a series of reinforcements of the base; by late January Khe Sanh's garrison comprised all three battalions of the 26th Marines; the 1st Battalion, 9th Marines; the troops of SOG's Forward Operating Base 3, equivalent to a rifle battalion; and the ARVN 37th Ranger Battalion.

"Pentagon East" proved little behind the marine commanders, if at all, in its belief that Hanoi aimed its offensive at Khe Sanh. When intelligence discovered specific VPA or NLF plans for other places, MACV estimated Hanoi would do Khe Sanh plus these things, never that the People's Army would do those things and not Khe Sanh.

There was yet another reason why William Westmoreland believed in the threat to Khe Sanh: he *wanted* to fight a battle along the border. Westy got his opportunity to make the case for a frontier fight in early December, when General Wheeler warned that some in Washington favored pulling back from the border and concentrating in the coastal plain, closer to the villages, the real focus of the pacification war. General Westmoreland replied on December 11. His dispatch argued that fighting near the border denied the enemy maneuvering room, prevented the People's Army and the Viet Cong from submerging in the population, and enabled MACV to make the best use of its firepower and reserves, which could grind down the adversary in the plains, then quickly shift forward when major battle impended.

What Westy did not mention in this message, MAC 11956, sent to Bus Wheeler on an "eyes only" basis, was his desire to mount an invasion of Laos. That depended entirely on preserving Khe Sanh as a jumping-off position. At Saigon on December 9, while mulling over what to tell Washington regarding border strategy, Westy had in fact set MACV staff specifically to review plans for operations York and El Paso, the Laotian invasion scheme. Supply difficulties forced the general to scale back the endeavor to something very similar to the previous High Port concept, a division-size thrust to Tchepone using U.S. troops. There was no possibility at all of carrying out the original El Paso, which had provided for two U.S. divisions plus one of ARVN's.

The El Paso plan had been developed by General Bruce Palmer, deputy commander of U.S. Army forces in Vietnam, together with senior planner Colonel John Collins. Palmer recounts that in 1966 and 1967 Westmoreland felt he lacked sufficient forces, both combat and logistics, to sustain the major cross-border offensive, but "when in 1968 there were forces available, the political climate at home would not permit such a move." In fact, when Westmoreland cabled Washington with a summary of the El Paso concept on January 8, 1968, the White House reaction proved so immediate and negative that Westy had to send a second message, explaining that his idea was merely a contingency plan. It was, declared General Westmoreland, a plan to "take advantage of a possible change in national policy" for an operation "that could be conducted no sooner than the end of the northwest monsoon in the late fall or early [w]inter of this year."

Despite Washington denials, however, it remained possible that MACV might be able to get permission for an invasion as exploitation or "hot pursuit" of an enemy defeated at Khe Sanh. Thus General Westmoreland wanted a fight at Khe Sanh both to smash the People's Army using American firepower in the sparsely populated borderlands, and as another gambit in his search for authority to cut The Trail. Khe Sanh might happen despite Hanoi's intentions rather than because of them.

One man who, in a very studied way, tried to reject the Dien Bien Phu analogy was the commander at Khe Sanh, U.S. Marine colonel David E. Lownds. As reporters flocked there in ever greater numbers, Lownds professed not to be reading the books that were all around him, or thinking the thoughts on everyone's mind. Of course, just looking up from the combat base toward the hills on every side, the comparison was plain to see, but Lownds nevertheless insisted there was none to be made. That was tough. Marine tough. And hard as the New England winters in which he had been reared. Colonel Lownds figured morale at Khe Sanh required that he assume a certain rhetorical posture, and he stuck to it. Later some marines swore they had seen copies of books about Dien Bien Phu in the colonel's quarters, but in public, marines hung together.

Colonel Lownds had been in command of the 26th Marine Regiment, and the combat base, since August 1967, when Khe Sanh remained a relatively quiet outpost on the border. Lownds had a good feeling for its role in MACV strategy. He had earned a Bronze Star in the 1965 American intervention in the Dominican Republic and other decorations from Korea and World War II, when he fought at Kwajalein, Saipan, and Iwo Jima. A reservist from Holyoke, Massachusetts, Lownds was recalled for Korea and then became a regular officer. Khe Sanh would be on his first Vietnam tour; in fact, it was his first assignment.

The sense of impending battle remained strong through the fall and winter of 1967. The Green Berets at Lang Vei strengthened their defenses, adding an underground command bunker and more internal subdivisions at the camp. For his part, Colonel Singlaub of the Studies and Observation Group ordered FOB-3 to relocate from an outlying position. The Forward Operating Base built a new compound right outside the wire of the marine post. Like Special Forces, FOB-3 constructed underground bunkers, complete with shower heads that must have been the envy of any marines who knew about them. Later Singlaub would not understand why marines never dug in as deeply as his own SOG troops. The reason was the marines lacked the heavy wood beams and other construction materials necessary for that kind of fortification and could not divert scarce air transport to bring in those materials—an example of just how limited Khe Sanh actually was as a platform from which to invade Laos. What the marines did do was bring up more troops.

Signs of the People's Army were plentiful. A team from the Marines' 3d Reconnaissance Battalion, patrolling past Hill 689 in Indian country, stepped off the path only to be passed by a big column of *bo dois* using the same track. Captain Richard Camp, in the field with his Lima Company of the 3d Battalion, 26th Marines, encountered not one but several enemy bivouacks, each big enough for a battalion, all recently occupied.

On January 2, in an incident pregnant with meaning for combat troops, marines on the Khe Sanh perimeter fired at faces in the rain at night, and the next morning found the bodies of several enemies who had been scouting out the defenses. Although Captain Harper Bohr, the intelligence officer for the 26th Marines, does not remember such a finding, the authors of a Marine Corps historical monograph on Khe Sanh record that one of the VPA bodies was that of a regimental commander. Bohr, and others, too, thought another of the dead might have been Chinese. All had been wearing American utility uniforms.

Expecting battle at Khe Sanh, General Westmoreland sent more troops to I Corps, deliberately accepting risks elsewhere. He also prepared one of those SLAM operations, this to be named Niagara, for its cascade of munitions onto the heads of a hapless enemy. Another key preparation, drawn directly from the McNamara Line technology, was to divert sensor fields to place them in the immediate vicinity of the combat base. People's Army troop movements set off the sensors, enabling Marine artillery and Niagara air strikes to counter several possible attacks. Target information officer Captain Mirza Munir Baig, previously coordinator of clandestine intelligence collection for marines along the DMZ, set up a miniature version of what Task Force Alpha had at Nakhon Phanom. Colonel Lownds made preparations of his own, such as an actual march out Route 9 to the border, furnishing data used to interpret the sensor readings. At first Baig had trouble turning readings into usable targets, but as the Khe Sanh siege wore on, he became quite adept, to the point that a couple of the VPA troop movements indicated by sensors could be entirely broken up by guns and planes.

General Tran Qui Hai opened the engagement on January 21, the day after American helicopters began sowing sensor strings around Khe Sanh. A marine patrol from one outpost, Hill 881 South, had stumbled into *bo dois* a few days before. Subsequently General Hai ordered bombardment of Khe Sanh with artillery from across the Lao border. This resulted in a fire at the combat base's main ammunition dump that ignited a substantial portion of the marines' stockpiled shells. Under cover of the confusion, VPA troops began assaulting Hill 861 as well as Khe Sanh village. The village fell, but marines successfully held their outposts, not just this night but also throughout the siege.

The encounter also brought to an end the strange existence of the Royal Laotian Army enclave at Ban Houei Sane. For years the Lao had continued their truce with the People's Army. It would be too much to say that Bataillon Volontaire (BV) 33 was a thorn in the side of the VPA, but the Lao presence was an inconvenience, if only because it invited other, more aggressive actions against The Trail. In early 1967, for example, a project to move U.S. Army heavy artillery (175-mm guns) forward to Khe Sanh had been intended partly to enable the United States to fire in support of Ban Houei Sane. That fall, ARVN colonel Ho Tieu of the Strategic Technical Directorate planned a visit to Laos to select points around BV-33 where he could send ARVN commandos. Ho Tieu wanted to deal strictly with the Lao military, who recognized this as a political question and insisted on involving Souvanna Phouma. As a Laotian officer told the CIA, "any agreement with the South Vietnamese to permit their participation in military operations in Laos would have the effect of legalizing the North Vietnamese military presences."

In mounting a credible threat against Khe Sanh, General Hai of the People's Army decided it was necessary to clear out the Ban Houei Sane enclave. On the night of January 23–24, 1968, VPA guns fired a barrage of about 150 shells (100 mm or larger) and followed up with an attack by three battalions backed by seven tanks. Lieutenant Colonel Soulang of BV-33 had no weapons to fight tanks and was outgunned anyway by the attackers. A Raven FAC on station that night, Captain Charles Rushforth, tried to send in B-57 bombers to help Soulang but was unable to tell friendly from enemy troops on the ground. By morning Ban Houei Sane had fallen. The People's Army 24th Regiment took at least 48 Lao prisoners who were sent to a camp near Muong Phine, while Soulang, with 519 soldiers and 2,270 civilians, crossed the border into Vietnam and took refuge with the Americans at Lang Vei. The Green Berets had the Laotians camp a little bit away from the Special Forces, at Lang Vei village.

The battle marked the first time during the war that the People's Army used tanks in combat. Though U.S. planes found tread marks in the ground the next day, and Soulang told Americans of the VPA armor, only the Green Berets at Lang Vei took him seriously enough to ask for antitank weapons to be sent to them. Up the chain of command the reports were not believed.

As the day of the lunar new year, Tet, approached, the Khe Sanh area fell silent. In contrast, Americans and Saigon officials found more and more hints that the Liberation Front or People's Army intended to attack other places. Near Nha Trang radio intelligence discovered enemy troops on the move. The same was true at Qui Nhon. At Pleiku the police capture of a Viet Cong safe house yielded tape recordings that were to have been played on the local radio station once captured. The recordings clearly referred to a general uprising.

The incoming intelligence had to be interpreted in the light of the evident threat to Khe Sanh. MACV did just that. On January 15 General Westmoreland told Washington he expected a big enemy attack before Tet—a 60 percent probability. When the shelling started at Khe Sanh, with coincident attacks on the village and Hill 861, Westmoreland reported the expected offensive had begun, and described it as working up to a full-scale attack on Khe Sanh by means of actions in Quang Tri and Thua Thien Provinces, then a "countrywide show of strength just prior to Tet, with Khe Sanh being the main event." As evidence appeared of threats to more places, Westmoreland added them to his list, but the contours of Hanoi's actions were still viewed as Khe Sanh plus whatever was being reported. On January 22, in an "eyes only" cable, Westy made explicit his belief in an enemy bid for decisive battle: "I believe the enemy sees a similarity between our base at Khe Sanh and Dien Bien Phu and hopes, by following a pattern of activity similar to that used against the French, to gain similar military and political ends."

In actuality, however, as Tet drew near, the *bo dois* around Khe Sanh hunkered down. Their attack on Ban Houei Sane was the last ground assault until after Tet. The Americans and ARVN waited breathlessly for something that did not happen. On January 27 ARVN sent Khe Sanh its last reinforcement, the 37th Ranger Battalion, while Westy induced South Vietnamese president Nguyen Van Thieu to cancel the Tet cease-fire in the I Corps area (and to shorten it elsewhere). But on Tet, at Khe Sanh, only a few mortar rounds fell on the combat base. The trouble was in the rest of South Vietnam.

At Khe Sanh the role of The Trail was direct, incontrovertible. Through the rest of Vietnam, though less visibly, The Trail still made possible a series of coordinated attacks unlike anything seen before in the Vietnam War. The attacks were on a truly massive scale, with the Liberation Front and the People's Army committing 67,000 to 84,000 troops; the maximum number of *bo dois* estimated at Khe Sanh was no more than 40,000 and the actual may have been closer to 25,000. There were attacks on all major cities, including Hue, Da Nang, and Saigon—in fact, on 166 cities and towns in all, on 39 of 44 provincial capitals, 71 district seats, every ARVN corps headquarters, several major air bases, and the military high command headquarters, several major air bases, and the military high command headquarters. With such a breadth of assaults there could be no doubt Hanoi and the NLF intended a major offensive. Given the timing of the lunar new year, the action became known as the Tet Offensive.

Making sure everything ran smoothly for a military operation this big proved too much for Hanoi and the NLF, who had previously conducted only a handful of efforts involving more than a single formation. At Tet it would be a matter of whole fronts acting in an integrated fashion. The scale of the offensive almost guaranteed there would be problems. In the event, the Tet forces attacked at a number of places a day too soon. These included Nha Trang, the very first attack recorded, Pleiku, Kontum, Qui Nhon, and Da Nang. All the premature attacks occurred in the regions of Interzone 5 or the B-3 Front. Some believe that Hanoi ordered a twenty-four-hour acceleration but that the order did not reach certain commands. Historian Ngo Vinh Long, on the basis of postwar Vietnamese sources, argues that the premature attacks were conducted by forces using an old calendar when Hanoi and the NLF were converting to a new one.*

Regardless of the reason for the fact that some forces attacked sooner, it had the effect of tipping the hand of the offensive. Most likely based on radio intelligence of VPA or NLF troops moving into attack position, MACV ordered an alert on January 30. The Seventh Air Force called a Condition

---

*At the June 1997 conference on missed opportunities in the Vietnam War, Vietnamese officers at a luncheon among military figures on both sides (plus this historian) confirmed that a calendar change lay behind their problems of timing at Tet.

Red state of readiness for its ground security teams at 5:32 P.M. that day. American troops were supposed to take special precautions, to secure their command posts, to cancel the scheduled Tet cease-fire. General Westmoreland reports he got on the telephone with each of his senior subordinates to pass the word. However, MACV does not appear to have had enough assurance of its information to inform ARVN and get Saigon forces on alert, too, and dispatches sent to Washington that day also betray a lack of confidence in the indications of an attack.

Nothing prepared the grunts, American of ARVN, for the scope of Tet; any claim that surprise was avoided can apply only to individual tactical situations, such as that at Pleiku. The proof was in the pudding. On the night of January 31, *even after the warning given by the enemy's premature attacks*, it was business as usual at "Pentagon East," MACV headquarters. A survey of the locations of key American officers and officials the night of Tet puts this point beyond doubt.

General Westmoreland was at home on Tran Huy Cap Street. There was shooting near enough to hear. Westy stayed put and near the phone to get the latest reports.

General Creighton W. Abrams, deputy MACV commander, was at his home down the street from Pentagon East. Abrams had retired for the night. Aides tried to avoid disturbing "Abe" because they knew he was going to need all the sleep he could get.

General Walter T. Kerwin, MACV chief of staff, was also at home that night. "Dutch" Kerwin shared a house in Saigon with SOG chief Colonel John Singlaub. A bullet or shell fragment came through Singlaub's window. Both officers, in their underwear, ran out of their upstairs bedrooms and met in the hall. They armed themselves and dressed. Singlaub's driver was gone for the night but left the car behind, and the SOG commander managed to drive himself to headquarters. Dutch Kerwin waited until morning, then was held up returning to MACV by an ambush on the road.

The MACV operations chief was marine major general John Chaisson, who had just returned to Saigon from home leave in Maine. Chaisson was awakened by shooting outside his window. He, too, was at home.

Major General Phillip B. Davidson was chief of the Combined Intelligence Center Vietnam, MACV's integrated intelligence operation with ARVN, as well as its J-2 intelligence branch. Davidson prepared to defend his house with orderlies and housemates. Colonel Daniel O. Graham, Davidson's estimates chief, was at one of the Bachelor Officers' Quarters facilities in Saigon, and was rousted from his bunk to form one of an ad hoc unit of field-grade officers to defend their area.

It was the same all over the American high command. In I Corps the top U.S. Marine commander was Lieutenant General Robert E. Cushman. He was in quarters at Da Nang. General William W. Momyer of the Seventh Air Force was at home, too. So was MACV pacification chief Robert W. Komer, and Ambassador Ellsworth Bunker, who had to be returned to the U.S. embassy the next day in an armored car with a heavily protected convoy.

As for the Vietnamese, President Thieu was with his wife's family in My Tho in the Mekong delta. Vice President Nguyen Cao Ky was at home within the ARVN command complex at Tan Son Nhut airbase. The chief of the ARVN Joint General Staff (JGS), General Cao Van Vien, was at home in Cholon, Saigon's twin city. Vien could not get across the city to the JGS until after dawn.

Who ever heard of a command headquarters, except one taken by surprise, that goes to sleep the night of a big attack?

One of the most spectacular actions at Tet was the assault on the U.S. embassy in downtown Saigon by a small group of Viet Cong sappers. That commando action amazed America and usually receives the most attention in accounts of Tet. But what happened at Tan Son Nhut, besides a good illustration of the importance of The Trail to Tet, was far more potentially damaging to the South Vietnamese and the American war effort.

In many ways Tan Son Nhut was a nerve center of the war, responsible for key functions of command and intelligence. Westmoreland's headquarters was here, as was the command of the U.S. Seventh Air Force, the South Vietnamese Joint General Staff, and Saigon's air force. In addition, a number of senior generals lived in an area on Tan Son Nhut or nearby. Air Marshal Ky and General Abrams headed the list, but there were others. The air base itself played host to reconnaissance aircraft, electronic planes, and transports that daily moved the pallets that made U.S. military activities in Vietnam possible. Among planes at the base were RF-4 and RF-101 photo planes; C-130 and C-123 transports, both U.S. and VNAF; rescue helicopters; and electronic warfare planes. Photo labs and technicians, interpretation experts, mapmakers, all were quartered at Tan Son Nhut. The Combined Intelligence Center Vietnam was also located on the base. A loss to any or all of these capabilities would trigger a real disaster.

The Liberation Front forces intended a serious battle in the Saigon area and prepared a strong attack against Tan Son Nhut. It was made the target of several subregions of the guerrilla forces. Under the supervision of General Hoang Minh Thai from the North, COSVN delegated General Tran Van Tra to manage operations, with General Tran Do in direct command. Tran Do made Tan Son Nhut airbase the objective of different forces. From the west came the so-called Vanguard Group 2 under Colonel Nguyen Van Nho. From the north a regular and a guerrilla battalion were each supposed to hit the edge of Tan Son Nhut, while from the northeast, Vanguard Group 1 was to approach from the direction of the Saigon River. Both the Vanguard units had the mission of striking the area of Tan Son Nhut that held the MACV and JGS headquarters, the South Vietnamese generals' billets, the ARVN Armed Forces Language School, and other facilities.

Lieutenant Bruce E. Jones was a young officer on duty with the special intelligence staff that had formed to monitor the Khe Sanh region for MACV. Jones had the overnight duty for the night of Tet. Senior officers scoffed when Jones expressed misgivings about security that night, but the reassurances were wrong. When the lieutenant went to a local restaurant for dinner, the skittishness and fears of the Vietnamese all but made it obvious to Jones that an attack was coming. His own ARVN counterpart at the Combined Intelligence Center believed there would be an attack on cities, Jones writes, including on Saigon. On Tet it came. At Tan Son Nhut. Only four guards were on duty outside MACV headquarters. Lieutenant Jones grabbed an M-16 rifle for a desperate defense of Pentagon East.

Colonel Nho's Vanguard came the closest to the American–South Vietnamese nerve center. Nho was an old revolutionary from Tan An, in the Mekong delta, who had joined the anti-French resistance as early as 1940. He remained fearless. Nho would put his lead battalion right up against the Tan Son Nhut perimeter fence at Gate 51. They would wait until someone entered, then charge. For the perilous job of decoy the Viet Cong found a taxicab. *Bo doi* Nguyen Tan Mieng volunteered to drive up to Gate 51 and pretend to be making a routine delivery. As the gate opened, a busful of sappers would speed up behind and the assault troops pile out to overwhelm the guards. Colonel Nho's plan almost worked.

This threat amounted to roughly 1,200 *bo dois*. About half the soldiers belonged to the NLF 267th Battalion; a quarter were People's Army men reassigned to the Liberation Front, what U.S. intelligence called VPA "fillers." Colonel Nho had another 300 men in his 269th Battalion, and there were 420 more in the NLF D16 Battalion, believed to consist mostly of fillers. The sapper unit, entirely People's Army, provided another small company. The Vanguard also had support from mortars of the 63d Artillery Battalion. Colonel Nho's strike units were accompanied, according to Vietnamese sources, by a handful of pilots and a small unit of aircraft mechanics to take advantage of any planes that could be captured at Tan Son Nhut.

Except for Colonel Nguyen Van Nho himself, and a few others, all the senior commanders involved, not to mention all those VPA fillers, had come down The Trail.

The U.S. Air Force had a regular base security detachment at Tan Son Nhut; ground attack was always considered possible. As recently as the night of January 27 the base had conducted a perimeter defense maneuver based on the assumption that the Viet Cong were attacking Gate 51. The exercise had been held at twenty-five minutes past midnight. Ironically, it had been called "Tet." On the night of the real Tet, the air force's 377th Security Police Squadron was the only unit at Tan Son Nhut in a full-alert posture.

At about 3:20 A.M. an ARVN general officer's car drove up to Gate 51 and sought entrance to the generals' compound. That was when the Viet Cong bus raced up behind, stopped, and disgorged a bunch of armed men. Some began to shoot, while others ran for the barrier. Colonel Nho's forces from across the road helped out with mortar shelling and throwing grenades. The NLF 267th Battalion came right behind the sappers.

The 051 Bunker was the main defensive position near the gate. It suffered a direct hit from one of a dozen mortars the Vanguard force had put in the Vinatexco textile plant across the way. Fourteen minutes after the start of the attack, the 051 Bunker reported the perimeter fence beyond it being breached.

Joe Urgo was one of the ground security men in the Tan Son Nhut forces. Several times he had stood duty in the 051 Bunker, and that night four of his friends were in it. Urgo was among the troops the security squadron formed into eight squad-sized (13-man) reaction teams. A reserve of 262 airmen were on call in the barracks, while other units at Tan Son Nhut contributed three 30-man intermediate reserve platoons to the defenses. A total of 457 airmen were on post all over Tan Son Nhut at the time of the attack. Urgo's security team reinforced the perimeter behind 051, but it was already too late. At 4:20 A.M. Tan Son Nhut reported that parts of its western perimeter had been overrun.

In fact the air base defenders were plenty lucky that night, for bad as it was, Colonel Nho's attack was only half the planned NLF effort. The other prong of the attack failed to make contact. That assault, coming from the north, miscarried when the E268 Regiment was hit by rockets as it approached the air base. Captain Huong Van Ba, who had infiltrated down The Trail several years before, recalled that the unit had orders to wait for a rear echelon, but the reinforcement never arrived. Ngo Vinh Long records that the change in timing for the Tet offensive caught rear-echelon forces a night's march farther away from Saigon than planned. American and ARVN reaction forces rapidly blocked routes into the city, making their arrival impossible. In any case, Captain Ba's regiment fought on for three days, then withdrew from the Saigon area with heavy casualties.

The lead element of the north-side attack, meanwhile, was again a sapper unit, and it had gone ahead to make an assault at Gate 4. At about 7 A.M. the attack penetrated the gate, but bogged down in the building of the Armed Forces Language School, and after a couple of hours some ARVN paratroopers with a few M-41 tanks arrived and sealed off the NLF attackers.

Crisis continued around Gate 51, where Colonel Nho's force got almost 700 yards inside the perimeter. At Gate 10, an inside barrier, the 267th Battalion came upon the entrance to MACV headquarters. A jeep of security airmen drove up just as the first guerrillas arrived, and their fire pinned down the Liberation Front long enough for guards to slam the gate shut and assume defensive positions. Lieutenant Jones and MACV staffers, armed as best they could, joined the defenders and kept the guerrillas in check.

Other NLF troops maneuvered to outflank the defenses, finally making a move toward the JGS complex. At about 5:00 A.M. the Vietnamese base commander ordered three tanks to counterattack in the Bunker 051 area. Inside fifteen minutes, two of the M-41s were destroyed by rocket-propelled grenades. The last tank retreated.

Luck was also with the Tan Son Nhut defenders in that Colonel Nho's follow-on forces failed to arrive. The NLF 269th Battalion stumbled into a firefight before it reached the base perimeter, ending up stymied by Saigon's 53d Regional Force company, one of the times a militia unit made a real difference. The D16 Battalion also failed to reach the forward positions of the assault troops.

At 6:30 A.M. help for Tan Son Nhut arrived in the form of the armored cavalry troop of the U.S. 25th Division from Cu Chi. Two companies of the ARVN 8th Airborne Battalion also played a key role in stopping the attack.

When General Cao Van Vien arrived at his office he telephoned countermanding orders that stopped the movement of two South Vietnamese marine battalions that were being sent to other sectors. The marines were used to clear out Tan Son Nhut. South Vietnam's chief of airborne troops then considered it a point of honor that his command clear out the last pockets of resistance, so that a lot more paratroopers would be committed at Tan Son Nhut as well. Gunship helicopters flown by Americans, plus flareships of the VNAF 33d Wing, also proved crucial in breaking up Liberation Front movements.

Counterattacking troops went after the 051 Bunker shortly after noon; at 5:00 P.M. Tan Son Nhut was declared secure. Colonel Nho's forces had suffered more than 400 dead that were counted, with total losses by American estimates at more than 600. The remnants fled to the countryside.

Unlike some of the other Tet battles in the Saigon-Cholon area, which went on for days, the fight at Tan Son Nhut ended pretty quickly. But the result could easily have gone the other way, and the outcome had not been cheap for the Allies. The U.S. Air Force had had 13 of its planes damaged, the VNAF 10 (some of the latter were hit at other bases, however). American casualties were 23 killed and 86 wounded, while South Vietnamese losses added another 32 killed and 89 wounded soldiers and airmen. A year later an air force magazine printed as a centerfold a painting of the 051 Bunker from behind. To Joe Urgo it brought back all the frustrations and senselessness of Vietnam, and of that night in particular. Soon after his discharge, Urgo joined Vietnam Veterans Against the War.

Hanoi and the Liberation Front incurred big losses at Tet, but their achievements should not be minimized either. In the matter of airfields, for example, Bien Hoa and Da Nang were hit in addition to Tan Son Nhut. And although those targets were separated by more than 400 miles, all the attacks began within thirty minutes of each other. The seven planes that were destroyed and fifty-five damaged in these attacks would be missed by the Allied troops fighting at Tet.

In general, perhaps because they had survived the blow, the Allies were inclined to exaggerate the degree of their success during Tet. General Nguyen Van Thieu set the tone himself. One day ARVN officers informed Saigon's president that they had killed the VPA's General Tran Do. Thieu, who had been a Viet Minh himself in the early days of the Vietnamese revolution, knew Tran Do and came to view the body. Afterward Thieu told Westmoreland that they had indeed killed General Tran Do. That news would have surprised Tran Do's *bo dois*, who were maneuvering under his orders at that very moment. Just as Tran Do lived to fight another day, so the Liberation Front and the People's Army survived their battles at Tet, not only at Saigon but elsewhere.

One of the officers in the vanguard groups that attacked Tan Son Nhut was Nguyen Van Nang, who had come South so long before, in the early days of The Trail, with the named Phuong Nam infiltration group. Tran Van Tra had been one of Nang's instructors in the guerrilla warfare course he took just prior to his trek. Now, with The Trail, both of them were among the Nambo forces, the ones in the Far South fighting for Saigon. The Trail, too, made the difference in the losses suffered in Saigon at Tet. Nang, who led a two-battalion group against Saigon's 6th Precinct and also suffered losses, reported that about a week afterward their subregion command received a thousand replacements from the North, plus another hundred from local forces in Duc Hoa district.

In some places, however, even The Trail proved unequal to the demands of the ambitious offensive. This was the case at Hue, the place (other than Saigon) that had the most sustained fighting. In Thua Thien and Quang Tri Provinces the Liberation Front's guerrilla forces were relatively weak, both because of successful U.S. Marine programs such as the Combined Action Platoons, and because of the greater emphasis on conventional warfare in the I Corps area adjacent to the DMZ. Documents captured in the summer of 1967 had pointed up this guerrilla weakness and speculated that the American and ARVN focus on intercepting traffic from the North was the reason why they did not try to destroy the understrength guerrilla units. In any case, when orders for Tet came down, officers of the local command, the Military Region Tri-Thien-Hue (MRTTH), were afraid they could not carry out the mission.

General Tran Van Quang, who was the regional commander, described the doubts the Party committee had had about the Tet order. Quang had been a militia specialist in the People's Army even before he became a guerrilla commander, and knew the difficulties of surfacing scattered forces to make a large-scale attack on ARVN and American regulars. After considering matters, the Tri Thien committee asked Hanoi for reinforcements and a postponement—by May or June they felt they could make a well-prepared attack on Hue. The additional troops requested amounted to the better part of a division, two infantry regiments, two artillery battalions, and an antiaircraft battalion, as well as 400 tons of ammunition. These were substantial demands, evidently carried to Hanoi by the region's top political cadre, Le Chuong, who made a trip *up* The Trail to settle matters with the General Staff and other Hanoi authorities. Hanoi radioed MRTTH to hold on, that Le Chuong would bring back new decisions. When the political cadre returned, there was a showdown at the cave in the Truong Son foothills that served as Tri Thien headquarters. Hanoi's orders were probably not what General Quang expected—the command was to go ahead and attack with its own resources. Quang was to seize and hold Hue, a city of 105,000, for five to seven days. Ngo Vinh Long writes that Hanoi described the task as a diversionary measure (like Khe Sanh) for what it saw as the main attack, the one in Saigon.

While hewing to its original orders, Hanoi apparently did soften on the question of reinforcements to Tri Thien. By mid-November, according to a Vietnamese agent working for the Americans, who elicited this information from a cadre present at some of MRTTH's high-level meetings, regional officers were talking as if they were definitely going to be reinforced with "a battalion which would be armed with modern weapons, supported by experts." At the Combined Intelligence Center Vietnam in Saigon, during the final days before Tet, the top American analyst for I Corps concluded that some People's Army units were leaving the Khe Sanh area, headed for Hue. At Khe Sanh itself, during the days of Tet some of the sensor strings around the combat base activated in a way that could have been recording VPA movements *away* from that place.

Though Tri Thien commanders may have felt they needed several more months to fully prepare for attack on Hue, they went ahead as ordered on Tet. The Hue operation, planned and executed quite carefully, opened with a barrage of 122-mm rockets aimed at Hue's Citadel and other targets. Two battalions of Colonel Nguyen Trong Tan's 6th Regiment followed to occupy points north of Hue's Perfume River, while two battalions of the People's Army's 4th Regiment maneuvered below the river. Other units took up blocking positions. All this began at 3:40 A.M. on January 31, twenty minutes after the start of the Tan Son Nhut fighting on the fringe of Saigon.

With few exceptions, the Tri Thien forces captured their objectives. For several days the People's Army effectively controlled Hue. More than 200 installations, buildings, even houses, figured as goals of the assault forces. Cadres worked from lists of individual people in various neighborhoods who were assessed to be Saigon government agents, functionaries, informers, and so forth. As the Americans and South Vietnamese gathered to recapture Hue, NLF security forces systematically swept up these alleged enemies of the revolution, many of whom disappeared, never to be heard from again. More than 3,500 citizens were missing by the end of the Tet battle, and 2,300 to 3,000 bodies were exhumed from mass graves discovered afterward. It has always been the position of Hanoi that these were civilians caught in the crossfire of the fierce battle of Hue. For example, Colonel Nguyen Quoc Kanh told an American journalist in 1988: "There was no case of killing civilians purposefully; those civilians who were killed were killed accidentally." During the battle Khanh commanded the 806th Battalion of the VPA 6th Regiment, which held a blocking position north of the city and then helped defend against the Allied counterattacks.

Still, the Liberation Front had Hue wired for sound. This battlefield had been prepared well. Just how well is shown by the experience of Nguyen Qui Duc, just a boy at the time. Duc's was a prominent family, his grandfather a mandarin who had served the Vietnamese emperor and the French. Duc's father was senior civilian adviser to ARVN I Corps commander General Hoang Xuan Lam, and deputy province chief for Thua Thien. The family actually lived in Da Nang and had only come to Hue to visit the grandparents for Tet. The night of Tet the cadres came for Duc's grandfather. They knew the father was visiting and that the family had had dinner at the mandarin's home two nights before.

Nguyen Qui Duc's father was among those taken away by the cadres, but he was not killed. The cadres told the man he would be taken to the countryside for a short period of reeducation. This would be the start of a long odyssey that began on The Trail. The Saigon official became one of a stream of Hue prisoners sent west. At first they went to camps in the liberated zone, in the Annamite foothills. The South Vietnamese, along with SOG's Joint Personnel Recovery Center, learned of the Hue prisoners and made attempts to free them. Beginning on February 23, two SOG Bright Light teams were put on alert for Duval Sands, one of these rescue efforts, but the weather never cleared enough to deploy. General Hoang Xuan Lam mounted a rescue of his own using a Ranger battalion, but the ARVN arrived too late. General Lam told the family that if the rangers had come a half hour sooner, their father would be home with them at that very moment.

As the battle for Hue continued to rage—it would last through the end of February—up at Khe Sanh the Route 9 front made a new series of attacks. In a major assault backed by PT-76 tanks, a VPA regiment captured Lang Vei Special Forces camp. This not only brought about a new disaster, it also forced Colonel Soulang and his Laotian Army refugees to retreat farther (right back to Khe Sanh), and it cleared Americans and their CIDG strikers from the Route 9 border crossing at Lao Bao. Some of the Hue prisoners, including a couple of Americans captured there, moved up the Vietnamese side of the Annamites to Lao Bao, where they crossed the border to pick up The Trail. The prisoners, including General Lam's civilian aide, continued up The Trail into the DRV.

"We are going where there is everything," they were told.

Where there is everything. The comment said it all, in terms of *bo dois'* images of their world. The sacrifices and privations of The Trail, of the war in the South, were endured for a new life. Though in reality the poverty of the land, the needs of the war, and the American bombing had resulted in many shortages in the North, no one could tell a *bo doi* that home and hearth was not the land of good and plenty.

Not all prisoners taken up The Trail reached the North. This fate befell Michael Benge, a civilian with the Agency for International Development stationed at Ban Me Thuot as deputy province adviser. Racing around the town to check on his various charges, Benge had just arrived at the compound of some missionaries when captured by a Viet Cong armed propaganda team. Benge spent five years in prisoner camps either inside South Vietnam or in the triborder area of northeastern Cambodia. Two American prisoners with him, Hank Blood and Betty Olsen, died from pneumonia and dehydration, respectively. Benge saw Montagnard strikers and ARVN soldiers killed for refusal to cooperate or for no evident reason at all. To reach the Cambodian camp, the party trekked up the Sihanouk Trail. Benge spent five years in captivity.

Much the same way as the Hue prisoners, wounded People's Army *bo dois*, emissaries of the southern commands on mission, anyone with business in the North was viewed with envy and told that wonders awaited them. There *were* these people, too. That came as a surprise to the Americans and the Saigon forces. Throughout the war the image that took hold, and that still exists today, is that the Old Man's Trail was a one-way street, conveying men and supplies to war, pumping the lifeblood for the conflict. The VPA's decision to move the Hue prisoners to the DRV would be routine, however, and the movement itself ordinary. Nguyen Qui Duc's father went by truck, entering the DRV panhandle and actually making most of his trip inside the Democratic Republic. The same was true of several Americans taken prisoner at Khe Sanh or Lang Vei, and of some German nurses apprehended mistakenly by Viet Cong outside Da Nang. These groups of prisoners all entered the DRV at the western end of the Demilitarized Zone, generally following the path of the very earliest part of The Trail, Vo Bam's Trail, which would gradually be improved to become a road the Americans knew as Route 912, joining Route 9 at Ban Dong, just inside Laos. We have not yet encountered a story of prisoners entering the North across Mu Gia Pass.

We do have evidence, in an April 1968 document captured later in the war, of a People's Army soldier using the Napé Pass to return home. This is the record of a *bo doi* who left his regiment in Laos, passing through the DRV panhandle to Ha Dong, where he entered the Politico-Military Training school. It is noteworthy in this case that the VPA cadre being repatriated was not wounded, sick, or in any way unable to continue fighting.

The more usual practice was that *bo dois* fought on until somehow precluded from participating in the war—thus the many instances in which *bo dois* on The Trail stayed at a way station clinic when they became sick, to continue the trek later. These men could recover to fight again. *Bo dois* who were repatriated often had been wounded so severely they could not return to their units. A couple of years later, American troops operating in western Quang Ngai Province overran one of three or four main hospitals serving Interzone 5. Records captured there indicate that in 1968 the hospital received 1,924 badly wounded *bo dois*. Of these serious cases, 154 soldiers died, 178 recovered to be sent to convalescent camps, another 195 returned to their units, but fully 1,397 were repatriated to the DRV. During 1969 the hospital would handle another 2,925 patients, and of them, 1,051 went home.

When trucks were available the People's Army wounded traveled by convoy. Otherwise they walked. The hardships of the trek South on The Trail were greatly magnified for a disabled person trudging North.

It is hardly surprising the *bo dois* should have felt the need to sustain themselves with visions of going where there was everything.

In 1969 American photoreconnaissance planes over Mu Gia Pass did indeed get pictures of columns of VPA wounded hobbling their way homeward.

As time went on, evidence accumulated that the DRV was also evacuating children up The Trail. These were often the children of Liberation Front cadre who were in danger living in a countryside vulnerable to harassment fire, both artillery and airpower. Captured documents reveal that in 1967 there were already more than 1,000 South Vietnamese children attending schools in Hanoi. Families who took in the children received extra rations and other amenities. In later years reports of children on The Trail increased significantly. They moved in groups of twenty-five to thirty, with guides from the way stations, always in the dry season.

From available records there is no way to gauge the volume of traffic up The Trail. Intelligence reports indicate, however, that the traffic began at a low level, perhaps in 1967, and gradually increased. A prisoner taken that year mentioned meeting groups headed North during his trek down The Trail. He estimated as many as 80 groups on the move of 15 to 30 persons each. By 1969, prisoners were talking of groups as large as 50 to 120 evacuees. Documents captured in Cambodia in 1970 indicate that 4,000 persons were sent North from just three straggler recovery regiments, the VPA units responsible for personnel administration on The Trail. One of these units dispatched no fewer than 1,200 evacuees in the last month before the Allied invasion of Cambodia. These data make it clear The Trail was a two-way street.

To return to the time of Tet, of the Year of the Monkey, 1968, or as the Vietnamese call it, Tet Mau Than, the Hue fighting became some of the fiercest of the offensive. General Tran Van Quang's demands for reinforcements were finally to be met from Khe Sanh, from the Route 9 Front, toward the end of February. Within two weeks the CIA was reporting these troop movements in Washington.

At Khe Sanh, where there was *no* attack on Tet, the immediate difficulty was refugees, primarily Colonel Soulang and his Laotian soldiers with their families, but also Bru tribesmen and others driven from the surrounding villages. According to Soulang's account to an American attaché, twenty-six of his men were killed in the Lang Vei battle that took place on February 7, some by People's Army gunfire, some by American bombs. The Royal Laotian Army commander told his men to break up into groups and make either for the border or for Khe Sanh combat base. Perhaps forty Lao were carried by helicopters to Khe Sanh, and these soldiers were immediately disarmed by the marines and put outside the Khe Sanh perimeter, where they took cover in shell craters. Soulang showed up a day or so later with seventy-four more Laotian Army survivors. They, too, were disarmed. The Americans gave them no food, and Soulang claims to have felt more like a prisoner than an ally. On February 8 a Special Forces major returned the Laotian weapons, but that was about it. Two days later, the Lao civilians stuck outside Khe Sanh decided to make for the border and disappeared.

Meanwhile, the soldiers of Bataillon Volontaire 33 remained an awkward inconvenience to Colonel David Lownds and his marines, not to mention a diplomatic embarrassment to the United States, South Vietnam, and Laos. At one point shortly after the fall of Ban Houei Sane, Ambassador Sullivan got the impression that the BV-33 survivors were being integrated into the Lang Vei defenses. He reacted acerbically: "Lao troops fighting North Vietnamese in [South Vietnam] gravely jeopardizes Lao neutrality." Sullivan had the same opinion of Lao fighting for Khe Sanh, though there was little chance David Lownds would agree to *that*. The alternative, leaving the Lao outside the Khe Sanh perimeter, was also not acceptable, however. At the beginning, MACV did not attempt evacuation of the Lao due to the combat situation in the Khe Sanh area, but Laotian leader Souvanna Phouma had already been told that MACV would remain alert to prospects for aerial movement, and would evacuate Soulang and his troops to Savannakhet as soon as practicable. The Laotian government went public to announce the fall of Ban Houei Sane the day before the initial Tet attacks.

Prime Minister Phouma returned to the subject of the BV-33 survivors in a conversation with Ambassador Sullivan the afternoon of February 6. By then a mass of refugees was gathering outside Khe Sanh's gates. At the time of the Lang Vei assault the crowd was already estimated at 6,000, and Colonel Lownds worried about whether he could conduct a battle over the heads of all these civilians. The fall of Lang Vei then drove the Laotian soldiers right into the mass of refugees, complicating the entire issue. On February 9 MACV decided to move the Laotians to Da Nang to get them out of the way, and the State Department asked the embassy in Vientiane whether Air America could move the evacuees on to their homeland. Instead, the Laotian military took up the task. American aircraft got 111 FAR soldiers, together with two women and a child, to Da Nang. Soulang left three officers at Khe Sanh to screen future arrivals, and himself went on to Saigon to make final arrangements. He returned to Da Nang, where Royal Laotian Air Force C-47s moved the entire group to Savannakhet on February 15.

After listening to Colonel Soulang's account of the Ban Houei Sane battle and its aftermath, especially the treatment of the Laotian soldiers and civilians outside Khe Sanh, the general commanding the FAR military region remarked that the Laotians "must consider South Vietnamese as enemy because of their conduct."

There are no sources available to shed light on the fate of the FAR soldiers and civilians who disappeared up Route 9 toward Indian country and The Trail.

At Khe Sanh Colonel Lownds had a similar problem with the commander of the 5th Special Forces Group, Colonel Jonathan A. ("Fred") Ladd. This time the issue was the CIDG strikers and Mike Force troops who had defended Lang Vei itself. Fred Ladd went up the chain of command to Westmoreland, bringing up the issue of a prospective invasion of Laos, arguing such an operation would be more difficult if the U.S. mistreated local people along Route 9, including tribesmen in his CIDG units. In fact, Colonel Ladd was almost desperate, for the Lang Vei battle had been very frustrating. Ladd had been up there just before the fight and recalls, "We could hear the tanks moving around." The 5th Group commander and SOG boss Daniel Baldwin went to marine general Robert Cushman to beg for antitank mines for Lang Vei. Cushman was willing to get the mines, but MACV refused to believe there was a tank threat, and no mines were supplied.

Since the summer of 1967, when Fred Ladd took over Special Forces in Vietnam, he had become something of a buddy to MACV deputy commander General Creighton V. Abrams. Abe shared Ladd's bungalow each time he went to Nha Trang on inspections, and also began stopping by on trips elsewhere. During these quiet visits Abrams and Ladd would sit on the porch, sipping martinis and playing with Ladd's dog. Colonel Ladd's argument about the effect of treatment of the population on a Laos invasion, very much a Westmoreland interest, probably owed something to Ladd's friendship with Creighton Abrams.

Green Berets usually hold up General Abrams as one officer who had no love for them, but they owe Abrams for his role in the battle of Lang Vei. General Westmoreland was at Da Nang at the time of the disaster; Westy's notes for that day record him as finding a lack of initiative, forcing the MACV commander to intervene to stiffen Cushman. Lieutenant Colonel Daniel L. Baldwin, leader of SOG's Command Control North, offered his troops for a relief column but needed choppers for an operation. Baldwin says Westy ordered the helicopters released to SOG for a Lang Vei rescue. Fred Ladd remembers it differently. "In Westmoreland's book he says he did all that," Ladd recollects, "but he didn't." Colonel Ladd insists that Westmoreland couldn't make up his mind to evacuate Lang Vei or to activate the contingency plan to relieve it.

The 5th Special Forces Group commander finally had to get General Abrams on the telephone. "I just can't get Westmoreland's attention long enough to do anything," Ladd told Abrams. "He's putting it off." Marine officers were also putting off Ladd on helicopters on grounds they might be needed for a marine evacuation. General Abrams then called marine air chief Major General Norman J. Anderson and personally ordered the choppers for the relief mission put at SOG's disposal.

Colonel Baldwin then tried to reach his field unit, Forward Operating Base (FOB)-3, to lead the recovery, but his helicopter malfunctioned and returned to Phu Bai. Baldwin ended up on the radio to Major George Quamo, FOB-3 commander, instructing him to mount the rescue. Fred Ladd also headed for Khe Sanh and made it in time to join the relief attempt. He met the Lang Vei survivors and accompanied them back to the combat base.

General Westmoreland agreed that the Mike Force and CIDG strikers could be flown out of Khe Sanh if they could be identified. An initial move brought out 104 Mike Force soldiers, 112 strikers, and 8 ARVN Special Forces troops. Follow-up efforts through the rest of February lifted out 90 more Lang Vei veterans plus another 91 Laotian survivors of Ban Houei Sane.

Once Laotian and Lang Vei survivors were being handled, the true dimensions of the problem became more apparent—there were *thousands* of

Bru tribesmen clustering as refugees around Khe Sanh. At Tet in some places in I and II Corps, the NLF or the VPA had attacked behind crowds of civilians forced to act as human shields. Colonel Lownds and his superiors worried that the same might happen at Khe Sanh. Lownds determined to shoot if he had to, but preferred to move the refugees. At Da Nang, I Corps commander General Hoang Xuan Lam directed that none of the Bru should be brought to the lowlands. When about 1,500 of the refugees tried to walk down Route 9 by themselves, it was the other side, the People's Army, who turned them back. On February 10 a column of refugees on Route 9 west of Khe Sanh was hit by air strikes when Ravens saw VPA *bo dois* interspersed among the crowd and suspected the peasants were working as porters.

In contrast with the overall situation with the refugees, at the FOB-3 compound Bru women were being paid to fill sandbags. Captain Lee Dunlap had tried Bru workers, and found them very dependable. Perhaps 100 women labored on sandbags alone. There were other Bru in SOG's Spike teams and its Hornet rifle company. A marine who had formerly done pacification work in Khe Sanh village questioned tribesmen as to what they would do if the People's Army attacked behind a curtain of their friends. He was surprised to hear Bru complacently say they would shoot without giving it a thought.

Differences with the Bru were just one of the things that distinguished the Studies and Observation Group at Khe Sanh from the marines. The SOG troops were spooky and hush-hush and ranged even more widely than marine scouts. There was also an unusually large presence directly due to the McNamara Line project. For several years Khe Sanh had been a launch site for FOB-1, the SOG command at Phu Bai, and that remained active. But that was small potatoes, far eclipsed by FOB-3, created in late 1967 for the express purpose of erecting the barrier. When Lee Dunlap arrived, he headed one of four Spike teams, and FOB-1 was at an old French fort near Khe Sanh village. Needing a bigger site for FOB-3, Colonel Singlaub considered moving to Lao Bao, right on the border, but that was just too risky. His choice was to relocate to the combat base. The new compound was dug in belowground—another feature distinguishing it from the marine combat base. Khe Sanh's Seabees did the construction, but an army major who was a civil engineer came in from the 1st Special Forces Group on Okinawa to supervise.

Emplacement of Dye Marker sensors in Laos would be cloaked under the innocuous phrase "Special Projects Effort" and be headed by Major George Quamo. Aside from sixteen Spike teams, Quamo needed a bigger reaction force and recruited a company among the Bru. Captain Dunlap began training the riflemen in December 1967, with sergeants from the Spike teams leading platoons of the Hornet Force. Another Army major, "Shaky" Campbell, outranked Quamo and had overall command of SOG elements at Khe Sanh, who numbered about 600 (131 of them Americans) in the spring of 1968. Marines' orders to go to ground as Hanoi's troops closed in triggered another difference with SOG. Colonel John Singlaub did not like having SOG men trapped in a static, defensive role. He kept them in the field. Just after Christmas 1967, a scout team grabbed two porters at the tail end of a VPA ammunition party. Lieutenant Colonel Baldwin, SOG chieftain for the northern provinces, was on the scene when Khe Sanh village fell, leading a patrol into the village that came back with many captured enemy weapons. Then, just before the People's Army assault on Ban Houei Sane, Captain Dunlap's reconnaissance team spotted the VPA soldiers taking position there. On its way back, the patrol stopped at Lang Vei to warn Special Forces. Studies and Observation Group officers insist that all their intelligence was passed along to the marines, in fact that the Spike teams debriefed in three places following each patrol.

Soon after FOB-3 and other volunteers made the rescue mission to recover Lang Vei survivors, a disguised explosive device was thrown into the FOB perimeter. Americans found the canister next to their positions in the morning. Major Quamo and SOG explosives specialists tied a rope around the thing and pulled it to see if it detonated, but were reluctant to try opening the device. Quamo decided to have it opened by experts at Command Control North; CCN might also have people who could read the Chinese markings on the device. Asking one of the VNAF helicopter pilots to fly him down, George Quamo left for Da Nang. Their H-34 helicopter never arrived. A lieutenant colonel named Barr took command of FOB-3 on April Fool's Day.

The MACSOG unit at Khe Sanh also used radio intelligence to good advantage. On one occasion they pinpointed a headquarters of a People's Army unit in Khe Sanh village simply because the *bo doi* working the radio mentioned they were being hit by gunship helicopters. By finding the only unit using attack copters at that moment, SOG identified the target, which Captain Larry Henderson believes was at least a regiment, if not the divisional leadership of the 304th Division. Since battalions from two different regiments of the 304th had made the Lang Vei attack, meaning higher-level coordination became a necessity, the bombing amounted to a significant hit on the enemy. There is evidence that at one point in the Khe Sanh campaign Hanoi *flew* new personnel into the theater—to Tchepone airfield, at night; some may have parachuted. This suggests that very important officers did have to be replaced in the People's Army command. At another time, Sergeant Herve Saal reports, the VPA were overheard getting ready for an assault on the main combat base, and a concentration of SLAM firepower pulverized the enemy force before it reached its assembly area. This incident marked the end of the Khe Sanh campaign, at least in terms of any threat to the marine base.

Since January 25, before Tet, when MACV redeployed the 1st Cavalry Division (Airmobile) to I Corps, its commander had had orders to plan an operation across Route 9 to restore ground transport to Khe Sanh and relieve the garrison. Once its airfield closed to the big C-130 cargo planes (from February 12 to 24), the flimsiness of Khe Sanh's aerial supply link became painfully apparent. Parachute delivery would be substituted, but overland shipment remained much preferable. Though the Cav played a role in the battle for Hue, screening the city to prevent more *bo dois* reaching there, it was Khe Sanh, not Tet, that brought the winged horsemen to I Corps.

The idea of a Khe Sanh relief was important to General Westmoreland. It became a fixture in the cables passing among MACV, CINCPAC, and Washington. By mid-February General Maxwell Taylor, now a personal adviser to President Johnson, would be questioning whether a certain brigade of reinforcements Westy was requesting for this Route 9 offensive would be enough to achieve the aims MACV advanced. Westmoreland got the troops he wanted, but the operation was much bigger than they. By March 2 Major General John J. Tolson, commanding the Cav, had a plan he could brief at Da Nang for generals Cushman and Abrams, whom Westy had now sent permanently to I Corps with an advanced echelon of MACV. A week later, when William Westmoreland came to Phu Bai for the official activation of MACV Forward, as it was called, several competing concepts were aired before the commander in chief. Marine leader Robert Cushman favored reopening Route 9 over the alternatives, which were clearing the A Shau valley or the coastal plain from Dong Ha up to the DMZ. Westy agreed. Major General William R. Rosson took charge of a provisional army corps MACV inserted at the bottom of Route 9. Including Khe Sanh's garrison, Rosson would command the 1st Cavalry, the equivalent of a division of marines, and an ARVN airborne task force. The offensive would be named Pegasus, for the winged horse of Greek mythology.

General Westmoreland insisted on a contingency plan for a brigade-size invasion of Laos in conjunction with Pegasus. Westy wanted to prepare for "hot pursuit" of a defeated Vietnam People's Army across the border into its lair on The Trail. On March 7 Da Nang hosted a meeting of U.S. officials in Vietnam, Laos, and Thailand. Ambassador Sullivan and his retinue flew over in a T-39 executive jet. The Vientiane envoy wanted to talk about plane and helicopter allocations, CIA guerrilla operations in lower Laos, the general military situation, and the particular problems of Lima Site 85, a top-secret aircraft guidance and targeting facility that, like SOG's "Eagle's Nest," had been plunked down squarely in the middle of Indian country and was now threatened by the Pathet Lao. Sullivan wanted to permanently assign the 56th Air Commando Wing in Thailand to support certain operations. If there was time, the conferees could talk about Muscle Shoals.

General Westmoreland wanted to talk about Laos and North Vietnam, specifically about invading them. To draw back Hanoi's divisions from Khe Sanh, Westy resurrected the idea of an amphibious operation north of the Demilitarized Zone. This one would be a feint. Aware of Washington objections to the above-the-DMZ option, the recommendations carefully said that study of the project ought to include "reexamination of earlier expressed fear that failure to follow through on such a feint might be termed a propaganda victory for North Vietnam." In addition, in connection with the projected Khe Sanh relief operation, William Westmoreland wanted to plan for "limited" ground incursions into Laos. In the agreed summary recommendations from the Southeast Asia Coordinating Committee, participants argued: "The use of Laotian territory by the enemy has reached a degree of seriousness where, despite the political problems involved, we should consider permitting limited military operations in Laos."

At his session with the marine and army planners compiling the details for Pegasus, General Westmoreland raised the possibility of extending a road up the Ba Long valley to connect inland with Route 9 in the vicinity of Ca Lu (see Map 7), which General Tolson had already picked as location for the Cav's main base. With true Cav swagger, the air assault troopers were going to call this "Landing Zone Stud." A road that hooked up at Stud was not feasible according to the top engineers, however. Back in Saigon, Westy instructed MACV planners to revise the plans for operation El Paso, updating them to use a smaller force for the Laotian invasion. With the Pegasus planners, Westy wanted arrangements for a brigade-size force of either Americans or ARVN troops that could hit targets close to the border, "conducted in such a way as to have no press exposure," against objectives "worthy of the political risks involved." Selected as potential targets were the People's Army base areas around Ban Dong; Co Roc, which incidentally, SOG had just identified as a major VPA base in addition to its role in the artillery bombardment of Khe Sanh; Lao Bao; and the head of the A Shau valley.

With these recommendations still under discussion in Washington, in mid-March General Westmoreland tried to get Ambassador Sullivan to agree in advance to the projected plans. It is fair to say that William Westmoreland did as much as he could to create conditions that would have enabled him to invade Laos in the spring of 1968.

Lyndon Johnson had many favorite sayings, earthy, salty, or just plain Texan. One concerned a camel and a tent and was really about incrementalism. LBJ used to say that if you let the camel's nose inside your tent, the rest of him would follow. That was exactly the story with MACV's contingency plans for Laos. At the White House, National Security Council staffer Marshall Wright had this to say about the proposals from the Da Nang conference:

> [They] seem to me to be based on the assumption that we can take additional military actions in Laos, and that otherwise the situation stays the same.
>
> That assumption is almost certainly incorrect. The enemy will certainly take steps to counter our ploy. They will attempt to destroy our forces introduced on their supply line. And they may very possibly use our action as a pretext for an assault upon major Laotian cities.
>
> In short, if we "hot up" the war in Laos we can expect with confidence that the enemy will do the same for he has consistently [shown] fewer inhibitions . . . than we have. . . . And he has the resources on the spot. Unless we are prepared to contemplate a major war in Laos

with the overt commitment of American resources we had better be very careful.

Colonel Robert N. Ginsburgh, the military liaison officer between the NSC and the Joint Chiefs of Staff, had to be alert to refer to the MACV proposal the right way ("Westy does not plan [to actually conduct] ground action in Laos") and to note how MACV was ready to *lower* the ante ("Westy would like authority for employment of one battalion").

Ginsburgh's main audience continued to be the national security adviser, Walt Rostow, not the president. Passing Westmoreland's proposals to Walt was preaching to the choir. Rostow forwarded Westy's plan for an offensive in I Corps to President Johnson on March 21, "to refresh your memory." His summary comment on Westmoreland's idea: "I believe he should be encouraged to move out, if anything, at an accelerated pace." Walt offered three strategic alternatives: a continuation of the 1966–1967 strategy, an emphasis on population control, or "a policy of forcing a decision from Hanoi and its allies." Rostow went on to write, "I feel in my bones that after the Tet Offensive, things can never be quite the same, and that a simple return to the 1966–1967 strategy will not wash." He demanded the pacification approach with faint praise: "It is conceivable that, after very careful analysis with Westy on the scene, some practical difference could be identified between the policy he has been following and a policy of so-called population protection."

Thus Rostow's preference for forcing a decision emerged clearly. The security adviser laid down three possibilities:

- mining the North Vietnamese harbors and trying to interdict the transport routes from China;
- invading the southern part of North Vietnam and blocking the transport routes from, say, Vinh, to both Mu Gia Pass into Laos and the roads to the DMZ; or
- moving into Laos on Route 9 and blocking on the ground the Laos transport routes into South Vietnam just south of the seventeenth parallel.

Any of those options would do for Rostow, who went on to discount the possibility of Soviet or Chinese intervention and recommend the options be staffed out and one of them implemented if a peace bid should fail.

General Westmoreland renewed his call for contingency authority to invade Laos on April 2, just as operation Pegasus took wing toward Khe Sanh. It also happened to be just prior to Westy's return to Washington for consultations. There is significance in the fact that the April 5 paper sent to LBJ by Deputy Secretary of Defense Paul H. Nitze, on talking points for the president's meeting with Westmoreland, did not even mention the Laos invasion contingency. Perhaps Nitze had thrown in the towel where Rostow refused to give up. As far as Lyndon Johnson was concerned, Laotian invasion had the mark of the devil upon it.

Khe Sanh's siege broke in the early afternoon of April 6, when a company of ARVN paratroops made contact with the combat base. In the meantime, stars had moved in the political firmament. Pressure and controversy had soured Lyndon Johnson, and the apparent contradiction between claims of success in Vietnam and the evident power of the enemy at Tet deepened his gloom. Johnson's problems multiplied when it emerged that the JCS (*not*, be it noted, Westmoreland) wanted to mobilize reserves and send 210,000 more troops to Vietnam. In the early primaries of the 1968 presidential campaign, LBJ did surprisingly poorly against Minnesota Senator Eugene J. McCarthy and New York senator Robert F. Kennedy, who both espoused ending the war. On March 31 President Johnson made a nationally televised speech in which he withdrew from the election, effectively retiring from politics. Johnson also halted the bombing of the three northernmost route packages in the Rolling Thunder campaign. General Westmoreland would be kicked upstairs—made army chief of staff. His successor as commander of MACV would be Creighton Abrams. Changes were visible everywhere, perhaps especially to the people of lower Laos, and of Quang Binh Province, DRV. On them, the bombs began falling faster than ever.

CHAPTER 11

Pinball Wizards
1968–1969

On the Thai bank of the Mekong River there was a market town named Nakhon Phanom. For years "NKP," as Americans liked to call the place, had had a prominent role in events in Laos, primarily due to the fact that it was on the river. Nakhon Phanom had ferry connections to Thakhek, the only place for miles on the Laotian side from which one could sustain forces in the central part of the panhandle. From NKP you could also take a boat up to Vientiane, or else downriver toward Cambodia and the sea. The promenade by the Mekong stood serene, the yellowed stucco buildings of the town testament to the prosperity of the place. Nakhon Phanom also sported the largest image of Buddha in all northeastern Thailand. That was only the tile adornment of a local temple, true, but still quite impressive. The stillness of the day was broken by the sounds of market, or boats, hardly ever the bark of guns.

That is, until the advent of The Trail. Then, the location of NKP so close to the whole arc of the route of Hanoi's lifeline, and the fact that it *was* a river town, made Nakhon Phanom supremely desirable as a military base. Americans came, to make the simple airstrip into a complex capable of accommodating jets, a facility that would conduct the war in Laos. The place was so well located for helicopter flights into the Laotian panhandle, Indian country, that MACSOG built its own compound at Nakhon Phanom from which to mount patrols against objectives on The Trail.

When Washington came to make up its mind in favor of a high-technology barrier to block The Trail, Nakhon Phanom loomed even larger for American planners. It would be the perfect command post and support point for the barrier effort. In the fall of 1967 Secretary McNamara approved deployment of the electronic portion of the barrier. It was to feature a nerve center that would collect data from sensors on the ground throughout the area of The Trail. The nerve center would use the data to target attacks on The Trail. McNamara selected Nakhon Phanom to be that nerve center. At NKP commanders would put together the big picture and make choices in the battle of The Trail.

An innocuously labeled entity known as Task Force Alpha formed to create the command center. Nicknamed Dutch Mill, the complex at Nakhon Phanom took shape behind the story that these Americans were managing data in behalf of the U.S. command. The vague cover story was technically true but not complete by half. An operations center (20,000 square feet) plus a communications facility (5,600 square feet) made up the heart of Dutch Mill, backed up by six 200-kilowatt diesel generators and a growing maze of antennae. Thai workers began building the complex in July 1967.

Brigadier General William P. McBride headed Task Force Alpha, supervising the scientists and engineers who, as recounted earlier, were moving quickly on the experiments that would validate the system. The original barrier concept provided that The Trail be blocked using passive weapons such as land mines, with the sensors revealing when the enemy had transited the blockade zone. This design quickly changed to a dynamic one wherein there would be no reliance on the barrier per se, but instead a real-time battle between forces dispatched on the basis of the sensor readouts and the Vietnamese on The Trail. After extensive study, on September 8, 1967, U.S. authorities divided the Steel Tiger area—that is, lower Laos—into a half-dozen sectors for the interdiction effort. The sectors were represented on large wall maps at Dutch Mill's operations center, where the movements detected by the Dye Marker sensors were posted and followed.

Analysts studied the road network, and great energy poured into finding each improvement or addition the Vietnamese made to The Trail. A whole new vocabulary became attached to the battle against Hanoi's lifeline. Beyond "choke points," there would now be "route segments" (the length of road between intersections), "flashers" (detected targets or lit-up sensors), "Panther Teams" (any unit of strike aircraft directed by a Raven FAC), and "Headshed" traffic advisories. The Nakhon Phanom command post got a new code name, Sycamore, as did the overall barrier system, henceforth called Igloo White.

The way the system developed was probably inevitable. It soon became evident that hitting targets from airplanes was far preferable to the passive barrier. In due course commanders also realized the other drawback of the linear barrier—designed to cross the neck of Indochina from east to west, Hanoi's troops and convoys trekking down The Trail spent relatively little time inside the barrier's main kill zone. Much more sensible was to reorient the barrier, adapting the sensor base to The Trail's own spatial dimensions. Like The Trail itself, Igloo White would have a northeast-to-southwest axis. The sensors were key, and as in antisubmarine warfare, separating true from spurious readouts would be critical. Moreover, the truly important intelligence would not be the current data, it would be to locate the opponent where he might be *at some later moment when you could position forces to engage him.* Pathway prediction and delay intervals were what made the route segments and choke points so vital. The entire system functioned exactly like a pinball machine; in truth the mavens of the electronic battlefield became pinball wizards.

Nakhon Phanom's mainframe computer was up and running, and the air force, the navy, and SOG were hard at work emplacing strings of sensors when the military situation in I Corps climaxed with the battle of Khe Sanh. The pinball wizards forged their techniques in the fires of Khe Sanh, and it was at that time, in early and mid-1968, that the Vietnam People's Army discovered the electronic battlefield and its sensors. Hanoi's *bo dois* answered with countermeasures. They confused Task Force Alpha's pinball wizards with false sensor returns—for example, driving herds of cattle up and down the paths near seismic sensors, or hanging buckets of urine in tree branches above chemical sniffers. Aside from fooling the sensors, the VPA strengthened its antiaircraft defenses. An innovation attributed to trailmaster Dong Sy Nguyen during this period would be the mobile anti-aircraft detachment. These units traveled The Trail alongside the most important convoys.

Striving to perfect their attack techniques, Americans incorporated every imaginable wrinkle into the pinball war. The long-serving Ravens of Tiger Hound, whose spotters had been the most effective interdictors of the Ho Chi Minh Trail for years, now became mainstays of the Panther teams. Dutch Mill data made the Ravens even better. Signals from sensors along The Trail, plus reports from radios all over Laos, were relayed to NKP and the air command at Udorn by three electronic aircraft that orbited over Laos in shifts. The planes with call signs "Hillsboro" and "Alley Cat" flew in daylight, the latter over central and upper Laos. "Moonbeam" took the night shift. Airborne command post C-130s exercised control over warplanes in the area, assigning them to Ravens as targets became available. The circle became complete once the Seventh Air Force delegated its authority for strike planes above The Trail directly to Task Force Alpha at Nakhon Phanom.

Laos became the main business of NKP, the primary base of the 56th Air Commando (later Special Operations) Wing. The unit flew a variety of aircraft meeting all the needs of warfare in Laos, both upper and lower, including Raven FACs, attack planes, and helicopters. In mid-1968 the air force reinforced Nakhon Phanom with its 633rd Special Operations Wing for even bigger efforts. More than $16 million would be spent to improve the base facilities at Nakhon Phanom.

In the spring of 1968 General Momyer of the Seventh Air Force ordered new studies of integrating the air capabilities used in the assault on The Trail. The system that endured went into action that October. At that time an intensive effort began that would be known as Commando Hunt. At NKP, Sycamore Control became the effective forward command post of the Seventh Air Force for purposes of the battle for The Trail. The pinball wizards had come into their own. For the remainder of the war Nakhon Phanom would call the shots, managing all the strike, FAC, gunship, and command aircraft assets flying over The Trail. The harnessing of sensor intelligence and time-sequenced attacks gave new meaning to the term "estimated time of arrival" and to the notion of predicting pathways.

A tremendous combat effort aimed at The Trail. In October 1968 the scale of air activity in lower Laos stood at 4,062 fighter-bomber sorties plus 271 by B-52s. In November, with the bombing halt over North Vietnam, the air campaign in Laos mushroomed to 11,492 fighter-bomber flights, with 661 more by B-52s. That meant about 400 sorties a day. Until May 1969, when the air forces had to mount a maximum effort inside South Vietnam, attack sorties along The Trail never dipped below 10,000 a month. Sorties never returned to 1968 (pre-bombing halt) levels until June 1970, when Cambodia became the main focus. In terms of raw numbers, during 1969 there were 110,000 attack sorties against The Trail, along with 5,567 Arc Light flights by B-52 bombers.

Commando Hunt reached stride between November 1968 and April 1969. Within a zone extending from Mu Gia Pass to the North, and the line roughly along Route 9 in the South, Task Force Alpha controlled the aircraft and emphasized its Panther Teams. Intelligence estimated that the People's Army possessed about 1,300 trucks within the Commando Hunt zone, of which perhaps 275 might be on the move on any given night. As early as December the forces engaging The Trail were claiming destruction of 27 trucks a day; that figure rose to 44 every day by April. The pinball wizards watched with glowing eyes as the pressures against The Trail mounted.

To a great degree it was the slow movers that made things possible for everybody else. The slower, piston-engined aircraft were better at ground attack (a slower approach to the target helped the pilot), at close air support; they carried the implements of war into all manner of airfields near the front. Then there were the Ravens. The Forward Air Controllers (FACs), for much of this period flying the oldest, slowest planes, served to link all the air assets to the environment around them. The FACs called the air strikes, and they often connected the grunts in the boondocks below with the rest of The 'Nam. The air strikes were the grunts' biggest aid and, of course, the best interdiction resource in the battle of The Trail. Ravens also informed higher command of events at the edge of the battle area, identified ground teams and downed pilots for recovery and rescue, found enemy targets, and had the most "loiter time," the longest interval in which they could maintain a presence over the battlefield.

Ravens had had a role in The Trail campaign from the start. Looking at the FACs' ability to find targets, anticipating further improvement by cooperating with scouts on the ground, before the end of 1965 the air force had FACs working with Project Delta. The first pilots to fly above Delta were extensively briefed at Nha Trang, then sent on actual recon missions. The FACs got an eyeful of what conditions would be on the ground. With the inception of MACSOG the need for spotters increased so much that pilot indoctrination became perfunctory. But like Tiger Hound, where the coming of the Ravens greatly benefited armed reconnaissance over The Trail, the scout team–airplane combination quickly showed its worth. Around

Bien Hoa in early 1966, an operation named Mallet brought remarkable success to Delta along with marked relief—two of nine recon teams involved were saved by FACs overhead. By late 1967, on an average day there were more than a dozen Ravens flying with SOG teams all over Vietnam. Jets were great when you needed them, but without the slow movers the work simply could not have been done.

This proved especially true in the delicate task of inserting Spike teams. Ravens controlled the missions, guiding helicopters to remote LZs where they would alight a scant moment, and heavily armed scouts would jump off and disappear into the woods. For SOG (and Delta) recon missions, the Ravens came to rely on a standard "package"—a word that is an artifact of the attitude taken toward strategy in Vietnam, more like an accountant than a general—of aircraft. This included the FAC himself; perhaps four helicopters (two gunships, a troop carrier, and a backup or rescue ship); and two or four strike aircraft, preferably slow movers themselves. Recon men had mixed feelings about the airpower devoted to them. On the one hand, it was good to have all that firepower; on the other, the mass of aircraft generated so much noise it became impossible to get into an area without tipping off everyone in the vicinity. Jack Singlaub was one who loathed the dependence on helicopters; he made sure to optimize SOG's precision parachute capability.

The numerous difficulties were well illustrated by Billy Waugh, who had once been with the launch site at Kontum but by 1967 was with FOB-1 at Khe Sanh. Sergeant Waugh was very conscious of People's Army area security; as a whole, MACSOG reported a marked increase in The Trail's active defenses. Gunshots almost always announced the arrival of a SOG recon team. The Spike teams then raced VPA reaction forces to complete their reconnaissance before the enemy closed in. Many patrols found firefights at, or only a short way from, their points of insertion; there were plenty of emergency extractions from hot LZs. Tactics such as staying off the radio, or faking a landing at several places before choosing the real LZ, ultimately were not good enough. Joe Garner, another fine SOG noncom, would end his tour frustrated that SOG was producing little good intelligence, merely diverting a certain number of VPA and Pathet Lao *bo dois.*

For a long time Fred Caristo, an officer with MACSOG's unit running operations against Hanoi, was convinced there must be spies among the Vietnamese commandos in training. Americans did everything they could to avoid spies in their midst, but the problem could not be eliminated because of the civil war aspect of Vietnam, where brothers, sisters, cousins, and uncles, fighting for different sides, could at any time reach out to each other across the chasm of violence. The Studies and Observations Group went beyond background checks and security clearances for its recruits, subjecting them to lie detector tests, making psychological profiles, detailed investigations, and even little traps and tests set for Vietnamese under training at Long Thanh. But the problem of "hostile penetration" could never be eliminated.

Captain Caristo devised elaborate countermeasures, and SOG adopted a program to fool Hanoi's security forces into thinking there were resistance networks they did not know about, or that SOG believed in commando teams that in fact it had concluded were being played back, controlled by Hanoi against the Americans. Retribution for spies could be devious. Once Caristo mounted an entire fake operation that put one commando thought to be an agent into the DRV. The man supposed he was part of a team but at the last moment, while boarding the aircraft, his comrades were replaced by blocks of ice. The agent and the ice were parachuted in, and that unfortunate had then to explain to People's Army officers the empty parachutes of other team members.

Though espionage penetrations at the level of the commandos were real enough, the true problem existed at the top. Certain arrests in Quang Tri just before Tet exposed ARVN officers as enemy spies. One of the men arrested had once been chief of staff of the South Vietnamese Special Forces. After the war, as it turns out, the Hanoi government presented a medal for bravery to another individual who had been a top aide to Saigon's prime minister, Nguyen Cao Ky. The procedure for Saigon government approval of contemplated SOG operations was for the list to be reviewed periodically by ARVN Joint General Staff head Cao Van Vien and the MACSOG chief. General Vien, Singlaub insists, had no requirement to involve anyone else in this process, but nevertheless had an informal arrangement with Air Marshal Ky under which he did run the proposals past the prime minister's office. The betrayal may have happened right there.

Be this as it may, Prime Minister Ky represented political authority in the South. The government, once taken over by ARVN's generals, would retain effective control over the army after the coup fever of the early and mid-1960s had passed. This meant, despite any arrangements with the Americans intended to preserve MACSOG security, that General Vien owed his job to Ky and another general, now president, Nguyen Van Thieu, neither of whom completely trusted the Americans. At the same time, ARVN's Special Forces had been involved in several of the early coup episodes. It was simply not realistic to suppose that Saigon was going to permit its generals, using ARVN Special Forces, to carry out secret operations without reference to political authority, *especially* projects dictated by Americans.

That Hanoi's penetration of the Saigon regime was thorough is clear—there is evidence that a senior aide to President Thieu also spied for the DRV. The informers would have been difficult to find, but worse, the CIA had *its own* agents in the entourages of both Vietnamese leaders, and may have had one or both offices bugged as well. American interest lay in *avoiding* security investigations of the top Vietnamese leaders. Adversary penetration of SOG plans thus had to be accepted as a given.

This is not to say that the Studies and Observation Group lacked resourcefulness, however. The most important initiative, beginning in 1967, would be a fresh program called STRATA (Short-Term Reconnaissance and Target Acquisition). The thing about STRATA was that it could be *unilateral,* that is, entirely American-controlled. Indigenous teams would be used, trained, and paid by SOG, but because all their operations would occur outside South Vietnam, and because none required Saigon cooperation, the Americans could dispense with the need for ARVN approval. Patrols went to a variety of predesignated target areas ranging from the Demilitarized Zone to as far north as Nghe An Province of the DRV. Jack Singlaub credits the inspiration for STRATA to Fred Caristo. Vietnamese linguist and intelligence specialist Sedgwick Tourison disputes that claim but does not detail an alternate version.

In October 1967 an early STRATA patrol ended in disaster, with all ten commandos missing, but the concept was validated and improved. That December, Special Forces Major George ("Speedy") Gaspard took over as STRATA operations planner. Gaspard streamlined the scout teams down to six to eight men. The two dozen missions run in 1968 concentrated on Quang Binh and the approaches to The Trail. More than half the patrols aimed at the DMZ and the border immediately above it, primarily road-watch expeditions lasting a couple of weeks each. Several teams were sent to grab prisoners, and one went to monitor a river. The last-named mission, STRATA 120, became the only patrol on Speedy Gaspard's watch to be lost without a trace. That still amounted to a big contrast with the Footboy program of agent teams into North Vietnam, in which capture seemed the norm. For STRATA 120 the crunch came in mid-May, with its final radio contact on the seventeenth. Three other STRATA teams suffered casualties in 1968, for a total of fifteen missing in action. Even with these losses, however, twenty-three of twenty-four STRATA patrols came back. Road watch furnished coverage of the roads to Ban Karai Pass for a cumulative total of about two and a half months in 1968, plus about a month on the routes into Mu Gia Pass. In addition, several STRATA missions scouted out the land on the Vietnamese side of Napé Pass.

Aside from STRATA, the Studies and Observation Group continued its other activity, the cross-border missions. A new code word was added, Nickel Steel, to cover forays into the immediate environs of the Demilitarized Zone. Prairie Fire and Daniel Boone further increased their pace as well. In the period from mid-1967 through mid-1969 the Studies and Observation Group spent $15.6 million in direct costs for Prairie Fire, plus more than $3.1 million on the McNamara Line sensor systems; there were also more than $6.2 million in direct costs for Daniel Boone operations. Until 1969 the Cambodian cross-border activities were funded through the 5th Special Forces Group, but after that its budget would be SOG's responsibility. Maritime and other actions against the DRV consumed a greater amount of SOG's budget, but the disparity diminished.

Cross-border operations continued at a high level and, as usual, the secret warriors had their troubles with American diplomats in Laos. Colonel Singlaub recounts that Westmoreland, encountering these difficulties, would order him to work it out with Ambassador Sullivan at the SEACOORD meetings in Udorn. Westy disliked Sullivan, according to Singlaub, and would contrive to be otherwise occupied when he could, leaving MACV to be represented by General William W. ("Spike") Momyer, commanding the Seventh Air Force. Momyer had orchestrated the massive application of aerial firepower that took place at Khe Sanh, and he had flown fighter-bombers over The Trail himself. Even from a fast mover, Spoke Mimyer had seen that the People's Army was adopting new measures to frustrate him—dispersing gasoline stocks in single barrels or small allotments all along the roads rather than big, juicy truck parks that Seventh Air Force planes could plaster. General Momyer knew he needed SOG to keep up the pressure on the ground so his planes could perform to best advantage. At the SEACOORD meetings Spike Momyer could be tough with Sullivan and wring concessions for Singlaub, continually faced with complaints from Vientiane, recounted earlier, about SOG operations. Colonel Singlaub recalls that the complaints always seemed to go out in cables to the whole world, while Sullivan's apologies, when discovering he had been wrong on one item or another, always seemed to come in the men's room or over drinks at the officers' club.

Due to the Tet Offensive and its aftermath, MACSOG's operations during 1968 would be conducted inside South Vietnam to an unusual degree. More than 40 percent of Prairie Fire missions, for example, including all its company-size Hornet Force missions, took place inside the border. In part this was due to requests from American combat leaders—General Westmoreland ordered a maximum effort into the A Shau valley by special warfare forces at the time of operation Pegasus, preparing a later offensive by elements of the 1st Cavalry Division. In the Central Highlands, 4th Infantry Division commander Major General Charles P. Stone asked MACSOG for missions into Indian country beyond Dak To and Kontum. Nevertheless, there were a total of 271 Spike team and 56 Hatchet Force missions into Laos or the Nickel Steel area.

The effects of the Tet fighting were even more marked in the Daniel Boone zone. With its main compound at Ban Me Thuot, Command and Control South (CCS) had 158 Americans and 1,070 indigenous troops. Between February and September 80 percent of the CCS operations took place inside Vietnam. Only in October, when 53 missions went into Cambodia, was the cross-border emphasis restored. During 1968 as a whole, CCS mounted 726 operations, of which 287 crossed into the actual Daniel Boone area of operations.

The perils of aircraft packages and dangers of LZs in Indian country are vividly demonstrated by the experience of Reconnaissance Team Maine, sent out to help prepare a SLAM mission in February 1968. The target, called Quebec-1, was a segment of the Sihanouk Trail behind the Chu Pong massif. The team launched their operation from FOB-2 at Kontum on February 19. Though the target area was close to the Laotian base at Attopeu, little help was to be expected from that quarter. Team Maine's leader, Staff Sergeant Douglas Glover, had premonitions about the mission and told a friend he had dreamed he was going to be killed. Glover was not quite a

"Fucking New Guy"—Vietnam vernacular for a brand-new arrival—but Quebec-1 would be only his third patrol. Glover's friend Staff Sergeant Fred W. Zabitosky, a twenty-six-year-old from Trenton, New Jersey, went out with RT Maine as assistant team leader. Radioman Percell Bragg and six Nung troops completed the force.

This operation was part of a special effort; General Westmoreland desperately wanted to know if the enemy was planning another wave of Tet attacks, so Colonel Singlaub laid on a set of five missions designed to get a quick fix on VPA troop movements and supply stocks in the main concentration areas. Targets could then be pasted by Arc Light, using new methods (inaugurated at Khe Sanh) under which the B-52s could be given targets at the very last moment, minimizing the lag between discovery and counteraction.

Team Maine boarded slicks of the 57th Assault Helicopter Company and headed for Laos. Landing on the LZ, they found themselves smack in the middle of a People's Army camp. Green Berets of MACSOG liked the imagery of their "Hornet Force" strike companies, but Team Maine, trapped inside a real hornets' nest, could have used the help of such units. Before the battle ended there would be twenty-two enemy assaults. The forward air controller became crucial, calling back flights of A-1E strike aircraft and getting some troop carrier helicopters to recover the SOG scouts. Sergeant Zabitosky fired weapons and kept down the *bo dois* as his teammates ran to the landing zone and took position. Zabitosky then led the defense in place of Glover, who concentrated on maintaining radio contact with the FAC, observing for air strikes.

A product of a broken family, Fred Zabitosky had run away to join the army at a tender age, and he liked the discipline of the service. It was discipline that pulled him through that dark morning in 1968, saving Team Maine. When Zabitosky reached the perimeter he managed the withdrawal as the choppers arrived. The first one got out all right, with Sergeant Bragg and several Nungs. The others crowded into a second slick, but it was hit by a rocket-propelled grenade as it climbed through 100 feet. The chopper shuddered, lost power, then crashed and caught fire. Burned, his rib cage and back smashed in the crash, Zabitosky nevertheless pulled the pilot and copilot from the wreckage and helped Nung survivors reach a nearby clearing, where Zabitosky managed to lug the wounded copilot, who weighed almost twice as much as he. A medical evacuation helicopter landed and took aboard the survivors. The first ship's door gunners and Sergeant Glover were killed. Later that day Team Texas mounted a Bright Light mission into the same area in an effort to recover the bodies of the dead. RT Texas, led by Sergeant "Pappy" Webb, counted 109 dead *bo dois*.

By one account, Team Maine had landed amid the headquarters and base camp of a People's Army division, an installation home to more than 2,000 of Hanoi's soldiers. Estimated by Vietnam's notorious "body count," the VPA losses have been put at Webb's 109 or at 145, either way a significant fraction of *bo doi* strength.

Sergeant Zabitosky was given the Medal of Honor for his bravery that day. The awards ceremony occurred more than a year later, after Richard Nixon had become president of the United States.

"I appreciate the project. I know what happened. I know where you were when you got it," Nixon told Zabitosky, "but unfortunately we have to write your citation as being in Vietnam."

Sergeant Zabitosky's citation reads simply that his men were operating "deep inside enemy-controlled territory" and makes no mention of MAC-SOG. However, the back side of his medal, where no one could see it, was engraved: "FOB-2, C & C Detachment, 5th Special Forces."

For all the wrenching anxiety of their mission, RT Maine, or at least most of them, came home. The same could not be said for other forays, other teams, and the prospect of getting caught in Indian country had to be terrifying. Not so lucky was Reconnaissance Team Asp, a CCS unit built around tribal Rhadé, which was diverted to I Corps by the war situation, and sent to place a wiretap northeast of Tchepone. The Spike team worked out of Heavy Hook, SOG's secure compound at Nakhon Phanom, so as to approach their target area from the rear. Team Maine entered without incident on March 27 and apparently placed their tap, but the next day called for an emergency extraction. There was no place to land a helicopter in the dense jungle, especially one of the big CH-3s come to rescue them. The chopper let down a ladder, and the Rhadé began to climb while their three American sergeants, George R. Brown, Charles G. Huston, and Alan L. Boyer, covered them. The last Rhadé, and Sergeant Boyer, were halfway up the ladder when it parted, either damaged or overstrained, and they fell back to earth. Boyer did not move. Brown and Huston were still shooting as the rescue chopper and its backups were forced to leave.

An immediate Bright Light mission by another team under Sergeant Charles Feller tried to recover the RT Asp men, but they found nothing. Some observers believe the rescue mission may have landed in the wrong place. Sergeants Brown, Huston, and Boyer were listed among Americans missing in action in the Vietnam War.

Scuttlebutt among those close to SOG was that Team Asp's wiretap worked. If so, Asp's sacrifice proved unique, for according to its command history for 1968, the Studies and Observation Group had only one wiretap that yielded exploitable intelligence that year. In all there were four wiretaps placed in Laos and Cambodia, plus two inside Vietnam.

As for overall losses, SOG's toll in 1968 amounted to 56 American dead, 214 wounded, and 27 missing in action. Vietnamese or other indigenous casualties numbered 133 killed, 481 wounded, and 55 missing. That was almost 1,000 casualties, a tenth of SOG's strength. In addition, 17 helicopters were lost in Laos, 3 in Cambodia, and 9 on SOG operations inside Vietnam.

Tet and its aftermath marked a high point for MACSOG in terms of open battle. At Hue the group's radio station, Voice of Freedom, was attacked. Its million-watt broadcast transmitter, only the second of that size in the world, was rendered useless when the Liberation Front broke key parts. Replacements had yet to arrive when Jack Singlaub left Vietnam at the end of his tour. Khe Sanh, of course, directly involved FOB-3, and that unit operated at a high level through operation Pegasus and the subsequent months, when marines conducted mobile operations radiating out from the combat base. The phase of mobile operations around Khe Sanh proved as costly as the siege itself, and FOB-3 was engaged in many of these actions. Then there was Kham Duc.

IN an earlier age Kham Duc had been one of the original border surveillance camps. As such, it had had extra-strong complements of CIDG and Mike Forces and fair success at keeping watch on the Annamite foothills. When the badly designed border camp A Ro closed in 1963, Kham Duc took its place. When MACSOG formed, Kham Duc was pressed into service as a launch site for scout missions into Indian country. Its temporary facility would be improved with a permanent one, located at one corner of the camp. Both the 5th Special Forces and SOG's Command and Control North considered Kham Duc an important position and took pains to defend it well.

In the spring of 1968 there was an engineer detachment at Kham Duc improving its airfield. The engineers had their own compound outside the main camp, as did the 137th CIDG Company, brought in for training and to increase available maneuver forces. Green Beret Detachment A-105 under Captain Christopher J. Silva ran Kham Duc, with about 50 Special Forces, Vietnamese LLDB, CIDG cadre, and interpreters. Troops included 440 Montagnards, 122 Americans in A Company of the 70th Engineer Battalion, and 125 total (22 of them American) in the SOG contingent. In addition, Kham Duc would be bolstered by a satellite position about four miles to the south, as the crow flies (though much farther on the ground), at a place called Ngok Tavak. Manning the satellite would be another Mike Force company of 122 Nungs led by Australian captain John E. D. White, with a dozen Australian, American, and Vietnamese cadre. Altogether there were nearly 900 troops in the sector.

Tet was quiet here. The Mike Force Nungs and Montagnards went about their business, while combat roiled through the rest of South Vietnam. The first signs of trouble were discovered by a FAC. This aerial observer reported *bo dois* at work on a road crossing the Vietnamese border, extending toward Route 14, the main thoroughfare of the Central Highlands. That was early in February. Photo planes returned pictures that confirmed the report. As the days stretched to weeks, the People's Army pushed its road northward, toward Ngok Tavak and, beyond it, Kham Duc.

The enemy was not *on* the road. Rather, the People's Army already inhabited Quang Tin Province, locale of both Kham Duc and its satellite. The VPA 2d Division provided the muscle here. The significance of the road lay in the great improvement it afforded the VPA in ability to supply forward units. That would enable the People's Army to threaten lowland towns, district seats, and ultimately Da Nang. For Hanoi's legions, Kham Duc and Ngok Tavak stood in the way of that possibility.

A key question for MACV was whether the VPA 2d Division would maneuver to the north, through Quang Tin, or perhaps turn south into the Central Highlands proper. Because Kham Duc was situated on the Quang Tin side, Colonel Jonathan Ladd's 5th Special Forces Group got the job of finding out if the *bo dois* were going to come that way. Jed White's 11th Mike Force Company went to Kham Duc as a fresh unit to pursue that mission.

Ngok Tavak began as nothing more than a forward base to let Green Beret patrols range farther into the jungle. Captain White's first misgivings were on the flight up to Kham Duc, whose airstrip had been built in the 1950s to bring in construction materials for a hunting lodge for Ngo Dinh Diem. White's entire company traveled on one C-130 aircraft. He worried about an accident. In mid-March the unit moved to Ngok Tavak, a mountain, under the peak of which stood an old French fort that became the base camp. Vietnamese leader Diem had been right about the hunting—game abounded. Venison became a staple in diets throughout the Kham Duc area. But finding the People's Army proved more difficult. More doubts rose when MACV stopped supplying Ngok Tavak by helicopter—choppers were too expensive in maintenance and wear. The C-7 Caribous that replaced them brought three-week loads (the helicopter visits had been every four days), which meant White's troops could no longer carry all their supplies. This was especially true once the Caribous brought a half dozen live pigs to tend. Ngok Tavak became a static post.

Until late April, patrols from Ngok Tavak returned with nothing but venison and hair-raising stories of tigers or herds of wild elephants. There were no settlements at all and no tribesmen to bring news from places farther afield, such as The Trail, just over the Laotian side of the border. Then one of White's patrols encountered three armed Montagnards. No one was hurt; the probable explanation was that the men had been scouts for the People's Army. From then on, indications piled up rapidly. A captured document associated a 559th Transport Group *binh tram* with the road the *bo dois* were building. Photographs showed the road made of dirt and three lanes wide. More documents revealed movement of the headquarters and a couple of units of the 2d Division toward Ngok Tavak and Kham Duc.

At the beginning of May the U.S. command decided to reinforce Ngok Tavak with an artillery platoon from D Battery, 2d Battalion, 13th Marine Artillery Regiment. Lieutenant Robert Adams brought up two 105-mm howitzers and thirty-three marines. Kham Duc also sent thirty-five men from a CIDG mortar unit. The morning after the strikers arrived, Captain White found all his camp's telephone wires out, along with many of those that controlled the detonation of claymore mines. After that the Montagnard unit was believed to be infiltrated with Viet Cong. Jed White asked Kham Duc to withdraw the strikers, but there were no aircraft to move them. The CIDG unit would be placed outside the main perimeter, where it could be observed and its defection would not cripple the defense. White's main problem with the marine artillery detachment was his desire to regain a mobile role for Mike Force. Once there were guns to protect, there could be no alternative to holding Ngok Tavak. In addition, the vegetation and height of surrounding hills meant guns could fire only at maximum elevation, which limited their usefulness anyway. Tim Brown, a marine with D/2/13, confirms that his unit fired only a couple of support missions in the days before the battle.

Captain White dispatched a fighting patrol toward the south, but it had gone only a few miles when ambushed. The troops had to split up to escape, fortunately with just one man lost. On May 6, and again on the eighth, patrols met the People's Army, the second time barely 1,000 yards from Ngok Tavak. Also on May 8, soldiers from Kham Duc captured a *bo doi* who said he was from the 1st Regiment of the VPA 2d Division. The prisoner revealed the division intended to hit Kham Duc but the operation had been postponed because heavy weapons were late arriving. Toward evening on the ninth, the CIDG platoon leader at Ngok Tavak went to Captain White and asked permission to go back to Kham Duc on foot. The Australian officer was happy to approve. He learned later the Montagnards had been in touch with the enemy even before leaving Kham Duc. They were told they had no chance to live if they stayed at Ngok Tavak, but when the CIDG tried to leave, they quickly fell into an ambush *bo dois* had set for Mike Force.

Chris Silva, boss at Kham Duc, came to Ngok Tavak late that afternoon to reason with the Montagnards. He was still there in the night when the attack came. Hanoi's soldiers struck the CIDG position first. The strikers bolted; *bo dois* swarmed at the French fort, where there was one gap in the wire covered by a single .50-caliber machine gun.

"Don't shoot! Don't shoot! Friendly! Friendly!" screamed men running toward the gap.

Defending marines held their fire long enough for the People's Army to take advantage. The perimeter was breached, the machine gun wiped out with a grenade. On the other side of Ngok Tavak, the parade ground, where Australian NCOs led two more platoons of Nungs, the VPA massed, but claymores stopped them in their tracks. Jed White eventually rallied his defenders here, and at dawn counterattacked into the French fort and restored the position. It was obvious to him Ngok Tavak could not be held.

Captain White asked for permission to withdraw, but the B Detachment at Da Nang, his superiors in the 5th Group chain of command, did not respond. With danger mounting by the minute, White decided to retreat on his own initiative. Airpower had saved his men in the first attacks—there had been warning from a FAC the previous afternoon, while an AC-47 gunship had turned up at a critical moment in the night—but there was no guarantee this could go on. White knew the dangers of the jungle, judging them fewer than those of remaining in place. A flight of CH-46 helicopters took out wounded and brought some men from the 12th Mike Force Company, but only two ships landed before the LZ became impossible. Da Nang now ordered Jed White to hold, informing him that reinforcements were en route to Kham Duc. The Australian finally decided he would retreat in the afternoon regardless of what Da Nang said, and that is what he did. Choppers picked up the survivors on a grassy knoll a couple of miles from the fort. Hanoi's troops stayed under cover and were nowhere to be seen.

At Kham Duc mortar shells were already beginning to pitch into the ground as C-130s disgorged the first of more than 700 soldiers, a composite task force of the Americal Division's 196th Infantry Brigade. The core of the force was Lieutenant Colonel Robert B. Nelson's 2d Battalion, 1st Infantry. Nelson assumed command of Kham Duc in place of the wounded Captain Silva, who had been trapped at Ngok Tavak and now was evacuated to a field hospital. The rest of the survivors appeared briefly at Kham Duc and were sent on to Da Nang the next day. A ground sweep around the border camp on May 11 found nothing, but that night an outpost would be bombarded, then attacked and overrun. Defenders held out inside bunkers until noon on May 12, when they were ordered to escape.

Higher command decided not to make Kham Duc another Khe Sanh. Marine general Robert Cushman had few reserves plus another Special Forces camp, at Thuong Duc, that was also threatened. There was an apparent Liberation Front buildup in the lowlands. All this formed part of a second wave of the Tet offensive, and there could be no telling where it would end. Cushman met with Fred Ladd of 5th Group, Americal Division commander Major General Samuel W. Koster, and General Creighton Abrams of MACV Forward, to make the decision.

Fred Ladd, sensitive to the importance of Kham Duc in the larger battle of The Trail, refused to give up the fight. Without Kham Duc, SOG's scouts would be starting their missions farther away from The Trail. In particular, helicopters would have grave difficulties flying into a whole section of lower Laos. Ladd insisted on Kham Duc's importance to MACSOG and warned of the propaganda value to Hanoi of a victory there. General Cushman overruled Colonel Ladd, worried about the new wave of Tet attacks. General Abrams backed Cushman.

The final decision was Westmoreland's, and he, too, wanted no part of a battle for Kham Duc. "In my opinion it had none of the importance or defensive potential of a Khe Sanh," Westy wrote later. He ordered evacuation. General John Chaisson, MACV's top operations expert, put this in a letter home: "The decision to evacuate was brought on considerably by the Khe Sanh experience."

After a slow start the morning of May 12, an airlift moved tremendous numbers of people out of Kham Duc, especially in its last hour. Two FACs and an airborne command post managed the fast movers' bombing and strafing in an effort to suppress antiaircraft. Dangers were unavoidable, though. Before the end of the day two C-130 transports and four helicopters had crashed. Some 256 persons, mostly civilians, died in the evacuation.

Meanwhile, that morning Lieutenant Colonel Daniel Schungel, Special Forces commander for I Corps, arrived from Da Nang. He had been at Kham

Duc only a couple of hours when the evacuation order came through. Schungel became the only high-ranking Green Beret officer present at both the fall of Kham Duc and that of Lang Vei, a somewhat dubious distinction. The People's Army began to close in on the base about noon. They then attacked the SOG compound. Though *bo dois* were in the outer fence wire by 2:00 P.M., the combination of small arms, artillery and mortar fire, plus air strikes, kept them at bay. By four-thirty the last defenders were boarding their planes out of Kham Duc.

In all the toll of the battle would be 299 casualties, more than a third American. Every single marine at Ngok Tavak was killed or wounded, and there were 31 missing, the largest number in any single action of the Vietnam War. Studies and Observation Group proved lucky: SOG suffered just three wounded. The greatest loss, however, would be diminished access to The Trail.

Kham Duc proved the high point for Hanoi of the second wave of Tet in the northern provinces of South Vietnam. Except for Saigon, where again there would be major fighting, mortar bombardments and rocket attacks dominated the action. Back when Hanoi planned Tet, at the headquarters cave of the Tri-Thien-Hue military region, General Tran Van Quang kept telling his aides they should think of Tet as a process, not a battle. The waves of Tet—and there would be a third one, in August 1968—show this was indeed Hanoi's intent. In August rocket and mortar attacks were again the highlights. Again, too, the Studies and Observation Group would become a target. One of the People's Army attacks aimed at the CCN compound outside Da Nang. This sapper attack ended with fifteen SOG Americans and sixteen South Vietnamese killed, while Hanoi's losses amounted to thirty-eight dead and nine captured.

Another MACSOG loss, equal to the impact of the withdrawal from Kham Duc, would be the abandonment of Khe Sanh itself. In the period after operation Pegasus, Colonel Stanley S. Hughes of the 1st Marine Regiment had held that combat base with four battalions, conducting more and more operations into the surrounding countryside. Both Cushman and General William R. Rosson of XXIV Corps, which now controlled the DMZ sector, preferred mobile warfare over defending Khe Sanh as a fixed position. A full battalion of infantry plus engineer troops were tied down just keeping Route 9 open to Khe Sanh, however. Those troops could be saved simply by relocating the forward supply point to Ca Lu, known to the Cav as LZ Stud, and then to Marines as Fire Support Base Vandegrift.

The plan to abandon Khe Sanh is dated June 12, 1968, the day after William C. Westmoreland left Vietnam to become army chief of staff. By itself that fact says a great deal about the reasons for Khe Sanh and the connection between the combat base and the project for an invasion of Laos. Creighton Abrams, the new commander of MACV, refused to be tied to Khe Sanh. As "Dutch" Kerwin put it in 1976, "General Abe did not see eye to eye with General Westmoreland on Khe Sanh. Now he never came out and said we ought to be out of Khe Sanh, but I know from my conversations with him that he felt we would be better off without Khe Sanh. . . . It was a tomb that we were locked in at Khe Sanh. Perhaps if General Westmoreland had stayed, we would still be at Khe Sanh."

President Johnson also wanted no more nonsense about defending exposed positions or pressures to invade Laos, and his military adviser Maxwell Taylor had been advocating a pullout from Khe Sanh since the height of the siege. It is likely that during a visit to Washington that Abrams made in March, the seed of the idea to get out of Khe Sanh was planted by LBJ himself.

One who objected would be Walt Rostow. When it came to executing the plans for the withdrawal, Walt warned the president that pulling out of Khe Sanh meant a serious problem—certainly of public relations and perhaps of substance. Since MACV had long harped on its tying down many VPA with just 6,000 Americans and Vietnamese, Rostow feared people would ask why that was not still a good idea. Couched in terms of image and politics, the things Rostow knew mattered to Lyndon Johnson, the argument for holding Khe Sanh had been squarely posed.

Though he often responded to political arguments such as Rostow's for Khe Sanh, President Johnson *refused* to step in and cancel MACV's withdrawal. The reasons almost certainly have to do with the relationship between LBJ and his new Vietnam commander, Creighton Abrams. No record apparently exists of private conversations Johnson had with Abrams when the latter briefly came to Washington in March 1968. Mutual esteem prevailed between the two men, however, and the president repeatedly sought Abrams's advice. He did so in the period after suspending Rolling Thunder for the northern part of the DRV, on the occasion of the second wave of Tet attacks, and before Johnson's full bombing halt in November 1968. General Abrams furnished the White House with copies of his views on overall strategy, as well as specific ideas on bombing tactics. Abrams, in fact, supported the end of the bombing of North Vietnam as a means of opening the door to negotiations while actually giving him *increased* firepower to use against The Trail in Laos. LBJ, now actively seeking negotiations, appreciated political support from Abrams. Walt Rostow followed the president's lead and began to focus on the details of preliminary talks under way between the United States and Hanoi in Paris.

At Khe Sanh, marines disposed of their supplies and equipment, blew up bunkers, and dismantled installations on the airfield. The Studies and Observation Group abandoned its FOB-3 base. The marines pulled back to Firebase Vandegrift at Ca Lu. The 5th Special Forces opened the nearby Camp Mai Loc, which was Lang Vei rebuilt, with 210 Mike Force troops, 114 CIDG strikers, 18 ARVN Special Forces, plus Green Beret Detachment A-101. Construction of the camp would be covered by a marine rifle company and accomplished by an engineer platoon with heavy equipment. Through the autumn MACSOG spent more than $250,000 at Camp Mai

Loc to replicate the launch site it had had at Khe Sanh. But Command and Control North finally used Mai Loc only a few months before making Quang Tri its primary DMZ base.

As for Khe Sanh, the last Americans left the combat base on July 6, 1968. A Baltimore newspaper printed news of the planned withdrawal, and the People's Army tried to block Route 9, but U.S. forces easily broke through the *bo dois* along the road.

Regardless of casualties at Khe Sanh or at Tet, by the summer of 1968 there had been practical effects other than Tet's political impact. American military figures and some analysts point only to Hanoi's casualties in seeing a victory for the United States. But Hanoi had achieved a *military* result independent of and in addition to its psychological success. The People's Army in 1968 succeeded in clearing the flanks of The Trail. In Laos, Hanoi guaranteed that achievement by putting more pressure on Attopeu and Saravane. By late spring U.S. officials were telling each other the VPA had enough troops deployed to capture Saravane anytime they wanted. The monsoon that year brought quiet sighs of relief.

The loss of Khe Sanh and Kham Duc transformed SOG's cross-border campaign. Ground support for the McNamara Line would be curtailed in favor of SOG's other missions. From Quang Tri and Mai Loc, Spike teams found it most practical to cover the DMZ and Tchepone area. Deeper forays posed increasing headaches. Without Kham Duc, similarly, SOG helicopter coverage of the Prairie Fire operational zone was reduced by about one third. The Studies and Observation Group tried to compensate by greater use of Dak Pek, in the Central Highlands, and of Nakhon Phanom in Thailand. Increased activity in the Central Highlands forced SOG to create an independent Command and Control Central at Kontum. Jack Singlaub left Vietnam in the summer of 1968. His successor, Colonel Stephen E. Cavanaugh, made all efforts to get SOG's reconnaissance teams across the borders again. During 1969 almost five hundred RT missions went into the Prairie Fire area alone, and fully a quarter of that effort in the vicinity of Tchepone. If SOG could not hit the entire Trail, at least it could act strongly against one part of it.

Meanwhile, the end also came for Lyndon Johnson. Americans, obliged to reconsider Vietnam due to the Tet Offensive and the evident power of Hanoi and the National Liberation Front to make attacks throughout South Vietnam, stopped supporting U.S. policy. The efforts of Rostow, Westmoreland, and others to make extravagant claims of progress to solidify public approval ratings backfired. The Joint Chiefs of Staff simultaneously asked President Johnson to mobilize reserves and send 210,000 more U.S. troops to Vietnam. Johnson demanded a policy review and engaged his friend, and McNamara's replacement at the Pentagon, Clark Clifford, to oversee the exercise. Clifford told the president he needed to project peace, not war, and advised rejection of the troop request. LBJ followed that advice and, as already noted, withdrew from American electoral politics. Johnson became a lame-duck president.

The antiwar movement had had a significant role in Lyndon Johnson's withdrawal from politics. Self-motivated antiwar activists worked in the campaign organizations of politicians who opposed Johnson. In turn, LBJ's poor showing in early 1968 political primaries had helped condition his thinking in March. The antiwar activists focused on electoral politics that year, as the civil rights movement turned in a very different direction, erupting in mob violence in a number of U.S. cities, including Detroit, Newark, Atlanta, and Washington, D.C., among others. These riots, sparked by the assassination of Dr. Martin Luther King, Jr., a few days after LBJ's speech of March 31, polarized the race issue and ended the nascent alliance between civil rights and antiwar movements. Conversely, antiwar demonstrations ebbed as activists got involved in the 1968 elections. Richard M. Nixon, the leading candidate in those elections, insisted he had a plan to end the Vietnam War. When Nixon won, the American public thought it had reason to suppose this was a step toward peace in Vietnam.

The shocks of 1968 included not only the King assassination but also that of Robert F. Kennedy, and the antiwar activists got a trauma of their own in Chicago at the Democratic National Convention that summer. Both those who had opted to work on election campaigns and the activists focused on protest ended up in an ugly confrontation with Chicago police. In the aftermath, protesters such as Tom Hayden, who until recently had been doing civil rights work in Newark, were left to find their way through the maze of confusion. "Around me the currents of protest seemed to be passing through a particle accelerator," Hayden later wrote. "My mind was on Vietnam as the central issue, the metaphor and mirror of our times, the moral and murderous experience that would mark our identity for the future." In speeches against the war, Hayden began asserting that the movement's goal should be to make it impossible for the next president to take office without promising to end the Vietnam War.

Richard Milhous Nixon seemed to promise that, but in office delivered something very different, a veritable escalation. Some observers argue that the antiwar movement, echoing its own increasing despair over the evident refusal of government to respond to dissent in America, became more disruptive. Were the activists taking a page from the struggle of African Americans? Certainly the group Students for a Democratic Society (SDS) reflected a mood to go for the jugular, but in 1968 SDS splintered, one faction spinning out leftward, leaving behind the core of antiwar sentiment. That core, the product of a multi-issue constituency, could never have agreed on a strategy of purposeful violence, even to end the war.

Nevertheless, in American politics and in the arena of the antiwar movement, Tet and 1968 brought changes as momentous as it had for MACV and the Studies and Observation Group. Changes in The World, no less than those in The 'Nam, would come full circle to affect the battle of The Trail. In the short run, however, President-elect Nixon and his new national security adviser, Henry A. Kissinger, occupied themselves arranging the transition to a new administration. Kissinger met with President Johnson on December 5. A week later, Johnson and Nixon met to discuss Vietnam.

By this time fitful talks had begun in Paris, and negotiators were even close to fitting in the Saigon government and the National Liberation Front as participants. Talks started under a formula that included President Johnson calling a halt to Rolling Thunder in return for tacit understandings that Hanoi would not do certain things in South Vietnam. In December, Nixon and Kissinger learned the latest—that Washington had evidence of nothing more than small-scale breaches of the bombing halt conditions, and had vigorously protested all it had heard of. Walt Rostow asked LBJ to tell Nixon that small units of Hanoi's troops were in the Demilitarized Zone, but then he referred to SOG's Nickel Steel operation: "We also run patrols into the southern half of the DMZ, in part to capture personnel and demonstrate in Paris that it is North Vietnamese and not NLF forces which are violating the DMZ." There was also talk of attacking enemy sanctuaries in Cambodia, of possible fighting around Saigon, of the resumption of bombing, and the latest pacification statistics.

In his final days at the White House, Walt Rostow showed he had not changed the views developed years before. *New York Times* reporters William Beecher, Peter Grose, and Hedrick Smith interviewed Rostow for his retrospective comments.

The reporters asked how the United States could have made Russia live up to promises to make Hanoi withdraw from Laos under the 1962 Geneva agreements. Dr. Rostow answered that Washington ought to have made this a very important diplomatic issue. Walt then said, "At a time when things were going rather well, we could have taken the kind of steps we took later."

"Send military forces?" the reporters asked.

"Yes," Rostow replied.

But when the *Times* followed up, asking whether Dr. Rostow meant sending military forces into Laos, the national security adviser hinted at a different predilection: "No, not into Laos."

Walt Rostow did not reveal explicitly his preference for an invasion of North Vietnam. Instead he became expansive: "I do think, taking the whole sweep of this problem, that if we put anything like the effort into the honoring of the 1962 accords that we later put into saving Southeast Asia when it was near collapse in 1965, that we would have been better off."

That statement, clearly provocative, challenged the journalists, who knew about the Kennedy administration policy debate over invading Laos with SEATO. One of the reporters asked if there had not been "a serious drive inside the administration in 1962 to take some of these steps."

"I don't want to go into that now," Rostow countered.

The security adviser wanted to make a charge but refused to discuss the specifics of it. When the reporters again pressed him, Rostow retreated to blandness: "My point is not to try to write history."

Needless to say, or perhaps necessary to say, is that public officials leaving office use this kind of exit interview precisely to try to define for history the issues on their watches, a sort of preemptive strike at opinion. That aside, Walt Rostow's January 1969 remarks are most important in demonstrating that the ideas of striking into Laos, and of invasion of the North, continued as live options right into the Nixon years. Casting about for different directions in Vietnam, President Nixon and his minions were perfectly willing to consider forceful ones. The combination of measures that became the Nixon strategy, confrontational and clever, set the stage for the pinball wizards of the Vietnam War.

CHAPTER 12

A Strategy of Force
1969–1970

Facing history for himself, Richard Nixon wrote that he entered office with three fundamental premises regarding Vietnam. He intended to prepare the American public for failure to achieve total military victory; to endeavor to keep U.S. commitments to Saigon; and finally, to end the war as quickly as was honorably possible. These were certainly important components of policy, but the account is incomplete, even disingenuous. Of escalation, in his memoir Nixon wrote, "It was an option we ruled out very early." Instead, Nixon reports, he wanted a bargain, "a fair negotiated settlement that would preserve the independence of South Vietnam." In turn, Richard Nixon's idea of a fair settlement, still following his own memoir, was what he initially offered at Paris—the DMZ as a real "boundary" between North and South, plus a simultaneous withdrawal of the United States and of the Democratic Republic from South Vietnam. No doubt this looks good on paper, but in reality, in 1969 there was no way to attain those terms, *except* through victory in Vietnam.

The Demilitarized Zone had never been a boundary and by international agreement was not supposed to be one. In claiming the DMZ as a border, Richard Nixon clearly aligned himself with those predecessors who had sought to justify the war in Vietnam and fight it, with men like Walt Rostow and Dean Rusk. This was not the road to accommodation. As for Hanoi abandoning the National Liberation Front by withdrawal from the South, absent a DRV defeat the likelihood of agreement on that point had to be negligible. Holed up in its base areas, sustained by The Trail, the Vietnam People's Army could afford to wait. The Nixon administration, facing steadily intensifying antiwar sentiment, had the clock ticking against it. Given that Richard Nixon had no intention of offering Hanoi incentives for a deal, the sole pathway to the outcome he desired would have been to defeat the Northerners.

National security adviser Henry Kissinger, in his second recounting of Nixon's Vietnam War, a book he titled *Diplomacy*, maintains solidarity with his former boss. "Nixon was eager to negotiate an honorable extrication," writes Kissinger, "which he defined as almost anything except turning over to the North Vietnamese Communists the millions of people who had been led by his predecessors to rely on America." These themes—that Nixon inherited the mess and that Nixon tried flexibly to negotiate a settlement—repeat what Henry wrote in his memoir *White House Years*. Kissinger would reiterate those arguments again on other occasions, such as the public discussion surrounding release of a movie titled *Nixon* by the Hollywood director Oliver Stone. The same themes would be echoed by subordinates such as NSC aide Peter W. Rodman, who writes, "The American commitment to Vietnam was an inherited fact. The task he faced was how to get out."

A theme is a leitmotif, though, and substance is different and more serious. Rather wistfully Henry Kissinger would say, in the Vietnam portion of *Diplomacy*, "Would that history were as simple as journalism." But Kissinger spent a major portion of his time in the White House sidling up to journalists, and then sequestered his papers at the Library of Congress and elsewhere under conditions preventing historians from gaining access to them. Kissinger has only himself to thank for his difficulties with history. The same is true for Richard Nixon, who fought tooth and nail any release of his papers, not just private but public ones, too, to the public domain. The result is that the internal records of the Nixon presidency have been very slow to emerge. Nevertheless, an increasing proportion of these records is coming to light, enough to suggest that Nixon and Kissinger will continue to have problems with history.

Peter Rodman argues that Richard Nixon during his election campaign simply said he had a plan to end the Vietnam War, and that the statement was somehow "transmogrified" into the notion that Nixon had a "secret plan" to end the war. This is undoubtedly correct. The antiwar movement came to fear that Nixon's secret plan was to end the Vietnam War through a military victory. This belief turned out to be substantially accurate also, for the perverse reason that Richard Nixon's plan to end the war was completely unrealistic. On the one hand, as Rodman and other participants make clear, Nixon intended to use American diplomatic links with Russia to get Moscow to induce Hanoi to agree with a settlement. As already seen here, however, Moscow had very limited influence in Hanoi and the motion that Russia could broker a Vietnam bargain was a pipedream. On the other hand, and even more problematical, Nixon's preferred offer had nothing to recommend it. Unless defeated militarily, in the field, Hanoi was never going to agree.

Thus, in effect if not a priori, the Nixon policy required a strategy of force. Indeed, what we now know of Nixon administration plans and maneuvers only strengthens that conclusion. As Nixon and Kissinger have both noted in different places, even before the administration took office, Nixon had ordered a review of Vietnam policy. As late as 1994 Henry Kissinger was still claiming that that review, embodied in National Security Study Memorandum (NSSM)-1, compared the courses of unilateral withdrawal, a showdown with Hanoi, or gradually shifting responsibility to the

Saigon government. Nixon, as we have seen, writes that the showdown option was abandoned very early. The reality is rather more complex.

Responding to NSSM-1, the various parts of the U.S. bureaucracy generally posed conditions to any American withdrawal, while holding out the potential for additional increments of force and/or forceful options. In its analysis of the reasons why Hanoi had agreed to negotiations, the State Department pointedly argued that, though the DRV might realize it was not winning, there seemed no sense of defeat in Hanoi, no notion that the war was being lost. In National Intelligence Estimate 50-68, the CIA denigrated the old saw of the "domino theory," and in its responses to NSSM-1 Langley noted, "The air campaign in Laos is not resulting in any sustained reduction of the capacity of the enemy logistic system." The CIA also maintained its long-standing position that the bombing of the DRV was ineffective, but it did not go so far as to argue the war was no longer winnable, if it ever had been. The Joint Chiefs and the Office of the Secretary of Defense, in contrast, insisted that airpower could be even more useful than heretofore believed, and they rejected withdrawals of American troops unless ARVN forces became more capable. The JCS went so far as to argue that conditions for a cessation of hostilities should include not only a cease-fire but also the "verified" withdrawal of the People's Army to the North, a verified halt of infiltration down The Trail, a repatriation of U.S. prisoners, substantial reduction of guerrilla terrorism, and a restored DMZ with "adequate safeguards," all seen as contingent on continuation of the U.S. effort.

The National Security Council's policy review revealed the U.S. government's divisions over Vietnam and essentially put Nixon in the position of being able to select his own course. Here there were two major alternatives. One was to continue the approach begun by the Johnson administration—strengthen the Saigon forces and begin unilateral withdrawals of U.S. troops while negotiating. This was favored by Melvin R. Laird, the new secretary of defense, who coined the term "Vietnamization" for it. The policy was also the favorite of the new secretary of state, William P. Rogers, and insiders called Vietnamization the "Laird-Rogers policy." The second alternative was to deal Hanoi a "savage blow" to force the DRV into concessions. That term, attributed to Henry Kissinger by his good friend British journalist Henry Brandon, defines the national security adviser's preference and was suggested soon after the 1968 election.

Richard Nixon in actuality adopted both policies. That is, it was necessary to do *something* on the ground in Vietnam, and the Laird-Rogers policy built on what was already in progress, while the Kissinger force option did nothing for the ground situation. There would be no stopping Vietnamization. Saigon leader Nguyen Van Thieu recognized that—as early as the New Year Thieu gave a speech anticipating American troop withdrawals from Vietnam. At a summit conference held at Midway Island on June 8, 1969, Thieu even gave Nixon advice on which U.S. units could be included in the first slice of the reduction. The memorandum of conversation for that meeting, however, also makes clear that Nixon still had in mind a savage blow—the way to overcome Hanoi's negotiating strategy, Nixon said, "is to set a deadline." Thieu agreed, and also "stated very frankly that there was a sagging of spirit in Saigon." That worried the U.S. president.

In his memoirs Richard Nixon makes this point at length:

> After half a year of sending peaceful signals to the Communists, I was ready to use whatever military pressure was necessary to prevent them from taking over South Vietnam by force. During several long sessions, Kissinger and I developed an elaborate orchestration of diplomatic, military, and publicity pressures we could bring to bear on Hanoi.
>
> I decided to set November 1, 1969—the first anniversary of Johnson's bombing halt—as the deadline for what would in effect be an ultimatum to North Vietnam.

Several entries in the diary of presidential chief of staff H. R. Haldeman show that the discussion was of the Kissinger policy, and also that Henry saw his approach as being in opposition to the Vietnamization policy of Laird and Rogers. Henry pushed his savage-blow idea vociferously—for example, on July 7 in the White House, and at an evening meeting on the presidential yacht *Sequoia*. A week later Nixon sent a secret letter to Ho Chi Minh warning of measures he would be obliged to take if Hanoi were not more forthcoming at the Paris peace talks. Ho replied in late August, shortly before his own death on September 3, refusing to make any concessions.

The next two months brought the climax of the force option, which came to be called operation Duck Hook. Nixon reviewed the general idea with Kissinger on August 28, with Bob Haldeman noting it "will be a tough period ahead if we go to it." At San Clemente, Nixon's California White House, the president walked along the beach with Haldeman and, after a hard day speechwriting, made a celebrated statement claiming credit for the force option: "I call it the Madman Theory, Bob. I want the North Vietnamese to believe I've reached the point where I might do *anything* to stop the war."

Existing accounts treat Duck Hook as if it were simply a theoretical construct, an idea of using force discussed more or less informally at the National Security Council and among NSC staff. In fact there was much more than that. The *coup de force* idea revolved around preferences of the Joint Chiefs of Staff and involved plans developed by the Joint Staff of the JCS. A group of eight officers of the Joint Staff, led by its operations director, Rear Admiral Frederic A. Bardshar, quietly crossed the Pacific and, after stopping at Honolulu for talks at CINCPAC, closeted itself at MACV to develop the plans. The code name for this little exercise was Pruning Knife, and as Bardshar put it in one of his cables, "We anticipate that the planning group will develop a sound military concept of action needed to achieve U.S. objectives . . . by force of arms."

Admiral Bardshar was a good choice for Pruning Knife, in that he was both an experienced combat commander and familiar with the operational environment of Southeast Asia. Until the previous summer Bardshar had been in charge of a carrier division on Yankee Station in the South China Sea, busily carrying out Rolling Thunder. Bardshar had been captain of the carrier *Constellation* during the Tonkin Gulf incident, had flown fighters and led a carrier air group in the Pacific during World War II, and had been on staffs with carrier units, NATO, the Mediterranean Fleet, and the Joint Chiefs. Just short of his fifty-fourth birthday, Frederic Bardshar had participated in the battles of the Philippine Sea, Leyte Gulf, and Okinawa, and he held multiple Silver Stars, Distinguished Flying Crosses, and Legions of Merit. In some ways, however, Pruning Knife would be his most delicate assignment.

There were at least four components to the Pruning Knife operational plans. One was an aerial offensive against the DRV at the rate of at least 532 sorties a day. This provided strikes against Hanoi's air force, its rail lines, bridges, and so on in the classic Vietnam style. A second component was the mining of Haiphong Harbor and other northern ports, planned down to the number of entry channels, the mines necessary to block each, expected weather, defenses to overcome, and alternate "modules," as they were called by Pruning Knife planners. Another scheme prepared under Admiral Bardshar provided for blocking Cambodian ports on the Gulf of Siam. Finally there was an outline plan for ground attacks into the Demilitarized Zone and the Democratic Republic. As the reporting cable (MAC 12563) summarized, on a top-secret "EYES ONLY" basis, "Ground operations into the DMZ and [DRV] will have a decided psychological impact on the enemy by demonstrating that they are no longer free to operate at will in the DMZ and that incursions may be made into [DRV] territory at any time."

While the Pruning Knife group made its way to Vietnam to assemble the plans on the spot, in Washington the senior officials went through the sheafs of ideas in their final deliberations. Henry Kissinger weighed in with a memorandum to Nixon on September 10, arguing that Vietnamization might not succeed in reducing American casualties until its final stages, that "the pressure of public opinion on you to resolve the war quickly will increase—and I believe increase greatly," and that time was running out faster in Washington than in Hanoi. This background was intended to sway Nixon into favoring Henry's "savage blow" option.

The issues were explored at length in a morning-long session of the National Security Council held in the Cabinet Room on September 12. This meeting included Ambassador Bunker; General Abrams; the CINCPAC, now Admiral John McCain; and top field commanders who came home for the council of war. Richard Nixon, who had made Vietnamization his own by calling it the "Nixon Doctrine," talked about making sure Asian boys fought Asian wars, but he also pressed for more forceful options the United States could take. After the main NSC session, Nixon walked over to the Old Executive Office Building, where he had a hideaway office, and talked some more with Bunker, Abrams, and McCain, along with General Earle Wheeler. During the private meeting the gloves came off and Nixon spoke of smashing Hanoi. These sessions provided important impetus for the Pruning Knife mission to Saigon.

A few days after returning to Hawaii, Admiral John McCain sent Wheeler a further dispatch, this on an "ABSOLUTELY EYES ONLY" basis. McCain spoke of actions in Laos in addition to those contemplated against the DRV. The CINCPAC, though he discussed the time-honored measures of improved coordination of military aid, and more top-level military advice for the U.S. ambassador, went far beyond those possibilities. McCain cabled:

> I RECOGNIZE THAT IT IS UNREALISTIC TO PLAN FOR THE COMMITMENT OF U.S. GROUND UNITS IN LAOS AND I WOULD NOT RECOMMEND SUCH ACTION EXCEPT IN VERY UNUSUAL CIRCUMSTANCES. HOWEVER, I HAVE FOR SOME TIME BEEN EXAMINING THE POSSIBLE EMPLOYMENT OF ASIAN THIRD COUNTRY FORCES TO FIGHT THE ASIAN WAR IN LAOS. USE OF THE ARVN AND POSSIBLY EVEN [SOUTH KOREAN FORCES], ON A QUICK STRIKING, CLEAN-UP AND GET OUT OPERATION IN THE SOUTHERN PANHANDLE OF LAOS HAS POSSIBILITIES AS A PSYCHOLOGICAL SHOCK ACTION.

With this cable, as well as the initial Pruning Knife messages in hand, on September 24 the Joint Chiefs of Staff had a working breakfast with the president. It was the first time Nixon had met with the entire Joint Chiefs, and while their subject was described as being the military budget, the plans for Southeast Asia were quietly discussed as well.

At Camp David on September 27 Richard Nixon told an assembly of Republican congressional leaders that he would not be the first president to lose a war, that Hanoi was mistaken to think he had little time left, and that the next thirty, then sixty, days would be critical.

Henry Kissinger made different comments in different places, leaving many confused as to what he truly thought. One NSC staffer quotes Kissinger saying, "I just can't believe that there is an organized society on earth that doesn't have a breaking point." By his own account Henry said little at the National Security Council on September 12, but in papers given Nixon on the tenth, the twelfth, and as late as October 30, Dr. Kissinger argued that Vietnamization would not work. The president, however, looking ahead to the nationwide televised speech he had already scheduled for November 3, began to change his own mind. Nixon agonized over the divisions in America, appreciated that Duck Hook would enrage the antiwar protesters, and made a connection between reducing the casualties in Vietnam and the political heat at home. Watching the weekly casualty reports, by early October Nixon could see that Laird's directives to Vietnam field commanders were indeed cutting the losses. On October 9, in a comment to Bob Haldeman, Kissinger remarked that he feared the president had ruled out his "savage blow" project. Speaking with Haldeman later in the day, Richard Nixon said he had not actually ruled out the Kissinger option but that the Laird-Rogers policy was beginning to look viable.

Meanwhile, the NSC staff was at work on an assortment of studies of the force option. Colonel—later General—Alexander M. Haig, who had started as an NSC military aide but who became Henry's deputy, handled military aspects in conjunction with Colonel William Lemnitzer, an NSC staff aide since before Tet, and Rear Admiral Rembrandt C. Robinson, Haig's successor as military assistant. Their Duck Hook study is still classified, and Haig did not even mention the episode in his memoir *Inner Circles*, but others believe he favored the attacks. William Watts, a Foreign Service officer who had worked on U.S. domestic issues during an assignment with Governor Nelson A. Rockefeller, arrived on the NSC staff at this time. Nixon happened to be at San Clemente, and Watts joined the presidential party in California. Out at dinner with Haig, Watts saw the atmosphere turn conspiratorial when the words "Duck Hook" dropped into the conversation. Though his task as NSC staff secretary was supposed to be largely administrative, Watts would be told to write a paper on the domestic political implications of Duck Hook. He found himself appalled. His opinion, rendered on October 13, was that pushing ahead would be a major error.

Lawrence Lynn, staff expert on systems analysis, critiqued Duck Hook from an operational standpoint, arguing the military had no reason to expect that these kinds of attacks would work any better than in the past. Lynn could point to CIA views, which remained as before: bombing was ineffective, plus the Pathet Lao and Hanoi had the power to threaten Laos at any time, and aggravating them could only crystallize that possibility. A draft speech flowed from the pens of Peter W. Rodman; Anthony Lake, later to become national security adviser to President William J. Clinton; and Roger Morris, subsequent biographer of both Richard Nixon and Al Haig. Lake and Morris separately joined in another memorandum rejecting Duck Hook on practical grounds. Only the NSC experts on Russian and Chinese affairs, Helmut Sonnenfeldt and John Holdridge, supplied opinions that bolstered the chances of the savage blow. Although Sonnenfeldt and Holdridge discounted the potential intervention of Hanoi's allies, Richard Nixon had yet to undertake the diplomacy that severed the triangle of Communist states from each other. Execution of the Pruning Knife options, especially the Haiphong mining, or the other isolation-of-the-battlefield measures—invading the DMZ and Laos—would very likely have brought in the Russians, at a minimum.

These studies inside the administration coincided with a new surge in the antiwar movement. During the initial months of Nixon's administration the protesters had been mostly quiescent as they waited to see what results would flow from Richard Nixon's plan to end the Vietnam War. But without movement on the Paris negotiations the frustration grew, particularly after April 1969, when the number of American combat deaths in Vietnam surpassed those suffered in the Korean War. A national moratorium was called for October 15, with a follow-up event for a month later.

Before the big demonstrations planned for Washington, the Students for a Democratic Society launched a deliberately violent protest in Chicago from October 8 to 11, the "Days of Rage." The SDS had been bloodied in this city the year before, and the "Chicago 7" leaders of the 1968 demonstrations were going up for trial. The Weathermen, the most militant faction of the splintered SDS, wanted to show up the contradictions of state power by means of open confrontation. The Days of Rage would be their theater, but also marked the effective end of SDS. Probably no more than 600 Weathermen and -women, and their hangers-on, were at this violent affair, but they attracted a great deal of attention.

The moratorium, when millions across the nation stopped business as usual for a day, framed the other end of the range of antiwar activism in America. The September 15 march on Washington that keynoted the moratorium proved huge—organizers spoke of up to a million demonstrators. The official police count would be 250,000, but the Nixon White House had its own photographs made, and as Bob Haldeman reveals, the White House crowd estimate was at least 325,000. If October had been huge, November would be humongous, as the November 15 march on Washington drew tremendous masses of protesters. Even the police count started at 600,000 that day.

At the White House, Henry Kissinger, who had been using the depths of antiwar sentiment to argue that the administration had little time left, needing to act immediately on Duck Hook, stepped back once Nixon accepted the Vietnamization strategy. On October 17, in the midst of the moratorium, Kissinger recommended *against* any immediate decision on Duck Hook. This was a way to drop advocacy of the savage blow quietly and without fanfare. Richard Nixon recast his November 3 speech to the nation as an appeal to public opinion, a device to gain room to move. Nixon's speech alleged the existence of a "silent majority" in favor of his war policy, and no doubt contributed to the massive turnout of demonstrators at the November 15 moratorium march.

In retrospect, both Richard Nixon and Henry Kissinger later regretted their failure to carry out Duck Hook. Telescoping the events of those war years, they pointed to the bombing and mining of 1972, which they believed successful, and wished it had been carried out in 1969. But *in* 1969, what William Watts feared was exactly right—the activists were frustrated enough to turn to violence, public opinion had begun its shift away from support of the war, and the Russians, not to mention the Chinese, had yet to be decoupled from Hanoi. Historian Tom Wells interviewed many of the key players for his important account of the impact of the antiwar movement. Their reflective views are as valid as Nixon's and Kissinger's and no doubt better informed. "The fact is that at that particular time the Chiefs' proposals would have been insane," recalls Lawrence Lynn. Here is Roger Morris: "It all had what I would call the 'Gallipoli syndrome' about it. It was a military and political fiasco which had taken on reality in these neatly typed papers somewhere in the Pentagon."

So Duck Hook was not to be. The top-secret JCS planning group came home from Saigon. Admiral Bardshar got another Gold Star to add to his Legion of Merit. And the military problems in Southeast Asia remained as before. Isolation of the battlefield had become a holy grail for military strategy in Southeast Asia, and this complement to pacification a route actually pursued, but the task had ramifications wider than anyone knew. Ultimately the search for the grail spread the war across new borders, and the aerial effort to cut The Trail turned Southeast Asia into a real-life version of a pinball machine.

"Kissinger, God knows what he supported" is what Admiral John McCain would tell an army colonel, in fact Earle Wheeler's son, who interviewed him in 1976. In contrast there could be little doubt where John McCain stood. The admiral had had little introduction to his post as commander in chief Pacific (CINCPAC)—merely stopping overnight in Washington en route from his command of U.S. naval forces in Europe to the Honolulu headquarters of CINCPAC. That move, in July 1968, and McCain's conversation with then secretary Clark Clifford, made for instant immersion in the difficulties of a theater command that spanned much of the globe. Admiral John S. McCain, Jr., son of an admiral of the same name (McCain's nickname in the navy actually was "Junior"), had sailed submarines in the Pacific during World War II, and surface ships off Taiwan during the Korean conflict, but his recent career had been bound up in the Atlantic and with NATO. Junior McCain had been the amphibious commander of the U.S. intervention in the Dominican Republic in 1965. Like Lyndon Johnson, who had gone overboard with claims of Communists in the Dominican events, McCain acquired something of a reputation for sticking red arrows on maps, but he was a competent naval leader.

Where McCain parted company with LBJ was over Rolling Thunder. When the president cast around for ways to stop the bombing in the fall of 1968, McCain didn't like it but knew writing on the wall when he saw it. The admiral made a fifty-cent bet with his chief of staff that President Johnson was going to stop Rolling Thunder. The day LBJ did that, Admiral McCain arrived at headquarters to find his staff chief, army general Clair Hutchinson, holding up a dispatch.

"Look at this, Admiral," Hutchinson said, handing over the cable.

Junior McCain took one glance, then shot back, "I won fifty cents from you!"

McCain took the half dollar and taped it to the corner of his desk. Over the months the coin got awfully rusty. The admiral would look at it on important occasions, when CINCPAC had to take a position or make a decision.

One issue that must have led to much coin-gazing was Hanoi's use of Cambodia to support the NLF and the VPA. This in essence posed a counterpoint to The Trail.

Cambodia had a coast on the Gulf of Siam, and a port called Kompong

Som, though, in that era, it had been renamed Sihanoukville for leader Norodom Sihanouk. The sea was the key for Hanoi, and the question was the extent to which it could use the sea to supply the South. In the earliest days of the war the National Liberation Front had actually received the majority of its outside assistance from the sea—estimates run up to 70 percent—partly because this route was easier than an overland trek, because large quantities could be moved at once, because there were no obstacles or defenses in the way of sea movement, and partly because NLF supply requirements were very low. Hanoi formed its 759th Transportation Group expressly to run supplies by sea to the South, and this unit used 100-ton steel-hulled trawlers plus conventional junks.

As the Americans and the South Vietnamese formed a junk force for coastal patrol, sea infiltration became more difficult. The United States later added surveillance aircraft, fast motor vessels, and even heavy warships such as destroyers in an effort to bar the southern coast to Hanoi's supply craft. During the course of the war several dozen of the steel-hulled trawlers were intercepted and sunk; only a couple are known to have gotten through. Thousands of junks were stopped and searched, hundreds seized or sunk. Of course, the traffic was impossible to stop, and there is no way of knowing how many (or how few) ships got through for each one that was stopped, but there *was* opposition to seaborne infiltration, *except* through Cambodia. Shipping supplies directly through Sihanoukville became the path of least resistance for Hanoi, one used with impunity as long as Cambodia remained neutral, and one that could be used for mass shipments by large freighters and oceangoing vessels.

The use of Sihanoukville, of Cambodian territory for NLF and NVA base areas, and of the more northerly Sihanouk Trail to link with The Trail through Laos, were all recognized from an early date. By 1966 the CIA was reporting evidence that the Liberation Front had been using Cambodia for four years or more. In December 1965 the CIA's Directorate of Intelligence undertook a full-scale monograph, "Cambodia and the Viet Cong," which concluded that the NLF had moved supplies through Cambodia but that the volume was small and did not involve complicity by Prince Sihanouk's government.

This understanding became the heart of a dispute involving Admiral McCain and CINCPAC, General Abrams and MACV, the CIA in Saigon and at Langley, and virtually everyone trying to isolate the battlefield in Vietnam. From before Tet it was a standard estimate of MACV intelligence that the enemy had a capacity to draw about twenty-five tons a day of supplies from Cambodia and Sihanoukville. At the time that NSSM-1 was compiled for the Nixon administration, MACV claimed it had evidence Hanoi had moved 10,000 tons through Cambodia between September 1967 and October 1968. These figures did not much bother the CIA—the military's own estimates of the capacity of The Trail in 1967 stood at almost *200* tons a day, while the number 10,000 was not very different from the figure 9,875, which represented the daily tonnage estimated in 1966–1967 multiplied by the thirteen months of the interval. The CIA itself was estimating VPA/NLF procurement in Cambodia at about 30 tons a day; the big difference was that Langley saw all but a small fraction (one tenth) of this tonnage as being foodstuffs and supplies bought directly from the local economy.

When Creighton Abrams took command in Saigon the Cambodia estimates were one of the matters that annoyed him. The MACV arguments over Sihanoukville supply in NSSM-1 were a reflection of Abrams's concern. In addition to their position on the amount of NLF/VPA supplies moving through Sihanoukville, MACV intelligence also insisted that this source fed *all* of the enemy forces in the Far South, the area the NLF knew as "Nambo," that included Saigon and the Mekong delta. According to MACV, The Trail only fed People's Army and NLF forces from the Central Highlands and in I Corps. The CIA absolutely opposed that claim. Admiral McCain sided with MACV.

Toward the end of 1968, after the election, there was an attempt to resolve the doubts over Cambodia and Hanoi. An interagency group of intelligence analysts, led by James C. Graham of the CIA's Office of National Estimates, traveled to Southeast Asia. Having looked at the evidence available in Washington, briefed at Honolulu on CINCPAC's holdings, they searched for data in Saigon, Hong Kong, and Bangkok. One member stopped in Vientiane on the way back, to get any material available there. The American group even had access to the views of the Australian attaché in Phnom Penh, who met with them while in Bangkok. The group also met with or consulted field commands including MACSOG, which compiled a report and did a full briefing based on its Daniel Boone missions, IV Corps, the 1st Cavalry Division (Airmobile), and the 25th Infantry Division. The Graham committee came back with the impression that the intelligence evidence available in the field did not differ much from what there was in Washington.

The overall conclusions nevertheless did not satisfy the military, either MACV or CINCPAC. Analysts from Langley and the State Department went beyond what they had been willing to say in October 1968, the last time these issues had been addressed, but the CIA remained unwilling to concede Sihanoukville as the sole source of supply for the Far South, or to agree on military estimates of the tonnage of the supply flow. The CIA and other members *did* agree to a conclusion they had rejected in 1965, namely that Cambodian army officers were involved in the traffic, heavily involved, and that Prince Sihanouk was probably aware of both Hanoi's supply flow and the corruption among his military. As for the sole-source argument, however, the Graham mission insisted that joint study by both the CIA and the Defense Intelligence Agency showed that sufficient supplies had reached the Central Highlands area and the Cambodian-Laotian-Vietnamese triborder area from the *North* (i.e., The Trail) in both 1967 and 1968 to support the fighting that had taken place.

At the CIA the chief of the Office of Economic Research, Paul V. Walsh, masterminded a very serious study of Sihanoukville's docking and unloading capability and the transport infrastructure of Cambodia. These conclusions bolstered the very small estimate the agency had made of the arms traffic. The Graham mission conceded that estimate was almost certainly low, but pointed to the gap between it and the MACV estimate as illustrating the difficulties of this intelligence question.

General Abrams conceded nothing. His chief of staff, Major General Elias C. Townsend, talked to intelligence chief Brigadier General William C. Potts, who stuck to the MACV estimate on Sihanoukville. Townsend recalls: "I continued to tell Potts to come up with his best estimates of the situation, that he put his best estimates to Abrams, and if he had any input that he wanted to get from those people [the CIA], put it in." Abrams rejected the conclusions of the Sihanoukville study. Admiral John McCain agreed.

The dispute brought a Saigon visit by Russell Jack Smith, the deputy director of intelligence for the CIA. Smith found young MACV intelligence officers very modest about their estimate. "When I pressed hard as to how they supported their estimate," the CIA official recounts, "modesty began to approach embarrassment. They had nothing else to go on; the figure they produced was a possibility." Saigon and Langley still had only the same data.

Difficulties over evaluating Hanoi's supply network brought a big push for new data in 1969. The Studies and Observation Group mounted a total of 454 Spike team forays into Cambodia that year, using the new code name Salem House. Though there were restrictions during one period due to South Vietnamese operations, and during another in an effort to negotiate release of some prisoners, the SOG effort was clearly substantial. The missions responded to a special committee called Vesuvius, formed by MACV intelligence for Cambodia. Officers at MACSOG also compiled a guidebook to Cambodian license plates and truck types to enable reconnaissance teams to distinguish NLF from Cambodian vehicle movements.

Before long, MACV's Vesuvius committee learned that lots of Hanoi's supplies were moving on trucks of two particular companies. One of them was Chinese-owned. Fred Ladd, who returned for a third Vietnam tour as chief military adviser in Cambodia, thought the interpenetration so extensive that the National Liberation Front leadership lived in villas in Phnom Penh and had offices downtown. Ladd remembers that when Cambodia eventually closed Sihanoukville port, there were more than a dozen Chinese ships there at that moment.

At CINCPAC Admiral McCain set the Naval Security Group to work recording messages to and from ships on the Sihanoukville run. The effort yielded data on the volume of shipping into the port. Naval attachés and Office of Naval Intelligence operatives in the Far East, who collected information on the flags and markings used by merchant ships, as well as their registration, noticed that North Vietnam was using certain Chinese ships, or perhaps Hanoi even had its own ships disguised as Chinese vessels.

The prize score came in Hong Kong. There, before the end of 1968, the CIA had tied certain businessmen to ships bearing major traffic to Sihanoukville. Constant attention to the companies involved resulted in recruitment of a spy with access to the warehousing records and bills of lad-ing of the shipments through Cambodia. The CIA discovered that the shipping through Sihanoukville was far more than its estimate; in fact, the real data were close to MACV's projection. Later, when the United States invaded Cambodia and the government of Prince Sihanouk was overthrown, replaced with one to the Nixon administration's liking, even more data on the DRV shipments became available. There are reports that the new dictator, Marshal Lon Nol, opened up to U.S. investigators an entire room containing records of the trucking companies involved.

With the American incursion into Cambodia in 1970, many documents were captured that put flesh on analysts' bare-bones picture of the operation of the National Liberation Front, and the Vietnam People's Army rear services administration. For one thing, it became known that, in addition to any of its other effects, the U.S. military buildup in Soviet Vietnam had affected NLF operations in Cambodia quite directly. The buildup and dollar spending that went with it inflated the Saigon economy, devaluing the currency, which affected the NLF because it collected taxes from many South Vietnamese. When these were exchanged for Cambodian currency, the money lost value; some local dealers even refused to accept Vietnamese notes. The NLF eventually profited by setting up an elaborate scheme for currency trading, but in the short run, purchasing in the Cambodian economy became more difficult and more expensive.

Other captured documents explained how the NLF with its notorious headquarters (which Americans called "COSVN" for the "Central Office for South Vietnam") had escaped: the enemy had been expecting the Cambodian invasion. Some showed the attack had been anticipated for months. The NLF and the VPA moved key installations ahead of the attack, partly due to that expectation, partly to the outbreak of warfare in Cambodia after Lon Nol took over the government and began fighting both the Cambodian Communists (Khmer Rouge) and the Vietnamese.

Some material afforded insight into the People's Army system. Americans learned the VPA had formed a new 470th Transportation Group, in Cambodia, exactly parallel to the 559th on The Trail. Mysterious units called "straggler recovery regiments" were revealed to be rear bases on the infiltration routes that rested and treated convalescent *bo dois* sickened or hurt during infiltration. Finally there was documentary confirmation that key combat units of the Liberation Front and People's Army had pulled back across the border in the summer of 1968 to lick their wounds after Tet. A crucial reason why the intensity of fighting had gone down in 1969 had been that the adversary main forces spent much of their time out of contact with the Americans.

This intelligence, as much as the quantities of supplies and equipment captured, would be the primary gains from the U.S.-ARVN invasion of Cambodia. Admiral McCain would be a fervid proponent of that invasion, and General Abrams, while not quite the advocate as the CINCPAC, was a willing executor. Lieutenant General Michael S. Davison had been McCain's chief of staff in 1969, at the time when Nixon ordered a secret B-52 bombing program in Cambodia, in an attempt to neutralize the NLF/VPA bases, and by the spring of 1970 was in command of II Field Force, the troop command that would carry out the invasion. Davison was in-country only about a week on April 21, touring his 25th Infantry Division, when he received a message that General Abrams had set out to visit him and was already en route. Davison rushed back, his helicopter landing just ahead of Abrams, and barely had time to rustle up a jeep for them to ride to headquarters. There General Abrams instructed Davison to plan the invasion and keep it very quiet. General Davison in turn delegated most of the detailed planning to a small circle from Major General Elvy B. Roberts's 1st Cavalry Division (Airmobile).

Meanwhile, this invasion concerned not just a U.S. troop command, but CINCPAC, the Joint Chiefs, even the White House, not to mention the South Vietnamese Army, whose III Corps would be in the assault alongside the Americans. A blizzard of cables burned up the wires between Washington and Saigon, including some out of channels from the White House directly to MACV. General Abrams managed this dovetailing of interests with great dexterity. For example, Admiral Thomas Moorer, who had taken over as chairman of the JCS, tells a story about Abrams and the ARVN in the Cambodian invasion. According to Moorer, Abrams visited a ranking ARVN commander to coordinate details—this may have been Nguyen Van Thieu, Cao Van Vien, or Do Cao Tri, Davison's counterpart as leader of the ARVN III Corps. In any case, Abrams informed the Saigon officer that the invasion was to go on a Thursday.

"I've been to my astrologer," countered the ARVN general, "and the astrologer says this is the worst day we could have picked. I can't go Thursday. I won't go Thursday. I want to go Saturday."

Abe was unable to move the South Vietnamese off their insistence. When he returned to MACV headquarters, however, General Abrams found a new Washington cable ordering a postponement until Saturday so the diplomats could properly inform Britain and France of the American moves. A MACV staff officer pointed this out, complaining that everything had been arranged with ARVN's lower echelons for invasion on Thursday and the postponement was impossible. Abe cooled his staff off; he then called the senior ARVN general to say MACV had been able to arrange the postponement the Vietnamese wanted. Finally, Abrams sent Washington a dispatch that the Vietnamese would be very disturbed by the postponement but he had gotten them to go along with it.

Washington never knew it was timing the Cambodian invasion according to a Vietnamese astrologer.

When the invasion began (actually it was a Friday, May 1, 1970), General Davison monitored the action from a helicopter as troops air-assaulted across the border. Davison saw the land pockmarked with bomb craters, unmistakably those of Arc Light strikes. That was how he learned of the secret bombing of Cambodia.

Perhaps the Nixon White House, too, ought to have consulted an astrologer before invading Cambodia. Alternatively, it would have helped to have thought through the political implications. In his November 3 speech the previous year, Richard Nixon had tried to conjure a majority opinion to back his Vietnam policy. Within days—on November 15, to be precise—there occurred the largest mass expression of opinion in a march or demonstration in U.S. history to that time. A half million people descended on Washington for an antiwar demonstration, and there was another tenth-of-a-million-size gathering in San Francisco. White House chief of staff Bob Haldeman went up that morning to survey the Washington protesters. "It was really huge," Haldeman, a seasoned operator, recorded, "very impressive. Weird around White House because they have a cordon around a two-block area, so no people, cars, or anything can get by the solid barricade of buses."

The presidential call for a decent interval in Vietnam in the November 3 speech, and the throwing down of a gauntlet to the protesters, had a certain short-term effect, and the president gained something from the backlash opinion of Americans horrified at antiwar tactics, student activism, or just youth culture. But Richard Nixon miscalculated the impact of his appeal; the mood of America had already shifted. Since the Tet offensive there had been a growing majority opinion on Vietnam, for the most part indeed silent, but its center of gravity favored ending the war. The fact that both Richard Nixon and Henry Kissinger maintained in retirement that they should have gone ahead with Duck Hook in 1969 shows that this miscalculation persists in retrospect. The antiwar demonstrators, who already represented an enormous opposition, were only the leading edge of the wave. Once ordered, invasion of Cambodia would predictably produce protests. Crossing a national border to invade a new country, which included any project to push through Tchepone to cut The Trail, executing Duck Hook, or invading North Vietnam, would all have been deliberate choices to confront the antiwar opposition.

A further wild card was that the movement had begun to spin off ever more militant factions. The Weathermen, the radicalized survivors of SDS, acquired the most notoriety after the "Brownstone Bombing," an incident on March 6, 1970, in which a town house on 11th Street in Greenwich Village, New York City, suddenly exploded, collapsing in a heap of rubble. Weathermen had been making bombs inside, and one had made the wrong electrical connection with a detonator. Three persons died in the building; two Weatherwomen escaped. A number of bombings throughout the United States would be attributed to Weathermen or other fringe groups, including more than one inside the Pentagon itself.

High political risk was evident in the Cambodia invasion decision, a risk to which Nixon and Kissinger were by no means oblivious. Kissinger suffered what amounted to a rebellion inside his own National Security Council staff, with several members resigning before Nixon made his final decision and announced it on television on April 30.

The predicted occurred. A demonstration had already been called to support Bobby Seale and other Black Panthers on trial in New Haven, and the

Cambodia invasion sparked the protesters. Other tumults followed. At Kent State University in Ohio, National Guardsmen were called out after the school's Reserve Officer Training Corps (ROTC) building burned down on May 2. Two days later, the Guard fired into a crowd of protesters and bystanders, killing four and wounding nine; another student was killed by Guardsmen at Ohio State. Days later, at Jackson State University in Mississippi, police gunfire killed two African American students at a war protest.

For a long time one theme of speakers at antiwar demonstrations had been that waging war in Southeast Asia meant waging war against the American people. The events at Kent State and elsewhere seemed to provide direct confirmation, resulting in a true firestorm. Misleading rhetoric about "outside agitators" to the contrary, college students were at the heart of the protests, and the heat melted down the tacit alliance that had previously existed between labor and the U.S. government. Though Nixon's cries for support turned out 60,000 construction workers ("hard hats") in a prowar demonstration, there were more than 4 million protesters at colleges all over the country plus another 130,000 people in a new march on Washington. Movement organizers sensed that the Washington demonstrators were ready to go beyond Gandhian nonviolence and later argued over whether a tactical error had been made in refusing to try and shut down the government.

This last is a key point: frustration at the U.S. government's determination to pursue a war in the face of popular will led the movement toward adopting more violent tactics. Where, in 1969, SDS Weathermen had been a splinter group, a persistent confrontation in 1970 and after would have made Weatherman tactics the standard. Richard Nixon's Vietnam policy brought America to the brink of internal rebellion.

After Kent State antiwar protesters sent out a call for student strikes and demonstrations, a strike central office was set up at Brandeis University. Within forty-eight hours of that strike call, more than a hundred colleges and universities had scheduled votes on a strike or had already gone out. Eventually 536 colleges would declare temporary or permanent strikes; of them, 51 never completed the spring 1970 semester. There were serious clashes between protesters and security forces at 26 universities, and the National Guard, as in Ohio, was called up to be sent to 21 of them. Fires and bombings damaged ROTC buildings at 30 schools. At Harvard, the Center for International Affairs (now called the John Kennedy School) was trashed; in other places, too, institutions held to be complicit with the war stood in great danger. The list could go on—University of Maryland, University of Michigan, Berkeley, Columbia, University of Wisconsin—these were only a few.

Richard Nixon called the students "bums" and talked about U.S. policy not being made in the streets. Here is Bob Haldeman's diary entry for May 6: "[The president] obviously realizes, but won't openly admit, his 'bums' remark very harmful." On May 8: "Media have built it up very big and it really is . . . the hard line was mainly from K[issinger] who feels we should just let the students tear it for a couple of weeks with no effort at pacification, then hit them hard." The White House bomb shelter, constructed to cope with a nuclear war with Russia, would be pressed into service as a command post monitoring the May 9 march on Washington. National Security Council staffers had to mingle with the antiwar protesters and crawl under the barriers of buses just to get to their jobs. Nixon's standing in the opinion polls fell in the wake of the Cambodia invasion.

Administration efforts to minimize damage, both in advance and afterward, had a major effect in Southeast Asia, especially in the war for The Trail. The main measure, to restrict the military operating area in Cambodia to a twenty-five-mile-deep zone, and put a time limit on the period during which the United States would fight in Cambodia—to characterize the invasion as an "incursion"—prevented American forces from effectively pursuing the adversary. Even had the elusive "COSVN" headquarters been found, it could not have been engaged. Subsequently the effort to dampen political fallout led to even faster withdrawals of U.S. troops from Vietnam. When next there was an invasion across a border, it would be the fabled invasion of Laos, but the Nixon administration issued strict instructions that no Americans participate in the combat. That would have consequences of its own. In the meantime, the battle for The Trail was in the hands of the pinball wizards.

On The Trail the rain of destruction peaked in 1969, when more than 433,000 tons of munitions fell on the land. The lessons of the air campaign also were learned well, so well that in 1970 Congress decided to hold hearings to explore the potential of the electronic battlefield. Defense analysts extolled the precision with which means could be allocated and results assessed through remote sensing methods. In Vietnam itself, before the end of the war sensor arrays would become standard equipment at bases all over. Meanwhile, young intelligence analysts such as Edward J. Drea, who served during 1970–1971, could marvel at the way the sensor signals were being used in real time to conduct actual attacks on Hanoi's lifeline.

What is essential to note, however, is not simply the use of the electronic battlefield technology, but the fact that these techniques were, and remained, coupled with a massive military effort. Though 1969 would be a peak, subsequent reductions were not necessarily perceptible—in 1970 there would still be 394,000 tons of explosives dropped on lower Laos, and in 1971 another 402,000. Obviously the numbers of aircraft sorties had to have remained substantial. Indeed, there were 74,147 in 1970, then 69,909 more flights during 1971. Arc Light targets were based on specific intelligence, sometimes from Task Force Alpha. The fighter-bombers were usually given secondary targets in advance, but instructed to hit them only if the pinball wizards failed to come up with more urgent or vital assignments.

Of course, the real score was and remained the biggest problem, figuring out what was really happening in the battle of The Trail. For example, at the rate of attrition of People's Army trucks claimed for December 1968, the VPA supply network should have been on the ropes in only a month and a half. But Task Force Alpha ran the initial Commando Hunt effort four times that long, and measurably increased its claimed effectiveness (by 50 percent), yet had *no* observable impact on The Trail. The system *could not have been working as advertised.*

As had been the case in earlier wars, and would be again in the Persian Gulf in 1990–1991, the assessment of bomb damage proved an impenetrable mystery. Pilot claims were and remained suspect. While Robert McNamara was still secretary of defense he had gone to the National Photographic Interpretation Center, an outside agency then run by the CIA, and asked them to quietly review every day whatever pictures there were that pertained to each pilot claim. The photo analysts reduced a lot of the claims. The supposed results should have put The Trail out of business, yet Hanoi's truck convoys continued to drive south every night.

Many heads were put together in the attempt to discern the reality underlying the daily reporting, and the effort became the focus of many a bureaucratic squabble. The Defense Intelligence Agency and the CIA, for example, worked out an agreed formula that discounted 75 percent of pilot claims to derive a more accurate figure. The air force disputed this affront to its brave crews. Truck number estimates were used in an elaborate model of Hanoi's transportation system to reveal the exact moment the People's Army would grind to a halt. Former intelligence officials recall that the computer model reached zero—where Hanoi was supposed to be out of trucks—no fewer than fourteen times. That was *years* before the end of the war! Eventually there would be nine Commando Hunt campaigns and thousands of tons of bombs. The trucks kept coming.

The contradictions could become glaring, as happened at Udorn, headquarters of the Seventh/Thirteenth Air Force, during this time under Major General Louis T. Seith. Naturally, details of truck "burns" on The Trail formed a major feature of the morning briefing, and the results often seemed quite good. But the photo planes flown to document claims just as frequently showed no damage. Staff officers started the joke that there was a "Great Laotian Truck Eater" somewhere back in the hills that devoured overnight the hulks of those vehicles destroyed by American airpower.

Some commanders proved more credulous than others. One time the morning brief specified as many as three hundred trucks demolished. "Gentlemen," the general reacted with glee, "what we have here is the end of North Vietnam as a viable fighting power."

That night, traffic on The Trail continued as usual.

Some thought the failures due to the inherent shortcomings of attack aircraft, and the solution to be reliance on the B-52s. The climax of the Arc Light effort came while the Seventh Air Force fought under General Lucius D. Clay, Jr. That was the fall of 1970 through summer 1971. Clay wanted to use the B-52s to shut down the passes across the Annamites, calculating this would force a halt to the supply trucks. Each of the passes—Mu Gia,

Ban Karai, and Napé—were hit by one or several cells of B-52 bombers in shifts around the clock. Starting in October 1970 the Arc Light effort concentrated almost entirely on southern Laos, with B-52 sorties over The Trail almost doubling, to 900 a month. At the same time, B-52 flights over South Vietnam dwindled to fewer than 100; during November a total of only 7 B-52 airplanes completed missions over South Vietnam. For the next half year, B-52s delivered more than 22,000 tons of bombs in lower Laos every month.

Aside from Arc Light, General Clay also presided over a new phase of enhanced air effort. With this overall expansion of the U.S. air campaign against The Trail, the proportion of munitions dropped by Arc Light actually fell—from roughly two thirds in the summer of 1970 to fewer than half the following February. Radio intelligence and the sensor systems were the primary sources for target selections, both for the B-52s and for the tactical aircraft.

Limiting factors remained what they had been since the dawn of armed reconnaissance, with a few new ones thrown in for good measure. Fast movers made up the bulk of attack sorties; they were less accurate than propeller-driven planes. Assessing damage from B-52 strikes remained forever difficult. Laotian authorities frequently punished bombing errors by erecting altitude restrictions, while the U.S. services imposed restrictions of their own. People's Army forces constantly deployed higher-caliber antiaircraft guns, and these, too, forced altitude increases on the Americans. Every altitude increase made bombing more inaccurate. Vietnamese countermeasures also reduced damage, while weather conditions could be dangerous for attackers as well. Area restrictions, again some from the Lao and others self-imposed, ruled out some targets altogether.

Air attack took three main forms, corresponding to People's Army movement tactics. The Arc Lights were most awesome in their destructiveness, and could hit without local warning, although Vietnamese officers insist their monitoring of U.S. communications furnished a basic notice. At night, when the Vietnamese truck convoys pushed ahead, big multiengine aircraft dominated the skies. Jet B-57 bombers served as both FACs and strike planes; large transports, successively including the C-47, the C-119, and the large C-130, were adapted into "gunships." In the daytime there were the Panther teams with the Ravens and their attack planes.

The gunships were something to see. In their first incarnation, the venerable "Dakotas," the World War II–vintage C-47s, the gunships earned renown. But six AC-47 gunships were lost over The Trail, and the press for bigger weapons and armor called for a heavier airframe. The AC-119 would be an interim, though honorable, contributor, but it was still only a twin-engine aircraft, not nearly as capable as the four-engine C-130, which arrived for its combat trials in September 1967. Dubbed the "Spectre," the AC-130 finally had radar, sensor readouts, 105-mm cannon, and gatling-type multiple machine guns. A pilot could expect to fly 120 to 150 missions during a tour. One typical crew finished its year with 228 confirmed truck kills. The Spectre was a wonderful aircraft—with one engine out, this C-130 was still able to climb 400 feet a minute. Both the Spooky (AC-47) and the AC-119 (until its AC-119K configuration) were rated as unsatisfactory fliers on one engine, given their loads and weight characteristics. At the end of 1969 the gunship force in Southeast Asia amounted to 7 AC-130s, 18 AC-119Ks, 18 AC-119Gs, and 2 AC-123Ks. The gunship program was one of those especially favored by defense scientists, including the President's Science Advisory Committee.

In addition to the gunships, the Americans had certain all-weather aircraft that flew missions at night, sometimes exclusively at night. Navy A-6 "Intruders," air force B-57 "Canberras," including those of the Royal Australian Air Force, the B-26K, and some attack aircraft were active this way. At Ubon after 1968 there were four Air Force squadrons flying in darkness who called themselves "Nightowls," such as the 497th Tactical Fighter Squadron with its F-4Ds. Lieutenant Colonel Stanley Clark, who commanded the 497th in 1968–1969, said, "I'm usually concentrating so hard on the ground, trying to find a light, or a target, or a bend in a road, I don't even know which direction I'm going, much less where I am." And again, "The ground is your enemy at night." Claims of destruction should be viewed with that in mind.

Stalwarts of the daylight air campaign were the Panther Teams. Here the FACs were key. The 23d Tactical Air Support Squadron flew from Nakhon Phanom and had the best touch with Dutch Mill and its pinball wizards. Their radio call sign, "Nails," suggested a tough bunch, and they were complemented by the pilots of the 20th Squadron at Da Nang, well known to American troops at Hue, Khe Sanh, and elsewhere as "Covey." Captain Thomas Yarborough flew the OV-10 "Bronco" with the 20th in 1970–1971. Covey was an intense assignment, with more takeoffs and landings at Da Nang than official statistics showed for Chicago's O'Hare International Airport. Following familiarization flights, Yarborough quickly found himself flying against the Ho Chi Minh Trail. From Da Nang one had to cross the Annamites to reach the Steel Tiger area, and that could be dangerous, especially for the O-2 "Bird Dog" aircraft some FACs used. Those planes had much less power than the OV-10s, twin-engine aircraft, and even the Broncos could be challenged by the mountains. The planes would climb in circles for a long time before crossing, often using the pass at Lao Bao. Weather would be dicey; the typical pattern was that clouds gathered above the mountains, lowering the ceiling for the FACs, whose planes lacked all-weather instruments. The clouds usually built to a thunderstorm in the afternoon, so a FAC caught out late in the day would be in trouble. Yarborough encountered that very situation at least once.

The antiaircraft threat displayed on a map in the Covey operations center at Da Nang chilled Yarborough. On the map every antiaircraft position was shown by a red circle denoting its range. Yarborough recalls: "The whole damn map was nothing but red circles!"

Still, intelligence watched closely, even drawing conclusions as to the behavior of individual People's Army gun crews. The FACs adjusted their flight patterns to the adversary to a considerable degree. For a flight the FAC would cross the Annamites while avoiding antiaircraft, then radio "Hillsboro," the orbiting airborne command post on duty. Yarborough notes the FACs would call in "the code phrase that let them know we were leaving South Vietnam and crossing into the secret political-military world of Laos."

A standard mission of June 1970 found Yarborough flying The Trail at a leisurely pace south, toward Chavane. He could see the town up ahead, and the point at the edge of a nearby meadow where a Vietnamese-built dirt road branched off toward the border and the nearest *binh tram*. Suddenly the pilot noticed four men on motorcycles. Yarborough chased them briefly, then turned the other way to see where the *bo dois* could have been coming from. Soon he summoned "Misty," a flight of F-100 fighter-bombers, to look over what he had seen. The sequel, which Yarborough relates in *Da Nang Diary*, his Vietnam memoir, is worth quoting at length:

> Misty executed a hard pull up to the north without saying a word. Since I knew he'd seen the target, it was impossible to keep my curiosity in check. "Misty, Covey 221. You saw it, didn't you? I saw the same thing, so just blurt it right out."
>
> A long pause filled the air before Misty answered me. "Covey, nobody's gonna believe this except you and me. I got a real good look at your target. Either I'm stone blind or that thing is an honest-to-god Bell telephone booth. The door was wide open and I bet there was change in the coin return. Is that what you thought it was?"
>
> "That's affirmative. You don't suppose the truck drivers call back home to Hanoi to talk to their wives on it, do you?"
>
> Misty mulled my question over for a few seconds, then answered, "If they do, I hope a strange man answers or else the bastards get a busy signal."

Back at Da Nang, the squadron intelligence office grilled Yarborough for literally half an hour on the size, color, shape, and everything else about the telephone booth.

On another mission, working with Ravens who staged at Ubon, the pilot with Captain Yarborough briefly set their plane down on the 4,000-foot dirt airstrip of Saravane, which happened to be controlled by the Vietnam People's Army, who had a 37-mm gun right in front of the flight operations building! The American plane made a touch-and-go takeoff to escape before VPA soldiers could fire on them. It was not that kind of stunt, but rather the fact he had taken fire, been damaged, and handled it well that set up Yarborough for assignment to Prairie Fire. He spent most of the remainder of his tour working with MACSOG to insert Spike teams on their perilous patrols. On July 10, which would be a sad day, Yarborough was involved when a team was lost on the crest of Co Roc Mountain.

American intelligence during this period achieved much better understanding of People's Army infiltration practices, and proved able to target some way stations at just the right time. One mission like this would be operation Tailwind, one of the biggest MACSOG strikes of 1970, aimed at *Binh Tram* 37 near Chavane at a moment when the VPA had moved large quantities of supplies into this area. The attackers were a Hatchet Force, a company-size unit from SOG led by Captain Eugene McCarley, with six-teen Americans and 140 montagnard strikers who left the Command Control Center compound at Dak To on board four helicopters. The important feature of their mission, however, would be the large amount of airpower that FACs used to blast the *binh tram* as soon as the Hatchet Force encountered resistance. Every helicopter in the lift force, as well as all four supporting AH-1G gunship helicopters, were hit by ground fire in the landing phase. During the extraction, thirty-six "sets" (a set usuallly comprised four fighter-bombers) of aircraft smashed the VPA opponents.

Operation Tailwind achieved notoriety in 1998 when one of its MACSOG platoon leaders alleged that nerve gas (sarin) had been used for the attack. It was typical for SOG to use tear gas, but sarin can poison the body through the skin, and the U.S. Army does not use it tactically—standards are to avoid areas so contaminated for thirty-two days. The Hatchet Force did not carry the protective suits needed in the presence of sarin, had no antidotes, and performed no postmission decontamination. In fact, returning team members went straight from the helipad for a drink. Moreover, former officials who managed army nerve gas stocks at the time recall no requests for sarin for MACSOG, and the unit's command history for 1970, which features this September 11 combat action, contains no mention of the nerve gas. The allegation itself was later said to be a "recovered memory." In addition, essential facts about Tailwind leaked within a month and were the subject of an Associated Press dispatch out of Saigon, and had nerve gas—or American deserters, who are also mentioned in these allegations—been part of the real Tailwind, that must have leaked as well. No one should doubt that at this time, four months after America's political meltdown over the invasion of Cambodia, such charges would have been highly controversial.

In any case, the Hatchet Force in operation Tailwind proved lucky. Though every American had some wound, many of them minor, montagnard casualties were only three killed and thirty-three wounded. A month later another SOG mission sent out by Command Control Center, RT Fer-de-Lance, would be lost without a trace.

In December 1970 came what the pinball wizards would celebrate as the most successful interdiction strike of the battle of The Trail. It started because the experts at Nakhon Phanom had gotten pretty good at reading their data. When trucks passed a sensor array and disappeared before the next one, it usually meant a truck park. On this occasion Task Force Alpha sent a FAC to follow up one such reading that had disappeared from the boards. It was near the village of Ban Bak, a People's Army supply center behind Chavane. No one had ever seen flak like at Ban Bak, but there had never been such lucrative targets either. The fighter-bombers and Ravens kept at it for days, from December 19 until bad weather closed down operations that Wednesday, the twenty-third. Damage seemed staggering—one secondary explosion that had to be either fuel or ammunition generated a mushroom cloud that rose to 8,000 feet.

That Christmas the 20th Tactical Air Support Squadron celebrated with an unusual "tree" in its officers' club, an acoustical sensor with wires stuck on for branches and makeshift decorations. It was odd but appropriate.

Yet, in spite of Ban Bak, of Commando Hunt, of Task Force Alpha and all the rest, the ants were still on the move. The *bo dois* on The Trail did not rest. American frustration at inability to seal off the southern battlefield now led to one hell of a gamble, nothing less than the invasion of Laos. The play of that card brought about the climax of the war on The Trail.

CHAPTER 13

No Plug in the Funnel
1971

After these many years, Tchepone just was not the same. Bui Tin, who saw the town at the beginning of the decade and again in the mid-1960s, came back in the early 1970s, in the guise of a reporter for the Vietnam People's Army (VPA) newspaper *Quan Doi Nhan Dan*. From his last visit Tin remembered the vibrant marketplace; it had been a surprise that at the height of conflict so many things were available so easily. Now that was gone, a casualty of war, along with most of the houses and buildings of the town. The citizens of Tchepone were still there, amazingly, for given the intensity of bombing to which they had been subjected, and the destruction of homes and placid way of life, it was surprising that more had not died under the weight of metal. Bui Tin found the reason—people now lived in the many caves throughout the region. The highlight of the trip was a pagoda, a new Buddhist pagoda, brightly decorated. Amid the misery and destruction people had found it in themselves to build something new. Upon reflection came the realization that a pagoda was a very practical thing; it was a token of hope for a new life.

New life was very much what Tchepone needed. According to figures kept by a district official, recited to an American visiting after the war, the bombing destroyed 6,557 houses and more than 5,000 storage structures. That was every house in the district. Although civilian dead numbered only about 1,500, they included the majority in four villages. Of local livestock, cows and water buffalo numbering perhaps 6,000, the bombing claimed 1,800. Postwar investigation showed that the Tchepone district had been the target of a greater tonnage of explosives than any German industrial city of World War II. An experienced journalist who had covered the war, and returned to Indochina years later, Henry Kamm was moved by what he witnessed in this shattered district and wrote this: "Tchepone became to many American and South Vietnamese military leaders what Moby Dick was to Captain Ahab—the object of an obsessive, destructive quest."

People's Army commanders were perfectly aware of their adversary's obsession; it was their units and facilities that were the aim of all this activity.

Tchepone would constantly be strengthened, even during the 1969–1971 period, when VPA infiltration down The Trail slumped and a great deal of what there was would be sent on to the Far South. Of about 70,000 *bo dois* who made their trek in 1969, American data suggest that perhaps 2,100 were destined for Tchepone, among slightly over 8,000 who reinforced base areas from A Shau northward.

While infiltration numbers were down, the People's Army sent a higher proportion of specialized manpower. The sappers, called *dac cong* in the VPA, were especially prominent, and were used ever more widely in the South, even as the number of attacks declined. The People's Army committed these small units of elite troops as a means of economizing its forces overall.

Corporal Le Dinh Thao figured among this flow. One of two hundred *dac cong* of the 14th Sapper Battalion, which came down The Trail with the 2150th Group, Thao got special training in climbing through barbed wire to destroy bunkers, command posts, and tanks, a technique praised as "flowers blowing up inside an enemy installation." To practice destroying tanks, the sappers worked with four T-54s borrowed from the VPA armor command. The unit left its training camp on May 10, 1969, marching for a day before joining the larger infiltration group, roughly twice its size.

From the Red River delta the 2150th Group took a train as far as Vinh. After marching for half a day, they switched to sampans. The next day it was trucks, mostly driven by women, which carried them to the Truong Son range. The remainder of their trek was by foot. Moving down the Vietnamese panhandle, the group sometimes slept with peasants in their villages, other times at military encampments. Crossing the Truong Son, the fresh *bo dois* came upon a column of people headed north. Guarded by six or seven soldiers with AK-47 rifles, this group included old men and women, several of them pregnant, and perhaps twenty kids. Le Dinh Thao befriended one nine-year old, who told him the children were the orphans of Liberation Front cadre, mostly from Quang Nam and Phu Yen Provinces in the South. While marching through Laos the 2150th Group later encountered a second, much smaller, party of children headed north. The main hardships occurred in Laos, where the *bo dois* got no canned pork or fish, nothing beyond rice, which they supplemented by hunting. Nearing Tchepone, they were obliged to ford the Sepon River no fewer than three times. Before the trek ended (in Cambodia), almost a third of the soldiers had contracted malaria, and several were left behind in Laos. On the other hand, during the time Thao remained with the party, the marchers never had to face American airpower.

Leaving in early June to commence its own infiltration, the 4th Sapper Battalion had completed training under direct supervision of the sapper high command located at Ha Dong City. About a week before departure, new officers and cadre arrived and assumed leadership of the 4th, their former cadre staying behind to train a new sapper unit. Like Le Dinh Thao, Private Nguyen Van Minh of the 4th Sappers began his journey with a train ride. Steam locomotives powered by coal pulled wooden freight cars, each bearing perhaps forty *bo dois*. Thereafter the sappers switched to trucks, twelve to fourteen men per vehicle, and these carried them south as far as Quang Binh Province. Minh's battalion crossed into Laos at the western end of the DMZ and passed through Ban Dong and Tchepone before heading for parts south. They eventually reached the K-9 way station in Tay Ninh in October 1969.

The entire area of Tchepone, with its *binh trams* and a hard defensive crust, created by two People's Army infantry regiments up against the border, had become a transition point for the trek south. It was in 1969 that workers and engineers completed the road Nguyen Van Minh's 4th Sappers used, the one that came west past the Demilitarized Zone. Use of that route enabled the People's Army to move troops farther before they entered the Laotian killing zone, and it also permitted easier transit of the Truong Son range. The importance of the area dictated strong efforts to defend it. Around Tchepone alone, CIA information in April 1969 located VPA troops north, northeast, east, south, and in the town, totaling two engineer and four infantry battalions and two independent companies, not counting the Pathet Lao 130th Antiaircraft Battalion, also believed to be in the vicinity. A new People's Army communications center and four ammunition depots were identified by radio intelligence and overhead reconnaissance.

Antiaircraft defense, naturally, remained a primary function of the troops assigned to the 559th Transport Group and manning The Trail. Colonel Dong Sy Nguyen, who continued to lead the trailmakers, kept up a stream of tactical innovations that matched the growing sophistication of America's pinball wizards. Radar control for 37-mm antiaircraft guns became widespread around the time of the siege of Khe Sanh. Soon 57-mm radar-controlled guns appeared as well. The first part of 1969 saw 85-mm and 100-mm air defense guns, too, initially at Ban Karai Pass, later all over. As of the end of Rolling Thunder, on November 1, 1968, the People's Army was estimated to have 200 large antiaircraft guns in Laos. A MACSOG report for 1969 asserts that the scale of the threat increased more than six times during that year, while Air Force reports put People's Army antiaircraft strength as of May 1970 at over 800 guns of all sizes. In early 1971 these large-caliber guns made up a big fraction of the 200 artillery pieces the People's Army were thought to have in the vicinity of Tchepone.

Given the extent of defenses, flying against The Trail was dangerous; perhaps not as much as inserting for a SOG patrol, but plenty dangerous nonetheless. For example, the U.S. Air Force introduced an advanced gunship, the heavily armed AC-130 Spectre, over Laos during 1968. The prototype aircraft came under fire during fifty-six of its first fifty-seven sorties. A Spectre would be hit for the first time on March 3, 1969, and the first AC-130 to be shot down was lost on May 24. The powerful gunships were staples of the Commando Hunt campaigns, with the combination of slow-moving Spectres and fast-mover F-4 Phantoms considered an especially lethal mix.

The diary of one antiaircraft *bo doi* of a unit in Saravane, published in

Quan Doi Nhan Dan in 1971, gives the flavor of the desperate contest between the fighters on the ground and those in the air. On February 15, 1970, the *bo doi* recorded, his unit hit a Spectre though it had but nine rounds to shoot. They were promptly told by higher command that their position would be attacked: "As forecast, this morning enemy aircraft appeared and dropped bombs." One delayed-action cluster bomb dropped in the gun position and Hoang, lead gunner, dashed to the bomb and threw it out of the emplacement. Hoang had been reading a book, the diarist records: "I don't know why, at that moment, I only thought that if the bomb exploded there it would have destroyed the book."

A few days later, the detachment leader and diarist Pham Dinh Cung became one more of the lost souls of this war, but his record was taken up by other *bo dois* who noted the final moments: "Yesterday, we were fighting all day long. When we had only 15 rounds left, the viewer on our gun was blown off by fragments of the bombs that simultaneously exploded near our position . . . engulfed in smoke. Comrade Cung jumped onto the gun base to replaced cannoneer number two . . . a fragment hit his chest."

Hoang Dinh Cang led the detachment on April 22 when there was an engagement with another AC-130 gunship that has remained controversial to this day. This Spectre was shot down, and press reports of the time note six crewmen killed, four missing, and one rescued with minor wounds. Lieutenant Colonel Charles S. Rowley, navigator on that flight, remains on the list of missing in action from the Vietnam War. Never previously cited is the account of this action by the Vietnamese diarist: "Last night, we knocked down another C-130, which crashed in the rear of a truck company. All the nine aggressor pilots aboard were killed. Some bodies were charred. Some bodies were thrown in one direction and the heads were thrown in another." Battle was a harrowing thing. After the antiaircraft unit's second combat against a Spectre, however, "The Armed Branch Station sent us a 50-kilogram pig as a reward."

Some of the most important people the antiaircraft gunners were trying to protect—and the ones U.S. airmen were trying to hit—were the drivers of trucks on The Trail, whom the *bo dois* took to calling "pilots of the ground." They can be seen in photographs, standing before their vehicles or huddled over half-disassembled engines, sometimes women, sometimes wearing padded body armor over their uniforms. By 1970 the trucks were moving in convoys, often battalion-size convoys of forty to sixty vehicles. The Trail had become a finely articulated transport system. Trucks most often crossed the Truong Son at the passes; troops now frequently made their way through Quang Binh and entered Laos west of the DMZ. The roads had many bypasses and numerous subsegments, controlled by area bosses who could reroute convoys based on the latest information on what route segments were open, which ones were closed by bombs or weather, and what the urgency farther on might be. Reporting points at intervals all along the roads sent up information on conditions around them, as well as how many trucks had passed by. The trail managers had what amounted to real-time data and could run The Trail as a complex switching mechanism. Nguyen Thanh Linh, gone to the South in 1965 but who ended up as one of the managers, recalls: "There was one main road that could be seen from an airplane. If you stood on the road, however, you could see many, many other roads that were not visible from the air. There was a network through the jungle, but all led back to the main road."

Than Minh Son, one of the drivers, who resettled in southern Vietnam after the war, remembers pushing every night for thirty or forty miles, the road barely discernible, lights dimmed and mounted beneath his truck to minimize visibility from the air. "We were attacked frequently by American airplanes," Son reminisced. "If ten out of a hundred trucks arrived safely, that was a great victory. If a bomb hit in front of us, we drove through the forest and made a new road." Son himself was wounded by shrapnel that creased his scalp, and he lost a brother and two cousins in the war. "When I smile or laugh a lot, I get a headache."

Journalist Nguyen Phuong Nam visited the 559th Group managers in 1970 to do stories on The Trail. Staying with one area boss, Nam was sharing the man's bed when bombers hit their dugout. The manager's leg was severed. Drenched in blood, Nam miraculously came out without a scratch. At the burial next morning *bo dois* told Nam he must have had the protection of Buddha. Perhaps it was the same with the town of Tchepone—the new pagoda was far more utilitarian than anyone knew. But the smile of Buddha was going to be tested, for the war was coming to Tchepone, on the ground, violently, directly, and soon.

Among Washington leaders and senior American commanders, Indochina was nothing if not a tar baby. It was like Jack Kennedy had said, at the height of the Berlin Wall crisis, making a play was like taking a drink; soon enough the effect wore off and you needed another. Like the alcoholic, too, who does not distinguish between *need* and *want*, Washington never questioned its "need" to prosecute the Vietnam War, even during the period of Nixon's Vietnamization. Thus, ultimately, the Cambodian invasion proved unsatisfying. For all the destruction wrought by the secret bombing of 1969–1970, and the supplies and documents captured in the 1970 invasion, plus all the casualties inflicted on the Liberation Front and the People's Army, the situation afterward remained that Hanoi's troops and irregulars held their base areas and could emerge at will. In Honolulu Admiral McCain still put red arrows on his maps, and those arrows still pointed at Saigon.

Like the Cambodia invaders, the pinball wizards had taken their best shot but had come up short. The electronic battlefield was functional, and by the summer of 1970 Commando Hunt had gone through four successive iterations, with every wrinkle and innovation brilliant commanders and clever scientists could devise. "Panther teams" of aircraft, gunship-fighter combinations, "Commando Bolt" real-time sensor responses, "flashers" using aircraft equipped with new radars that indicated moving targets, novel sensors, different mixes of munitions, everything. Yet the best intelligence data and systems analysis on The Trail indicated that in the campaign season from November 1969 through June 1970 the People's Army had put something more than 63,000 tons of matériel in at the top of their network, and gotten about 20,000 tons out at the bottom. That was without the use of Cambodian ports or anything infiltrated by sea. At the conventional estimate of 15 tons per day as a supply requirement, Hanoi needed to move only 5,475 tons to supply its armies for an entire year. The Cambodian invasion increased the intensity of combat for the People's Army, and thus its consumption, but that military campaign could not be maintained in the face of opposition in the United States, and anyway there was no way to be confident the adversary was being pushed anywhere near his limits.

The canvass for options began in Washington, not Saigon, where General Creighton Abrams was fully occupied managing Vietnamization. Nixon, in his efforts to pour oil onto troubled political waters, had announced a further U.S. withdrawal of 150,000 troops at the height of the Cambodian invasion. The administration's private intention, Henry Kissinger makes clear, was to hold withdrawals during 1970 to no more than 60,000, with the rest to come out the next year.

In August defense secretary Melvin Laird informed the White House that budget constraints were such that the larger portion of the withdrawal would have to be completed in 1970, with the last 60,000 to come out by May 1971. According to Laird, this course had been recommended not only by General Abrams, but also by the Joint Chiefs of Staff.

Further withdrawals put a premium on strategy. The intervention in Cambodia also meant the United States had accepted a responsibility to shore up its confederates in that country, and that, too, had to fit into the puzzle. On August 17 Kissinger circulated a White House directive ordering a policy review for Southeast Asia. Called National Security Study Memorandum (NSSM)-99, the review was to produce a strategy for the long term. Kissinger supposed this ambitious undertaking could be completed rather quickly—a Cambodia paper within three weeks, the full study in six. Instead, the Cambodia paper came to monopolize the efforts of Washington officials, until it was split off from the other project in October as NSSM-89. Discussions on both continued for months.

What is of great importance is the range of options offered in the initial phase of NSSM-99. Several envisioned various degrees of activity the United States would support in Cambodia by Cambodian, Thai, and/or South Vietnamese forces. The ARVN incursions into Cambodia, of which operation Chenla II is probably the best known, were clearly underwritten by NSSM-99. The National Security Council paper also contained one option, "Strategy 4," which provided for troops on the ground to block lower Laos. The variants on this option ranged from intensified local Laotian and CIA covert warfare activities, already consuming about $42 million a year; to adding ARVN, Cambodian, and Thai commando raids on top of Prairie Fire; to full-scale operations into Laos by ARVN forces of regiment size and larger. That last force variant grew as discussions about NSSM-99 continued.

Henry Kissinger presents divergent rationales for the Laos operation in the accounts he has given of it. In the memoir *White House Years*, Kissinger writes that a dry-season offensive was necessary in 1971 to disrupt Hanoi's supply buildup; to give the DRV further incentive to negotiate in Paris, where a process of open and secret peace talks had become routinized; and to reduce a "battalion deficit," a shortfall in ARVN military power expected to reveal itself when next Hanoi threw its armies into an offensive. In Kissinger's more recent study *Diplomacy* he argues differently: "Without challenging the North Vietnamese logistics bases, no conceivable American withdrawal strategy could have worked." Henry puts this in the context of Cambodia, but it applies perfectly to The Trail and, as Kissinger also tells us, his own idea for a 1971 offensive was in fact to invade Cambodia anew.

Kissinger is misleading as to the timing of this planning, writing in *White House Years* that his preference for a Cambodia operation changed only after a visit to Saigon by deputy national security adviser Alexander M. Haig. That trip, on which Haig took other NSC staff members, happened between December 11 and 18, 1970. But more than a month earlier, on November 4, the president had ordered a full canvass of alternatives, and on the sixth a National Security Council meeting on Vietnam occupied most of the morning at the White House. Nixon reiterated the order on November 28, shortly after the unsuccessful raid on Sontay, near Hanoi, by MACSOG commandos seeking to free American prisoners.

At the request of Joint Chiefs chairman Moorer, as early as November 10 Admiral McCain had offered two plans from his catbird seat in Honolulu. One was the NSSM-99 option of coordinated operations among Cambodian, Thai, and ARVN forces along their own borders. The other, which Mc-Cain deemed contingent on the Laotian government abrogating the 1962 Geneva accords, consisted of an operation in lower Laos by combined ARVN, Thai, and Laotian troops. McCain followed in early December by asking General Abrams in Saigon to begin planning, together with ARVN's Cao Van Vien, for major ARVN ground incursions into lower Laos with maximum U.S. air support. On December 8, still prior to Haig's departure, Bob Haldeman relates that Kissinger voiced opposition to any Tet truce. Henry's reference to both Cambodia and Laos in this connection has a dual-edged quality since, by his own admission, Kissinger was already pondering a dry-season offensive.

Most telling of all is what happened at MACV on December 8. Creighton Abrams called a staff conference among top commanders that day at "Pentagon East." His intelligence chief, Brigadier General William C. Potts, briefed the latest data on The Trail, while Abe made a point of going around the room to establish what opportunities there might be for offensive action. Then Abrams sent his commanders back to their posts, each to quietly plan the outline of an operation in their area. No one else was to know. Two days later, with Al Haig about to arrive, MACV bosses listened to the results. On December 12, in his cable 15808 to McCain, General Abrams offered

> a coordinated air-ground attack . . . to sever the enemy [line of communication] at Tchepone . . . and to deny to the enemy the logistic corridor vital for continued prosecution of the war. . . . A multiregimental task force will attack to seize the Tchepone area, conduct operations within Base Area 604 to destroy enemy stockpiles and facilities and block major routes both north and south of the Tchepone area.

The offensive would consist of four phases and last for about three months, beginning with a preparatory attack by U.S. troops to clear the region west to the border and to reopen Khe Sanh, followed by ARVN seizure of Tchepone, a third phase there, then a withdrawal southeast through Muong Nong and Co Roc (which Americans called Base Area 611) to the A Shau valley. Admiral McCain cabled Washington in his turn that the operation would be "an excellent opportunity to strike the enemy where he least expects it, to destroy his resupply effort at the heart of the system."

This outline plan was the work of Lieutenant General James W. Sutherland, a pipe-smoking University of Alabama graduate who had been a friend of Abe's since both served at Fort Knox after World War II. Sutherland had also been a unit commander in the 3d Armored Division when Abrams was assistant division commander in the 1950s. Now General Sutherland led the U.S. XXIV Corps, which had replaced the marines as the top-echelon U.S. command in the South Vietnamese I Corps. Sutherland believed that the last week of January or beginning of February would be the ideal time for the contemplated offensive.

When the invasion came it was put about that the plan, code-named Lam Son 719, was a South Vietnamese initiative. These events show that cannot have been true. Kissinger's memoir also tries to put the onus on Abrams and Ellsworth Bunker in Saigon, plus Nguyen Van Thieu, claiming the suggestion was made *during* Haig's trip. Leaving aside Abrams for the moment, it is true that Ambassador Bunker favored a Laotian operation, and had been on record since Westmoreland's Southpaw project of 1967. Meeting with Walt Rostow, Bunker had described himself as a "strong supporter" of Southpaw. But there is no record of Bunker, or Thieu, not to mention Abrams, bringing up the Laos initiative without prompting. Conversely, there *is* a record of Abrams, prior to Cambodia, being prompted to propose that operation so the idea would not appear to be coming from Washington. In addition, it is known that Al Haig was extremely upset subsequently with how Lam Son had been handled by MACV, which suggests a certain proprietary interest in the invasion. Further, General Westmoreland was army chief of staff at this time and told associates later that *he* was not consulted prior to Lam Son, though having proposed so many similar actions, Westy might have been considered an ally for proponents. That, too, is consistent with White House initiative in the Nixon administration, but inconsistent with Lam Son as a MACV enterprise. Lewis Sorley, biographer of Abrams, is reluctant to rule out the general as originator of the Laos plan. Although this issue cannot be resolved before declassification of additional records, existing evidence suggests that, like Cambodia, Creighton Abrams was prompted to deliver an option the White House could take credit for if it worked, and let him sink for if it did not.

Wherever the Laos option came from, the White House accelerated its interest. On December 15, with Haig still in Saigon, presidential chief of staff Haldeman's diary quotes Kissinger: "He thinks that any pullout next year would be a serious mistake because the adverse reaction to it could set in well before the '72 elections." With Al Haig's return on December 18, Haldeman's diary shows Nixon and Kissinger fully up to speed. Here the chief of staff refers directly to Nixon: "He had Henry in and just sort of sat and chatted. . . . They also got into our operating plan in Laos where they're going to move the South Vietnamese in for a major attack operation." On December 22 Bob Haldeman records: "Henry came up with the need to meet with the P[resident] today with Al Haig and tomorrow with Laird and [JCS chairman] Moorer because he has to use the P[resident] to force Laird and the military to go ahead with the . . . plans, which they won't carry out without direct orders."

The military were not the only ones who had trouble with the Laos plan. Any invasion carried with it the same political-diplomatic drawbacks that had always attached to military action in lower Laos. This had been clear from the outset in the NSSM-99 process. As early as July 16, 1970, an interagency ad hoc group on Laos, in reporting on the political impact of proposed paramilitary operations, advised that Souvanna Phouma was an ally worth preserving: "Souvanna has consistently said that the only foreign ground forces in Laos were those of North Vietnam." When the CIA's Hmong tribal forces in northern Laos needed heavy support, Kissinger was explicitly reminded, Souvanna had gone to Thailand and lobbied for the dispatch of artillery batteries and other covert aid, then denied the Thai presence when it was reported in the press.

Politics in Laos remained as delicate as always, according to the political impact paper, which pointed out how Souvanna, again as he had on previous occasions, refused to associate himself with Saigon leader Nguyen Cao Ky's call for a Southeast Asian alliance or joint operations in Laos by ARVN, Cambodian, and Thai troops. On the other hand, Souvanna himself had originated a request that the United States assist certain Thai special forces active in the Bolovens Plateau area of lower Laos. The U.S. embassy in Vientiane, now under Ambassador G. McMurtrie Godley, vetoed the project on both political and military grounds. Souvanna's neutralist public persona could be shattered, in this view, even by paramilitary operations short of large-scale invasion. The paper argued: "A Lao government which was not able to protect the interests of the ethnic Lao in the Mekong valley would probably not be able to maintain itself in power even if the US should continue to support it." As for an offensive by ARVN along the lines of Lam Son 719: "Souvanna would be inclined to oppose such operations, and he might even conclude that they would lead to such an open escalation of the conflict that he would prefer to resign. . . . Regardless of the public position which Souvanna might take . . . he would be considered as having acquiesced . . . and his 'neutralist credentials' would correspondingly suffer."

These arguments were echoed by State Department officials when Kissinger began talking about an offensive into Laos. Henry relates that Nixon moved the plan forward by successively gaining the support of Laird and then William P. Rogers, his secretary of state, after Laird made a Saigon trip with Admiral Thomas P. Moorer (January 11–15). But once Kissinger began holding detailed planning sessions of his crisis unit, the Washington Special Action Group (WSAG), and Rogers had heard the views of his in-house experts, agreement evaporated. Undersecretary of State U. Alexis Johnson, superbly skilled at bureaucratic maneuvers in Henry's opinion, "began to surface objections that did not challenge the decision but would have delayed its implementation indefinitely." The objections? Johnson thought Souvanna Phouma ought to be consulted in advance of any invasion. "It was," Kissinger writes, "a strange argument."

In fact, the objection was the opposite of strange—the United States had maintained its relationship with Souvanna throughout the war precisely by such private soundings. The just-cited report of the ad hoc group on Laos had raised this very necessity in analyzing the lower Laos options. When Secretary Laird met President Thieu during his own Saigon visit, on January 11, Thieu's only reservations had had to do with public justification for the Laotian invasion, and Thieu had worried in particular that Souvanna could not appear to reject or disapprove the ARVN invasion. When Ambassador Godley did meet with Souvanna, the Laotian prime minister had wanted to know why an offensive like this could not be made farther south, down by the "Sihanouk Trail" and behind Vietnam's Chu Pong massif. Prime Minister Phouma also stated that the size of the ARVN operation would be a problem for him; he expected ARVN to withdraw within a week or two. If he said nothing, the Laotian leader adverted, the Chinese might move against him in northern Laos. Sure enough, Souvanna warned, he would publicly protest an ARVN operation into Laos. When the time came, Phouma declared that it was Hanoi's troops who were the problem in Laos, but he went on to protest Saigon's moves as advertised.

Alex Johnson recalls of Laos: "The action was ill-conceived from the start. It required an unproven group of soldiers to strike at an objective that the enemy would defend stoutly in a region where it had superior logistics. I argued against the operation in the WSAG and Rogers argued against it with the president, but Nixon and Thieu ordered it."

Actually the diplomatic problem posed by Johnson and Rogers came close to saving the Nixon administration from this debacle. The Pentagon suddenly expressed interest in decoupling the initial, U.S. phase of the invasion, from the rest. That would take place entirely within Vietnam, and the rest could be canceled if necessary. On the afternoon of January 27 General Abrams recommended cancellation of the operation and said MACV would take that action shortly after midnight of the twenty-ninth. Admiral McCain reluctantly concurred, but both commanders emphasized the value an operation would have. In Washington Admiral Moorer asked for more detailed arguments that could be used by the president that day. Moorer got the material, and he and Laird used it when Nixon met with them, Rogers, and Helms at the White House. Rogers continued to warn of the Laotian political situation, possible Chinese reactions, and an uproar in Congress and the press, but he was argued down. Nixon directed that the initial phase go ahead as planned, reserving to himself further decisions. When Mel Laird got last-minute jitters and asked Moorer, on January 29, for possible alternatives to a Laotian invasion, he would be told there was "no direct substitute for the Tchepone operation in terms of anticipated results and effect on the enemy." What the JCS chairman offered—paramilitary action by CIA irregulars in Laos or additional activities in northeastern Cambodia—were paltry substitutes.

Then there was the CIA. As Kissinger writes more than once, Richard M. Helms could be ignored because Nixon had no use for the CIA, or the agency had no place giving policy advice, or because Nixon knew Helms would not leak after he had his say. Helms did object; according to Kissinger, "[Helms] turned out to be the only adviser to raise serious questions." In fact, a coordinated intelligence community study released on December 14, 1970, pointed out that the People's Army had strong forces in lower Laos, with its largest concentration around Tchepone, along with formidable air defenses, especially dense in the vicinity of Tchepone. Another CIA memorandum, prepared on a close hold basis at Kissinger's request, evaluated the probable VPA response to an attack with U.S. air support but without ground forces. According to a postwar study of intelligence effectiveness in the Vietnam War, the January 21 memorandum "was remarkably accurate with respect to the nature, pattern, and all-out intensity of the [VPA] reactions." At WSAG, meanwhile, Richard Helms "pointed out that the proposed operation had been frequently considered in the past and had always been rejected as too difficult."

Helms happened to be perfectly correct. The Kissinger memoir professes surprise: "Later I learned that four years earlier our then Vietnam commander, General William Westmoreland, had thought that such an operation would require two corps of *American* troops. Though he was now a member of the Joint Chiefs of Staff, no such view was submitted to the White House in 1971." It is difficult to decide whether the greater professional failure of Henry Kissinger and his national security system lay in planning a full-scale invasion without bothering to ascertain what similar things had been considered in the past, or in moving ahead with a ground offensive without reference to the army chief of staff. Since the CIA raised this very issue before the Laotian offensive began, Dr. Kissinger's protestations that he only learned later ring quite hollow.

Then there is the question of American participation. As has been seen here at length, since the beginning of cross-border operations the issue of unilateral American versus American-Vietnamese, versus Vietnamese-only efforts had been a thorny one. Long before 1971 the conclusion had been reached—and not just by MACSOG—that only American or combined operations had much chance of success. Now it happened that the political imbroglio created by the Cambodia invasion of 1970 had already led to the imposition of restraints on the Nixon administration. An amendment to the defense authorization law sponsored by Senators John Sherman Cooper and Frank Church prohibited American troops in either Laos or Cambodia. Pentagon and State Department lawyers thrashed out their understanding of the prohibition in the course of work on NSSM-99. The message to the White House was clear: not only American ground troops but also advisers with ARVN units would be prohibited from entering Laos if the Lam Son offensive went ahead. The men making up their minds about Lam Son knew there was no question of full U.S. support, as is indicated by the terms of reference Kissinger gave the CIA for its estimate on Hanoi's response to an offensive toward Tchepone. The ARVN, absent its U.S. advisers, would not even be up to its own standards of effectiveness.

Finally there is the matter of what Hanoi knew about the Tchepone operation. If DRV intelligence agencies had penetrated the offices of Thieu and Ky, as previously suggested, the intention to invade Laos could have been known as soon as mid-December, when Al Haig met with the Saigon leaders. If that were not enough, Americans put deliberate straws in the wind, such as Admiral Moorer of the Joint Chiefs, who referred to invading Laos as an option in a late December interview with the *New York Times*. Unnamed senior administration officials were also quoted in the press as expecting a high point in the fighting even greater than in 1970. In addition there were references to an increase—some talked about a doubling—of infiltration down The Trail. That suggested an American focus specifically on lower Laos, which was the part of The Trail the United States could reach.

Beyond simple open sources there were other avenues for Hanoi to gain knowledge of Lam Son. General Abrams took good precautions; on his staff few knew what was up, Jim Sutherland was sworn to secrecy, no wider circles were brought into the planning until a go-ahead from the JCS on January 7, no messages or documents were circulated except by hand of officer. Security on the American side was first-rate. With ARVN it was not. Haig had met in Saigon with Thieu and Ky; there were also contacts between Abrams and ARVN Joint General Staff chief General Cao Van Vien. The ARVN I Corps commander, Lieutenant General Hoang Xuan Lam, was not permitted to discuss the offensive with Jim Sutherland of XXIV Corps until December 29, but a week before that, Sutherland learned, Lam had breached security right in front of him. The two had been standing in the waiting area at Phu Bai airfield, expecting Nguyen Cao Ky and a visiting troupe of entertainers with Bob Hope. Alongside them were numerous other officers, including ARVN 1st Division commander Brigadier General

Pham Van Phu, his U.S. senior adviser, and so on. In Vietnamese, Lam and Phu began talking about the upcoming operation.

At a much less exalted level, Captain Craig McMullin was a photo interpretation specialist with the intelligence section of I Corps. A Dallas boy and graduate of Texas Christian University, McMullin had arrived in Vietnam to find himself assigned to the Phoenix program. McMullin insisted on work in his specialty and ended up at I Corps (later he discovered he had been traded for two lieutenants and a refrigerator). Anyway, in late December ARVN captain Do Van Loi came to him with a request for aerial photographs of the region from the Laotian border to Tchepone and down to the Bolovens. On the ARVN side the word was around.

Not only was the request unusual, but also the extensive order would be filled in less than a week. McMullin thought back later on and realized as soon as that happened he ought to have realized something was up.

Cao Van Vien had long advocated this kind of attack to cut The Trail. The JGS chief had even made his arguments in speeches and in an article published in a U.S. Army magazine. Early in January Abrams came to Vien with confirmation of a go-ahead from Washington. General Vien, according to another Saigon officer's account of the Tchepone offensive, at first wanted ARVN paratroops to drop into the town, then attack eastward and meet troops coming up Route 9. He ordered Colonel Tran Dinh Tho, the JGS chief of operations, to look for suitable drop zones in the Tchepone area. But later Vien abandoned this concept of the offensive without even mentioning it to the U.S. commander. Vien's discussions with President Thieu have gone unrecorded.

Accounts are that the basic plan for Lam Son was completed by January 13. A couple of days later Colonel Tho and his counterpart, MACV J-3 major general Donald Cowles, flew up to Da Nang to brief Generals Sutherland and Lam. At I Corps headquarters Lam's chief of staff, Colonel Cao Khac Nhat, was kept out of the meeting. Later Nhat took Colonel Tho aside and asked him, "why exclude me from the meeting? I have already completed the operational plan!" Colonel Nhat pulled the Saigon operations chief into his private office and laid out his ideas, using a general situation map.

There could be little doubt that knowledge of Lam Son was out there. On January 16 when Sutherland and Hoang Xuan Lam went to Saigon to present their plan to Abrams and Vien, the American general recalls: "By then I knew, and so did General Abrams, that the [Vietnam People's Army] had been alerted that something was going on." By January 25 XXIV Corps and MACV had positive intelligence that Hanoi *did* know about the Laos invasion. That information was sent to Washington; there was nothing kept from the president and Henry Kissinger. Nixon aide Bob Haldeman records, under date of January 26, "Hanoi has our plan we've discovered." There was still time to call off Lam Son; Saigon leader Thieu gave his final approval only that day. Instead Nixon and Kissinger pushed ahead. Haldeman on the rationale: "We can draw them into a monumental trap and then move ahead and bomb them."

Beginning on January 28, intelligence started coming in showing the People's Army moving some of its troops, especially those opposite the U.S. 101st Airborne Division, back into Laos.

Whom the gods would destroy they first fill with giddy arrogance. The battle of The Trail stepped to its climax with the inexorability of a Greek tragedy.

One of the more interesting documents captured during 1969 had been a calendar notebook recovered from the body of a soldier bearing an AK-47 assault rifle. The notebook belonged to one "Comrade Tin." Intelligence associated the alias with General Le Trong Tan, and the *bo doi,* killed by a patrol from the 2d Battalion, 1st Infantry, ARVN 1st Division, must have been one of Tan's escorts. The Tan notebook recounted how the People's Army general had gone to Hanoi from the front, where he held a senior post in the Tri-Thien-Hue military region. Unlike most, General Tan could afford to travel by automobile, and left toward the end of March, his first stop at Station 34. As had long been true, crossing Route 9 was one of the most dangerous parts of any trip, north or south, and it was no different for Le Trong Tan. The day General Tan's group made its crossing, it was caught in a U.S. air strike. One of his bodyguards was killed, but Tan's party escaped further damage. They arrived in Hanoi thirteen days after leaving the front.

In keeping with the widespread reliance by the People's Army on aliases and *noms de guerre,* the Tan notebook used these to identify the persons he met in Hanoi. A few were relatively transparent. "Uncle," who gave general instructions, more likely than not was Ho Chi Minh, widely known as "Uncle Ho." Then there was "Brother Sam"—General Hoang Sam was chief of the Rear Services Department of the People's Army, the man in charge of getting the supplies that were sent down The Trail. Tan's strategic instructions were provided by "Quang," who may have been Van Tien Dung or indeed Giap, or, less likely, Le Duan. In any case, what was significant would be instructions that actually anticipated seeing an end to the war, and foresaw that the United States would come to some agreement with Hanoi—all efforts should be directed at compelling the United States to withdraw from Vietnam. To that end, General Tan was to assert control over territory in the rural and mountain regions of his command, as well as plant agents among the ARVN forces and in the cities. Tan was instructed to rebuild his forces so they would be as strong as before the Tet Offensive. Before leaving for the South again, in late May, Tan had final discussions with the high command regarding his own relations with the leaders of the Route 9 Front.

According to the captured notebook, Hanoi leaders expected the outcome to emerge within a year. Although that timetable was never met, the strategy of avoiding major battles during the U.S. withdrawal, and then seeking an end to the conflict, is implicit in the course laid down for General Tan. In the autumn of 1970 Tan was appointed to lead the 70B Corps, a large field command that comprised troops of both the Route 9 Front and the DRV's Military Region 4, which controlled Quang Binh and the panhandle. The result of Hanoi's strategy would be that 70B Corps units were near full strength when the ARVN invaded Laos along Route 9. Le Trong Tan would be the top *bo doi* in the field against the South Vietnamese. Fate had put one of the People's Army's finest leaders in charge at a key moment in the war.

General Le Trong Tan had been born in 1914, a time when many Vietnamese—the French called them "Annamites" then—were enlisting patriotically in a colonial army that helped France win World War I. His birthplace is variously listed as Haiphong, Dong Hoi, or Hoai Duc district on the outskirts of Hanoi. Working as a laborer in central Vietnam, Tan joined the Viet Minh at the end of World War II and was soon a People's Army cadre at Hanoi. He rose steadily, becoming deputy commander of the VPA 312th Division when it was formed, then succeeding to divisional command, leading the Viet Minh troops who invaded Sam Neua Province of Laos in 1953. A year later, at Dien Bien Phu, Tan's division made some of the most arduous attacks and were triumphant. General Tan went to Russia afterward for advanced military studies, and headed the VPA infantry school and military training system. He had gone South under the alias "Ba Long" and served with COSVN from 1966 to 1969, eventually becoming chief of staff, before his assignment to Tri-Thien-Hue.

After the war Tan would go on to become deputy chief and chief of the People's Army General Staff and vice minister of national defense. His reputation was sterling. Bui Tin, for example, writes this of General Tan: "An officer of great talent and virtue. He was highly respected throughout the army as a general who was always in the forefront of the battle wherever it was hottest. . . . General Tan was an officer who studied the details of every campaign and applied this experience to his own command strategy. He had no other passions. He did not drink, not even beer."

All of this says much for Le Trong Tan's skill and perceptiveness. Bui Tin records that he once asked Tan what he would have done to win the war if he had been an American general. Tan replied, saying of the Americans: "If they had been wise they should at a certain point in time have cut a specific section of The Trail and taken over that area. Then we would have been stuck. We would never have been able to fight and win as we did. If they had been brave enough to do so, they would at least have severely disrupted our strategic network." General Tan believed the Americans had had the strength for such an operation between 1965 and 1967, which is a matter of judgment, since the U.S. forces were just deploying at that time. Le Trong Tan also spoke without reference to the logistical factors entailed, of which much has been said here and still more is to be shown. In addition, the comment does not take into account the political equation, which offered a risk of Chinese or Russian intervention during the early years, and the danger of meltdown in the United States in the later ones. The limiting factors were real.

Nevertheless, it is most significant that a People's Army commander agrees with Americans ranging from Rostow to Westmoreland that cutting The Trail was the thing to do. It happens that Tchepone was the only suitable piece of real estate on which to execute that intention, because only there, along the mountain fastness of the Vietnamese border, was there an access to the sea. Unfortunately for those who put so much stock in the notion of cutting The Trail, the physical obstacles remained as formidable as the Vietnamese adversaries.

Major General Raymond G. Davis took command of the 3d Marine Division in the summer of 1968, after the harrowing siege of Khe Sanh. The 3d held the portion of Vietnam just below the Demilitarized Zone (DMZ), including the erstwhile McNamara Line and the lowlands of Quang Tri Province. That meant the division was also the principal American unit responsible for Route 9. Bragging rights assumed during Davis's tenure included the claim that Route 9 had been pacified and that it had been developed into an all-weather thoroughfare. To make his point, in the same way Bill Colby used to do to show pacification was working, Davis drove alone in a jeep at night from Quang Tri over to Ca Lu. But the full story of Route 9 was more checkered, and would be of crucial import to the eventual invasion of Laos.

The road itself dated from the French period and had not been much maintained after World War II. A French column on its way into Laos to restore colonial administration in that country had used Route 9 in 1946; that had in fact been the largest military movement on the road right through to the times of Saigon leader Ngo Dinh Diem. Roadbuilding, already recounted, figured among Diem's passions, and he had had plans for Route 9. The dreams never amounted to much because they intersected with Hanoi's march South and the opening of The Trail. The security situation swiftly worsened with the onset of the Viet Cong insurgency, to the point that major construction on Route 9 became foolhardy. Until September 1964 the road was a one-lane dirt job usable only by jeeps and light trucks. That autumn the way was no longer considered secure. The Special Forces camp then at Khe Sanh henceforth received all its supplies by air; the road deteriorated.

A most notable feature about the marine sweeping operation of 1966 called Virginia was that the unit involved marched back from Khe Sanh following Route 9. A chaplain recorded: "We did see traffic signs which looked rather ludicrous since they were now practically in the middle of the jungle. Bridges over scenic chasms gave mute evidence of past hostility since some of them had been blown by charges and were just hanging on by a few inches of steel." It is also significant that coffee planters who grew crops around Khe Sanh preferred to market their beans at the Mekong valley town of Savannakhet, the Laotian terminus of Route 9, instead of trying the much shorter trip down to the Vietnamese coastal plain. This occurred despite the presence of Hanoi's troops at Tchepone, by the way, and no doubt has something to do with Bui Tin's memory of thriving coffee shops in Tchepone town when he visited there in the mid-1960s.

Khe Sanh stood forty miles from Dong Ha, the lowland ville where Route 9 joined Highway 1, but it might as well have been on the moon. Only in the spring of 1967 did U.S. Marines decide they had spare engineer resources to reopen the road. The most basic restoration of necessary bridges took three weeks. Marine boss General Lew Walt was ecstatic when Khe Sanh finally became accessible by road. Starting in late March, "Rough Rider" truck convoys traveled to Khe Sanh for the first time. Rough was indeed what the ride was—a truck could not even turn around anyplace in the twenty-mile stretch between Ca Lu and Khe Sanh. Route 9 remained a back country lane. The period of open communications did not last very long either. That summer the high command's attempt to move heavy artillery to Khe Sanh ended with the ambush of a covering infantry unit. The convoy halted at the last possible place—Ca Lu. Once again considered dangerous, Route 9 closed after a final "Rough Rider" convoy on August 3, 1967.

In 1968, the year of the siege, Route 9 would be reopened in the course of the Pegasus relief operation. Even below Ca Lu, several culverts and a bridge had to be restored, and between there and Khe Sanh the 11th Combat Engineers and 7th Engineer Bridge Company had to clear landslides, fill numerous craters, build ten new bridges, and repair three old ones. For a few months, while the 1st Marine Regiment engaged in mobile operations, Route 9 supplied the patrol base that Khe Sanh became, but then remaining installations were destroyed in August. After that the forward edge of the battle area became Ca Lu itself, which marines knew as Firebase Vandegrift, and nearby, Camp Mai Loc with Special Forces Detachment A-101.

The way of the road is evident in the experience of John Lindquist, a Wisconsin marine who served in 1968–1969 with the motor transport and logistics companies of the 3d Division. Lindquist went on no fewer than eighty-eight truck convoys up Route 9, sometimes as a driver, others as a radioman. Improvements were being made in the road, and Lindquist admired the work of the engineer and Seabee units that labored on it from December 1968. They used defoliants to clear a space more than 200 yards wide on each side of the road, and huge Rome plows to take out the remaining brush. At the post of Thon Son Lam, more familiar to Americans as the "Rockpile," the engineers installed a rock crusher, and gravel from this machine would then be spread on the road to pack the shoulders and as a base for pavement.

Well enough. But the improved part extended west not much past Cam Lo, and the pavement ended just after the Rockpile, which was actually built right on the road and had to open its gates each time a convoy went through. A typical truck convoy consisted of forty-five to sixty vehicles, though there could be small special details of only a few or even one truck. The convoys would form up in the "Dust Bowl" at Dong Ha, wait for the signal, then set off. Along the improved stretch, land mines could be detected by seeing where the dirt had been disturbed, but the adversary still could put out claymores or explosive charges in culverts, so a sweep had to precede each convoy, then a check vehicle. On a bad day you could see

where the People's Army planned to ambush the convoy, and their anticipated escape routes, by looking at places the security teams had detonated
mines they found. Past the Rockpile, "Route 9 was such a little piss-ant
highway, just a lane and a half," Lindquist recalls. "The jungle would actually touch my face as we drove by."

Firebase Vandegrift was set in a little valley next to Ca Lu. There were a
couple of saddlebacks on the ridge behind it, then the A Shau valley. With all
the potential for trouble, and the People's Army base areas beyond the usable
road, Lindquist felt nervous even though he sat atop a sandbag in his truck.
The marine finally volunteered for a garbage detail to escape the convoys.

Marines continued to maneuver in the foothills below the DMZ, hump-
ing out over the ridges west and north of Vandegrift and Camp Mai Loc.
With their penchant for naming things, the marines were wary of "Rocket
Valley" and "Mutter's Ridge." There were operations such as Virginia Ridge,
Idaho Canyon, Herkimer Mountain, and Arlington Canyon. In due course
the 3d Marine Division stood down, to return to the World as part of the
withdrawal program. After November 1969 the U.S. Army took over, with
the 1st Brigade, 5th Division (Mechanized) the major American combat
unit. Increasingly the ARVN troops of I Corps furnished the bulk of military
manpower.

Camp Mai Loc continued as the forward base in the Annamite foothills.
In April 1970, coincident with a round of intense fighting farther south, at
Dak Seang in the Central Highlands, the People's Army hit Mai Loc. Behind
rockets and mortar shells the VPA sent 100 sappers against the Special
Forces camp. The sappers broke in at several points, hurling demolition
charges, firing rocket-propelled grenades, doing their best against the CIDG
strikers, a number of whom were veterans of the debacle at Lang Vei.
Within a couple of hours the 5th Brigade had reinforced Mai Loc with
twenty tanks and armored personnel carriers and the VPA sappers were
driven back, but the loss tally told its own story: 6 Green Berets were killed
and 13 wounded; among CIDG strikers, who numbered 250, there were 21
dead, 8 wounded, and 26 missing; only 29 of Hanoi's sappers were confirmed killed. The toll was an illustration of the efficacy of People's Army
sapper assault tactics. Not too long afterward, Camp Mai Loc was closed out
and Detachment A-101 joined the stream of withdrawals from Vietnam.
The ARVN deployed Rangers and regular troops to hold Mai Loc as a conventional strongpoint. Needless to say, no effort was made to maintain the
road past Ca Lu. When the time came for the Laotian invasion, Route 9
would be a restoration project before it could be a supply route.

The alert came in the middle of the night for Alpha Company of the 1st
Battalion, 11th Infantry. Alpha had spent the past two months at Mai Loc,
radiating pickets into the Annamite foothills, toward Ca Lu and more exotic places. Captain Philip Bodenhorn actually had his men out that night.
Now they were on notice for an air assault into Khe Sanh. The rest of the

battalion would be coming from Quang Tri; deploying from barracks, they had a relatively easy time of it. Alpha Company had to recall its men for a hurried muster, boarding helicopters for the combat lift. Bodenhorn had already garnered four Purple Hearts in slightly more than half his Vietnam tour; he privately agreed with men in his unit who groused that this sounded like trouble.

Khe Sanh! That fabled place, graveyard for many men and certain generals' dreams, now lay squarely within Indian country. Except for MACSOG and the marines' Force Recon, no Americans had been on the ground around Khe Sanh for many months. The idea of going there now at first seemed folly. When Bodenhorn learned more, the operation made more sense. Alpha Company would be part of a much bigger push. Lieutenant Colonel Raymond E. Farrar's entire battalion would lift into Khe Sanh to secure the airfield of the old combat base. While 1/11 Infantry did this, two more battalions, 4/3 Infantry and 3/187 Airborne, would assault into landing zones along Route 9 to protect the advance up the road. As the airmobile plan unfolded, Lieutenant Colonel Richard Meyer's 1st Battalion, 77th Armor would punch right up Route 9 from Dong Ha to Ca Lu, where the former Firebase Vandegrift would be reactivated, initially for guns from the army's 108th Artillery Group, later as a supply base. From Vandegrift armored cavalry troops and engineers in combined task forces would refurbish the road. To speed up that process, advance parties of engineers and troops would land by chopper farther up the road, where they could begin preparations to replace bridges and culverts.

This was operation Dewey Canyon II, the initial phase of the Laotian invasion. The effort was entirely American, and it would still have been possible to call off the ARVN cross-border offensive intended to follow. Once General Abrams had reassured Washington he expected American casualties to remain relatively low, however, Richard Nixon exhibited no qualms about pressing ahead. As a security measure, Dewey Canyon II took the same name as an operation the marines had conducted a couple of years earlier in the A Shau valley, and in radio traffic places involved in the new operation were given cover names of locations in the A Shau. Admiral Moorer of the Joint Chiefs actually thought the code name Dewey Canyon too reminiscent of old-style Vietnam search-and-destroy operations and tried to get it changed, but MACV and other commands saw no need and gave no further thought to such niceties.

Under General Sutherland of XXIV Corps, the tactical commander on the American side was Brigadier General John G. Hill, who led the 1st Brigade, 5th Infantry Division (Mechanized). A decorated veteran of combat in Korea who enjoyed "Jock" Sutherland's confidence, Hill planned Dewey Canyon carefully, and his brigade had been reinforced heavily to conduct it. Hill's own troops included an armored and two infantry battalions, an armored cavalry squadron, an artillery battalion, a ranger company, and other units. For Dewey Canyon General Hill had two extra infantry battalions, another armored cavalry squadron, and one more artillery battalion. This brigade amounted to the equivalent of two, in all perhaps 7,000 troops. On top of that, XXIV Corps asked the U.S. Marines for engineers and transport, and additional Americans were lent from that source. Most important, the 101st Airborne Division (Airmobile), which had succeeded to the mantle of the Cav, supplied the bulk of helicopters for the offensive.

American officers and men expected a tough fight to break through to Khe Sanh, much less clear the zone out to the Laotian border. Instead, contact would be sporadic and light. On Route 9, called the "Gold" axis of advance in XXIV Corps plans, three huge D-7 bulldozers of A Company, 7th Engineers, spearheaded the column. In the darkness the driver of the lead dozer couldn't see enough to clear the brush ahead and asked to use his lights. Armor commander Colonel Meyer approved; the troops progressed, lights blazing, with no ill effect. Meyer took the precaution of calling for a curtain of artillery fire north of Route 9, however. Such was the density of the early morning *crachin* and the noise of the vehicles, that the barrage could neither be seen nor heard. The men on the Gold axis made almost four miles before morning.

The air assaults began at 8:30 A.M. and were complete before midafternoon. At Khe Sanh the landing, anticipated with fear, went in without incident. Captain Doug MacLeod, battalion surgeon for the 1/11 Infantry, rappelled into the landing zone with the first wave. Later MacLeod remarked wonderingly, to a military reporter, "We thought we would get some contact—at least a few mortar rounds or a sapper probe." But no People's Army *bo dois* were seen during the entire day. Only in the rear, at Mai Loc and at Firebase Fuller, which were rocketed, did there seem to be any reaction. It was not until the fourth day, February 2, in a raid near the old Lang Vei Green Beret camp, that D Troop of the 2nd Squadron, 17th Cavalry encountered an installation of forty or fifty VPA bunkers that showed evidence of having been occupied twelve or twenty-four hours earlier.

The road restoration was crucial. Men of the 14th and 27th Combat Engineer Battalions, along with the 7th, and the specialized companies attached to them, did work without which the rest of Lam Son would have been impossible. Engineers and helicopters cooperated to place preassembled bridges at necessary points. On the "Gold" axis alone, and just between Vandegrift and Khe Sanh, eighteen bridges and twenty culverts had to be replaced. Route 9 was open to Khe Sanh on February 1. The next day a tracked vehicle made it as far as Lang Vei. On February 5 American troops completed clearing Route 9 all the way to the Laotian border. "Those goddamn tankers, they get all the credit," complained engineer surveyor Steven Hill, "but all they do is drive over the roads we build for them. If we didn't go ahead of them with all those bridges, they wouldn't do anything but jump in and out of their little holes!"

In actuality, the tanks of 1/77 Armor retained their base at Ca Lu throughout Dewey Canyon, providing the heavy force for Firebase Vandegrift and the road security for Route 9.

Among the engineers' other achievements, one of the most remarkable became the carving out of a second road north of Route 9. Following existing tracks and river valleys, the new road began at the Rockpile and formed axis "Brown" in the plans. Called the "Red Devil Road," the path was primitive but could be made better. It crossed 20 streams or marshy areas and almost 2 miles of dense forest in an overall length of 15 miles. The first part, ascending the Annamite foothills for a vertical rise of 475 yards, involved an impressive 27 percent grade. The Red Devil Road opened as the Vietnamese phase of Lam Son kicked off. It increased supply capability at Khe Sanh by permitting trucks to return for new loads without using Route 9. Throughout the operation engineers built or improved a good 50 miles of roadway.

Equally important was the airstrip at Khe Sanh itself. Aerial photography during the period of preparations for the offensive showed the strip needed several weeks of work, but the Americans decided to level an area right next to the old strip for a new runway, an "assault" airstrip. A quick survey right after U.S. troops helicoptered into the place on January 30 confirmed this plan. Work began immediately. An air force officer arrived on February 1 to watch over the work by army engineers. Two days later, word was put out for public consumption that the new strip was open, but in fact the engineering work went on until 5:00 P.M. on February 4. At that time the air force made a test landing with a C-130 transport, using the opportunity to insert an airfield control group for the field, which they expected to handle forty to sixty C-130 landings a day. The Herky Bird transport also carried 834th Air Division commander General John H. Herring Jr. In front of the brass the C-130 sank into the ground, making ruts five inches deep. Fortunately the plane's powerful engines were able to pull it into the air again, but now everyone was on notice that the ground at Khe Sanh would have to be compacted before aircraft operations began. Meanwhile, more than 200 bundles of aluminum plating were estimated necessary to repair the adjacent airstrip from 1968. The assault airstrip eventually reopened on February 9 and the marine strip on the fifteenth.

Meanwhile, the final, fatal decisions were made, again in Washington. Ambassador Ellsworth Bunker participated at the White House on February 2 when the die was cast. That morning Kissinger circulated a five-page memorandum to the NSC principals summarizing considerations in proceeding with the invasion, including the State Department objections that Secretary Rogers had aired. In the afternoon Rogers attended, along with Laird, Moorer, Dick Helms, Al Haig, and Kissinger, as Richard Nixon made his final choice. According to Kissinger, no new arguments emerged, but that is a broad formulation covering everything from an assertion that no one raised any objection to a record that everyone restated previously expressed views. Kissinger also recounts that late that night he asked the president to review again the desiderata on Laos. If so Kissinger, who favored the invasion, was keeping his flanks covered. Nixon forged ahead, issuing orders to proceed with the further phases of the planned operation.

By now things were beginning to happen automatically. The Montagnards in this district—40,000 Bru tribesmen—were removed from the border area. Some were sent as far away as Pleiku and Kontum, crammed into big American planes with a few belongings. Speaking of airlift, there would be major lifts in connection with offensive preparations, more than 600 flights. Most went to Quang Tri or Dong Ha, an unused strip reactivated for the occasion; almost all the sorties were of the large C-130s. The ARVN Airborne Division in its entirety moved from Tan Son Nhut. American supplies and specialists flew in from Bien Hoa.

On January 29 ARVN general Hoang Xuan Lam established a forward headquarters at Dong Ha. Simultaneously, Jock Sutherland set up a XXIV Corps command post at Quang Tri. The ARVN's 1st Armored Brigade and its 1st Infantry Division started northward up Highway 1. On February 3 American helicopters carried three full battalions of the ARVN 1st Ranger Group into an LZ close to the Laotian border. The rangers set up a couple of firebases west and northwest of Khe Sanh to cover the attack up Route 9. On the fifth, the Rangers were joined by guns of the U.S. 64th Artillery. Saturday, February 6, brought ARVN formations right into the Khe Sanh region. A task force composed of the 1st Armored Brigade and the 1st Brigade of the Airborne Division entered its assembly area, screened by U.S. armored cavalry troops. Behind them the 3d Regiment, plus the headquarters of the 1st Regiment, both of the ARVN 1st Infantry, reached Khe Sanh. That afternoon the Airborne Division's 2d Brigade arrived at Dong Ha-Quang Tri.

A critical aspect of the preparations, fuel, became a true headache at this time. The delay opening Khe Sanh airstrip meant that aviation fuel for the helicopters to move ARVN troops into Laos was not there. The plan had been that the limited capacity of Route 9 could be restricted to supplies for ground forces. By February 5 General Sutherland already felt that a lack of large (1,200-gallon) tanker trucks had become his thorniest resupply problem. By the eighth, when Lam Son jumped off, the situation had assumed emergency proportions. Only the diversion of big U.S. choppers to carry loaded fuel blivets directly to the helicopter fields at Khe Sanh enabled the slicks to get off the ground for the Lam Son air assault. The fuel crisis would be further complicated that very day—at 2:00 A.M. a fuel convoy moving west on Route 9 was ambushed, with six of the big tankers destroyed or damaged. The ambush was a demonstration, if one were needed, of just how vulnerable the overland transport routes were.

American B-52 bombers mounted eleven Arc Light strikes on previously identified targets as the offensive swept into Laos on February 8. Artillery began firing in support of the attacks at 8:00 A.M. A half dozen ARVN battalions figured in the initial helicopter lifts. The lead element of the invasion, across the border on the ground at 7:12 A.M., was an engineer platoon from the armor-airborne task force, checking Route 9. It was a fateful day.

There were no surprises in Laos. Some participants told journalists later that the Vietnam People's Army (VPA) and Pathet Lao forces had been stronger than expected, but that was just not true. On January 12, 1971, in an "eyes only" cable (MAC 00335) sent to General Sutherland over Abrams's signature, MACV intelligence chief Bill Potts had put the cards on the table. Potts furnished a new evaluation of VPA strength in lower Laos to inform the tactical planning for the invasion. The MACV intelligence was quite plain: within the Laotian military region corresponding to the invasion area, Pathet Lao and People's Army strength was put at 42,000. Of these there were 5,000 VPA and 5,000 Pathet Lao in combat units, with the rest working for *binh trams*, ten of them, termed "a potentially significant fighting force." Higher command resided in a front headquarters and nine regimental or larger command posts. Most importantly, "it appears that the bulk of the enemy's combat units in the region are located in the vicinity of Tchepone."

As important as the front-line troops was the question of the reinforcements that could be brought to bear. The MACV experts believed the VPA could bring in two additional divisions from the DRV, as well as up to twenty battalions brought back out of I Corps fighting areas. These estimates were believed and refined at XXIV Corps and the 101st Airborne Division, which provided the helicopter firepower and lift used by the invasion forces. The XXIV Corps appreciation was that the adversary might be able to bring up as many as seven fresh regiments (i.e., more than the equivalent of two full divisions) within twenty-one days. Because the Dewey Canyon phase of the operation began a full week before the actual invasion of Laos, the VPA were on notice of the attack. Intelligence quickly developed evidence that VPA troops were already on the move.

General Le Trong Tan began his arrangements to combat the offensive in January, even before Dewey Canyon. *Bo dois* of the 24B Regiment, VPA 304th Division screened Route 9 northeast of Ban Dong, while the 64th Regiment of the 320th lay to the south of the road. At Ban Dong itself, Binh Tram 33 was on alert. A Viet Cong regiment, the 1st of the 2d VPA Division, usually deployed in the southern part of I Corps, was on the march to the Tchepone area. Headquarters of General Tan's 70B Corps began moving toward the battle area late in January. On February 6 the 1st Viet Cong Regiment was already nearing Ban Dong, while the 812th of the VPA 324B Division neared the towering Co Roc massif, which dominated the battlefield to the south. As of February 8 the forces opposing the ARVN were already increasing and were estimated at 22,000, some 13,000 of them combat troops.

Some of this, but only some of it, proved visible to the secret warriors of MACV's Studies and Observation Group. One SOG reconnaissance team on a road-watch patrol managed to stay in the field for a month, starting from the end of December 1970. In addition there was a Hatchet Force platoon atop Co Roc Mountain at the beginning of February. Missions in general, however, were at a low ebb due to orders from Washington. Concerned with political backlash, Secretary Laird and others wanted no Americans in Laos when the Lam Son invasion began. Laird was convinced reporters would try to find evidence of U.S. soldiers in Laos and that any contradiction of administration claims that there were none would become a major setback.

The Joint Chiefs of Staff's exclusion order, which came through on February 5, did permit continued ARVN-led patrols. In a sense this became part of Vietnamization, for the prohibition left the field to the South Vietnamese. Eventually the change would be reflected in code names as well, for Prairie Fire would transition to the Vietnamese Phu Dung.

Nevertheless, there were still Americans at risk in Lam Son 719. There were plenty of U.S. aircraft in the sky above the troops. Sergeant Joe Kline, crew chief of a UH-1 Huey, of the 101st Aviation Battalion, the Kingsmen, recalls a definite air of history about Khe Sanh. Even though air activity hardly got started until late morning, due to the time it took the *crachin* to burn off, soon "Khe Sanh was easily visible from the air for distances of more than thirty miles due to the large cloud of red dust being generated by all the helicopter traffic." Just reciting nicknames of the various 101st Division helicopter companies flying out of Khe Sanh gives some idea of the numbers of aircraft involved in the invasion. Besides Kingsmen there were the Toros, Blue Max, Commancheros, Black Widows, Dolphins, Phoenix, Lancers, Hawks, Ghostriders, and Redskins. All were army units, either transport "slicks" or gunships. Heavy-lift helicopters, observation ships, marine choppers, and so on made more. And, of course, there were the Ravens and the fast movers. Plenty of Americans were at risk in Laos; in fact, more than 200 would be killed there.

Co Roc filled the skylines as a chopper passed the border. Below lay a feature, a line of escarpment generally following the border, the Sepon River, and bending back toward Tchepone, that would become critical in the Laotian campaign.

Battalions of the ARVN 1st Division set themselves up at LZs Delta and Hotel along the escarpment; soon they would be establishing firebases to screen the southern flank of Route 9. Helicopter pilots were familiar with the dangers of small-arms fire from Vietnam, but for the most part they did not fly in areas where substantial VPA forces were a constant presence, and there were very few heavy antiaircraft weapons, so most flights took place at 500 feet or less. In Laos the brass decided to fly the choppers at 3,000 feet or higher, which eliminated the small-arms threat but put helicopters at a prime engagement altitude for heavy flak. Aircrews did not like that. The general situation was further complicated in that, as SOG troops could have told the planners, most LZs in Laos were not big enough to land more than one or a few choppers at a time. That meant loose, trailing aircraft formations, not tight flights, were absolutely necessary. Flak gunners underneath a flight path could find targets all day long.

The earliest American helicopter lost went down the very first day of Lam Son. Its pilots were warrant officers Paul Stewart and Thomas Doody. The ship sustained heavy damage and had been clawing through the air toward Khe Sanh when its tail boom separated and it went in. No one survived the fiery crash.

Frank G. Wickersham was a hot young marine pilot with Squadron HML-367. He remembered Khe Sanh from the 1968 battle, when he had piloted a transport chopper all over the sector below the DMZ. After that campaign, things had become so quiet that one day, inserting a marine reconnaissance patrol, they had been able to have a tiger hunt, with the helicopter using its prop wash to drive tigers into the guns of the men on the ground. In 1971, Wickersham remembers, the area was so dangerous that his unit became involved when army heavy helicopters refused to lift artillery into the battle zone. Marine CH-53s were asked to do the job, but they, in turn, needed flak suppression support, which brought in HML-367, which had AH-1G gunships. Wickersham participated in the latter part of the campaign, for he was one of a handful of pilots with Colonel Paul ("Tiny") H. Niesen attached to HML-367 to field-test the new AH-1J "Sea Cobra." Captain Wickersham quickly found himself flying ten to fifteen missions a day over Laos—keeping the log for sorties, the copilot's job, quickly became ridiculous. These were supposed to be recorded for such purposes as awarding air medals, and the rules were that each crossing of a border should be recorded as a sortie. On one of their first days over Laos, Wickersham looked at his copilot's log and said, "From your record we earned *ten* Air Medals today!"

Like Joe Kline, Frank Wickersham felt the press of the past. His primary refueling point was at Lang Vei; another time they put in guns on top of Co Roc; he saw a lot of places familiar from the 1968 battle. "It was like flying into history," Wickersham recalls.

As for sorties, the marines finally came to the device of counting each load of fuel that was used up as a sortie. Officially, within a month the press was being told U.S. helicopters had flown more than 145,000 sorties.

Flying into Co Roc Mountain, Wickersham saw no trace of the caves that the Marines at Khe Sanh in 1968 had supposed were full of VPA artillery. In fact, the insertion of ARVN guns and infantry atop Co Roc went entirely without incident. There were also many flights out toward Tchepone, not as escort for slicks but to scout and strike enemy forces on the move. "Tchepone was still a village," Wickersham recalls, "but it was almost like a ghost town."

For those in quest of the grail, the high commands out to cut The Trail, Tchepone beckoned, ghost town or not. At 11:00 A.M. on February 8 President Nguyen Van Thieu released an official statement on Lam Son 719. Thieu denied that his invasion constituted "an act of aggression of the Republic of Vietnam against the friendly nation of Laos," and also insisted "this is not an expansion of the war." Rather, "This is an operation limited in time and in space, with the clear and unique objective of disrupting the supply and infiltration network of the Communist North Vietnamese."

Just who would be disrupted remained to be seen. On his scout missions to Tchepone, Frank Wickersham kept spotting Hanoi's troops coming up, even to the south of Route 9. He was amazed at the amount of equipment displayed—tanks, trucks, guns—almost too many to count. Scouts were making these sightings from the very first day of the invasion. There was indeed going to be a battle royal in lower Laos.

* * *

In the style of great endeavors in military history, a central feature of Lam Son 719 was the armored attack along Route 9. The operational group carrying out this portion of the plan consisted of the 1st Armored Brigade reinforced by two ARVN airborne battalions. As the armor crossed the border west of Lao Bao (see Map 8), artillery at that place fired in support, and more guns moved up behind to increase the concentration in the Lao Bao area. Things looked good the first day, with the ARVN making about nine kilometers, almost six miles. Together with heliborne insertions of flanking forces on both sides of the road, by dusk on February 8 the Army of the Republic of Vietnam had thrust a seemingly solid wedge across the border and toward The Trail.

On the second day, it began to rain. Although some accounts are written as though this made little difference to the armored group, General Nguyen Duy Hinh, author of a U.S. Army monograph on the Laotian invasion, reports that February 9 was "a day of marking time." The first major objective on the road was Ban Dong, just a dozen miles inside Laos, and the armor did not close in on it until late in the afternoon of the third day. The plan had been for ARVN paratroops to make a combat assault into Ban Dong from helicopters and join with the troops attacking from the road to capture the place, but the weather did not clear for a long time. It was at about 5:00 P.M. on February 10 that the ARVN 9th Airborne Battalion hit the landing zone at Ban Dong, linking up with the armor a couple of hours later. Ban Dong had fallen. There was little trace of the enemy, however, and the *binh tram* logistics unit that had long been the core of Hanoi's presence at Ban Dong must have withdrawn in good order.

From that moment the invasion of Laos began to bog down. South Vietnamese ranger and airborne troops holding flanking positions above the road encountered significant Vietnam People's Army forces for the first time. Although Lieutenant Colonel Phat's 3d Airborne Battalion captured six VPA trucks laden with ammunition and uncovered some caches, the troops grew more cautious amid signs of the enemy.

What happened along Route 9 was of a piece with the evolving situation. The ARVN military region and I Corps commander, General Lam, pleased with performance so far, determined to extend the invasion into its second phase, sending reinforcements to new positions preparatory to further advance by the armored group. At Ban Dong, Colonel Nguyen Trong Luat, commanding the 1st Armored Brigade as well as the operational group as a whole, ordered his men to ransack the countryside. For two days ARVN detachments combed the roads and trails that converged at Ban Dong for Hanoi's supply caches.

Colonel Luat occupied a good jumping-off point for a further advance toward Tchepone. After days of searching, however, Luat stayed put, his troops merely tinkering with their dispositions. Nguyen Trong Luat was a hero to some Vietnamese, dating from the battle of Plei Me in 1965, where he had commanded a motorized force that, like that in Laos, stood in grave

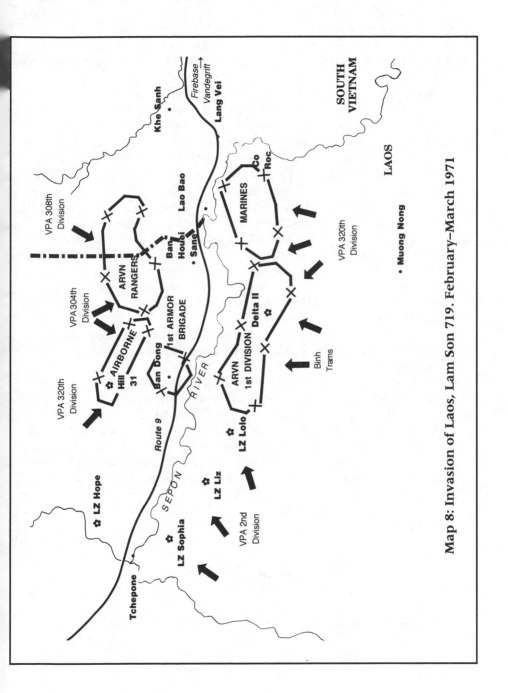

Map 8: Invasion of Laos, Lam Son 719. February–March 1971

danger of ambush, but Americans held differing opinions of Luat's leadership. The senior adviser to the South Vietnamese armored command saw Colonel Luat as a good officer, while General Sutherland of XXIV Corps viewed him as an incompetent martinet. In any case, in 1965 Luat had stopped for a critical interval following initial contact with the enemy, and at Ban Dong in 1971 he did the same thing.

In Colonel Luat's favor it must be noted that the stretch of Route 9 in Laos was in an even worse state of disrepair than the part of the road in Vietnam, already described as abysmal. A subordinate, Lieutenant Colonel Bui The Dung, who led the 11th Armored Cavalry, told journalists a couple of weeks later, "This is not tank country." That was certainly true, yet when Luat received orders to send a task force to help ARVN troops completely away from the road, who were under pressure in one of the flanking fire support bases, the tank reinforcements crossed country more rugged than along Route 9. It was a question of attitude. When reporters asked Bui The Dung whether a halt in the operation presaged an attempt to get out, the attitude showed: "Try to get out, yes," remarked Lieutenant Colonel Dung, "There's no reason to stay in bad country . . . when you cannot move."

Rather than a line marking one phase of a triumphal progress to Tchepone, Ban Dong became a firebase, a static position denoting the farthest extent of the ARVN advance into Laos.

Off the Vietnamese coast, meanwhile, proponents of invading the North had their day in the sun, sort of. Admiral McCain had pressed for months for an amphibious hook above the Demilitarized Zone, and in the context of the Laos operation this became a feint attack to deceive Hanoi. General Abrams insisted he had no troops to use in such a deception, so McCain ultimately fell back on his own resources. A landing force built around the 3d Battalion, 9th Marines held rehearsals off Da Nang, then sailed up toward Vinh. From February 12 through the first week of March the force simulated assaults on North Vietnam. Amphibious commanders actually planned a raid by two marine companies to destroy the airfield at Vinh. Planes from carriers flew missions nearby, and the amphibious ships sent the kinds of messages they would have used in a real invasion. The naval group reported being watched closely by North Vietnamese radar, and intelligence detected some VPA troop movements as well. But the adversaries never came to blows here.

Real warfare could be found in Laos. A conference at Dong Ha on February 14 among Generals Abrams, Sutherland, Vien, and Lam became the prelude to the next stage of battle. Top U.S. officers worried that ARVN firebases, supposed to secure the advance against flank threats, were instead slowing down the campaign. Creighton Abrams had already told Can Van Vien that troops should be sent against Tchepone as quickly as possible. The generals determined to accelerate Lam Son 719 by having the ARVN 1st Division occupy a series of hills south of Route 9, after which ARVN paratroops would go after Tchepone. The generals expected the latter attack within three to five days. Instead, on February 19, when President Thieu visited I Corps, General Lam reported the flank firebases held by ARVN rangers under heavy pressure, making any thrust by the Airborne Division foolish.

Vietnam People's Army forces were building up rapidly. The VPA's General Le Trong Tan also knew just what to expect. Two days into the invasion, the ARVN had lost a helicopter carrying American reporters but also senior I Corps staff officers, carrying annotated maps plus codes and communication instructions. Hanoi's information continued to be quite good.

On February 11 prisoners taken near Ban Dong revealed the presence of the 64th Regiment of the VPA 320th Division. The rangers had already run into the 88th Regiment of the 308th, the People's Army elite, the "Iron Division" of Dien Bien Phu. Several more regiments of the VPA 2d Division were also closing in, from the direction of Tchepone. As early as February 14 there were reports of VPA tanks, at first just light PT-76 vehicles, but soon Soviet- and Chinese-made T-54s and T-55s, whose 100-mm armament outgunned the M-41 tanks with Colonel Luat's ARVN armored brigade. The *bo dois* were strong.

At Ham Nghi, a few miles southwest of Khe Sanh, coordination center for the American advisers prohibited from entering Laos, the feeling of foreboding grew. Captain McMullin with I Corps intelligence heard no more about follow-up attacks toward the Bolovens plateau.

Le Trong Tan had no intention of defending passively against the invasion of Laos. Despite heavy American air support, including many Arc Light strikes plus a daily average of hundreds of fighter-bomber and gunship helicopter sorties, *bo dois* were making increasingly fierce attacks. Initial targets were the bases held by the ARVN 21st and 39th Ranger Battalions, assaulted repeatedly. On February 20 Fire Base Ranger North was overrun, its survivors escaping surrounding *bo dois* to reach Ranger South. Though more than 600 VPA soldiers were estimated killed, the threat grew worse, and on February 24 Ranger South was itself abandoned.

Hanoi's forces now focused on the strongpoints north of Route 9 held by the ARVN airborne division. It was these that Colonel Luat's tanks were ordered to help. A task force of the 17th Armored Cavalry with the 8th Airborne Battalion started out toward Fire Support Base 31. Two and a half miles north of Ban Dong they encountered and captured a PT-76 tank and a couple of Russian trucks. Another element of the same force found four-inch-diameter pipes—in fact, three different pipelines—and captured documents later suggested there were pipelines throughout the Vietnam People's Army base areas. Hanoi's supply network embodied in The Trail had become as sophisticated in its own way as any American logistics system.

The pipeline discovery actually led Washington to an embarrassment that did nothing to improve the credibility of the Nixon administration. Existence of the pipeline came as no surprise—it had been seen in aerial photography as early as July 1968 and had been the subject of a MACV intelligence study in December 1970. Construction had been monitored as Hanoi pushed the pipe from Vinh through Mu Gia Pass and into lower Laos. The giveaway in the overhead photography came when interpreters found the jungle pattern disrupted—by *bo dois* trying to lay pipe in straight trenches—and the discovery was then verified by CIA scout teams, who cut a section of the pipeline fifteen miles below Mu Gia Pass in the spring of 1969. Intelligence later detected pipelines entering Laos across the Ban Karai and at the western edge of the DMZ also, and it was this latter line that the ARVN found during the Laos invasion. South Vietnamese tank troops tore up several hundred yards of the pipelines, and in Washington on February 24 Secretary of Defense Melvin R. Laird and air force general John W. Vogt held a press conference at which they displayed a three-foot section of Russian-made pipe taken from Laos. The problem arose when leaks revealed that the pipe shown had not been taken by *any* of the troops in Lam Son 719. Within days senior Pentagon officials had admitted as much, while trying to retain a fig leaf, which close observers dismissed, that the pipe had been taken by a South Vietnamese clandestine mission prior to the invasion. Washington had been forced into a backhanded admission that it ran secret operations into Laos, blowing MACSOG's cover for its activities Prairie Fire and Nickel Steel, the reality of which U.S. officials had been denying for years.

Meanwhile, in Laos the 3d Airborne Brigade of the South Vietnamese Army learned too late just what an anthill had been kicked over. Colonel Nguyen Van Tho's brigade held two positions, Firebases 30 and 31, taken the first day of the invasion. The former, on Hill 655, held by the ARVN 2d Airborne Battalion, had been emplaced in the morning and its guns then used to shield seizure of Hill 456 by the 3d Airborne Battalion along with brigade headquarters. Colonel Tho's troops hunkered down.

Bo doi general Le Trong Tan began concentrating troops against the ARVN airborne almost immediately. From Hanoi General Van Tien Dung also traveled to the front to supervise the battle of Laos. The paratroop positions were carefully probed. On February 26, the ARVN captured Mac Thang Long, a platoon leader in the People's Army 25th Sapper Battalion. The sappers had had a company scouting Firebase 30 for five days already. Platoon leader Long told the South Vietnamese that his unit had been struck by air twice while moving up and that morale was low. However, the 25th Sappers were mostly stout men from Nam Dinh and Ha Bac Provinces in the North, had appeared in Quang Binh just two months before, and had only just moved up, with a clear counterattack mission. Mac Thang Long may not have been leveling with the paratroops about morale among his sappers.

Consolidation of the ARVN firebases depended on helicopter lifts greatly affected by the rapidly increasing scale of Hanoi's antiaircraft defenses. Where base construction might typically consume upward of 15,000 sandbags, for example, at Firebase 31 just a third of that number arrived. The defenses could only be proofed against 82-mm mortar shells. The People's Army opponents would soon be shooting much larger 100-mm, 122-mm, and 130-mm artillery rounds. The danger was real.

When an ARVN armored task force discovered the pipeline, it had been en route to clear the area around Firebase 31. The task force stopped when hit by the 36th Regiment of the VPA 308th Division, backed by tanks. South Vietnamese armor not only failed to reach Firebase 31 but also had to fight two battles just to make it back to Ban Dong. Admitted losses were three tanks, over two dozen other vehicles, and more than two hundred casualties. Saigon forces claimed to have killed a thousand *bo dois* and wiped out twenty-three tanks, including half a dozen heavy T-54s. This was the first time the ARVN had faced the T-54 tank in combat.

Another effort to succor Firebase 31 would be a heliborne assault mounted by the ARVN 6th Airborne Battalion, Colonel Tho's last reserve. This attempt miscarried due to Vietnam People's Army tactics—*bo doi* antiaircraft gunners held their fire as the slicks alighted on the landing zone, then opened up as the helicopters were disgorging troops. Unable to maneuver, the choppers suffered. The remainder of the 6th were shifted to another LZ. Even a prelanding Arc Light strike had not suppressed this opposition. After 100 casualties the 6th Airborne had done nothing to break up the VPA units assembling to attack Firebase 31.

On a dismal Thursday, the end came for Colonel Tho's brigade. Le Trong Tan massed the 24B Regiment of the 308th, backed by PT-76 light tanks, and opened the attack with a midday artillery bombardment. There were no American forward air controllers on the scene because the available FAC had copied the wrong map coordinates and flown elsewhere. Guns firing from Ban Dong and Hill 655 to support the firebase were not enough. When a FAC did reach the area, the first flight of F-4 fighter-bombers he directed destroyed a number of VPA tanks. That did not prevent *bo dois* from assaulting from the north and east with twenty more tanks. In less than a hour the ordeal of the 3d Airborne Brigade was over. Colonel Tho, his artillery and operations staff officers, the battalion commander, all were captured along with other Red Berets. Only a few escaped to friendly positions.

That was on February 25. Two days later, the scene shifted to south of Route 9, where General Pham Van Phu's ARVN 1st Infantry Division withdrew from a firebase called Hotel 2 after the place became too hot to hold and valuable helicopters were lost. For public consumption President Thieu was talking about the Laotian invasion as a Dien Bien Phu for Hanoi; General Phu had actually been at Dien Bien Phu as a young company commander in the Vietnamese 5th Airborne Battalion, and he would have been slower to make that comparison. A Northerner by birth, Phu had five sons and spoke of going back, but never again as a prisoner—at the end, in 1975, he would commit suicide rather than face prison camp. Despite abandoning LZ Hotel, General Phu's troops fought hard for their string of firebases on the southern flank.

Among its other effects, the Laotian invasion revealed serious shortcomings in the high command. For "Jock" Sutherland this operation had begun on an auspicious note—it started on his birthday. But General Sutherland had no command authority over ARVN and, it turned out, rather little influence with I Corps commander General Hoang Xuan Lam. The latter did not lead effectively. Lam permitted his armor commander, Colonel Luat, to ignore orders and play off I Corps and the Airborne Division commands against each other. Senior ARVN officers would also observe later that the weakness of the I Corps forward command post at Ham Nghi had been a factor in the collapse of Firebase 31. Lam did nothing to oblige top staff officers to leave the headquarters at Dong Ha, which left Ham Nghi with only junior people. Though Lam himself often visited Ham Nghi during the day, when he was not there or his attention could not be captured, the staff at Ham Nghi had no authority to act. On February 27, in fact, this situation became the subject of a dispatch from General Abrams to Sutherland: "I AM CONCERNED WITH THE ADEQUACY OF GENERAL LAM'S CONTROL ELEMENT AT KHE SANH. IT DOES NOT APPEAR ADEQUATE IN STAFF STRENGTH OR ORGANIZATION FOR THE TASK OF CONTROLLING AN OPERATION OF THE SIZE AND COMPLEXITY OF LAM SON 719."

Nguyen Van Thieu took a hand at this point with orders that the Vietnamese marine division should relieve the airborne at the front. Whatever his other limitations, Hoang Xuan Lam was a good cavalryman, a graduate of the French Army cavalry school Saumur. Not only could he see the difficulty of switching the marines for the airborne in the midst of battle, but it was also true that the marine division had never before fought as a single formation. In addition, the ARVN's inability to forge ahead and seize Tchepone was becoming an obvious failure. On February 28 General Lam flew to Saigon, meeting with Thieu that afternoon to propose an alternative. Lam's concept was for Pham Van Phu's infantry to extend toward Tchepone while marines inserted into the line behind them, taking over firebases vacated by the 1st Division. Extra armored cavalry would be borrowed to make up losses, and a marine brigade would be placed in I Corps reserve. President Thieu approved.

On March 1 the Saigon leader and his chief of staff, General Vien, met with Abrams and U.S. ambassador Ellsworth Bunker to describe the new wrinkles in planning for Laos. American assistance would be crucial to carrying out a heliborne assault in the Tchepone sector. The requirements magnified already enormous demands on the Americans of the 101st Airborne Division, whose choppers suffered daily as they tried to be all things to all people in Laos. By mid-February the division's air component, stretched to the limit, stood in danger of breaking. Major General Thomas M. Tarpley, the 101st boss, had little knowledge of helicopters, nor did his deputy, Sidney Berry. At MACV Creighton Abrams and his staff put their heads together and came up with Jack Hemingway, a brigadier who was perhaps the army's leading expert on rotary wing aircraft. Hemingway came to reinvigorate the 101st aircraft maintenance efforts. Throughout Vietnam the army also sought extra mechanics and sheet metal workers who could repair damage. A new forward echelon of the army's top-level aviation command deployed to Quang Tri to help keep the slicks and gunships in the air.

Beginning on March 5 General Phu's 1st Division leapfrogged a series of firebases into landing zones extending into the area of Tchepone. The stage was being set for the climax of the Laotian incursion. Unfortunately for ARVN and the Americans, Hanoi's troops had now massed on both flanks of the South Vietnamese incursion, and General Le Trong Tan rapidly completed preparations to hurl his *bo dois* at the South Vietnamese positions. Both sides were about to roll the dice.

A number of the intelligence staffs professed wonder at the rapidity with which the Vietnam People's Army was able to concentrate against the Laotian invasion. There was no surprise, however, for the scouts of the Studies and Observation Group. For a long time MACSOG Spike teams had been used to patrols that were a race against the adversary's response. Lam Son 719 seemed the same thing on a much grander scale. "All of the Prairie Fire pilots and most of the SOG troops smiled nervously and began fidgeting," Tom Yarborough reports. "The consensus of opinion was that the ARVN troops were in for a tough time." To make light of the situation, just before Americans kicked off with the precursor Dewey Canyon II, a few Command and Control North (CCN) guys made a sign that read "Welcome to CCN country." Yarborough flew as forward air controller for the mission to Khe Sanh in which the commandos planted their sign right next to the old runway.

In a way, the lark of a mission to Khe Sanh proved a high point for SOG in terms of participation in the invasion. There were both political and military reasons for this. On the political side, legal strictures now existed against the presence of American troops in both Laos and Cambodia, and the U.S. command went out of its way to prevent any occasion for sin. As General James Sutherland put it, "I made doubly certain that no American got out of a helicopter on the ground inside Laos."

This did not stop people from claiming to have seen Americans, of course, and both ABC and CBS Radio networks broadcast reports of American ground troops taking part, while on February 11 ABC reported that the body of a dead American disguised in a South Vietnamese uniform had been evacuated from inside Laos. In Saigon, MACV authorities knocked the reports down hard. "That's not true," declared a spokesman, "not a bit of it."

Given the frustrations voiced, not only by MACSOG scouts but also by the numerous advisers and communications specialists normally with ARVN units, who were kept back at the Vietnamese border, there is little reason to doubt these assertions.

There was also a practical military reason why SOG missions were not flown into Laos. The massive airlift requirements of the invasion, a strain even on America's aviation assets, demanded that every possible helicopter be pressed into the service of Lam Son 719. Jock Sutherland asked that choppers dedicated to CCN activities be diverted into the stream for Laos. This was approved. As pilot Tom Yarborough puts it, "Like a giant sponge,

Lam Son 719 continued to soak up men and equipment." For MACSOG, "During the month of March we couldn't have mounted a team insertion if we'd wanted to. The teams were ready; the FACs were ready; the Covey riders were ready. The missing vital element proved to be helicopters."

The situation persisted long enough that on March 17 Major General Donald Cowles, the MACV operations chief, sent XXIV Corps a message in which he insisted, "IT IS HIGHLY DESIRABLE THAT WE GET SOG BACK INTO [Base Area] 611, BA 614, AND THE LAOTIAN SALIENT." In dry cables Cowles's import was clear: "WOULD APPRECIATE YOUR GUIDANCE SOONEST AS TO WHEN YOU FEEL THAT YOU CAN RELEASE COBRA AND SLICK REQUIREMENTS TO SOG IN CONSIDERATION OF CURRENT I CORPS OPERATIONAL CONCEPTS." As it turned out, the diversion of helicopters from CCN lasted another two weeks.

The MACSOG effort never did return to what it had been. During the period immediately prior to the invasion roughly eight reconnaissance teams had conducted patrols in support of the original offensive concept (Silver Buckle), and there were an unknown number of missions to assist Dewey Canyon II. Typical of these were the Spike teams sent into the Muong Nong area (Base Area 611) on January 16 and 18. Both had been engaged instantly and both had had to be extracted within a half hour or less. One team tried a dozen different landing zones and actually attempted five insertions. In Base Area 611, CCN aircraft tried simulating the landing of teams or supply bundles and, as had happened years before in the program of sending agents into the DRV, the secret warriors began trying to make *bo dois* believe in the presence of notional scout teams in their base areas.

Once the invasion began, with the exception of Americans manning the communications relay station perched high atop a Laotian mountain, the prohibition against U.S. nationals applied to SOG members. Henceforth the South Vietnamese Strategic Technical Directorate, now including ARVN's Special Forces, carried out the cross-border forays. Vietnamese-led teams seemed less effective to SOG, and in April MACV asked Washington for authority to resume American-led Spike teams in Laos, but the moment had passed. Colonel John K. Sadler, commanding SOG, would never have that authority again. Though there are indications Americans may have crossed the border a couple of times, it would not be like the old days.

In addition, the tactical focus of SOG operations also changed, with a much greater effort devoted to Cambodia (539 scout missions through March 1972, as opposed to 432 by CCN forces). American losses, mostly in Command and Control North activities, numbered 16 dead, 68 wounded, and 11 missing. The toll for STD included 73 killed, 255 wounded, and 74 missing in action. After March 1972 the Studies and Observation Group stood down, replaced by a smaller unit advising the STD.

To return to Lam Son 719, as the invasion continued and the impracticality of a further ARVN advance to the Bolovens plateau or into Muong Nong from the rear became evident, more attention centered on the A Shau valley. Command and Control North began to work this area, inserting a

Spike team along each side of the valley in late February. One was Reconnaissance Team Python under Captain James Butler, which soon found itself in a serious firefight, and had to be pulled out under fire on February 20. The other Spike team would be evacuated four days later because the diversion of helicopters to Laos precluded regular support for the men in the field.

Raven pilot Tom Yarborough had been in the RT Python fight as air controller. He comments tellingly, "For all practical purposes, the Prairie Fire mission died on the west wall of the A Shau valley" with a FAC who went down. At a higher level, the commander of the 101st Airborne Division, General Thomas Tarpley, made a similar point in his later debriefing: "Unless these operations produce more hard intelligence, the level of risk to . . . personnel and the division's supporting aviation assets makes these operations of questionable value as a valid intelligence source."

The secret missions had been eclipsed by the big unit war. Now everything was up to the Army of the Republic of Vietnam and the American helicopters carrying them to Tchepone. As Nixon and Kissinger must have known, while the Laotian invasion was no more than a glimmer in their minds, the ARVN was a very weak reed on which to rest a war strategy.

Helicopter pilots, Ravens, fast and slow movers, infantry, artillerymen, all depended on the radio to a huge degree. In general, radio offered good flexibility, the opportunity to assign different frequencies to different purposes and communicators, so there were different "nets" for tactical commanders, airmen, and so on. The Laos invasion made radio different in two ways. First, due to the absence of American advisers with the troops on the ground, South Vietnamese were the observers on the ground and with the FACs. This created difficulties even on ARVN nets, but on the air nets, where the *lingua franca* was English, there was massive confusion. Marine gunship pilot Frank Wickersham heard communicators completely unable to communicate. Ironically, the problem ameliorated as helicopters were shot down—that is, American crews on the ground awaiting rescue often took over on the radios, and when they did, things improved. The other big difference with radio concerned the "guard" frequency, a radio band no one was supposed to use except for emergency situations such as reporting a "Mayday," an aircraft shootdown. In Laos there was so much traffic on the guard bands they became just another tactical frequency.

With that backdrop, the deep-penetration air assaults to Tchepone magnified everything. There were 120 slicks in the Tchepone lift on March 6, plus command choppers, gunships, medevac helicopters, scouts, FACs, and strike aircraft. Talk about confusion, the lift force had to depart Khe Sanh ninety minutes early when Hanoi's *bo dois* began to pitch artillery shells into the vicinity of the combat base.

No one harbored illusions as to the ease of this combat assault. On March 3, when Firebase Lolo appeared eight miles southeast of Tchepone, after a similar air assault, no fewer than eleven choppers had been shot down and forty-four damaged. The succession of LZs extending toward Tchepone had each involved dangers, first Lolo, then Liz, finally Sophia, fewer than three miles from the town. Two battalions of the ARVN 1st Regiment with eight 105-mm guns were soon in place at Sophia to cover the next assault.

The big attack came at a landing zone buoyantly code-named Hope, two and a half miles northeast of Tchepone. It was entrusted to the 2d Regiment of the 1st Division, brought up for the purpose from its sector near the DMZ, where it had been replaced by Americans of the 101st Airborne Division. The fresh ARVN troops presumably offered the best prospect for brushing aside *bo doi* defenders. Leading the assault were the "Black Wolves," the regiment's 2d Battalion under Major Hue Ngoc Tran. Called "Harry" by his American friends, Tran was among ARVN's finest officers and had been wounded four times. It was Tran, then in charge of the 1st Division's scout company, who had recaptured the Citadel at Hue during the Tet Offensive of 1968. Now Tran was at the scene of the ARVN's greatest moment.

A few minutes ahead of the slicks were scout helicopters of the 2d Squadron, 17th Cavalry, timed to reach the Tchepone vicinity just as the fast movers let up on their attacks. The area had already been subjected to preparatory Arc Light strikes. Next came the "aerial rocket artillery," choppers heavily armed with rockets for close air support, whose use had been pioneered by the 1st Cavalry Division. The 4/77 Aerial Rocket Artillery, created from the organic air unit of an infantry division, flew first into the fray. Captain Jake Benjamin of the 4/77 encountered heavy flak for the first time in the Tchepone lift: "Balls of smoke began to appear in the air. . . . At first no sound came through the heavy plastic canopies . . . but as they drew closer, sound grew. It seemed thick enough to land on." Frank Wickersham also saw the rocket-armed Cobras over Laos. "The army guys were very brave and fearless, but I saw enough of them get shot down," Wickersham observes. He did not think much of Laos as a combat laboratory.

Wickersham and the marine choppers flew escort for the lift force, then bore off to the south on a "skunk hunt," lingo for an observation mission. He saw Vietnam People's Army troops on the march, and called the target up the chain of command, but none of the FACs would take it on, so no one went to paste these adversaries. Wickersham's own rules of engagement were that he could not fire until fired on, and the *bo dois'* guns remained silent. This was one of the times "Wick" believes he ought to have violated standing orders.

Among the troop carriers, the first big CH-46 Chinook into LZ Hope exploded in a ball of fire from an antiaircraft hit. The second was damaged. But more and more ships came in and deposited their squads of ARVN infantry. Jim E. Fulbrook, piloting one of the smaller UH-1s, his call sign "Chalk 47," with the 71st Assault Helicopter Company, numbered among thirteen choppers damaged that day. It would be the only time in 1,420 hours logged on combat missions in Vietnam that Fulbrook got hit by the enemy. His good fortune Fulbrook attributes partly to luck but mostly to the fact that he flew at very low altitude, giving VPA antiaircraft crews minimal time to respond. In Laos, however, his altitude for the approach had been set by orders. Frank Wickersham agrees with Fulbrook on the tactic of low-level flying, incidentally, observing that crews in Laos, after a few days at low level, were ordered to high altitude, where they suffered losses, and then back to low level again, which he found far preferable.

At LZ Hope Major Tran soon had a significant force on the ground. Once his unit set up a perimeter, more slicks brought up the 3d Battalion, 2d Regiment. The two battalions sent search parties to the north and east. Tran's troops encountered a major stockpile of 122-mm rockets, in another place a heap of bodies left by an Arc Light, in a third a couple of tank hulks burned out in an air attack. Initially there was little fighting on the ground. On March 8 Major Tran's 2/2 Infantry entered Tchepone itself. He would be promoted to lieutenant colonel for the feat, which marked the high-water mark of the offensive against The Trail. Tchepone, of course, stood barely twenty miles inside Laos.

Exultant ARVN officers gushed to reporters about exploitation of their success, among other notions bruited about, talking of attacks out to the VPA supply center at Muong Phine, farther up Route 9. But already ARVN's flank had begun wavering south of Tchepone. General Le Trong Tan ordered new attacks focused on the firebases Liz, Sophia, and Lolo, reportedly named for the movie stars Elizabeth Taylor, Sophia Loren, and Gina Lollobrigida. At Lolo pressure grew heavier by the hour, as Frank Wickersham could have warned from his skunk hunts. "During the heavy fighting around [Firebase] Lolo," said ARVN's General Pham Van Phu, "I called for B-52 strikes within 300 yards of my unit." Almost 1,700 *bo dois* were estimated to have died in the Lolo battle. Yet after March 8 there was increasing difficulty supplying Lolo, and the firebase would be evacuated a week later. The ARVN rear guard on the withdrawal, 4th Battalion of the 1st Infantry, suffered catastrophic casualties, with just 32 survivors picked up by helicopters.

Back on March 9 there had been a key meeting in Saigon at the Presidential Palace in which Generals Vien and Lam advised Nguyen Van Thieu that the invasion should be stopped ahead of schedule. The weather, never as good as on the Vietnamese side of the mountains, was worsening; supply lines were poor; the Hanoi forces had greater reinforcement capacity than the ARVN itself. According to the account Cao Van Vien gave Abrams, which the MACV commander promptly passed in a dispatch to Jock Sutherland, the decision provided for ARVN to continue operations in the area of The Trail for another seven to ten days; in particular, the 2d Regiment would continue to work the Tchepone area for one to three more days. "MY UNDERSTANDING," reported General Abrams, "IS THAT AFTER THE SEVEN TO TEN DAY OPERATIONS DESCRIBED AN ORDERLY WITHDRAWAL WOULD BE EXECUTED."

In fact the 2d Regiment had already begun departing Tchepone, climbing the ridge south of the town that morning toward Firebase Sophia. It would not return. Hue Ngoc Tran's 2/2 Battalion instead ended up at a firebase called Delta I.

Generals Vien and Abrams briefly discussed an alternative for which the MACV commander pushed hard. That was the notion of reinforcing the Laotian drive with the ARVN 2d Division, the last big unengaged force in I Corps. The South Vietnamese Joint General Staff chief put the 2d Division on a dangle—Vien would be willing to send in the troops if MACV put the 101st Airborne Division's ground units into Laos. Abrams would have none of it, but agitated for sending the ARVN division to Laos anyway, to prolong the Lam Son operation. In the 2d Division's actual sector, at and south of Da Nang, ARVN commander Brigadier General Nguyen Van Toan and his opposite number, U.S. 23rd Infantry Division commander Major General James L. Baldwin, on their own initiative made the arrangements necessary to effect the takeover that would free the ARVN troops to deploy to Laos.

Creighton Abrams pressed buttons everywhere in an attempt to jump-start the Laotian offensive. According to biographer Lewis Sorley, Abe had put the option of reinforcement to General Vien as early as March 6, before the ARVN even reached Tchepone. After President Thieu's decision on the ninth, Abrams redoubled his efforts. On March 11 Thieu had Abrams and Ambassador Bunker to the Presidential Palace to detail his decision to them directly. General Abrams made his case for reinforcement to Thieu in person. Back at Pentagon East, the MACV commander cabled Washington to get the Nixon administration to light a fire under Thieu. As a result, Kissinger's staff asked the JCS its opinion in the matter. The army chief of staff, General William C. Westmoreland, felt the necessary forces could not be assembled. Here, in Laos, and now, was the battle for The Trail for which Westmoreland had pressed so eagerly and so long. But rather than pull out the stops, as Abrams was doing, Westy appears to have undercut his former deputy. A share of the responsibility for the outcome rests on Westmoreland's shoulders in consequence.

General Abrams tried another tack by requesting extension of his authority to support the ARVN operation in Laos, which had originally been given only through April 5. At CINCPAC Admiral McCain backed the request. Washington approved only continued discussions with the Saigon government. The official history of the Joint Chiefs of Staff shows that "Admiral Moorer . . . the President, and Dr. Kissinger all wished to avoid the appearance of a premature withdrawal from Laos." In a cable on March 11 to McCain and Abrams, Moorer warned against

SUCH A MOMENTUM IN [South Vietnamese] MOVEMENT TO THE EAST [i.e., toward the Vietnamese border] THAT THEY APPEAR TO BE BUGGING OUT. . . . WE MUST BE CAREFUL TO GUARD AGAINST ALLEGATIONS FROM THE PRESS AND OTHERS THAT THE [ARVN] ARE BEING FORCED TO RETREAT.

Despite these earnest desires, however, the warlords of Washington refused to take the measures to keep Saigon's army in Laos.

What the war managers did do, then and after, especially after, was jockey to place blame for the events of Lam Son 719. Richard Nixon, in his memoir, writes that "the American command in Saigon failed to respond to . . . unexpectedly intense . . . combat with the necessary increase in air power." Henry Kissinger claims the U.S. military gave him six different dates for when they expected to reach Tchepone, and failed to explain why they had to do that particular thing, as opposed to any of several other strategic alternatives—as if Kissinger had not himself been in on the launching of this strategy. Kissinger also disapprovingly cites several messages from General Abrams or Ambassador Bunker that discussed why things were not going better. Most interestingly, in the context of the question whether Thieu could reinforce Laos with ARVN's 2d Division (although erroneously calling it the 3d), Henry claims that "we"—that is, Washington—"had been urging [Thieu] to commit" the troops for more than ten days. In fact there is no currently available evidence that anyone other than Creighton Abrams pressured Saigon on this score.

Dr. Kissinger's deputy, then brigadier general Alexander M. Haig, also got an earful on the subject of Laos. One day Nixon called Haig into his office, where the general found the president closeted with political crony John Connally. Nixon told Haig to pack a bag—he was to fly to Saigon and relieve Abrams of command. Haig was floored. Nixon here spoke of sending a one-star general out to replace a four-star who was arguably the most skilled general officer in the U.S. Army. Nixon persisted; Lincoln had fired George McClellan, he could do the same with Abrams. Haig advised the president to sleep on it. Nixon finally settled for sending Haig out on an inspection trip.

As for Kissinger, Haig heard from him, too. "Well, Al," Haig quotes Henry saying, "your military finally got what it wanted and they've _____ it up!"

The Haig inspection took place just as the ARVN tide in Laos began to recede. In his own memoir Haig recounts finding that ARVN had been permitted to go into Laos with less support, particularly in gunship helicopters, than would have been the norm for a U.S. operation, and with artillery positioned too far away. Of course, gun positions depended on the border if the United States was not to enter Laos—a political decision—and the ARVN had moved out of range. As for helicopters, there were more than 600 under control of the 101st Airborne Division; Abrams had given them ships from units all over Vietnam. The raw airpower used in Laos was enormous, too: over 8,500 tactical air sorties plus 1,358 by Arc Light bombers for a total of more than 52,000 tons of delivered bombs. That represented a greater weight of munitions than delivered by Rolling Thunder on the area of North Vietnam above the DMZ (Route Package 1) *in all of 1967.* Senior officers at Lam Son remarked there were so many bombs exploding it was impossible to see the sun set in the afternoons due to the dust in the air.

Admiral Thomas Moorer has this to say about Richard Nixon's attitude in regard to bombing, in particular Arc Light:

> He had been accustomed to looking at the air strike program for the day and, of course, it was put on a little chart and they put it in little rectangles which indicated the bomb areas. . . . He would get the idea sometimes that he would wipe out every individual around, say, any of the areas under attack simply by laying down . . . these bomb zones.

There were occasional arguments over the optimal uses of airpower, including at least one in which General Abrams put through a direct call to the White House only to discover that Admiral Moorer already sat in Kissinger's office. Such disputes did not make Abrams the culprit for what happened in Laos, however. The MACV commander had made the best of what he was saddled with, laboring hard for success in Laos.

Vu Thuy Que could have told the Nixon administration something about the efficacy of bombing. A thirty-four-year-old officer in a Vietnam People's Army unit in Laos, Que was slapped to the ground by the concussion of explosions in one of the bombings. His head hit a rock and he was buried, living only because he was dug out by his men. There were many like Que—without doubt the bombs inflicted losses—but like him, other *bo dois* kept after the ARVN troops, and once it became apparent the South Vietnamese were mostly responding woodenly, VPA morale surged despite U.S. firepower. This time Le Trong Tan's soldiers also had guns and tanks, and it was the ARVN who were at the end of a vulnerable supply line. Beginning with Firebase Lolo, there was no stopping Hanoi's momentum.

CHAPTER 14

The Road Turns South
1971–1975

While wishful thinking persisted in both Washington and Saigon, by March 11, 1971, the handwriting was on the wall. That day Nixon aide Bob Haldeman made a clear record of the state of play at the White House. Henry Kissinger showed concern, Haldeman told his diary, "the Vietnamese now have decided to pull out as quickly as they can because they're afraid that the North Vietnamese are massing for a big attack and . . . their guys are going to get trapped and slaughtered." Kissinger wanted the ARVN to hang on for another three weeks or so—officially to increase their haul of captured supplies, but other reasons were just as important. At the White House, officials spoke of timing the ARVN pullout to coincide with a major statement on Vietnam the president was already planning for April, to make the occasion "one big 'ending the war'-type deal." Left unstated was the concern Admiral Moorer expressed that day, that the appearance of a bugout from Laos would have disastrous consequences. The most people around the White House would admit to was the political danger to President Nguyen Van Thieu, who faced an election scheduled for later in the year.

In Saigon that day, Thieu himself proved less than forthcoming with Abrams and Bunker. This pattern of questionable honesty had become ingrained in Nixon administration policymaking on Vietnam and now, with the chips down and Saigon paying in the same coin, the losers were the soldiers at the front in Laos. The pattern continued. On March 16 Admiral Moorer told Secretary Laird the ARVN had completed two phases of their plans and were proceeding to the third. In fact Phase II of the Lam Son *plans* provided for *extension* of the offensive, while the truth was that the South Vietnamese withdrawal had begun. Similarly, I Corps commander General Lam met on the sixteenth with American general Sutherland and told him that the ARVN would continue its "Phase III" until April 10 or 15. When Jock Sutherland learned that Lam's version of Phase III included *no* provision to continue blocking the roads or get into Base Area 611, the Americans knew that "offensive" had ceased to be the proper description of the ARVN operation.

Admiral Moorer drew the appropriate conclusions in a Joint Chiefs of Staff cable (no. 6505) on March 17: "THE REDEPLOYMENT . . . AS OUT-LINED . . . COULD ADD FUEL TO THE CURRENT PESSIMISTIC REPORTS CLAIMING A ROUT OF VIETNAMESE UNITS FROM LAOS . . . WE RUN THE RISK OF LOSING MOST OF OUR HIGH-LEVEL POLITICAL SUPPORT FOR PROSECUTING LAM SON TO A SUCCESSFUL CONCLUSION, AND OF UNDERMINING WIDESPREAD CONFIDENCE IN THE SUCCESS OF VIETNAMIZATION." To prevent that possibility Moorer was now willing to press for South Vietnamese reinforcement of the invasion, but it was too late for that.

On the ground Le Trong Tan's *bo dois* kept up the pressure. Improved weather on March 16 did not stem the tide in spite of 13 Arc Light strikes and more than 200 fighter-bomber sorties, plus 637 by gunship helicopters. There were more than 1,300 flights by transport choppers, among other things beginning an evacuation of the 3d Regiment of General Phu's division. The firebases near Tchepone, abandoned by the ARVN, swarmed with pursuers. Antiaircraft guns in the areas of firebase Delta and of Ban Dong endangered supply flights. Ngoc Tran's 2/2 Infantry, maneuvering around Delta, came upon a huge People's Army encampment emptied by an Arc Light attack. Tran's riflemen figured the camp contained more than 130 buildings, bunkers, sheds, and even underground installations, but barely 18 bodies were found. That evening Khe Sanh was shelled and 4 Americans were killed.

At the border, where two U.S. artillery battalions were firing in support from Lao Bao, counterbombardment by the People's Army became a daily occurrence. The same proved true at Khe Sanh, where the record air deliveries of supplies in early March proved to be the peak. The air force had planned to open an airstrip at Tchepone for C-123 lifters, but the ARVN's inability to capture and hold that place scrubbed the project. Stocks at Khe Sanh were permitted to decline. Major Charles Lutz, commanding the forward supply echelon at the combat base, where forklift work at the airfield came courtesy of the U.S. Marines—Company C, 1st Marine Shore Party Battalion—estimated the average haul at 225 tons a day. That compared to 750 tons by road up Route 9. The combined total still represented a significant constraint—had the ARVN been able to deploy its 2d Division through Khe Sanh, it is by no means clear that the enlarged force could have been supplied.

Meanwhile, the climax came along the ridgeline south of Route 9. The important firebases there were held by the 1st Infantry Division and by the 147th and 258th Vietnamese Marine Brigades. Hanoi's troops scented opportunity as the ARVN pulled back units that had covered the raid to Tchepone. At firebases called Moon, Brown, and Delta I came pitched battles, as a result of which the allies claimed to have completely knocked out two VPA regiments, inflicting 3,000 casualties on a force of 4,200 in the People's Army 29th and 803d Regiments. But South Vietnamese losses proved heavy, too. Though the 258th Marine Brigade got out of Laos fairly easily, the 147th suffered more than 300 dead and twice that many wounded. Almost 100 South Vietnamese Marines were missing.

Pham Van Phu's 1st Division, stretched to the limit, came close to collapse. At a command conference General Lam held at Ham Nghi on the evening of March 18, Phu joined other ARVN division commanders recommending withdrawal as quickly as possible. General Phu's anxiety startled other officers, who had never seen him display such an attitude. Speaking to reporters, Phu admitted Route 9 no longer served to supply his men in Laos, and also that he had evacuated firebase Brown, where medevac helicopters were taking heavy fire. Colonel Nguyen Van Chung, leading Phu's 2d Regiment at the front, later told American reporters that maneuvering had been difficult. "We had to be very mobile and could not stay in any one place too long," Chung said. "We did not want to give the enemy time to bring in large forces to surround our troops and to use his heavy artillery."

Exactly what that meant is evident from the experience of the Black Wolves, Harry Tran's 2d Battalion of Chung's regiment. Tran kept his men in good order as they fell back from Delta I, but resupply proved virtually impossible as 2/2 Infantry hacked through the jungle. Every so often the ARVN soldiers stumbled into more *bo dois* and there would be a sharp exchange of fire. When a helicopter flew up to act as command chopper for Lieutenant Colonel Tran, he had to wave it off. The troops were reduced to drinking their own urine in place of water. On March 21 the end came for 2/2. The battalion fell into an ambush. Harry Tran, wounded, lost parts of four fingers of his left hand and ended up in captivity. He would spend almost thirteen years in Hanoi's prisons; eventually Tran emigrated to the United States and rejoined his family, and he earned the U.S. Silver Star medal for his bravery in combat.

So progressed the withdrawal. Al Haig, by now in Vietnam conducting his inspection for Nixon, confirmed Washington's worst fears. Kissinger quotes Haig's reporting cable: "MY VISIT TO I CORPS HAS CONVINCED ME THAT THE ISSUE NOW IS NOT FEASIBILITY OF REINFORCING AND REMAINING IN LAOS, BUT URGENT NEED TO IMPRESS UPON ARVN THE NECESSITY OF MOVING OUT ONLY WITH FULL CONCENTRATION OF US FIREPOWER IN AN ORDERLY AND TACTICALLY SOUND FASHION."

Haig's military jargon looked measured on paper but belied the reality. So did the assertions, since repeated, that only a few South Vietnamese soldiers were affected by the sense of panic. No ARVN troop wanted to be the last man left across the border, and every soldier could see the antiaircraft fire, the trouble the choppers were having getting to them. Every time a helicopter landed, there was a danger it might be the last to get through. The photographs of ARVN soldiers clinging desperately to helicopter skids, and stories of how chopper crews had had to lighten their loads by ejecting men at the point of a gun were real. Yes, the pictures were of only a few units, but then the reporters were only permitted to be with those formations. If generals like Pham Van Phu could be shaken, and war heroes such as Hue Ngoc Tran and Nguyen Van Tho captured, prospects for ordinary Vietnamese could hardly be bright.

With so much hinging on the helicopters, the system proved sorely strained. Jack Hemingway worked wonders, and more than 500 mechanics and repairmen were funneled in to augment maintenance for the 101st Airborne Division, but demand remained ahead of supply. Official returns show more than 700 helicopters damaged over Laos, a number greater than the entire chopper force at the start of the campaign. The figure of 107 helicopters lost is an undercount, because ships were not counted as lost unless they could not be recovered, and ships were counted as recovered even if all that could be salvaged was metalwork showing the aircraft number. The proportion of "damaged" choppers that had truly been destroyed reduced the workload for mechanics, but not enough to make their job an easy one.

The fate of the tank spearhead shows the sheer difficulty of conducting a ground offensive into Laos. Colonel Nguyen Trong Luat, with his 1st Armored Brigade task force, had never succeeded in going much past Ban Dong. The reasoning that Laos was not tank country said something about the realism of MACV's plans for an invasion ever since Westmoreland's time, for the high shoulders lining Route 9 had not changed. America's own air campaign had contributed to the poor going, for the many tons of bombs heaped on The Trail had left numerous craters to trap unwary vehicles.

Colonel Luat hunkered down at Ban Dong and by late March transformed the place into a fortification, using his mobile forces to man static defenses. There were three main strongpoints to the place. Three quarters of a mile west of the Ban Dong road junction—the armor's forwardmost position—lay Bui The Dung's group with the 11th Armored Cavalry and the 8th Airborne Battalion. About a mile northeast of the junction stood a complex housing the command of the 1st Airborne Brigade, its 9th Battalion, and the 4th Armored Cavalry. Another paratroop battalion, the 1st, occupied advanced positions beyond the strongpoint. Finally, Colonel Luat with 1st Armored Brigade headquarters plus the 7th and 17th Armored Cavalry squadrons camped right on Route 9, straddling the road junction. In all there were nearly three thousand ARVN troops backed by 105-mm and 155-mm howitzers and M-41 tanks.

Beginning on March 17 *bo dois* started actively squeezing the Ban Dong defenses. Harassment from shelling kept ARVN off balance while People's Army units drove back patrols circulating around the positions. *Bo dois* observing Colonel Luat's strongpoints on the morning of the nineteenth saw preparations for withdrawal; their warnings triggered a sustained effort to roll up the ARVN units. Guns of the 675B Artillery Regiment began a two-hour bombardment, a big firepower concentration by Hanoi's standards. A village with neat rows of lodges on stilts, corrugated tin rooms shimmering in the sun among luxuriant coconut groves, Ban Dong was destroyed. "All that remained," according to a Liberation Front journalist, "was a drab gray of soil littered with hundreds of carcasses of crumpled trucks and aircraft." At midmorning VPA troops began ground attacks. Le Trong Tan hurled major forces at Ban Dong—the VPA 2d Division along Route 9 from the direction of Tchepone, elements of the 308th and 324B from the north. Tanks of the 202nd VPA Armored Regiment accompanied several units. Air strikes wiped out four VPA tanks quite quickly, blunting the assault long enough for Colonel Luat's men to pull out. One *bo doi* unit had been sent to infiltrate Ban Dong junction and Firebase Bravo, known in earlier days as the village of Ban Houei Sane, where the ARVN's 2d Airborne Brigade held open Route 9. Paratroops with the ARVN rear guard had some tough moments while Luat's armor lit out on the road.

The withdrawal of 1st Armored Brigade became an epic in the tale of the Laotian operation. Covering the rear, the 1st Airborne Battalion would be in heavy fighting on March 19, sustaining almost 20 dead plus other casualties. Colonel Luat's tanks made the initial retreat, to an LZ called Alpha, without too much trouble. Allied airpower inflicted major losses on Hanoi's armor. Then March 20 came, the peak day for U.S. support. On that day there were 11 Arc Light strikes, 270 fighter-bomber sorties, and another 1,388 sorties by helicopter gunships. Near Ban Houei Sane, however, Luat's lead elements encountered an ambush in which they lost 4 M-41 tanks, with almost 100 casualties to the 11th Armored Cavalry and the 8th Airborne. *Bo dois* prisoners revealed that more ambush positions had been set up astride Route 9. As a result, the 1st Armored Brigade commander determined to head off cross-country and find a place to ford the Sepon River, avoiding altogether the dangerous final segment of road.

Colonel Luat left Route 9 in darkness, during the night of March 21. Sure enough, there were no enemies in sight. The column worked its way through the forest until noon the next day, when the leading vehicles came out on the west bank of the Sepon about a mile from Route 9. A scout helicopter helped Luat find a fording place, then CH-54 "Sky Crane" helicopters lifted in a couple of bulldozers, while other choppers brought Luat chainsaws and gear to clear away jungle. While preparation proceeded, Colonel Luat threw the 9th Airborne across the Sepon to ensure that the opposite bank of the river was safe. Aircraft meanwhile found VPA tanks coming up Route 9 behind the ARVN, clearly trying to catch up. That afternoon and into the night air attacks and artillery halted Hanoi's forces while ARVN made ready. Early on the morning of March 23 the 1st Armored Brigade column pushed across the Sepon. It regrouped that afternoon, in plain sight of the VPA on Co Roc Mountain, on the parade ground of the old Lao Bao prison.

Nguyen Trong Luat later told Nguyen Duy Hinh, the ARVN's historian of the Laotian operation, that "had his unit not taken to the jungle to seek a way out, he did not believe a single vehicle could have made it back to Vietnam." Luat's American advisers joined the armored brigade now that it had regained Vietnamese soil. Luat still had 20 tanks and more than 50 armored personnel carriers, but even more tanks, and more than 100 vehicles in all, had been left behind in Laos. The halt at Lao Bao prison to regroup unwittingly gave Saigon's Colonel Luat something in common with his enemies.

Hanoi's Le Duc Tho and Generals Vo Nguyen Giap and Nguyen Chi Thanh had also spent time at Lao Bao during colonial days, inside the prison, looking out. The determination shown by those former prisoners had much to do with the perils Colonel Luat's armor had faced getting out of Laos.

As the South Vietnamese armored troops recoiled from Ban Dong, an incident on the other side of the border demonstrated anew how brittle U.S. forces had become. Once again Route 9 would be the focus; in fact, the action took place between Lang Vei and Lao Bao. Convoys on the road had previously been ambushed, and on the morning of March 20 several parties of "lurps," the storied long-range reconnaissance patrols, were choppered in to scout this stretch of roadway. One of the scout patrols came under fire after it found and detonated two mines, so the lurps called for help. Brigadier General John Hill alerted the 3/187 Infantry of his brigade to respond, but the best-placed unit was actually Lieutenant Colonel Gene L. Breeding's 1/1 Cavalry. Breeding in turn gave the mission to Bravo Troop of his squadron.

So far, so good. Bravo's commanding officer, Captain Carlos A. Poveda, had two of his platoons on line, and hustled down Route 9 toward the reported ambush. Suddenly the mechanized soldiers came under fire. A couple of vehicles took damage, and half a dozen men were killed or wounded. Poveda called in artillery and air, then withdrew, covering with fire from his own armored personnel carrier. The "track," as these carriers were called in The 'Nam, ran over a mine and became disabled, with one crewman wounded. They were stuck as the rest of the troop retreated. To complicate matters, they were joined by the crew of a chopper that had been damaged and had landed nearby. When other members of Bravo Troop realized the situation, two tracks came back up Route 9 to evacuate Poveda's survivors. *Bo doi* fire remained strong.

Regaining friendly positions, Captain Poveda realized that the disabled track contained marked-up maps and signal instructions that could help the People's Army maneuver in the Khe Sanh vicinity. His boss, Colonel Breeding, wanted that stuff back and also wanted to recover the APC and helicopter. Breeding ordered an attack up the road to regain the equipment. Captain Poveda, a well-regarded unit leader, proved unable to get the men to go back into the maelstrom of fire. Specialist Randy Thompson, killed in action a few days later, would be widely quoted as saying that the reason for the order was not a good one, but Thompson had also claimed, "I never heard a direct order. They asked us to go and we refused." Bravo's platoon sergeant, Billy Griffen, himself willing to go back in, nevertheless backed the men: "They did take a good beating down there. They were down. They were tired."

General John Hill, listening in on the radio net as the trouble developed, decided he would relieve Poveda of command. The captain should not have been trying to lead his unit while manning the rear-guard position. Hill awarded no medals for the action, but took no further disciplinary action against Bravo Troop. However, Breeding's 1/1 Cavalry would be replaced on road watch on this critical section of Route 9 by the heavier 1/77 Armor.

In his handling of the Bravo Troop incident, Brigadier General Hill may have felt eyes looking over his shoulder. Not only had his brigade sector become important due to the Laos invasion, but also the general had already come under scrutiny. During the early days of the invasion a senior MACV chaplain, visiting the front and talking with grunts there, came away with the impression that Hill hovered near the end of his tether. When Abrams mentioned these doubts to Jock Sutherland, the XXIV Corps commander invited the MACV commander to come up to see for himself. Following one of their meetings, Abrams and Sutherland choppered to Khe Sanh to get a firsthand impression of John Hill. Sutherland supported his brigade commander, and Creighton Abrams seemed satisfied. The episode proved ironic for Brigadier General Hill, however, who had been a young company commander in the Korean War when his father led the 9th Infantry Regiment there—the elder Hill had been relieved by a division commander who considered he had lost control in the face of North Korean invaders.

Such was the media interest in the Laos invasion that when the incident with Bravo Troop occurred, it was discovered and reported within days. Army chief of staff Westmoreland immediately asked General Abrams for an evaluation, and MACV went to XXIV Corps for Sutherland's comments before responding. John Hill would be exonerated. Later in 1971, having returned to the United States after his assignment, Brigadier General Hill immediately volunteered for another tour in Vietnam.

The deeper meaning of the Bravo Troop incident had to do with the disappearing combat edge of American forces. Like ARVN soldiers, none of whom wanted to be the last man killed in Laos, Americans knew that the United States was withdrawing from Vietnam, and none wanted to be the last to die in that war. Discipline problems had been growing ever since the Johnson administration; drug use had become pervasive, and soldiers such as those of Bravo Troop had begun to question their orders. Most ugly of all, unpopular or incompetent officers were in danger of "fragging," the term likely deriving from the use of fragmentation grenades on some of these occasions—that is, being attacked by their own men. There had been almost 100 of these fraggings in 1969 and more than 200 in 1970. Some senior officers at the time of the Cambodia invasion already harbored doubts whether they could depend on their men for the operation. Good officers kept their men busy—often in the field—and retained grunts' confidence by being realistic and reasonable. It is instructive that a number of American senior officers and former battalion commanders, at a panel discussion of Vietnam twenty-five years after the Laos invasion, divided about evenly over whether they thought U.S. troops could have been depended on for an offensive at the time. In 1971 these were live fears. U.S. units were fragile, as Bravo Troop showed itself to be, and an American offensive to cut The Trail most likely impossible for this reason alone.

Hanoi, aware of these trends in U.S. forces, played on them. *Bo dois* at the front were told if they did not know already; in the period of the Laos invasion, for example, *Quan Doi Nhan Dan* ran an article on demoralization among American troops on January 29, 1971. Some Vietnam People's Army attacks during the Lam Son operation also focused on Americans, their supply system, or the positions they held to free ARVN soldiers for the offensive in Laos. That February, positions of the formerly infamous McNamara Line were mortared or shelled no fewer than twenty-three times. Intelligence identified the 19th, 25th, 31st, and 33rd VPA Sapper Battalions in the zone of Khe Sanh and Route 9 during this time frame. On March 8 and again on the twenty-first there were sapper attacks on Firebase Vandegrift that aimed at supply dumps supporting Lam Son 719. A number of fuel blivets were destroyed along with 36,000 gallons of JP-4 jet fuel and 8,600 rounds of 20-mm ammunition.

At Khe Sanh a significant attack occurred during the early morning hours of March 23. The People's Army assault force would later be identified as the 2d Company, 15th Engineer Regiment. The *bo dois* were discovered as they infiltrated the perimeter just north of the old marine airstrip, along a sector held by Delta Troop of the 2/17 Cavalry. Mortars and rocket-propelled grenades supported the attackers, who fought for more than four hours. Fourteen *bo dois* died and one was captured. Two of the air cavalrymen's copters were destroyed and four more were damaged; three Americans were killed.

That proved to be the day Colonel Luat's ARVN armor escaped from Laos. In fact the last South Vietnamese troops left Laos on March 24, weeks ahead of the time until which Vietnamese leaders insisted they would stay. President Thieu, as ARVN troops pulled out, declared he would be going back, to make raids into Base Area 611, the Muong Nong-Co Roc complex, which had gone untouched. After intense Arc Light and fighter-bomber strikes, on March 31 the reinforced scout company of the ARVN 1st Division landed in the Muong Nong sector from choppers of the U.S. 2/17 Cavalry, spending a little more than a day on the ground with only light contact with the enemy. Again on April 6 the 1st Division scouts tried their luck at a point a little farther south. This time they spent only a few hours on the objective. These became the final ground attacks of the Laotian offensive.

In the air the South Vietnamese withdrawal received important protection, not only from fighter-bombers and B-52s but also from the gunships, the vaunted Spectre AC-130s and improved AC-119Ks. In a total of 239 sorties the gunships rendered great services, including accounting for the majority of VPA tanks destroyed from the air. Gunships and B-52s were the targets when Hanoi upped the ante on its Trail defenses—moving surface-to-air missiles into position at the Mu Gia and Ban Karai passes, whence they could engage the U.S aircraft over Tchepone. In February and again in March, when SAMs were fired American fighter-bombers responded by attacks on the SAM sites inside North Vietnam. Gunships recorded four instances of SAM firings in March and April. In May 1971 one of Hanoi's MiG fighters engaged a U.S. aircraft over Laos for the first time. By the spring of 1972 there would be SAM sites near Tchepone itself. One perverse effect of the Laotian invasion was that it induced Hanoi to build up The Trail's defenses more than ever.

Some of the airpower issues came to the fore at the White House on the afternoon of March 26, 1971, when the president gathered top advisers to review events in Indochina. Nixon opened by insisting that air sortie rates in Vietnam had to be kept high at least through the 1972 presidential elections, even if it became a budgetary problem. Henry Kissinger seconded that demand and added that the ARVN needed to be improved to the point where it could move divisions from one corps area to another without difficulty. Admiral Moorer briefed the group that over half of Hanoi's battalions committed against the invasion (seventeen of thirty-three) had been put out of action.

At the White House meeting on March 26 Richard Nixon asked if the military expected to evacuate Khe Sanh. Moorer replied that forces in place at the combat base would merely be thinned out; he anticipated Khe Sanh would be held through May. In fact the press carried initial reports of U.S. withdrawal from Khe Sanh the very next day. The last Americans left Khe Sanh, and its base facilities were blown up (for the second time in four years), on April 6. Tanks of the 1/77 Armor were carefully spaced at two-mile intervals down Route 9 to help protect the departing convoy. The ARVN's 4th Armored Cavalry Squadron and its 77th Ranger Battalion furnished the rear guard. It is of a piece with the whole experience that the big convoy ground to a halt for two and a half hours when a single truck broke down on one of the many Route 9 bridges. No better illustration of the shoestring quality of the invasion strategy was possible.

On March 24, 1971, as the last ARVN troops fled Laos, Richard Nixon gave an exclusive interview to Howard K. Smith of ABC News, in an effort to counteract the public perception that the Laotian invasion had been a failure. Nixon spent a full day at the White House preparing for the televised interview, and on the air gave figures representing claims for enemy losses, equipment captured and destroyed, ARVN performance, and so on. Two weeks later, in a speech reporting to the nation on Indochina, Nixon asserted that the Laotian invasion had been a success. How little his thinking changed over the years is indicated by the fact that Richard Nixon used many of the same figures in a 1985 book he titled *No More Vietnams*.

Some of the statistical claims bear comment. One is the assertion, most likely drawn from Pentagon records of which ARVN battalions rated as "combat-effective," that only four of twenty-two ARVN battalions did poorly in Laos. In reality four ARVN battalions did not rate as combat-effective because they had been almost totally destroyed, not because they performed poorly. Actually, units such as the 2/2 Infantry, 3d Airborne, 4/1 Infantry, and 39th Rangers performed among the best of any of the South Vietnamese.

Conversely, the 1st Armored Brigade rated combat-effective despite suffering a crippling 50 percent loss. There were at least a half dozen other ARVN battalions that had to be rebuilt after Lam Son 719 by South Vietnamese accounts, and these, too, are not reflected in the raw statistic or in Nixon's assertions. The ARVN Airborne and 1st Divisions overall suffered about one third losses in Laos; the ranger group that had been engaged, over one half. These were not the casualties of a victorious army.

Nixon's figures for enemy weapons destroyed include 3,754 individual weapons; 1,123 crew-served weapons; 110 tanks; and for ammunition, 13,630 tons. These numbers actually correspond to figures put out by the Saigon embassy in Washington, contained in the biweekly *Vietnam Bulletin* of March 17, 1971. Final figures provided by ARVN general Nguyen Duy Hinh were considerably higher: 5,170 weapons, 1,963 crew-served weapons, 106 tanks. Some figures might not have been accurate; for example, the United States verified only 88 VPA tank losses. Moreover, *South Vietnamese* and American equipment losses were significant, too: 2,500 individual weapons; more than 500 crew-served weapons; 71 tanks. The South Vietnamese claimed to have destroyed 98 radios; after the invasion, they asked to replace 1,517 radios of their own. *Vietnam Bulletin* even padded its statistics with items such as four electric generators seized, not to mention three water pumps. A long-standing and standard measurement of progress in the Vietnam conflict was to cast a ratio between weapons lost and those captured. By that measure the Laos invasion hardly ranked as a success.

Not many would agree that the Laotian invasion stands as a great military victory. Among serving officials, Dr. Kissinger later wrote that the plans "in no way accorded with Vietnamese realities"; Alex Johnson saw it as "ill-conceived from the start." Former Vietnam intelligence chief General Phillip B. Davidson called Laos the "raid too far." Colonel Do Ngoc Nhan judged the invasion "further evidence of our erroneous evaluation of the enemy capability." General Nguyen Duy Hinh, whose official monograph for the U.S. Army put Lam Son 719 in the best possible light, nevertheless finds that Saigon and Washington "really missed the chance for a big victory . . . on a battleground which was decisive for the outcome of the war." Hinh further states that "our enemy had once more proved that his war machinery was effective . . . [and that] he was determined and capable enough to muster his force for the protection of his vital area."

Discovering this required no invasion of Laos or attempt to block The Trail. Hanoi had long since said as much, in public. In Hanoi in 1966 Australian journalist Wilfred Burchett had interviewed General Nguyen Van Vinh of the People's Army. Here is Vinh's comment:

> They speak glibly of offensives through Laos. But where are they going to get the troops? What do they think we will be doing meanwhile? And the Pathet Lao? . . . How can they dream of pushing through a couple of hundred miles of jungle and mountains in Southern Laos

and occupying it? That might look very attractive on the maps they print in their newspapers. Perhaps it is of comfort to the U.S. public. But in fact they cannot do it.

During the actual invasion in 1971, William D. Morrow Jr. was an officer with Advisory Team 162, which worked with the ARVN Airborne Division. He spoke later of the People's Army: "Tough, well disciplined, and motivated . . . tactics were excellent. . . . My last experience with [the VPA] was Lam Son 719 into Laos. The results of that excursion speak for themselves. My personal observation—the [VPA] would have defeated any army that tried that invasion."

The Vietnam People's Army troops under Le Trong Tan undoubtedly incurred tremendous losses during the Laotian fighting. Whether the toll amounted to nine thousand, thirteen, or nineteen, all numbers that have been used, does not really matter. More important by far would be strategic and tactical impact. The indicators there pointed the other way. Truck traffic estimates remained high following the Route 9 campaign, averaging 2,500 a month, numbers previously seen only during peak periods. Documents captured in both Laos and Vietnam included directives to local forces enjoining them to exploit the victories of Laos—the exuberant tone could not be missed. When General Lam's I Corps went ahead with its consolation operation into the A Shau valley, Hanoi's *bo dois* struck back hard. One riposte, in the northernmost Central Highlands, would be a fierce battle for Firebase 6, an outpost near Dak To.

Across the border in lower Laos, Hanoi's forces completed clearing the flanks of The Trail. During 1970 they had captured Attopeu and Saravane once and for all. Now, in the spring of 1971, a new unit appeared in the People's Army order of battle, the 968th Division, and that force began an offensive into the Bolovens plateau. Royal Laotian government troops were driven from several fortified positions, starting with Paksong in the heart of the Bolovens. An RLG counterattack in June failed to dislodge the *bo dois*. A more extensive offensive in the fall recaptured both Paksong and Saravane for a couple of months, but both were again in Hanoi's hands before the end of the year. Seesaw warfare continued for another year, but the Vietnam People's Army retained the advantage.

In the Tchepone sector the People's Army began a new series of improvements following the Lam Son 719 battles. Though the VPA seemed to have faded away—an American slick pilot who carried MACSOG/ARVN STD teams into landing zones here saw nothing during several missions—Hanoi's basic position became more secure than ever. It was the summer of 1971 before Saigon's STD commandos again made forays directly into the Route 9–Tchepone region, and their reports were disquieting. The road, the commandos found, suddenly seemed in rather good condition. Equally disturbing, there were double-wire lines on telephone poles strung quite close to the Vietnamese border. The forces of Hanoi were confident enough to begin preparing border crossings of their own.

What also belied the claims of victory in Laos would be the state of the South Vietnamese polity. Richard Nixon anticipated an election in 1972, but Nguyen Van Thieu faced one later that very year, 1971. Though Thieu juggled the electoral politics and arrested or prevented from running candidates who might have posed a real threat, he still felt constrained to mount some kind of election campaign. The swing through Hue became the occasion for an incident that illustrates the atmosphere in the South. Thieu's entourage flew into the Hue Citadel in helicopters and then drove to the province leader's compound in highly decorated jeeps, sort of a parade. Don Walker, an American pacification adviser at Hue, noticed that Thieu's bodyguards, hanging on the sides of the jeeps, were too tall for Vietnamese. He decided they might be Nungs or Koreans. The fact that Nguyen Van Thieu did not depend on Vietnamese for his personal security had to be significant.

A couple of hours later, after conferences with provincial officials, Thieu emerged for what had been styled as a victory celebration for Laos. Its main feature would be the flyover of a large formation of helicopters right up the Perfume River. Standing next to a group of Vietnamese civilians, Walker heard them comment that what the choppers needed to be realistic was ARVN soldiers hanging from the skids. Walker recalls, "It was the damndest thing I ever saw."

Whatever its impact in The 'Nam, the Laotian operation simultaneously revealed important changes in The World. On the foreign policy side the changes favored Nixon administration strategy. On the domestic side, however, political protest intensified, with adverse consequences for the White House. The net effect would be that the constellation of restraints on Washington changed, but that United States strategy in Vietnam remained subject to them.

In terms of the delicate diplomacy of Vietnam, U.S. negotiations with Hanoi were deadlocked throughout the period. What changed was the relationship between Hanoi and its allies in Beijing and Moscow. The transformation owed something to Hanoi's bilateral relations but also to Nixon administration initiatives.

First to the Hanoi relationship. As new data become available about the other side in the Cold War, it is evident that Hanoi's alliances were by no means stable during this period. In fact, the relations of the Democratic Republic of Vietnam with China had begun to sour. Due to the Cultural Revolution the Chinese increasingly turned inward, but Beijing had never been entirely comfortable with Hanoi in any case. Chinese authorities were frustrated that the DRV pursued its own strategy and showed little proclivity to follow Beijing's advice. The Tet Offensive in 1968 constituted a marked departure from Chinese preferences, which were for protracted guerrilla war. The death of Ho Chi Minh in the fall of 1969 also broke the symbolic union of Ho and Mao and with it an important rationale for Beijing's support of Hanoi.

Another factor in the transformation would be the sharpening dispute between China and Russia. For some years the dispute had been primarily ideological, but in the spring of 1969 Chinese and Russian troops openly fought over the border between the two countries. Beijing increasingly saw improvement of relations with the United States as a way to gain leverage over the Russians. For a number of years the United States and China had been conducting secret talks in Warsaw aimed at settling differences between the two countries. During 1970 both Richard Nixon and Mao Zedong publicly expressed interest in a summit conference. Private messages set up channels for further contacts.

Chinese People's Liberation Army (PLA) troop strength in Vietnam peaked at 170,000 men. In March 1969, just prior to the outbreak of Russian-Chinese border incidents, there were sixty-three PLA regiments in the Democratic Republic, embodied in sixteen divisions and totaling 150,000 troops. Antiaircraft units were mostly equipped with 37-mm and 85-mm guns and served six to eight months before rotating home. From that time PLA forces, just like Americans, were progressively withdrawn from the war theater. The halt in the bombing of the DRV, whatever negative effects some claim for it, very much eased Beijing's path in pulling out of North Vietnam. Present knowledge is that the last PLA units left in 1971, and forces at that time already stood at a much reduced level. In all 320,000 PLA troops served in Vietnam. Beijing's public data are that the PLA suffered about 1,100 dead and 4,300 wounded in the Vietnam War.

At the time of Cambodia the Chinese continued to show a degree of solidarity with the DRV. Mao Zedong in fact raised the specter of nuclear weapons to counter U.S. escalation. By the time of the Laotian invasion, Beijing's response would be played in a much lower key. There was a statement of support from Mao, a pro forma denunciation in *People's Daily*, and at least one large demonstration—press reports of many thousands—in Canton. But China took no concrete action. In effect Beijing had been decoupled from Hanoi, and the risk of Chinese intervention, unlike in the mid-1960s, minimized.

In their diplomacy, Nixon and Kissinger told Moscow they were measuring the general progress of Soviet-American relations against developments in specific areas, such as Vietnam. This policy of "linkage" became a signature of the Nixon administration, though Moscow resisted it. Russian officials were aware that they could not "deliver" Hanoi—that is, they could not force the DRV into an agreement on U.S. terms. Nor did the Russians have any inclination to do so. They could not miss the signs of rapprochement between Washington and Beijing, but Moscow had a different game to play. Russian officials knew from Hanoi that Chinese aid to the DRV had slackened, so continuation of strong Russian aid cemented the relationship with the Vietnamese. Dangling opportunities before the United States for nuclear arms control and other measures of détente prevented complete Chinese success in their play of an American card.

At the same time, Russia had no intention of going to war over Vietnam at this late date, and there is no doubt that leader Leonid Brezhnev and senior aides such as Andrei Gromyko saw benefits from accommodation with the United States. Russian backing for Hanoi in the instance of the invasion of Laos thus remained rhetorical only. For its part, Washington saw this as a success in defusing the threat of Russian intervention in Indochina. Subsequent Russian eagerness for a summit with the Americans only reinforced the dynamic.

Washington's successes in foreign affairs failed to give Richard Nixon a free hand in Vietnam because Americans increasingly viewed his war strategy as downright dangerous. The first day of the invasion, a demonstration took place outside the South Vietnamese embassy in Washington. Across the nation fifty thousand marched a few days later, including a "mill-in" in New York City that forced police to close off Times Square, plus the biggest winter march yet in Boston. Few colleges went on strike, but the antiwar movement concentrated on planning major demonstrations for April. Concern at the risk the war would be internationalized with this crossing of another border was shown in opinion polls: a majority—46 to 41 percent—disapproved of Richard Nixon's handling of the Vietnam War. This represented a reversal of the standard pattern, in which opinion tended to rally around the flag in the immediate aftermath of any crisis. Moreover, opinion solidified. In April the Harris poll found a majority who agreed with the statement that the Vietnam War was morally wrong, and a substantial majority—60 to 26 percent—who favored continuing U.S. withdrawal *even if* that led to the collapse of the Saigon government.

Public attitudes were quite visible to American soldiers in The 'Nam, even in the early days of the offensive. At Khe Sanh, in the first flush of success with Dewey Canyon II, reporters asked soldiers if Americans were going to invade Laos. "We going into Laos?" shot back Darrel Hogan, a sergeant from Kentucky. "Hell, no. You want to start a war back in the States?"

That was exactly what portended. Steering committees working toward the spring demonstrations split over how militant these should be. Antiwar activists ending up planning two distinct marches on Washington, a mass demonstration for April 24 and a deliberate confrontation set for May 3, called "Mayday." Nancy Zaroulis and Gerald Sullivan, two chroniclers of protests against the war, capture the mood very well in this quote from one activist:

> I'll tell you what this Laos thing means. We've used every straight political tactic there is, and there has been no response from the government, none at all.
>
> Now the time has come to say to the government that either you stop the war or we'll stop you. So I intend to go to Washington in the spring and in an absolutely disciplined, nonviolent way . . . bring the

tactics of the civil rights movement ten years ago into today's antiwar movement.

As far as discipline is concerned, the military is the very model of this quality, and a wild card in the spring of 1971 would be materialization of a grunt antiwar organization. The Vietnam Veterans Against the War (VVAW), building since 1967, had carried out various protests at Ohio State, at Valley Forge, and on both coasts, but Laos put the vets on the national stage with a major mobilization. The special characteristics of VVAW actions had always been creativity and discipline, and these were in evidence when the vets came to Washington. Almost two thousand participated.

Two days before VVAW members descended on Washington, the Nixon administration went to court to revoke their permission to camp on public lands. The vets came anyway. Washington police were reluctant to enforce the court order, which would be overturned by a federal appellate court. The Justice Department went to the U.S. Supreme Court in an effort to reinstate the order. By April 18, a full week ahead of the scheduled mass demonstration, nine hundred vets were already in the nation's capital. Their numbers swelled. Beginning on April 19, veterans testified before Congress—a notable political birth for John Kerry, former naval officer in the Mekong delta and a future U.S. senator from Massachusetts. The vets ranged the spectrum of the American military involvement in Vietnam. One VVAW leader had been a young crewman in the airlift the United States mounted to help France at Dien Bien Phu. Veteran demonstrators included men who had been with the Leaping Lena cross-border mission, marine units that had crossed the Laotian border to ambush People's Army truck convoys, units that fought on the McNamara Line, advisers, paratroopers, lurps, "rear-area mothers," a true cross section of the Vietnam experience.

In Washington the vets lobbied legislators, presented "guerrilla theater" skits, marched on Arlington National Cemetery, and demonstrated at the U.S. Supreme Court, where more than 100 were arrested. The spectacle of the arrests did nothing to help the Nixon administration. U.S. Supreme Court justices restored the court order prohibiting the VVAW encampment, but vets voted that night to stay, giving rise to headlines such as "VETS DEFY TOP COURT." Bob Haldeman's diary makes clear that discussion of what to do went right up to the president. Nixon ordered Attorney General John N. Mitchell not to use police or evict the vets. Under pressure from the Supreme Court, the Justice Department finally returned to the federal district court to ask that the prohibition be terminated, and it was.

The climax of the VVAW's demonstration, in obvious allusion to the Laotian invasion called Dewey Canyon III, came on April 23, a day ahead of the antiwar movement's mass march. On that day vets protested outside the U.S. Capitol. Many brought their service medals. In a calculated gesture that took some people's breath away, one veteran after another walked up to the barriers surrounding the Capitol and flung his medals over the fence.

One spectator watching this happen was Colin Powell, the army officer who would rise to be chairman of the Joint Chiefs of Staff in the Persian Gulf War two decades hence. Powell had been an ARVN adviser in the early days, with an infantry battalion at A Shau before that place became a Special Forces border camp. On a second tour, as a major, Powell had been a staff operations officer. He had learned the insanity of Vietnam early, Colin Powell recounts, and though still proud of his uniform, "I understood their bitterness."

The next day, thousands more demonstrators flooded Washington, seemingly a reinforcement for the veterans' protest. Between 200,000 and 500,000 Americans went to the same place, the steps of Congress, with the same demand to end the war. Richard Nixon fled to Camp David, but as in 1970, the White House had been fortified, ringed with buses, machine guns dug in on the lawn.

At this moment Saigon foreign minister Tran Van Lam and the president of its senate, Nguyen Van Huyen, happened to be in Washington. Ambassador Bui Diem takes up the story:

> I took advantage of the opportunity to show them around, allowing them to see . . . the flood of hatred and rage that had regularly washed the capital over the past several years. We drove through the streets in my unobtrusive beige Buick, skirting the main crowds but getting good close-up views of the ragged clothes and bitter faces of demonstrators and the stolid rows of police and National Guardsmen. Huyen and Lam were profoundly shocked. . . . Neither had been spared my briefings and reports over the years. But apparently my words had not adequately conveyed the emotion loose on America's streets.

Indeed, come Mayday, that proved exactly the case, when for two days Washington became the scene of a running battle between demonstrators and security forces, who resorted to wholesale arrests of anyone they could apprehend. Robert F. Kennedy Stadium in Washington, pressed into service as an ad hoc jail, would be packed. About 50,000 are believed to have participated in Mayday, and arrests, many of perfectly innocent bystanders, were between 8,000 and 12,000. The U.S. government would later be forced to pay compensation and vacate criminal records when the Mayday arrests were found to be violations of due process.

The Nixon administration never regained the high ground in public opinion. By 1972, when Hanoi launched its own offensive in Vietnam, protests, leafleting, and dissent in myriad forms were daily events in many American cities. Washington would be virtually an armed camp. One resident who lived at the edge of Georgetown, beyond which there was some parkland, was not surprised to find U.S. troops camping out there at the time of Mayday, when the army in fact deployed 10,000 active and National Guard soldiers. What amazed the man was that weekend after weekend the troops were back in the park. Reflecting on this period much later, a senior army general recalled that the army had had to deploy the equivalent of a combat division to Chicago, to Washington several times, to Miami, two divisions to Detroit. There was literally no way, he concluded, to have continued the Vietnam War. Richard Nixon's determination to strike across borders, into Cambodia and then into Laos, contributed mightily to the national upheaval that made the general right. Now, with Saigon and Washington having shot their bolt and failed, Hanoi was going to ride The Trail South. By now doubtless no one in Washington remembered what DRV prime minister Pham Van Dong had said at the dawn of the war. His side, he had warned, would be in Saigon tomorrow.

Air America pilots who had helped support the Laotian invasion with supply runs from their Thai bases groused that the brass had it all wrong—the proper thing would have been to mount the Lam Son offensive from the Mekong valley. The CIA contract people thought the whole attack would have been much easier that way. Of course, the logistics infrastructure to support such a course did not exist, quite apart from the matter of where the troops would have come from—if ARVN or Thai, there would have been major diplomatic difficulties with the Royal Laotian government, which itself lacked the resources for an effort of this kind. However, it was not MACV or Saigon that took the point, it was Hanoi. In concert with the Vietnam People's Army's move into the Bolovens plateau, *bo dois* also drove west along Route 9 itself, stopping only when they had captured Dong Hene, just thirty miles from Savannakhet. The threat to the Mekong valley became explicit, quieting any voices that demanded an attempt against The Trail from that direction.

Not differing in kind from the clear-and-secure operations familiar to plenty of American soldiers, the VPA effort formed only part of a more extensive program. In the midst of the huge ARVN offensive going on all around them, the trailmakers actually laid 240 miles of new roadways—and those were only the ones U.S. intelligence found out about. For the first time, roads were discovered in Laos that were surfaced in asphalt. It would not be long before the Vietnam People's Army had more miles of blacktop in Laos than Saigon had on Route 9 on its side of the border.

Truck traffic evidence also remained disturbing. Traffic always declined with the approaching monsoon season, but in 1971, sightings remained high. Reporter Peter Osnos would be told in late May that 600 trucks a day were moving through Ban Karai Pass; that amounted to twice the level of 1970. Official statistics actually were higher than that at the beginning of the month, though sightings declined to a couple hundred a day toward June. Even as the monsoon hit, trucks were still being seen at a rate of more than 1,000 a week. These supply movements occurred in the face of the final phase of Commando Hunt V, with the pinball wizards doing their best to close The Trail. From April to June 1971 there were more than 20,000 fighter-bomber sorties, plus more by B-52s, flown in lower Laos.

The fast movers dispensed 53,000 tons of bombs, Arc Light another 67,000. Air activity continued at a lesser rate through the summer rains.

American authorities attribute Hanoi's strong supply push to the VPA's need to make up for supplies and equipment lost during the Laotian invasion. The estimate in Washington, for which Kissinger credits solid analytical work by his NSC staff, would be that any offensive by Hanoi had been delayed for at least a year. The NSC analysis owed much to CIA projections. Days after the last ARVN troops left Laos, the CIA on March 29 served up an extensive projection taking enemy losses and estimated supply and infiltration capacity of The Trail and comparing these across a range of nine possible strategies. Only for the cases of a Hanoi focus on lower Laos, or a VPA low profile overall, were troops and logistics judged adequate as of mid-1971. Central Intelligence Agency analysts believed that Hanoi would attain a capability to assume an offensive posture in I Corps and the Central Highlands by early 1972, but that would require additional infiltration of 160,000 *bo dois*, and supply might still constrain the People's Army. As for the possibility of a Tet-like nationwide offensive, that would require infiltration of 300,000 troops, with manpower and logistics levels that probably could not be met before late 1973. Langley repeated the gist of these projections in a national intelligence estimate of April 29, 1971, the last NIE on Vietnam the intelligence community would compile during the American phase of the Indochina War. The NIE predicted a Thieu victory in the upcoming elections (an easy call), reasonably good chances for the ARVN in 1971, an increase in Hanoi's military activity as U.S. elections approached in 1972, but nothing that would rise to the level of the Tet Offensive. As late as January 7, 1972, a CIA intelligence memorandum declared: "One thing Hanoi cannot do in the remaining months of this dry season; it cannot launch a nationwide military offensive on anything approaching the scale of Tet 1968."

At tranquil Nakhon Phanom, astride the muddy Mekong, the pinball wizards of Task Force Alpha planned new wrinkles for Commando Hunt VII, the operation they would mount during the 1971–1972 dry season. In spite of Richard Nixon's comments at the White House the previous spring, budget limits had forced the military to scale back the planned air campaign. Money had been allotted for only 8,000 fighter-bomber sorties a month. To make up for that, while economizing forces, the pinball wizards came up with the notion of "blocking belts." These were nothing less than a return to the old McNamara Line concept of an aerial barrier, saturated with area-denial weapons such as mines, with constant efforts to keep selected choke points closed, and specially seeded with sensors to alert the wizards when Hanoi's trucks did manage to get through.

Three barriers were envisioned for Commando Hunt VII. The northernmost, called the Tchepone belt, had actually been aligned along an east–west axis at roughly the latitude of Ban Karai Pass. There was a central belt aligned through Ban Bak, and a southern one through Chavane. Between the belts, armed reconnaissance, Panther teams, and the Spectre and AC-

119 gunships would reign. Seeding of the barriers began about a month before the dry season.

Hanoi's trailmakers had been busy, too. The focus on lower Laos that resulted from the Lam Son battles led the People's Army to further increase its antiaircraft defenses along The Trail. The numbers were in dispute between Task Force Alpha and the high command of the Seventh Air Force. Alpha estimated antiaircraft strength at 600 or 700 already, rising to 1,500 before the end of Commando Hunt VII. The key flying command, the Seventh Air Force, saw the enemy as having less than half this strength, rising from about 350 to about 550 during the campaign. The sides to this dispute agreed that Hanoi's defenses were more effective than ever, partly due to the introduction of new high-velocity ammunition. Eighteen aircraft would be lost to gunfire, including one of the big AC-130 gunships.

Most ominous of all, the People's Army extended its surface-to-air missile (SAM) defenses. During the previous campaign the SAMs had already been in evidence, with fifty missile firings against U.S. aircraft detected, and a total of eight SAM battalion sites located. The threat increased tremendously in 1971–1972. Both the Ban Karai and Mu Gia passes were placed off-limits to B-52 flights after SAM firings in those places. Soon after the start of the Easter offensive of 1972, a SAM site appeared on the hallowed ground of Khe Sanh.

Coincident with the beginning of the ground campaign in Vietnam, on the night of March 29 another Spectre gunship, flying about eleven miles northwest of Tchepone, would be knocked out of the air by a SAM. Half a dozen other gunships, both AC-130s and AC-119s, were damaged that month. According to Vance Mitchell, one of the AC-119K pilots and a friend of the crew shot down near Tchepone, only two of these gunships had been lost during the entire battle of The Trail up to 1971, but then five airplanes went down in the last year of the war. Following the Tchepone shootdown came a painful decision to restrict the gunships to less threatening environments, which meant fewer vital targets. The best weapon in the U.S. interdiction campaign had just been neutralized at the outset of the biggest enemy offensive of the war.

Henry Zeybel, who served during the same period as an AC-130 sensor operator, knew that the Spectre gunships in 1971–1972 were the most sophisticated of the war. In terms of claimed destruction, the gunships delivered peak performance at that time. Zeybel and his buddies heard briefings indicating they were kicking the hell out of Hanoi's truck inventory and supply throughput. The Vietnamese had had to ask Russia for 9,000 more trucks plus China for another 3,000. Pilot Mitchell agrees that if the Seventh Air Force had had 100 more gunships, the battle of The Trail could have been won. Unfortunately, the truck claims were as suspect as ever, and the air force would have had to have decided years earlier if there were going to be 100 more gunships in 1971–1972. Given air force attitudes, as well as the demands on it for airlift, there was minimal chance that the service would have diverted that much aircraft production. Meanwhile, over

The Trail, the defenses developed independently of *any* American decisions; the close-out time frame would have been the same.

The point would be driven home again on April 9, when a flight of marine A-6 bombers off the carrier *Coral Sea* flew armed reconnaissance toward Tchepone. It was dusk as the planes spotted some trucks and went in. Captains Clyde Smith and Scott Ketchie had just begun their third pass when the tail of their Intruder exploded in a ball of fire. Both ejected. Ketchie disappeared; Smith would be rescued after four harrowing days stranded in Indian country. The rescue forces reckoned Clyde Smith's position as within range of *two* SAM sites, antiaircraft guns, and fewer than five minutes from North Vietnamese MiG fighters at a base in the DRV's panhandle. Rescue forces were further strained at that moment because another aircraft survivor, Lieutenant Colonel Iceal Hambleton, who would spend twelve days on the ground, had been shot down in his EB-66 above Cam Lo. That plane also fell victim to a SAM.

These air operations were in response to the new People's Army offensive, begun at the end of March. The attack would be as big as Tet, massive but different, an offensive the VPA was not supposed to be capable of. Attacks along the DMZ smashed through the strongpoints of the McNamara Line in Quang Tri Province. The ARVN 3d Division, recently formed to make up Kissinger's "battalion deficit," would be effectively destroyed. Hue panicked but would be saved as ARVN's I Corps rallied under fresh leadership—General Ngo Quang Truong not only restored the front but also later battered his way back into Quang Tri City. In the Central Highlands the People's Army overran the base camp of the ARVN 22d Division—one of those sites selected by Saigon potentate Ngo Dinh Diem during his road-building days. The People's Army went on to assault Kontum, saved only by hard fighting, spearheaded by Montagnards, long disparaged by lowland Vietnamese. Near Saigon, *bo dois* swarmed across the Cambodian border, taking Loc Ninh outright and laying siege to An Loc, which became a legendary battle of the 1972 campaign. Among the cannon the People's Army used shelling An Loc were 105-mm and 155-mm howitzers they had captured from the ARVN during the Laotian invasion.

This offensive amounted to a conventional military operation, not some guerrilla strike. Troop and supply needs were greater, yet interdiction failed to halt the VPA. Perhaps the ants were ants no more, but tigers; certainly their road had turned South. In fact, *bo dois* added another 310 miles of roadways to The Trail during Commando Hunt VII, and intelligence now estimated the ranks of the 559th Transportation Group at an astounding 96,000 troops. These *bo dois* moved the supplies and reinforcements in the face of 170,552 tons of bombs dropped in Commando Hunt VII, almost two tons for each Vietnamese soldier.

With the outset of the Easter offensive the weight of U.S. airpower would inevitably be drawn away from The Trail. South Vietnam became the major focus. After May 8, when the United States mined Haiphong Harbor, the Democratic Republic also became the target of renewed bombings. The number of air sorties thrown against The Trail in the last nine months of 1972 diminished, amounting to fewer than the pinball wizards had had to play with in any previous operation. The total tonnage of munitions added up to 22,000. The B-52s dropped 364,000 tons of bombs on South Vietnam that year, and another 98,000 in the North. Fighter-bombers expended 188,000 tons of bombs over South Vietnam plus 118,000 tons in the North. Of course, the bombing of North Vietnam's panhandle in Operation Freedom Porch contributed to reducing supplies entering The Trail, but as had been the case in Rolling Thunder, the actual impact remained indeterminate. The much-vaunted Christmas bombing of Hanoi, operation Linebacker II, would be primarily for political effect.

No longer the lifeline of desperate men and women, The Trail became the highway to victory. It was during the 1972 fighting season that negotiations in Paris moved off dead center. These led to a cease-fire in Paris in January 1973 that formalized U.S. withdrawal from the Vietnam War. The Paris agreements cemented the aerial stand-down over The Trail that VPA defenses had imposed by military action. There would be one instance in which the United States sent bombers over Laos in the spring of 1973, to dissuade Hanoi from sending more troops and tanks South, as it had done. But Hanoi disputed what was meant by the right to "replace" troops and equipment under the Paris agreements, while the Nixon administration's hands were increasingly tied by the Watergate political scandals.

Hanoi and Saigon continued their Vietnam War on a lesser scale. It became known as the "war of the flags," as each side demonstrated control of territory by flying flags over villages. This remained a war of posts and alarums for almost two years, an interval in which the contestants measured progress by single hamlets or ranger camps, and accused the enemy of cease-fire violations in lengthy lists of provocative incidents. American, South Vietnamese, Liberation Front, and DRV officials met weekly at a compound outside Saigon to resolve dubious claims even as this low-level warfare went on all around them.

By late 1973 The Trail would no longer be a trail, except perhaps at its furthermost reaches. Blacktop two-lane highway extended from the mountain passes all the way to the Chu Pong massif. By 1974 the paved roads went right into the Central Highlands from the Laotian side, and in the Far South one could travel on paved road all the way to Tay Ninh Province. Indeed, this is exactly what happened when Hanoi decided to try its hand again at a military offensive for the spring of the following year. The fabled oil pipeline also now extended to Loc Ninh.

One Vietnamese who made the trip *North*, up The Trail, in 1974, was Truong Nhu Tang, a senior official in the provisional government that had been set up by the NLF. Tang was to go abroad as an ambassador for the Liberation Front, and he began the journey at Loc Ninh in a Chinese-made jeep. Tang traversed roadbeds that were mostly hard-packed dirt or macadamized, and met *bo dois* working with the *binh trams* as long as eight to ten years without seeing home. The way stations were like villages every sixty miles or so. There was a constant rush of traffic, Tang recounts, "not much different from what I would later experience heading into the suburbs of an American city during rush hour." At one point they passed a truck convoy loaded with the carcasses of crashed American airplanes. At night an eerie and beautiful spectacle bedazzled travelers, "an endless stream of flickering headlights tracing curved patterns against the wilderness, as far in both directions as the eye could see."

As a VIP, Truong Nhu Tang spent his nights at a series of luxury cottages that had first been built at Politburo orders when the DRV had to house former Cambodian leader Norodom Sihanouk, who had allied himself with Hanoi after his 1970 overthrow, and had made his way down The Trail to his homeland. These luxury cottages had actually been known to the Americans of MACSOG—Medal of Honor winner Franklin Miller mentions one he encountered.

A standard journey up The Trail—made by both Truong Nhu Tang and People's Army planner General Hoang Van Thai—involved a trip through Tchepone and Khe Sanh. General Thai, on his way from COSVN to Hanoi to consider the next stage of the war, was given a detailed tour of the Khe Sanh battlefield. Both Tang and Thai proceeded down Route 9 to the sea— the road was open now, but for the other side—then straight up the coastal highway. Truong Nhu Tang flew the rest of the way from Dong Hoi; General Thai would be followed by General Tran Van Tra, called home for a later stage of the consultations. Tra again traveled through Tchepone and Khe Sanh, all the way to Hanoi by motorboat and automobile. This had clearly become the preferred itinerary for Vietnamese on the move. Tran Van Tra, who had worked with Vo Bam in the early days of opening The Trail, found himself amazed at the changes wrought in the land, and comforted by the protection they enjoyed: "On one hill after another there were cleverly camouflaged gun emplacements and antiaircraft proudly and imposingly pointing skyward."

Tra is less forthcoming about his return trek to COSVN headquarters, but by that time the traffic had become massive. Hanoi sent 100,000 troops down The Trail in 1973, and another 80,000 during the first half of 1974. Route 9 into Ban Dong, which had given the ARVN so much trouble during their 1971 invasion of Laos, was now three lanes wide. Master of The Trail Dong Sy Nguyen, soon promoted major general, promised that for the first time People's Army units would be carried by trucks the whole distance from their points of departure in the North to the front in the South; 26,000 troops moved this way in 1974. The roads were macadam or paved all the way to the South Vietnamese border. In addition to the *bo dois*, 22,000 tons of supplies moved down The Trail in 1974. Though ammunition remained short in many categories, the reliability of The Trail became an important reassurance for Hanoi in approving the offensive it was eventually to carry out the next year. Initially conceived as a limited attack, the 1975 offensive led to the fall of Saigon and the end of the war.

Another VPA general who trekked South for the final offensive would be Van Tien Dung. The essence of a Very Important Person, General Dung would have overall command of the attack. His travel party was disguised as "Detachment A-75," and began with a plane to Dong Hoi. Waiting there would be Dong Sy Nguyen with a bunch of cars from the 559th Group. Past Quang Binh there were many potholes left from the Americans, but at the DMZ the Ben Hai River served as an avenue west by boat. Nguyen assigned his deputy, Colonel Phan Khac Hy, to accompany Dung's group all the way to the Central Highlands. En route they passed the VPA 316th Division, the entire unit mounted in 500 trucks. It was the first time the People's Army had moved such a huge formation by motorized transport. The roads of The Trail, General Dung enthused, were like "strong ropes inching gradually, day by day, around the neck, arms and legs of a demon, awaiting the order to jerk tight."

The orders came soon, and it was Van Tien Dung who gave them. People's Army *bo dois* attacked first at Ban Me Thuot, cradle of the American Montagnard program, later a base for MACSOG. This is not the place for an account of the spring of 1975, when the ARVN reeled back in retreat and then suddenly disintegrated. Suffice it to say that the collapse of Saigon began in the Central Highlands, spread to I Corps, then to the capital region, and that in the space of two short months events took their course. Tragically, the end would be a disorderly evacuation capped by another of those icon images of the Vietnam War, the last helicopter on the roof of the U.S. embassy in Saigon. So much, contributed by so many, turned into so little.

By that time, Hanoi's difficulties were the problems of a conventional war. Fueling and supplying distant, mobile armies; trucks and equipment to motorize large bodies of troops; these were the problems of a mature military power. One of the ultimate ironies of the Vietnam War is that the struggle to forge The Trail, and the herculean efforts to keep it open in the face of a concerted effort to close it, became a key part of Hanoi's evolution to a modern, relatively sophisticated military machine, one much closer to the American adversary than the primitive guerrilla forces the United States had had so much trouble deciding how to fight. A second irony—Hanoi's own decisions in moving prematurely to a general uprising played an important role in forcing the People's Army to resort to the conventional military mode. A third irony, perhaps the most poignant, resided in the fact that the transformation of the war happened at the very time that political dissent had made it impossible for the United States to pursue a conventional war in Southeast Asia. The Nixon Administration's attempt to forge ahead despite obstacles brought America closer to civil war than it had been at any time since 1861.

In all these developments The Trail, and the battle for it, had been the fulcrum. Forged by man in the face of a hostile, unexplored nature, The Trail became a true lifeline. Hanoi's retrospective statistics tell the story. The Trail and its tendrils added up to 12,000 miles of road. About a million *bo dois* made the trek South. Tonnage moving along The Trail grew from a hundred tons a week by 1963 to over ten thousand in 1970. There were five main roads, twenty-nine branch roads, and many, many cutoffs and bypasses. People's Army fighters, men and women, defused 56,750 unexploded bombs and destroyed 12,6700 magnetic ones, not to mention 81,500 antipersonnel mines, and took 1,196 prisoners from aircrews and commando missions, as well as the ill-starred Lam Son 719. The total volume of materials moved down The Trail in 1974, Hanoi tells us, was twenty-two times what moved in 1966.* By any standard of human endeavor and achievement, what happened on the Ho Chi Minh Trail must rank high among the works of men and women.

For Vietnamese another matter worth pondering is the place of this experience in the national pantheon. The leaders of the American war were tempered in the war against France, the war that ended at Dien Bien Phu. The Trail became the crucible for a generation of Northerners, and Saigon's fight to avoid downfall that for many more, not least among them the *Viet kieu*, the expatriates who left Vietnam. On one side or the other, the experience of The Trail, alternately romanticized or denigrated, formed the people of today's Vietnam. In recent years there has been a move toward redefining the experience on the Vietnamese side, presenting more of the pain and suffering and less the heroic aspects of The Trail. Related to this is the increasing Vietnamese concern over the several hundreds of thousands of persons missing in action from the American war. Hanoi's decisions were not always right, Saigon's not uniformly wrong. Ultimately, the trail makers worked harder to keep their eyes on the prize beyond the horizon, threading purposefully among the obstacles. For that Hanoi would be crowned with victory.

*In the 1990s a Vietnamese account of The Trail became available in the United States, a source that specified that a total of 1,777,027 tons of supplies had been moved down the Truong Son route from 1965 to 1975. Several American analysts have used this figure as if it existed in a vacuum, to allege that Hanoi massively supplied the war in the South. The raw number of tons, however, must be pictured in the light of the growth in the *volume* of shipments, as denominated here and also illustrated at various places in this narrative. In addition, the tonnage should be seen in the light of the shift in the Vietnamese war effort to rely on more conventional forces. Many more supplies were necessary to fuel the war effort in 1972 or in 1975 than had been necessary during 1966. Finally, the number 1,777,027 as a tonnage does not necessarily represent such a great quantity as military logistics go. For the period 1965 to 1975 that works out to 487 tons a day, which amounted (Hanoi acknowledges) to 70 percent of the supply requirements for a force consisting of up to a dozen VPA regular divisions plus the entire Viet Cong. U.S. Army staff manuals for this period envision a requirement for roughly 50 pounds a day of supplies to keep a soldier in the field. At that rate the 184,000 U.S. troops in Vietnam at the end of 1965 were consuming 4,600 tons of supplies a day, more than *ten times* Hanoi's average. By 1968 the U.S. daily requirement would be up to 13,700 tons.

None of Hanoi's achievements, on the other hand, should detract from the efforts against The Trail by American and South Vietnamese warriors. These allies bent every nerve to break Hanoi's umbilical cord, and strained their brains to innovate technologies and tactics equal to the task. For all the scorn heaped on the McNamara Line, the sensor systems and weapons created to support it proved the foundation of the much more valuable electronic battlefield. As the battle of Khe Sanh demonstrated vividly, the sensors made a big difference to the security of bases throughout South Vietnam for the remainder of the war. Similarly, technologies created to fight The Trail, such as low-light vision systems and moving-target array radars, transformed the use of tactical airpower. The problems of the interdiction campaign, such as the difficulty of hitting individual bridge spans, gave birth to "smart bombs," weapons with terminal guidance whose use greatly improved accuracy on target. For the United States, the fruit of defeat on The Trail would be reaped in the brilliant success of these same technologies in the war against Iraq, the Persian Gulf War of 1990–1991.

On the ground, the troops of the Studies and Observation Group, of the ARVN's Strategic Technical Directorate, of the CIA's special guerrilla units, and the occasional U.S. Marine or ARVN regular units permitted to enter into the battle of The Trail did their level best. Their heroism was legion. Their mission was impossible. The land, the techniques for insertion and extraction, the close organization of the territory by Hanoi's *bo dois*, all made it necessary to settle short of success. More commandos would not have changed the structure of the situation. Because The Trail had been in place and become ramified long before the creation of the commando forces, reduction in the political constraints limiting SOG forays would also have failed to alter the essential structure of adversary advantage.

Figures such as Walt W. Rostow and William C. Westmoreland, who pressed constantly against the restrictions impeding U.S. operations, exercised an influence that requires some comment. After the appearance of a Vietnam memoir by Robert S. McNamara it became suddenly fashionable to saddle this former secretary of defense with the responsibility before history for the Vietnam debacle. As Pentagon chief, however, McNamara mostly responded to proposals brought to him by others. More often than not, it was civilian strategists such as Rostow, or military commanders such as Westmoreland, who were the innovators and initiators. This was specifically true with suggestions for ways to neutralize The Trail. Not only did the proposals that were implemented fail, but also these involved major escalations for the United States in Vietnam, dragging America farther into an unwinnable war. There is responsibility enough for Vietnam that it can be shared.

Unlike the warfighters of a later day, who based themselves on Vietnam experience and evolved a vision of decisive warfare, the best and brightest of Vietnam never attained unanimity on the spectrum of rebellion to regular war that characterized the Indochina conflict. This meant that as the influence of one or another of the Vietnam warfighters waxed or waned, the basic U.S. approach to the war changed also. American strategy acquired a halting, start-and-stop quality. Certain figures in key positions, such as national security advisers Walt Rostow and Henry Kissinger, were also able to play on the fears and hopes of the presidents they saw at close range, in a way that added to the disorienting progress of strategy. There is responsibility to be apportioned for that, too.

The main prescription of the Vietnam warfighters has been and is the lower Laos barrier/invasion. Paradoxically, many of the same individuals who perceive this barrier system as a perfect strategy also disparage the McNamara Line, which had in fact been the practical application of that idea. Significantly, this barrier-line idea, which bears his name, represents one of those few cases where McNamara himself was innovator and advocate.

Nevertheless, critics of the McNamara Line were right. The early rejection of extending the ground strongpoints of the McNamara Line across Laos to the Thai border is a telling commentary on the practicality of the concept. Moreover, even if, by dint of grunts' incredible exertions plus amazing feats of logistics, a barrier system *had* been put in place across lower Laos, there would have been no way to prevent Hanoi from simply shifting its trail activity farther west, into Thailand, much as the original Ho Chi Minh Trail had bypassed the Demilitarized Zone of Vietnam. This simple fact reveals the bankruptcy of the barrier system as a perfect strategy for victory in Vietnam.

Emplacing the barrier system, beyond all else, required an invasion of Laos. Aside from the nightmares of supply entailed, and the vulnerability of troops dangling at the end of this lengthy supply line, the possibility of such a strategy was always obvious. Hanoi's generals commented publicly, and Robert McNamara secretly, on what could happen to such an invasion. American armies would have been necessary to give an invasion some chance of success. But the dynamic on this issue was set in the early years of the struggle: A ground intervention big enough to be effective would have been risky politically. Moreover, at first the physical capability for such a move was entirely lacking. In the SEATO Plan 5 period, international diplomacy added obstacles to the political ones. Washington's fears of a Russian or a Chinese entry into the war became a controlling factor. Both Russia and China lent substance to that misgiving, by sending advisers and troops or technicians to North Vietnam, and by their agreements with Hanoi on military matters. Warfighters such as Rostow, who insisted on Vietnam as a Cold War crisis while simultaneously discounting response by the Cold War adversaries under any circumstances, were walking a very dangerous path.

During the middle phase of the Vietnam War, the era of the U.S. military buildup, General Westmoreland squarely posed the invasion option for President Johnson but was rejected. The international aspects of an invasion, of either Laos or North Vietnam, remained important, but the corps-size force Westmoreland needed for that offensive had become far more sensitive in view of the worsening domestic opposition to the Vietnam War. Meanwhile, on The Trail the fulcrum of the war had already begun turning against the United States.

By the last stage of the conflict the antiwar movement had acquired so much preponderance, and the political consensus against the war had hardened to such a degree, that the U.S. forces necessary to give an invasion some chance of success could not be used. Worse, the changed domestic climate brought about a deterioration in the quality of the U.S. forces themselves that called into question their ability to perform in the invasion the warfighters wanted. When South Vietnamese troops did what the Americans could not, what happened went exactly as Hanoi's generals had publicly predicted. Both in prospect and in retrospect the ground barrier across Laos amounted to dumb strategy. *Only* the warfighters are responsible for that.

The antiwar movement did not lose the Vietnam War. Hanoi's ability to sustain the Viet Cong in the face of all Westmoreland's attrition operations turned the tide. The Trail made that possible. On the political side, American presidents failed to build domestic support at an early date. The halting U.S. strategy and the lack of evident progress then frittered away much of the political support there was. Again the warfighters bear a share of the responsibility here. Finally, the war was not Washington's to lose; Hanoi *won* the war, by dint of its actions and forces; it was not simply handed the victory.

On the subject of political constraints, a favorite argument of the warfighters, that Washington ought to have ignored the Laotian government and the 1962 Geneva accords, also falls short. Events showed again and again that Souvanna Phouma's Laotian government was positively useful to the United States. American military capabilities in lower Laos were limited by practical matters of available forces and supply capacity that had nothing to do with the 1962 accords. Discarding Geneva would have let officials feel better—they would be unfettered, just as was Hanoi—but U.S. ability to act in lower Laos would have improved only marginally. On the other hand, the political cost of abrogating Geneva would have been enormous, involving disintegration of the Laotian government that helped the United States; an international perception of Washington as aggressor; and, especially in the early years, a danger of countervailing foreign intervention in the war by Russia, China, or both. The latter possibility, most disturbingly, meant that a U.S. action could afford an opportunity for its Cold War enemies to heal their ideological rift.

The most rational adaption of the barrier idea became that of the pinball wizards. Interdiction from the air avoided the pitfalls of the ground strategy. Orienting the axis of the barrier to the length of The Trail extended the zone of maximal destruction. Resources devoted to the attempt were also enormous. Between 1964 and 1972 fighter-bombers flew 426,000 sorties against lower Laos alone, with B-52s adding more than 30,000 more. The 1.7 *million tons* of bombs they dropped were the equivalent of more than a dozen Hiroshimas. Lower Laos plus Rolling Thunder added up to a greater tonnage of munitions than used in all the strategic bombing of World War II.

Arguing that all these bombs were dropped without much thought— that is, that bombing would have been more effective if better directed—

also fails. The battle of The Trail peaked in 1969–1970, under Task Force Alpha's pinball wizards. Close to half the sorties flown and munitions expended were during those years, specifically 198,000 aircraft sorties and 827,000 tons of explosives. Of the remainder, close to half the residual totals were run up in 1971–1972, also under the pinball wizards, when 449,000 tons of bombs fell in lower Laos. With the electronic battlefield in place after 1968, and the innovations of the Commando Hunt campaigns, the American forces waging the battle of The Trail were as well directed as they ever would be.

Advocates of blocking The Trail as the war-winning strategy that should have been pursued speak as if this were something that was never tried, certainly not done, hardly thought about. The opposite is true. From day one, as seen here in great detail, generals and leaders in both Saigon and Washington considered one scheme after another to cut The Trail. Closing off the Vietnamese border, denying passage through Laos by use of passive weapons, commando raids, armed reconnaissance, directed air attack, gunship surveillance, aerial barriers, finally outright invasion—all were tried in the effort to choke The Trail. Moreover, each course was pursued with all the cleverness and creativity of a highly sophisticated military machine and its technical experts. The truth never was that the warfighters failed to engage The Trail in battle. The truth is that the warfighters lost their gambit.

The rise and fall of the warfighters' stratagems is perversely evident from the fate of Tchepone, and the corridor Route 9 forms back to the Vietnamese coast. In the early years, when the invention of ways to combat The Trail continued in full swing, so did Hanoi's effort to improve its network. Tchepone flourished. Toward the end, when the strategists settled upon, first the pinball wizards' air campaign, then the invasion, Tchepone was destroyed. In the ground campaign of 1971, Ban Dong, too, was demolished. Inhabitants, like those of the North Vietnamese panhandle under the bombs of Rolling Thunder, were reduced to living in caves.

Today the district of Tchepone furnishes mute testimony to the ferocity of the battle against The Trail. The Communist successor government in Laos requires special permits to enter this part of the country but will grant them for a certain fee. A number of Westerners have made the trip, usually by car from Savannakhet. The road has deteriorated once again—in the monsoon season the trip is virtually impossible. The zone of The Trail, far enough away from the scrap metal markets to make claiming its provender unprofitable, is littered with the detritus of war. A short distance off the main routes, on both sides, lie the wrecks of trucks, tanks, and aircraft.

Roughly 5,000 Lao live in the town of Tchepone now. Travelers describe crude wooden shacks cobbled together. The village of Ban Dong, with a few tin roofs, is a little better off. Robert Shaplen and Henry Kamm, among the finer journalists to have covered the Vietnam War, both visited Tchepone in the after years. They found huts perched precariously on the lips of bomb craters, peasants striving to make the best of land pockmarked by explosions, children and water buffalo regularly falling victim to still-live munitions.

In the area of Vietnam that was the Demilitarized Zone and the Mc-Namara Line the story is the same. In the district of Khe Sanh an average of one person a day is killed by explosives left over from the war. Down in the coastal plain, between Quang Tri and Vinh Linh of the former North Vietnam, the daily average is two. A memorial cemetery to the soldiers and workers killed along the Ho Chi Minh Trail is located near Khe Sanh. It contains more than ten thousand remains. There are seventy-eight other, smaller graveyards scattered the length of the former route. The battle of The Trail claimed an enormous number of victims and still does. These days, when the mines left in the ground from more recent conflicts, such as those in Angola and Afghanistan, have become a matter of public concern, Laos and the former DMZ of Vietnam remain on the list of the most dangerous places on earth. And, to come full circle, all this destruction did nothing to drain the guerrilla sea in which swam the Viet Cong.

The perfect strategists hark after a lost past. Refusing to acknowledge what happened then, they learn little from the experience. Robert Mc-Namara, at least, has admitted he was mistaken. Yesterdays are past, not to be regained by perfect strategies, denial, or refighting the Vietnam War. Far preferable is reconciliation. American veterans of the Vietnam War are increasingly taking this path in their lives, as in the case of Wilson Hubbell, who had been stationed at Qui Nhon during the great Tet Offensive. Hubbell returned in 1995 to encounter a former *bo doi* most probably on the other side of the same firefight. The old enemies sat down and drank tea together. "I feel like the war is over," Hubbell said later. For the perfect strategists the war can never end.

AFTERWORD

Anh Hung (Elder Brother Hung)
who was once a PAVN grunt

by David Connolly

I told him that I was wounded in our war.
He said that made us brothers,
for he also bore the mark of pain.

I asked was the pain worth winning the war?
He only saw that too many, on both sides,
have suffered, and still do.

I told him we tired of the death for no gain.
He only knew war, his whole life, and accepted
it as the buffalo does the plow.

I asked if he volunteered as I had done.
He said he did, but would rather
have taught children to read and write
than to fight and die.

NOTES

Abbreviations That Appear in the Notes

CDEC   Combined Documents Exploitation Center

CF   Country File

CFVN   Country File Vietnam

CHECO   Contemporary Historical Examination of Current Operations
         (a research project of the Pacific Air Force)

CICV   Combined Intelligence Center Vietnam

FRUS   *Foreign Relations of the United States*

JCS   Joint Chiefs of Staff

JFKL   John F. Kennedy Library, NARA

JFKP   John F. Kennedy Papers

LBJL   Lyndon Baines Johnson Library, NARA

LBJP   Lyndon Baines Johnson Papers

M&M   Meetings and Memoranda Series

NARA   National Archives and Records Administration

NLP   Nixon Library Project, NARA

NSF   National Security File

SNIE   Special National Intelligence Estimate

USAMHI   U.S. Army Military History Institute

US-GVN   United States–government of Vietnam

Chapter 1. "Plainly a Gateway to Southeast Asia": 1954–1960

page

4   "useful analogy" et seq.: Memo, McGeorge Bundy to Lyndon B.
         Johnson, June 30, 1965 (declassified July 17, 1980). Lyndon Baines
         Johnson Library: Lyndon B. Johnson Papers: National Security
         File [hereafter abbreviated LBJL:LBJP:NSF]: Memos to the presi-
         dent: Bundy, box 4, folder: "Bundy, v. 11."

5   "every new road": Letter, Ngo Dinh Diem to Frank E. Walton and Donald Q. Coster, June 24, 1960. Department of State: *Foreign Relations of the United States 1958–1960,* Vietnam, vol. I. (Washington, D.C.: U.S. Government Printing Office, 1986, p. 507 [This series will hereafter be abbreviated *"FRUS"* with appropriate dates and volume numbers. Because these published records are relatively widely available, in the notes that follow the author attempts to cite *FRUS* wherever possible, even in cases where the original document is in his possession].)

8   "completely rotten" et seq.: Nguyen Dinh Thuan remarks at luncheon, April 8, 1960. *FRUS* 1958–1960, Vol. I, p. 383.

8   "we will be in Saigon tomorrow": Pham Van Dong remark to Georges Picot, September 12, 1959. *FRUS,* ibid., quoted p. 309.

9   "We will drive the Americans": Cable, Elbridge Durbrow–Christian Herter (Saigon 278), March 7, 1960. *FRUS,* ibid., quoted p. 301.

9–10   "Under instructions from the . . . Party" et seq.: Vo Bam, "Opening the Trail," *Vietnam Courier,* 1984–1985, May 1984, quoted p. 9.

10   "special trail": Ibid.

10   "This route must be kept": Quoted, ibid.

13   "ALL GOODS DELIVERED SAFELY": Ibid., quoted p. 12.

17   "The Communists have started a major offensive": State Department Memorandum of Conversation, April 4, 1960. *FRUS,* 1958–1960, vol. I, p. 361.

17–18   "I recalled we had not been able to control bootleggers": Cable, Durbrow–Herter (Saigon 2622), March 10, 1960. Ibid., p. 327.

18   "Support from North Vietnam appears to have increased": Central Intelligence Agency, Special National Intelligence Estimate [hereafter cited as "SNIE"] 53.1–50 August 23, 1960. Ibid., p. 539.

18–19   "The Viet Cong infiltrate": Military Assistance Advisory Group Vietnam, Report, November 30, 1960. Ibid., p. 699.

19   "Better utilization": Ibid.

20   "Plainly a gateway to Southeast Asia": Arthur Schlesinger Jr., *A Thousand Days.* New York: Fawcett Books, 1967, quoted p. 303.

Chapter 2. Ants and Elephants: 1961–1962

page

23   "For the Annamite": Arthur Dommen, *Conflict in Laos: The Politics of Neutralization,* rev. ed. New York: Praeger, 1971, quoted fn., p. 342.

24   "Vietnamese grow rice": James Markham, "Letter from Laos: The Ho Chi Minh Trail Is a Highway Now," the *New York Times Magazine,* August 25, 1974, quoted p. 12.

25   "They were playing both sides": John Prados and Ray W. Stubbe, *Valley of Decision: The Siege of Khe Sanh.* New York: Dell Books, 1993, quoted p. 63.

26   "old reliables" et seq.: Tran Van Tra, *History of the Bulwark B2 Theater,* vol. 5: *Concluding the 30-Year War* (Foreign Broadcast Information Service Translation). Joint Publications Research Service Publication 82783, February 2, 1983, p. 103.

26   "It really was a trail": Bui Tin, *Following Ho Chi Minh: Memoirs of a North Vietnamese Colonel* (translated by Judy Stowe and Do Van). Honolulu: University of Hawaii Press, 1995, p. 47.

26–27   "The Party Central Committee has discussed": Vo Bam, "Opening the Trail," op. cit., quoted p. 14.

27   "climbed mountain slopes and forded streams": Ibid.

27   "In early 1964 it was easier": Bui Tin, *Following Ho Chi Minh,* p. 47.

29   "volunteer fire department": John F. Kennedy speech to American Friends of Vietnam, Washington, D.C., June 1, 1956, in John F. Kennedy, *The Strategy of Peace.* New York: Popular Library, 1960, p. 92.

30   "his language defined the mood": Arthur Schlesinger, Jr., *A Thousand Days,* p. 495.

30   "This is the worst yet": Ibid., quoted p. 299.

30–31   "1961 promises to be" et seq.: Memo, Edward Lansdale to Robert S. McNamara, January 17, 1961. U.S. Congress, House of Representatives, Committee on Armed Services. "Report: United States–Vietnam Relations 1945–1967." Washington, D.C.: U.S. Government Printing Office, 1972, vol. 11, p. 1. [This publication is one of three versions of the seminal "Pentagon Papers," each of which has significant and informative differences. It will hereafter be cited as "US-GVN Relations" with appropriate volume number].

32   "the extremely rugged nature": Memo, Colonel E. F. Black, April 28, 1961. US-GVN Relations, vol. 11, p. 59–60.

32   "Lansdale-Gilpatric proposal": Anon., *Senator Mike Gravell Edition of The Pentagon Papers.* Boston: Little, Brown, n.d. [1972], vol. 2, p. 443. [Hereafter this will be cited as "Gravell Pentagon Papers" with volume number.]

33   "Our lightly held defensive positions": Letter, President Ngo Dinh Diem–John F. Kennedy, June 9, 1961. John F. Kennedy Library: John F. Kennedy Papers: National Security File: Country File [Henceforth cited as JFKL:JFKP:NSF:CF]: box 193, folder: "Vietnam, General, 7/1/61–7/4/61."

33   "recently occupied": "Memorandum of Conversation with the President," June 14, 1961. *FRUS,* 1961, vol. I, p. 173.

34 "a SEATO operation of a Lebanon type": Memo, Walt W. Rostow to John F. Kennedy, April 13, 1961. *FRUS, 1961–1963*, vol. XXIV, p. 126.

34 "We must seriously consider": Memo, Robert W. Komer to McGeorge Bundy, May 4, 1961. *FRUS, 1961*, vol. I, p. 123.

34 "long open flank" et seq.: Memo, Sterling J. Cottrell to John McConaughy, July 8, 1961. Ibid., p. 201.

35 "cross their border substantially" et seq.: Memo, Walt W. Rostow to Dean Rusk, July 13, 1961. *FRUS, 1961*, vol. I, p. 206.

35 "defense against further guerrilla infiltrations" et seq.: Paper, General Maxwell D. Taylor, July 15, 1961. Ibid., p. 223–224.

36 "the battle in South Vietnam" et seq.: Paper, Walt W. Rostow and Maxwell D. Taylor to John F. Kennedy, July 21, 1961. Ibid., pp. 241, 249.

36 "The immediate military danger": Memo, Maxwell D. Taylor to John F. Kennedy, July 26, 1961. Ibid., p. 243.

36 "We must decide" et seq.: Memo, Walt W. Rostow and Maxwell D. Taylor to John F. Kennedy, July 27, 1961. Ibid., p. 249.

36 "new military alternative" et seq.: McGeorge Bundy, Memorandum of a Discussion, the White House, July 28, 1961. Ibid., p. 253.

37 "it is somehow wrong": Memo, Walt W. Rostow to John F. Kennedy, March 29, 1961 (declassified November 17, 1975). JFKL: JFKP: NSF: CF: 193, f.: "Vietnam, General 1/61–3/61."

37 "direct action against North Vietnam": Memo, Walt W. Rostow to U. Alexis Johnson, June 23, 1961. JFKL: op. cit., f.: "Vietnam, General 6/18–6/30/61."

37 "limited military operation[s]": Memo, Walt W. Rostow to Dean Rusk, July 13, 1961, op. cit.

39 "probably not relax" et seq.: Gravell Pentagon Papers, II, quoted 77–78.

40 "border/coastal patrol system": U.S. Embassy, Saigon Country Team, Basic Counterinsurgency Plan, January 4, 1961. *FRUS, 1961*, vol. I, p. 9.

40 "It is suggested": Cable, Maxwell D. Taylor to John F. Kennedy, October 25, 1961. Ibid., p. 428.

40 "General, we won't be needing you": Frederick Nolting, *From Trust to Tragedy*. New York: Praeger, 1988, quoted p. 36.

41 "movement by units occurs" et seq.: Memo, William J. Jorden to Maxwell D. Taylor, September 27, 1961. *FRUS, 1961*, vol. I, pp. 310, 311–12.

Chapter 3. The Watershed: 1962–1963

page

44   "They're not easy to manage": Anon., *The Ho Chi Minh Trail.* Hanoi: Red River Publishing House, 1982, pp. 106–7.

45   "the new-type war of the enemy" et seq.: Letter, Le Duan to Southern Bureau of Lao Dong Party, July 1962. Anon., *Letters to the South.* Hanoi: Su That Publishing House, 1985, p. 56.

46   "as dangerous as it became": Bui Tin, *Following Ho Chi Minh*, op. cit., p. 47.

48   "The Border Patrol Force is doing well": Thomas A. Parrott, Minutes of Meeting of Special Group (CI), May 17, 1962 (declassified May 6, 1997). JFKL:JFKP:NSF: Meetings and Memoranda Series [hereafter cited as "M&M"]; b. 319, f.: "Special Group (CI) 4/6/61–6/7/62."

51   "As the Montagnard trail watchers": Vietnam Working Group, Visit Report, Visit to Vietnam October 18–November 26, 1962. *FRUS*, 1962, vol. II, p. 775.

51   "expressed doubt that": Cable, Maxwell Taylor to Dean Rusk, September 11, 1962. JFKL: JFKP: NSF: CF, b. 194, f.: "Vietnam, General 9/62."

52   "we wanted an agreement": Dean Rusk (as told to Richard Rusk), *As I Saw It.* New York: Penguin Books, 1991, p. 429.

54   "must put forces opposite Hanoi" et seq.: Roger Hilsman, Memorandum for the Record, May 10, 1962. JFKL: Hilsman Papers, Country File: b. 1, f.: "Laos 5/1/62–5/10/62."

54   "holding and recapture": McGeorge Bundy, Memo, Presidential Meeting on Laos" (NSAM-157), May 24, 1962. US-GVN Relations, b. 12, pp. 467–68.

54   "The debate was taut and tense": Roger Hilsman, *To Move a Nation.* New York: Delta Books, 1967, p. 149.

55   "but felt it was unwise militarily to introduce": William H. Sullivan, Memorandum of Conversation, Contingency Planning for Laos, June 12, 1962. *FRUS*, 1961–1963, vol. XXIV, p. 843.

55   "The Defense Department is not currently pursuing": Ibid., p. 844.

59   "We must have the capability" et seq.: U.S. Mission to Saigon, *Vietnam Documents and Research Notes*, no. 96, "The Vietnam Workers' Party's 1963 Decision to Escalate the War in the South," Saigon, July 1971, pp. 7, 13, 15, 16, 18.

59   "essentially all the infiltrators": CIA, United States Intelligence Board Memo D-24.7/4, Infiltration and Logistics—South Vietnam,

October 28, 1965. LBJL: LBJP: NSF: CFVN, b. 50–1, f.: "Southeast Asia, Special Intelligence Material, vol. 8 (10/65–12/65)."

Chapter 4. The Battle Joined: 1963–1964

page

62   "Rostow took a position": Merle Miller, *Lyndon: An Oral Biography.* New York: G. P. Putnam's Sons, 1974, quoted p. 413.

62   "Air Marshal" and SEATO Plan Six: David Halberstam, *The Best and the Brightest.* New York: Random House, 1972, p. 61.

62   "You know, you don't sleep quite so well": Halberstam, quoted p. 160.

63   "They are the scavengers": Walt W. Rostow, "Countering Guerrilla Attack," in Frank M. Osanka, ed. *Modern Guerrilla Warfare.* New York: Free Press of Glencoe, 1962, p. 466. This version initially appeared in *Army* magazine in September 1961. The June 13 speech actually bore the title "Guerrilla Warfare in Underdeveloped Areas" and had been personally approved by John Fitzgerald Kennedy.

63   "I believe it is in the common interest": Walt W. Rostow, Memo, Suggested Language, May 9, 1962. LBJL: Walt Rostow Papers, b. 13, f.: "Southeast Asia."

63   "quietly": Hilsman, Memorandum for the Record, May 10, 1962, op. cit.

63   "Mikoyan and Laos": Memo, Walt W. Rostow to Dean Rusk, November 28, 1962 (declassified August 19, 1993). LBJL: Rostow Papers, op. cit.

64   "It is evidently Ho's policy": Memo, Walt W. Rostow to Dean Rusk, July 4, 1963 (declassified August 13, 1987). LBJL: Ibid.

64   "if we are to have a showdown": Ibid.

64   "is explicitly based on the fact" et seq.: Memo, Walt W. Rostow to Dean Rusk, November 1, 1963 (declassified August 19, 1993). LBJL: Rostow Papers, op. cit.

64   "the problem of the illegal crossing": Draft Memo, Walt W. Rostow to Dean Rusk, February 7, 1964 (declassified August 19, 1993). Ibid. Also see the April 3, 1964, paper from Rostow to Harlan Cleveland in the same file.

64   "forces are converging" et seq.: Memo, Walt W. Rostow to Dean Rusk, January 10, 1964 (declassified August 19, 1993). Ibid.

65   *"we could trigger"* et seq.: Memo, Walt W. Rostow to William P. Bundy, May 19, 1964 (declassified August 19, 1993). Ibid. The italics are Walt Rostow's.

65   "diplomacy can only be truly effective": Memo, Walt W. Rostow to
        William P. Bundy, June 11, 1964 (declassified August 13, 1987).
        Ibid.

65   "deeply dangerous game": *Department of State Bulletin*, March 16,
        1964, p. 399.

65   "The President doesn't know": Lyndon B. Johnson statement to
        Walt Rostow, telephone tape transcript, March 4, 1964, 6:05 P.M.
        LBJL: LBJP: Telephone series.

65   "We should begin a series": Undated fragment of a memorandum
        (c. May 1964), Walt W. Rostow (declassified August 19, 1993).
        LBJL: Rostow Papers, op. cit.

66   "our only real choice": Memo, Walt W. Rostow to Dean Rusk, May
        17, 1964 (declassified August 19, 1993). Ibid.

66   "The Trigger: A 'Dear Brutus' View," title of May 19 Rostow memo
        quoted on p. 137.

66   "intermediate ranges of military action" et seq.: Memo, Walt W.
        Rostow to William P. Bundy, May 24, 1964 (declassified August
        19, 1993). LBJL: Rostow Papers, op. cit.

66   "Unless U.S. forces are located": Memo, Walt W. Rostow to Lyndon
        B. Johnson, June 6, 1964 (declassified March 28, 1988). LBJL:
        LBJP: NSF: CFVN; b. 52/3, f.: "Southeast Asia Memos, vol. II(4)
        5/64–6/64."

67   "a serious politico-military scenario" et seq.: Memo, Rostow to
        Rusk, November 28, 1962, op. cit. (the "Mikoyan and Laos" paper).

67   "in almost a year": Walt W. Rostow, *The Diffusion of Power, 1957–
        1972: An Essay in Recent History.* New York: Macmillan, 1972, p. 288.

67   "I do have the personal feeling": Letter, Walt W. Rostow to Freder-
        ick E. Nolting, September 5, 1962. *FRUS, 1961–1963,* vol. II, p. 616.

68   "I regarded continued use": Rostow, *Diffusion of Power,* p. 288.

68   "The challenge we face" et seq.: Lyndon B. Johnson speech, Au-
        gust 5, 1965. *Department of State Bulletin,* August 24, 1964, p. 261.

68   "worth considering whether": Memo, Walt W. Rostow to Dean
        Rusk, August 10, 1964 (declassified August 19, 1993). LBJL: Ros-
        tow Papers, b. 13, f.: "Southeast Asia."

69   "was recognized as having" et seq.: Robert S. McNamara with
        Brian VanDeMark, *In Retrospect: The Tragedy and Lessons of Vietnam.*
        New York: Times Books, 1995, p. 156.

69   "the key to failure": Norman B. Hannah, *The Key to Failure: Laos
        and the Vietnam War.* Lanham, Md.: Madison Books, 1987, passim.

69–70   "there was still no consensus" et seq.: McNamara, *In Retrospect,*
        pp. 145, 155.

70   "there was a wide range of opinion": Maxwell D. Taylor, *Swords into Plowshares*. New York: W. W. Norton, 1972, p. 321.

70   "was over a year . . . in preparation": Paul M. Kattenburg, *The Vietnam Trauma in American Foreign Policy, 1945–1975*. New Brunswick, N.J.: Transaction Books, 1980, p. 122.

70   "during my first year in the White House": Lyndon B. Johnson, *The Vantage Point*. New York: Holt, Rinehart & Winston, 1971, p. 119.

70   "This irony said much": Robert McNamara, *In Retrospect*, p. 159.

70   "On balance . . . I recommend against": Memo, Robert S. McNamara to Lyndon B. Johnson, March 16, 1964. Gravell Pentagon Papers, III, 504.

71   "Rostow Thesis" and "by applying limited": Study, Analysis of the Rostow Thesis, undated (declassified December 5, 1993). LBJL: Rostow Papers, b. 13, f.: "Southeast Asia."

71   "Alternatives for Imposition" and "the report recognized": Robert H. Johnson, "Escalation Then and Now," *Foreign Policy* no. 60, Fall 1985, pp. 135, 139.

72   "negotiations therefore were seen": Ibid., p. 133.

72   "it will be more difficult for us": Walt W. Rostow to Dean Rusk, February 12, 1964 (declassified August 19, 1993). Rostow Papers, op. cit.

72–73   "U.S. policy is to see to it" et seq.: George C. Herring, ed., *The Secret Diplomacy of the Vietnam War: The Negotiating Volumes of the Pentagon Papers*. Austin: University of Texas Press, 1983. The American talking paper is quoted from p. VI.C.21–24; Pham Van Dong is quoted from p. VI.C.8 (my translation).

73   "not only with North Vietnam" and "powerful friends": King C. Chen, "North Vietnam in the Sino-Soviet Dispute, 1962–1964." *Asian Survey*, vol. 4, no. 9, September 1964, quoted p. 1035. Cf. the *New York Times* for May 11, 1964.

73   "the Chinese and North Vietnamese seek": CIA, Special National Intelligence Estimate [hereafter cited as "SNIE"] 14.3-63, The Impact of the Sino-Soviet Dispute on North Vietnam and Its Policies, June 26, 1963 (declassified March 28, 1990), p. 1. LBJL:LBJP:NSF: NIE Series, b. 5, f.: "14.3 North Vietnam."

73   "dramatic new Chinese Communist intervention": CIA, SNIE 50-64, Short Term Prospects in Southeast Asia, February 12, 1964 (declassified March 28, 1990), p. 2. LBJL: Ibid.

73–74   "the DRV probably could not sustain": CIA, SNIE 14.3-64, The Outlook for North Vietnam, March 4, 1964 (declassified March 31, 1987). Ibid.

74   "preparatory and low-scale actions" et seq.: CIA, SNIE 50-2-64,

Probable Consequences of Certain U.S. Actions with Respect to Vietnam and Laos, May 25, 1964 (declassified July 2, 1986), pp. 2, 3. LBJL: LBJP: NSF: CFVN, b. 52/3, f.: "Southeast Asia Memos II(4) 5/64–6/64."

74　　"in all probability Chou En-lai" et seq.: Department of State, Bureau of Intelligence and Research, Memo RFE-55, Chinese Communist Interview on War in Southeast Asia, August 5, 1964. LBJL: LBJP: NSF: CFVN; b. 54, f.: "Southeast Asia Memos (B), v. III, 6/64–8/64."

74–75　　"The Chinese people absolutely will not sit idly by" et seq.: Allen S. Whiting, *The Chinese Calculus of Deterrence.* Ann Arbor: University of Michigan Press, 1974, quoted pp. 173–74.

75　　"U.S. imperialism went over": Ibid., quoted p. 175.

76　　"Chinese intentions and capabilities": Thomas L. Hughes, "The Power to Speak and the Power to Listen," in Thomas M. Frank and Edward Weisband, eds., *Secrecy and Foreign Policy.* New York: Oxford University Press, 1974, p. 36–37.

76　　Joint Chiefs of Staff paper (JCSM-174-64): Paper of March 2, 1964. *FRUS, 1964–1968,* vol. I, pp. 114–118.

76　　"essentially a Chinese Communist enterprise": Memo, Walt W. Rostow to Dean Rusk, January 7, 1963. LBJL: Rostow Papers, b. 13, f.: "Southeast Asia."

76　　"with Ho (and implicitly, Mao)": Memo, Walt W. Rostow to Dean Rusk, July 4, 1963. Ibid.

76　　"I assume . . . that Ho and Mao": Memo, Walt W. Rostow to Dean Rusk, February 15, 1964 (declassified January 8, 1993). Ibid.

76　　"what role nuclear weapons might play": Memo, Walt W. Rostow to U. Alexis Johnson, March 9, 1964 (declassified August 19, 1993). Ibid.

76　　"help deter": Memo, Walt W. Rostow to William P. Bundy, May 19, 1964, op. cit.

76　　"Mao's basic doctrine" et seq.: Paper, Walt W. Rostow to Lyndon B. Johnson, June 6, 1964, op. cit., pp. 12, 13.

77　　"Our goals in Vietnam": Lyndon Johnson, *The Vantage Point,* p. 119.

78　　"The situation is very disturbing": Memo, Robert S. McNamara to Lyndon B. Johnson, December 21, 1963. Gravell Pentagon Papers, III, pp. 494–495.

78　　"WE BELIEVE POTENTIAL IMPORTANCE": Cable, Leonard Unger to Dean Rusk (Vientiane 682), December 14, 1963 (declassified December 5, 1995), LBJL: LBJP: NSF: CF: Laos, b. 265, f.: "Laos, vol. 1."

79 "graduated military pressure" et seq.: McNamara memo of December 21, 1963, op. cit.

79 "to a limited degree" and "enhance U.S. management": CIA, Cable CAS 2441, November 14, 1963 (declassified June 28, 1991). JFKL: JFKP: NSF: CF: b. 132, f.: "Laos, General 10/63–11/63."

79–80 "if the U.S. government is prepared": CIA, Cable 2439, November 14, 1963 (declassified June 28, 1991). JFKL: Ibid.

79 CIA Cable 2440, cited here, originated on November 14, 1963 (declassified June 28, 1991). JFKL: Ibid.

80 "out of a clear blue sky" et seq.: Military Assistance Command Vietnam, MACSOG Documentation Study, July 16, 1970 (declassified August 4, 1992), Appendix D, p. D-8. [Hereafter cited as "MACSOG Study".] The author is indebted to Jack Kull for this valuable document.

81 "action against North Vietnam": Summary Record of 524th NSC Meeting, March 17, 1964. *FRUS, 1964–1968,* vol. I, p. 171.

81 "Vietnamese cross-border" et seq.: Memo, Robert S. McNamara to Lyndon B. Johnson, March 16, 1964. *FRUS,* op. cit., p. 159.

82 "received nothing in return": Brigadier General Soutchay Vongsanavh, *Indochina Studies: RLG Military Operations and Activities in the Laotian Panhandle.* U.S. Army: Center for Military History, 1981, p. 30.

84 "This was the one thing": Donald Duncan, "The Whole Thing Was a Lie!" in *A Vietnam Primer,* ed. the Editors of *Ramparts* magazine. San Francisco: *Ramparts,* n.d. (c. 1969), p. 82.

84 "much more than we had": MACSOG Study, Appendix D, p. D-9.

86 "My domain has always been": Douglas Pike, *PAVN: People's Army of Vietnam.* New York: Da Capo Press, 1986, quoted p. 349.

88 "We believe that none": Memo, John McCone to Lyndon B. Johnson, July 28, 1964. *FRUS, 1964–1968,* vol. I, p. 586.

89 "a logical follow-on" et seq.: Memo, Thomas J. Corcoran to Michael Forrestal, November 12, 1964 (declassified July 23, 1987). LBJL: LBJP: NSF: CFVN; b. 54, f.: "Southeast Asia Memos vol. 4 (8/64–8/65)."

89 "We could develop a series" et seq.: Thomas J. Corcoran draft paper, "Option V," n.d. [November 12, 1964]. Ibid.

Chapter 5. Dark Road Ahead: 1964–1965

page

91 "Action against North Vietnam" et seq.: John T. McNaughton draft paper, "Action for South Vietnam," November 6, 1964. *The Penta-*

gon Papers as Published by the New York Times, ed. Neil Sheehan et al. New York: Bantam Books, 1971, pp. 365–366.

92   "the working group is agreed" et seq.: Memo, William P. Bundy, Project Outline, November 7, 1964. Gravel Pentagon Papers, III, pp. 588–590. Cf. *FRUS,* 1964–1968, vol. I, p. 302.

92   "we are putting forces into place": Letter, Walt W. Rostow to Robert S. McNamara, November 16, 1964. New York Times Pentagon Papers, pp. 418–419.

92   "massive . . . to deal with any escalatory response": Memo, Walt W. Rostow to Dean Rusk, November 23, 1964. Gravell Pentagon Papers, III, p. 646.

93   "We will join at once" et seq.: National Security Council, Position Paper on Southeast Asia, December 2, 1964 (declassified September 14, 1977). LBJL: LBJP: NSF: NSC Staff Files, b. 2, f.: "Memos for the President vol. 7."

93   "It was agreed to continue our stone-walling": Memo, Chester L. Cooper to McGeorge Bundy, December 19, 1964 (declassified February 3, 1988). LBJL: LBJP: NSF: CF: Laos, b. 269, f.: "Laos, Memos vol. 13 (12/64–1/65)."

94   "I didn't know there was going to be a war" et seq.: Bill Mauldin, "Vivid Picture of the Attack on Pleiku—And Who Ordered It," *Life* magazine, February 19, 1965, p. 32.

95   "Pleikus are like streetcars": David Halberstam, *The Best and the Brightest.* New York: Random House, 1972, quoted p. 533.

95   "sustained reprisal": Memo, McGeorge Bundy to Lyndon B. Johnson, February 7, 1965. New York Times Pentagon Papers, pp. 423–427.

97   "I soon sensed that": Maxwell D. Taylor, *Swords into Plowshares,* p. 341.

97   "It is far-fetched": Cable, William Sullivan to Dean Rusk (231100Z April 1965), quoted in Jacob Van Staaveren, *The United States Air Force in Southeast Asia: Interdiction in Southern Laos 1960–1968.* Washington, D.C.: Center for Air Force History, 1993, p. 72.

98–99   "Laos was really more of a geographical expression": William H. Sullivan Oral History (JFKL), June 16, 1970, p. 4.

101   "I saw no possibility": William C. Westmoreland, *A Soldier Reports.* New York: Dell Books, 1980, p. 164.

101   "While accepting the strategic goal": Ibid., p. 169.

101   "Lao believe our methodical bombardment" et seq.: Cable, William H. Sullivan to Dean Rusk (Vientiane 1712), April 21, 1965 (declassified August 27, 1981). LBJL: LBJP: NSF: Memos to the President, b. 3, f.: "Bundy v.10 (Apr. 15–May 31, 1965)."

101   "only to avoid capture" et seq.: Cable, William C. Westmoreland to
             U. S. G. Sharp (MACSOG 9621), March 27, 1965 (declassified Au-
             gust 18, 1992). LBJL: LBJP: NSF: CF: Laos, b. 270, f.: "Laos, Cables,
             vol. 15, 4/65–1/66."

102   "Both [the] Air Attaché and I": Cable, William H. Sullivan to Dean
             Rusk (Vientiane 2054), June 21, 1965 (declassified February 14,
             1984). LBJL: LBJP: NSF: Memos to the President, b. 3, f.: "Bundy,
             vol. 11 (June 1965)."

103   "Higher authority approved the concept": Cable, Joint Chiefs of
             Staff to CINCPAC (no. 3924), October 12, 1965 (declassified Sep-
             tember 2, 1992). LBJL: LBJP: NSF: CF: Laos, b. 270, f.: "Laos, Ca-
             bles, vol. 15, 4/65–1/66."

104   "ARVN Special Forces operations in Laos": Cable, Military Assis-
             tance Command J-32 (no. 4315), May 28, 1964 (declassified No-
             vember 24, 1980). LBJL: LBJP: NSF: CFVN, b. 52/3, f.: "Southeast
             Asia Cables, vol. 3 (5/64–6/64)."

104   "the firing ranges were totally inadequate": MACSOG Study,
             Annex Q, p. B-q-8.

105   "told us you didn't care": Sedgwick Tourison, *Secret Army, Secret
             War.* Annapolis, Md.: U.S. Naval Institute Press, 1995, quoted p. 98.

105   "If you had a . . . problem" et seq.: MACSOG Study, p. B-q-22.

105   "did not provide enough depth": Ibid., p. C-b-30.

106   "they could navigate" et seq.: Ibid., p. B-q-23.

107–108   "There was no actual control" et seq.: Ibid., p. B-s-7.

115   "The war of aggression in the South": Letter, Le Xuan-Comrade
             Xuan [General Nguyen Chi Thanh], May 1965. Le Duan, *Letters to
             the South,* p. 103.

117   "A lot of guys went to Vietnam": *New York Times,* June 14, 1994,
             p. D20.

117   "This was Indian country": Colonel Charles A. Beckwith and Don-
             ald Knox, *Delta Force.* New York: Harcourt Brace Jovanovich, 1983,
             p. 50.

118   "I don't think I'd ever met": General H. Norman Schwarzkopf with
             Peter Petre, *The Autobiography: It Doesn't Take a Hero.* New York:
             Bantam Books, 1992, p. 114.

119   "I was the first off" et seq.: Peter Arnett, *Live from the Battlefield.*
             New York: Simon & Schuster, 1994, pp. 153, 157.

119   "The truth is": Ibid., quoted p. 254.

120   "Please get the microphones out of here" et seq.: Schwarzkopf, *It
             Doesn't Take a Hero,* quoted pp. 120–121.

Chapter 6. The World and The 'Nam

page

124   "Our two parties and countries": Qiang Zhai, "Beijing and the Vietnam Conflict, 1964–1965," in *Cold War International History Project Bulletin* (nos. 6–7), Winter 1995–1996, quoted p. 235.

124   "It is our policy": Chen Jian, "China's Involvement with the Vietnam War, 1964–1969." *China Quarterly* no. 142 (June 1995). Ms. copy, quoted p. 15.

124   "We will unhesitatingly rise in resistance" et seq.: Qiang Zhai, repr. p. 236. *Peking Review* printed the text of Zhou's statement in May 1966, leading American observers such as Allen S. Whiting to date the message at that time, but the publication of Chinese foreign affairs documents on Vietnam, and of Zhou Enlai's papers, both confirm the 1965 date.

126   "Available evidence to date": Attachment to CIA Memo, Richard D. Kovar to Chester L. Cooper, July 30, 1965 (declassified October 14, 1976). LBJL: LBJP: NSF: CFVN, b. 50/1, f.: "Southeast Asia Special Intelligence vol. 7."

126   "a possible change" et seq.: Central Intelligence Agency (OCI), Intelligence Memorandum SC 11269/65, October 17, 1965 (declassified October 9, 1976). Ibid.

126   "border defense/coastal security mission" et seq.: CIA (OCI), Intelligence Memorandum SC 11391/65, October 20, 1965 (declassified September 16, 1992). Ibid.

126   "fair chance" et seq.: CIA, Special National Intelligence Estimate 10-3-65, February 11, 1965 (declassified September 10, 1993). LBJL: LBJP: NSF: NIE Series, b. 1, f.: "10-65, Communist States."

126   "We think it unlikely": CIA, SNIE 10-3/1-65, February 18, 1965 (declassified September 8, 1994). Ibid.

127   "put the United States under various new pressures" et seq.: CIA, SNIE 10-5-65, April 28, 1965 (declassified August 9, 1994). Ibid.

127   "It is likely that Hanoi": CIA, SNIE 10-6-65, June 2, 1965 (declassified September 8, 1994). Ibid.

127–128   "almost certainly would counter in the northwest" et seq.: CIA, SNIE 10-10-65, September 10, 1965 (declassified September 8, 1994). Ibid.

128   "splintered the intelligence community": Ted Gittinger, ed., *The Johnson Years: A Vietnam Roundtable*. Austin: Lyndon B. Johnson School of Public Affairs, University of Texas, 1993, p. 63.

128   "I am not the village idiot": Thomas Hughes interview, March 8, 1997.

130   "seeking to wean Hanoi away" et seq.: Memo, Department of State (George C. Denny), February 1, 1965 (declassified July 31, 1979). LBJL: LBJP: NSF: International Meetings Series, b. 29, f.: "McGeorge Bundy Trip to Saigon 2/4/65, vol. III (1 of 2)."

130   "underscores both the USSR's desire": CIA, Intelligence Memorandum OCI/0341/65, February 1, 1965 (declassified October 20, 1976). LBJL: Ibid.

130   "At a minimum": Memo, Department of State (Lindsey Grant), February 5, 1965 (declassified July 31, 1979). Ibid.

131   "It so happened that the Americans": Georgi Arbatov, *The System: An Insider's Life in Soviet Politics.* New York: Times Books, 1992, p. 117.

131   "Kosygin bitterly resented": Anatoli Dobrynin, *In Confidence.* New York: Random House, 1995, p. 136.

132   "The situation was absurd": Ibid.

134   "This declaration ought to have been taken seriously": Andrei Gromyko, *Memoirs.* Garden City, N.Y.: Doubleday, 1989, pp. 184–185.

135   "the U.S. aggressors" et seq.: Staughton Lynd and Thomas Hayden, *The Other Side.* New York: New American Library, 1966, quoted pp. 118–119.

136   "You've got to learn from the South": Terry H. Anderson, *The Movement and the Sixties.* New York: Oxford University Press, 1995, quoted p. 138.

Chapter 7. Squeezing Hanoi: 1965–1966

page

140   "were nothing more than those of prudence": Admiral Ulysses S. G. Sharp, *Strategy for Defeat,* p. 91.

141   "General Kinnard's ideas" et seq.: William C. Westmoreland, History Notes, August 29, 1965. LBJL: Westmoreland Papers, b. 6, f.: "History File vol. 1 (29 August–4 September 1965)."

141   "The Army hadn't moved a full division": J. D. Coleman, *Pleiku: The Dawn of Helicopter Warfare in Vietnam.* New York: St. Martin's Press, 1989, p. xi.

142   "The trail from our hatchway": Robert Mason, *Chickenhawk.* New York: Penguin Books, 1984, p. 55.

142   "it seemed like the guy": Matthew Brennan, ed., *Hunger-Killer Squadron.* New York: Pocket Books, 1992, p. 2.

143   "The secret of our troops' movement": N. K. Kha, "Pleime (19 October–27 November 1965)," in Nguyen Khac Vien, ed., *Face to Face with the Enemy.* Hanoi: Foreign Languages Publishing House (Vietnamese Studies no. 54), 1978, p. 41.

144   "tracer fire you could land on": Philip D. Chinery, *Life on the Line.* New York: St. Martin's Press, 1980, p. 33.

145   "simulate the imminent approach": General Vinh Loc, *Why Pleime?* Pleiku, Vn.: privately printed, August 1966, pp. 99–100.

147   "They say the creek": Matthew Brennan, ed., *Hunter-Killer Squadron,* pp. 4–5.

148   "I flew right through camp after camp." Matthew Brennan, ed. *Headhunters.* New York: Pocket Books, 1988, p. 42.

149   "a bloody nose for the ARVN general reserve": Westmoreland History Notes, cited by Harold C. Moore and Joe Galloway, *We Were Soldiers Once . . . and Young.* New York: Random House, 1992, quoted p. 307.

150   "I have just been assigned": General Vinh Loc, op. cit.

154   "philosophy that any U.S. spokesman": Cable, William H. Sullivan to Dean Rusk (Vientiane 1116), April 25, 1966 (declassified February 19, 1992). LBJL: LBJP: NSF: CF: Laos, b. 271, f.: "Laos, vol. 16."

158–159   "air and other direct pressure": memo, Walt W. Rostow to William P. Bundy, August 5, 1965 (declassified August 19, 1993). LBJL: Walt Rostow Papers, b. 13, f.: "Southeast Asia."

159   "optimum": Memo, Rostow to Dean Rusk, September 8, 1965 (declassified August 18, 1992). Rostow Papers, op. cit.

159   "waterborne logistics craft": William C. Westmoreland and U. S. G. Sharp, *Report on the War in Vietnam (as of 30 June 1968).* Washington, D.C.: U.S. Government Printing Office, 1969, p. 22.

160   "There were two ways": Da Nang combat pilot who wishes to remain anonymous.

Chapter 8. Indian Country: 1966–1967

page

183   "the vast majority of . . . . infiltrators": Military Assistance Command Vietnam (Combined Intelligence Center Vietnam [hereafter cited as CICV]), The North Vietnamese Soldier in South Vietnam, October 3, 1966, p. 34. University Press of America: Microfilm Records of MACV, reel 27.

193   "I also had girlfriends": Martha Hess, ed., *The Americans Came.* New York: Four Walls Eight Windows Press, 1993, p. 29.

194   "The period of writing": Kenneth B. Richburg, "The Ho Chi Minh

Trail Revisited: Vietnam's Death March." *Washington Post,* April 26, 1990, quoted p. A33.

194   "So many facts": Ibid.

194   Sources for the fiction discussed: Bao Ninh, *The Sorrow of War.* New York: Random House, 1995. Anon., *The Ho Chi Minh Trail.* Hanoi: Red River Publishing House, 1982. Anon., *Portrait of the Vietnamese Soldier.* Hanoi: Red River, 1984. Interview with Kevin Bowen, Joiner Center, University of Massachusetts. English translations of Bao Ninh's novel continue to be hawked frequently in the streets of Vietnamese cities.

194   "He went South, and I got injured": Martha Hess, *Then the Americans Came: Voices From Vietnam.* New York: Four Walls/Eight Windows Press, 1993, quoted p. 211.

195   "traffic goes on" et seq.: Vu Can and Nguyen Khac Vien, eds., *With the Fighters of Quangbinh-Vinhlinh.* Hanoi: Foreign Languages Publishing House (Vietnamese Studies no. 9), 1966, pp. 10–11 and passim.

195   "We were bombed nearly every day" et seq.: Martha Hess, ed., *Then the Americans Came,* pp. 25, 34, 36.

197   "The Americans made the correct choices": *The Washington Post,* April 26, 1990, quoted p. A-37.

203   "strong-minded American ambassadors with Napoleonic ambitions" et seq.: General John K. Singlaub Oral History, U.S. Army Military History Institute (Carlisle Barracks).

Chapter 9. Forks in the Road: 1967

page

205   "working stiff, not a thinker": John Prados, *Keepers of the Keys.* New York: William Morrow Publishers, 1991, quoted p. 164.

207   "I said I doubted": Cable, William H. Sullivan to Dean Rusk (Vientiane 513), January 3, 1966 (declassified June 7, 1984). LBJL: LBJP: NSF: Memos to the President, b. 6, f.: "Bundy vol. 18, January 1–11, 1966."

207   "remote" et seq.: Bob Brewin and Sydney Shaw, *Vietnam on Trial.* New York: Atheneum, 1987, quoted p. 132.

207   "not practical at this time": Ibid., quoted p. 133.

208   "hold the area hostage": Walt W. Rostow, *The Diffusion of Power,* p. 513.

208   "the idea reminds me of a fox": Wilfred Burchett, *At the Barricades.* New York: Times Books, 1981, quoted p. 226.

208   "Let them try!": Ibid., quoted p. 227.

208   "It is necessary to prepare": CIA (Foreign Broadcast Information
            Service), *Asia and Pacific Supplement*, April 14, 1967 (FBO/73/67/
            015), p. 28. Cf. Patrick A. McGarvey, ed., *Visions of Victory*. Stan-
            ford, Calif.: Hoover Institution Press, 1970, repr. p. 195.

208–209   "We have adequately prepared": General Vo Nguyen Giap, *Big Vic-
            tory, Great Task*. New York: Praeger, 1968, pp. 101–102.

209   "the landing would have been": William Broyles Jr., *Brothers in
            Arms*. New York: Alfred A. Knopf, 1986, quoted p. 97.

209   "On balance, I thought this a more effective way" et seq.: Walt W.
            Rostow, *Diffusion of Power*, p. 513. William Westmoreland is quoted
            from his "History Notes, 10–30 April 1967," from the entry for
            April 27 (Westmoreland Papers, b. 11, f.: "History File vol. 15.")

210   "When we add divisions" et seq.: Gravell Pentagon Papers, vol. IV,
            quoted p. 442.

210   "I will proceed": William C. Westmoreland, History Note, April 27,
            1967, op. cit.

211   "real Indian country": Richard D. Camp with Eric Hammel, *Lima-
            6: A Marine Company Commander in Vietnam, June 1967–January
            1968*. New York: Atheneum, 1989, p. 61.

211   "*Ground actions in Laos*": Memo, Robert S. McNamara to Lyndon B.
            Johnson, May 19, 1967 (declassified June 9, 1989). LBJL: LBJP:
            NSF: CFVN; b. 81/2, f.: "Vietnam 3E(1)b Future Military Opera-
            tions 6/65–12/67." Italics in the original.

212   "It could be extremely difficult for the President to decide": Memo,
            William J. Jorden and Robert N. Ginsburgh to Walt W. Rostow,
            September 7, 1967. LBJL: LBJP: NSF: CFVN; b. 81/2, f.: "Vietnam
            3E(1)a Future Military Operations 6/65–12/67."

213   "an iron-curtain counterinfiltration barrier": Joint Chiefs of Staff
            (History Division), *The Joint Chiefs of Staff and the War in Vietnam,
            1960–1968* (declassified June 14, 1994), Pt. 1, Ch. 35, p. 21. [Here-
            after cited as "JCS History" with dates.]

213   "visible, fixed, long-term": Memo, J-3 to Joint Chiefs of Staff (TP
            58-65), November 8, 1965. JCS History 1960–1968, op. cit.

214   "Specifically he wanted to know" et seq.: Cable, William H. Sullivan
            to Dean Rusk (Vientiane 6419), April 18, 1967 (declassified Au-
            gust 11, 1991). LBJL: LBJP: NSF: CF: Laos; b. 271, f.: "Laos, vol. 17."

215   "remains an open question": Cable, Dean Rusk to William H. Sul-
            livan, April 19, 1967 (declassified January 23, 1992). LBJL: Ibid.

215   "watertight" et seq.: Cable, William H. Sullivan to Dean Rusk (Vi-
            entiane 7071), May 15, 1967 (declassified April 22, 1992). Ibid.

218   "the more I struggled": Richard S. Greeley, "Stringing the Mc-
            Namara Line," *Naval History* magazine, vol. 11, no. 4, August 1997,
            p. 66.

219 "had better bring another 200,000" et seq.: Cable, William H. Sullivan to Dean Rusk (Vientiane 433), July 24, 1967 (declassified April 22, 1992). LBJL: LBJP: NSF: CF: Laos, b. 271, f.: "Laos, vol. 17."

221 "I'm beginning to wonder" et seq.: John Prados and Ray W. Stubbe, *Valley of Decision: The Siege of Khe Sanh.* New York: Dell Books, 1982, quoted p. 76.

221 "If we could combine": Cable, William H. Sullivan to Dean Rusk (Vientiane 7403), May 29, 1967 (declassified April 22, 1992). LBJL: CF: Laos, op. cit.

222 "Vehicle traffic has ground virtually to a halt": Cable, William H. Sullivan to Dean Rusk (Vientiane 7638), June 9, 1967 (declassified November 8, 1991). Ibid.

222 "The rainy season has arrived": Memo, Walt W. Rostow to Lyndon B. Johnson, June 15, 1967 (declassified July 31, 1991). Ibid.

222 "all knowledgeable Lao": Cable, William H. Sullivan to Dean Rusk (Vientiane 7946), June 27, 1967 (declassified May 26, 1994). Ibid.

222 "The unusual cloud formations" et seq.: Memo, Donald F. Hornig to Walt W. Rostow, May 23, 1967 (declassified April 7, 1993). LBJL: LBJP: NSF: CFVN; b. 85–89, f.: "VN(3)P Project COMPATRIOT, 5/67–7/67."

223 "to express his deep concern": Robert McNamara and Brian VanDeMark, *In Retrospect,* quoted p. 216.

224 "I reacted to the horror": Ibid.

224 "I consider this an unprecedented victory": *New York Times,* November 20, 1965.

224 "The effect on the antiwar movement": Thomas Powers, *The War at Home.* New York: Grossman Publishers, 1973, p. 90.

225 "Something . . . is wrong": Anon., *The Vietnam Hearings.* New York: Vintage Books, 1966, p. 33.

225 "It is not McNamara's war" et seq.: Ibid., pp. 51, 21.

226 "Lyndon Johnson covered the entire Congress": Dean Rusk, *As I Saw It,* p. 546.

226 "The U.S. presence rested on a bowl of jelly": McNamara, *In Retrospect,* p. 222.

226 "Murderer!": Ibid., quoted p. 258.

227 "Gettysburg Address": Memo, Walt W. Rostow to Lyndon B. Johnson, June 3, 1966. LBJL: LBJP: NSF: Memos to the President; b. 8, f.: "Rostow vol. 5 (May 27–June 10, 1966)."

229 "Johnson was constantly concerned": Richard Helms quoted in Tom Wells, *The War Within.* Berkeley: University of California Press, p. 154.

230   "Can you imagine?": Paul Hendrickson, "McNamara: Specters of Vietnam," *Washington Post*, May 10, 1984, quoted p. B1.

233   "For us, you know": Stanley Karnow, "Giap Remembers," *New York Times Magazine*, June 24, 1990, quoted p. 60.

234   "The present time is the era of revolutionary storms": Vo Nguyen Giap, *Big Victory, Great Task*, p. 58.

234   "present mobilization level" et seq.: Ibid., pp. 90, 94.

235   "will have a very great adverse effect": Ibid., p. 49.

236   "to annihilate a major U.S. element": Military Assistant Command Vietnam (CICV): Combined Documents Exploitation Center, CDEC 11-1591-67, November 14, 1967 (declassified November 1979); attached to note "Dak To Captured Document," n.d. LBJL: LBJP: NSF: CFVN; b. 143–57, f.: "Press Releases on Captured Documents."

236   "the decision to stage": White House retyped copy of Cable Paris 25/1625Z November 1968 (declassified November 5, 1991). LBJL: LBJP: NSF: CFVN: b. 138, f.: "Memos to the President re Bombing Halt, vol. 7 (11/21/68–1/13/69)."

237   "No well-fortified barrier": Giap, *Big Victory, Great Task*, p. 99.

Chapter 10. Fire in the Night: 1968

page

241   "I don't want any damn Dinbinphoo!": John Prados, *The Hidden History of the Vietnam War*. Chicago: Ivan R. Dee Publishers, 1995, from Hugh Sidey, "The Presidency: A Long Way from Spring," *Time* magazine, February 12, 1968, quoted p. 16.

243   "when in 1968 there were forces available": General Bruce Palmer Jr., *The 25-Year War*. Lexington: University Press of Kentucky, 1984, p. 106.

243   "take advantage of a possible change in national policy": Cable, William C. Westmoreland to Earle Wheeler (MAC 00686), January 15, 1968 (declassified May 9, 1984). LBJL: Westmoreland Papers, b. 13, f.: "History File vol. 28."

246   "any agreement with the South Vietnamese": Cable, CIA to White House Situation Room (102049Z), October 10, 1967 (declassified July 8, 1992). LBJL: LBJP: NSF: CF: Laos, b. 271, f.: "Laos vol. 17."

246   "I believe the enemy sees a similarity": Cable, William C. Westmoreland to Earle Wheeler (MAC 00967), January 22, 1968 (declassified December 16, 1983). LBJL: LBJP: NSF: NSC Histories; b. 47, f.: "March 31 Speech, vol. 2."

254   "a battalion which would be armed with modern weapons": Military Assistance Command Vietnam, CICV Intelligence Report

6-028-6244-67 December 14, 1967 (declassified June 12, 1989). LBJL: LBJP: NSF: CFVN: b. 153, f.: "CDEC Bulletins, vol. 2."

254 "There was no case of killing civilians purposefully": John Prados, *The Hidden History of the Vietnam War*, quoted p. 155.

255 "We are going where there is everything": Nguyen Qui Duc, *Where the Ashes Are*. Reading, Mass.: Addison-Wesley, 1994, quoted p. 63.

258 "Lao troops fighting North Vietnamese": Cable, William H. Sullivan to Dean Rusk (Vientiane 4042), January 25, 1968 (declassified July 25, 1991).

258 "must consider South Vietnamese as enemy": John Prados and Ray W. Stubbe, *Valley of Decision: The Siege of Khe Sanh*. New York: Dell Books, 1993, quoted p. 384.

258–259 "We could hear the tanks moving around": Colonel Jonathan Ladd Oral History, U.S. Army Military History Institute (Carlisle Barracks).

259 "In Westmoreland's book": Ibid.

259 "I just can't get Westmoreland's attention": Ibid.

262 "reexamination of earlier expressed fear" et seq.: Memo, Copy of Saigon 22495, March 19, 1968 (declassified March 17, 1988). LBJL: LBJP: NSF: NSC Histories, b. 48, f.: "March 31st Speech vol. 4, Tabs LL–ZZ and a–k."

263 "conducted in such a way as to have no press exposure": Ibid.

263–264 "[They] seem to me": Memo, Marshall Wright to Walt W. Rostow, March 25, 1968 (declassified December 2, 1992). LBJL: LBJP: CF: Laos, b. 272, f.: "Laos, vol. 18."

264 "Westy does not plan [to actually conduct] ground action in Laos" et seq.: Memo, Robert N. Ginsburgh to Walt W. Rostow, n.d. (March 1968), and handwritten note, idem., n.d. (April 1968). LBJL: Ibid.

264 "to refresh your memory" et seq.: Memo, Walt W. Rostow to Lyndon B. Johnson, March 21, 1968 (declassified May 2, 1988). National Security Archive: McNamara Collection.

Chapter 11. Pinball Wizards: 1968–1969

page

276 "I appreciate the project": Jim Graves, "SLAM Mission into Laos," *Soldier of Fortune* magazine, vol. 6, no. 6, June 1981, quoted p. 50.

276 "FOB 2, C & C Detachment": Ibid.

279 "Don't shoot! Don't shoot! Friendly! Friendly!": After Action Report, 5th Special Forces, Mobile Strike Force, Company C, "Ngok

Tavak," May 16, 1968, quoted p. 2. The author is indebted to Tim
Brown for a copy of this document.

280   "In my opinion it had none of the importance": William C. West-
            moreland, *A Soldier Reports*, p. 473.

280   "The decision to evacuate": Ronald H. Spector, *After Tet*. New York:
            The Free Press, 1993, quoted p. 170. Chaisson's letter home was
            on May 14, 1968.

281–282   "General Abe did not see eye to eye": General Walter H. Kerwin
            Oral History (Abrams Project; USAMHI).

284   "Around me the currents": Tom Hayden, *Reunion: A Memoir*. New
            York: Random House, 1988, p. 205.

285   "We also run patrols": Memo, Walt W. Rostow to Lyndon B. John-
            son, December 12, 1968 (declassified June 26, 1984). LBJL: LBJP:
            NSF: Memos to the President, b. 43, f.: "Rostow vol. 110."

285   "At a time when things were going rather well" et seq.: Walt W.
            Rostow Interview, *New York Times*, January 5, 1969, p. 14.

Chapter 12. A Strategy of Force: 1969–1970

page

287   "It was an option we ruled out very early" et seq.: Richard Nixon,
            RN: The Memoirs of Richard Nixon. New York: Warner Books, 1978,
            vol. 1, pp. 430, 432.

287–288   "Nixon was eager to negotiate" and "Would that history were so
            simple": Henry A. Kissinger, *Diplomacy*. New York: Simon & Schus-
            ter, 1994, p. 675.

288   "The American commitment": Peter W. Rodman, *More Precious
            Than Peace*. New York: Charles Scribner's Sons, 1994, p. 124.

288   "transmogrified": Ibid.

289   "The air campaign in Laos": National Security Study Memoran-
            dum 1, Vietnam Progress, February 21, 1969. Repr. *Congressional
            Record*, May 11, 1972, p. E5009.

289   "savage blow": Henry Brandon, *Special Relationships*. New York:
            Atheneum, 1988, quoted p. 248.

290   "is to set a deadline" et seq.: National Security Council, Memoran-
            dum of Conversation, June 8, 1969 (declassified August 24, 1995).
            National Archives and Records Administration: Nixon Library Pro-
            ject [hereafter cited as NLP]: White House Central Files: President's
            Office File: Memos to the President, b. 1, f.: "Beginning June 7,
            1969."

290   "After half a year": Richard Nixon, *RN*, vol. 1, p. 486.

290   "will be a tough period ahead": H. R. Haldeman, *The Haldeman Di-
             aries: Inside the Nixon White House*. New York: G. P. Putnam's Sons,
             1994, p. 83.

290   "I call it the Madman Theory": H. R. Haldeman with Joseph Di-
             Mona, *The Ends of Power*. New York: Dell Books, 1978, quoted
             p. 122; emphasis in the original.

290   "We anticipate that the planning group": Military Assistance Com-
             mand Vietnam, Cable MAC 12408, September 23, 1969 (declassi-
             fied September 25, 1989). U.S. Army Military History Institute
             (hereafter abbreviated USAMHI), Carlisle Barracks. Creighton W.
             Abrams Papers, box "1969–1970."

291   "modules": Cable, Frederic Bardshar to Earle Wheeler (191630Z),
             September 19, 1969 (declassified September 25, 1989). Abrams
             Papers, op. cit.

291   "Ground operations into the DMZ": Cable, Bardshar to Wheeler
             (MAC 12563), September 25, 1969 (declassification date NA).
             Abrams Papers, op. cit.

291   "the pressure of public opinion": Memo, Henry A. Kissinger to
             Richard M. Nixon, September 10, 1968. Repr. Kissinger, *White House
             Years*. Boston: Little, Brown, 1979, pp. 1480–1482.

292   "ABSOLUTELY EYES ONLY" et seq.: Cable, John McCain to Earle
             Wheeler (160446Z), September 16, 1969 (declassified September
             25, 1989). Abrams Papers, op. cit.

292   "I just can't believe": Tad Szulc, *The Illusion of Peace*. New York:
             Viking Press, 1978, quoted p. 156.

294   "The fact is that" et seq.: Tom Wells, *The War Within*, quoted p. 358.

295   "Kissinger, God knows what he supported": Admiral John McCain
             Jr., Oral History (Abrams Project, USAMHI).

295   "Look at this, Admiral" et seq.: Ibid.

298   "I continued to tell Potts": Lieutenant General Elias C. Townsend
             Oral History (Abrams Project, USAMHI).

298   "When I pressed hard": Russell Jack Smith, *The Unknown CIA*.
             Washington, D.C.: Pergamon-Brassey's, 1989, p. 210.

300   "I've been to my astrologer": Admiral Thomas H. Moorer Oral His-
             tory (Abrams Project, USAMHI).

301   "It was really huge": Haldeman Diary, entry for November 15, 1969.
             H. R. Haldeman, *The Haldeman Diaries*, p. 108.

302   "[The president] obviously realizes": Haldeman diary entry for
             May 6, 1970. Ibid., p. 161.

302–303   "Media have built it up very big": Haldeman diary entry, May 8,
             1970. Ibid., p. 162.

304   "Great Laotian Truck Eater": and "Gentlemen, what we have here":

Earl H. Tilford Jr., *Setup: What the Air Force Did in Vietnam and Why.* Montgomery, Ala.: Air University Press, 1991, quoted p. 212, n. 47.

306 "I'm usually concentrating so hard": *New York Times,* December 16, 1968, quoted p. 3.

306 "The whole damn map": Colonel Tom Yarborough, *Da Nang Diary.* New York: St. Martin's Press, 1991, p. 35.

307 "the code phrase that let them know": Ibid., p. 36.

307 "Misty executed a hard pull up": Ibid., pp. 71–72.

Chapter 13. No Plug in the Funnel: 1971

page

311 "Tchepone became to many": Henry Kamm, "On the Ho Chi Minh Trail: New Villages and Old Bombs," *New York Times,* January 30, 1990, p. A8.

312 "flowers blowing up": Interrogation of Le Dinh Thao (CICV 6-029-0500-70), May 23, 1970. Texas Tech University: Douglas Pike Collection, unit 2, f.: "Military Activity 5/69."

314 "As forecast, this morning" et seq.: Khanh Van, "We Followed the Convoys to the Front," Pt. 8. *Quan Doi Nhan Danh,* March 13, 1971 (CIA/JPRS trans.).

315 "There was one main road": *Washington Post,* April 26, 1990, quoted p. A33.

315 "We were attacked frequently": *New York Times,* March 1, 1995, quoted p. A10.

317 "battalion deficit": Henry Kissinger, *White House Years,* pp. 987–989.

317 "Without challenging": Kissinger, *Diplomacy,* p. 695.

318 "a coordinated air-ground attack": Cable, Creighton W. Abrams to John S. McCain (MAC 15808), December 12, 1970. JCS History 1971–1973, quoted p. 16.

318 "an excellent opportunity": Cable, McCain to Wheeler (150236Z), December 15, 1970. Ibid., quoted p. 17.

318 "strong supporter": Memo, Walt W. Rostow to Lyndon B. Johnson, November 21, 1967, 3:50 P.M. (declassified March 11, 1986). LBJL: LBJP: NSF: CFVN: b. 127, f.: "Vietnam [March 19, 1970 Memo] (1)."

319 "He thinks that any pullout next year" et seq.: H. R. Haldeman, *The Haldeman Diaries,* pp. 221, 222, 224.

320 "Souvanna has consistently said" et seq.: Memo, Jonathan Moore to Henry A. Kissinger, July 16, 1970 (declassified December 1, 1995), with attached paper "Political Impact in Laos of Proposed

Paramilitary Operations in South Laos." National Security Archive: National Security Directives collection.

320   "began to surface objections" et seq.: Kissinger, *White House Years,* 997.

320   "The action was ill-conceived from the start": Ulysses Alexis Johnson and Jef O. McAlister, *The Right Hand of Power.* Englewood Cliffs, N.J.: Prentice-Hall, 1984, p. 533.

321   "no direct substitute for the Tchepone operation": Memo, Admiral Thomas Moorer-Melvin Laird (CM-544-71), January 29, 1971. JCS History 1971–1973, quoted p. 24.

321   "turned out to be the only adviser": Kissinger, *White House Years,* 996.

321   "was remarkably accurate": General Bruce Palmer, "U.S. Intelligence and Vietnam," *Studies in Intelligence,* vol. 28 (special edition), 1984 (declassification date NA), p. 87. I am in debt to Lewis Sorley for this source material.

321   "pointed out that the proposed operation" et seq.: Kissinger, *White House Years,* ibid.

323   "Why exclude me from the meeting?" Major General Nguyen Duy Hinh, *Indochina Monograph: Lam Son 719.* U.S. Army: Center for Military History, n.d. [1979], quoted p. 34.

323   "By then I knew": Lieutenant General James W. Sutherland Oral History (Abrams Project, USAMHI).

323   "Hanoi has our plan we've discovered" et. seq.: H. R. Haldeman, *The Haldeman Diaries,* p. 239.

325   "An officer of great talent and virtue": Bui Tin, *Following Ho Chi Minh,* op. cit., p. 141.

325   "If they had been wise": Bui Tin, "Vietnamese View of Early American Efforts," p. 4. Paper presented at the conference "Vietnam 1954–April 1965" hosted by the Robert McCormick Foundation, March 7, 1996.

326   "We did see traffic signs": John Prados and Ray Stubbe, *Valley of Decision,* op. cit., quoted p. 49.

328   "Route 9 was such a little piss-ant highway": John Lindquist interview.

330   "We thought we would get": *Pacific Stars and Stripes,* February 5, 1971.

330   "Those goddam tankers": *New York Times,* February 5, 1971, p. C11.

333   "a potentially significant fighting force" et seq.: Message, Creighton Abrams to James Sutherland (MAC 00335), January 12, 1971 (declassified October 4, 1985). James W. Sutherland Papers at U.S. Army Military History Institute (Carlisle Barracks).

334   "Khe Sanh was easily visible from the air": Joe Kline, "Taking Fire," *Vietnam* magazine, vol. 4, no. 5, February 1992, p. 20.

335   "From your record" et seq.: Frank Wickersham interview.

335   "an act of aggression of the Republic of Vietnam" et seq.: "President Thieu's Message on Vietnamese Operations in Laos," February 8, 1971, in *Vietnam Bulletin*, vol. 5, no. 7, February 15, 1971, pp. 3, 2.

336   "a day of marking time": Nguyen Van Hinh, *Lam Son 719*, p. 68.

338   "This is not tank country" et seq.: *Mainichi Shimbun*, February 24, 1971.

342   "I AM CONCERNED": Message, Abrams to Sutherland (MAC 02079 EYES ONLY), February 27, 1971 (declassified October 4, 1985). Sutherland Papers, op. cit.

343   "All of the Prairie Fire pilots" et seq.: Tom Yarborough, *Da Nang Diary*, op. cit., pp. 229–230.

343   "I made doubly certain": Sutherland Oral History, op. cit.

343   "That's not true": *Pacific Stars and Stripes*, February 14, 1971.

343–344   "Like a giant sponge": Tom Yarborough, *Da Nang Diary*, p. 256.

344   "IT IS HIGHLY DESIRABLE": Message, Major General Donald Cowles to Sutherland (MAC 02741 EYES ONLY), March 17, 1971 (declassified October 4, 1985). USAMHI: Sutherland Papers.

345   "For all practical purposes": Tom Yarborough, op. cit.

345   "Unless these operations produce more": Senior Officer Debriefing, Major General Thomas M. Tarpley, n.d. (declassified December 31, 1978), p. 38. USAMHI.

346   "Balls of smoke began to appear": Bob Rosenburgh, *Snake Driver: Cobras in Vietnam*. New York: Ivy Books, 1993, p. 154.

346   "The army guys were very brave": Frank Wickersham interview.

347   "During the heavy fighting": U.S. Air Force: Project CHECO, *Report: Lam Son 719, 30 January–24 March 1971: The South Vietnamese Incursion into Laos*. USAF, 1971 (declassification date NA), quoted p. 119.

347   "MY UNDERSTANDING": Message, Abrams to Sutherland (MAC 02455 EYES ONLY), March 9, 1971 (declassified October 4, 1985). USAMHI: Sutherland Papers.

348   "Admiral Moorer . . . the President": JCS History 1971–1973, Part 1, quoted p. 49.

348   "SUCH A MOMENTUM IN": Message, Moorer to McCain and Abrams (JCS 6049), March 11, 1971. JCS History, quoted ibid.

349   "the American command in Saigon": Richard Nixon, *RN*, vol. 1, pp. 617–618.

349   "we . . . had been urging": Henry Kissinger's *White House Years*, p. 1008.

349 "Well, Al" et seq.: Alexander M. Haig with Charles McCarry, *Inner Circles.* New York: Warner Books, 1992, quoted p. 274.

350 "He had been accustomed": Admiral Thomas Moorer Oral History (Abrams project, USAMHI).

Chapter 14. The Road Turns South: 1971–1975

page

351 "the Vietnamese now have decided" et seq.: H. R. Haldeman, *The Haldeman Diaries,* p. 256.

352 "THE REDEPLOYMENT . . . AS OUTLINED": Message, Moorer to McCain and Abrams (JCS 6505), March 17, 1971. JCS History, op. cit., quoted pp. 51–52.

353 "We had to be very mobile": *Pacific Stars and Stripes,* March 24, 1971.

353 "MY VISIT TO I CORPS": Kissinger, *White House Years,* quoted p. 1009.

354 "All that remained": Anon., "Ban Dong Assaulted," *South Vietnam in Struggle,* April 1, 1971, p. 7.

355 "had his unit not taken to the jungle": General Nguyen Duy Hinh, *Lam Son 719,* p. 118.

356 "I never heard a direct order" et seq.: *Pacific Stars and Stripes,* ibid.

360 "in no way accorded": Kissinger, *White House Years,* p. 992.

360 "raid too far": General Phillip B. Davidson, *Vietnam at War.* Novato, Calif.: Presidio Press, 1988, p. 617.

360 "further evidence of our erroneous evaluation": Colonel Do Quoc Nhan, "Initiative in the Vietnam War," *Military Review,* August 1972, p. 85.

360 "really missed the chance": Hinh, *Lam Son 719,* pp. 171–172.

360–361 "They speak glibly": Wilfred R. Burchett, *Vietnam North.* New York: International Publishers, 1966, quoted p. 135.

361 "Tough, well disciplined": Michael Lee Lanning and Dan Cragg, *Inside the VC and the NVA.* New York: Ivy Books, 1992, quoted pp. 263–264.

362 "It was the damndest thing I ever saw": Don Walker interview.

364 "We going into Laos?": *New York Times,* February 5, 1971.

364–365 "I'll tell you what this Laos thing means": Nancy Zaroulis and Gerald Sullivan, *Who Spoke Up?* New York: Holt, Rinehart & Winston, 1985, quoted p. 347.

365 "VETS DEFY TOP COURT": *Chicago Sun-Times,* April 22, 1971, p. 1.

366 "I understood their bitterness": Colin Powell with Joseph E. Persico, *My American Journey.* New York: Ballantine Books, 1996, p. 149.

366   "I took advantage of the opportunity": Bui Diem with David
       Chanoff, *In the Jaws of History*. Boston: Houghton Mifflin, 1987,
       p. 286.

368   "One thing Hanoi cannot do": General Bruce Palmer, *U.S. Intelli-
       gence and Vietnam*, op. cit., quoted p. 91.

372   "not much different from what I would later experience" et seq.:
       Truong Nhu Trang with David Chanoff and Doan Van Thai, *A Viet
       Cong Memoir*. New York: Harcourt Brace Jovanovich, 1985, p. 242.

372   "On one hill after another": General Tran Van Tra, *History of the
       Bulwark B2 Theater: vol. 5, Concluding the 30-Years War*. CIA/JPRS
       Translation 82783, February 2, 1983, p. 103.

373   "strong ropes inching gradually": General Van Tien Dung, *Our
       Great Spring Victory*, trans. John Spragens, Jr. New York: Monthly
       Review Press, 1977, p. 15.

379   "I feel like the war is over": *New York Times*, March 1, 1995, quoted
       p. A10.

Afterword

381   The poem "Anh Hung" is by David Connolly, from his collection
       Lost in America. Woodbridge, Conn.: Vietnam Generation Press,
       1994, p. 63. Used by permission of the author.

INDEX

NOTE: Vietnamese names are alphabetized uninverted by their family name. It is customary, however, to refer to people by the last element of their name.

A-1E fighter-bomber, 186
A-1H Skyraiders/A-4C Skyhawks, 110
Aaron, Harold R., 108
Abrams, Creighton W., 141, 248, 249, 259, 262, 291, 338; and Bravo Troop incident, 357; and Cambodia, 296, 297, 298, 299, 300, 321; and Laos offensive, 317–18, 319, 322, 329, 333, 338, 342, 347–51; as MACV commander, 265, 280, 281–82; and Vietnamization, 316
AC-47 gunship, 186–87, 305, 306
AC-119 gunship, 305, 306, 358, 369
AC-130 Spectre, 305–6, 313, 314, 358, 369
Adams, Robert, 278
A-Detachments (U.S. Special Forces), 57, 143, 161
aerial photography, 32, 190; armed flights over Laos, 92–93, 99, 103, 110–11, 156, 158; strategic reconnaissance, 196–97, 206; of Trail supply movements, 111; U-2 aircraft, 78, 80, 196; of VPA pipeline into Laos, 339–40
Agency for International Development (U.S.), 255
air activity, 32, 116, 155–63, 195–97, 359, 377–78; all-weather aircraft, 306; antiaircraft units, 88, 313–14, 352, 363, 369, 370; armed reconnaissance, 92–93, 99, 110–11, 156, 158, 196–97, 206; defoliantion chemicals, 161; ferocity of, 159; first U.S. plane downed over Laos, 66, 67, 68; Franco-Indonesia war, 3; Leaping Lena project, 82–84; Mekong valley airfields, 39; numbers (1966), 163; slower aircraft effectiveness, 270–71; SOG support teams, 153–54; surface-to-air missiles, 132, 133, 358–59, 369–70; tactical technology, 375; total tonnage dropped, 377; U.S. bomb shortage, 159; U.S.-Chinese skirmish, 124; U.S. goal, 155–56; U.S. reprisal interdictions, 95–96, 110, 111, 131, 132, 195; U.S. strike mistakes, 162, 191; U.S. two main types of, 155; VPA supply runs, 24, 26–27, 41–42, 56, 60 See also B-52 bomber; helicopters; Rolling Thunder; Steel Tiger; *specific aircraft and air forces*; *under specific place names*
Air America, 24, 67, 258

Airborne Rangers (ARVN), 31, 79, 117–20, 150–51
airmobile concept. *See* 1st Cavalry Division; helicopters
Allen, Richard B., 116
Alliance for Progress, 61
Alpha-1 target, 152–53
Alpha Company (U.S.), 328–29
Alsop, Joseph, 65
American Friends of Vietnam, 29
amphibious operations, 209, 210, 212, 262, 338
Anderson, Norman J., 259
Andropov, Yuri V., 130
"An Dung" operations, 88–89, 133
Anh Hung (Elder Brother Hung), 381
An Khe, 140
An Loc, battle of, 370
Annam. *See* Interzone 5
Annamite Mountains, 15, 16, 23, 28, 43, 48, 51, 54, 56, 59; barrier construction, 215, 217; barrier sensors, 220; Camp Mai Loc base, 328; mud creation, 220, 221; U.S.-built Red Devil Road, 331; VPA prisoners' camps, 255; weather patterns, 182; *See also specific passes*
antiaircraft units, 88, 313–14, 352, 363, 369, 370
antiwar movement (France), 3
antiwar movement (U.S.), xv, 134–38, 223–31, 362, 364–67; and Cambodian invasion, 301–3; disorganization of, 230; marches and protests, 138, 227–29, 294, 301, 302, 364–67; militant faction, 301–2, 364–65; national moratorium (1969), 293–94; and Nixon administration, 287, 288, 292, 293–94, 364–65, 373; self-immolations, 223–24; and Tet Offensive, 283–84, 301; as war policy influence, 373, 377
ant simile, 4, 27–29, 181, 196, 309
Aptheker, Bettina, 136, 137
Aptheker, Herbert, 135–36
Arbatov, Georgi K., 130–31
Arc Lights (B-52 strikes), 151, 152, 158, 159, 162, 192, 194, 196, 239, 270, 275, 303–5; Laotian invasion support, 332, 339, 346, 347, 349, 352; Trail attacks, 368

Army of the Republic of Vietnam (ARVN), 5, 7, 11, 13, 88, 185; border control force, 31, 33, 40, 41, 42, 47, 49; Cambodian invasion, 300, 316; casualties, 22, 115; cross-border missions, 88–89; cross-border training, 104–8; desertions, 226; Duc Co battle, 116–21; and Easter offensive, 370; final blow to, 373; high command shortcomings, 341–42; Ia Drang counteroffensive, 149–51; and Indian country, 152; and Laos invasion, 206, 316–20, 322–23, 325, 328, 332, 334, 335, 336, 338–43, 345–50, 358, 359–60; Laotian pullout, 348–49, 351–56; Laotian secret agreement, 25, 81; Montagnard recruits, 47, 48, 49, 51, 58; North Vietnamese spies among, 271–72; performance report statistics, 359–60; Plei Me battle, 144–47; Ranger scouting parties, 18; strength increases, 18–19, 31–32, 35, 47–48; and Tet Offensive, 247, 248, 249, 250; U.S. advisers, 35, 41, 322; U.S. financial aid, 18, 30, 31–32, 33, 47, 206; Viet Cong as threat to, 17, 21, 22, 93, 94–95; VPA ambushes of, 109–10; *See also* LLDB; I Corps; Strategic Technical Directorate; II Corps; *specific units*
Arnett, Peter, 117, 119, 120
A-Ro, 58–59, 115, 277
ARVN. *See* Army of the Republic of Vietnam
A Shau valley, 13, 51, 58–59, 115, 186, 191, 193, 202, 206, 274, 366; as Laotian offensive focus, 344–45, 361; U.S. mud making, 221; VPA attack, 185–86; VPA traffic to, 238
assassinations, 15, 59, 64, 68, 284
Associated Press, 308
Attopeu, 7, 24, 162, 186–87, 206, 207, 222, 283; VPA capture of, 361

B-3 Front command (Central Highlands), 193, 247
B-52 bomber, 116, 117, 155, 160, 358; fire power, 151; Laos base, 158; SOG Hornet Force, 202; tonnage dropped in 1972, 371; *See also* Arc Lights
B-57 bomber, 305
Baig, Mirza Munir, 245
Baldwin, Daniel, 250, 261
Baldwin, James L., 348
Ball, George, 4, 62, 64, 69, 70, 92, 96
Bam, Colonel. *See* Vo Bam
Ban Bak, 308, 309, 368
Ban Dong, 24, 190, 256, 263, 313, 333, 352; battle destruction of, 336, 338, 339, 354–55; current condition, 378
Ban Houei Sane, 23–25, 82, 161, 190–91, 355; VPA attack on, 245–46, 247, 258, 259, 261

Ban Karai Pass, 153, 187, 191, 195, 222, 238, 273, 305, 358–359; VPA anti-aircraft defense, 313, 369; VPA pipelines into Laos, 340; VPA truck traffic through, 367
Ban Me Thuot, 48, 49, 86, 94, 144, 274; VPA 1975 attack on, 373
Bardshar, Frederic A., 290–91, 295
Barr, Colonel (U.S.), 261
Barrel Roll operations, 92–93, 102, 110
barrier plan. *See* McNamara Line
Base Area 611. *See* Muong Nong
Bataillon Volontaire 33 (Laos), 161, 245, 246, 257–58
Bear Cat (airstrip code name), 104, 107
Beckwith, Charles A. ("Chargin" Charlie), 117, 142–47
Beecher, William, 285
Beijing (government). *See* China
Benge, Michael, 255–56
Ben Hai River, 10, 11, 157, 373
Benjamin, Jack, 346
Bennett, John, 142–43
Berry, Sidney, 342
bicycles, 2, 27, 44, 45, 85
Bien Hoa, 89, 92, 101, 252, 271
Big Victory, Great Task (Giap), 208–9, 234, 235–36, 242
binh tram units, 112, 188–94, 202, 220, 221
Blackburn, Donald D., 97, 153, 155
Blackjack operations (SOG), 200
Black Panthers, 301
Black Wolves. *See* 2d Battalion (VPA)
Blair, John D. IV, 185
"blocking belts," 368
Blood, Hank, 255
Bodenhorn, Philip, 328–29
bo dois. See Vietnam People's Army
Bohr, Harper, 245
Bolovens Plateau, 7, 24, 41, 52, 57, 60, 103, 186, 207, 319; VPA offensive, 361, 367
bombing. *See* air activity
borders; Cambodian-Vietnamese, xiv, 20, 28–29; Chinese-Soviet dispute, 363; Chinese-Vietnamese, 124; Laotian-Vietnamese, xiv, 20, 23, 34; MACV clearance plan, 210–11; significance to different groups, xiv–xv; surveillance camps, 58–59; Trail's route along western, 13, 151; U.S. aerial photography, 78, 80; U.S. efforts to seal, 19–20, 32, 33, 35–41, 48–49, 51, 54, 58, 70, 81; VPA security measures, 188, 190; *See also* cross-border operations
Boun Oum, Prince, 53
Boyer, Alan L., 276
Braden, Ted B., 83
Bragg, Percell, 275
Brandon, Henry, 289
Bravo Troop incident, 356–58
Bray, David, 148

Breeding, Gene L., 356–57
Brezhnev, Leonid I., 130, 132, 364
Bright Light (SOG), 153, 154, 200, 255, 276
Brink Hotel (Saigon), 93
Broe, William V., 31
Brown, George R., 276
Brown, Tim, 279
Broyles, William, 209
Bru tribe, 11, 190, 258, 260, 332
Buddha, 311, 315
Buddhists, 183, 223
Bui Diem, 366
Bui Long Bac, 85
Bui Phung, 84
Bui The Dung, 338, 354
Bui Tin, 26, 27, 44, 45–46, 56, 232, 311,
    325, 326
Bui Van Cuong, 150
Bundy, McGeorge, 54, 70, 90, 93, 131, 137,
    224; Franco-Vietnamese war analogy,
    4; as hardliner, 68; Kennedy adminis-
    tration post, 34; McNamara and, 212;
    Pleiku attack response, 95; resignation
    from Johnson administration, 205; Ros-
    tow as national security successor, 159
Bundy, William P., 36, 64–65, 69, 92, 100
Bunker, Ellsworth, 248, 291, 318, 331,
    342, 348, 349, 351
Burchett, Wilfred, 308, 360
Busby, Horace, 68
Butler, James, 345
Butt Stroke (amphibious plan), 212
BV-33. See 33rd Volunteer Battalion

C-47 aircraft, 186–87, 305
C-123 "Provider" aircraft, 107, 161, 186
C-130 aircraft, 305–6, 331, 332
Cabell, Charles P., 7–8
Calgon, 220–21
Ca Lu (Firebase Vandegrift), 263, 281, 282,
    326–30, 358
Cambodia, 295–303; ARVN incursions,
    316; and Franco-Vietnamese War, 16,
    25; Hanoi supply runs, 296–98; and Ia
    Drang battle, 148, 150; legal bar to
    U.S. troops in, 322, 334, 343; Nixon
    port blockage plan, 291; SOG missions
    into, 153, 199, 200, 273, 274, 297,
    298, 344; Trail link, 155, 191; U.S.
    bombings of, 270, 299–300, 315; U.S.
    invasion of. See Cambodian invasion as
    separate listing below; Viet Cong training
    camps, 28–29; Viet Minh border bases,
    7; Vietnamese border, xiv, 20, 28–29;
    VPA transportation group, 191
Cambodian invasion (1970), xv, 299–303,
    315, 317, 322, 367
Cam Lo, 327, 370
Camp, Richard D., 211, 244
Campbell, "Shaky," 260
Camp Fay, 108
Camp Holloway, 119

Camp Mai Loc, 282–83, 327, 328, 330, 335
Cam Ranh, 140, 227
Cao Khac Nhat, 323
Cao Van Vien, 206, 249, 252, 272, 300,
    317, 322, 323, 338, 342, 347, 348
cargo planes. See air activity
Caristo, Fred, 271–72, 273
Carper, William C. III, 105, 106
Cav. See 1st Cavalry Division
Cavanaugh, Stephen E., 283
CCN. See Command and Control North
cemeteries, 46, 379
Central Highlands, 7, 24, 25, 37, 101; Cen-
    tral Intelligence Agency and, 88, 97,
    126; as conflict center, 56, 115, 116,
    328; Delta project effectiveness, 108;
    Easter offensive, 370; flights into, 56;
    1st Cavalry Division in, 140, 141–51;
    Green Beret buildup, 57–58; Ia Drang
    valley battle, 146, 147–51, 283; MAC-
    SOG Command and Control base, 283;
    MACSOG missions, 274; Montagnards,
    47, 48; North Vietnamese B-3 Front
    command, 193, 247; Northwest Fron-
    tier Force concept, 40–41, 47; Plei Me
    battle, 143–47; Route 14 through, 5,
    6map, 7, 277; Trail paved roads to,
    371; Viet Cong and, 15, 16, 95; village
    defense program, 49–51; VPA troop
    action, 109–10; as Westmoreland
    focus, 140
Central Intelligence Agency (U.S.), 6–8, 17,
    24, 41, 48, 51, 61, 97, 108, 196, 197,
    272; antiwar movement study, 230; on
    Cambodia-Hanoi supply links, 296,
    297–99; on Chinese activities, 126–29;
    on Chinese/Soviet intervention poten-
    tial, 54, 73–74, 130; Combat Intelli-
    gence Team, 79; covert activity in Laos,
    34, 57, 102; covert operations in
    North, 77–78, 79; Defense Department
    ties, 30; on domino theory, 289; infil-
    tration network estimates, 18, 20;
    Laotian invasion objections, 321, 322,
    367; Laotian strategy, 37, 39, 40, 52,
    69; South Vietnamese commando
    force, 31; on Soviet aid to Hanoi, 130,
    132–33; special guerrilla units, 375;
    on Trail bombings, 88, 304; Trail pro-
    jections, 368; Trail-watch program, 51,
    78, 79, 92, 101, 102, 157, 187, 193;
    Viet Cong activity reports, 39; Village
    Defense Program, 48–49, 50, 58; See
    also Special National Intelligence
    Estimates
Central Military Command (North Viet-
    nam), 10, 11, 14, 25–26
Chaisson, John, 248, 280
Changsha Province, 124–25
Chap Le, 95
Chavane, 60, 308, 368
chelating chemicals, 221

chemical warfare, 161, 220, 221
Chenla II, 316
Chen Yi, 53, 74, 75
Chicago 7, 294
China, 123–29; and Cambodia, 298; intervention possibility, 54, 77, 126–27, 128, 207, 208, 225, 229, 264, 325, 376; and Korean War, 197; as Laotian neutrality signatory, 53; North Vietnamese relations, 8, 73–77, 86, 123–29, 133, 294, 362–63; and North Vietnamese war strategy debate, 231, 232, 233; protracted war advocacy, 233; Soviet split, 129, 132, 233, 363; as threat to Southeast Asia, 37, 39, 64, 76; troops in Vietnam, 161, 363; Vietnam intervention terms, 125; Vietnam War role, 73–77, 133, 161
"choke points," 268
Cholon, 249, 252
Chou En-lai. *See* Zhou Enlai
Christopher, Warren, 230
Chu (Vietnamese sapper), 193
Chu Dang Chu, 11, 13
Chu Huy Man, 143, 146, 147, 148, 149, 150, 151, 152, 193
Chu Pong, 117, 121, 143, 146, 147, 149, 150, 154, 191, 203, 274, 371
Church, Frank, 322
CIA. *See* Central Intelligence Agency
CIDGs. *See* Civilian Irregular Defense Groups
CINCPAC (Commander in Chief Pacific), 18, 79, 81, 86, 96, 104; and Cambodian invasion, 300; and 1st Cavalry operations, 140; and SOG operations, 153, 202, 219; Trail bombing division, 156; *See also* McCain, John; Sharp, U.S. Grant
Citadel (Hanoi), 109
Civilian Irregular Defense Groups, 50, 51, 57, 83, 103, 106, 116, 143, 161, 185, 190; Camp Mai Loc losses, 328; at Kham Duc, 277, 278–79; and Tet Offensive, 258, 259
Civil Rights Act of 1964, 70, 136
civil rights movement (U.S.), 136, 137, 223, 228, 284, 365
Clapton, Eric, 241
Clay, Lucius D., Jr., 304–5
Clifford, Clark, 226, 283, 295
cluster bombs, 158
coastal patrol system, 40, 296
coercive diplomacy, 61, 62
Colby, William E., 40, 49, 50, 79, 326
Cold War; Kennedy focus on, 29, 30; Laos in context of, 29–30, 68; Rostow views on, 61, 62; Vietnam in context of, 30–31, 68, 73, 77, 229, 289, 362–64, 376, 377
Collins, J. Lawton, 38
Collins, John, 243

colonialism, 4
Combined Intelligence Center Vietnam (Saigon), 249, 250, 254
Command and Control North, 261, 277, 281, 283, 343, 344–45
Command and Control South, 274, 276
Commander in Chief Pacific. *See* CINCPAC
Commando Hunt campaigns, 269, 270, 304, 309, 313, 315–16, 367, 368–69, 370, 378
Commando Lava operation, 221
Communications Data Management System. *See* Dutch Mill
Communist governments. *See* China; Lao Dong Party; North Vietnam; Soviet Union
Communist Party of Laos, 15
Communist Party of the Soviet Union, 134
Communist Party of the United States of America, 135–36
Compatriot project (rainmaking), 222–23
Congress, U.S., 224–25, 226, 322
Congress for Racial Equality, 136
Connally, John, 349
Connolly, David, 381
Con Thien, 201–2; battle, 190, 208, 219–20
Cooper, Chester L., 53, 93
Cooper, John Sherman, 322
Cooper-Church Amendment, 322
Coral Sea (aircraft carrier), 95–96, 110, 370
Co Roc Mountain, 191, 263, 318, 333–35, 355
Costello, Nancy, 116
counterinsurgency, xiv, 18, 30, 34, 35, 38, 39, 54, 140
Covey operations, 306
Cowles, Donald, 323, 344
Craig, William T., 51
cross-border operations, 92, 97, 101–8; in Cambodia, 153, 273, 274, 298; initial U.S. plan, 80–84, 88–89, 90; Leaping Lena failure, 82–84, 89, 92, 104, 117, 365; public revelation of, 228; SOG losses, 276; SOG resources, 200; SOG teams, 151–55, 198–203, 271–76, 283; South Vietnamese Special Forces, 344; Sullivan opposition, 103, 273–74; Tet effects on, 274–77, 283; training program, 103–8; unilateral American vs. South Vietnamese participants issue, 322; U.S. backhanded admission of, 340; *See also* Daniel Boone; Forward Air Controllers; Prairie Fire
Cuba, 132
Cuban Missile Crisis (1962), 129, 131
Cu Chi, 252
Cultural Revolution, 362
Cushman, Robert E., 237, 248, 259, 262, 280, 281
Custer, George, 148

D16 Battalion (NLF), 250, 252

dac cong (sappers), 312–13
Dak Pek, 283
Dak Seang, 328
Dak To, 7, 17, 110, 116, 149, 152, 193,
    222, 308; battle, 193, 235, 236, 361
Dalton, Roy C., 161
Da Nang, 81, 93, 193, 338; airfield hits,
    110, 252; air traffic, 306, 307; blockage
    of paths to, 58; as French air base, 3; as
    MACSOG center, 108, 160; Tet attack
    refugees, 260; Tet attacks on, 247, 248,
    256, 281; as Tiger Hound's main base,
    160; VPA troop movements to, 239, 278
Da Nang conference, 262–64
Da Nang Diary (Yarborough), 307
Dang Vu Hiep, 94, 131
Daniel Boone (SOG mission), 153, 199,
    200, 203, 273, 274, 297
Dao Vu, 193
Davidson, Phillip B., 248, 360
Davis, Raymond G., 326
Davison, Michael S., 299–300
DeBruin, Eugene, 24
Defense Communications Planning Group,
    214
Defense Department, U.S. *See* Pentagon
Defense Science Board (U.S.), 237
defoliants, 161, 220, 327
Delta project, 82–84, 89, 104, 108, 142–43,
    198, 270; Duc Co battle, 117–21; Khe
    Sanh patrols, 190; Plei Me battle,
    144–47
Demilitarized Zone (DMZ), xiv, 5, 6map, 7,
    16, 190; barrier construction, 212, 213,
    215, 216map, 217, 219; defense esti-
    mates, 40; land mines remaining in,
    379; Nixon ground strikes plan, 291; as
    Nixon settlement boundary, 287; SOG
    activity in, 154, 273–74, 283; Tally Ho
    operation north of, 162; Tet attacks on,
    247; Trail crossing of, 10, 11, 13, 14,
    256; U.S. reprisal bombings north of,
    95–96; U.S. troop defense line, 39; Viet
    Cong divisions, 15, 41; VPA advances,
    236, 370; VPA pipeline, 340
Democratic Republic of Vietnam. *See* North
    Vietnam
Depuy, William E., 149
de Silva, Peer, 79
Detachment A-101 (U.S. Special Forces),
    327, 328
Detachment A-105 (U.S. Special Forces),
    276
Detachment A-113 (U.S. Special Forces), 49
Dewey Canyon II operation (Laos),
    329–30, 333, 343, 344, 364
Dewey Canyon III (antiwar demonstra-
    tion), 365
Dexter, Ronald J., 202
Dickson, Edward A., 95
Diem, President. *See* Ngo Dinh Diem
Dien Bien Phu, 1–5, 15–16, 25, 33, 43, 66,

69, 85, 143, 325, 365, 374; significance
    in Vietnam War, 236, 241–42, 244,
    246, 341; VPA "Iron Division" at, 339
Diffusion of Power, The (Rostow), 67, 68
Dinh Khanh, 118
Diplomacy (Kissinger), 287–88, 317
"Division Commander's Story, A" (Mau),
    194
DMZ. *See* Demilitarized Zone
Doan Van Quang, 89
Dobrynin, Anatoli, 131, 132
Do Cao Tri, 300
domino theory, 289
Dong. *See* Pham Van Dong
Dong Ha, 169, 327, 329, 332, 338
Dong Hene, 367
Dong Hoi, 14, 95, 110, 157, 162, 195, 373
Do Ngoc Nhan, 360
Dong Sy Nguyen, 84, 269, 313, 372, 373
Doody, Thomas, 334
Do Van Loi, 323
Dow Chemical Corporation, 220
draft protests, 227
Dragon's Jaw bridge, 156
Drea, Edward J., 303
Drell, Sidney, 220
drug use, 357
DRV. *See* North Vietnam
Duc Co, 149, 150; battle, 116–21, 143, 144,
    145, 241
Duck Hook (proposed operation), 290–95,
    301
Duell, Mike, 157
Dulles, Allen, 31
Doumer Bridge (Hanoi), 109
Duncan, Donald, 82–84, 106, 228
Dung, Lieutenant Colonel (ARVN), 338
Dunlap, Lee, 260
Durbow, Elbridge, 17–18, 19
Dutch Mill surveillance center (Task Force
    Alpha), 218–19, 268, 269, 270, 303–4,
    306, 308, 368, 369, 378
Duval Sands, 255
Dye Marker (barrier code name), 217, 219,
    260–61

8th Airborne Battalion (ARVN), 252, 339,
    354, 355
8th Battalion, 66th Regiment (VPA), 149
8th Cavalry (U.S.), 148
8th Light Infantry Battalion (RLA), 24
11th Air Assault Division. *See* 1st Cavalry
    Division
11th Armored Cavalry (ARVN), 354, 355
11th Combat Engineers (U.S.), 327
11th Infantry (U.S.), 328
11th Mike Force Company (U.S.), 278
XVIII Airborne Corps (U.S.), 140
18th Medical Battalion (VPA), 184–85
18th Regiment (VPA), 110, 181, 190
83rd Special Operations Group (VNAF),
    107

88th Regiment, 308th Division (VPA), 339
E268 Regiment (VPA), 251
803d Regiment (VPA), 352
806th Battalion (VPA), 254
808th Battalion (VPA), 109
812th Battalion, 324B Division (VPA), 333
834th Air Division (U.S.), 331
Eagle's Nest (communication site), 199–200
Easter offensive (1972), 366, 367, 368, 369, 370–71
Eisenhower, Dwight D., 29–30, 31
Eisenhower administration, 7, 35, 38, 61
Eldest Son project (SOG), 203
electronic warfare, 218, 220–23, 237, 268–69, 303–9, 375 (*see also* sensors)
elephants, xiv, 24, 44, 46, 181, 221
Ellsberg, Daniel, 229
El Paso plan, 210, 211, 243, 263
Emerson, Henry, 117

1st Airborne Brigade (ARVN), 354, 355
1st Armored Brigade (ARVN), 332, 336, 354, 355, 360
1st Battalion, 5th Cavalry (U.S.), 149
1st Battalion, 7th Cavalry (U.S.), 148
1st Battalion, 9th Marines (U.S.), 220, 242
1st Battalion, 11th Infantry (U.S.), 328–29
1st Battalion, 77th Armor (U.S.), 329
1st Brigade, 5th Infantry Division (Mechanized) (U.S.), 328, 329
1st Brigade, 101st Airborne Division (U.S.), 140
1st Cavalry Division (Airmobile, U.S.), 115, 121, 139, 140–42, 147, 151, 206, 207, 212, 235, 274, 297; "aerial rocket artillery," 346; Cambodian incursion, 300; first night air assault, 148; and Khe Sanh, 261–62; move into Central Highlands, 146–51; serious losses, 149
1st Division of People's Volunteers (China), 125
1st Infantry Division (ARVN), 332, 334, 341, 343, 346, 347, 352, 353, 358
1st Marine Battalion (South Vietnam), 119
1st Marine Regiment (U.S.), 281, 327
1st Observation Group (ARVN), 31, 42, 104
1st Radio Battalion (U.S. Marines), 237
1st Regiment, 2d Division (VPA), 279, 333
1st Squadron, 9th Cavalry (U.S.), 147
4/77 Aerial Rocket Artillery (U.S.), 346
4th Armored Cavalry (ARVN), 354, 359
4th Battalion, 1st Infantry (ARVN), 347, 359
4th Infantry Division (U.S.), 193, 200, 206, 274
4th Regiment (VPA), 254
4th Sapper Battalion (VPA), 312–13
Fifth Brigade (U.S.), 328
5th Interzone. *See* Interzone 5
5th Marine Battalion (South Vietnam), 119
5th Special Forces Group, 57, 106, 108, 117, 142, 145, 160, 200–201; Camp

Mai Loc, 282–83; cross-borders operations, 273–76; and Kham Duc, 277, 278, 280; and Tet Offensive, 258–59
14th Combat Engineer Battalion (U.S.), 330
14th Sapper Battalion (VPA), 312
40th Regiment (ARVN), 95
48th Regiment (VPA), 183
49th Infiltration Group (VPA), 43–44
52d Aviation Battalion (U.S.), 119, 150
52nd Regiment (VPA), 183
53d Regional Force Company (Saigon militia), 251
56th Air Commando Wing (U.S.), 262, 269
57th Assault Helicopter Company (U.S.), 275–76
426th Sapper Regiment (VPA), 239
470th Transportation Group (VPA), 191, 299
497th Tactical Fighter Squadron (U.S.), 306
559th Transportation Group (VPA), 56, 278, 299, 315, 373; antiaircraft defense, 313; network of way stations, 45–46; reorganization, 112; strength estimates, 84, 370; Trail defense, 188, 190; and Trail inception, 14–16, 20, 26, 44; Trail maintenance and improvements, 191, 193
F-4 Phantom aircraft, 313
FACs. *See* Forward Air Controllers
Faith, Don, 198
Fall, Bernard B., 242
Farm Gate, 54, 91, 95
Farrar, Raymond E., 329
FAR troops. *See* Royal Laotian Army
FBI, 225, 230
Feller, Charles, 276
Felt, Harry D., 57, 86
Firebase 6, 361
Fire Base 30, 340, 342
Fire Base 31, 339, 340, 341
Firebase Bravo, 355
Firebase Brown, 352, 353
Firebase Delta I, 348, 352
Firebase Fuller, 330
Firebase Liz, 347
Firebase Lolo, 345–46, 347, 350
Firebase Moon, 352
Firebase Sophia, 347
Firebase Vandergrift. *See* Ca Lu
Fire Break (Laos invasion plan), 207
First Team (U.S. Army), 115, 141, 147, 151
Fisher, Bernard D., 186
"flashers," 268
flexible response policy, 31, 35–36
flooding (induced), 220, 222
FOB. *See* Forward Operating Base
Footboy (SOG project), 153, 200, 201, 273
Force Reconnaissance battalions (U.S. Marines), 198, 244
Forrestal, Mike, 89, 99
Fort Benning, Georgia, 139, 140, 142

Forward Air Controllers (FACs), 159–62, 196, 202, 238–39, 270–71, 280, 282; and daylight campaigns, 306–7; *See also* Ravens

Forward Operating Base (FOB)-3 (SOG), 243, 259–60, 261

fraggings, 357

France, 17, 70, 72

Franco-Vietnamese War (1945–54), 1–5, 10, 16, 29, 33, 86, 109, 182; Royal Laotian Army creation, 23–24; significance to U.S. policy planners, 4–5, 66, 241; significance to Vietnamese, 27–28, 374; supply lines, 2–3, 11, 13, 25; *See also* Dien Bien Phu

Freedom of Information Act (U.S.), xv

Freedom Porch operation, 371

French Expeditionary Corps, 86

French Indochina War. *See* Franco-Vietnamese War

Fulbright, J. William, 224–25, 230

Fulbrook, Jim E., 346

Full Cry plan (Laos), 206–7

Garner, Joe, 51, 271

Garwin, Richard R., 220

Gaspard, George ("Speedy"), 273

Gavin, James W., 242

Geneva accords (1954), 4, 5, 8, 10, 72

Geneva accords (1962); barrier seen as violating, 213; China and, 74; Harriman and, 30, 52–53, 98–99; net effect of, 55–56; objectives and results, 98–99; Rostow policy and, 63–68; Russia and, 5, 63–64, 71–72; signatories, 53; and U.S. subsequent policy, 69, 82, 103, 285, 377

Gia Lam, 109, 184

Giap, General. *See* Vo Nguyen Giap

Gilpatric, Roswell, 31–32, 34, 40

Ginsburgh, Robert N., 264

Glover, Douglas, 274–75

Godley, G. McMurtrie, 319, 320

Golden Eagle operation, 103

Graham, Daniel O., 248

Graham, James C., 297–98

Great Britain, 36

Great Society, 70, 77

Greek Civil War, 64

Greeley, Richard S., 217, 218

Green Berets (U.S. Special Forces), 63; A Shau camp defense, 185, 186; Camp Mai Loc, 327, 328; Central Highlands buildup, 57–58; cross-border operations, 80, 103, 104, 106, 108, 228; Duc Co battle, 116–20, 241; high command, 57; Indian country operations, 151–63; and Kham Duc, 277, 281; and Khe Sanh battle, 244; Khe Sanh camp, 25, 58–59, 116, 326; Ladd and, 258–59; Lang Vei camp, 190; Montagnard program, 49–52, 58, 60; NLF/VPA

pressure against, 115; Plei Me camp siege, 143–47; risk-takers, 117; and SOG operations, 200, 201; and Tet Offensive, 255; Trail patrols, 52; *See also* Delta project

Griffen, Billy, 356

Gromyko, Andrei, 134, 364

Groom, John F., 160

Grose, Peter, 285

Group 559 (VPA), 18

Group 959 (VPA), 18, 53–54, 56

guerrilla warfare; bases, xiv–xv, 7; and Hanoi's war strategy, 231; infiltrator profile, 43–44; outside aid to, 19; potential attack route, 5–7; tactics, 15, 22; theories on, 19, 30, 31, 45, 64, 232–33, 234; *See also* counterinsurgency; infiltrators; National Liberation Front; Viet Cong

Gulf of Siam, 7, 295, 296

Gulf of Tonkin, 3, 184, 209; Chinese policy, 123; incidents, 55, 68, 74, 75, 85, 88, 99, 109, 124, 129

Ha Dong, 256, 312

Haig, Alexander M., 293, 317, 318, 319, 322, 331, 349, 353

Hainan Islands, 124, 126

Haiphong, 3, 35, 37, 206; U.S. bombing of, 196; U.S. harbor mining plan, 291, 293; U.S. mining of harbor, 370–71

Halberstam, David, 62, 95

Haldeman, H. R. (Bob), 290, 292, 301, 302, 317, 319, 323, 351, 365

HALO technique, 199

Hambleton, Iceal, 379

Ham Nghi, 339, 342, 353

Hancock (aircraft carrier), 93, 95

Hannah, Norman B., 60, 69, 81

Hanoi (as government). *See* North Vietnam

Hanoi (city), 3, 15; ambience, 109; bombing during Kosygin visit, 96, 130–31, 195; bombing intensity (1967), 196, 206; children evacuees to, 257; Christmas 1972 bombing, 371; three American visitors, 134–36, 223

Han Trinh Province, 113

Hardnose project, 51, 78, 79, 92, 101, 102, 157

Harkins, Paul D., 40, 51

Harriman, W. Averell, 30, 52–53, 54, 56, 64, 67–68, 69, 98, 99

Harvard University, 226, 302

Hatchet Force missions (SOG), 274, 308, 333

Ha Tinh Province, 28, 113, 185, 196

Havens, Ritchie, 241

Havoc forces (SOG), 153, 200

Hayden, Tom, 134, 135, 137, 284

Haymaker forces (SOG), 153, 200

Headhunters (U.S. Army scouts), 147, 148

Headshed traffic advisories, 268

Heavy Hook (Nakhon Phanom), 276

Hector I and II (ARVN commando teams), 187

helicopters; and assault missions, 139, 144, 147; and Kham Duc base, 280; and Laotian evacuation, 352, 353, 354, 362; and Laotian offensive, 330, 332, 334–35, 340, 342–46, 349; and Saigon evacuation, 373; SOG losses, 276, 283; and SOG missions, 152, 153–54, 199, 200

Helms, Richard M., 229, 230, 321, 331

Hemingway, Jack, 342, 354

Henderson, Larry, 261

Hendrickson, Paul, 230

high-altitude teams, 199

High Port plan, 207, 210, 243

Hill, John G., 329–30, 356–57

Hill 456, 340

Hill 861, 245

Hill 881 South, 237, 245, 246

hill tribes. See Montagnards

Hilsman, Roger, 54, 56, 64, 69, 74

Hmong tribe, 69, 102, 319

Hoa Binh, 182

Hoang Minh Thao, 193

Hoang Dan, 237

Hoang Dinh Cang, 314

Hoang Minh Thai, 249

Hoang Van Thai, 26, 236, 372

Hoang Xuan Lam, 217, 255, 322, 323, 332, 336, 338, 339, 347, 353, 361; on Laotian offensive phases, 351; leadership limitations, 342

Ho Chi Minh, 5, 8, 9, 27, 64, 76, 134, 232, 324; as "Asian Tito," 137; birthplace, 184; Chinese visit and talks, 124–25; death of, 362–63; and invasion speculation, 308; Nixon threat to, 290; presidential palace, 109

Ho Chi Minh Trail; achievements of, 374; air attacks on, 46, 97, 194, 195–97, 238–39, 270–71, 303–9, 313, 315, 367–68, 370, 371, 377–78; airmobile harassment of, 140, 141; antiaircraft defenses, 313–14, 369; area map of, 12; armed reconnaissance strikes against, 93, 99, 110–11, 156, 158; and ARVN commando plans, 41, 42; bicycle supply loads down, 2, 27, 44, 45, 85; bombing advocates, 66, 88, 89–90; bombing damage repair, 191; bomb-proofing proposal, 45; border troop defenders, 188; Cambodian trail link. See Sihanouk Trail; capabilities, 226; clinic way stations, 256; condition in 1973, 371–72; condition in 1998, 378–79; cutting efforts and failures, 325–26, 378; damage estimates vs. continued supply runs, 304; defense/security measures, 186–88, 269, 313, 358–59, 369–70; as difficult target, 151–52;

electronic countermeasures, 220–23, 268–69, 303–9, 375; enlargement and improvements, 25–27, 44–45, 60, 72, 80, 82, 84, 86, 87map, 111–13, 114map, 156–57, 181, 188, 191, 192map, 193, 361–62, 367–68, 370, 371–72; FACs action against, 159–62; first infiltrators down (1959), 13, 14; first VPA casualty, 18; forging of, xiv, 10–16, 22; hardship conditions, 15, 23, 26, 43–44, 111, 157; improvisations and ingenuity, 181–82, 220, 223, 269; increased movement down, 27, 45–46, 56, 109–10, 111, 113, 121, 156–57, 181–83, 185, 196, 208, 312, 372; intelligence inklings of, 17, 33; intelligence reports on, 41, 63, 77–78, 80, 82, 83–84, 102–3, 155, 157, 191, 193, 226, 238, 268, 307–8; Khe Sanh's proximity, 242, 247; Kim Lu supply warehouse, 15; Laos section, 15–16, 23–27, 55–56, 155, 191; as Laotian invasion objective, 323; length of, xiv, 374; as literary subject, 194; massive traffic on, 372, 374; McNamara barrier plan, 212, 268–70; mechanized equipment introduced on, 193; memorial cemetery, 379; as metaphor and microcosm, xv; as military attack coordination factor, 247; most successful interdiction strike on, 308–9; movements northward, 255–57, 312, 371–72, 374; narrowness of, 27, 44; natural obstacles on, xiv, 16, 23, 28, 43, 44, 46, 111, 157, 220; North Vietnamese policy split on, 44–45; paved roadways, 371, 372; personal stories of, 193–95; porters, 84–85, 112, 113; prisoner marches northward, 255–56, 374; raids on. See cross-border operations; relay stations, 13, 45–46, 371–72; SAMs defense, 133, 134, 358–59, 369–70; as secret operation, 10–11, 13–14, 18, 26, 112; significance of, xiii, xv, 151, 373–75, 376, 377–78; SOG reconnaissance teams, 151–55, 160, 161, 197–203; South Vietnamese link, 191, 193; Soviet policy and, 133–34; strategic importance of, 325–26; supply movements South, 111, 316, 339, 368, 372, 374; and Tet Offensive, 236–39, 250, 253, 283; total tonnage shipments, 374; trailmakers, 84; trailmakers's journeys down, 26, 27, 45–46; truck convoys, 314–15, 367; U.S. limited attack proposal, 77; and U.S. Nakhon Phanom base, 267–69; U.S. road-watch teams, 52, 78, 79, 92, 101, 102, 157, 187, 193, 238, 273; U.S. weather modification, 220–23; as victory highway, 371–74; VPA and Pathet Lao control of, 56; See also infiltrators

Hogan, Darrel, 364
Holdridge, John, 293
Holm, Richard, 157
Holmes, David H., 162
Hon Gay, 124
Hong Kong, 81, 298–99
Hong Ky, 116
Hoover, J. Edgar, 225
Hornet Force missions (SOG), 153, 154, 200, 202, 260, 274
Hornig, Donald F., 220, 222
Ho Thieu, 88, 105, 245–46
Hubbell, Wilson, 379
Hue, 15, 16, 58, 81, 236, 362; A Shau approach to, 185; Easter offensive attack on, 370; Tet attack on, 247, 253–57, 261, 276–77
Hue Ngoc Tran ("Harry"), 346, 347, 348, 352, 353, 354
Hughes, John C., 94
Hughes, Stanley S., 281
Hughes, Thomas L., 74, 75–76, 128, 130
Humphrey, Hubert, 96, 131
Huong Van Ba, 157, 251
Huston, Charles G., 276
Hutchinson, Clair, 295
Huu Mai, 1, 2–3

Ia Drang (river), 144, 149
Ia Drang valley, battle of the, 146–51, 158, 198, 206, 207, 224, 226; as factor in Hanoi war strategy, 231
Igloo White (code name), 268
Illinois City (code name), 217
Inchon landing, 209
India-4 (target), 155
India-China war (1962), 129
Indian country, 151–52, 161–62, 163, 181–203, 237, 239, 274–76, 277
indigenous peoples. See Montagnards; specific tribes
Indochinese war. See Franco-Vietnamese War
Infiltration Group 53 (VPA), 109
infiltrators, xiv, 5, 8–9, 27–29, 56, 59–60; ants as simile for, 4, 27–29; as core of Vietnam War, 19; early successes in villages, 21–22; first down Trail, 13, 14; Green Beret preventive programs, 51; Hanoi's revised strategy (1964), 85, 109; improved conditions for, 157; increases along Trail, 27, 45–46, 238; Laotian responses, 24; McNamara Line against, 212–20; original plans, 11, 13; personal examples, 27–29, 85, 86; profile of, 43–44; seaborne arm, 14; South Vietnamese interception, 15, 18–19, 33; U.S. intelligence of, 18, 20, 78; U.S. intelligence profile of, 183–84; U.S. plans to counter, 39–41, 63–67, 68, 70; VPA units, 109–10, 181, 182, 196; See

also guerrilla warfare; Ho Chi Minh Trail; Viet Cong
Inner Circle (Haig), 293
Institute for Defense Analysis, 213
insurgency theories, 19, 232–33, 234
International Control Commission, 66, 72, 112, 155
International Day of Protest (1965), 138
International Voluntary Services, 49
Interzone 5 (Annam), 10, 11–13, 25, 45, 110, 116, 143, 256
Iowa team. See Team Iowa

Jackson State University, 302
Jarai tribe, 58
JASON Group, 213
Johnson, Harold K., 100–101, 139, 140, 141, 198
Johnson, Lyndon B., 133, 158, 196; and antiwar movement, 134, 135, 137, 226–27, 230, 284; and barrier plan, 217; bombing halts, 134, 135, 224, 265, 282, 285, 295; and bombing of North Vietnam, 96, 130–31, 132, 138, 196, 206; and cross-border operations, 81, 90; and Dien Bien Phu, 4, 241; domestic programs, 70, 77, 136; economic development offer, 135; escalation ambivalence, 70–71, 77, 90; escalations, 92, 95–97, 115, 210, 234; free action zone widening, 198; ground troops decision, 110–11, 126, 127; and Harriman, 69; information control, 226–27; and Laos invasion plan, 206–7, 263, 264, 282; and Laotian Trail bombing plan, 88, 90; and McNamara, 230; memoir, 226–27; and North Vietnam invasion proposals, 207–10, 212; NSAM-358 document, 214; political concerns, 70, 77, 92, 95, 210, 224, 265, 282; public opinion and, 115, 137, 227, 228–29; and rainmaking operation, 222–23; and reprisal raids, 95–96, 99; and Rostow, 65, 68, 76–77, 159, 205; Saigon team, 100; Soviet relations, 129, 131; threats against, 227; withdrawal from politics, 265, 283; Zhou warning to, 124; See also Johnson administration
Johnson, Robert H., 64, 71, 72, 74
Johnson, U. Alexis, 100, 320, 360
Johnson administration, 61–84, 88–90, 91–103, 110–11, 115, 130–31, 139–63, 205–31, 262, 289, 376; bombing escalation advocates, 158–59, 205–6; escalation alternatives, 91–93; and French failure in Vietnam, 4; groundwarfare alternatives, 206; ineffectiveness of war policies, 206; manipulation of public opinion, 225, 226, 228, 283; muddled approaches, 219; Vietnam policy differences, 69–72, 207, 208

Joint Chiefs of Staff (U.S.), 55; and amphibious invasion proposal, 210; barrier plan criticisms, 213, 214, 215, 219;
and bombing of North Vietnam, 96;
and bombing of Trail, 88, 89, 156; and
Cambodian invasion, 300; on Chinese
threat, 76; cross-border operation approval, 103; on Dien Bien Phu, 241;
force emphasis in war policy, 289, 290;
and Laotian invasion, 334, 348; and
MACSOG, 97, 160; mud and rainmaking approval, 221, 223; and Nixon
policies, 292, 295; and Taylor-Rostow
plan, 35, 36, 37, 39; on terms for ending war, 289; troop requests, 92,
100–101, 265, 283; troop withdrawals,
316; and U.S. airmobile action, 140;
See also Taylor, Maxwell D.
Joint Task Force 728 (Pentagon), 214, 217
Jones, Bruce E., 249–50, 251
Jorden, Willim J. (Bill), 41, 42, 46–47
Jungle Jim (U.S. air unit), 41, 54

Kamm, Henry, 311, 378
Karnow, Stanley, 233
Karozov (Russian ambassador), 129
Kattenburg, Paul M., 69, 70, 71, 89
Katu tribe, 115
Kaysen, Carl, 212–13
Kearns, Chuck, 155
Kelly, Francis J. ("Splash"), 200
Kennedy, John F., 136, 315; assassination
of, 59; counterinsurgency strategy, 30;
flexible response policy, 31; inaugura-
tion persona, 29; national security ad-
visers, 35, 36, 37, 48; and Rostow, 61,
63, 67; Southeast Asian policy, 29,
30–31, 35–37, 39, 40, 41, 52–53, 54,
55; South Vietnamese relations, 33
Kennedy administration, 29–42, 46–49,
52–60, 98; foreign affairs lineup, 62;
Laotian policy, 34, 69, 285 (*see also*
Geneva accords); national security ad-
visers, 34–35, 61; public trust of, 227;
Rostow and, 61–68; significance of
Taylor-Rostow mission, 38; Viet Cong
strength estimates, 22; Vietnamese
strategy failures, 47
Kennedy, Robert F., 100, 265, 284
Kent State University, 302
Kerry, John, 365
Kerwin, Walter T. ("Dutch"), 248, 281–82
Ketchie, Scott, 370
Kha (as term), 51
Kham Duc, 58–59, 89, 97, 102, 108, 201,
222; as MACSOG launch point,
151–52, 160, 277–78, 280; MACSOG
loss of, 283; and Tet Offensive, 277–81;
U.S. evacuation of, 280–81
Kha tribe, 23, 27
Khe Sanh, 11, 15, 33, 43, 88, 89, 116, 153,

191, 202, 210; air strip, 331, 332; barrier sensors, 219, 254, 260, 261, 270,
277, 375; Dien Bien Phu parallels, 242;
fall of village, 261; Green Berets' camp,
25, 58–59, 110, 155, 244, 326; land
mines remaining in, 379; and Laotian
invasion, 318, 329, 330, 331, 332, 334,
342, 343, 352, 359, 364; refugees from
Tet attacks, 257–60; relief operation,
262–64; road access, 327, 331; SOG
activities, 160–61, 260–61, 275, 277;
SOG pullout, 281–83; Tet siege of,
254–56, 261–62, 265, 269, 277, 280,
281, 334–35; as Trail stopover, 372;
Trail victims' memorial cemetery, 379;
U.S. pullout, 359; VPA assault on, 358;
VPA deceptive moves against, 236–37,
238, 241, 242, 243–47; VPA destruction
of U.S. outposts, 190, 211; VPA SAM
site, 369; VPA shelling of, 161, 352
"Khe Sanh Front," 239
Khmer (people), 51
Khmer Rouge, 299
Khrushchev, Nikita, 30, 67, 129
Kien Giang, 231
King, Jerry, 52
King, Martin Luther, Jr., 228, 284
Kingsmen (U.S. air battalion), 334
Kinnard, Harry W. O., 139, 140, 141, 142,
147, 149, 206
Kissinger, Henry A., 223, 226, 284–85, 295;
on antiwar movement, 302–3; on
Hanoi offensive signs, 368; and Laos
operation, 316–23, 331, 345, 348–51,
360; memoir, 321, 349, 360; Soviet
policy, 363; Vietnam strategy state-
ments, 287–89, 290, 291, 292–93, 294,
301, 359, 376
Kline, Joe, 334
Kolesnik, N., 133
Komer, Robert W., 205, 248
Kompong Som. *See* Sihanoukville
Kong Le, 98
Kontum, 110, 116, 193, 200; as ARVN fron-
tier force base, 40–41, 58, 89; Easter of-
fensive attack on, 370; as MACSOG
base, 283; Tet attack on, 247; as Tiger
Hound launch site, 160; Viet Cong ac-
tivity, 16
Kontum-Pakse highway, 7, 17
Korean War, 98, 100, 133, 152, 197–98,
209, 293, 357
Koster, Samuel W., 280
Kosygin, Alexei, 96, 130–31, 132, 195
Krulak, Victor H., 79

Ladd, Jonathan (Fred), 201, 258–59, 278,
280, 298
Laird, Melvin R., 289, 290, 292, 293, 316,
319, 320, 321, 331, 333, 340, 351
Lake, Anthony, 293

Lam, General. See Hoang Xuan Lam
Lam Son 719 (code name). See Laotian invasion
Landing Zone Albany, 149
Landing Zone Delta, 334
Landing Zone Hope, 346, 347
Landing Zone Hotel, 334
Landing Zone Stud, 281
Landing Zone X Ray, 148–49, 224
land mines, 32, 378–79
Lang Vei, 244, 246, 330, 356; battle, 190; Camp Mai Loc as rebuilding of, 282–83, 335; fall to VPA, 255, 256, 258–60, 261, 281
Lansdale, Edward G., 30–32, 33, 36, 38, 39, 40
Lao Bao, 23, 37, 86, 255, 336, 352, 356
Lao Bao prison, 23, 231, 355–56
Lao Dong Party, 8, 9, 15, 21, 26, 44–45, 132; Ninth Congress, 59; pro-Chinese wing, 73, 86; VPA troop membership, 183; war policy resolutions, 86, 231–32, 235
Laos; air activity, 66–68, 158, 191, 202, 265, 269, 270, 303, 305, 313, 377, 378; air activity restrictions, 162; air interdiction strikes, 93, 97, 110, 111, 156, 162, 163; armed reconnaissance flights over, 92–93, 99; Attopeu base, 186–87; as B-52 bomber base, 158; Ban Houei Sane's strategic position, 25; barrier construction, 212–15, 218–19, 260–61, 273; cease-fire (1962) lapses, 53–54; Communist successor government, 378; first U.S. plane shot down over, 66, 67, 68; French war strategy, 1, 3, 16; Green Beret tribal recruits, 51–52; internal political factions, 9, 15, 23–25, 29, 53, 56, 98; invasion of (1971). See Laotian invasion as separate listing below; invasion proposals (1967), 206–7, 210–12, 214, 219, 243, 258, 262–63, 281, 285, 286, 376; land mines remaining in, 379; legal bar to U.S. troops in, 322, 334, 343; neturalist government, 34, 53, 128, 319; neutralization negotiations, 39–40, 52–54 (see also Geneva accords (1962); neutralization and partition proponents, 98–99; North Vietnamese border patrols in, 188; secrecy of U.S. activity in, 154, 155; South Vietnamese concerns, 7–8; South Vietnamese scout teams in, 57; South Vietnamese secret agreement, 81–82; strategic location, 20; Tchepone's strategic importance, 27; Tet Offensive effects, 255, 257–58, 283; Trail route through, 15–17, 23–28, 85, 86, 110, 155, 181, 191, 256, 314; U.S. FACs program, 158–62; U.S. interventionists, 63, 66, 68, 72, 76, 80–81 (see also subhead invasion pro-
posals above); U.S. policies, 29–30, 35–37, 39, 48, 54–55, 63, 66, 68, 69, 72, 76, 78–79, 80–81, 97–102, 157–58, 273–74; U.S. weather modification, 220–21, 222; Viet Cong bases, 36; Vietnamese border, xiv, 20, 23, 24; VPA antiaircraft defense, 313; VPA presence in, 16, 24, 25, 41, 56–57; See also cross-border operations; Pathet Lao; Royal Laotian Air Force; Royal Laotian Army
Lao Theung, 51–52, 102, 157, 187
Laotian invasion (1971), xv, 303, 309, 316–25, 328–50; Abrams's attempts to restart, 348; air power, 330, 331, 332, 334–35, 339, 340, 342, 345–46, 349–50, 352, 355, 358–59, 367; antiaircraft defenses, 340, 352; armored attack along Route 9, 336–38; ARVN limitations, 341–42, 359–60, 362; ARVN losses, 352–53, 355; ARVN pullout, 347–48, 351–56, 358, 359, 362; assessment of, 376, 377; Hanoi's prior inklings of, 322–23; Hanoi's strategic response, 324–26, 339, 343, 349, 350, 352, 354–55, 359; Hanoi's troop losses, 361; initial phase, 328–29, 331, 333, 343, 344; map, 337; Nixon's statistics on, 359–60; pipeline discovery, 339–40, 341; planning for, 316–23; subsequent assessments, 349–50, 360–61; U.S. antiwar protests, 364–65, 367; U.S. Bravo troop incident, 356–58; U.S. troops-in-Laos prohibition, 322, 334, 343, 344, 364
Lao tribe, 97
"Lao wind," 43
Larsen, Stanley R., 147
Lartéguy, Jean, 4
La Theung (people), 51
Layton, Gilbert, 49
Leaping Lena mission, 82–84, 89, 92, 104, 106, 117, 228, 365
Le Chuong, 253
Le Dinh Thao, 312
Le Duan, 10, 14, 15, 45, 59, 73, 86, 115, 211, 324; Chinese high-level talks, 124; visit to Soviet Union, 132; war strategy, 232, 233
Le Duc Tho, 232, 233, 236, 356
Leftwich, William G., Jr., 119, 120
LeMay, Curtis E., 160
Lemnitzer, Lyman D., 36
Lemnitzer, William, 293
Leonard, Theodore, 80, 82, 84
Le Trong Tan, 324–26, 333, 339, 340, 341, 343, 347, 350, 352, 361; Ban Dong assault, 354–55
Lima Site 85, 262
limited-war theory, 61, 71
Lindquist, John, 327–28
Linebacker II operation, 371
Lingle, Terry K., 107–8

Liu Shaoqi, 124
LLDB (ARVN Special Forces), 50, 82–84, 89, 116; cross-border operations, 103–8, 344; at Kham Duc, 277; Khe Sanh base, 161; spies among, 272
Locke, Fred, 220–21
Loc Ninh, 236, 370, 371
Lodge, Henry Cabot, 68, 71, 80
Long Thanh, 103–8, 153
Lon Nol, 299
Lost Platoon, 148–49
low-light vision systems, 375
Lownds, David E., 244, 257–58, 260
LSTs (large landing ships), 209
Lubinitsky, G., 133
Lucky Dragon (U-2 program), 196
Luc Luong Dac Biet. *See* LLDB
Lutz, Charles, 352
Lynd, Staughton, 135, 136, 137, 223
Lynn, Lawrence, 293, 294
LZ. *See* Landing Zone

M-41 tanks, 119, 121
MAAG. *See* Military Assistance Group
MacArthur, Douglas A., 98, 100
MacLeod, Doug, 330
MACSOG (Studies and Observation Group), 82, 88–89, 92, 97, 208; air wing, 153–54, 308; anti-espionage measures, 271–72; autonomous position, 100; Cambodian forays, 153, 199, 200, 297, 298, 344; Camp Mai Loc base, 282–83; cross-border operations training, 103–8 (*see also* cross-borders operations); effectiveness vs. restrictions on, 203; establishment of, 80; heroic role played, 375; highly classified status, 154, 201; Joint Personnel Recovery Center, 255 (*see also* Bright Light); Kham Duc launch point, 151–52, 160, 277–78, 280; Khe Sanh launch point, 160–61, 260–61, 275, 277; Khe Sanh patrols, 190; Khe Sanh replacement, 282–83; limited role in Laotian invasion, 333, 343–44; losses (1968), 276; Meadows as legend with, 152; Nakhon Phanom base, 267–69; nerve gas use allegations, 308; personnel recruitment, 201; reconnaissance teams. *See* Spike teams; reputation, 152; Singlaub as commander, 197–201, 273–74; Sontay raid, 317; STRATA progam, 272–73; strength of, 108; tactical focus change, 344; and Tet Offensive, 255, 259, 274, 276–77, 281; Tet-related losses, 278–83; Tiger Hound as mirror, 160; Trail patrols, 103, 187; *See also* Nickel Steel; Prairie Fire; Spike teams
Mac Thang Long, 340
MACV. *See* Military Assistance Command Vietnam

Mai Loc. *See* Camp Mai Loc
Maine team. *See* Team Maine
malaria, 16, 44, 312
Mallet operation, 271
Malony, Mike, 157
Mandatory Declassification Review, xv
Mao Zedong, 19, 76–77; guerrilla warfare formula, xiv–xv; Hanoi relations, 124, 363; Ho Chi Minh talks, 124–25; Nixon contacts, 363; protracted war advocacy, 233; Soviet talks, 130
Markham, James, 24
Martin, J. Graham, 203
Mason, Robert, 142
Mataxis, Theodore C., 93–94, 95, 118, 119–20, 144
Mauldin, Bill, 94
Mayday protest (1971), 364–65, 366
McBride, William P., 219, 268
McCain, John, 291, 292, 295, 296, 297, 298, 299; amphibious attack on North Vietnam advocacy, 338; and Laos invasion, 315, 317, 318, 321, 348
McCarley, Eugene, 308
McCarthy, Eugene J., 265
McCone, John, 74, 88, 97
McGarr, Lionel C., 32, 40, 47, 115
McGhee, George, 62
McKean, William ("Bulldog Bill"), 117, 144, 145, 185
McMillan, William G., 220
McMullin, Craig, 323, 339
McNamara, Marg, 224
McNamara, Robert S., 77, 80, 82, 100, 139, 221, 304; and antiwar movement, 223–24, 226, 229–30; on Ball, 69; barrier plan. *See* McNamara Line; bombing policy, 95, 156, 195; and Bundy, 212; and Chinese threat, 76; departure from Defense post, 230; as diplomacy advocate, 70; and Lansdale memo, 30; on Laos invasion option, 211, 219, 376; restrospective views on Vietnam policy, 4–5, 137, 212–13, 226, 233, 235, 375, 379; technological orientation, 212, 220; Trail bombing proposal, 88, 90; and Vietnam involvement, 4, 31, 55, 65, 70–71, 78, 79, 96, 226, 229
McNamara Line (barrier plan), 212–20, 226, 245, 260, 283, 326; assessment of, 376; costs, 217; as electronic warfare testing ground, 375; Igloo White code name, 268; land mines remaining from, 379; Nakhon Phanom as command post, 267–69; new "blocking belts," 368–69; physical description, 213; sensors, 218–19, 220, 267, 273; VPA destruction of, 370; VPA reactions to, 219–20, 237, 358
McNaughton, John T., 91, 100
Meadows, Richard J. (Dick), 152, 155, 199
Mekong Delta, 5, 11, 17, 21, 23, 28, 34, 35;

Mekong Delta (*continued*)
  airfields, 39; Rostow's proposed occupation of, 64, 66; U.S. defense plans, 55, 69; VPA threat to, 367
Mekong River, 135, 267
Mertel, Kenneth D., 142
Meyer, Edward C., 141
Meyer, Richard, 329, 330
MiG-19 (aircraft), 75
Mike Forces (SOG), 198, 200, 258, 259, 277, 279
Mikoyan, Anastas I., 67, 68
"Mikoyan and Laos" memo (1962; Rostow), 63–64, 67
Military Assistance Advisory Group (U.S.), 19, 212
Military Assistance Command Vietnam (U.S.), 51, 79, 80, 82, 88, 94, 96, 97, 101, 102, 104, 120, 121, 159, 183, 188, 261; Abrams command, 265, 281–82; airmobile division, 115, 140–41; amphibious invasion plans, 323; and barrier construction, 215; and Cambodian/Hanoi link, 296, 297, 298, 299; and Cambodian invasion, 300; Khe Sanh withdrawal, 281–83; and Laotian invasion (1971), 317–19, 321, 323, 333, 348; and Laotian invasion proposal (1967), 207, 263–65; Laotian pipeline study, 339–40; LSTs, 209; and permissible activities over Laos, 191; and SOG operations zone, 153; and Tet Offensive, 243, 246, 247, 249–50, 251, 258, 259, 262, 278; troop increases, 210, 226, 234–48; Westmoreland's reassignment from, 265, 274, 281; York operation, 210–11; *See also* Westmoreland, William C.
Military Region Tri-Thien-Hue (MRTTH), 253–54
Miller, Franklin, 372
Minh Loi, 194
Minh Nhat Phung, 21
Mitchell, John N., 365
Mitchell, Vance, 369
Mitre Corporation, 217, 218
mobile strike forces, 50–51
Momyer, William W. ("Spike"), 248, 269, 274
Mon (people), 51
monsoons. *See* rainstorms
Montagnards, 47–52, 58, 94, 103, 115, 119, 120, 149, 332; defined, 48; at Kham Duc, 277, 278, 279; and Kontum defense, 370; South Vietnamese recruitment of, 47, 48, 49, 51; U.S. recruitment of, 40, 40–41, 48, 50–51, 57, 58, 60, 108, 185; in Vietnam People's Army, 143; *See also* Civilian Irregular Defense Groups
Moore, Harold G., 143, 148, 149
Moorer, Thomas, 300, 317, 319, 320, 321,

331, 348, 359; on ARVN pullout from Laos, 351, 352; on Nixon's response to Arc Light bombings, 349–50
Morakon, Pete, 116
Morris, Jim, 201
Morris, Roger, 293, 294
Morrison, Norman R., 223–24
Morrow, William D., Jr., 361
Moses, Robert, 136, 137
mudmaking, 220–21
Mu Gia Pass, 24, 25, 28, 43, 44, 56, 78, 153, 162, 189map; *binh tram* units, 188; CIA road-watch teams, 102, 157; as proposed U.S. bombing target, 88, 304–5; U.S. air interdiction strikes, 110, 156, 158, 162, 195, 196; U.S. rainmaking, 222; U.S. road-watchers, 187, 238, 256, 273; VPA antiaircraft units, 190, 369; VPA pipeline through, 339–40; VPA SAMs defense, 358–59
Munich crisis (1938), 62
Muong Nong (Base Area 611), 80, 83, 86, 191, 318, 335, 351; ARVN attack, 358; Spike teams and, 344; U.S. bombing attack, 239; as U.S. proposed bombing target, 88
Muong Phine, 86, 88, 93, 102, 157, 347
Muong Sen, 86
Muscara, Carmen, 41
Muscle Shoals (barrier electronics), 218, 237
Myers, Wayne D., 186
Myrdal, Gunnar, 62

9th Airborne Battalion (ARVN), 336, 354, 355
9th Infantry Regiment (ARVN), 357
9th Marines (U.S.), 220, 242, 338
19th Border Defense Battalion (VPA), 24
91st Airborne Ranger Battalion (ARVN), 144, 147
95th Regiment (VPA), 109–10, 185
919th Military Air Transport Squadron (DRV), 26–27, 56, 60, 86
923rd Border Battalion (VPA), 188
925th Border Battalion (VPA), 188
927th Local Force Battalion (VPA), 24, 188
968th Division (VPA), 361
Nakhon Phanom, 157, 218, 245, 306; as MAKSOG base, 267–69, 276, 283, 308, 368–69
Nambo tribe, 253
Nam Dinh, 183, 184
Nam Ha Province, 184
Nam Tha, 53–54
napalm, 88
Napé pass, 88, 110, 153, 158, 196, 256, 273, 305
Na Phao, 188
National Liberation Front, 15, 47, 135, 191, 287; Cambodian operation, 295–99; campaign against Green Beret camps, 115; children evacuees to Hanoi, 257,

312; creation of, 22; forces expansion policy, 59; and Giap's war strategy, 233; Hanoi relations, 77, 86, 111; infiltrator assignments by, 28–29; Montagnards and, 49, 50, 58; rapid growth (1960–1963), 29, 56; Soviet relations, 129, 130; strengthening of, 77; and Tet Offensive, 236, 247, 249, 250–53, 254, 276; *See also* Viet Cong
National Security Action Memoranda (U.S.), 31, 41, 81, 214, 226
National Security Council (U.S.), 34–35, 41–42, 80, 89, 368; cross-border operations, 81, 82; hardliners, 68; Johnson's advisers, 159; Kennedy's inner group, 48, 51, 61, 62–63; and Laotian invasion plan, 331; and Nixon policy alternatives, 289, 291–92, 293, 301; and sustained bombings, 96
National Security Study Memorandum (NSSM)-1, 288–89, 296, 297
National Security Study Memorandum (NSSM)-99, 316–17, 319, 322
NATO. *See* North Atlantic Treaty Organization
naval action. *See* seaborne activity
Naval Ordinance Testing Station, 221
Naval Security Group, 298
Nelson, Robert B., 280
nerve gas (sarin), 308
New Left, 135, 137
Nghe An Province, 183, 184
Ngo Dinh Diem, 5–9, 16, 32, 81, 278; assassination of, 59, 63, 68; birthplace, 231; distrust of Montagnards, 51; failure to supply border force, 47; and infiltrators from North, 20, 45; opposition groups, 22, 223; roadbuilding projects, 5, 7, 17, 48, 116, 326, 370; and Taylor-Maxwell mission, 38–39; unpopularity of, 29, 33; U.S. financial aid to, 18, 33; U.S. support of, 29, 30, 41, 52
Ngo Dinh Nhu, 49, 50, 52, 57, 59, 63
Ngok Tavak, 277–79, 280, 281
Ngo Quang Truong, 150, 370
Ngo Vinh Long, 247, 251, 254
Ngu (Vietnamese woman), 193
Nguyen Cao Ky, 106–7, 214, 215, 249, 272, 319, 322
Nguyen Chi Thanh, 86, 231, 232, 236, 242, 356
Nguyen Danh, 11, 13, 16
Nguyen Dinh Thuan, 7–8, 17, 33, 47
Nguyen Duc Mau, 194
Nguyen Duong, 10
Nguyen Duy Hinh, 336, 355, 360
Nguyen Huu An, 149
Nguyen Khac Huynh, 235
Nguyen Khac Vien, 195
Nguyen Khanh, 68, 71, 81, 82
Nguyen Minh Chau, 10
Nguyen Phuong Nam, 315

Nguyen Quang Sang, 194
Nguyen Qui Duc, 254–55, 256
Nguyen Quoc Kanh, 254
Nguyen Tan Mieng, 250
Nguyen Thanh Linh, 313
Nguyen Thanh Mai, 193, 195
Nguyen The Chat, 195
Nguyen Trong Luat, 145, 146, 150, 336, 338, 339, 342, 354, 355–56, 358
Nguyen Trong Tan, 254
Nguyen Van Chung, 353
Nguyen Van Doanh, 110
Nguyen Van Huyen, 366
Nguyen Van Minh, 312–13
Nguyen Van Nang, 27–29, 253
Nguyen Van Nho, 249, 250, 251
Nguyen Van Thieu, 214, 247, 249, 252, 300; election race, 351, 362, 368; and Laotian invasion, 318, 320, 322, 323, 335, 338–39, 341; Laotian invasion halt, 347, 348, 349; Laotian invasion strategy, 342; North Vietnamese spies on staff, 272; and Vietnamization policy, 289–90
Nguyen Van Tho, 340, 341, 354
Nguyen Van Toan, 348
Nguyen Van Vinh, 9–10, 13, 232; on Laotian invasion, 360–61
Nguyen Viet Sinh, 85
Nguyen Xuan Hoang, 209
Nhan Dan (newspaper), 73, 130
Nha Trang, 37, 57, 82, 83, 104, 107, 117, 201; as first Tet attack target, 247; as MACSOG center, 108, 270; signs of VPA movements, 246
Nhuan (Vietnamese woman), 193
Niagara operation, 245
Nickel Steel (SOG), 273–74, 285, 340
Niesen, Paul H. ("Tiny"), 335
Nitze, Paul H., 264
Nixon (film), 288
Nixon, Richard M., 226, 276; and air strike program, 350; and antiwar movement, 292, 294, 301, 302–3, 364–65, 366, 367; bombing of Cambodia, 299–300; Chinese negotiations, 363; election in 1968, 284–86; and election of 1972, 359, 362; and Laotian invasion, 319, 321, 323, 329, 345, 359; on Laotian invasion, 349; stated objectives in Vietnam, 287; statements vs. reality, 288–89, 291–92; statistical Vietnam success claims, 351, 359–60; Vietnam policies, 289–93; view of CIA, 321
Nixon administration, 287–309, 315–25, 328–50, 368, 376; and air power, 359–60; and antiwar protests, 365–66, 373; Cambodia and Laos invasions, xv, 299–305, 315–25, 331, 338–41, 345, 348–50, 351, 353, 364, 367; China policy, 362; congressional restraints on, 322; Laird and Rogers vs. Kissinger

Nixon administration (*continued*)
policies, 288–93; "linkage" outlook,
363–64; peace negotiations, 362; rainmaking project, 223; Soviet relations,
363–64; troop withdrawals, 316; war
escalation, 284, 285–86
NLF. *See* National Liberation Front
Nolting, Frederick, 38, 40, 49, 67
No More Vietnam (Nixon), 359
Norodom Sihanouk. *See* Sihanouk, Prince
Norodom
North Atlantic Treaty Organization, 33–34,
100
North Vietnam; American antiwar movement and, 134–36; bombing of (1972),
371; bombings of. *See* Rolling Thunder;
Pruning Knife; and Cambodia, 295–96;
Chinese relations, 8, 73–77, 123–29,
133, 231, 233; Chinese relations
changes, 362–63; covert CIA penetration program, 77–78; escalations of war,
86, 109–15; final offensive (1975),
373–74; land reform (1955–57), 8; as
Laotian neutrality agreement signatory,
53; offensive (1972). *See* Easter offensive; post-French war policy, 8; propaganda, 195, 197, 231; protracted war
strategy, 59, 231, 287; SOG teams
within, 273; Soviet aid, 132, 132–34;
Soviet relations, 8, 96, 129, 130–31,
132, 134, 231, 233; spies among South
Vietnamese regime, 272; supply line inception, 9–10 (*see also* Ho Chi Minh
Trail); terms for "just" Vietnam solution,
73; Trail's significance to, xiii–xiv; U.S.
diplomatic warnings to, 72; and U.S.
proposed strategic invasions of, 35, 68,
207–10, 285, 286, 338, 376, 377; and
U.S. proposed sustained bombing of,
91, 92, 95, 291–93; U.S. rainmaking
over, 222–23; war strategy, 231–33,
373; *See also* DRV Air Force; reunification; Viet Cong; Vietnam People's Army
Northwest Frontier Force, 33, 40–41, 47
Nosavan, General. *See* Phoumi Nosovan
Nouphet, Colonel (Laotian commander),
102
NSAM. *See* National Security Action
Memoranda
NSC. *See* National Security Council
NSSM. *See* National Security Study
Memorandum
nuclear warfare, 35, 64, 76, 136, 364
Nung tribe, 50, 58, 89, 108, 153, 161, 185,
186, 202, 275, 277
Nuttle, David A., 49

I Command (U.S.), 238, 245, 247
I Corps (ARVN), 116, 185, 208, 217, 253,
254–55, 260, 262, 269, 276, 318, 323;
Haig inspection report, 353; Truong

leadership, 370; weakness of Ham
Nghi post, 342
101st Airborne Division (U.S.), 140, 198,
324, 330, 333, 334, 342, 345, 346,
348, 349, 354
101st Regiment (VPA), 110
108th Artillery Group (U.S.), 329
130th Antiaircraft Battalion, 313
137th CIDG Company (U.S.), 277
147th Vietnamese Marine Brigade, 252
155th Assault Helicopter Company (U.S.),
144
173d Airborne Brigade (U.S.), 120, 193
196th Light Infantry Brigade (U.S.), 280
Office of Strategic Services (U.S.), 197
oil pipeline. *See* pipeline
oil strikes, 204, 205
"Old Man's Trail", xiii
Olsen, Betty, 255
Operation. *See* key word
"Option V" idea, 89
Osnos, Peter, 367
Ouang Binh, 16

pacification programs, 32, 50–51, 226, 243,
264, 326 (*see also* Village Defense
Program)
pacifism, 136, 223
Pakistan, 124
Paksane, 34, 51
Pakse, 17, 24, 34, 55, 82
Paksong, 361
Palmer, Bruce, 243
Panther Teams, 268, 270, 305, 306, 315, 368
parachute teams, 199
Parrot's Beak, 29
Pathet Lao, 23, 24, 51, 53–54, 56, 67, 84,
86, 98, 102, 161, 187, 313; and ARVN
invasion of Laos, 332–33
peace moves; Abrams and, 282; deadlocked
negotiations, 362; Hanoi political fac-
tions, 232; Hanoi's four-point proposal,
135; and Laos operation, 317; Mc-
Namara's negotiations recommenda-
tion, 230; Nixon's settlement terms,
287, 288; talks inception, 285
Pegasus operation, 262–64, 274, 277, 327
Peitun-Yunnani air base, 75
Pentagon (U.S. Defense Department); anti-
war protests outside of, 223-24, 228,
229–30; cautious approach, 55; Special
Operations Office, 30; on U.S. troops in
Laos or Cambodia, 322; Vietnam policy
reviews, 31–32; *See also* Laird, Melvin R.;
McNamara, Robert S.
Pentagon Papers, 32, 36, 229
People's Army. *See* Vietnam People's Army
People's Daily (newspaper), 74–75
People's Liberation Armed Forces, 22
People's Liberation Army (China), 75, 76,
363

People's Republic of China. *See* China
People's War, People's Army (Giap), 233
Perfume River, 254, 362
Persian Gulf War (1991), 118, 149, 304, 366, 375
Pham Dinh Cung, 314
Pham Tien Duat, 194
Pham Van Dong, 8, 9, 72–73, 125; delegation to Russia, 130; meeting with three Americans, 135; as pro-negotiations, 232; warning on war's outcome, 367
Pham Van Phan, 43–44
Pham Van Phu, 323, 341, 342, 343, 347, 352, 353
Phan Khac Hy, 373
Phan Khac Tue, 188
Phan Trong Tue, 84, 111–12, 113, 191
Phong (watchmaker), 1
Phong Nam Group (VPA), 28
Phouma. *See* Souvanna Phouma
Phoumi Nosavan, 23, 34, 52, 53–54, 81, 82, 98
Phu Bai, 260, 262
Phuong Nam, 253
Phu Tho, 11
Phu Yen Province, 312
Pike, Douglas, 209
Pincushion project, 51
pipeline, 339–40, 341, 371
PLA. *See* People's Liberation Army
Plain of Jars, 23
Pleiku, 37, 56, 113, 116, 149, 193, 210; and Dien Bien Phu, 141; Duc Co battle, 116–20; Plei Me battle, 144–47, 151; and Tet Offensive, 246, 247, 248; Viet Cong attack on, 94–95, 115, 130–31
Plei Me, siege of, 143–47, 148, 149, 152, 224, 336, 338
Plei Mrong, 57–58
Policy Planning Council (U.S.), 54, 62
Ponomarev, Boris, 129
Popeye (rainmaking code name), 221–22
porters, 84–85, 112, 113, 146
Port Huron Statement, 137
Potts, William C., 298, 317, 333
Poveda, Carlos A., 356
Powell, Colin, 366
Powers, Thomas, 224
Practice Nine (barrier project), 214, 215, 217, 221
Prairie Fire (SOG), 198–99, 200, 201, 218–19, 273, 274, 283, 307, 340, 343, 345
Presidential election of 1964 (U.S.), 70, 77, 91, 92
Presidential election of 1968 (U.S.), 210, 265, 268
Presidential election of 1972 (U.S.), 359, 362
Project. *See key word*
Protestant missionaries, 11, 116
Pruning Knife (operation), 290–91, 292
psychological warfare, 32–34, 61, 208

PT-76 light tanks, 341
public opinion, 115, 137, 226, 227; distrust of Nixon's Vietnam policy, 364, 366–67; growing majority antiwar sentiment, 224–25, 283, 294, 301, 303, 377; Johnson administration manipulation of, 225, 283; *See also* antiwar movement
"Puff the Magic Dragon" (AC-47), 186–87
Pushkin, Georgi, 67
Pye, Lucien, 62
Pyle, Jesse, 94

Quakers, 136, 223
Quamo, George, 259, 260, 261
Quan Doi Nhan Dan (newspaper), 311, 314, 358
Quang Binh Province, 14, 16, 78, 109, 111, 208, 313, 314; as Giap's and Diem's birthplace, 231; SOG reconnaissance, 153, 273; U.S. bombing effects on, 195, 196, 265; VPA buildup, 208; VPA occupation, 277–78, 325
Quang Nam Province, 16, 41, 110, 312
Quang Ngai Province, 16, 18, 27, 49, 256
Quang Tin Province, 58–59, 278
Quang Tri City, 370
Quang Tri Province, 11, 40, 43, 109, 110, 155, 326; and Easter offensive, 370; land mines remaining in, 379; and Laotian invasion command post, 332, 342; MACSOG base, 283; and Tet Offensive, 246, 253, 272
Quebec-1 (target code), 274–75
Qui Nhon, 95, 131, 142, 149, 246, 247
Quyet Thang Training Center, 104

radar, 32, 75, 313, 315, 375
radio communications, 199–200, 345
Radio Hanoi, 73, 77
rain forest, 28, 43
rainmaking, 220, 221–23
rainstorms, xiv, 13, 43, 111, 157, 182, 221, 222, 367
Ramparts magazine, 228
RAND Corporation, 54
Ranger (aircraft carrier), 95
Ravens (Tiger Hound FACs), 159–62, 196, 197, 239, 246, 260, 268, 269, 270–71, 305, 307
Reconnaissance Teams. *See* MACSOG; Team *headings; specific code names*
Red Devil Road, 331
Red River, 109
Red River Delta, 109, 125, 182, 183, 184, 312
Republic of Vietnam. *See* South Vietnam
Resolution 12 (Lao Dong Party), 232
Resolution 13 (Lao Dong Party), 235
Resolution 15 (Lao Dong Party), 9
Reunification Hotel (Hanoi), 134
"Reunification Trail" (Ho Chi Minh Trail), 13

reunification of Vietnam; capture of Saigon as goal, 19; DRV diplomatic proposals, 9; as Geneva 1955 agreement provision, 4; as infiltrators' goal, 27; as North's prime objective, 20, 73
Rhadé tribe, 40, 49, 276
Ridgway, Matthew B., 242
Road 547 (South Vietnam), 191
roads, 3, 43; Diem building project, 5, 7, 17, 48, 116, 326, 370; Laotian improvements, 112–13; North Vietnamese passages into South, 25–26 (*see also* Ho Chi Minh Trail); projects in North Vietnam, 113, 125; U.S. intelligence on, 32; *See also* Route *headings*
Roberts, Elvy B., 300
Robinson, Rembrandt C., 293
Rockefeller, Nelson A., 293
"Rockpile" (Thon Son Lam), 327, 331
Rodman, Peter W., 288, 293
Rogers, William P., 289, 290, 293, 320, 321, 331
Rolling Thunder (bombing operation), 96–97, 109, 131, 162, 265; Christmas-New Year pause, 134, 224; CIA assessment, 289; civilian effects, 195, 378; destruction claims, 159; goal of, 156; Hanoi propaganda reports, 195; intensification advocates, 158–59; Johnson approval, 206; Johnson halt of northern regions, 265, 282; Johnson's full halt of, 282, 285, 295, 363; Laotian bombing comparison, 349; McNamara's recommendation to halt, 230; numbers and destruction claims, 163, 196–97; protest marches against, 138; Route Package 1 target, 195–96; as sustained operation, 96, 101, 125–26, 130–33, 158–59, 195, 291; tonnage dropped, 377; U.S. aircraft lost, 125–26; VPA antiaircraft defense, 313
Romine, Richard E., 202
Romney, George, 226
Rosson, William B., 52, 262, 280
Rostow, Walt Whitman, 61–68; aggressive policy, 34–35, 36, 41, 54, 55, 61–68, 71, 72, 76–77, 158–59, 229, 282, 285–86, 287, 375, 376; bombing strategy, 205–6; career background, 61, 62, 205; on Dien Bien Phu, 241; influence on Vietnam policy, 375, 376; information manipulation, 228, 283; invasion of Laos advocacy, 54, 76, 264, 318; invasion of North Vietnam plan, 207–8, 209–10, 212, 214; Johnson administration post, 205, 227; Kennedy administration post, 34; mission to Vietnam, 37–42, 46, 63; papers on Vietnam, 30, 36, 37, 71, 76–77; policy break with Lansdale, 38; policy themes, 64–65; policy thesis, 71, 89; restrospective 1969 remarks, 285–86; U.S. ground

forces in Vietnam advocacy, 92; and weather-modification projects, 222
Route 9, 11, 25, 26, 32, 56, 88, 103, 109, 153, 162; armed reconnaissance mission over, 93; armored attack along, 336–38; ARVN activity, 33; barrier parallel to, 213, 215; Bravo troop incident, 356–58; defoliation of, 161, 327; Green Beret post, 58–59; history, 326–28; Laotian border crossing, 23, 24; and Laotian invasion (1971), 323, 325, 326, 328, 329, 330, 332, 333, 336–38, 352, 353, 355; and Laotian invasion plans (1967), 206, 207, 263; and Laotian invasion withdrawal, 354, 355; Laotian terminus, 326; MACV attack plan across, 210–11, 262; position of, 5, 6map, 336map; primitive conditions, 211, 327, 338; refugees, 260; Trail's crossing of, 13, 15, 256, 324, 372; U.S. blockage plan, 100–101, 127–28; U.S. improvements, 326–28, 330–31; and U.S. Khe Sanh pullout, 359; VPA activity, 41, 190, 367; and VPA attacks on Khe Sanh, 255; VPA widening of, 372
Route 12, 111, 188
Route 14, 16–17, 145, 277–78; position of, 5, 6map, 7
Route 15, 43, 44
Route 19, 95, 110, 117, 120
Route 23, 93
Route 110. See Sihanouk Trail
Route 912, 256
Route Package 1 (Vinh Linh/Quang Binh), 195–96
"route segments," 268
Rowley, Charles S., 314
Roy, Jules, 242
Royal Laotian Air Force, 86, 88, 91–92, 102, 155, 156, 160, 161
Royal Laotian Army, 15, 23-24, 25, 33, 162, 186, 187, 191; Ban Houei Sane enclave, 245–46; Tet attacks on, 255, 257–59
RT. See Team *headings*
Rushforth, Charles, 246
Rusk, Dean, 33, 34, 35, 46, 69, 77, 132; aggressive policy, 55, 70, 287; and barrier plan, 215; and cross-border operations, 80–81; hard line on China, 128, 225; Laotian agreement, 52, 53, 68; rejection of Trail bombing, 89–90; and Rostow, 62, 63, 64, 67, 68, 71, 72, 76, 159; Senate Foreign Relations Committee testimony, 225; and Sullivan, 98, 99, 100, 219; as Vietnam policy defender, 225, 226
Russell, Clyde, 80, 97, 104, 107
Russia. *See* Soviet Union

II Corps (ARVN), 47, 58, 94, 95, 115, 116–20, 121, 131, 144, 146, 149–51

2d Airborne Brigade (ARVN), 355
2d Air Division (U.S.), 159
2d Battalion, 8th Cavalry (U.S.), 147, 148–49
2d Battalion, 1st Infantry (U.S.), 280
2d Battalion, 2d Infantry (ARVN), 359
2d Battalion (Black Wolves; VPA), 110, 147, 239, 346, 353
2d Brigade, 1st Cavalry (U.S.), 150
2d Brigade, 1st Infantry (ARVN), 332
2d Brigade, Airborne Division (ARVN), 332
2d Division (ARVN), 348, 349, 352
2d Division of People's Volunteers (China), 125
2d Division (VPA), 126, 277–78, 279, 333, 339, 355
2d Regiment, 1st Division (ARVN), 332, 346, 347–48
2d Squadron, 17th Cavalry (U.S.), 346
6th Airborne Battalion (ARVN), 341
6th Battalion (VPA), 110
6th Regiment (VPA), 254
Seventh Air Force (U.S.), 75, 221, 247–48, 269, 274, 304, 369
7th Armored Cavalry (ARVN), 354
7th Cavalry (U.S.), 148
7th Engineer Bridge Company (U.S.), 327, 330
7th Signal Battalion (VPA), 113
17th Armored Cavalry (ARVN), 339, 346, 354
61st Division (PLA), 125
63d Artillery Regiment (VPA), 250
63d Division (PLA), 125
64th Regiment (VPA), 333, 339
66th Regiment (VPA), 148, 149
68th Artillery Regiment (VPA), 238
70B Corps (VPA), 324–25, 333
70th Battalion (VPA), 24, 26
70th Engineer Battalion (U.S.), 277
70th Transporation Group (VPA), 113
71st Assault Helicopter Company (U.S.), 346
71st Transportation Group (VPA), 113
72d Transportation Group (VPA), 113
77th Armor (U.S.), 329
77th Ranger Battalion (ARVN), 359
603rd Battalion (VPA), 14, 18
621st Infiltration Group (VPA), 85
633rd Special Operations Wing (U.S.), 269
711st Group (VPA), 113
759th Transportation Group (VPA), 296
Saal, Herve, 261
Sadler, John K., 344
Saigon (as government). *See* South Vietnam
Saigon (city), 201; capture as North Vietnam's goal, 19; fall of, 372, 373; and Tet Offensive, 237, 241, 247, 248–53, 254; as Trail's intended terminus, 13; Viet Cong hotel bomb explosion, 89, 93
Sale, Kirkpatrick, 138
Salem House (code), 298

SAMs (surface-to-air missiles), 132, 133, 358–59, 369–70
Saravane, 24, 51, 57, 206, 283, 307; anti-aircraft unit, 313–14; VPA capture of, 361
sarin (nerve gas), 308
Savannakhet, 11, 23, 24, 25, 34, 37, 55, 81, 82, 102, 206, 258, 378; Lao Theung and, 51–52; as Laotian Route 9 terminus, 326; RLAF headquarters, 161
Scherbakov, Ilya, 129
Schlesinger, Arthur M., Jr., 30
Schumaker, Robert H., 95
Schungel, Daniel, 280–81
Schwarzkopf, H. Norman, 118, 119, 120–21, 150
Science Advisory Committee (U.S.), 220
SDS. *See* Students for a Democratic Society
Seaborn, Blair, 66, 72, 73, 89, 135
seaborne activity; amphibious, 209, 210, 212, 262, 338; ARVN naval patrols, 32, 111–12; Cambodian coast, 296; infiltration system, 14, 18; as Trail supply route alternative, 17, 111
SEACOORD meetings, 100, 101, 162, 203, 221, 273–74
Seale, Bobby, 301
SEALS (U.S. Navy), 198
SEATO Plan 5 and 5 Plus, 34, 36, 37, 39, 40, 54, 55, 61, 69, 285, 376
Sedang tribe, 50, 56
Seith, Louis T., 304
Senate Foreign Relations Committee, 224–25
Seno outpost, 34, 86
sensors, 218–20, 242, 245, 316, 368; and base security, 375; effectiveness of, 303, 309; emplacement in Laos, 260–61; and Khe San area, 254, 260, 270; Nakhon Phanom command center, 267, 268, 269; VPA countermeasures, 220, 269
Sepon River, 23, 312, 334, 355
Seventeenth Parallel, 37, 39, 63, 100
Shackleton, Ron, 49
Shaplen, Robert, 378
Sharp, U.S. Grant, 96, 100, 102, 103, 140, 153, 207, 221; amphibious invasion plan, 212; and antiwar movement, 228; and barrier plan, 213, 215, 217; freedom of action pleas, 158, 228, 229
Shining Brass (cross-border operations), 101–3, 108, 152; SOG reconnaissance teams, 152, 153–55, 161, 198; Tiger Hound as aerial complement, 160
Sihanouk, Prince Norodom, 296, 297, 299, 372
Sihanouk Trail (Route 110), 155, 187, 191, 193, 203, 221, 238, 296; Hanoi supply movements through, 296–97; SLAM mission, 274–75
Sihanoukville (formerly Kompong Som), 295–96, 297, 298–99

Silva, Christopher J., 277, 279, 280
Silver Buckle plan, 344
silver iodide, 220, 223
Simons, Arthur ("Bull"), 206
Singlaub, John K. ("Jack"), 108, 155,
    197–201, 203, 208, 220, 244; and
    cross-border operations, 271, 272,
    273–74, 275; and STRATA program,
    273; and Tet attack, 248, 260–61; tour
    end, 277, 283
Sino-Soviet conflict, 129, 132, 233, 363
Sisler, Ken, 199
SLAM mission (SOG), 201–2, 203, 245,
    261, 274–75
smart bombs, 375
Smith, Clyde, 370
Smith, Edward B., Jr., 119
Smith, Hedrick, 285
Smith, Russell Jack, 298
SNIEs. See Special National Intelligence
    Estimates
SOG. See MACSOG
Soldier Reports, A (Westmoreland), 219
Song Ca flooding project, 222
Song Ma, 156
Sonnenfeldt, Helmut, 293
Sontay raid, 317
Sorley, Lewis, 319
Sorrow of War, The (Ninh), 194
Soulang, Colonel (RLA), 246, 255, 257
Souphanouvong, Prince, 53, 54, 56
South China Sea, 54
Southeast Asia Coordinating Committee,
    97, 160, 263 (see also SEACOORD
    meetings)
Southeast Asia Treaty Organization, 33-34,
    100; Laotian secret agreement, 81–82;
    See also SEATO Plan 5 and 5 Plus
Southpaw project, 318
South Vietnam; assassinations of Diem and
    Nhu, 59, 63, 68, 348; Buddhist monk's
    self-immolation, 223; coastal patrol re-
    quest, 17–18; coups, 59, 64, 68, 107;
    final collapse, 373-74; guerrilla resis-
    tance. See Viet Cong; National Libera-
    tion Front; infiltration of. See infiltra-
    tors; and Laotian neutrality, 319; North
    Vietnamese trails into, 25, 191, 193
    (see also Ho Chi Minh Trail); operations
    against former Viet Minh, 8–9; out-of-
    country operations, 81–82; Tet perva-
    sive attacks on, 247–48; Thieu election
    campaign, 362, 368; U.S. aid and rela-
    tions, 4, 30–32, 35, 41, 77; See also
    Army of the Republic of Vietnam; Viet-
    namese Air Force; Vietnamese Marines
South Vietnamese Strategic Technical
    Directorate, 344
Souvanna Phouma, 78, 93; approval of bar-
    rier, 214–15, 219; approval of U.S. in-
    terdiction strike targets, 110, 158; and

Laotian invasion plans, 319, 320; neu-
    tralist government, 34, 53, 54, 55;
    South Vietnamese agreement, 81, 82;
    Sullivan and, 98, 99, 103, 221; and
    Vietnamese conflict, 246
Soviet Union, 77, 129–34; Chinese split,
    129, 132, 233, 363; internal politics,
    129–30; intervention possibility, 54,
    133, 134, 207, 208, 229, 264, 293,
    325, 376; as Laotian neutrality agree-
    ment signatory, 53, 57; as Nixon policy
    factor, 288, 293, 363-64; North Viet-
    namese relations, 8, 96, 129, 130–31,
    132, 134, 294; and North Vietnamese
    war strategy debate, 231, 232, 233; as
    threat to Southeast Asia, 29, 30, 39;
    and U.S. Hanoi bombing raids, 130–31;
    and U.S. Laos policy, 67–68, 71–72,
    364; U.S. relations, 129, 130–31, 134;
    See also Cold War
Special Forces, South Vietnamese. See LLDB
Special Forces, U.S. Army. See Green Berets
Special Group (U.S.), 48
Special Guerrilla Units (Laos), 187
Special National Intelligence Estimates
    (SNIEs), 18, 37, 54, 73, 74, 289; on
    B-52 raid implications, 158; on Chi-
    nese intervention possibility, 126–27,
    128; Thomas Hughes's dissents, 128
Spectre. See A-130 Spectre aircraft
Spike teams (SOG), 151–55, 160, 161,
    198–99, 200, 202, 260, 271, 273–76,
    283, 298; and Laotian offensive,
    343–45; See also Nickel Steel; Prairie Fire
Stages of Economic Growth, The (Rostow), 61
Starbird, Alfred D., 214, 215, 217, 218, 237
Starlight Scopes, 239
State Department, U.S.; intelligence ana-
    lysts, 56, 74, 75–76, 128, 130; Intera-
    gency Working Group on Vietnam, 69,
    71; Laotian invasion objections, 320,
    321, 331; 1961 white paper on Viet-
    nam, 46–47; Policy Planning Council,
    54, 62, 69; on U.S. troops in Laos or
    Cambodia, 322; Vietnam recommenda-
    tions, 89; See also Rogers, William P.;
    Rusk, Dean
Station 5 (Ho Chi Minh Trail), 15
STD. See Strategic Technical Directorate
Steel Tiger (bombing operation), 110, 111,
    156–59, 162, 163, 202, 206, 268
Steptoe, Bill, 25
Stewart, Paul, 334
Stilwell, Richard S., 141
Stockton, John B., 147, 148
Stone, Charles P., 274
Stone, Oliver, 288
STRATA (Short-Term Reconnaissance and
    Target Acquisition), 272–73
Strategic Air Command (U.S.), 160, 162
Strategic Exploitation Service (ARVN), 104

Strategic Technical Directorate (ARVN), 104, 105, 108, 187, 375
Students for a Democratic Society (U.S.), 137, 138, 284, 294, 301, 302
Studies and Observation Group. See MAC-SOG
Sullivan, William H., 97–103, 162; and barrier construction, 214–15, 217, 219; and Geneva negotiations, 53, 54, 98–99; imperious persona, 203, 205; and Laos invasion plan, 206–7, 262, 263; on mud and flooding operations, 221, 222; opposition to cross-border operations, 102–3, 273-74; and permissible activities in Laos, 153, 154, 157–58, 191; and Tet Offensive, 258
Sung Lam, 237
Sunrise operation, 50
surface-to-air missiles. See SAMs
Sutherland, James W. ("Jock"), 318, 322, 323, 329, 331, 332, 333, 338, 341–42, 343, 347, 351, 357
Swank, Emory, 162
"Switchback" operation, 51
Sycamore (code name), 268, 269

III Corps (ARVN), 300
3d Airborne Brigade (ARVN), 340, 341, 359
3d Antiaircraft Battalion (U.S.), 75
3d Armored Task Force (ARVN), 119, 121
3d Battalion (VPA), 146
3d Battalion, 2d Regiment (ARVN), 347, 370
3d Battalion, 9th Marines (U.S.), 338
3d Force Reconnaissance Battalion (U.S. Marines), 190, 244
3d Marine Division (U.S.), 206, 326, 327, 328
3d Military Region (VPA), 208
3d Regiment, 1st Infantry (ARVN), 332, 352
12th Air Division (U.S.), 75
12th Battalion (RLAF), 24
13th Marine Artillery Regiment (U.S.), 278, 279
20th Air Commando Squadron (U.S.), 154, 306
20th Tactical Air Support Squadron, 309
21st Ranger Battalion (ARVN), 144, 145, 339
22nd Division (ARVN), 105, 370
23d Tactical Air Support Squadron (U.S.), 306
23rd Infantry Division (U.S.), 348
XXIV Corps (U.S.), 281, 318, 323, 329, 330, 332, 333, 344, 357
24B Regiment, 304th Division (VPA), 333, 341
24th Regiment (VPA), 41, 181, 246
24th Special Tactical Zone (ARVN), 117, 118, 119
25th Engineer Battalion, 188
25th Infantry Division (U.S.), 252, 297, 300

25th Sapper Battalion (VPA), 340, 358
26th Marine Regiment (U.S.), 242, 244–45
27th Combat Engineer Battalion, 330
29th Regiment (VPA), 352
32nd Regiment (ARVN), 17
32nd Regiment (VPA), 113, 118, 121, 143, 146, 154; entrapment in Ia Drang battle, 150
33rd Regiment (VPA), 143, 144, 146, 147, 148, 150
33rd Volunteer Battalion (RLAF), 24, 25, 191
33rd Wing (VNAF), 252
36th Regiment, 308th Division (VPA), 341
37th Ranger Battalion (ARVN), 243, 247
38th Artillery, 308th Division (VPA), 238
39th Ranger Battalion (ARVN), 339, 359
258th Marine Brigade (South Vietnam), 352–53
267th Battalion (NLF), 250, 251
269th Battalion (NLF), 250, 251
301st Battalion (VPA), 11, 13, 14, 15, 16
304th Division (VPA), 41, 237, 261, 333, 341
305th Division (VPA), 10
308th Division (VPA), 238, 339, 341, 355
312th Division (VPA), 325
316th Division (VPA), 143, 373
320th Division (VPA), 182–83, 184, 237, 333, 339
324B Division (VPA), 355
325th Division (VPA), 85, 109–10, 113, 185
330th Division (VPA), 28, 43-44
338th Division (VPA), 28, 182
341st Division (VPA), 11
377th Security Police Squadron (U.S. Air Force), 250
2150th Group (VPA), 312
T-54 tank, 341
Tailwind operation, 308
Tally Ho program, 162, 196
Ta Minh Kham, 28
tanks, 119, 121, 339, 341, 354
Tan Son Nhut airbase (Saigon), 150, 237, 332; Tet attack on, 249, 250–53, 254
Tarpley, Thomas M., 342, 345
Task Force Alpha (surveillance center). See Dutch Mill
Task Force Alpha (Vietnamese marines), 119
Tay Bac, 143
Taylor, Maxwell D., 50–51, 80, 140; aggressive policy, 35–36, 41, 54, 68, 70, 81, 82; as Johnson adviser, 262, 282; as U.S. ambassador in Saigon, 94, 95, 96–97, 99, 100
Taylor-Rostow mission (1961), 36, 37–42, 46, 61, 63
Tay Nguyen Front, 143
Tay Ninh Province, 28, 313, 371
Tchepone, 14, 33, 37, 54, 58, 80, 83, 207, 210; airfield, 27, 156; ARVN abandonment, 347–48, 352; and barrier plan, 215, 219; blocking belt, 368–69;

Tchepone (continued)
current conditions, 378–79; Green Beret patrol, 52; intense bombings/destruction of, 156, 311–12, 345–46, 347, 378; Khe Sanh's proximity, 242; in Laos invasion plan, 318, 321, 322, 323, 335, 338, 342, 343, 345–46, 347, 349; location, 23–26, 28; as major Viet Cong base, 41, 313; North Vietnamese supply flights into, 41–42, 60; Rostow's occupation advocacy, 63, 66, 68, 76; SOG reconnaissance scouts, 104, 283; as suitable place for Trail cutting, 326; as Trail stopover, 372; U.S. bombings of, 156, 311; as U.S. proposed bombing target, 88; U.S. weather-modification operations, 221, 222; as VPA and Pathet Lao base, 86, 109, 161, 190, 238, 321, 333; VPA SAMs sites, 358, 359, 370; VPA traffic to, 238; VPA Trail improvements, 361–62
teach-ins, 136–37, 138, 224, 225
Team Asp, 276
Team Echo, 78
Team Fer-de-Lance, 308
Team Iowa, 151–53, 155, 199
Team Maine, 274–75, 276
Team Montana, 154, 198
Team Ohio, 154
Team Python, 345
Team Romero, 153
Team Ruby, 78
Team Texas, 275
Tet Offensive (1968), 95, 195, 224, 241–65, 277–82, 299, 301; effects on cross-border operations, 274–77, 283; factors behind, 232, 233–36; political/ psychological effects, 283, 284, 362; premature attacks, 247, 248; preparations, 236–39, 248; prisoners, 255–56; refugees, 247, 257–60; scale intensity, 247–48; second wave, 280–82; strategy, 241, 247, 281; Trail effects, 283; U.S. delayed responses, 247–48
Thailand, 23, 39, 40, 55, 157, 262; and barrier plan, 213, 218; border protection, 34, 35; as proposed 1st Cavalry base, 140, 141, 207; U.S. troops in, 30, 54, 69; See also Nakhon Phanom
Thai Special Forces, 103
Thakhek, 34, 54, 267
Thanh, General. See Nguyen Chi Thanh
Thanh Hoa Province, 11, 28, 111, 156, 157, 182, 195, 196
Than Minh Son, 315
Thao Ma, 86, 88, 102, 160
Thompson, Llewellyn, 96, 131
Thompson, Randy, 356
Thong Nhat Hotel (Hanoi), 134
Thon Son Lam ("Rockpile"), 327, 331
"Threat to the Peace, A" (Jorden 1961 report), 46–47

Thua Thien Province, 11, 16, 40, 116; and Tet Offensive, 246, 253, 255
Tiger Hound program (FACs), 159–62, 202, 238, 269
Tiger project, 77, 78, 79–80, 88, 103, 105, 106, 108
tigers, xiv, 46
To Dinh Kanh, 146
Tolson, John J., 262, 263
Tonkin Gulf incident. See under Gulf of Tonkin
Tonkin Gulf Resolution of 1964, 55
Tourison, Sedgwick, 273
Townsend, Elias C., 298
Tran, Colonel (VPA), 185, 186
Tran Chanh Ly, 157
Tran Danh Tai, 184–85, 186
Tran Dinh Tho, 323
Tran Do, 232, 249, 252–53
Tranh Hoa, 195
Tran Khac Kinh, 57
Tran Luong, 10, 15
Tran Qui Hai, 239, 245, 246
Tran Sam, 84
Transportation Group (VPA), 14
Tran Van Ho, 104–5, 108
Tran Van Lam, 366
Tran Van Quang, 253–54, 257, 281
Tran Van Tra, 26, 249, 253, 372
Tri Thien, 254
Trojan Horse, 80
trucks, 85, 111, 112, 157, 185, 193–94, 238, 239, 270, 305; antiaircraft protection, 314–15; continued runs on Trail, 304, 361, 367, 372; U.S. Marine Route 9 convoys, 327–28; VPA large troop movements, 373
Truong Chinh, 59, 232
Truong Nhu Tang, 371–72
Truong Son mountains, 15, 106, 113, 253; passes as bombing targets, 156, 158; VPA crossing, 157, 187, 188, 312, 313, 314
Truong Son Strategic Supply Route. See Ho Chi Minh Trail

U-2 flights, 78, 80, 196
Uncertain Trumpet, The (Taylor), 35
Unger, Leonard, 78, 79, 80, 81, 86, 100
University of California at Berkeley, 136–37
Urgo, Joe, 251, 252
U.S. Air Force, 32, 54, 91, 95, 160, 249; Tet attack on Tan Son Nhut air base, 249, 250–53
U.S. antiwar movement. See antiwar movement
U.S. Army, 153-54, 328
U.S. Army Special Forces. See Green Berets
U.S. government. See specific agencies, personalities, and presidential administrations
U.S. Marines, 220, 237; Combined Action Platoons, 253; differences with SOG,

260–61; foothill operations below DMZ, 327–28; and Hue, 153; and Khe Sanh, 242–43, 244, 282; large losses at Ngok Tavak, 281; Virginia operation, 190, 326
U.S. Navy, 209

Vance, Cyrus, 159, 230
Van Eiweegen, Earl S., 119
Vantage Point, The (Johnson), 226–27
Van Tien Dung, 124, 125, 182, 232, 235, 239, 340, 373
Vesuvius (MACV committee), 298
Vien, General. *See* Cao Van Vien
Vientiane. *See* Laos
Viet Cong; attack on Pleiku, 94–95, 115, 130–31; attacks in ARVN II Corps region, 93–95, 116; attacks on Green Beret camps, 57–58; attack on U.S. embassy, 249; Bien Hoa air base strike, 91; Cambodian base area, 28–29, 295–96; casualties, 22; CIA reports on, 39; CIDG infiltrators, 190; equipment and supply system, 13, 16, 377; guerrilla activities, 5, 15, 16, 17, 234; Hanoi's support for, 7, 9, 14, 45, 46–47, 71, 110; as Hanoi war strategy factor, 231; indigenous roots, 21–22; infiltrators, 17–19, 21–22, 28, 33; Laotian bases, 36, 41; and Laotian invasion, 333; Liberation Front infrastructure, 22; massacre of Sedang tribe, 50, 56; Montagnard members, 49; origination of name, 9; shelling of U.S. bases, 89; spying activity, 21; strength estimates, 22; and Tet Offensive, 250; U.S. analysis misunderstandings of, 32
Viet Minh, 10, 27–29, 50, 109, 143, 325; independence fight against France, 1–5, 16, 86; infiltration back into South, 5, 43–44; Saigon government's operations against, 8–9; *See also* Viet Cong
Vietnam Bulletin, 360
Vietnam Day teach-in (1965), 136–37
Vietnamese Air Force, 41, 106–7, 108, 252; helicopter activity, 153, 154, 199
Vietnamese Marines, 119, 150
Vietnamese Special Forces. *See* LLDB
Vietnam Information Group, 228
Vietnamization, 289–90, 291, 292, 294, 315, 316, 334
Vietnam People's Army; air transport, 26–27, 41–42, 56, 60; aliases and *noms de guerre*, 324; antiaircraft defenses, 306–7, 313–14, 340, 352; assault on Camp Mai Loc, 328; border concentrations, 103; Cambodian operation, 295–99; communications techniques, 187; control of Trail, 56; as conventional military machine, 373; demographic profile, 183–84; and Eagle's Nest, 199, 200; final offensive (1975),

372–74; first soldier to die on Trail, 18; first use of tanks, 246; focus on U.S. troop demoralization, 358; French war action, 25; Green Beret's first encounter with, 52; as Hanoi war strategy factor, 232, 234; infiltrators into South, 85, 86, 161, 238; intervention in South, 109, 116–21, 155, 161; Laotian bases, 158; Laotian invasion responses, 336, 339, 341, 343, 361; and Laotian invasion warnings, 322–24, 332–33; as Laotian military advisers, 53–54; Liberation Front assignees, 250; and McNamara's barrier strategy, 219–20; medical resources, 44, 184; offensive (1972). *See* Easter offensive; sappers, 312–13, 328, 340, 358; SOG scout team encounters, 152–53, 154, 155; SOG supply sabotage, 203; Soviet advisers, 132–33; tanks, 339, 341; Tet Offensive troop commitment, 247; Trail sweeps, 186–88; training units, 182–83, 184; troop buildups, 113, 115, 156–57; troop movements South, 113, 116, 121, 149, 181, 182, 208, 239; troop recalls, 182; troops in Laos, 16, 24, 25, 56–57; *See also* Ho Chi Minh Trail; Tet Offensive; *specific battles, leaders, and units*
Vietnam Veterans Against the War, 228, 230, 252, 365
Vietnam War; assessment of options, 375–79; border sealing as key aspect of, 19–20; border surveillance camps, 58–59; as combat laboratory, 32, 375; congressional restraints on, 322, 333; escalation debates, 71, 72–73, 89–90, 205–10, 233–34; escalations, 95–98, 109–15, 131, 210, 234, 284, 285–86, 375; first airman Congressional Medal of Honor recipient, 186; first U.S. planes lost, 24; Franco-Vietnamese War as background, 4, 66; Hanoi strategies, 59, 231–37, 243, 324–25; Ho Chi Minh Trail as metaphor and microcosm, xv; language of, 123; missed opportunities, 1997 conference on, 235, 247; nationalism as factor, 4–5; underlying threads of, 19; U.S. aims statement (1964–65), 93; U.S. full-scale movement into, 4, 96–98, 100; U.S. mounting losses, 224, 293; U.S. public opinion polls, 115, 137, 225, 226, 228–29; U.S. strategic inconsistencies, 375–76; U.S. troop discipline problems, 356–58; U.S. troop involvement, 92, 96–97, 228–29, 234; U.S. troop withdrawals, 316, 328; U.S. veterans, 227–28, 379; U.S. weather modification, 220–23; *See also* antiwar movement; Tet Offensive; *specific battles and personalities*

Vietnam Workers' Party. *See* Lao Dong
  Party
Village Defense Program, 48–51, 55, 58
Vinh Linh, 11, 13, 14, 112, 162; land mines
  remaining in, 379; naval shelling, 196;
  Rostow invasion plan, 208, 210; U.S.
  bombing effects, 195–96; VPA buildup,
  208
Vinh Loc, 118, 144, 145, 146
Virginia operation, 190, 326
VNAF. *See* Vietnamese Air Force
Vo Bam, 9–18, 20, 22, 25, 26, 27, 29, 44,
  57, 256, 372; on effects of U.S. Trail
  bombing, 197, 198; 559th Transportation Group, 14, 15, 16, 26, 29, 56, 84,
  112; first trail trek, 51; second trail
  trek, 27
Vogt, John W., 340
Voice of Freedom (radio station), 276–77
Vo Nguyen Giap, 86, 112, 113, 239, 324,
  356; background, 231; Chinese high-
  level talks, 124, 125; and Franco-
  Vietnamese War, 2–3, 236; Moscow
  visit, 132; and Tet Offensive, 235–37,
  242; on threatened invasion of North
  Vietnam, 208–9; war strategy theory,
  45, 232, 233, 234, 237; Zumwalt's later
  discussions with, 211
VPA. *See* Vietnam People's Army
Vu Can, 195
Vu Thuy Que, 350
Vu Van Don, 112
Vu Xuan Chiem, 112
VVAW. *See* Vietnam Veterans Against the
  War

Walker, Don, 362
Walsh, Paul V., 297–98
Walt, Lewis, 217, 327
War on Poverty, 70
War Resisters' League, 137–38
Washington Special Action Group, 320,
  321
Watts, William, 293, 294
Waugh, Billy, 199, 271
Weathermen, 294, 301, 302
weather modification, 220–23
Webb, "Pappy," 275
Wells, Tom, 294
Westmoreland, William C., 80, 88, 92, 95,
  96, 221, 239, 283; and antiwar move-
  ment, 228; attrition strategy, 151; and
  barrier plan, 213, 217, 219; border
  strategy, 243; and cross-border opera-
  tions, 101–3, 155, 162, 198–201,
  273–74; Dien Bien Phu as strategy in-

fluence, 242, 246; and Duc Co battle,
  120, 121; and 1st Cavalry use in Central Highlands, 139–40, 147; and 5th
  Group command, 160; freedom of action pleas, 228, 229, 375; ground war
  proposals, 97, 100, 101, 115, 206, 207;
  and Ia Drang battle, 149, 151, 224; on
  Kham Duc evacuation, 280; Khe Sanh
  defense, 190, 243, 245, 262, 281–82;
  and Laotian invasion (1971), 318, 321,
  348, 357; Laotian invasion proposal
  (1967), 206–7, 210, 211, 214, 243,
  258, 262–63, 264, 376; misreading of
  VPA strength, 208; and North Vietnam
  invasion proposal, 209–10, 212, 376;
  reassignment, 265, 274, 281; and
  Shining Brass operation, 155, 198; and
  SOG operations zone, 153, 198, 203;
  and Tet Offensive, 246, 247, 249, 252,
  258, 259, 274, 275; and Tiger Hound
  program, 159–60; on Trail interdiction
  success, 198; troop requests, 209, 210,
  214, 226, 227, 234
Wheeler, Earle ("Buzz"), 100, 210, 213,
  230, 243, 291, 292, 295
White, John E. D. ("Jed"), 277, 278–80
White House Years (Kissinger), 288, 317
White Star project, 51
Whiting, Allen S., 74
Wickersham, Frank G., 334–35, 345, 346,
  347
Williams, Samuel T. ("Hanging Sam"), 17,
  115
wiretaps, 276
women, 113, 193–94, 314
Woods, Randall Bennett, 225
World War II, 62, 80, 94, 99–100, 197;
  bombing tonnage, 377; soldiers' jar-
  gon, 123
Wright, Marshall, 263–64

Xuan Mai, 28, 182
Xuan Thuy, 75

Yankee Team operation, 92, 99
Yarborough, Thomas, 306, 307, 343–44,
  345
Yarnell, Steve, 142, 147
Yen Bay, 125
York operation, 210–11, 243

Zabitosky, Fred W., 275–76
Zeybel, Henry, 369
Zhou Enlai, 74, 75, 124
Zierdt, William H., 144
Zumwalt, Elmo R., 211